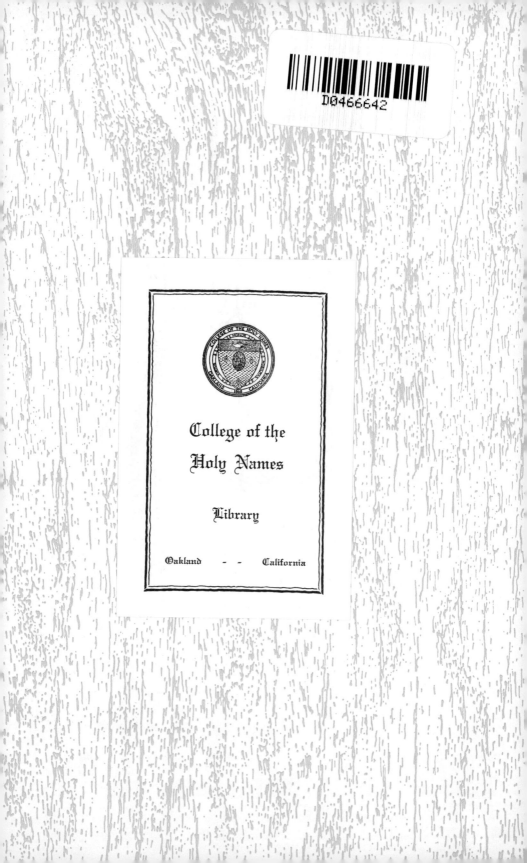

URBAN STUDIES

URBAN STUDIES

An introductory reader

Edited by
Louis K. Loewenstein

THE FREE PRESS *New York*
COLLIER-MACMILLAN LIMITED *London*

The Free Press
A Division of The Macmillan Company
866 Third Avenue, New York, New York 10022

Collier-Macmillan Canada Ltd., Toronto, Ontario.

Library of Congress Catalog Card Number: 79-136272

Printing Number 2 3 4 5 6 7 8 9 10

Contents

v

List of contributors

JOHN E. BURCHARD, Dean Emeritus, Massachusetts Institute of Technology, Cambridge, Massachusetts

HANS BLUMENFELD, Professorial Lecturer, Department of Urban and Regional Planning, University of Toronto, Toronto, Canada

JAMES S. COLEMAN, Professor, Department of Social Relations, Johns Hopkins University, Baltimore, Maryland

DAVID A. CRANE, Professor, Urban Design Program, Graduate School of Fine Arts, University of Pennsylvania

JOHN W. DYCKMAN, Chairman, Department of City and Regional Planning, College of Environmental Design, University of California, Berkeley, California

BERNARD J. FRIEDEN, Professor, Department of Urban Studies and Planning, Massachusetts Institute of Technology, Cambridge, Massachusetts

RALPH A. GAKENHEIMER, Visiting Professor, Department of Urban Studies and Planning, Massachusetts Institute of Technology, Cambridge, Massachusetts

HERBERT J. GANS, Professor, Department of Urban Studies and Planning, Massachusetts Institute of Technology, Cambridge, Massachusetts, and Faculty Associate, Joint Center for Urban Studies of MIT and Harvard

JANE JACOBS, Writer, Toronto, Canada

LOUIS K. LOEWENSTEIN, Acting Director, Urban Studies Program, San Francisco State College, San Francisco, California

KEVIN LYNCH, Professor, Department of Urban Studies and Planning, Massachusetts Institute of Technology, Cambridge, Massachusetts

DANIEL P. MOYNIHAN, Counselor to the President, The White House, Washington, D.C.

LEWIS MUMFORD, Writer, Amenia, New York

THEODORE R. SIZER, Dean of the Faculty of Education, Harvard University, Cambridge, Massachusetts

WILLIAM L. C. WHEATON, Dean, College of Environmental Design, University of California, Berkeley, California

ROBERT C. WOOD, President, University of Massachusetts, Boston, Massachusetts

Acknowledgements

Grateful acknowledgement is made for the use of the following material:

"The Pattern of Urbanization," excerpted from *Urban and Rural America: Policies for Future Growth*; A report by the Advisory Commission on Intergovernmental Relations, Washington, D.C., April, 1968.

"The Valuable Inefficiencies and Impracticalities of Cities," excerpted from *The Economy of Cities*, by Jane Jacobs. © Copyright 1969, by Jane Jacobs. Reprinted by permission of Random House, Inc., and Jane Jacobs.

"Form and Structure of the Metropolitan Area," by William L. C. Wheaton, from *Environment for Man*, edited by William R. Ewald, Jr. © Copyright 1967, by Indiana University Press. Reprinted by permission of Indiana University Press and William L. C. Wheaton.

"The City As It Is and As It Might Be," excerpted from *Building the American City*; the report by the National Commission on Urban Problems, Washington, D.C., December, 1968.

"Toward a National Urban Policy," by Daniel P. Moynihan, from *The Public Interest*, Volume XIX (Fall, 1969); and from Chapter I of *Toward a National Urban Policy*, edited by Daniel P. Moynihan. © Copyright 1969, by Daniel P. Moynihan, © National Urban Affairs, Inc.; © Copyright 1970, by Basic Books, Inc., Publishers, New York. Reprinted by permission of *The Public Interest*, Basic Books, Inc., and Daniel P. Moynihan.

The Kerner Commission Report (Summary), from the Report of the National Advisory Commission on Civil Disorders, Washington, D.C., 1968.

"Poverty in Cities," by Daniel P. Moynihan, from *The Metropolitan Enigma*, edited by James Q. Wilson. © Copyright 1968, by The President and Fellows of Harvard College; © Copyright 1967, by Chamber of Commerce of the United States of America. Reprinted by permission of Harvard University Press and Daniel P. Moynihan.

"Housing Conditions in Urban Poverty Areas," by Allen D. Manvel, extracted from Research Report No. 9, prepared for the consideration of the National Commission on Urban Problems, Washington, D.C., 1968.

"The Schools in the City," by Theodore R. Sizer, from *The Metropolitan Enigma*, edited by James Q. Wilson. © Copyright 1968, by the President and Fellows of Harvard College; © Copyright 1967, by Chamber of Commerce of the United States of America. Reprinted by permission of Harvard University Press and Theodore R. Sizer.

Equality of Educational Opportunity (Summary), by James S. Coleman, *et al.* A report for the United States Department of Health, Education, and Welfare and for the Office of Education, Washington, D.C., 1966.

"The Financial Crisis of our Cities," extracted from "Financing our Urban Needs," reprinted from *The Nation's Cities*, the magazine of the National League of Cities (March, 1969). © Copyright 1969. Reprinted by permission of *The Nation's Cities*.

"Impact of the Property Tax," by Dick Netzer, extracted from Research Report No. 1, prepared for the consideration of the National Commission on Urban Problems, Washington, D.C., 1968.

"Housing and National Urban Goals: Old Policies and New Realities," by Bernard J. Frieden, extracted from *The Metropolitan Enigma*, edited by James Q. Wilson. © Copyright 1968, by The President and Fellows of Harvard College; © Copyright 1967, by Chamber of Commerce of the United States of America. Reprinted by permission of Harvard University Press and Bernard J. Frieden.

"The Shape of the Nation's Housing Problems," extracted from *A Decent Home*; the report of The President's Committee on Urban Housing, Washington, D.C., December, 1968.

"The Failure of Urban Renewal: A Critique and Some Proposals," by Herbert J. Gans, from Volume XXXIX, No. 4 (April, 1965), *Commentary*, and from Chapter 18 of *People and Plans*, by Herbert J. Gans. © Copyright 1965, by the American Jewish Committee; © Copyright 1968, by Basic Books, Inc., Publishers, New York. Reprinted by permission of *Commentary*, Basic Books, Inc., and Herbert J. Gans.

"Home Remedies for Urban Cancer," from *The Urban Prospect*, by Lewis Mumford. © Copyright 1962, by Lewis Mumford. Reprinted by permission of Harcourt Brace Jovanovich, Inc., Martin Secker and Warburg, Ltd., and Lewis Mumford.

"Urban Transportation Planning: An Overview," by Ralph A. Gakenheimer, from *Taming Megalopolis*, edited by H. Wentworth Eldredge. © Copyright 1967, by H. Wentworth Eldredge. Reprinted by permission of Doubleday & Company, Inc., and Ralph A. Gakenheimer.

"Transportation in Cities," by John W. Dyckman, extracted from Volume CCXIII, No. 3 (September, 1965), *Scientific American*. © Copyright 1965, by Scientific American, Inc. Reprinted by permission of *Scientific American* and John W. Dyckman.

"The Public Art of City Building," by David A. Crane, from Volume CCCLII (March, 1964), *The Annals* of The American Academy of Political and Social Science. © Copyright 1964, by The American Academy of Political and Social Science. Reprinted by permission of The American Academy of Political and Social Science and David A. Crane.

"The Pattern of the Metropolis," by Kevin Lynch, from Volume XC, No. 1 (Winter, 1961), *Daedalus*. © Copyright 1960, by The American Academy of Arts and Sciences. Reprinted by permission of *Daedalus*, Journal of the American Academy of Arts and Sciences, and Kevin Lynch.

"The Culture of Urban America," by John Burchard, from *Environment and Change*, edited by William R. Ewald, Jr. © Copyright 1968, by Indiana University Press. Reprinted by permission of Indiana University Press and John Burchard.

"Criteria for Judging the Quality of the Urban Environment," by Hans Blumenfeld, from *The Quality of Urban Life*, Volume III, *Urban Affairs Annual Reviews*, edited by Henry J. Schmandt and Warner Bloomberg, Jr. © Copyright 1969, by Sage Publications, Inc. Reprinted by permission of Sage Publications, Inc., and Hans Blumenfeld.

ROBERT C. WOOD

Foreword

By any conventional index of intellectual history, the "urban studies" this volume samples came of age in an unprecedentedly short period of time. Claiming only limited lineage to past disciplines —architecture, planning, perhaps sociology and more dubiously state and local government—the field has traveled the conventional academic path from concept production to program adaptation in the one extraordinary, exhausting decade of the Sixties.

If the tenets of Keynesian economics, accelerated by the Great Depression, found their way into the practices of the U.S. Treasury in the Thirties, the time record of urban-oriented disciplines has been as fast, and the intellectual challenges more formidable. It is barely ten years since the first major interdisciplinary analysis of metropolitan behavior dissected the New York Metropolitan Region. Now, provoked by the civil disorders devastatingly portrayed in Watts, Newark, and Detroit, the nation has urban legislation on the books and urban prescriptions in the library unparalleled since the New Deal. The achievement in time is all the more impressive, given the assortment of disciplines, the flotsam and jetsam of theoretical contracts, the amalgam of philosophies that had in one way or another to be comprehended.

It is this book's singular achievement to represent these special characteristics of the urban field more faithfully than any other that I know. By organization and by selection, Louis Loewenstein has captured the contemporary nature of urban analysis (no selection here is before 1961); its ubiquity (from pitiless descriptions of human degradation to the design characteristics of physical beauty); and the rapid pace of transformation from diagnosis to practical application (the frequency of governmental reports as a measure of political attention). He has also exercised extraordinary discernment in choosing from the considerable volume of urban critique and commentary that now abounds. The polemical aspects of urban studies are appropriately restrained; the empirical emphasized; the functional issues balanced.

What emerges from Loewenstein's skillful composition—and what the reader might look for in addition to knowledge about and appreciation of the scope of urban affairs—is an implicit commentary on the contemporary process of urban policy formation. More specifically one detects some of the perils of forced-draft development, when academic proposals may become political realities before they have been substantially verified on accepted professional grounds. Alternatively, it is apparent that many of the documents, even the governmental ones, lack any of the practical political considerations that make or break their chances for implementation.

However the record of the Sixties is read, that hot-house alliance between politician and professor must certainly be acknowledged. What began in the campaigns of Adlai Stevenson, flowered perhaps in the election of John Kennedy, persevered in the administration of Lyndon Johnson, and continues with President Nixon needs recognition as a new dimension in decision-making. In the last ten years, ideas traversed the route from initial concept to proposal in law to program to activity with increasing rapidity. In the last five years, if the Poverty and Model Cities Programs are representative, the extent of political compromise with the original measure was extraordinarily slight.

This process, if it is to become part of the national scene, places special responsibility on the innovator. A scholar, accustomed to write and talk in the wistful hope that someone, someday, may be listening, now finds his ideas snapped up by idea-hungry and credulous Senatorial speech-writers. Members of a Presidential Commission, often treated as window-dressing and an excuse for Executive delay in the past, now discover their words taken with instant sincerity by the national press and frequently the prelude for action.

These circumstances that foreshorten the distance between

thought and action place a new importance on thought. The hastily conceived, spritely offered proposition has the danger of becoming law. The quickly assembled cluster of facts can be mistaken for the truth. Responsibility becomes as important a quality in the development of strategy as brilliance.

These injunctions are especially in order in urban affairs, where the boundary conditions are ill-defined and the relevant disciplines many. The reader will want to reflect in Section One on the rigor of reasoning and the foundation in fact of the descriptions made of urban phenomena. When a field of study can change so drastically *between* decennial censuses, the interim extrapolation and the partial sample become critical techniques. How much have we observed over the period of urban development in the United States; how accurately have we reported; what confidence in the reliability of our findings can we establish?

More important than descriptive accuracy perhaps is the specificity of definition and the adequacy of causal explanations. By "urban crises" and "urban problems" do we mean the contemporary disadvantages of the American black now living increasingly in cities; the housing conditions of the urban poor; the public diseconomies that arise from the concentration of economic activities in urban regions (which yield private economies); the fiscal plight of large municipalities; the fragmentation of the local policy process; or the pollution of air and water in areas of congestion?

Or should we more abstractly, but perhaps more usefully, define urbanity as a pattern of human density—a large number of people in a limited physical space. More specifically, that condition of density also involves a high velocity of interaction devoted increasingly to exchange of information. It is sustained by sophisticated technology. The net effect of the congestion and the interactions is such that the properties of both the people and environment affected are measurably effected. That is, they deviate from national norms. This kind of formulation clearly loses the dramatic quality inherent in the "crisis" approach to urban affairs. It may gain in precision and comprehensiveness of analysis.

Beyond definitions, the quality of causal explanations deserves special emphasis in urban studies. For example, parts of the Kerner Commission Report suggest that white racism, as a psychological and political phenomenon, lies at the heart of the urban problem (an attitude conditioned by three hundred years of history, and overlayed with implacable indoctrinations of one generation of white Americans after another). Yet, the chief recommendations of the Commission are economic and resource-oriented in character:

more funds for housing; more funds for local government; more funds for welfare; more funds for jobs. All these programs may be timely—but their relation to psychological and political needs for superiority and power remain, to say the least, obscure. Explicit treatment of cause and effect too often seem missing in the present literature.

Yet when all the defects and inadequacies of present urban studies are acknowledged, the awkwardness that stems from rapid evolution and the misinterpretations that occur in transmission to policy, the benefits of scholarship continue to outweigh the losses by far. If urban policy suffered in the Sixties from incomplete observations, inadequate data, simplistic projection, unguarded inferences, it nevertheless advanced significantly. Moreover, most of the advances occurred because knowledge, thought and reasoning—not folk wisdom, intuition and prejudice—underlay the programs. The urban renewal programs of the 1950's (testimonials to conservative reactions to the process of suburban diffusion) were re-evaluated and replaced. Protestant ethic and its conviction that the poor are immoral gave way to the more benign assumptions of the Poverty Program. Professionally constructed housing subsidy programs, based on knowledge of the *economics* as well as the business of industry, began to work in that complex and frustrating field. New concepts of political participation and institutional change were launched, with results still incompletely understood but essentially positive.

Professor Loewenstein's book faithfully records these accomplishments of urban analysis and these contributions to a better urban life. So the reader should be critical and skeptical as he approaches these selections; suspicious of the sweeping generalizations that occasionally appear and dubious of the most ambitious recommendations. Nevertheless, he should take heart that these intellectual efforts were made; the field of urban studies established; and the tradition of reason and empiricism continued. Given similar progress in the Seventies, the certainty and accuracy of urban analysis ought to expand substantially. As it does so, the quality of urban life in America will inevitably improve.

Robert C. Wood

LOUIS K. LOEWENSTEIN

Introduction

The emerging field of urban studies presents several paradoxes to anyone interested in understanding its scope and content. First, much of the subject matter is problem-oriented. That is to say it is concerned with phenomena known variously as urban troubles, urban problems, or urban crises, depending upon one's sense of urgency and commitment. Yet in this eighth decade of the twentieth century one is constantly reminded that everything affects everything else— that we live in a closed system of interdependencies. Therefore a problem orientation appears to be an oversimplification since we now recognize that all the various elements of urbanism are interwoven. We cannot separate or extract one strand from the urban fabric without disrupting the entire system.

Another seeming contradiction exists in the fact that the intellectual roots of urban studies lie in both the traditional academic disciplines and less orthodox fields. Urban studies have evolved from aspects of city planning, sociology, and economics, on the one hand, and from black and ethnic studies, social welfare, and even interdisciplinary social sciences on the other hand.

For a number of reasons, however, urban studies can be distinguished from other disciplines as a unique area of inquiry. As suggested above, for example, the focus of urban studies should be on problem solving, generally through the creation of viable policies, and not on the development of theoretical constructs. Second, the frame of reference of urban studies is the city and not the region, state, or nation. By city is meant a range of areal concern from the neighborhood or community to the metropolitan area. Another consideration is that urban studies relates to the "here and now." It generally does not look to other countries for analogues since its substance is particularly American. Furthermore, there is little or no historical precedent or experience to fall back on since the urban system is peculiar to our time. Finally, urban studies is characterized by being at the interface binding together such courses as urban geography with urban sociology and urban economics. Moreover, it joins this subject matter to such contemporary issues as inner-city race relations, violence in the ghettos, and the efficacy of the antipoverty programs.

In view of the disparate factors it should not be surprising that the selections offered in this reader may appear to be both divergent and incongruent and yet occasionally repetitious. This repetition occurs because questions of poverty cannot be divorced from questions of housing, which in turn will overlap matters of urban renewal which are related to matter of finance, and so forth. It is also important to remember that the field of urban studies is changing rapidly. It is not an exaggeration to mention that if this reader had been prepared a year ago or if it were to be assembled a year from now, it would include different works. Every effort was made to present the "classics" in the field; nevertheless, the rate of change is so rapid and the subject matter so new, it is inevitable that significant new reports and other articles are bound to supersede much of the material in this book. It should also be borne in mind that this reader makes no pretense of being "balanced." Obviously some areas of interest are more germane or important to those interested in urban affairs than are other subjects. As a consequence some topics have been singled out for inclusion while others have been excluded. At the center of the urban scene one finds the poor nonwhite ghetto resident and hence he has received special attention in this reader. Because of limitations of space or treatment elsewhere, such study areas as metropolitan government, crime and violence, or new towns and suburban morphology are not represented in this book.[1]

Other criteria for selecting articles for this reader are worthy of mention. First, each piece had to be readable, that is, well written,

1. See, for example, *Urban Government: A Reader in Administration and Politics*, edited by Edward C. Banfield (New York: The Free Press, 1969).

easily understood, and not pedantic. Each selection had to contribute to our understanding of the trends and forces underlying contemporary American urban problems. Finally, each essay had to be of lasting, if not everlasting, significance. For this reason extracts from five major federal reports have been included even though the presentation of official documents in such a reader is an unusual departure from the conventional anthology. We feel, however, that it is time not only to recognize these terminal studies but also to give them wider distribution than they would ordinarily receive through normal channels. Moreover, it is generally conceded that these official reports have improved over the years in both style and content so that they now compare favorably with the better academic studies. Indeed, as one wag recently expressed it: "As the problems have gotten worse, the government reports have gotten better."

This reader is divided into two major sections. The first portion is intended to provide an overview of the field through six articles which portray the nature of urban studies by emphasizing its complex interrelationships. The second part presents discussions about eight specific issues of contemporary significance: poverty, education, finance, housing, urban renewal, transportation, urban design, and the quality of urban life. Two articles on each issue are offered in order to give divergent viewpoints and to convey some notion of the range of ideas concerning each topic. In some cases the reader may find diverse perspectives reflected in the works of different authors on the same subject while in other instances government documents are contrasted with the thoughts of scholars.

Although no one article can incorporate all the issues and ideas with which urban studies is concerned, the first selection is designed to acquaint the reader with the broad range of topics which are individually treated in more depth later in this anthology. It, therefore, sets the stage for much of what is to follow. This essay, "The Pattern of Urbanization," is extracted from a definitive study on Urban and Rural America which was prepared by the Advisory Commission on Intergovernmental Relations. It is concerned with the continuous migration from rural areas to cities, chronicling historical development and the resultant regional population patterns. The reader is also introduced to the basic economic functions of urban places, the core city-suburban dichotomy in metropolitan areas, the special problems of race and sprawl, and finally to population growth forecasts. The dynamics of mobility are analyzed in detail in this study.

The economic aspects of cities are reconsidered in the second piece, "The Valuable Inefficiencies and Impracticalities of Cities," by Jane Jacobs. Mrs. Jacobs first acquired fame following the publication of her classic book *The Death and Life of Great American Cities*, which dealt with the need for human scale in city building to be realized through diversity, complexity, and heterogeneity in neighborhoods. In the selection in this reader, Mrs. Jacobs re-emphasizes these qualities, but she focuses on the dogma of ortho-dox economists and their view of the urban system. Conventional wisdom in urban economics states that urban growth and develop-ment is based on an excess of exports over imports.

This favorable balance of trade enables some metropolitan areas to prosper at the expense of others. Mrs. Jacobs attacks this folklore. She argues that the growth of urban places is due to the abundant interdependencies and opportunities for choice found in cities, to slack in the urban system, and most importantly, to the diversity of economic elements which come together in one place— the urban market. Mrs. Jacobs selects waste disposal as a case study to show that in the near future new technologies will be available to allow waste to be economically recycled, both to eliminate pollutant elements and to retain inherently useful economic commo-dities. Thus, Mrs. Jacobs views the city as an incubator of new products and services which can be created because of the vast range of skills, talents, and creative energies which are to be found in urban areas.

In the next article, Dean William L. C. Wheaton re-examines the changing functions of cities. In "Form and Structure of the Metropolitan Area," he points out that in the future new life styles will result in innovative arrangements for housing, places of em-ployment, and recreation areas. He describes new patterns of high and low density origin and activity zones, considers the possibility of new towns with attendant open space, and concludes that techno-logical advances in communication and transportation processes will foster both greater concentration and greater dispersion. Therefore, the metropolis of the future will be, in Wheaton's words, "one of huge size, of vast extent, of great diversity, of rigid change, and to the extent that it is open to future change, of indeterminate form."

The contemporary city, however, presents quite a different picture. The next selection is extracted from the introduction of the final report on the National Commission on Urban Problems whose chairman was Paul Douglas. This is the first of three blue-ribbon panel studies which have been included in this text. All three were commissioned by former President Lyndon Johnson in 1967 to inquire into major social and housing problems threatening

American society. This chapter, entitled "The City As It is and As It Might Be," highlights the Commission's response to President Johnson's mandate. This charge was to "conduct a penetrating review of zoning, housing and building codes, taxation and development standards . . . [and] to recommend the solutions, particularly the ways in which the efforts of the Federal Government, private industry, and local communities can be marshalled to increase the supply of low-cost, decent housing." The study, *Building the American City*, indicated ways in which housing programs could be improved, building codes and land-use controls modernized, housing costs reduced, and governmental taxation and finance measures overhauled and made more realistic. The portion of the study which has been included in this anthology not only summarizes these findings and recommendations, but also is designed to introduce the reader to the growing literature and wealth of information which has been developed on this subject.

The concluding sentence from the Douglas Commission selection which states: "We are confident that the Nation can rededicate itself to these goals that have been the touchstones of progress and success" is a fitting transition to the next article, "Toward a National Urban Policy." This selection by Harvard urbanologist Daniel P. Moynihan, Counselor to President Richard Nixon, shows how to make these goals operational by formulating ten proposals as a basis for federal governmental action. Although no programs have yet emanated directly from such a policy statement, this set of guidelines paves the way for direct national intervention and continuous participation in the solution of urban problems. Moynihan's statement is significant because it is the first enunciation of an urban policy at the federal level. Further, it is noteworthy that such a policy statement originated during a Republican administration rather than under Democratic auspices since Democrats heretofore have been considered to be traditionally more concerned than Republicans with urban affairs.

The final introductory selection is the summary of the Report of the National Advisory Commission on Civil Disorders, more familiarly known as the Kerner Commission report. In the summer of 1967, racial disorders of unparalleled magnitude struck Newark, Detroit, New Brunswick, and more than twenty other cities, setting off, in the Commission's words, "a chain reaction in neighboring communities" and unsettling the typical white middle-class Americans' belief in racial progress. After noting that " . . . the American people are baffled and dismayed by the wholesale looting and violence that has occurred both in small towns and great metropolitan centers," President Johnson directed this Commission to answer three basic questions:

1. What happened?
2. Why did it happen?
3. What can be done to prevent it from happening again?

This Commission responded forthrightly to this charge and made a number of recommendations for national action in the fields of employment, education, welfare, and housing which stand as landmarks of progressive public policy. The three opportunities confronting the city—pursuing present patterns, a ghetto enrichment policy, or such a policy plus integration of the suburbs—represent hard choices for the American public to face and accept. The committee's rationale for pursuing the third alternative is set forth in this synopsis along with its answers to the three questions originally posed by President Johnson.

The second part of the reader begins with a discussion of one of our basic societal ills—urban poverty. Daniel Moynihan's thoughts on this subject are contrasted with a survey by the National Commission on Urban Problems dealing with housing conditions in poverty areas. Moynihan notes that poverty in the United States is now largely an urban phenomenon, whereas it was once essentially agrarian. It is also concentrated among Negroes and other ethnic minorities and is closely associated with large and broken families. The poverty condition is exacerbated by the fact that the poor are seeking employment in a job market which is increasingly becoming more alien to them, and they are frustrated by a social welfare system which is not responsive to their needs. As a consequence, pockets of poverty have emerged and subsequently engulfed entire neighborhoods and districts. According to the Douglas Commission study, poverty areas now comprise twenty-three percent of the central cities' land area; to complete the circle, these areas account for seventy-nine percent of all the housing units which are occupied by non-whites.

Few would deny that our urban schools are in trouble and that they are not meeting the needs of the community. In the next essay, Dean Theodore Sizer analyzes the reasons for this failure and offers a program to make schools more responsive to these needs. After reviewing the educational reform movement, Dean Sizer makes the point that "educational policy is largely shaped by clusters of interest groups and bureaucrats. Most boards of education and school committees react to ideas rather than create them." He then suggests how to change this situation by "teaching people alternatives and providing them the means to act upon them." In the remainder of his article "The Schools in the City," Dean Sizer first outlines a strategy to accomplish this objective and then interprets the findings of a pivotal study entitled "Equal Educational Opportunity," generally known as "The Coleman Report." This report compares the effects of social and economic class on the educational progress of whites and Negroes. Dean Sizer's assessment is followed by a summary of the study. This abridgment was included to enable the reader to familiarize himself with this important piece of research and to evaluate this document and compare his reactions with Dean Sizer's.

Frequently overlooked as both a major cause and a major effect of our urban predicaments is the cities' lack of capital and operating funds. "The Financial Crisis of Our Cities" was chosen as the next selection to illuminate the fiscal condition of urban areas. This article, however, differs from most of the other essays in this book in two respects: It is written in a more popular style, and it abstracts a discussion by a panel of experts. The more colloquial mode contrasts with the complex subject matter, while the contributions of some thirty-three authorities give a dimension to the subject which would be lacking if the ideas of only one author were expressed. As this article notes, property taxation is the principal instrument for raising revenues at the local levels. Local governments depend on this source for about eighty-seven percent of their tax revenue. Yet, as the next selection points out, the property tax is generally inferior to several possible alternatives. This piece, extracted from a special report of the Douglas Commission, suggests that more viable forms of revenue production are user charges, local income taxes, land value taxes, and land value increment taxes. Financing some municipal functions at a higher level of government, i.e., the county, region, or state, is also considered in view of the more efficient tax collection procedures and the more equitable apportionment of expenditures which such an upgrading procedure would offer. The reasons put forth for considering these alternatives reiterate much of the argument posed in the companion piece in this section, but they are given special import here since they emanate from the prestigious National Commission on Urban Problems.

The current status of America's housing conditions is examined in the next two articles. The selection by Bernard Frieden focuses on housing problems confronting the poor and minority groups. It analyzes the nature and dimensions of these problems, the progress that has been made in dealing with them, and housing policies that may bring faster results. Professor Frieden hypothesizes that, "although there has been substantial improvement in American housing since World War II, there are disturbing signs that progress so far has exposed a hard core of remaining issues that call for new approaches. In addition, housing policies that have worked in the past are now coming into conflict with other national objectives." Mechanisms to ameliorate these conflicts are offered by the President's Committee on Urban Housing, which was headed by Edgar Kaiser. This committee was asked to " . . . find a way to harness the productive power of America . . . to the most pressing, unfulfilled need of our society . . . to provide the basic necessities of a decent home and healthy surroundings for every American family now imprisoned in the squalor of slums." It responded by suggesting a number of programs designed to produce at least twenty-six million new and rehabilitated housing units in a decade. In the Kaiser Committee's judgment such a goal could be realized in part by increasing housing subsidies to the poor, by involving the private sector more directly in these subsidized housing schemes, and by expanding the public housing and rent supplement programs. The summary portion of this study included here explains how the federal government can use these tools to narrow the gap between the aspirations of the poor and the realities of the housing market.

These recommendations stem in part from a rather widespread dissatisfaction with the urban renewal process as a means of producing housing for the poor. Perhaps the first to popularize this uneasiness was Herbert Gans, whose article "The Failure of Urban Renewal: A Critique and Some Proposals" is the next selection. Of all the essays in this reader, it is probable that Gans' contribution comes closest to being a classic, having already appeared in at least three other anthologies since its initial publication about four years ago. Professor Gans contends that what is required is an approach that "coordinates the elimination of slums with the reduction of poverty." Gans, however, is not the only critic of urban renewal, As indicated above, Jane Jacobs has also been one of the more articulate commentators on this program. Her opinions on this subject are contained in her book, *The Death and Life of Great American Cities*, which acts as a point of departure for the next selection, "Home Remedies for Urban Cancer," by Lewis Mumford. Mr. Mumford reacts to Mrs. Jacobs' comments with humor and wit, attributes not especially common among writers on urban affairs. Mr. Mumford's humanist view of the city emerges through this satire, which is rare in the literature of urban studies.

Along with housing and urban renewal, "The Transportation Problem" is especially visible and vexatious. The next two selections were chosen because they lucidly discuss the complexities of this subject. In the first, "Urban Transportation Planning: An Overview," Ralph Gakenheimer examines the objectives of the urban transportation system and makes the distinction between increasing accessibility and expediting traffic flow. He explains transportation planning techniques and introduces the reader to computer-based models, to the impact of technologies, and to other areas of concern which will affect future transportation decisions. In "Transportation in Cities," John Dyckman shows how urban transportation is concerned not only with moving people and goods into, out of, and through the city, but also with the spatial organization of all human activities within the metropolitan area. Dr. Dyckman gives considerable attention to the "peak hour" problem, to alternative models of travel, and to differing transportation strategies and concludes that, "if major changes are to be achieved in the present condition of transportation, deliberate individual and collective decisions on the whole question of the quality of urban life must first be made."

Concern for the quality of urban life is also the principal focus in the remainder of this reader. The first selection in the section on urban design, "The Public Art of City Building" by David Crane, is an eloquent plea for higher design standards and a greater commitment to aesthetic considerations on the part of all governmental agencies. Crane believes that urban design is a matter of both individual buildings and entire districts and that public design activities should embrace all levels of city building. In the next article, "The Pattern of The Metropolis," Kevin Lynch considers the forms of urban areas. He makes a distinction between five types of spatial organization: the dispersed city, the urban galaxy, the core city, the urban star, and the ring, and relates these different physical patterns to differences in life styles and human values. Lynch suggests that the pattern of the metropolis will significantly affect such personal factors as choice, interaction, cost, comfort, participation, growth and adaptability, and continuity; and he explains how public policies can encourage different types of spatial arrangement to enhance urban livability.

The final section in this reader focuses on the quality of urban life itself. The central purpose of improving the environment and upgrading the skills and talents of the citizenry is, after all, to make urban life better. John Burchard's discourse on "The Culture of Urban America" is a personal attempt to describe and enumerate some of those factors which comprise urban amenities. He cites twenty-four elements and then ranks sixteen American and foreign cities in terms of the degree to which these places appear to him to possess these features. The final article, by Hans Blumenfeld, sets out to establish "Criteria for Judging the Quality of the Urban Environment." As his point of departure, Blumenfeld takes Aristotle's dictum that "men come together in cities for security; they stay together for the good life," and then he returns to many of the topics mentioned elsewhere in this reader—the city as an economic machine, accessibility and transportation, the recycling of waste, urban renewal, the physical form of urban areas, places of privacy and activity—to show the impact of the physical environment on this "good life." It is, perhaps, fitting and proper that in this concluding article Blumenfeld should demonstrate this interrelationship, for in the final analysis, in urban studies as elsewhere, everything is related to everything else.

The scope and content of urban studies

I ADVISORY COMMISSION ON INTERGOVERNMENTAL RELATIONS

The pattern of urbanization

To describe the United States as an urban nation is to state the obvious. To tick off aggregate statistics indicating urban growth is to quote the first or second paragraph of nearly any speech or article dealing with a major domestic problem. To describe the first item on the nation's agenda of unfinished domestic business as "the urban crisis" is merely to state a truism. To explain the stresses and strains of contemporary intergovernmental relations in terms of competitive and collaborative approaches toward meeting the urban challenge, while less usual, is becoming more commonplace.

Yet, there is a widespread contemporary debate over the impact, direction and future course of urbanization in America and much of it indicates significant disagreements, and no little confusion, concerning the multi-dimensional features of this primary conditioner of American social and economic life.

In this first chapter of the Report [of the Advisory Commission], the contours of the urbanization process are sketched—first, by chronicling the historical development and evolving regional patterns of this process. The multi-faceted mosaic of the urban landscape is then probed by focusing on the core city-suburban dichotomy in metropolitan areas, the broader configuration of urban places in metropolitan and nonmetropolitan areas, the contrasting growth rates and basic economic features of urban places by area and region, the special problems of race and sprawl, and the metropolitan mirror of the future. The dynamics of mobility and migration are treated next with a view to tracing the patterns of movement, determining the relationship between migration and urban concentration, assessing the factors prompting or retarding movements, and examining the links between poverty and mobility. The relationship between urban growth and rural difficulties is then examined. . . . Finally, a short recapitulation of the major findings relating to intrametropolitan differences (developed in the Commission's earlier report, *Fiscal Balance in the American Federal System*) will be presented in order to place the earlier rural-urban analysis in proper perspective and to fit a vital piece into the mosaic of urban America.

In short, we are concerned here with the paradoxes of:

the emergence of an urban nation in a country that has a rural bias against cities;

greater urban growth, but declining older big cities;

the most dynamic expansion emerging in a broad geographic crescent that involves regions and states which until recently had a strong antiurban tradition;

large and small enclaves of poverty in both rural and urban areas, which are byproducts of urbanization and the economic advances it symbolizes; and

big urbanization with many nonpublicized elements of balance, but with economic and demographic results that threaten the qualitative balance, the balance between big and small, which also is a part of the American federal system.

REGIONAL GROWTH

A brief historical summary

In this chapter, we are concerned with one basic aspect of urbanization—the spatial distribution of people and their concomitant economic and social activities. Attention is centered on urban areas, where increasing proportions of Americans live, and where new patterns are emerging and becoming firmly established. Yet, given the diverse pattern of recent urbanization and the resulting difficulty of drawing a clean line between "rural" and "urban" areas, the former and its population will be fully considered. Our basic purpose at the outset is to sketch the historical evolution of the present geographical pattern of urbanization.

In 1790, when the newly formed national government first instituted a system of comprehensive censuses, 95 percent of the 3.9 million people were rural and some 85 percent were agricultural. The first century of the nation's existence under the constitution (1790–1890) witnessed a population increase of about 35 percent or more each decade. It was a period of heavy population increase and marked economic expansion. A record wave of immigration occurred prior to the Civil War, which exceeded that of the latter half of the previous century. The population reached 25 million in 1850, double this figure by 1880, and reached 75 million in 1900. It was not until the latter half of the 19th Century, that rates of natural increase began to decline. On the other hand, the economic problem of labor scarcity, along with other factors, provided the impetus for a third great wave of immigration from Europe.

The movement of population within the country during this period was more than simply a trek west. There was also a further intensification of urban development in the older sections of the east. Between 1890 and 1900, the beginnings of a major migration from agricultural to the "more abundant life" in urban areas got underway. This movement began even as the nation developed the most productive agricultural economy the world had yet seen. By 1900, 40 percent of the population were living in urban places of 2,500 or more, and more than 60 percent of the economically active population were working outside of agriculture.

The Southeast, Great Lakes, and Middle Atlantic regions experienced the greatest absolute increases in population during the long span extending from 1870 to 1960. The rates of increase, however, were highest in the Mountain, Southwest, and Far West divisions. The aggregate for the four Eastern regions (i.e., New England, Middle Atlantic, Great Lakes, and the Southeast including Arkansas and Louisiana) exceeded the national percentage increases in only a few decades, and then only at slightly above average rates.

A high rate of population growth occurred before 1910 in the Plains region, but subsequently its rates fell below the national average. In the early 20th Century, there were fewer in-migrants than out-migrants in Iowa and Missouri and by 1920 Minnesota, Nebraska, and Kansas followed a similar pattern. The proportion of national population residing in the Plains States has declined by 4 percent since 1910. The Far West, Southwest, and southern Mountain States have absorbed most of the "westward" movement of population in recent years.

On the whole, the least densely populated parts of the country experienced the most rapid relative growth between 1870 and 1960. Absolute population increases, however, were heaviest in the Middle Atlantic, Great Lakes, and Southeast regions. The larger share of the population then continued to cluster in areas east of the Mississippi, but to a lesser degree than was the case nine decades ago. The four eastern regions of the country contained 85.5 percent of the nation's population in 1870, 74 percent in 1910, 71 percent in 1950, a little over 69 percent in 1960, and 68.5 percent in 1966. The Far West, Southwest, and Mountain regions experienced the greatest relative expansion in terms of their share of the national population.

Overall, nearly the same pattern emerges if regional growth is measured in terms of employed labor force rather than population. The shares of the national labor force compare quite closely with the population percentages for all regions, with the Southeast providing the greatest deviation due to the influence of high birth rates.

The regional pattern of urban growth

Every census since 1870 reveals a positive increase in the total proportion of population living in urban areas. This dynamism paralleled the country's industrialization, and had a profound effect on the urban-rural pattern of population settlement and on regional population patterns. . . .

Table 1-1 provides the ten-year rates of increase of urban population by region. The rates of urbanization generally are significantly greater in the States comprising the Southwest, Mountain States and Far West than those for the States east of the Mississippi River. There are exceptions, of course, in the Southeast, and specifically, Florida. A comparison of the rates of urbanization and the proportion of urban residents to total U.S. population is provided in Table 1-2. Even though the west claims the most rapid percentage increase in total population, the great bulk of the nation's urban population still resides in the four eastern regional divisions.

THE URBAN MOSAIC

Population statistics provide a back-drop for the striking fact of 20th Century life—the population explosion in metropolitan America. In every decade except the 1930's, there has been an enormous growth in metropolitan areas (using the new Census definition of Standard Metropolitan Statistical Area—SMSA). Metropolitan population growth has exceeded nonmetropolitan

Table 1-1—Decennial Rates of Increase of Urban Population, by Region, 1870-1960

Region	1870–80	1880–90	1890–1900	1900–10	1910–20	1920–30	1930–40	1940–50	1950–60
United States[1]	41.0	56.5	36.4	39.3	29.0	27.3	7.9	20.6	25.4
New England	35.7	13.8	32.5	25.3	17.0	12.3	1.7	7.8	13.2
Middle Atlantic	34.7	39.6	35.0	34.6	22.7	20.7	4.8	8.0	8.4
Great Lakes	56.2	66.0	41.2	33.2	35.7	28.7	3.9	14.5	20.9
Southeast	16.2	63.8	37.1	48.3	36.0	39.3	18.6	33.5	38.2
Plains	53.1	106.2	27.7	31.3	22.2	17.6	7.9	17.1	22.8
Southwest	133.5	135.2	165.9	118.3	63.6	55.0	19.4	52.3	56.6
Mountain	351.5	197.9	51.6	68.6	23.8	14.7	18.1	31.0	34.8
Far West	89.1	94.1	37.4	112.1	45.1	60.3	14.9	43.6	51.3

[1] Excluding Alaska and Hawaii.

Source: Harvey S. Perloff, Edgar S. Dunn, Jr., Eric E. Lampard and Richard F. Muth, "Regions, Resources and Economic Growth" (Baltimore, Maryland: The Johns Hopkins Press, 1960), p. 20. Table adapted and updated by ACIR. To achieve comparability, the former definition of "urban" has been used throughout.

Table 1-2—Rank Order of Regions by Rate of Increase in Urban Population and Regional Proportions of U.S. Urban Population, 1870-1960

	1870 80% rate	1870 proportion	1900 10% rate	1910 proportion	1940 50% rate	1950 proportion	1950 60% rate (using former defin.)	1950-60 (current defin.)	1960 proportion (using former defin.)	1960 (current defin.)
(1)	Mt.[1] 351.5	MA 43.4	SW 118.3	MA 35.3	SW 52.3	MA 28.0	SW 55.6	(52.2)	MA 24.3	(25.0)
(2)	SW 133.5	GL 19.7	FW 112.1	GL 22.9	FW 43.6	GL 22.5	FW 51.3	(53.5)	GL 21.7	(21.2)
(3)	FW 89.1	NE 15.5	Mt. 68.6	NE 11.4	SE 33.5	SE 14.4	SE 38.2	(40.6)	SE 15.9	(16.2)
(4)	GL 56.2	SE 11.0	SE 48.3	SE 10.2	Mt. 31.0	FW 10.3	Mt. 34.8	(44.8)	FW 12.5	(13.5)
(5)	Pl. 53.1	Pl. 7.3	MA 34.6	Pl. 9.2	Pl. 17.1	Pl. 7.9	Pl. 22.8	(23.8)	SW 8.8	(8.2)
(6)	NE 35.7	FW 2.2	GL 33.2	FW 5.7	GL 14.5	NE 7.8	GL 20.9	(24.8)	Pl. 7.7	(7.3)
(7)	MA 34.7	SW .7	Pl. 31.3	SW 3.3	MA 8.0	SW 7.1	NE 13.2	(13.1)	NE 7.0	(6.4)
(8)	SE 16.2	Mt. .2	NE 25.3	Mt. 2.0	NE 7.8	Mt. 2.0	MA 8.4	(15.7)	Mt. 2.2	(2.2)

[1] Regional designations: NE (New England); MA (Middle Atlantic); GL (Great Lakes); SE (Southeast); Pl. (Plains); SW (Southwest); Mt. (Mountain); FW (Far West).

Source: Harvey S. Perloff, Edgar S. Dunn, Jr., Eric E. Lampard, and Richard F. Muth, "Regions, Resources and Economic Growth" (Baltimore, Md.: The Johns Hopkins Press, 1960), p. 21. Table updated by ACIR.

growth in every decade since 1900. Projections for 1975 indicate that this growth will continue at about 25 percent per decade.

Central city-noncentral city dichotomy

Between 1900 and 1920 central cities grew more rapidly than their surrounding areas (see Figure 1–1). This growth reflected the large

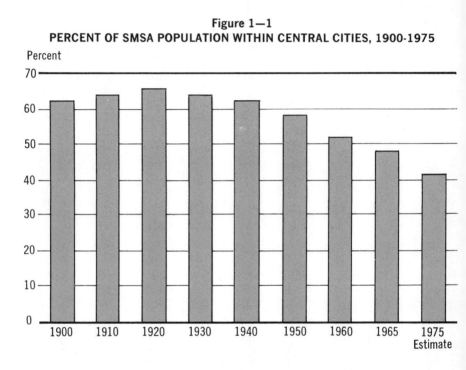

Figure 1—1
PERCENT OF SMSA POPULATION WITHIN CENTRAL CITIES, 1900-1975

immigration from both rural areas and foreign countries. By 1930, adjacent urban areas outside the central city began to play a more significant role in terms of urban growth, mainly because of changing modes of transportation and because these areas had not been incorporated into the legal limits of the central city. The growth of these areas soared after World War II. Central city growth fell to about two-thirds of the amount of the outside central city growth between 1930 and 1950, to about one-third between 1950 and 1960, and it is projected to fall to about one-sixth the amount from 1965 to 1975.

To some extent these figures on population growth understate the relative decline of the central city in that they ignore annexation. Since 1950, overall central city population growth has largely been a product of annexation.[1] If the 1950 boundaries are used as the basis for jurisdictional enumeration, central cities in all size categories experienced relatively minor increases or even declines over the decade 1950–60. As Table 1–3 shows, the nearly 11 percent

Table 1–3—Population Growth in Metropolitan Areas With and Without Central City Annexations, by Size of Area, 1950–1960

Size of area	Total change (percent)	Change without annexations (percent)
All SMSA's:		
Central cities	+10.8	+1.5
Outside central cities	+48.5	+61.7
Total	+26.4	+26.4
SMSA's population of:		
3,000,000 or more:		
Central cities	+1.0	+.6
Outside central cities	+71.3	+72.2
Total	+23.2	+23.2
1,000,000 to 3,000,000:		
Central cities	+5.6	−2.2
Outside central cities	+44.8	+52.7
Total	+25.0	+25.0
500,000 to 1,000,000:		
Central cities	+21.4	+4.8
Outside central cities	+57.4	+81.1
Total	+36.0	+36.0
250,000 to 500,000:		
Central cities	+16.2	+2.2
Outside central cities	+36.2	+51.9
Total	+25.6	+25.6
100,000 to 250,000:		
Central cities	+24.4	+4.6
Outside central cities	+27.6	+54.5
Total	+25.8	+25.8
Under 100,000:		
Central cities	+29.2	+8.6
Outside central cities	+10.9	+69.9
Total	+24.4	+24.4

Source: U.S. Bureau of the Census, "U.S. Census Population: 1960. Vol. 1, Characteristics of the Population." Part A. Number of Inhabitants.

increase in central city population for this period is only 1.5 percent, if annexations are excluded. The outside central city growth increases from 48.5 percent to 61.7 percent with this exclusion. Annexation also explains some municipal population growth in earlier decades. Cities that have increased their population without annexation frequently have had considerable undeveloped land within their borders. In recent years, such municipalities have been located primarily in the South and West and had effected earlier annexations.

1. Advisory Commission on Intergovernmental Relations, *Fiscal Balance in the American Federal System* (in process).

Although metropolitan areas in the various size categories have grown at about the same rate (with the exception of those in the 500,000–1 million class), there have been and are dramatic differences in the intrametropolitan distribution of this growth. Central city growth has taken place primarily in the smaller metropolitan areas, while the outside central city jurisdictions of the large metropolitan areas generally have grown more than the outlying regions in smaller metropolitan areas and at a faster rate. The growth picture then clearly is one of major contrasts between the central city and the regions outside the central city of the large metropolitan areas (500,000 plus).

In analyzing metropolitan area growth, the rural component of the area outside the central city should not be overlooked, since it conditions all central city-outside central city comparisons. This component, however, involves a population that is urban oriented in character. For all SMSA's in the United States in 1960, nearly one-fourth of the population outside the central city was rural. There were enormous variations, however, between various large metropolitan areas. Among the 37 largest SMSA's in 1960, for example, the rural portion of the population outside central city ranged from 1.2 percent in the Patterson-Clifton-Passaic SMSA to 45.5 percent in San Antonio, although this involved a small number of people in the latter case. The next largest percentage of rural population outside the central city area was in the San Bernardino-Riverside-Ontario SMSA with 38.9 percent; this portion was absolutely and relatively large.[1] . . .

Regional distribution of urban places

A breakdown by regions further emphasizes the heterogeneity of the national pattern but also the relatively greater growth rate of medium and large size urban categories.

In Table 1–4, independent urban concentrations have been grouped by population class and by regional divisions. . . . The data for these smaller areas are only approximations and are not wholly comparable to the larger metropolitan areas. They are adequate, however, for the present purpose.

For the United States as a whole, the percentage increase for 1960–1965 is nearly 10 percent for all urban areas (20,000 to 1,000,000 or more). There is considerable diversity, however, in the rates of population growth among the various sized urban areas, the greatest growth being in the 500,000 to 1,000,000 classification (12 percent). By way of contrast, the smaller categories (20,000 to

2. *Ibid.*

150,000) are growing at a rate below the national increase; indeed, *the smallest growth rate occurred in the smallest population class.*

The remaining population classifications grew at rates more or less paralleling the national average. Nonetheless, even though the largest urban concentrations had a growth rate only on a par with the national average, they accounted for no less than 52.9 percent of the total increase in Urban Area (UA) population between 1960–1965. As indicated by the following distribution, the proportion of the total increase going to the other population classifications was far less: 500,000 to 1,000,000—13.8 percent; 250,000 to 500,000—10.8 percent; 150,000 to 250,000—7.2 percent; 50,000 to 150,000—9 percent; and 20,000 to 50,000—6.3 percent.

Total UA population change for the five-year period was well below the national average in three regions, New England, Middle Atlantic, and East North Central, and somewhat below the average in the West North Central region. The East South Central division had a rate comparable to that of the nation. Above average growth was registered in the remaining regions with the lower South Atlantic, Mountain, and Pacific divisions making the greatest gains. It should be emphasized that percentage population changes for regions presents a rough picture which obscures a wide range of intraregional variation among urban areas.

Turning to the regional growth patterns for different size UA's, the smallest category (20,000 to 50,000) produced above national rates of growth in five regional divisions: the lower South Atlantic, East South Central, West South Central, Mountain, and Pacific regions. In short, small urban areas have been growing at greater than average ratios in the broad geographic curve that begins in Virginia, swings down through the Old South and Southwest, and ends up on the West Coast. Medium-size urban categories (50,000 to 250,000) follow exactly the same Southeast to Pacific arc in terms of regions having greater than national growth areas. Moreover, with but two UA subcategory exceptions, the regional rates of increase for these medium-size urban areas were greater than their counterparts in the 20,000 to 50,000 class.

Comparison of regional growth rates for the larger urban concentrations (250,000 to 500,000 and 500,000 to 1,000,000) reveals a somewhat similar geographic pattern of above-average increases. Only the lower rates for the East South Central division prevents an exact duplication of the same crescent-shaped pattern that emerged for the smaller categories. Finally, for the largest group (one million and over), a slightly different regional clustering arises with those in the upper and lower South Atlantic, West South Central,

Table 1-4—Urban Areas: Rate of Growth 1960–65 by Population Size and Region[1]

[Population figures in thousands]

Region and item	20,000 to 50,000	50,000 to 100,000	100,000 to 150,000	150,000 to 250,000	250,000 to 500,000	500,000 to 1,000,000	1,000,000 or more	Total
UNITED STATES:								
Number of UA's	365	127	48	48	43	23	24	678
Population—1960	10,390.9	7,858.8	5,442.7	8,394.1	13,569.1	14,497.4	66,435.1	126,588.1
1965	11,175.5	8,511.0	5,898.5	9,287.0	14,900.0	16,210.5	72,975.0	138,957.5
Percent increase, 1960–65	7.6	8.3	8.4	10.6	9.8	11.8	9.8	9.8
New England:								
Number of UA's	19	9	4	3	4	2	1	42
Population—1960	504.5	539.7	504.6	505.7	1,598.3	1,626.5	3,372.8	8,652.1
1965	514.0	571.5	514.5	534.0	1,684.0	1,735.0	3,540.0	9,093.0
Percent increase, 1960–65	1.9	5.9	2.0	5.6	5.4	6.7	5.0	5.1
Middle Atlantic:								
Number of UA's	53	14	6	6	5	2	4	90
Population—1960	1,571.7	958.5	711.9	1,236.0	1,563.4	1,182.7	22,579.5	29,803.7
1965	1,599.5	980.0	746.0	1,246.0	1,656.0	1,250.0	23,990.0	31,467.5
Percent increase, 1960–65	1.8	2.2	4.8	0.8	5.9	5.7	6.2	5.6
East North Central:								
Number of UA's	58	28	14	8	6	5	5	124
Population—1960	1,627.8	1,702.7	1,598.1	1,493.4	2,026.8	3,258.9	15,250.5	26,958.2
1965	1,714.5	1,804.5	1,683.0	1,629.0	2,149.0	3,600.0	16,285.0	28,865.0
Percent increase, 1960–65	5.3	6.0	5.3	9.1	6.0	10.5	6.8	7.1
West North Central:								
Number of UA's	39	8	5	2	4	—	3	61
Population—1960	1,140.7	493.5	579.9	310.6	1,303.1	—	4,518.4	8,346.2
1965	1,223.0	532.0	626.5	330.0	1,395.0	—	4,925.0	9,031.5
Percent increase, 1960–65	7.2	7.8	8.0	6.2	7.1	—	9.0	8.2

South Atlantic, Upper:								
Number of UA's	11	3	1	2	1	—	2	20
Population—1960	373.5	175.0	126.6	445.0	318.7	—	3,690.1	5,128.9
1965	372.0	177.5	121.0	449.0	355.0	—	4,215.0	5,689.5
Percent increase or decrease (—) 1960–65	—0.4	1.4	—4.4	0.9	11.4	—	14.2	10.9
South Atlantic, Lower:								
Number of UA's	57	18	5	13	6	2	2	103
Population—1960	1,572.8	1,120.4	542.3	2,260.5	1,868.2	1,035.2	2,223.1	10,622.5
1965	1,761.0	1,280.0	593.5	2,552.0	2,138.0	1,180.5	2,730.0	12,235.0
Percent increase, 1960–65	12.0	14.2	9.4	12.9	14.4	14.0	22.8	15.2
East South Central:								
Number of UA's	26	10	3	2	4	3	—	48
Population—1960	755.0	611.5	343.0	346.4	1,288.2	1,987.9	—	5,332.0
1965	828.0	648.5	431.0	387.0	1,403.0	2,150.0	—	5,847.5
Percent increase, 1960–65	9.7	6.1	25.7	11.7	8.9	8.2	—	9.7
West South Central:								
Number of UA's	46	16	4	5	6	4	2	83
Population—1960	1,268.4	1,052.0	470.5	830.7	1,692.9	2,573.0	2,274.0	10,161.5
1965	1,372.5	1,138.5	523.0	949.0	1,861.0	2,900.0	2,770.0	11,514.0
Percent increase, 1960–65	8.2	8.2	11.2	14.2	9.9	12.7	21.8	13.3
Mountain:								
Number of UA's	22	7	3	3	3	1	1	40
Population—1960	657.0	397.5	293.5	400.2	919.5	619.6	858.3	4,145.6
1965	719.5	461.0	339.0	555.0	1,115.0	810.0	1,035.0	5,034.5
Percent increase, 1960–65	9.5	16.0	15.9	38.7	21.3	30.7	20.6	21.4
Pacific:								
Number of UA's	34	14	3	4	4	4	4	67
Population—1960	919.5	808.0	272.3	565.6	990.0	2,213.6	11,668.4	17,437.4
1965	1,071.5	917.5	321.0	656.0	1,144.0	2,585.0	13,485.0	20,180.0
Percent increase, 1960–65	16.5	13.6	17.9	16.0	15.6	16.8	15.6	15.7

[1] Urban Areas (UA's) are Rand McNally "Metropolitan Areas" (RMA's) and Urban Concentrations.

Source: Derived from published and unpublished data developed by Rand McNally & Company.

Mountain, and Pacific regions expanding at a rate exceeding the national average for the five-year period.

Turning to the regions that uniformly produced below average growth rates for the various UA categories, another interregional arc emerges, swinging from rural Maine through the southern New England—Middle Atlantic—Great Lakes manufacturing belt, continuing through the wheat producing regions of the Plains States, and ending up in rural North Dakota.

While the foregoing stresses the relatively greater growth rates of the southern and western sectors (the lower South Atlantic, East and West South Central, Mountain, and Pacific States), certain striking facts relating to absolute population figures also stand out. They contained more than half of the Urban Area population living in the middle range of cities (50,000 to 1,000,000) although they accounted for only 39.4 percent of the total population in Urban Areas (20,000 and above). This seeming paradox mainly reflects the fact that these two geographic sectors contain only 27.4 percent of the urban population living in areas of one million or more.

Cities—their basic economic functions

An economic classification of cities provides additional insights into the nature of the urbanization process, especially when it includes a breakdown according to size, regional location, and metropolitan status. While a number of studies provide an economic classification of cities, most of them rely exclusively on census data describing the traits of persons residing in urban jurisdictions. For the purposes of this brief analysis, the approach developed by the International City Managers' Association in its *Municipal Year Books* will be relied upon, since it focuses on the economic activities actually going on in the various municipalities.

Over the past 20 years or more, the ICMA has presented an economic or "functional" classification of cities over 10,000 population in various editions of its *Municipal Year Book*. The 1967 edition of the *Year Book* contains classification data based on the 1963 Manufacturers and Business census in conjunction with data from the 1960 Census of Population.[3]

3. Richard L. Forstall, "Economic Classification of Places Over 10,000 1960–63," *The Municipal Year Book, 1967*, International City Managers' Association, pp. 30–65, which is a revision of four classifications previously published by the International City Managers' Association in its *Municipal Year Book :* Grace Kneedler Ohlson, "Economic Classification of Cities," 1945, pp. 30–38, 48 and Table IV; Victor Jones, "Economic Classification of Cities and Metropolitan Areas," 1953, pp. 49–57, 69, and Tables II and IV; Victor Jones and Andrew Collver, "Economic Classification of Cities and Metropolitan Areas," 1960, pp. 67–79, 89–90, and Tables IV and VI; and Victor Jones, Richard L. Forstall, and Andrew Collver, "Economic and Social Characteristics of

The number of cities and other places of 10,000 or more classified by ICMA totals 1,849. These urban communities were divided
into functional types, on a basis of the dominant economic activities
carried on within their corporate limits. The survey determined the
economic classification for nearly all of the types of cities by the
number of persons employed in four main categories: manufacturing, retail trade, wholesale trade, and selected services. The "aggregate employment" or combined total of the four categories does not
include employment in mining, transportation, public administration, and other such activities not reported by the Census of
Manufacturers and Business. The comparatively few cities (122)
in which these activities constituted the dominant economic effort
were determined by labor force data from the 1960 Census of
Population.

While fully recognizing that this approach does not reveal the
full profile of each municipality surveyed, it is the most sophisticated
method available and has produced a classification system that has
been extensively relied upon for more than two decades. Under this
ICMA system, the following economic municipal types emerge:

Manufacturing—where 50 percent or more of the aggregate
employment is in manufacturing and less than 30 percent in retail
trade;

Industrial—where 50 percent or more of the aggregate work
force is in manufacturing and over 30 percent is in retail trade;

Diversified-Manufacturing—where employment in manufacturing is greater than that in retail employment, but less than 50 percent
of the total employed in the four major categories;

Diversified-Retailing—where employment is greater in retailing
than manufacturing, but manufacturing accounts for at least 20
percent of the total in the big four;

Retailing—where retail employment is greater than manufacturing or any other component of the aggregate work force, and manufacturing is less than 20 percent;

Dormitory—where aggregate employment is less than 67 percent
of the resident labor force engaged in activities cited above and
below.

A small group of 122 are classified as "specialized cities" in the
survey and include those in which some unusual economic activity
forms the principal support of the community, such as:

Urban Places" and "Economic and Social Classification of Metropolitan Areas," 1963,
pp. 31-37, 85-113, and Tables I and III.

Wholesaling—where employment in this trade constitutes at least 25 percent of the aggregate employment;

Mining—where the resident labor force in mining is greater than that in manufacturing or retail trade;

Transportation—where the resident labor force in transportation is greater than that either in manufacturing or retail employment;

Resort—where the employees in entertainment, recreation, and personal services, but not in private households, total more than the manufacturing or retailing employment;

Government—where the resident labor force in public administration and armed forces outnumbers the combined manufacturing and retail employment and is greater than any other category and also where public personnel exceed the military;

Armed Forces—where the resident armed forces constitute more than 50 percent of the resident labor force, or outnumbers the combined employment in manufacturing and retailing and is more than 20 percent of a city's total population;

Professional—Where the resident labor force in professional activities (other than health and education) exceeds manufacturing or retail employment;

Hospital—where the hospital labor force surpasses that in either manufacturing or retailing;

Education—where educational employees outnumber those in the two major sectors;

Service—where employment in selected services is at least 30 percent of the aggregate and where a city does not qualify for any other category.

Table 1–5 shows the number of cities over 10,000 population by regions and SMSA's classified by basic economic function. The Northeast region contains 560 (30.3 percent) of the cities tabulated; the North Central region, 547 (29.6 percent); the South 453 (24.5 percent); and the West 289 (15.6 percent).

Cities classed as manufacturing constitute the most common single type, comprising 569 out of the total of 1,849 cities surveyed. With the exception of specialized city types, the smallest number were found in the industrial category and most of these were relatively small urban places. Diversified-manufacturing cities, the fourth largest group, were more strongly represented among large cities than smaller ones, with 15 of the 27 over 500,000 population falling in this category. The third largest class—the diversified-retailing cities—numbered 249, but included only four in the over

Table 1–5—Functional Classification of Cities Over 10,000 and SMSA's by Region,[1] 1963

Economic function	North-east	North Central	South	West	Total	SMSA's
Manufacturing	245	201	90	33	569	98
Industrial	28	30	10	6	74	7
Diversified—Manufacturing	61	63	85	25	234	62
Diversified—Retailing	34	55	103	57	249	43
Retailing	16	36	74	71	197	7
Dormitory	156	133	53	62	404	0
Specialized: total	20	29	38	35	122	9
Wholesaling	5	2	5	6	18	0
Services	0	0	2	3	5	0
Mining	0	3	4	3	10	2
Transportation	1	1	2	2	6	0
Resort	0	0	1	2	3	2
Government	1	1	4	2	8	1
Armed Forces	7	2	6	4	19	2
Professional	0	0	0	2	2	0
Hospital	0	1	0	0	1	0
Education	6	19	14	11	50	2
Total	560	547	453	289	1,849	226

[1] Regions are defined as follows:
Northeast: Connecticut, Maine, Massachusetts, New Hampshire, New Jersey, New York, Pennsylvania, Rhode Island, Vermont.
North Central: Illinois, Indiana, Iowa, Kansas, Michigan, Minnesota, Missouri, Ohio, Nebraska, North Dakota, South Dakota, Wisconsin.
South: Alabama, Arkansas, Delaware, District of Columbia, Florida, Georgia, Kentucky, Louisiana, Maryland, Mississippi, North Carolina, Oklahoma, South Carolina, Tennessee, Texas, Virginia, West Virginia.
West: Alaska, Arizona, California, Colorado, Hawaii, Idaho, Montana, New Mexico, Nevada, Oregon, Utah, Washington, Wyoming.
Source: ICMA, "The Municipal Year Book, 1967" (Chicago, Illinois, 1967), p. 40.

500,000 population bracket. Retailing cities, the fifth largest class, are concentrated in less industrialized regions and include smaller municipalities. The 404 dormitory cities, the second largest, are made up largely of suburban communities in which local employment is subordinate to commuting. Most of these are small with only 53 numbering over 50,000 in population.

The ten categories making up the specialized cities totaled about 7 percent of the cities classified. The three largest clusters in this special group are the college towns—totaling 50; the wholesaling cities—numbering 18; and the armed forces communities (19). It should be noted, however, that 54 other cities had armed forces residents constituting more than 20 percent of the working force.

The ICMA study also reveals important differences in the regional distribution of the different functional types. Eighty percent of the manufacturing cities are in the Northeast or North Central regions, accounting for 44 percent and 37 percent of their respective totals. Similarly, more than three-quarters of the industrial cities are found in these two regions. On the other hand, manufacturing and industrial cities combined account for only 22 percent of the cities in the South and only 13 percent in the West. Cities in the diversified-manufacturing category are more evenly distributed among the regions, accounting for 9 to 12 percent of those in three of the regions and 19 percent of all cities in the South.

Few cities in the diversified-retailing and retailing categories are found in areas where manufacturing and industrial centers are common. On the other hand, thirty-eight percent of all the cities in the South and 44 percent of those in the West were in these two categories. In both cases, they form the most important single functioning grouping.

Dormitory cities were most common in the Northeast and North Central regions, constituting 28 percent and 22 percent of the respective totals. Such communities comprised a much smaller proportion of Southern and Western cities.

Specialized cities are somewhat more common in the West (12 percent of all cities) and the South (8 percent), than in the Northeast (4 percent) or North Central regions (5 percent.) Cities in the education subcategory are most frequent in the North Central division and, surprisingly, more armed forces communities are found in the Northeast than in any other region. The frequency distribution of cities in the other *specialized* categories reveals no particular regional pattern.

Of the 226 SMSA's shown in Table 1–5, nearly half (46 percent) are classified as manufacturing or industrial. A little over one-fourth (27 percent) are in diversified-manufacturing and slightly less than one-fifth (19 percent) in diversified-retailing. Only 3 percent are in retailing, while the specialized categories account for only 4 percent of the metropolitan areas surveyed.

In general, the economic classification of SMSA's parallels that of cities of 100,000 or more. Two qualifications should be noted however: more SMSA's fall in the manufacturing category than large cities per se, and somewhat fewer in the diversified-manu-facturing group.

The sharply contrasting regional patterns of the manufacturing, industrial, and dormitory functional types prompted Rand McNally researchers to explore the regional and subregional variations in greater depth.[4] They found that the dominant region for manu-facturing, industrial, and dormitory cities is a manufacturing belt, comprising the Northeast and Great Lakes States, plus Minnesota, Iowa, St. Louis and suburbs in Missouri, Kentucky, West Virginia,

4. *Ibid.*, pp. 41–42.

Maryland, Delaware, and the District of Columbia. Involving more than the Northeast and North Central regions as defined by the Census, this area includes 512 (80 percent) of all manufacturing or industrial cities, and 289 or 72 percent, of all dormitory cities. Manufacturing or industrial cities comprise 65 percent of all cities in this northern crescent, when dormitory cities are excluded. This high proportion is maintained in nearly all sections of the region, though transition areas in which manufacturing-industrial cities are not as common appear on the western edge (southern Illinois, Iowa), the southern rim (Kentucky, West Virginia, Maryland), and in areas of the Northeast (upstate New York).

The southeastern section of Virginia, the Carolinas, Georgia, Alabama, and Tennessee has 67 manufacturing or industrial cities, or close to half of the nondormitory cities surveyed in this special analysis. Dormitory cities, in contrast, number only 15. This region then has many highly industrialized small cities, but few large metropolitan complexes and few large incorporated suburbs. Dormitory suburbs are relatively uncommon.

With only one manufacturing city, Florida has a lower percentage for this category than any other State east of the Mississippi. Seven of its 49 cities, however, are classed as dormitory in basic function. While highly urbanized, industrial development clearly is much less prominent in Florida than resort, commercial, and defense activities.

The South Central region, comprising Mississippi, Missouri (except for metropolitan St. Louis) Arkansas, Louisiana, Kansas, Oklahoma and Texas, has only a little over 10 percent of its cities in the manufacturing or industrial categories. The diversified-retailing city is typical for this region. As in the Southeast, large suburbs are not common, though some (14) have developed in the area's large and rapidly-growing metropolitan complexes.

The Northern Great Plains (including Nebraska) and the Mountain States (except for Nevada) comprise a vast region for 10 States. Not one of the 97 cities over 10,000 in this combined area falls in the manufacturing or industrial group, however. Urban centers in this area are usually regional trading centers having little manufacturing. Its six dormitory cities are adjacent to a few of the major metropolitan centers.

The Pacific Coast, including Nevada's few cities, has 49 of its 218 cities in the manufacturing-industrial categories. But a marked contrast emerges between the Los Angeles-San Francisco Bay metropolitan areas and the rest of the region. In these two major metropolitan areas, the proportion of manufacturing-industrial cities amounted to 43 percent, comparable to that in the Southeast. Like other metropolitan areas across the country, a high proportion (40 percent) of all cities within the two areas fall in the dormitory class. This reflects the restrictive annexation laws in California and concomitant fragmentation of local government. In the remainder of the Pacific region, there are only seven manufacturing or industrial cities, a lower proportion than for any other area, save for Florida and the Plains-Mountain group.

To sum up, manufacturing is the dominant economic activity of a high proportion of individual cities in the Northeast and Midwest. A moderate concentration of manufacturing-oriented communities is found in the Southeast and in the Los Angeles and San Francisco urban areas on the West Coast. Few are found in the rest of the country, with almost none in Florida, the Great Plains, and the Mountain region.

The ICMA analysis also disclosed significant variations in city-size for the various economic types.[5] Diversified-manufacturing cities tend to be very large, with nearly half of the cities over 250,000 assigned to this category. Only 21 percent in the 100,000 to 250,000 bracket and 15 percent in the 50,000 to 100,000 class have this functional designation. Large cities then rarely get that way without substantial manufacturing. Witness the fact that only one *retailing* city had a population over 250,000. Large cities also "tend toward an approximate balance between the various economic activities—a balance less likely to be found among smaller cities."[6] Middle-size cities (50,000 to 250,000) on the other hand, account for a greater share (about 37 percent) of the *manufacturing* category. Only 30 percent of those below 50,000 fall in this functional class and 28 percent in the over 250,000 bracket.

On the basis of these various findings, it appear that cities with significant manufacturing activities combined with a balanced blend of other economic pursuits tend to be large. Cities dominated by manufacturing tend to be medium-sized. Cities serving as local retailing or specialized centers, with little to moderate industry, tend to be small as do cities that serve as dormitory communities.

Finally, in terms of the location of these functional types in the intricate mosaic of urban America, central cities—as might be expected—are far more likely to be of the diversified-manufacturing type (and rarely retailing), than suburbs or separate "urban places." Manufacturing as such is found commonly in all three urban categories. Diversified-retailing, retailing, and specialized activities

5. *Ibid.*, p. 42.
6. *Ibid.*

tend to be more characteristic of the independent urban centers ("nonmetropolitan urban places"), while the dormitory function, not surprisingly, falls heavily to the suburban group.

The problem of sprawl

The earlier analysis of central cities, suburbs, "metropolitan remainders," and "nonmetropolitan urban places" (along with annexations) at least suggests that the process of urbanization does not always produce a painless, planned, and productive land use pattern on the urban perimeter.

The term "sprawl" is frequently used to describe much of the land development now taking place at the periphery of expanding urban areas. This pattern is characterized by substantial bypassed tracts of raw land between developing areas and a scattering of urban development over the rural landscape. As Jean Gottman put it: "Where two cities are close together the intervening rural space becomes covered with new developments. This kind of leapfrogging sprawl outflanks some farms while it covers others."[7]

Sprawl may occur with three types of physical development.[8] It may result from a very low density development of a large area, where single family homes are built on lots of two to five acres, or more. This low density sprawl consumes large amounts of land that some argue should be developed at higher density ratios. A second form results from more intensive development extending out from built-up areas along major highway routes. Space between the strip development is underdeveloped and public service costs usually are more expensive to provide in strip sprawl than in low density urban sprawl. Finally, sprawl also is characterized by leapfrog developments where relatively compact urbanization takes place, but surrounded by substantial undeveloped land. Such development usually requires the greatest initial capital expenditures for urban services.

Sprawl is not a static phenomenon. Each year approximately 400 to 500 thousand acres, most of which are in the outskirts of metropolitan areas, are withdrawn for urban land uses.[9] While this land consumption is only roughly 0.034 percent of the total area of the continental United States, unplanned development, scattered in

7. Jean Gottman, Megalopolis, *The Urbanized Northeastern Seaboard of the United States* (New York, New York: The 20th Century Fund, 1961), p. 247.

8. Robert O. Harvey and W. A. V. Clark, "The Nature and Economics of Urban Sprawl," *Land Economics* (February, 1965), p. 2.

9. Based on H. Landsberg, L. L. Fischman, and Jos. L. Fisher, *Resources in America's Future*, published for Resources for the Future (Baltimore, Maryland: The Johns Hopkins Press, 1963), Table 18–14, p. 371.

random and leapfrogging fashion over the countryside, destroys natural open space needed for the growing demand for recreation and other purposes. Furthermore, it spirals public service costs for sewer and water lines and school bus transportation, and frequently destroys any possibility for an efficient and economic mass transit system. Marion Clawson has succinctly summarized the case against sprawl:[10]

(1) A sprawled or discontinuous urban development is more costly and less efficient than a compact one. . . . (2) Sprawl is unesthetic and unattractive. (3) Sprawl is wasteful of land since the intervening land is not specifically used for any purpose. (4) Land speculation is unproductive, absorbing capital, manpower and entrepreneur skills without commensurate public gains. . . . (5) It is inequitable to allow a system in which the new land occupier is required to shoulder such a heavy burden of capital charges or debt merely for site costs —costs which in large part are unnecessary and avoidable.

Other writers, however, point out that sprawl is a form of normal growth that occurs at a particular point in time. Such scatterization, they argue, actually may provide flexibility in urban development and encourage efficient adaptation to change. Uniform compactness of development "should no longer . . . (be) . . . accepted unquestioningly as a planning ideal, and scatter . . . no longer categorically rejected as a device of the devil."[11]

Robert O. Harvey and W. A. V. Clark suggest that another important characteristic of sprawl—the choice of different housing opportunities relative to other alternatives—must be considered, notwithstanding its alleged and real costs.[12]

Sprawl, by any definition, refers to settled areas no matter what their characteristics may be. Accordingly, at the time the sprawl occurred, the cost was not prohibitive to the settler. It provided a housing opportunity economically satisfactory relative to other alternatives. If sprawl were in fact economically unsound, it would occur only by the action of housing seekers artificially restricted from free compacted markets, but who could and would pay a premium for freedom to be found only in the sprawl. Sprawl occurs, in fact, because it is economic in terms of the alternatives available to the occupants.

The fact that a number of public services may be lacking, or that the journey to work has been lengthened is apparently of little concern to most of us. As Raymond Vernon observes:[13]

10. Marion Clawson, "Urban Sprawl and Speculation in Suburban Land," *Land Economics* (May, 1962), pp. 99–111.
11. Jack Lessinger, "The Case for Scatterization: Some Reflections on the National Capital Regional Plan for the Year 2000," *Journal of the American Institute of Planners* (August, 1962), p. 159.
12. Harvey and Clark, *op. cit.*, pp. 8–9.
13. Raymond Vernon, *The Myths and Reality of Our Urban Problems* (Cambridge, Massachusetts: Joint Center for Urban Studies, 1962), p. 1.

. . . for all the course of protests, however, most Americans seem strangely unaroused. Each year they buy a few hundred thousand picture windows, feed a few hundred thousand more lawns. The decay of the central city barely concerns them; the cries of strangling congestion stirs them only briefly; even the issue of mounting taxes, an exposed nerve in the structure of local politics, does not seem to have the capacity to bring them shouting into the streets. . . . The striking disparity between the literature of protests and the lethargy of the citizen is a riddle which demands an answer. What I shall contend in substance is that the clear majority of Americans who live in urban areas look on their lifetime experience as one of progress and improvement not as retrogression; that they see their lot as being better than that of their parents and confidently expect the children to do a little better still.

Nevertheless, increasing population pressure has been and is spoiling the dream. Some suburban communities have reacted by adoption of insular policies. To stem population growth these communities have adopted land use controls that, in effect, build fences around the large central cities. Some suburban zoning practices have tended to bar lower cost housing by increasing residential minimum lot sizes to the point where only upper middle income families can afford the houses built on them. Such policies tend to produce fiscal disparities among local jurisdictions in metropolitan areas. No fiscal prognosis of suburban areas is valid, however, that lumps together all suburban jurisdictions. Anyone familiar with the fiscal landscape of suburbia is keenly aware of the fact that it does not present a uniform picture of affluence. On the contrary, suburbia fairly bristles with contrasts between rich, poor, and balanced jurisdictions;[14] although it is true that suburbia contains much of the wealth and income of the nation.

The battle against sprawl has been joined in a few communities across the country. These jurisdictions offer a method or strategy of attack. Some suburban localities have adopted cluster-zoning techniques to preserve open space for the community and to cut costs for the homeowner and builder. Others have adopted planned-community zoning techniques to permit a mixture of residential uses and also to allow commercial and even industrial uses on the same tract. Privately developed new communities such as Reston, Virginia, and Columbia, Maryland, also are advanced as an alternative to sprawl.

Another approach is directed toward reforming the real estate tax which presently and generally under-assesses vacant land, encouraging speculation. Proposals for tax reform are many and varied, but most focus on the market mechanism and seek to make private building decisions work for orderly planning and development.

14. *Fiscal Balance in the American Federal System, op. cit.*

Whatever course is chosen to encourage better urban land development and to discourage further sprawl, two factors having significant bearing on future urbanization policy should be recognized.[15]

(1) The present pattern of land use development results from the individual action of many decisionmakers—consumers, builders, landowners, developers, financial institutions, industry, commerce, and public agencies. If the urbanization process is to be structured in ways different from the past, the perceptions and expectations of each factor will have to be affected, if not changed.

(2) Public bodies have a residue of as yet unutilized powers to influence the growth and structure of an area. Programing and development of public facilities creates an envelope within which urbanization takes place. The timing, location, and scope of public investment decisions influence, if not shape, the physical form of the region.

Urban projections

Population projections for the United States anticipate an increase of approximately 83 percent by the end of the century. According to one study, by the year 2000 the total U.S. population is expected to reach 314 million persons.[16] This increase will be sustained largely by natural increases with only one-tenth to one-eighth of the net national population growth coming from immigration. In terms of race, the nonwhite population will increase by 123 percent, the white by 67 percent. The total white population is projected to drop from 89 percent to 85 percent of the total population in 2000 while the nonwhite will increase from 12 percent to 15 percent.

As shown in Table 1–6 this population growth will continue to be almost wholly urban, as it has for the past two decades. The rural population will account for only 15 percent of the total population or approximately 48 million. Although net migration will continue to swell the ranks of people in urban and metropolitan areas, current and future growth will largely come from the natural increase of people living in these areas. In other words, the country's metropolitan areas already contain a built-in factor to sustain great future growth.

Present projections for individual metropolitan and urbanized areas suggest that a major share of all national population growth will fall to the largest urban areas.[17] Projected data for separate areas indicate that 27 urbanized areas will hike their population by over

15. Marshall Kaplan, *Implementation of the Baltimore Regional Plan Alternative* (Baltimore, Maryland: Regional Planning Council, 1965), p. 10.

16. Jerome P. Pickard, *Analysis of Past and Future U.S. Population Growth Trends with Emphasis on Urban and Metropolitan Population*, processed (September–October, 1967).

17. *Ibid.*

Table 1-6—Past and Projected Population, United States, Urban and Rural, by Color, 1950–2000

| | Population in thousands | | | Percent | |
	TOTAL	*WHITE*	*NONWHITE*	*WHITE*	*NONWHITE*
1950 Census	151,326	135,150	16,176	89.3	10.7
Urban	96,847	86,864	9,983	89.7	10.3
Rural	54,479	48,286	6,193	88.6	11.4
Percent urban	(64.0)	(64.3)	(61.7)	—	—
1960 Census	179,323	158,832	20,491	88.6	11.4
Urban	125,269	110,428	14,840	88.1	11.9
Rural	54,054	48,403	5,651	89.5	10.5
Percent urban	(69.9)	(69.5)	(72.4)	—	—
1967 estimate	197,900	174,000	23,900	87.9	12.1
Urban	144,000	125,800	18,200	87.4	12.6
Rural	53,900	48,200	5,700	89.4	10.6
Percent urban	(73.0)	(72.0)	(76.0)	—	—
2000 projection	314,000	267,000	47,000	85.0	15.0
Urban	266,000	223,000	43,000	83.8	16.2
Rural	48,000	44,000	4,000	91.7	8.3
Percent urban	(85.0)	(83.5)	(91.5)	—	—

Sources: U.S. Bureau of the Census. U.S. Census of Population: 1960. General Population Characteristics, United States Summary, Final Report PC(1)-1B. (Washington: Government Printing Office, 1961.) Table 43. 1967 estimate from U.S. Bureau of Census publication P-25, No. 381 and 384. Year 2000 estimate from aggregated data in Jerome P. Pickard "Dimensions of Metropolitanism," Urban Land Institute Research Monograph: 14 (Washington, D.C. 1967).

65 million during the remainder of the century and thereby be responsible for more than three-fifths of the net national increase. These 27 include all of the 18 largest future metropolitan centers (each with a population of two and one-half million or more by 2000) along with nine other areas that are presently projected to have population gains of 750,000 or more.

In terms of regional focus, the South and West will benefit most from this growth and with the establishment of new metropolitan areas. The older metropolitan belt stretching from the northeast to the upper Mississippi will experience less dynamic urban growth. This futuristic treatment of metropolitan areas should not obscure the estimate that a sizeable urban population will reside outside of metropolitan concentrations of more than 100,000 persons—approximately 12 percent of the total in year 2000.

Finally, some forecasters see in this future urbanization pattern a tendency toward megalopolitan concentrations. Before describing these estimates, however, it should be noted that these projections are based on the continuance of certain existing trends; they tend to ignore other existing trends, notably in the South (outside of Florida) and the Southwest. *Most important, for purposes of this Report, they presume the maintenance of a basically laissez-faire role by government and industry with respect to future urban growth patterns.*

According to Urban Land Institute projections, 131 million people, 55 percent of the U.S. population, will live in four great urban regions by 1980 and, by 2000, over 187 million or 60 percent of the country's population.[18] These four major urban regions, it is estimated, will absorb most of the population growth from the present to year 2000.

The largest region will be a 500 mile corridor containing 67.9 million people along the Atlantic Seaboard, stretching from Boston to Washington, D.C. The second chain of cities extending nearly one thousand miles from Utica, New York, west to Chicago and north along the western shore of Lake Michigan to Green Bay, Wisconsin, will contain 60.8 million people. Linked with the East Coast megalopolis, this will form a Metropolitan Belt—a super-megalopolis of 128.7 million people. A Pacific Coast complex will consist of 44.5 million people, located along a 500 mile distance between San Francisco through Los Angeles to San Diego. Finally, the fourth major urban region will be comprised of 13.8 million people all within Florida. This belt of urban cities will extend 350 miles along the Atlantic coast between Jacksonville and Miami and will move westward across the Florida Peninsula to the Tampa-St. Petersburg metropolitan areas.

Another 52 million people will be living in 14 smaller urban regions and five metropolitan areas, according to Urban Land Institute projections. These smaller urban regions added to the four great regions will total 241 million persons or 77 percent of the population. These regions will occupy 11 percent of the nation's land* which is likely to be 30 times more densely populated than small town and rural areas.

THE DYNAMICS OF MOBILITY AND MIGRATION

The evolving drama of American urbanization—indeed the very settlement of the continent itself—has been critically influenced and enriched by developments relating to mobility and migration. *Contrary to popular impression, the proportion of Americans who moved from their state of birth during the decade 1950–1960 was not greater than ever before.* The census figures for more than a century indicate only slight shifts over each decade in the percentage of persons living in a State other than that of their birth:[19]

18. Jerome P. Pickard, *Dimensions of Metropolitanism*, Urban Land Institute Research Monograph 14 (Washington, D.C.: 1967), p. 23.
   * Excluding Alaska and Hawaii.
19. Ben J. Wattenberg and Richard M. Scammon, *This U.S.A.* (New York, New York: Pocket Books, 1960), p. 136.

	Percent		Percent
1850–1860	11	1910–1920	7
1860–1870	8	1920–1930	7
1870–1880	7	1930–1940	4
1880–1890	6	1940–1950	9
1890–1900	7	1950–1960	9
1900–1910	7		

Recent decennial interstate migration figures are slightly higher than they were during the period of 1860–1940 but do not match pre-Civil War levels. The dip in the rate of movement during the Depression years probably can be attributed to the fact that many persons had no money to move and, more important, no place to move to with any hope of better employment opportunities. The decade beginning with World War II, however, began a mobility trend which continued up to the last census.

The interstate figures conceal the full extent of migration, however. If all the moves made from year to year are considered, we find recently that for *each year one in every five Americans shifts his place of residence*. These moves can be classified on a distance scale beginning with those within a county over to those between non-contiguous States. Intracounty moves usually involve a change of residence within commuting distance of a given job. Intercounty shifts outside of metropolitan areas however usually involve a change to a new job. This type of move is defined by the Bureau of the Census as migration and is described as an intra-State movement. Moves between States are of two different kinds—those where migrants move to contiguous States and those where relatively long distances are travelled—between noncontiguous States. However, with growth of interstate metropolitan areas, even some of this interstate movement loses its significance.

The recent record reveals a surprising stability in the rates for various types of movement. Figure 1–2 depicts this record for the past 18 consecutive years for which the relevant data have been collected. It shows that about two-thirds of the moves are within the same county; less than one-sixth are to another county in the same State; and less than one-sixth are to another State. Mobility, then, is mostly short distance movement, but the short distance from a core city across the line to a suburb can be a light year in terms of political, fiscal and social significance.

Patterns of movement

The census data from the annual surveys show a consistent pattern

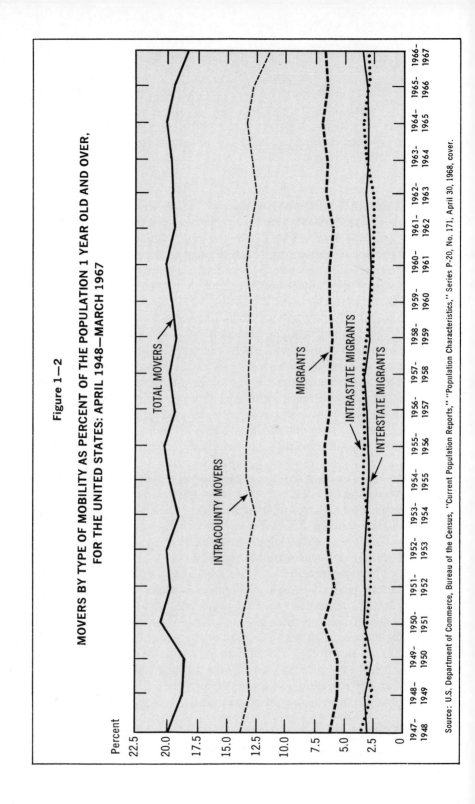

Figure 1–2

MOVERS BY TYPE OF MOBILITY AS PERCENT OF THE POPULATION 1 YEAR OLD AND OVER, FOR THE UNITED STATES: APRIL 1948–MARCH 1967

Source: U.S. Department of Commerce, Bureau of the Census, "Current Population Reports," "Population Characteristics," Series P-20, No. 171, April 30, 1968, cover.

of net migration into the West. In recent years, however, there appears to be some evidence that this has declined in volume. For the period between 1964 and 1966, net migration figures for the West indicate an annual average of about 150,000 as compared with a yearly figure of about 500,000 for the 1960 to 1964 period.[20] The overall mobility rate, however, was still higher in the West than in the South, Midwest, and Northeast regions.

The annual surveys show men to be slightly more mobile than women and nonwhites to be more mobile than whites. Yet, the migration rate—that is, the rate for longer distance moves—is higher for the white population. The relatively high migration rate for white persons completing one or more years of college and for professional workers suggests some relationship between higher socio-economic status and migration. On the other hand, unemployed men also had a relatively high rate of migration.

In terms of age groups, young adults (18–34 years) have a much higher total mobility rate than persons 35 years or older. Surveys for 1964–1966 show that young adults have a mobility rate of 34 percent as compared with 12 percent for the older group. Young adults also move greater distances than their seniors. With reference to racial groups, the total mobility rate for the four year period for nonwhite population was 24 percent and for the white population, 19 percent. The higher rate for Negroes, however, was largely a matter of local moves with 82 percent of the nonwhite migrants making intracounty shifts in contrast to only 64 percent of the white movers. Yet, those nonwhites who moved between noncontiguous States tended to move greater distances than their white counterparts—reflecting the continuing migration of nonwhites from the South to northern and western urban centers.

The 1960 Census data show that slightly more than 25 percent of the native population have moved from one State to another at least once in their lifetime[21] (as opposed to 9 percent who moved to another State during the 1950–1960 decade). The former figure includes children too young to have moved frequently. Overall, there has been remarkably little long-term change in *lifetime* migration as gauged by Census. In 1850, the lifetime movement patterns of native born Americans indicated that 76 percent resided in the State of their birth. The 1960 figure was only 1.5 percentage points smaller.

20. U.S. Department of Commerce, Bureau of the Census, Bureau of Labor Statistics, *Population Characteristics*, Current Population Report, Series P-20, No. 156 (December 9, 1966).

21. *Social Security Bulletin*, "Geographic Labor Mobility in the United States: Recent Findings," Vol. 30, No. 3 (March, 1967), p. 15.

The lifetime mobility of persons moving from one labor market to another, of course, is much higher and is probably greater than that for the last century—although the comparable data are nonexistent. Nearly seven out of ten family heads are now living in a labor-market area other than the one in which they were born, according to the University of Michigan Survey Research Center.[22] Yet only 21 percent of these household heads were living 1,000 miles or more from their place of birth. The Survey Research Center found that 20 percent of all moves were returns to a place where the family had once lived, including 9 percent to their place of birth. Survey respondents were asked whether they would stay in their present locale or move away, if they had the choice. Twenty percent indicated they wanted to move, and about half said they actually expected to in the following year. Those who actually moved, however, totaled only 5 percent.

Migration and urban concentration

Urban populations are transformed by two means: natural change and net (in or out) migration. Natural increases, as Table 1–7

Table 1-7—Components of Population Change, Metropolitan Area, 1960–1965

[All population data in thousands]

Area[1]	July 1, 1965 population	1960–65 total population change	Natural increase	Net migration	Net migration as percent of growth
All metropolitan areas,[2] total	129,993	+11,025	+8,589	+2,436	22
11 largest growth areas	51,353	+5,092	+3,142	+1,950	38
14 intermediate growth areas	17,555	+1,805	+1,222	+583	32
23 medium growth areas	17,684	+1,669	+1,259	+410	25
48 growth areas, subtotal	86,592	+8,566	+5,623	+2,943	34
11 largest slow growth areas, subtotal	10,437	+276	+597	−321	−54
141 smaller growth[3] or decline areas, subtotal	32,964	+2,183	+2,369	−186	−8

[1] Definitions: Largest Growth Areas: Metropolitan areas (or consolidated metropolitan areas) with population increase of 200,000 or more in the 1960–65 period; Intermediate Growth Areas: Population increase 100,000 to 199,000; Medium Growth Areas: Population increase 50,000 to 99,000. The largest slow growth areas are based on population size and represent the 11 largest metropolitan areas in 1965 population which had population growth less than 50,000 or declined in population: Pittsburgh, Buffalo, Milwaukee, Louisville, Providence, New Haven–Waterbury–Meriden, Albany–Schenectady–Troy, Toledo, Akron, Birmingham, and Worcester.

[2] All metropolitan and metropolitan county areas, including Middlesex and Somerset Counties, New Jersey, as defined to the end of 1966.

[3] Rochester, New York includes only Monroe County. The other three metropolitan area counties are included in the smaller growth areas.

Source: Jerome P. Pickard, "Analysis of Past and Future U.S. Population Growth Trends with Emphasis on Urban and Metropolitan Population," October 1967, Mimeo.

22. *Ibid.*, p. 17.

indicates, accounted for more than three quarters (78 percent) of metropolitan population growth during the period 1960–1965, while net migration accounted for 22 percent of the aggregate net growth. The proportions differ significantly with the 65 percent–35 percent breakdown for the preceding, 1950–1960 decade. The growing significance of the natural increase component can be explained in terms of the larger total part of the population that the metropolitan sector is assuming. Moreover, as we move through the final third of the century, this trend will accelerate, unless there is a dramatic shift to net out-migration from metropolitan areas.

During the five years 1960–65, the largest metropolitan growth areas (as defined by Jerome Pickard) steadily had net migration rates above the average for all other areas. The big eleven had population increases ranging from a low of 205,000 for Dallas to over 1.1 million for Los Angeles–Orange County and of the total increase of 5.1 million a little less than two-fifths (38 percent) resulted from net in-migration gains. It should be noted that these figures resulted, despite the fact that two of these areas—Detroit and Chicago— experienced out-migration losses of 55,000 and 3,000 respectively during this period. All told, the nine other areas* accounted for over four-fifths (81 percent) of all net migration during 1960–1965 to all metropolitan areas. Since these nine were the same areas that had the largest population growth during the 1950–1960 period, it seems clear that dynamic population growth and heavy in-migration are closely related.

Population gains for the 14 "intermediate" and 23 "medium" growth areas also benefited from net migration (32 percent and 25 percent of growth respectively), but obviously not to the extent of the fastest growing. The 11 "largest slow growth areas" and the 151 in the "smaller growth or decline" category, however, suffered net migration losses (54 percent and 8 percent of growth respectively) for the five-year period.

Detailed analysis of all the metropolitan areas experiencing a population gain of 50,000 or more during the years 1960–1965 reveals a varying migration pattern. Yet, certain trends stand out:

> In-migration accounted for a smaller proportion of the growth in metropolitan areas in the Northeast and Great Lakes areas. Only six of the 25 largest and intermediate growth areas were in these regions and of these only the New York–Northeastern New

* Los Angeles–Orange County; New York–northeast New Jersey; San Francisco–Oakland–San Jose; Washington, D.C.; Philadelphia; Houston; Miami–Fort Lauderdale; San Bernardino–Riverside; Dallas.

Jersey and Philadelphia areas benefited moderately from in-migration—with net migration ratios of 26 percent and 19 percent of total population growth respectively. Ten of the 23 "medium growth areas" were located in these two geographic divisions and five of these had modest migration ratios (20 percent of growth or more).

The overall population gains for 28 metropolitan areas, located in the South, Southwest, Mountain States, and Pacific Coast, came to 4.7 million or 43 percent of all metropolitan growth for the five-year period. This gain for these 28 also accounted for 55 percent of the total for the three high growth categories. Two and four-tenths million—or 51 percent—of the 4.7 million was derived from net migration gains. Moreover, as a proportion of the net migration total for the 48 high growth areas, this 2.4 million represents 81 percent and with reference to all net migrations to all metropolitan areas, it represents more than 99 percent. Finally, all but three of the four regions' 16 areas in the largest and intermediate growth categories had net migration ratios of 50 percent of growth or more.

The large metropolitan areas in three States—Florida, Texas and California—generally had very high net migration percent-ages for the 1960–65 period. Eleven areas, located in these States were among the 25 in the "largest" and "intermediate growth" categories; of these, only one (San Diego) had a ratio of net migration to total population growth of less than 50 percent. Of the four from these States in the "medium growth" bracket, two surpassed the 50 percent mark, but two fell below it (Orlando—48 percent and San Antonio—17 percent).

Only three other large growth centers (in the largest and inter-mediate groupings) had high (50 percent or more) net migration ratios: Washington, Atlanta, and Phoenix. And only one other in the "medium growth" bracket had a comparable net migra-tion proportion: Huntsville, Alabama. . . .

URBAN-RURAL CONTRASTS

The rural exodus

A major dimension of urbanization involves the tremendous changes in rural America. The heavy out-migration from the farms as a place of living and working is well known. In 1790, 95 percent of the population lived in rural areas; by 1860, the proportion had dropped to 80 per cent; and by 1900 to 60 percent. The first census showing the country had become predominantly urban was in 1920 when the urban population numbered 54.1 million as compared with 51.5 million rural (49 per cent). In absolute terms, however, the rural population grew steadily from 3.7 million in 1790 to a 61.1 million in 1950, using the old definition of urban, or 54.4 million, using the current one. Today less than 30 percent of us live in rural areas (using the current definition) and less than one-fourth of these 54 million rural residents live on farms and earn their livelihood from agriculture. In short, despite significant shifts within the rural population, this sector today has tended to stabilize slightly below the 1950 figure.

From 1920 to 1940 the urban population increased by 38 percent, while rural residents increased only by 11 percent. The nonfarm rural rate of growth was nearly as high as the urban. Only a slight decline in the number of rural farm people occurred, since the Depression retarded off-farm migration.[23] During World War II and the years immediately following, urban growth more than doubled its previous level, while the overall rural population increased by 3.7 million. From the 1940 level of 30.2 million, the farm population was down to 23 million by 1950. On the other hand, the nonfarm population, most of whom have little or no connection with agriculture, increased their share of the rural total by more than 10 percent during the decade—to reach the 60 percent level. In the 1950's, the urban rate of growth reached high levels while the rural population declined by a half million (using the new definition of urban), despite the continued substantial growth of the nonfarm rural sector.

Fully accurate comparisons with earlier data are difficult to make because of the radical change in the definition of the farm residents used in the 1960 census, which enumerated 15.6 million rural (farm) residents, or about one-third less than the 1950 figure.* In 1966, it was estimated that there were 11.6 million farm residents —a further decline caused by technological changes in agriculture, nonfarm employment, and other factors producing out-migration.

The substantial growth in urban population, however, does not mean that vast areas of the country are being bulldozed over with housing tracts and highways. The greater part of the densely developed northeastern seaboard, for example—a stretch from

---

23. *Rural People in the American Economy, op. cit.*, p. 32.

* In 1960, farm residents were determined by using a definition based on criteria of land acreage and value of agricultural products sold. Formerly, farm residents were determined on the basis of the respondent's opinion as to whether his house is on a farm or ranch. The figure of 15.6 million is the annual average from 1960 derived from the Current Population Survey of the Bureau of the Census. The enumerated farm population in the 1960 census was 13.5 million.

southern New Hampshire to northern Virginia—is not urban in actual land use. There are more "wide open spaces" in America today than at any time since the closing of the frontier in the late 19th Century.[24] More land today is classified as "forest and woodland, not grazed" than for many years. The agricultural revolution has caused a drop in the population density in rural areas, even as it is rising everywhere else. Moreover, fewer acres are under cultivation today than previously even though farms are getting larger.

When the changes in the number of farm people are viewed in local and regional terms, a picture of even greater fluidity arises. Many rural regions, as well as individual counties, have experienced sharp population losses. From 1950 to 1960 nearly half of the counties in the nation lost population and the overwhelming majority of these were rural in character. As Figure 1–3 indicates, regions of heavy decline included the interior coastal plain of the lower south from Georgia through Texas and the continuous area of the Great Plains. The Allegheny Plateau, much of the Ozarks, and other upland country of Arkansas, Oklahoma and Missouri also dropped in rural population in the 1950's. Finally, the marginal corn belt areas of Iowa and Missouri had rural losses of up to 10 percent.

At the same time, there were areas of sizeable rural increase. Many of these grew from net migration as well as from natural increase. Increases in rural populations in the 1950's were found in state economic areas of Florida, California and Nevada and in many of the outlying areas of large industrial centers of the lower Great Lakes and Atlantic seaboard. Nevertheless, many of these areas showing a rural growth had large farm population reductions. Agriculture is not the major rural activity in these areas and only the increase in nonfarm rural people offsets farm losses. The revival of rural growth in these areas generally is not associated with the traditional rural primary industries, but with manufacturing and commuting to urban employment.

The net migration from the farms has produced many problems of both rural and urban adjustment in recent years. For example, the rural population has a larger proportion of children under 15 (33.4 percent of the rural population) than the urban population (30.1 percent of the urban population), as well as a higher proportion of those in the 15 to 19 year bracket. Yet, there is a relative shortage of persons in the 20 to 64 year age group as a result of migration from rural areas. This is particularly acute in the most mobile age group, those in the 20–44 category. Rural persons 65 years old and over comprise only a slightly larger proportion of this population

24. *Ibid.*, p. 8.

Figure 1—3

RURAL POPULATION CHANGE FROM 1950 TO 1960
By State Economic Areas

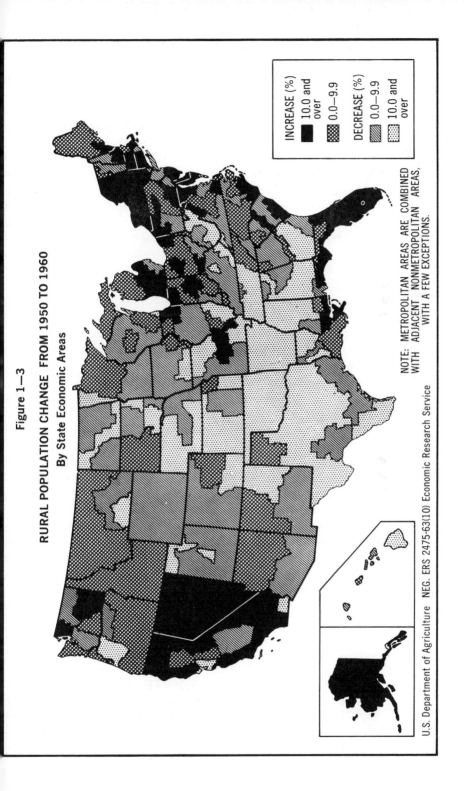

INCREASE (%)
■ 10.0 and over
▨ 0.0—9.9

DECREASE (%)
▨ 0.0—9.9
▨ 10.0 and over

NOTE: METROPOLITAN AREAS ARE COMBINED WITH ADJACENT NONMETROPOLITAN AREAS, WITH A FEW EXCEPTIONS.

U.S. Department of Agriculture   NEG. ERS 2475-63(10) Economic Research Service

than those in urban areas, but the large proportion of children bring the average age of the rural population down to about 3 years less than that of the urban sector. These and other factors combine to produce significant disparities between rural and urban America. . . .

INTRAMETROPOLITAN DIFFERENCES

The preceding treatment of rural–urban contrasts demonstrated that significant disparities exist between the people and communities in these two broad divisions. In population growth, income levels, educational and health facilities, housing, and the incidence of poverty, the rural sector in every instance was in a more disadvantaged position. Yet disparities involve more than urban-rural differences. . . . Within the metropolitan areas of the nation, significant interlocal differences exist and these comprise another dimension of urbanization that merits recapitulation here.

The major findings relating to metropolitan disparities as they emerge from the Commission's study of *Fiscal Balance in the American Federal System* are as follows:[25]

The central cities, particularly those located in the industrial Northeast and Midwest, are in the throes of a deepening fiscal crisis. On the one hand, they are confronted with the need to satisfy rapidly growing expenditure requirements triggered by the rising number of "high cost" citizens. On the other hand, their tax resources are increasing at a decreasing rate (and in some cases actually declining), a reflection of the exodus of middle and high income families and business firms from the central city to suburbia.

The concentration of high cost citizens in the central city is dramatically underscored by public welfare statistics. For example, 27 percent of Maryland's population is located in Baltimore, yet 72 percent of Maryland's AFDC expenditures is to be found in that city. In a like fashion, Boston, with 14 percent of Massachusetts' population, accounts for 40 percent of that State's AFDC expenditure.

A clear disparity in tax burden is evident between central city and outside central city. Higher central city taxes are reinforcing the other factors that are pushing upper income families and business firms out of the central city into suburbia.

On the educational front, the central cities are falling farther behind their suburban neighbors with each passing year. In 1957 the per pupil expenditures in the 37 large metropolitan areas,

25. *Fiscal Balance in the American Federal System, op. cit.*

surveyed in depth, favored the central city slightly—$312 to $303 for the suburban jurisdictions. By 1965, the suburban jurisdictions had forged ahead, far ahead—$574 to $449 for the central cities. This growing disparity between the central city and suburban school districts takes on a more ominous character in light of the fact that the central city school districts must carry a disproportionately heavy share of the educational burden—the task of educating an increasing number of "high cost" under-privileged children. Urban children then who need education the most are receiving the least.

To make matters worse, State aid to school districts actually aggravates this situation by favoring the rural and suburban districts.

On the municipal service and custodial front, the presence of "high cost" citizens, greater population density, and the need to service the needs of commuters force central cities to spend far more than most of their suburban neighbors for police and fire protection and sanitation services. The 37 largest central cities had a non-education municipal outlay of $232 per capita in 1965—$100 greater than their suburban counterparts.

While these findings may not be too startling, they clearly reinforce the hunch, held by many, that the public finance-public services outlook for most large central cities is somewhat bleak. Moreover, they tend to demonstrate that core cities and numerous rural jurisdictions have far more in common than first glance would have it. Finally, the root cause of the problems facing both of these widely separated sectors is the same: recent migration, urban growth and technological developments have drained their most productive resources.

SUMMARY OBSERVATIONS

To summarize and highlight this tracing of the American pattern of urbanization, the following findings should be noted:

In recent years, metropolitan areas experienced the greatest population gains. Yet, using either the SMSA or Rand McNally definition, central cities enjoyed some growth in the smaller SMSA's but only minor increases or actual declines (especially when annexations are excluded) in medium, large, and giant metropolitan areas.

Noncentral city areas in metropolitan areas, on the other hand, have had dramatic percentage and absolute increases, especially in the 500,000 plus SMSA categories. The Rand McNally analysis reveals that metropolitan suburbs (incorporated suburbs of 10,000 or more) expanded by 13.9 percent (omitting annexations) compared to a 3.5 percent hike for central cities from 1960–1965; while "metropolitan remainders" experienced the greatest proportionate growth.

Using Rand McNally figures, urban places of 10,000 or more outside of metropolitan areas of 100,000 or more grew at slower rates than metropolitan suburbs and remainders, but faster than central cities; the remaining nonmetropolitan areas (towns below 10,000 in population, rural villages, and farms) had the lowest percentage increase of any of the Rand McNally categories.

The relative growth rates of "Urban Areas" of 20,000 or more clearly recall that the smaller categories (20,000–50,000 and 50,000 to 100,000) fell below the national average for all urban areas between 1960–1965; those for "urban areas" in the medium, large, or giant brackets show a proportionate hike comparable to or greater than the national average, with those in the 500,000 to 1,000,000 class having the most rapid relative increase of all.

In terms of the total urban population increase during the period 1960–1965, the giants in the one million plus category accounted for more than half and those in the 250,000 to 1,000,000 bracket for nearly one-fourth of the total.

Regionally, with the exception of the one million plus group, urban areas with the highest rate of population growth generally were located in a broad geographic crescent beginning in Virginia, swinging through the old South and Southwest on to the West Coast. Urban areas, again except for the one million and over category, having uniformly below national average percentage hikes formed another interregional arc beginning in Maine; extending through Southern New England, the Middle Atlantic States and Great Lakes; and swinging through the Plains States to terminate in North Dakota.

Classification of municipalities according to their basic economic characteristics reveals a high proportion of manufacturing and industrial cities in the Northeast and Great Lakes areas; a moderate concentration of manufacturing-oriented communities in the Southeast and in the Los Angeles-San Francisco urban areas; and almost none of these types in the Prairie States, Mountain Region, and Florida.

In terms of size, cities with significant manufacturing combined with a balanced blend of other economic activities tend to be large; cities with manufacturing primarily, medium sized; and cities serving as local retailing or specialized centers, with little or moderate manufacturing, small.

Migration has been a major factor in the growth of large metropolitan areas, with nine such areas accounting for four-fifths of all net migration to all metropolitan areas during 1960–1965; in regional terms, migration benefited such areas in the Northeast and Great Lakes areas least over this period, while 28 such complexes in the South, Southwest, Mountain States, and Far West accounted for 43 percent of all metropolitan gains and more than half of their growth came from net migration gains (accounting for 99 percent of all net migration to metropolitan areas).

Motivational research suggests that improved economic opportunities are significant in prompting migration, but better education and job skills were common background traits of the migrating unemployed; moreover, while areas of high economic activity attract in-migration, areas of low-level activity do not necessarily encourage gross out-migration at higher rates than for other areas; blue collar workers, the less well educated, many Negroes, and older people do not move to another location simply because of the chance of economic betterment; several factors, largely noneconomic in nature, sustain movement among these groups; the migration from low-level economic areas usually depletes disproportionately the most productive sector of their work force.

One special dimension of urbanization involves the heavy increase in the Negro proportion of the population of central cities in SMSA's—a jump from 12 to 20 percent between 1950–1966; the percentages are much higher for central cities in the 250,000 plus metropolitan area bracket.

Another special dimension of urbanization is the relatively stable level of America's rural population since 1950—yet the farming sector continues to drop, with a particularly sharp loss of 4 million between 1960 and 1966.

Urban-rural comparisons of population growth, educational and health facilities, housing, and income levels suggest major disparities for every index with rural America consistently in the disadvantaged position.

A final distinguishing feature of current urbanization is that within metropolitan areas another set of disparities emerges with central cities confronting much greater public finance-

public service problems than suburbs and metropolitan remainders.

Future projections indicate an urban population increase of
approximately 83 percent by the end of the century; the rural
population will account for only 15 per cent of the 314 million
total and non-whites will increase their share of 15 percent; the
lion's share of the population increase will occur in the largest,
fastest growing urban areas with 27 giants adding over 65 million
to their population (or more than three-fifths of the total); the
regional breakdown suggests that the South and West will
experience the greatest gains.

The valuable inefficiencies and impracticalities of cities[*]

INTRODUCTION

People who think we would be better off without cities, especially without big, unmanageable, disorderly cities, never tire of explaining that cities grown too big are, in any case, inefficient and impractical. Certainly, as we all know, the most routine and ordinary activities— getting people to work, moving goods around, keeping trees alive, making space for school playgrounds, disposing of garbage— absorb ridiculous amounts of energy, time and money in cities, as compared to towns and villages. And it does seem as if big cities are not necessarily efficient for producing goods and services. Factories move to the outskirts and the suburbs, and to small and distant towns, often for reasons of efficiency.

All this is true. Cities are indeed inefficient and impractical compared with towns; and among cities themselves, the largest and most rapidly growing at any given time are apt to be the least efficient. But I propose to show that these grave and real deficiencies are necessary to economic development and thus are exactly what makes cities uniquely valuable to economic life. By this, I do not mean that cities are economically valuable in spite of their ineffici-

* From THE ECONOMY OF CITIES, by Jane Jacobs. © Copyright 1969 by Jane Jacobs. Reprinted by permission of Random House, Inc.

ency and impracticality but rather because they are inefficient and impractical.

Efficiency as it is commonly defined—and I do not propose to change its definition, which is clear and useful—is the ratio of work accomplished to energy supplied. We can speak of high or low rates of efficiency because, in any given instance, we have two relevant factors to measure; input of energy, and quantity and quality (value) of work accomplished. We can compare the measurements in one instance with measurements in other instances.

But these particular measurements are not relevant when development work is wanted. A candy manufacturer, reminiscing to a *New Yorker* reporter about the first candy bar he developed as a shipping clerk in a candy factory, recalls, "I showed it to my boss and he was very happy. 'How many of these can you make in a minute?' he asked me. 'In a *minute?*' I said. 'It took me four months to make this one!'" Suppose it had taken him eight months? Or two months? That measurement has nothing to do with the operating efficiency envisioned by his boss.

EFFICIENCIES IN DEVELOPMENTAL WORK

Efficiency of operation, in any given case, is a sequel to earlier development work. Development work is a messy, time-and-energy-consuming business of trial, error, and failure. The only certainties in it are trial and error. Success is not a certainty. And even when the result is successful, it is often a surprise, not what was actually being sought.

A low rate of efficiency in production work means that the person or organization doing the work is going about it ineptly. But the exorbitant amounts of energy and time and the high rates of failure in the process of developing new work do not mean the development work is being done ineptly. The inefficiency is built into the aim itself; it is inescapable. There is no systematic way to evade it. The president of Du Pont, a company that has tried to systematize its development work to the highest degree possible, has told a *Fortune* reporter that only about one out of 20 of those research projects that the company decides to develop further after initial exploratory work turns out to be useful to the company. The fact that an organization engages in large-scale production, which is what makes a large organization large, and that it produces very efficiently too, does not mean that the efficiency spills over into development work.

Indeed, development work is inherently so chancy that by the law of averages chances of success are greatly improved if there is

much duplication of effort. The U.S. Air Force's analytical organization, the RAND Corporation, having been assigned to study
how waste could be eliminated in the processes of military development work, came to the conclusion that although duplication
of effort was theoretically wasteful, it was not wasteful empirically.
For one thing, the report said, different people brought different
preconceptions to development work and there was no way of
telling in advance which might prove fruitful or where it might lead.
Eminence or reputation or even past success was not a reliable
indicator. The report cited as an illustration the fact that in 1937
when the jet airplane engine had already been developed in Britain,
a committee of distinguished aeronautical experts in the United
States, to whom this event was not yet known, studied the possibilities of jet propulsion, and came to the conclusion that it was not
practicable. It was their recommendation that attempts to develop
jet propulsion be dropped. The RAND researchers said that they
had found definite waste, and a lot of it, in the development work of
the military establishments; it was the great waste of administrative
man-hours and energy devoted to trying to eliminate duplicated
effort.

At least as long ago as 2500 B.C. there were cities of "terrible
efficiency," according to the archeologist Stuart Piggott in *Pre-
historic India*. He was referring to Mohenjo-daro and Harappa,
the twin capital cities of an ancient empire of the Indus. Mohenjo-
daro and Harappa were marvelously developed, to a point. But at
some time before 2500 B.C. development work had halted. They
added no new goods and services from that time on, it seems, nor
did they make any improvements in their old products. They simply
repeated themselves. Their production must have been stupendous.
The same standardized bricks were used in truly staggering quantities, not only in the cities themselves but throughout the scores of
towns in the empire. The same wonderfully accurate stone weights,
in multiples and fractions of 16, were turned out endlessly. And the
voracious wood-fired kilns belonging to the two cities mass-produced
so many identical pottery cups that Piggott speculates it may have
been the custom to drink from a cup and then break it. One suspects
that they had more cups than they knew what to do with.

But while other people were developing the spoked wheel and
the light chariots made possible by spoked wheels, Harappa and
Mohenjo-daro kept turning out only clumsy, solid wheels and cumbersome, heavy wagons. While other people were learning to
strengthen bronze weapons and tools with a thickened central rib,
and to make the heads of these with hollow hafts so handles could

be fitted into them, Harappa and Mohenjo-daro kept turning out only one-piece, flat, easily broken implements. At length the Indus River at Mohenjo-daro became a lake of mud.* The mud flows engulfed the city and undermined many buildings. The people seem to have been incapable of any response that involved changed ways of doing things, or new ideas. After every mud flood they rebuilt exactly as before, with their interminable bricks, and the quality of the work deteriorated steadily until it was no longer done at all. The mud floods cannot be described as the "cause" of Mohenjo-daro's decay because a similar decline was evident in the other city of Harappa and throughout the empire, alongside a similar, endless repetitiveness of old work. The response to the mud floods was merely one dramatic symptom of the all-pervading stagnation.

WAYS TO MEASURE CITY GROWTH

If we were to measure the economic development rate of a city, we could not do so just by measuring its output in a year or any group of years. We would have to measure, rather, the additions of new work to its older output, over a period of time, and the ratio of the new work to the older work. Then, to speak of a low or a high development rate, we could compare the rates of addition of new goods and services during different periods and the rates of addition among different cities.

A city's ability to maintain high development rates is what staves off stagnation, and allows the city to continue to prosper. The fact that a high development rate must be maintained is obviously little understood, nor does it seem understood that efficiency fails to make a city prosper. The commissioners of the housing agencies of New York City sincerely believe that they have been benefiting the economy of the city by reducing the numbers and varieties of New York's enterprises in the cause of efficiency for those retained. One of these commissioners boasts with pride that each store permitted in the plans for the new Lower East Side, a section that was rebuilt under the city's auspices, replaced an average of 40 older stores wiped out by the construction. By such means, he reports, the

---

* Just why is uncertain. Dr. George F. Dales of the University of Pennsylvania, an archeologist who has been making recent excavations at Mohenjo-daro, theorizes that subterranean volcanic activity and shifts of rock strata downstream from the city dammed the river and caused an upwelling of mud and silt. I suspect that a contributory cause was the immense destruction of forests, unremitting over a period of more than five centuries, to feed the mass-production brick and pottery kilns. This must have caused drastic erosion and silting.

city is being made efficient. Of course the Lower East Side, once fabulously productive in developing work, is now almost an economic desert. But the commissioner is quite right: it does have more efficient stores.

Is it not possible for the economy of a city to be highly efficient, and for the city to excel at the development of new goods and services? No, it seems not. The conditions that promote development and the conditions that promote efficient production and distribution of already existing goods and services are not only different, in most ways they are diametrically opposed. Let us consider a few of them.

Breakaways of workers—especially very able workers—from existing organizations promote the development of new work as well as the creation of new organizations. But breakaways are not good for the parent company; they undermine its efficiency. To the company or companies in control, one of the advantages of a company town is that breakaways are not feasible there. And in any settlement where breakaways are inhibited, by whatever means, the developmental rate must drop, although the efficiency of already well established work is apt to climb. Rochester, New York, used to be a city in which immense numbers of breakaways occurred. So many Rochester breakaways were creative and successful, particularly in the development of a great variety of fine scientific and advanced technological equipment, that during a period in the late 19th and early 20th centuries it would have appeared that Rochester was destined to become one of the country's most economically creative and important cities. But George Eastman, of Eastman Kodak, put an end to that. One reason that enabled him to establish his company was that Rochester businesses were already doing highly advanced work in precision manufacturing and in the making of optical and other scientific products. Once Eastman had developed Kodak into a strong company (a rapid progress, in part owing to Eastman's own development work and in part due to his purchases of other camera and film companies), Eastman fought breakaways from his company with every means at his command; and he was successful. He entangled in long and bitter lawsuits the men who had the temerity to try to leave him and form their own enterprises. And as Eastman Kodak, an efficient organization, came to dominate the economic, the political and even the cultural life of Rochester, breakaways from its other industries also dwindled.

In the more than half a century since Eastman made Rochester into an efficient company town, only one other enterprise there, Xerox, has created notable new work. Xerox started as a small photo-supply company, named Haloid, that had formed before Eastman dominated the city. Possibly because it was so small and obscure, it managed to exist "in the shadow of Eastman," as the city's historian, Blake McKelvey, has put it. Then, shortly after World War II, Haloid added the new work of making photo-copying paper and machines for using it. The Xerox process had not been invented by Haloid, but Haloid bought rights to it—as so often happens in such cases—after the innovation had been turned down by many large companies. Xerox's success, great as it has been, has not transformed Rochester back into a vigorous, developing city. It would take many organizations and people adding new work to old, and much diversity of development, to accomplish that.

Now consider for a moment the question of suppliers of bits and pieces of work to other producers. Many relatively small suppliers, much of whose work duplicates and overlaps, are indispensable to a high rate of development. But they are not efficient, neither in respect to their own work nor the operations of the producers who buy from them. For example, during the years when the automobile industry was developing in Detroit, those who tried manufacturing cars were very numerous; nobody knows exactly how many there were, but there were more than five hundred, possibly more than seven hundred. And the suppliers of bits and pieces of work to these producers were even more numerous. Indeed, some of those suppliers became automobile manufacturers themselves; Buick, for instance, began with sheet-metal work, Dodge with supplying engines. But a multiplicity of small, duplicating, overlapping suppliers was not an efficient arrangement for the three huge manufacturers who came to dominate the Detroit industry. Supplying parts to them became, beginning in the 1920's, a "simple" business. According to a report on the industry made by *Fortune* in 1946, it was "at times brutally so. . . . Prices are low, profit margins narrow and volume requirements high. Together these mean mass production with consequent heavy investment in plant and machine tools. Second, the list of customers is extremely small. Loss of a single account can frequently be catastrophic. . . . Finally, the market for original equipment parts is precisely the market for automobiles, no more and no less." This is not a portrait of supply industries that can engage in development work, but it is a portrait of highly efficient suppliers.

Consider also the conflict between development and efficiency as it applies to the work of investing development capital and supplying working capital. The most efficient way to invest capital (whether by government, by semipublic, or by private lenders and investors—it does not matter) is through a relatively few large investments and loans, not through many small ones. If small loans are made, it is most efficient to consolidate them, in effect, by making them only for purposes that have already become standardized and routinized. To put capital into the purchasing of enterprises that produce goods and services already developed is more efficient than to put it into development of new enterprises and new work. Also, it is efficient to invest development capital in a sure thing— if in new work, then in new work for which customers are guaranteed in advance. It is efficient, for example, for banks to lend to enterprises, even small ones with experimental products, if the borrowers have contracts for military development work from governments. The companies' development expenses will be covered in this way and the companies enjoy the possibility of large production contracts later.

But for a city to develop new work at a high rate means that its enterprises must have access to much inefficiently dispensed capital: many, many small loans and investments, a high proportion of them out of the routine, still other, relatively large, loans for swift expansion of goods or services that seem to be working out experimentally but which must go into larger-scale production to become practicable—although it is not a certainty they will be. And both kinds of investments must be available from a variety of sources because preconceptions infuse the businesses of investing and lending money as surely as they do other endeavors. Not everyone sees the same investment opportunities in the same ways. Not everyone glimpses an opportunity.

Consider too the physical arrangements that promote the greatest profusion of duplicate and diverse enterprises serving the population of a city, and lead therefore to the greatest opportunities for plentiful divisions of labor upon which new work can potentially arise.* It is most efficient for large construction firms to produce monotonous multiples of identical buildings; it is most efficient for architects to design multiples of identical buildings. Super-blocks are more efficient than smaller blocks because there are fewer crossings and traffic can flow more efficiently; when there are fewer streets, utilities can be distributed more efficiently and of course the maintenance of streets costs less.

---

* For reasons I have analyzed at length in *The Death and Life of Great American Cities*, enterprises serving city consumers flourish most prolifically where the following four conditions are simultaneously met: 1) Different primary uses, such as residences and working places, must be mingled together, insuring the presence of people using the streets on different schedules but drawing on consumer goods and services in common; 2) small and short blocks; 3) buildings of differing ages, types, sizes and conditions of upkeep, intimately mingled; and 4) high concentrations of people.

APPROACHES TO CITY BUILDING

Back in 1961 New York City proposed rebuilding the neighborhood in which I live. The idea was to wipe out virtually everything occupying the land and to mass produce a new "neighborhood," formed for the most part of identical, large buildings. Had the plan been to construct identical, small buildings it would, in essence, have been the same approach. The idea was to satisfy similarities of need, similarities of use, and to impose—by means of clearance— similarities of sites to accommodate the mass production construction. This was to have cost an estimated $35 million. Owing to the wholesale destruction of existing dwellings, it would have resulted in a *net* gain of only about 300 dwelling units. It would also have resulted in a loss of 156 businesses, employing about 2,500 persons. Some of these might have relocated elsewhere, at an additional economic cost not included in the $35 million. Most would have represented a total loss; that is, they would have disappeared from the economy.

This scheme was defeated. Residents and property owners in the neighborhood, through their civic organization, the West Village Committee, thereupon hired a firm of architects and planners and instructed them to work out a different kind of scheme. New buildings, gardens and public sidewalk plazas were to be added into vacant sites, abandoned plots, and makeshift parking lots in the neighborhood without destroying a single existing dwelling or requiring the removal of any business, other than random and makeshift parking.

The architects met these requirements by working out an ingenious scheme for three different sizes of relatively small buildings (for the most part, of 10 apartments each), that could be fitted into existing vacant and abandoned sites individually and in combinations. The buildings themselves were capable of many differentiaations: apartments, shops, and workshops, all of varying sizes. This scheme, costing an estimated $8.7 million (instead of $35 million, both at 1964 prices) provided a net increase of 475 dwelling units (instead of 300) and destroyed no businesses.

But numerous small enterprises, just by existing, are in conflict with the economic efficiency of a city's large and well-established enterprises. The student newspaper of Columbia University, back in February 1964—more than four years before the great eruption of student protest concerning the University's expansion and building policies, among other things—was complaining editorially as follows:

In the original quadrangle of the campus . . . the University constituted a dead
center of academic buildings, separated from the neighborhood and lacking its
total life. But this center was small. . . . As Columbia has expanded, the central
area has grown. The policy has been to build new structures as close to the old
ones as possible. The justification has been the convenience of adjacent classrooms and offices [i.e., efficiency of university administration]. But with expansion . . . stores and services had begun to disappear. . . . The disappearance of
variety saps the life of the community. The lack of stores and services adds
another problem. As buildings are demolished, many of the comforts of student
life—a good restaurant or a convenient laundry, for example—become available
only with difficulty.

Just by being present and in the way, other enterprises thus
conflict with the efficiency of the University—not, to be sure, the
University as a body of students and faculty, but the University
as an administrative enterprise. But here is the point: the administrators determine what is efficient for the University and what is
not.

Just by being present, many small enterprises conflict in still
another way with the efficiency of large enterprises. One of the
great advantages of a company town, for the company, is that there
are few alternative ways for people to earn their livings. But this does
not promote economic growth.

Consider, also, the conflict as it affects individuals who might
add new work to old. From the viewpoint of efficiency, a man or
woman trained to specific work, and good at it, is best kept at that
kind of work as long as needed. But from the point of view of
economic development, a man or woman trained to specific work
is most valuable if he adds something new to that work—if he
changes what he does. Of course he may fail.

Thus, one of the social preconditions for economic development
is not so much the opportunity for a person to change his work
(and his class) from that of his father, as is often supposed, but
rather the possibility of changing radically his own work and his own
place in society during his own working life. This is not the same as
being given the opportunity to train for work that has already
been established by others and to engage in it, even though the
change is a step upward. China, during its long stagnation, exempli-
fied the institution of the public talent hunt. Poor peasant boys of
exceptional talent could compete for prestigious places in the bureaucracy, the occupations at the top of the economic heap in China,
and could become members of the upper class in consequence.
This was useless as far as economic development was concerned,
for the talented boys were simply moving from one kind of well-
established work to another kind of well-established work.

STAGNATION EVILS

Practical problems that persist and accumulate in cities are symptoms of arrested development. The point is seldom admitted. It has become conventional, for instance, to blame congested and excessive automobile traffic, air pollution, water pollution, and noise upon "rapid technological progress." But the automobiles, the fumes, the sewage, and the noise are not new, and the persistently unsolved problems they afford only demonstrate lack of progress. Many evils conventionally blamed upon progress are, rather, evils of stagnation.

Consider, for example, the problem of mechanical noise. Noise has become so pervasive in large American cities that the phrase "noise pollution" has been coined to suggest its positive harmfulness. When mechanical noise first became a problem, an evasion of the problem was arrived at: zoning noisy industries into special areas. The practice did not combat the noise, only shunted it aside. In the meantime, mechanical devices increased while methods for diminishing the problem went undeveloped. The solution, of course, is new goods and services. Francis Bello, *Fortune*'s specialist on technology, has listed some of them: equipment that sets up opposite, cancelling patterns of sound; mounts that eliminate vibrations; new acoustical materials and treatments. He wrote back in 1955 that these devices for countering noise at its sources had been feasible for some time, but had gone undeveloped. They remain undeveloped. Excessive noise is not a problem of progress, but evidence of stagnation. The same can be said of the problem of over-dependence on automobiles. The problem and all its far-reaching consequences grow worse, but not because of progress.

Solutions to most of the practical problems of cities begin humbly and when humble people, doing lowly work, do not also solve problems, nobody is apt to solve humble problems. It is instructive to examine the curious difference in ancient Rome between the water supply to the city and the water supply within the city. The aqueduct system was begun early and was improved and elaborated by Roman engineers through the centuries as the city grew larger and more complex. Fountains and hydrants brought plentiful water from distant sources to most quarters of the city. But otherwise, Rome's plumbing was almost as primitive as that of a village. Not that the Romans were incapable of plumbing work—the large public baths had water piped in, and systems for circulating and heating it; the rich had intricate and clever water clocks, and waterworks in the gardens of their villas—but apart from rather minimal supplies to the first floors of some residences of the wealthy, Rome's utilitarian water needs were amazingly neglected. Water for dwellings, shops and almost all public buildings was brought in by hand labor. The *aquarii*, the slave water carriers, were the lowest and most hapless of workers. Juvenal called them the scum of the slave population. The slaves themselves were not free to develop their work by building plumbing systems nor could they even experiment with such possibilities.

The drainage situation was similar. The sewers of Rome were begun by 500 B.C. and they too became marvels of engineering. But, according to Jerome Carcopino in *Daily Life in Ancient Rome*, although a few houses in Pompeii were sensibly connected to the drainage system (including connection of upstairs latrines), "the drainage system of the Roman house is merely a myth begotten of the complacent imagination of modern times." Slaves carried out waste water and sewage. When some people in an economy are forestalled from solving practical problems, but others doing other work are not, the solutions to practical problems become strangely lopsided and problems accumulate.

FUTURE TECHNOLOGIES TODAY

Let us now look a little way into the future. If we observe the acute practical problems of cities in highly advanced economies today, we may be able to glimpse some of the forms economic growth could take in the highly advanced economies of the future—whatever such economies may prove to be. Waste disposal will do as an example, for in many different forms—air pollutants, water pollutants, garbage, trash, junk—wastes have created highly acute problems for large cities. They cause lesser problems, which are nevertheless chronic and unsolved, outside of cities.

Although the cities of the United States are making little or no progress in coping with wastes, hints and clues to solutions do appear. What they portend, I think, is not waste "disposal," but waste recycling. Odd little news items about wastes crop up. *The New York Times* describes an apparatus produced by a Japanese manufacturer that bales assorted trash and garbage, compacts it under hydraulic pressure, and encases the resulting dense, solid block in asphalt, cement, vinyl, or iron sheeting, depending on what is wanted. Bacteria are killed in the process. The blocks can be made in almost any shape desired, for use in building. Those sheathed in metal can be welded together. According to the company's American representative, who was interviewed by *The Times*, the process—apart from the usefulness of its product—is 50 to 75 per cent cheaper than incineration. The largest machine the company produces can handle 3,000 tons of waste in 24 hours; the smallest, 150 tons in 24 hours. The same company produces an older apparatus for pressing stripped automobile bodies into solid, small blocks for economical handling as scrap—manufacturing to which the company logically added its new device.

A manufacturer in Washington, D.C., advertises a device to be installed in buildings in place of a garbage incinerator. It reduces the bulk of garbage and trash by about 75 per cent for purposes of collecting it easily and economically. The containers filled with compacted garbage are supposed to be removed by a trash collecting contractor, and empties left in their place. This of course is not, in itself, a method of recycling waste, but it hints at the sort of auxiliary systems that will be needed for getting some wastes from their places of production to points of processing.

Here and there, garbage is being processed into compost. *The Times*, which seems to employ someone deeply interested in garbage, has described a little factory in Brooklyn, New York (run by the proprietor and a part-time helper), that converts restaurant garbage into light-weight, pulverized, dehydrated garden compost. The income from the sale of the compost is clear profit—the proprietor of the plant pays his costs by means of the silver he retrieves from the garbage and sells back to the restaurants. St. Petersburg, Florida, has a considerably more elaborate plant that handles unsorted garbage and trash. First the material goes through a magnetic separator to remove metal, which is sold as scrap; then the rest of the material is ground up, soaked, digested (by bacteria), dried and screened to yield a compost that is inert—it has no nutritive value left—but is useful for soil conditioning, a job that chemical fertilizers cannot do. It is a small plant, handling only 100 tons of refuse a day. Its products do not pay for its operation, but that is one of the most interesting things about it. The difference between its income from sales and its costs is paid by the municipality in the form of a fee of $3 per ton for disposing of the garbage and trash, an arrangement that the municipality finds economical. One glimpses how waste recycling can be made economically feasible even while it is still in a primitive and experimental state.

The conventional approach to the problems of air pollution is to ban, or attempt to ban, fuels that contain high volumes of pollutants like sulfur dioxide. I suspect this is a futile effort. Of course it can reduce pollution from given smokestacks, but as the number of smokestacks increases, the pollution increases accordingly, even though higher grade fuels are used. One is dealing with a problem by simply attempting to "subtract" it, an approach that seldom works. A much more promising idea was described in a technical article in *Public Service Magazine* of September, 1964, by a vice-president of the Pennsylvania Electric Co. of Johnstown, Pennsylvania. He reports that a test was run in one of that company's coal burning plants, beginning in 1961, to capture sulfur dioxide in the stacks and convert it to sulfuric acid, which of course is one of the most basic and heavily used chemicals in modern economies. In the test, 90 per cent of the sulfur dioxide was captured from ordinary, low-grade bituminous coal containing about a three per cent sulfur content. In a 24-hour day, this amounted to about 1,050 tons of sulfuric acid at a 70 per cent concentration, which at the time of the test had a delivered market price of $8 to $10 a ton. The cost of capturing and converting it was $7 a ton. In effect the process amounts to a new way of mining sulfur for sulfuric acid. The same approach, in principle, has been used rather widely to capture particulate air pollutants such as fly ash and soot, both of which are recycled. Fly ash is used to make cinder block. But there remains, I should think, enormous opportunity for capturing and recycling various gases which are not only dangerous in the air but also potentially valuable.

CITIES AS MINES

One of the oldest forms of waste recycling is the reprocessing of waste paper. One producer of book papers advertises that its papers are more resistant to deterioration from humidity and temperature changes than paper made from new pulp, and accompanies these advertisements with striking photographs of New York City, which it calls its "concrete forests." This fancy, that the city is another kind of paper-yielding forest, is rather apt; but the metaphor of the waste-yielding mine may be more comprehensive. For in the highly developed economies of the future, it is probable that cities will become huge, rich and diverse mines of raw materials. Such mines will differ from any now to be found because they will become richer the more and the longer they are exploited. The law of diminishing returns applies to other mining operations; the richest veins, having been worked out, are gone forever. But in cities, the same materials will be retrieved over and over again. New veins, formerly overlooked, will be continually opened. And just as our present wastes contain ingredients formerly lacking, so will the wastes of the advanced economies of the future yield up ingredients we do not now have. The largest, most prosperous cities will be the richest, the most easily worked, and the most inexhaustible mines. Cities that take the lead in reclaiming their own wastes will have high rates of related development work; that is, many local firms will manufacture the necessary gathering and processing equipment and will export it to other cities and to towns.

How will the mines be organized? First, it is useful to distinguish between two great classes of wastes; those that are carried by water, and all others. Leaving aside the water-borne for the moment, consider the fact that all other wastes must be collected from their points of production by people. This is true even of the wastes that now go into the air. It is impossible to "control" air pollution. That is to say, it is practical only to trap pollutants before they get into the air—to prevent air pollution. Such captured wastes, like the sulfuric acid at the electric plant, have to be collected by somebody, just as any other non-water-carried wastes must be, and sent on from their point of collection to processors or reusers. The sulfuric acid produced at the electric plant illustrates what I think is the main difficulty in waste recycling but also the great opportunity to organize the new industries. The production of the sulfuric acid at the electric plant is not sufficiently large to interest the electric company itself in going into the business of stockpiling acid, finding various customers, and shipping it. Yet the acid is worth collecting; indeed, in this case, a chemical company contracted to pick it up at the electric plant and pay for it. In large cities, the multitude of other fuel users who now float off sulfur dioxide into the air—hospital heating plants, factories, apartment houses—produce even less of it, taken individually, than an electric plant does, although in sum their production is enormous. They are not about to add thousands upon thousands of little chemical distributing businesses into the economy, out of their own chemical wastes. In the same way, somebody, who has old machinery to get rid of seldom finds it worth his while to hunt up a reuser of that particular apparatus. The job is better done by somebody who mines old machinery from many different factories. Even he may not be the one who finds the ultimate reuser; he may be a middleman collector who sorts what he collects and resells it to specialists who know the markets for various categories of second-hand machinery.

When waste recycling is at a primitive stage, as it is at present, the collector of second-hand machinery, the collector of waste paper, the collector of restaurant garbage all engage in feasible occupations, but not of the sort necessary if waste recycling is to develop much.

Picture so simple an establishment as a single household and its wastes. Imagine that one serviceman calls who is interested only in old metal, another who is interested in waste paper, another in garbage, another in discarded wood furniture, another in used-up plastics, another who wants old books (but only if their bindings have gilt letters; another serviceman is interested in the others), and so on. A family would be driven crazy by this traffic, let alone by the necessity of separating and storing for various intervals the various wastes. An economy in which wastes have become an acute problem is precisely an economy in which this sort of thrift is a nuisance to the producers of wastes and not worth their while.

WASTE AS AN ADVANTAGE

But diversity of wastes can in fact be advantageous, if properly handled. The more highly developed waste recycling becomes, the more valuable is this very diversity of materials. The aim must be to get all the wastes possible into the system—not only those that are already valuable at a given stage of development, but also those that are only beginning to become useful and those that are not yet useful but may become so.

A type of work that does not now exist is thus necessary: services that collect all wastes, not for shunting into incinerators or gulches, but for distributing to various primary specialists from whom the materials will go to converters or reusers. The comprehensive collecting services, as they develop into big businesses, will use many technical devices. They will install and service equipment for collecting sulfuric acid, soot, fly ash and other wastes in fuel stacks, including gasses that, at present, cannot yet be trapped. They will supply and handle containers for containerized wastes and will install fixed equipment such as chutes, probably by employing sub-contractors. Who will develop the comprehensive collecting services? My guess is that the work, when it does appear, will be added to janitorial contracting services—a kind of work, itself, that as yet hardly exists except for the benefit of relatively few institutional and other large clients, and is not notable for yielding development work. But in economies where people doing lowly work are not hampered from adding new work to old, we may expect that just such lowly occupations as janitorial work will be the footholds from which complex, prosperous, and economically important new industries develop.

Comprehensive collectors of wastes may at first derive their incomes like the St. Petersburg trash and garbage processing plant which gets a $3 fee per ton for handling wastes and derives the rest of its income from sale of its products. As proportions of unused wastes become smaller and the income derived from the sales becomes larger, comprehensive collectors will compete for the privilege of doing the collecting work free, just as some collectors of profitable special wastes now do. Eventually they will compete for collection rights by offering fees for waste concessions, again just as some collectors of special wastes now do.

Water-borne wastes present quite different problems and possibilities. Although water does the initial collecting work, water is difficult to mine. Current methods of treating sewage and obtaining its products—purified water and residues—are very expensive, cumbersome and slow, and they require large spaces considering the yield. Sewage treatment plants are consequently few compared with the need for them. Waters polluted by industrial wastes are similarly expensive to mine. The paper industry of the Soviet Union is now polluting the waters of Lake Baikal in Siberia, an action that Soviet conservationists warn will be disastrous to the freshwater life in the lake, life that is unique for having evolved, during long ages past, in isolation from life in other bodies of water. The justification for this vandalism, like the justification for the destruction (which has already been accomplished) of almost all life in Lake Erie by sewage and industrial wastes, is that treatment to remove the pollutants—or to divert them into other bodies of water, at best an evasion,—is too expensive.

Thus the first priority in dealing with water-borne wastes, in view of the difficulty of mining them, is to keep them out of the water to begin with, if at all possible—to collect them in some other way. This is indeed possible with some water-borne wastes: those that are in the water only and solely because the water is a means of carrying them away from the point of production. Human excretions are in this category; to carry these wastes away by flowing water is extraordinarily primitive. It is amazing that we continue to use such old-fashioned make-shifts. Excrement in sewage complicates the handling of all city waste waters, including even the run-off from rainstorms, and exacerbates all the problems of public health connected with water pollution.

Economies that develop in the future will, I think, turn to the use of chemical toilets.* The residues in the toilets will be collected

* These, of course, already exist but have not been developed except for use in situations where water is very scarce or where connecting it to toilets is impractical. Chemical toilets for standard use will probably not be developed or manufactured by existing manufacturers of bathroom fittings. It was not the makers of iceboxes who developed electric refrigerators, nor makers of coal stoves who developed the electric

like any other non-water-borne wastes. In effect they will be ash—"burned" to small amounts of dehydrated and sterilized phosphates and nitrates—collected about once a year from any given household toilet, more often from public facilities. Other kinds of wastes that will be kept out of water are analogous: they are in the water only because it is now the economical medium for carrying them, in lieu, often, of comprehensive waste collecting services; garbage from food-packing plants is an example.

So-called heat pollution, resulting when hot water is dumped into streams and lakes, leads to highly complex deterioration of water because of the destruction of cleansing biological cycles. This damage will cease in economies that continue to develop, because the hot water will be piped and recycled to yield its heat and so save fuel. Still other industrial wastes in water will diminish, or at worst increase less rapidly than they now do, because of their own recycling. For instance, reuse of paper somewhat reduces the effluents from paper making, which are most severe in the pulping operations. Aluminum reducing causes much water pollution, but recycling waste aluminum causes less. And still other processes that currently pollute waters will decline owing to obsolescence. Vehicles using electricity will indirectly reduce water pollution from oil refining, for example.

CONCLUSION

In the past, when acute city practical problems have been solved, the solutions have not been an economic burden upon their societies. On the contrary, solutions have increased true economic abundance, true wealth. Of course more workers have been needed to do previously undone work, but the costs of doing undone work have not been at all analogous to adding unproductive bureaucracies, nor the costs of maintaining idle people on welfare. Just so, we may expect that the solving of pollution and other problems arising from wastes, while requiring many workers, will not be an economic burden upon the developing economies where such problems are, in fact, solved. On the contrary, all the wealth extracted from recycled wastes, plus pure air and pure water, will represent increases in true abundance. Indeed, much of the new work, we may expect, will wholly or partly support itself even during its difficult trial, error, and development stages.

stove business; no more should we expect makers of flush toilets to develop practical chemical toilets of the future.

3 WILLIAM L. C. WHEATON

Form and structure of the metropolitan area*

INTRODUCTION

The founders of city planning in the United States, men of enormous vision, largely failed to perceive the influences which democracy, technology, and affluence would exercise on the city of the future, its scale, its form, and its modes of expression. They failed to anticipate the influence which the automobile, the horizontal assembly line, or the widespread availability of electric power and means of communication would exercise to virtually destroy the old, compact city, draw from its central district most of the retailing and manufacturing functions which had historically sustained it, and spread the metropolitan area over countless square miles at low density. Men of vision though they were, these great leaders largely embraced design philosophies now wholly repudiated, the classic and revivalist notions of the nineteenth century, the Renaissance forms and architectural formalism. They ignored the inspirations of St. Elia, of Garner, or of Sullivan and Wright, which were more relevant to the future. Nor did these founders fully appreciate the extent to which social objectives would replace the traditional concerns of government. Though they were active participants in

* Reprinted from ENVIRONMENT FOR MAN edited by William Ewald Jr., by permission of Indiana University Press.

movements for social and political reform, the directions that those reforms would take half a century later in the search for full employment, social security, public health, mass education, and racial equality were rarely foreseen.

There is no reason for believing that our vision of the future of metropolitan areas will prove to be substantially better than those of our forebears. Perhaps because we are conscious of their frailties in forecasting, we may be more cautious. Perhaps we have a slightly better sense of historical evolution, but any of us looking at the record of the past must be exceedingly humble in looking at the future.

Today we believe that half a century from now the population of the United States will exceed 500 million people. If this proves true, we will have 500 to 1,000 metropolitan areas as now defined. The largest of these, the East Coast New York region, will contain perhaps 50 million people and will be part of a larger region exceeding 100 million people. There may be several other metropolitan areas with 25 million population. Presumably 85 to 95 per cent of the population will be urban. Further, it is now possible to foresee a day when the average family may have an income of $15,000, when ten years of productive work may yield the equivalent of a normal lifetime's work in today's terms, with all that this portends for consumption and for work. If these forecasts prove to be true, they will work vast changes in the nature of society and the functions of urban areas. Our concern today is to try to anticipate some of these changes and to suggest how they may affect the form and structure of metropolitan areas.

In approaching this broad and nebulous topic we will first discuss the functions of the city and its life styles. Then we will deal with some of the more important physical elements of the city.

CHANGING FUNCTIONS OF METROPOLITAN AREAS

Half a century ago, Frederick Jackson Turner was noting the closing of the American frontier as a fact which would redirect the attention of society to urban development, alter the labor market in many ways, and ultimately affect the American way of life. A quarter of a century later, when the urbanization of America was already at full flood, Louis Wirth could write a seminal article on "Urbanism as *a* Way of Life."[1] But even Wirth did not anticipate the enormous rate of population growth which has subsequently occurred, its concen-

1. Louis Wirth, "Urbanism as a Way of Life," *American Journal of Sociology*, 44, July, 1938.

tration into urban areas, the depopulation of the countryside as a result of increases in agricultural productivity, and thus the overwhelming urbanization which now characterizes our society. Whereas in all previous times urbanism was the way of life of a minority, and the basic population was rural or small-town, within these two generations urbanism has become *the* way of life of an overwhelming majority of the population. Whereas formerly people moved to the city to perform special or unusual functions, leaving the reservoir of population on the land, today that reservoir lives in cities, functioning or otherwise, and urban ways of life are characteristic of modern societies.

This observation should force us to reconsider the functions of the city, for the facts will compel that reconsideration in any event. If the city is to become the reservoir for population, it may have to sustain large populations who have no traditional function. Where we have traditionally dealt with the economic, political, cultural, or military functions of the city, perhaps a major function of the city of the future will be sustaining the population, enabling it to consume. We already have retirement communities and resort communities, whose chief functions are consumptive. We have poverty communities, which are distinguished largely by the fact that they are not able to consume enough. We are currently engaged in token efforts to retrain or redirect the residents of these communities toward employment, at the same time recognizing that if we were to succeed we might merely increase the number of employable unemployed.

Sociologists formerly assumed that the city was a mechanism for acculturation, that it would assimilate migrant populations, raise them in middle-class value systems, and incorporate them into the economic system. Today sociology suggests that assimilation may no longer function toward these ends. Acculturation and assimilation may not be inevitable. Instead, internally spawned heterogeneity may generate a variety of life styles, as Janet Abu-Lughod notes in a fascinating paper.[2] This tendency is already evident in our styles of work and leisure, and in the functions of the home. If we extrapolate these trends the functions of the metropolitan area of the future may be both different in nature and differently distributed.

The traditional functions of work, home, and play will remain, of course, though in changing forms and proportions. We all recognize the shifts which have occurred in the composition of

2. Janet Abu-Lughod, "The City Is Dead—Long Live the City: Some Thoughts on Urbanism" (Berkeley: Center for Planning and Development Research, University of California, 1966).

employment. Agriculture has declined from the prevailing occupation in America to that of less than 10 per cent while agricultural output has multiplied. Manufacturing next became the dominant force in the economy, but in recent years output has increased steadily while employment has declined. It is not inconceivable that a small fraction of the population will, in the future, produce all of the products required by consumers. Construction remains a large employer, but its rationalization cannot be deferred indefinitely. Services are currently expanding, including government services. They offer the prospect for continued growth, but within services rationalization and mechanization proceed apace, even into hitherto backward areas like education. Many services can be largely replaced by manufacturing, as disposable clothing may someday largely eliminate laundries, or as laundromats have already shifted much of this function away from the home.

Under the circumstances, the composition of employment, its duration, and its definition are subject to radical future changes. We are already talking about the thirty-and the twenty-hour work week. When incomes double, however, some of the population will prefer two twenty-hour week jobs, to keep busy and increase income. Others may prefer to work six months and play six. Still others may prefer to work very hard for ten or fifteen years so that they can retire at forty and indulge in other activities for the rest of their lives. The professions will never get any rest. The very nature of their work makes them completely dedicated to it. Finally, there are those who prefer to "work" very inefficiently, or at a leisurely pace, but for long hours. Some small shopkeepers and artists seem to fall in this class. Their "work" is in fact a way of life, engaging them for many hours, containing elements of leisure, and often producing relatively low compensation.

With "surplus" population having "surplus" time the very definition of work will change, as it is already changing. We will pay people to go to school, to keep them out of the labor market as well as to instruct them. This can be extended indefinitely, providing the individual with an exhilarating sense of accomplishment while keeping him busy. Community organization efforts, the leadership of certain creation activities, and all kinds of rites, formerly regarded as voluntary activity, may become defined as "work" and be paid. Some of these occupations may be humble. The Parisian street sweeper receives a modest stipend to hold a broom and occasionally flush the street. He has a secure and continuing occupational and social status from this activity. Others such as artists are highly paid and honored for what is defined as work but may for others be play. We can readily redefine many activities as work, provide compensation and status for them, and in the process change the functions of the city and its subareas. When a quarter or a third of the population can produce all the essentials of life, those of the remainder who desire a function will find it, and society will support the activity in one way or another, and honor it.

Leisure is the obverse of work, as De Grazia has noted.[3] The portion of life devoted to it will increase radically. Already we can see that what we now call retirement may encompass more than half of the adult years. Much leisure activity is energetic— as in gardening or sports, the pursuit of arts or crafts, travel and exploration. These activities are socially sanctioned and rewarded. Perhaps, as the competition for space increases, we will reward space-economizing forms of leisure. There may be prizes for those who sit at home and read most, or who put in the most elapsed hours looking at TV, or acquire the most perfect tan. Neighborhood and community rites and ceremonies, which consume time and energy in socially accepted ways, may be at a premium. Dancing in the streets should become more common.

We all recognize the enormous demands for space which will be generated by increased leisure of the active recreation types. We will need hundreds of thousands of miles of highways for leisure driving, countless square miles of beaches, lakes and rivers, parks and playgrounds, and hundreds of new forms of destinations and service places. But we will also require hundreds of new cities to accommodate these needs, quite possibly a quarter of all new urban growth. There would be cities with no visible means of support—existing solely to accommodate the lives of those who have no active productive functions as now defined.

The last of the traditional triumvirate of functions is the home. It was once the center of almost all activities. Many of its functions, e.g., education, recreation, and health, have been transferred to specialized institutions. For some of the population this trend may continue—the home may be merely a place for sleeping and the storage of personal property. For the student living in a dormitory, or a resident nurse in a hospital, or the child in a summer camp, this may be true today. Thus a home may be merely a point of departure. For many others the home may develop far more functions. It may be the center of work for those engaged in the arts or crafts, for salesmen, some professions, or neighborhood services. It may

3. Sebastian De Grazia, *Of Time, Work and Leisure* (New York: Twentieth Century Fund, 1962).

become the center of leisure for those who prefer gardening, or crafts, or for those of lowered mobility.

The most important historic function of the home, of course, has been as a place for child-rearing. This function has expanded as adolescence and education have been extended, but it has also contracted as many educational, recreational, and maintenance functions have become institutionalized. At some time in the near future all nations must adopt population policies which must have the effect of reducing the average size of child-rearing families or of reducing the proportion of such families, or both. Presumably the consequences of these efforts will be a shift toward smaller homes, and an increase in the proportion of dwellings designed, located, and priced to serve single persons and couples without children. Very similar effects have been historically associated with rising incomes and education. The two factors may reinforce each other. Leo Grebler long ago pointed out that only half of the potential number of households actually occupied their own dwellings.[4] With rising incomes this proportion should be increased steadily, too, by an increasing proportion of dwellings for single or two-person occupancy.

An increasing proportion of the population owns more than one home. Resort areas for summer occupancy have been expanding at an astonishing rate. Winter resorts and communities are burgeoning. An increasing number of families have country homes and city apartments. Many station their families in the country, suburbia, or a small town house to which the breadwinner commutes for weekends, or every other day, living meanwhile in a city apartment. The redefinition of work and leisure, and the changes in their proportions, will create great incentives for extensions of these patterns of living.

Finally I should note two other features of our styles of life which will influence metropolitan form and structure. First, more people will change their style of life during their lifetime than heretofore. We are accustomed to think of youth, adulthood, and old age as the primary types, and one or two communities as the locus of life. In the future we might think of childhood at home, adolescence at college, young married at college, young adult with or without children, mature adult without children, retired and able-bodied, retired and impaired. In addition to these different periods of life we will have more families choosing suburban, urban, exurban, and rural locations. We will have families who choose to live in different

---

4. Leo Grebler *et al.*, *Capital Formation in Residential Real Estate*, National Bureau of Economic Research (Princeton: Princeton University Press, 1956), Chapter V.

regions or countries for periods of their lives. In short, the number and types of home and location a normal family may occupy will increase. Second, we may discover that people have a wide range of tolerance of change. Some may be able to tolerate frequent change, but others may require considerable locational permanence, may have a low propensity to move, despite their enhanced possibility of movement. I will return to this theme later.

CHANGES IN FUNCTIONAL AREAS

We now turn to the effect of these forces, intangible as they are, upon the form of the metropolitan area. Planners have traditionally described metropolitan form in terms of central cities, suburban areas, urban-rural fringe zones, greenbelts, and new towns. We have described the form of the metropolitan area in terms of contiguous growth, sprawl or noncontiguous growth, linear forms, radial forms, and satellite forms. Within the developed areas we have described central business districts, regional subcenters and neighborhood centers, and neighborhoods. We have distinguished between modes of transportation and their form-giving influence, particularly rail and automobile transportation, and we have terminology dealing with the separation or mixture of land uses in the fine grain. This has been the terminology of city planning dealing with the form of the metropolitan area.[5]

During the last half century some of this language, or the dimensions which we attribute to it, has changed notably. When Ebenezer Howard wrote about new towns he described a community of 30,000 people. When the program was adopted by the British government a new town had become 60,000 people. When those towns were finished, they included 80,000 people. In the new plans for southeast England and for Paris, they were conceived as cities of 300,000 or more. Thus the scale of the concept of a new town or a satellite community has grown with the urban population and the metropolitan area until the term means something quite different from the original concept.

Similarly, our concept of the metropolitan area is being subjected to rapid change. We have scarcely begun to analyze the meaning of the megapolitan area, much less to adapt our language to this new reality. For this reason, I propose to discuss some of the

5. There is also another catalogue of terminology which deals with the detailed physical composition of subdistricts, zones, or buildings. This language is largely architectural and is in considerable degree, though not entirely, separate from the language in which the form of the metropolitan area is described.

terms which we use to describe metropolitan areas, selecting those in which the most dramatic changes appear to be in prospect.

Few things are more fixed in our language than the idea of a central business district. There must be only one. It must have such a high proportion of certain types of activity that it dominates a metropolitan area. But such districts were once dominated by retail trade. Few are today. Today a central business district means an office, managerial, and financial center, which need not coincide with a retail center. New York City clearly has two central business districts on Manhattan Island. Los Angeles has grown prodigiously and prosperously without ever developing a classical central business district. The East Coast megalopolis has a dozen or more, depending upon the definition that we choose. It seems clear that in a city of 50 million there will be numerous high-density zones of a character quite different from the central business district as it is now known.

High density

These high-density zones will probably ultimately consist of single or linked structures containing residential, office, and retail facilities for several hundred thousand people. We already have buildings housing 10,000 or more employees. We already have 100-story structures containing both offices and apartments. We already have examples of employment densities and residential densities exceeding 10,000 persons per acre and in the range of $\frac{1}{4}$ to $\frac{1}{2}$ million persons per square mile. If these conditions exist today and are accepted as tolerable in places like Manhattan, Chicago, and Hong Kong, it is not unreasonable to suppose that as the urban population triples and as the size of the largest metropolitan areas moves into the 25 to 50 million range, we will see many such high-density zones.

Constitution Plaza, Penn Center, the Shinjuku district of Tokyo, are crude or primitive expressions of this kind of zone. It is regrettable that we do not have anywhere in the world a good example of a planned building complex for 100,000 people capable of accommodating the daily movements of goods and people which would be necessary in such a complex. No one will question that such a complex is technically possible, or that it could be designed and built to be an exceedingly attractive, exciting, and economically efficient place in which to live and work. In a four-block length of Sixth Avenue in New York City the equivalent of such a complex has been built within the last five years in the most primitive form imaginable. It consists of eight skyscraper office buildings and hotels. If that complex had been built on top of a ten-story parking lot with aerial ramps to the surrounding freeway system, mechanical walkways between buildings at the 20th and 40th-story levels, and mechanical circulation from the underground subway serving it, we would today have the kind of high-density zone of which we will have many examples in the future.

Note that in describing this type of zone, I am not using the traditional terminology of central business district, because I am describing both a residential and a work place and one which may contain all of the other service facilities of a very large city of several hundred thousand people. Further, such high-density zones may have specialized functions. In any event, we must open our eyes to the possibilities that densities will reach far beyond anything we have heretofore considered acceptable and that when attained, such high densities will be of a different character from those which we have heretofore known or described.

Other activity zones

Aside from these zones of ultra-high density, other types of activity zones of moderately high density appear to be emerging. Typically they contain mixed uses, and do not fit neatly into our descriptions of either industrial districts or regional centers. At the Valley Forge Interchange there is emerging a huge development accommodating 25,000 industrial employees, a million square feet of retail space, a thousand acres of parking lots, expressways, and thoroughfares, and not a single dwelling. The Los Angeles airport is rapidly becoming the largest office building and hotel district on the West Coast, far more convenient for business meetings than any other place in the western million square miles of the country. Airports will doubtless be major metropolitan area form givers in the future because of their propensity to generate these and other activities.

We are seeing the emergence of other activity centers of a city building scale. Man-made resort, recreation, and convention centers are now beginning to burgeon at an unprecedented rate. As the natural recreation sites diminish in number, wholly man-made resort cities will emerge: Disneyland and Las Vegas are illustrations. There will doubtless be some permanent World's Fairs. The two most important types of activity center now on the horizon, however, are institutions of higher education and hospitals. The proportion of the population that participates in higher education is rising sharply. With increased college attendance and continuing increases in vocational and nonvocational education, the number of major centers of educational activity in our metropolitan areas will double and double again. A metropolitan area of a million population may well expect to have several new educational complexes of the

15,000–25,000 student size. Each can generate a population of two or three times the student population.

There will be a similar explosion in health facilities. With increased longevity, the launching of medical insurance, and the expansion of our concepts of health and treatment, community and metropolitan health centers of much larger size, accompanied by specialized housing, specialized retailing, recuperative, and recreation facilities of new types will undoubtedly become major activity centers. We may expect, then, a major increase in the types of activity center and in their number, size, and complexity, and in the types of urban areas which they generate.

Low-density origin zones

At the other end of the scale many forces seem to reinforce the development and maintenance of very low-density, mixed-use zones which may eventually be the characteristic form of land use in megalopolitan areas, filling a large part of the space between higher-density zones. In planner terminology it is called sprawl or scattered development. It consists of low-density residential uses mixed with minor retail facilities, planned industrial districts, and scattered, inoffensive industry. I cannot envisage that the traditional concepts of separation of land use over large areas will apply to such low-density zones. They rarely do today. The detailed separation of land use at the street scale will prevail so that industrial and commercial traffic does not penetrate and impair residential areas. But otherwise the forces of the market, the adoption of performance standards, the need to reduce journeys to work and shopping, and the changes in our concepts of home and work place are likely to alter so that we will accept a much higher degree of mixture of uses than we have been accustomed to in the past.

For this reason, maybe we shouldn't call these low-density zones "neighborhoods" or "residential areas" at all, but instead adopt some more neutral terminology like "origin zones." Such a terminology would recognize that many residential areas could include attractive places for work and local retail areas, that a large proportion of any population is locally employed in service industry, that under some circumstances it may be easier to bring work to people rather than to take people to work, and that especially as the volume of movement out of origin zones builds up in major metropolitan areas, it will become desirable to maintain the highest possible degree of residence, work, and recreation within the origin zone.

Within these zones, of course, we will have neighborhoods of varied types. During the last half century we have accumulated a vast amount of knowledge of the human ecology of the city. Hundreds of studies have portrayed the social structure, geographic distribution, behavior, and values of different populations in different areas.[6] This literature reveals the immense and growing variety of life styles in our society. We have some who live out their lives within a neighborhood in the heart of a metropolis, scarcely ever moving outside a small orbit. Herbert Gans has aptly called them the urban villagers. At the other end of the scale we have cosmopolitan and jet-set types who breakfast in New York, lunch in Los Angeles, and dine in Chicago almost weekly, who may live in Washington but have more friends in San Francisco or Boston.

In the face of this knowledge our traditional concept of the neighborhood is fatally deficient and is in the process of being replaced. Traditionally, we have considered high, low and medium-density areas, and single or mixed dwelling type areas, and little else that is relevant. Surely the work of the sociologists and anthropologists tells us more. We need neighborhoods for the villager and the cosmopolitan, for youth, for the aged, and for mixed age groups, neighborhoods of high and low density, of single and mixed dwelling type, socially homogeneous and mixed, economically stratified and economically mixed, central, suburban and rural, stable and changing, historic and contemporary, neighborhoods for those who prefer anonymity and for those who like community, for the poor as well as the rich, for the mobile and the stable.

Thus there are at least a dozen dimensions by which we could characterize a neighborhood, and there are several hundred possible types of neighborhood. Further, we have the analytical and diagnostic techniques by which we can measure, approximately, the composition of the population with respect to its desire or need for each of these characteristics.[7] From such an analysis we could plan for the far richer and more diverse types of neighborhood which the future metropolis will require, and future affluence demand.

More is at stake here than merely meeting market demand. The pace of change is such that many in the population cannot bear it with equanimity.[8] They need the stability and continuity of an

6. Cf. the work of Bennett Berger, W. B. Dobriner, Walter Firey, Herbert Gans, Charles Seelye, Lloyd Warner, and William H. Whyte, Jr., for example.

7. Greenleigh Associates, *Diagnostic Survey of Tenant Households in West Side Renewal Area of New York City* (New York, 1965); *Home Interview Study of Low-Income Households in Detroit, Michigan* (New York, 1965); and Arthur D. Little, Inc., *Renewal Attitudes Study, City of San Francisco* (Cambridge, 1965).

8. Marc Fried, "Grieving for a Lost Home," in Leonard Duhl, ed., *The Urban Condition* (New York: Basic Books, 1963), and other chapters of the same. Cf. also Alvin L. Schorr, *Slums and Social Insecurity* (Washington: U.S. Department of Health, Education and Welfare, 1963).

environment which will persist at least a generation. Some require the social security of a stratified neighborhood, the comfort and ease that come with living with like people. This may be true of many middle-class families who have just made it to suburbia, and also true of many low-income families among minority groups. Others may desire change and diversity. Their needs may be easier to meet. The very stability of social life requires that we take a new look at the neighborhood, and try to plan to meet a wider range of needs. Such a reexamination will surely reveal that the classic "mixed" neighborhood was at best an obscure ideal with many internal contradictions. At worst, as Isaacs has noted, it was an excuse for some form of segregation. Perhaps it is fortunate that there has been such an enormous gap between the planners' traditional ideal and its realization.[9]

Among the types of neighborhood there are several that demand special attention because of their novelty or seeming difficulty. We have both new and old neighborhoods, even whole cities, composed almost exclusively of elderly adults—a forbidding prospect, but a reality. We have neighborhoods consisting almost wholly of youths— around colleges. In the future we may have whole cities of youths built around new universities. We seem to be building whole neighborhoods around hospitals and health facilities—neighborhoods for the sick, the recuperating, and their caretakers. We are getting seasonal or second-home neighborhoods, whole communities which are inhabited part of the year. We shall have many more, enough perhaps for a quarter of the population. We need new neighborhoods with built-in employment opportunities, for urban villagers of all types. If some of these types sound unfamiliar or repulsive, they are nevertheless here, and will surely multiply in the future as urban society beomes larger, more heterogeneous, and more affluent.

On the fringes of the metropolitan area another phenomenon is emerging—the unfarmed zone. Recently a ranch containing 80,000 acres has been subdivided in southern California into such an area. Some of it is divided into conventional 2½-acre lots. Still more is in 20 to 40-acre farmlots, including an area zoned for small, highly mechanized dairy farms and another for uneconomic orchards. The largest area is being sold off in lots of 40 to 200 acres, for country estates, horse raising, and other gentleman farmer pursuits. Sales are brisk. Soon the buyers will qualify for federal subsidies not to plant their farms, not to market their cattle. Most will have farm

9. Reginald R. Isaacs, "The Neighborhood Theory: An Analysis of Its Adequacy," *Journal of the American Institute of Planners*, Vol. XIV, No. 1, Spring. 1948.

losses to write off against income taxes, and all will wait for future capital gains, when this area, an hour and a half from Los Angeles, is further subdivided for higher density urban uses. In the affluent world of the future there will be millions of families seeking such places—as a refuge from the city, as a tax gimmick, and as a long-range, self-supporting speculation.

New towns

New towns or new cities have a vital role to play in this new kind of metropolitan area. The present lively and growing interest in new communities has yet to produce anything approximating the classical idea of a new community, or any approximation of the many new cities of Europe. The present projects under private sponsorship are necessarily limited by the housing market and density preferences which prevail in their local areas. They are limited by the restrictions imposed upon them by local governments. They are limited in their financial capacity to install overhead investment in advance of development. They are limited by their inability to control or directly influence the provision of transportation facilities to nearby or central employment centers. Despite these limitations, one or two may make significant contributions in urban design and amenity. One or two may make significant advances in the provision of community facilities, or in the range of dwelling types offered, or other features. None, of course, can market to a very wide spectrum of incomes, especially in the lower-middle income ranges. Despite these limitations, these pilot projects deserve support because they help to awaken the American people to new possibilities and standards.

The United States alone among the major nations of the world has failed to adopt and implement some sort of new towns policy. As a consequence, we have no examples of the convenience, amenity, and economy characteristic of the high-quality new city design performance found in the Scandinavian countries. We particularly need planned new cities to set design standards for a population which has come to accept scattered, unorganized growth as the norm. We have few distinguished examples of how beautiful an urban area can be. Thus we urgently need 50 to 100 standard-setting models. With even a dozen demonstration new cities in the next decade we might logically expect the merit of those performances to attract the national support required to create a national policy. Such a policy would attract a moderate share of all future building, to ease the pressure for scattered development, to provide substantially better environments, often at higher densities than can otherwise be provided, and to permit some real tests of the economies of planned cities.

Despite these hopes, here, as abroad, the expansion of existing communities will continue to account for most metropolitan growth. Further, we will see great variety in the size, composition, and location of new cities. Some will emerge as wholly new cities, based upon new recreation or retirement markets, new technologies, new exploitable resources. A half-dozen new cities in these forms have developed in the postwar years. Most new cities will occur as satellites to existing metropolitan areas, some at moderately great distances from the center and many nearly contiguous to it, separated from the area by natural landmarks, parks, or other relatively narrow open space zones. Certainly there is no single pattern which we can point to as a natural prototype for the United States.

Open space

In the terminology for describing the metropolitan area we also need a category which might be labeled "zone separators." Open space performs many functions in the metropolitan region which we are only beginning to treat. It provides corridors for movement, scenic beauty, agriculture, climatic or thermal protection, hydrological functions, recreation space, and reserve space for future urbanization. In no area of planning have we so miserably failed to develop a full set of concepts and to devise the means for regulation and control. The two failures are undoubtedly related. Until we can distinguish the purposes of open space, we will probably fail to secure public consent to regulation.

All too often we have taken refuge in the traditional idea of the greenbelt. If it made some sense to Ebenezer Howard in the nineteenth century, it makes very little today. While we can readily get along without abstract notions about greenbelt, we must at the same time recognize that important ecological functions are performed by open space and that we have long neglected the study of urban physical ecology. The bays, the river valleys and the hilltops, the forests and the fields, perform essential hydrological, climatic, and other functions which we have scarcely begun to define and measure. They maintain and control the flow of water essential to the civilization of the urban area. In many areas they moderate the climate, purify or humidify air, and in other ways maintain thermal controls in the metropolitan area. We can guess, though we cannot prove, that filling San Francisco Bay would raise the temperature of the metropolitan area by five to ten degrees and blanket it with a layer of smog which would cost tens of millions annually. But these arguments will command little support until they can be scientifically demonstrated and measured.

Another form of open space consists of public park and recreation areas. Although our methods of estimating the requirements for these may be inadequate, they constitute an essential part of the open space system of the metropolitan area. In most metropolitan areas the natural sites for regional parks were delineated many years ago. In most metropolitan areas we have failed to acquire those sites systematically. The resurgence of national interest in this subject currently offers some hope that we will now proceed to acquire them.

But public open space does not now, and probably will never comprise more than a small share of the open space required in the metropolitan region. Some of it is required to provide visual breaks in an otherwise continuous and often dreary developed region. Some of it will be required to make movement in the open space corridor more efficient, safer, and pleasanter, especially when 90 per cent of our recreation activity is recreation driving. Some of it will be required for the thermal and hydrological effects which I have mentioned. Many of these requirements can be accommodated under private ownership, but subject to both police power and other types of control.

I see no major reason why future expressways should not be used to create scenic corridors within the metropolitan region and on a two to four-mile grid. More than a generation ago, the Merritt Parkway demonstrated that a corridor 600 to 1,000 feet wide could be landscaped to create the impression of countryside, forests, and woods even while it traversed a densely developed urban area. It is ridiculous to propose the preservation of greenbelts or mile-wide scenic corridors if the purpose is to provide visual recreation. That purpose can be efficiently achieved with comparatively narrow rights of way properly landscaped. If there are those who desire to see rural land uses, cows can be stationed in the highway corridor to simulate the traditional image of the countryside without wasting useful urban land. We might even install plastic cows and sheep to create a simulation of the desired rusticity. Since the user pays or should pay for the highway facility, and is the primary beneficiary in terms of both safety and pleasure, it should be reasonable to pay for scenic expressway corridors from highway funds, and to insist that all future expressways conform to such standards.

Farm belts are another matter. Many commercial farm areas are not the pleasant state of nature that they were once considered. In fact, farm areas can be dangerous and unpleasant for urban dwellers.

They contain unpleasant smells, odoriferous fertilizers, and dangerous insecticides which increasingly render them hostile or unpleasant to the nonagricultural population. Far from a pleasant refuge from the city, cultivated areas are becoming areas from which nonagricultural residents should be excluded for the protection both of the agriculture and of the urban dweller.

Agricultural uses, however, virtually never pay an economic return comparable to urban uses. While there is no impending shortage of agricultural land which would justify alarmist demands for agricultural zones, the protection of the urban dweller from agricultural dangers requires the development of such zones, and the long-range protection of agricultural soils from speculative sterilization in nonagricultural uses may soon justify such zones.

The motivation for owning and holding land will increase mightily in the next two generations. As population and affluence rise and as the pace of change in an urban society increases, we may expect millions of families to desire the emotional security and the lifetime continuity of owning a place of refuge from urban tension and change. We may expect millions of families to be able to afford to indulge this desire as hundreds of thousands now do. Presumably they could readily usurp agricultural uses and sterilize millions of acres of land which might otherwise serve agricultural purposes. Under these circumstances it would be reasonable to limit nonagricultural holdings of this semirecreational type to nonagricultural areas.

Thus, between the scenic uses, the movement corridor uses, the ecological functions, the recreation uses, and the farm uses of land, we may find concepts for defining those spaces within and around the urbanized region which should be preserved at ultra-low density or in their scattered condition. Ian McHarg in Pennsylvania, Phillip Lewis in Wisconsin, and Garret Eckbo in California have begun to define metropolitan open space in these terms.[10] As studies of this type are extended and refined, I have little doubt that we will develop both the scientific basis and the legal justification for creating a network of linked open spaces which will serve to provide that minimal separation between activity zones which is justified and which will help to give form to the metropolitan area and to provide the separation necessary for identity in an otherwise urbanized landscape.

10. Wallace-McHarg Associates, *Plan for the Valleys* (1963); Phillip H. Lewis, *Recreation and Open Space in Illinois* (University of Illinois, Sept. 1961), and Eckbo, Dean, Austin & Williams, *Urban-Metropolitan Open Space Study*, prepared for the California State Office of Planning, Sacramento, Nov., 1965.

TRANSPORTATION LINKS

The links between origin zones and activity zones are the media of transportation, communication, and goods or energy movement. Here technological developments have already reshaped the metropolitan area twice in this century, first toward higher densities and greater concentration, and more recently toward lower densities and greater dispersion. We customarily think of the shift from rails to roads as a major dispersing element, but the automobile-generated dispersal could never have been effective without universally available electric power, telephone, and radio, the development of household equipment to replace services, and the like. The link modes are therefore important: rail, highway, wire, wireless, pipelines and other forms of tubes, air, water, and ground. New classes of vehicles like hydrofoils and hovercraft open new transportation possibilities. New control devices present interesting prospects for vehicle guidance and volume control.

Manifestly there are enormous possibilities for substitution in these linkages. The automobile has replaced rails for virtually all intrametropolitan movement of persons outside of a dozen cities. The airplane and the automobile have eliminated intercity rail travel in most of the United States. Facsimile may replace newspapers. Video phone and linked computers can replace many business trips. Atomic power can replace transmission lines. Pipelines can replace tank cars and ships. The garbage grinder can obviate the garbage truck. It is important to note that technology affects not only the home-work relationship but also the location of industry and employment and of course the nature of the activities located.

Here we can consider only a few of the most important of these potentialities, and our judgment of them may be wide of the mark. The automobile, bus, and truck will continue to be the major mode of movement in metropolitan areas of up to two million population. They work now with remarkable efficiency, and could be improved substantially with better highway and parking facilities, safety devices, and pollution prevention devices. The automobile will have to be further constrained when we have 250 million cars. One would guess that the volume and direction of automobile movement will be widely controlled by computer and that the driver will be required to reserve freeway space as is now done with airline reservations. On major facilities automatic control of vehicles will prevail.

As one approaches any major high-density activity center in those areas, the degree of social control will perforce increase, the degree of individual control will be reduced, the degree of collective ownership or use will be increased, and that of individual ownership or use decreased, the proportion of mass transit will be increased. Vehicles entering major high-density zones may be equipped with homing devices so that they will go away by themselves, be stored, and reappear upon demand and after reasonable notice. Individual ownership of the vehicle will probably be much more costly, if permitted at all, than collective ownership. Payment of a rental charge would entitle the user to services on a system of collectively-owned small vehicles which were available upon demand at many points within the system and were charged on an actual utilization basis. In at least a dozen of the larger metropolitan areas only fully automatic tracking vehicles like the Starr car will be permitted. These will permit individual guidance and control at the low-density destination and mass control at high volumes in the high-density destination. The automobile is not going to disappear, in short, but it will be radically modified and controlled, pooled and rented, and, in high-density areas, supplemented by other facilities.

At present, only 2 or 3 per cent of the population flies regularly and only about 10 per cent has ever flown. Yet airports have become major shapers of the metropolitan area and major forces determining the growth or decline of whole metropolitan areas. Since it seems inevitable that within the foreseeable future the proportion of the population that flies regularly will multiply manyfold, and the proportion that has flown will increase several-fold, one would guess that the form-shaping effects of air travel have only begun to be felt. We are only at the beginning in vertical take-off craft and helicopter service, and local travel by air is therefore in its most primitive stages. The control mechanisms for modest volumes of local flights are largely in existence in the space and defense programs and will surely be applied to permit much larger volumes of local air travel. Even though local air travel may not serve the huge volumes required by high-density zones, since both air and land modes will operate and exist side by side, it is clear that pricing, licensing, and other volume controls must be devised as technical capacity restraints become operative.

In mass transit we are beginning to see a resurgence of rail transit by means of subsidy. This has been stimulated by the belated recognition that the central city cannot survive without efficient mass transit. Japan already has a 225-kilometer-per-hour train system which functions superbly and which is planned to operate at even higher speeds. The East Coast Corridor Study is now exploring other possibilities, including the revival of the pneumatic subway, a train-like vehicle which would have center to center speeds exceeding those of air travel. Sooner or later, of course, we must solve the problems of travel to the airport to enable air travel to be competitive or even humane.

The terminals and stops on high-density, high-speed transportation systems have yet to be fully exploited. The Pan American building on top of Grand Central Station is not an accident. When the 200-mile-an-hour railroad is finally installed, it will generate many ultra-high-density activity centers, and many ultra-high-density residential centers. An interesting and unresolved enigma is whether other changes of mode points can ever achieve the volumes to justify, or the technologies to permit, high-density development.

CONCLUSION

The functions of the metropolitan area are changing rapidly. As the functions change, the form and structure of the metropolitan area must also change. A new technology, a new affluence, new forms of corporate and governmental organization, and changing public values—all of these acting in combination are creating metropolitan areas whose size, geographic extent, and variety exceed anything previously envisaged by man. Metropolitan areas of the future may reach 100 miles in any direction and contain populations larger than those of many nations. It would be foolish to attempt to forecast in detail the effect of these changes upon form and structure.

But further, our life styles are changing, becoming more varied and different. Read the Utopias again, the Utopias which have shaped so much of our thought about the future. In the main, they present pictures of relatively single-valued systems, of societies more monolithic than our present one, of static or closed societies, ill adapted to change and innovation.[11] If there is any virtue in the American society it is in the promise that it will remain open. Democracy, the free market, and receptivity to change have produced something here that no one could have envisaged at the turn of the century. Having embarked upon receptivity to change as a sort of national principle, we would be ill advised at this late date to seek others, especially the more fixed and stable ones of the Utopias.

American metropolitan areas are not headed toward Ebenezer Howard's tidy little new towns surrounded by countryside. While we may have several—indeed, we may hope that we could have many—the new communities we build will certainly contain popula-

11. Thomas Reiner, *The Place of the Ideal Community in Urban Planning* (Philadelphia: University of Pennsylvania Press, 1963).

tions of 100,000 and are more likely to contain populations of a quarter of a million. They will be larger than the whole metropolitan areas with which Howard was concerned. Nor will our metropolitan areas be those envisaged by Bellamy, with their solid middle-class values—everyone nice, tidy, polite, well dressed, and well ordered. They will not even be Wirth's metropolitan areas of acculturation and assimilation. Instead, they will be characterized by a wide variety of values and ways of life, hopefully organized so that each can explore its own destiny in contiguity to others, or perhaps in the same physical space. Certainly we will have many, perhaps mostly, nonspatial communities. Nor will our metropolitan areas be the cities of empire arranged in grand geometric order by Burnham. That order has already been dissolved by the free-flowing form of the expressway, by the disintegration of the ordered central business district, by the asymmetrically-centered skyscraper technology. The new centers and subcenters will have a far different order, a different rhythm, a different technology, and a different purpose.

Our metropolitan areas of the future will not even resemble the garden metropolises of Le Corbusier, of ordered skyscrapers standing in a park. We will have many pieces of Le Corbusier, as we do today, in Chicago, in New York, and in Los Angeles. But the parks envisaged are in fact a surrounding landscape of single detached houses. Similar areas of the future may reach higher densities than he envisaged and still remain only fragments of the metropolitan area—model points in a changing metropolis. Nor, finally, will our metropolitan areas be Wright's Broadacre City, though they will contain hundreds, indeed thousands, of square miles of relatively low-density urbanized area, mixing industrial, commercial, and residential uses much as he envisaged them and linked primarily by automobiles.

No, the metropolis of the future will be one of huge size, of vast extent, of great diversity, of rigid change, and to the extent that it is open to future change, of indeterminate form. Many of these forms will be new, the ultra-high-density nodes, central districts, outlying highly accessible residential districts, and outlying highly accessible specialist activity districts. These will be linked with ultra-high-speed transportation and communications systems. Both will exist in zones of relatively low density, as measured by the standards of the past. They will also be linked by networks of public and private open space sufficient, we hope, to maintain a viable natural ecology. We will have new cities, many of them representing new styles of life and some, perhaps, to replicate for those who desire it relatively fixed examples of old styles of life. Because we need both stability and change, we will have areas for conservation and areas constantly being renovated or renewed, areas for the citizen whose neighborhood is the world, and areas for the urban villager.

Our concepts of metropolitan planning have been evolving rapidly. They have been expanded, have become enriched, and are becoming more open. They still, however, fail to provide for the flexibility which must characterize the future, for the degree of local choice which will surely be maintained to preserve what is left of the tradition of local democracy. Nor do our metropolitan plans embrace the geographic scope of the metropolis of the future or its administrative form. We are embarked upon a period of very rapid evolution in professional thought to devise new methods of foreseeing the forms which the future will generate and to accommodate our present actions and our proposals to that scale of change.

4 NATIONAL COMMISSION ON URBAN PROBLEMS

The city as it is and as it might be

INTRODUCTION AND SUMMARY

The anger of the slums is that of people disinherited from our society.

"You *know* what our slums look like! You *know* we need help there! We have rats, roaches, plaster falling from the walls, we have two-family flats rented out to four and five families with children, and sometimes no bathroom!" The young woman from the slums of East St. Louis was angry and accusing. There we were, she said, prying around looking at poor folks. She obviously felt that our interest was purely academic and clinical.

She couldn't have been more wrong. That afternoon of hearings in East St. Louis really hurt. And it was not the first time it hurt either. The National Commission on Urban Problems heard the same anger from hundreds of slum-dwellers all over the country in 1967.

At the outset of its formation in January 1967, the Commission knew what slums were. Like others, most of the Commission members had seen them and had read about them, but from a distance. We traveled to the slum areas of two dozen cities across the United States and heard from citizens—and the experts—in all of them. We could have stayed in Washington and gathered statistics, but statistics do not tell enough about a slum.

One has to see and touch and smell a slum before one fully appreciates the real urgency of the problem.

We walked the streets and talked with residents of the most notorious ghettos of the country. Names that are now becoming familiar to all Americans—Harlem, Watts, Hough, South Central, the Hill in Pittsburgh, the Hill District in New Haven, the North Side of Philadelphia, the West Side of Chicago, the East Side of Cleveland, and East St. Louis. We talked with people of all walks of life and all shades of involvement with the problems. Black and white, rich and poor, the administrators, the activists, the militants, and the concerned citizens. The experience was vivid and moving.

We saw the face of the deteriorating central city and the awesome pattern of suburban sprawl in southern California. We saw the face of redeveloping urban America—the Southwest of Washington, Lake Meadows, and Hyde Park in Chicago, Dixwell in New Haven, Society Hill in Philadelphia, Roxbury in Boston, downtown Baltimore, and the new face of urban Atlanta.

We saw rural renewal in Grand Prairie, Texas, and the private renewal of areas that are just in the earliest stages of graying in Arlington, Texas.

The civil disorders of the hot summer of 1967 followed us and preceded us. We saw the ugly, burned-out urban streets that were still smoldering in some places, and we sensed the tension and the anxiety in communities that would erupt not too long after our being there.

To say that the urban problem is essentially a problem of big-city slums is not only simplistic, to a large degree it is erroneous. A slum is a geographic place with buildings and other facilities in varying stages of deterioration, but people as well as houses, stores, streets, and lots make slums. And what is happening in the slums and the rest of the central city cannot be separated from the kind and pace of growth in the suburbs.

The people in the slums are the symptoms of the urban problems, not the cause. They are virtually imprisoned in slums by the white suburban noose around the inner city, a noose that says "Negroes and poor people not wanted." It says this in a variety of ways, including discriminatory subdivision regulations, discriminatory fiscal and planning practices. In simple terms, what many of these practices add up to is a refusal of many localities to accept their share of housing for poor people. But the problem is more than that.

The urban problem can be described as the big-city slum, and as the white suburban noose, but also as all the problems of growth and population shifts and sprawl and public expenses connected with them. A far bigger *proportion* of Negroes—and of American Indians, Puerto Ricans, and Mexican-Americans—are subjected to poverty and to miserable housing than holds true for whites. But a far bigger *number* of whites are poor and in bad housing. Some point to the proportions and say the urban problem is entirely a racial issue. Others who point to the numbers say it has little to do with race. Both miss important dimensions of what is happening. And what is happening threatens the future of our metropolitan areas.

Much of the problem has resulted from a lack of political commitment on the part of the larger society to do anything really constructive for and about the disinherited, the aliens within our culture.

Many Americans find it curious that slums should be such a problem, or the symptom of our biggest domestic problem. Why now? they ask. Slums have been a historical fact in every major city. The forebears of almost all Americans who are now in the middle class came through one urban slum or another, before moving into the mainstream of the larger society.

The imagery of a "mainstream" is useful in understanding the present slum problem. Like the waters that feed a big river, the rural poor trickle in from the fields and the hills. Time was when they paused in slack water (the slums) before moving out into the mainstream. Today the poor are still pouring into the slack water, although at a slower rate, but now there's a dam at the other end, so great numbers appear fated to stay in the slums unless they get help.

That dam, holding back the slack water, is a complex mixture of many things. One major component of it seems to be the present middle-class culture which is alien and even hostile to today's rural poor. Those in this cultural mainstream speak a different language and have different values.

But it is more than cultural. As the Commission investigated housing and building codes, land-use policies, governmental arrangements, Federal housing programs, and local and Federal taxes that affect city growth patterns, we found a web of urban matters, often ignored and equally often misunderstood, which combine to deny decent housing, job opportunities, and minimum urban services to the poor.

A generation and more ago there were plenty of jobs that simply took brawn, jobs slum-dwellers could easily do. Most of the new job openings our society creates are white collar jobs and highly skilled jobs, jobs that take at least a high school education. However, you can't fully explain the current crisis by pointing out that most of those jobs are now done by machines. It's far more complex than that.

Our society is designed to assure most of us available alternatives to where we live, how we live, and what we do. Big-city slum-dwellers do not have this freedom of choice. They are denied a full range of opportunities in education, jobs, and housing. Mainstream Americans take those opportunities for granted and slum-dwellers know this. They know how the more prosperous half lives and they aspire to the same way of life. The fact that they cannot achieve this way of life is a source of much of their anger and bitterness.

We on the Commission are acutely aware, even more so than when we first met in January 1967, that this report itself will not change a slum or build a single unit of adequate housing. But a report can move people and government to action, action specifically designed to change a slum.

From a cottonfield in the South, big cities look like the only chance left to the rural poor, but city slums become prisons for the disinherited when they arrive.

The tide of migration from the rural South into the big cities lies at the heart of many of our urban problems today. In the 1950's Arkansas, West Virginia, Mississippi, and South Carolina lost more than one-fourth of their nonwhite population, while millions of nonwhites poured into our central cities.

Obviously, underlying the move of both whites and nonwhites from the rural South was the mechanization of farming that has changed all agriculture in the last generation. The most popular speculation concerning the move frequently has been exaggerated: that big-city welfare payments drew in the poor. New York State's welfare payment to a family of four is more than five times higher than Mississippi's payment. It is not enough in itself to support a family although it is far better than what is available in Mississippi. But most experts agree that the real reason behind the migration was just plain gumption. Families with gumption got up and got out of areas where there were no longer any jobs for them, or where share-cropping and tenancy conditions made holding a job on a farm meaningless.

What attracted the migrants was the gleaming hope of a better life that our bustling industrial complexes have always held out to the poor and the downtrodden. So they poured into our big northern and western metropolitan areas. Many have indeed caught on in city life and we should not ignore that fact. In March 1967, for example, the average Negro family in the metropolitan areas had an annual income of $5,300 as compared with an average of $2,900 for those who remained behind in the nonmetropolitan areas.[1] But many did not get jobs and what happened to them was commonly tragic. The able-bodied men often could not find jobs in the alien culture. To qualify for welfare it was necessary in many cities for the family to break up. Many welfare practices sapped the slum-dweller's incentive to find a job and hold his family together. If the father of a family on welfare got a job, most of what he earned was deducted from his family's welfare payments. In effect, he may have been taxed up to 100 percent on his earnings. So he faced a hard choice: Quit the job or abandon his family? Important reforms now are finally being made in such upside down welfare rules.[2]

Starting with slavery, the Negroes' treatment and place in society have had the effect of weakening the status of the Negro male and, therefore, the family life of Negro citizens. And any number of studies have shown that, without the man, the family tends to fall apart.

Of about 8.4 million people now on welfare in the United States less than 80,000 are employable adult men. There are, however, a great many employable adults among the 1,278,000 mothers on welfare, but adequate day-care centers for their children are almost nonexistent.[3] No welfare program in the country has the budget for enough day-care centers to permit all the able-bodied mothers on welfare to earn by working outside the family.

Then, too, if any of those now on welfare are to enter the mainstream, they must be assisted by programs which permit them to learn basic skills and the rudiments of reading, writing, and arithmetic. Our failure to assimilate the nonwhite slum-dweller into the larger society is particularly shocking in light of the fact that we recognize the problems of assimilation for another group of people: Cubans entering the United States are provided—by the Department of Health, Education, and Welfare—medical and psychiatric services, family counseling services, employment counseling services, plus financial assistance. For them, welfare is a national program.

1. Negro Population, March 1967. Bureau of the Census Series P-20, No. 175, October 23, 1968. (The corresponding figures for whites were $8,500 and $6,500, respectively.)

2. The year 1968 witnessed two major advances in the welfare field. The Supreme Court in a decision knocked out the "man-in-the-house" rule, applied in 18 states, and the Department of HEW promptly required compliance with the court's interpretation that a family otherwise eligible for welfare aid could not be denied assistance because of the presence of an adult male in the home. Secondly, a job incentive plan was instituted, with a number of states carrying it out on an optional basis before it was to become mandatory for all states in July, 1969. Under this plan, the first $30 of monthly wages and 30 percent of the remainder are exempted from income taxation. (Many experts urge an exemption of the first $50 and 50 percent of the remainder.)

3. HEW data as of March, 1968.

For poor American citizens, it is still a State by State or local matter. Before the refugee family moves North, East, or West, efforts to locate jobs, housing and neighborhood contacts are worked out by the staff of HEW's Cuban refugee programs.[4] For the poor American family, few such services are provided.

The accomplishments of this program for Cubans are outstanding and indicate what can be done once the Nation commits itself to solving a specific problem.

The uneducated and unskilled American rural migrant family needs even greater help than the typical Cuban refugee who arrives here with a good education and with job skills. Yet no institution responds to the massive migration of native rural families moving North, East, and West from the South. It is more difficult to locate and hence to deal with these migrants since they come from thousands of separate sources and go to a myriad of places instead of, like the Cubans, funneling through a few distributing points such as Miami. But more should and could be done to locate, train, and assimilate them.

The economic picture for the migrant is often a grim one. Non-white slum-dwellers live with an unemployment rate that is at least twice as high as for whites. For some groups such as teenagers it amounts to 25 percent or more. Female heads of poor families experience a rate as high as 50 percent. In 1968, the unemployed generally, and especially the jobless Negroes, were concentrated in the Nation's largest metropolitan areas. In some big-city slums only about half of the adult men have full-time jobs and about one-fifth of those with full-time jobs earn less than $60 per week.

It is true that real incomes per household in most central cities are steadily increasing, but this is not true in some of the worst slum areas. And the cost of living for the poor often rises faster than incomes. The gap between wages and basic costs for the person in poverty is often astronomical.

Even though Americans below the poverty level fell from 39 million to 26 million in the 8 years from 1958 to 1966, a phenomenal record, we still have a long way to go to close the gap. Available employment of the type for which slum adults might qualify is generally not available in the slum. In a recent year, 63 percent of all construction permits for industrial buildings were issued for locations outside central cities. On the other hand, 73 percent of office building construction permits were issued inside central cities. Central cities increasingly are becoming white-collar employ-

4. See *Hearings Before the National Commission on Urban Problems*, vol. 5, 1968, pp. 333–46.

ment centers while the suburbs are becoming the job employment areas for new blue-collar workers. This is ironical in view of the fact that low-paid blue-collar workers, especially if they are Negroes, live in the central cities while the white-collar workers are increasingly living in the suburbs. Traveling to work becomes increasingly difficult for both. Whites and blacks, white collars and blue collars, pass each other by as they come and go from work.

The problem is further compounded by the fact that a slum-dweller's dollar buys a lot less for him than it will for the average middle-class American. The American standard of living is inextricably bound to our system of credit. The uneducated and unemployed are more often victims, rather than beneficiaries, of the credit system. Lacking a credit rating, the poor are driven to those institutions which specialize in high-risk loans at a very high cost to the consumer. Then, too, the band of residential segregation around the ghetto, aptly termed the white noose, coupled with increased immigration and a natural population growth, generates a greater demand for living space—however badly deteriorated or rat infested —at relatively high cost.

Perhaps the most potentially explosive problem we face in our cities is the fact that the increase of nonwhites in central cities is accompanied by just as big a movement of whites from the center city to the suburbs. The result is an almost unyielding pattern of segregation.

For instance, an on-going Chicago survey takes an annual count of specific blocks which contain more than 25 percent Negro population. In 1950 there were 1,080 such blocks. Between 1950 and 1960 an additional 1,344 blocks shifted from less than 25 percent Negro to more than 25 percent Negro. From 1960 to 1961 1,101 more blocks similarly shifted. Thus the *rate* of transition from white to nonwhite occupancy actually increased from 2.6 blocks per week to 3.5 blocks per week.

Negro isolation could become even more serious than it is today. Projections based on recent experience[5] show that, between 1960 and 1985, central cities could lose 2.4 million or 5 percent of their whites, but gain 10 million nonwhites, a 94 percent increase. This means that nonwhites would move up from 18 to 31 percent of the population of the Nation's central cities (see Fig. 4–1).

If the Negroes continue moving into the suburbs at the present rate, their projected number will jump from 2.8 to 6.8 million. But

5. Patricia Leavey Hodge and Philip M. Hauser, *The Challenge of America's Metropolitan Population Outlook—1960 to 1985*, National Commission on Urban Problems, 1968.

the number of suburban whites will also more than double, from 52 to 106 million. So the additional Negroes will be all but lost in a sea of whites, as their proportional increase will move from only 5 to 6 percent of the total suburban population by 1985.

These are projections, not predictions. They show the direction in which we have been heading, a shift toward greater racial stratification. But we should not fool ourselves that solutions are easy. It will take massive efforts to reverse the past trends and the momentum behind them.

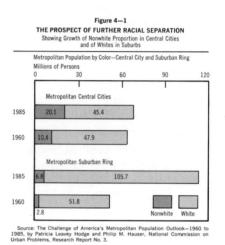

Figure 4—1
THE PROSPECT OF FURTHER RACIAL SEPARATION
Showing Growth of Nonwhite Proportion in Central Cities
and of Whites in Suburbs

Source: The Challenge of America's Metropolitan Population Outlook—1960 to 1985, by Patricia Leavey Hodge and Philip M. Hauser, National Commission on Urban Problems, Research Report No. 3.

In State legislatures and in the Congress there are strong indications now that the old rural-city rivalry is being replaced by a rural/suburban-city rivalry. This new suburban and rural coalition until now has significantly limited the ability of urban legislators to change the nature of statutes and programs which affect the central city, and it also reinforces suburban exclusiveness, and the power blocs behind it. This reinforcement, in effect, exacts a subsidy from the central city by imprisoning low-income families and poor families in the central city and sharply limits the dispersion of low-income families to the suburbs.

The overwhelming majority of the future nonwhite population growth is likely to be concentrated in central cities unless major changes in public policies come about. But one searches in vain to find current programs of Federal, State, or local governments aimed at significantly altering this tendency.

Slums in our big cities, which are now in the midst of social decay, may well become social and economic disaster areas.

It is entirely possible that a greater concentration of Negroes in the central cities would be accompanied by an increase in tension and violence. If this violence is met by repressive measures there could be a further polarization of blacks and whites, and the flight of more and more businesses, and therefore, jobs, from the city.

The suicidal consequences that such a possibility suggests are not pleasant to contemplate. They threaten our country.

Our big cities are hard up, costs of local government are skyrocketing, and representation for the poor in slums is almost nonexistent.

The lowest income groups are attracted to the inner city slums because that is often where the oldest urban housing is offered at the lowest rents. It needs to be stressed that the weekly rents are often low only because so many people are crowded into such small and poorly equipped space; figured on a per house or per room basis, or as a percentage of investment, the rents received by the owner may be quite high indeed.

The concentration of low-income families places an inordinate burden on each central city to provide welfare services, expanded police protection, and other costly public services. Yet the departure of many middle- and upper-income residents and many industries to the suburbs weakens the central city tax base. The conversion of neighborhoods from middle-income to low-income occupancy, which occurs when slums expand, also reduces the prosperity of retail businesses, thereby further depressing the local tax base. So center cities experience a sharp rise in demand for revenue at the same time that their ability to produce revenue is either static or declining. The result can be, and sometimes is, death for a neighborhood or the slow strangulation of the city itself.

City services cost money. In 1962, the per capita expenditure of local governments averaged one-third more in metropolitan areas than elsewhere. However, the main reason for higher public expenditure in cities is that urban life requires public provision of some services that, under rural conditions, need not or cannot be supplied, like street cleaning, and public sewerage systems. Also cities call for increased intensity of other kinds of public services such as fire protection.

Percentage ratios of per capita expenditure show four functions—public housing and urban renewal, nonhighway transportation, refuse collection and street cleaning, and parks and recreation—for which spending is over 200 percent higher in metropolitan areas than elsewhere. In three functions—police protection, fire protection, and sewerage—the urban level averages from 100 to 200 percent higher. Public welfare, libraries, water supply, health and hospitals, and interest on debt show the urban level averages from 35 to 90 percent higher. Only metropolitan-area spending on streets and highways is well below local public per capita expenditure elsewhere for this purpose.

Urban government expenditure is now running at an annual rate of about $370 per capita, or about one-tenth as much as the average per capita income of metropolitan area residents. In the 20 years following World War II local government expenditure increased 571 percent, or at a much faster rate than gross national product (up 259 percent). Metropolitan areas account for nearly three-fourths of all local public spending.

More than 40 percent of urban government spending is for education—mainly for elementary and high schools, but including some expenditure for local colleges and junior colleges. Social welfare functions take about one-sixth of the total and about one-tenth goes to water supply and sanitation, a tenth to highways and other transportation, and a tenth to police and fire protection, with all other urban expenditure making up the remainder.

Local taxes provide about one-half of all the funds needed to finance urban government services, with the balance supplied by intergovernmental revenue and local nontax sources, such as service charges and benefit assessments. Our 38 largest metropolitan areas, with 41 percent of the Nation's population, account for about one-half of all local government finances. In 1966, local government revenue in these 38 areas averaged $351 per capita, or 44 percent higher than in the rest of the country. Direct Federal grants made to urban governments are not yet major revenue sources. While these grants have been rising rapidly, the 1962–66 increase in Federal aid to the major metropolitan areas accounted for only $346 million of the added $7.8 billion of annual local government revenue. Local property taxes provided $2.7 billion of that increased revenue.

The property tax is the largest single source of urban government financing. Property taxes are widely criticized because they are so regressive, inequitably levied and poorly administered in almost every municipality in the United States. Even so, in response to needs, the property tax yield has been rising strongly. Nationwide, State-local property tax revenues in 1967 totaled $27.7 billion—against $19.1 billion 5 years earlier—with metropolitan areas accounting for about three-fourths of the total.

Slums are expensive to city administrations. Normally, their costs reflect high welfare, police, and fire department activity. In other services, such as schools, garbage and trash removal, snow removal, street surfacing and repair, replacement of old and inadequate water and sewer lines, the slums, where additional expenditures are badly needed, are usually on the bottom of the priority lists (if they manage to get on the list at all) in competition with other city neighborhoods.

Large cities have great problems of keeping the streets clean, but in the slum neighborhoods sanitary conditions generally are intolerable. Practically all can be characterized by junk- and garbage-filled lots, abandoned cars, broken bottles, and scattered debris. Whether this is the fault of the city, of the landlords, of the tenants, or of people from other neighborhoods who use these neighborhoods as their dumps is a futile argument. All are involved. No one group can really solve the problem without the cooperation of the others. Too often the people living in a block try to spruce it up but get discouraged because the city or the landlords do not do their part. City sanitation departments similarly become indifferent if their genuine effort produces little visible difference.

A common characteristic of an evolving slum is a mixture of land uses not conducive to a neighborhood of homes. One small neighborhood we saw in Philadelphia had seven junk shops, two slaughterhouses and 10 bars within its boundaries. Planning often fails to weed out such land uses. Many "nonconforming" uses, recognized as incompatible to an area, are permitted because they existed before residential zoning began. Others, although disallowed under a zoning plan, creep in as "variances," the planning term for exceptions to the rules. Most cities require that a notice be posted for a number of days prior to a hearing for the issuance of a zoning variance. Perhaps no one in the neighborhood understands the meaning of the notice, or if the notice is understood, the loss of a day's pay to protest the granting of a variance is generally considered too high a price to pay for being a good citizen. The unemployed members of slum communities conceivably could attend the hearings but they lack experience and the respect from officialdom to accomplish much in this field. So the hearing proceeds without effective local opposition, usually resulting in the granting of the variance. Variances and nonconforming uses help mightily to create and perpetuate slums.

The problems raised by all of the foregoing are monumental and basic. Take the lack of fiscal resources, political representation, and general neglect in slum areas. Couple those facts with the middle class moving to the suburbs and a new rural/suburban political coalition. All of those facts could hasten the time when the only strong voice that would speak for the slums would be the Federal Government, at best a distant and indifferent parent. And that voice would be represented in Congress by an even smaller percentage of representatives than the slums have today.

Coping with metropolitan area problems is incredibly complex because of the proliferation of local governments, all with differing viewpoints, within those areas.

Right after World War II, middle-class America accelerated its flight to the suburbs so fast that thousands of square miles of farmland were turned into housing developments virtually overnight. The pace of that rush has not yet noticeably slowed. To serve the urban needs of this new suburbia, new units of local government were created by the thousands. These included more than newly incorporated rural villages; they included all kinds of special districts to provide schools, garbage collection, water supply, street lighting, sewage treatment and the like. If all these units of government were laid out on a map, every metropolitan area in the country would look as if it had been "nonplanned" by a mad man. These crazy-quilt metropolitan areas actually are the work of sane human beings, well-intentioned in their work, but often reaching for the easy, expedient, and politically popular solution.

The U.S. Bureau of the Census defines a metropolitan area as "an integrated economic and social unit with a recognized large population nucleus." As of 1967, the Census Bureau recognized 228 such areas in the United States. They are called "standard metropolitan statistical areas" or SMSA's. Generally, an SMSA consists of one or more entire county areas, primarily nonagricultural and closely related to a central city, or cities, of 50,000 or more. (In New England, SMSA's consist of groups of cities and townships rather than of entire counties.)

Nearly two-thirds of all Americans live in metropolitan areas. Slightly less than half of all metropolitan area residents live in the central metropolitan cities, but most of the increase in SMSA population is taking place in the outlying-ring territory, suburbia.

In 1967, our metropolitan areas were served by 20,745 local governments, or about one-fourth of all local governments in the Nation. This means 91 governments per SMSA—an average of about 48 per metropolitan county. But these averages cover great variations. There are 20 SMSA's with fewer than 10 local governments each—13 in the South, five in New England, and two in the

West. At the other extreme are such SMSA's as Chicago, with 1,113 local governments (186 per county); Philadelphia, with 871 (109 per county); Pittsburgh, with 704 (176 per county); and New York, with 551 (110 per county).

The overwhelming majority of these local governments are relatively small. For example, two thirds of the municipalities in SMSA's have a population of less than 5,000 and one-third of the total number have fewer than 1,000 residents. Similarly, of the 3,225 townships in SMSA's, over two-thirds have a population of less than 5,000. Most of the SMSA special districts also involve only small-scale operations. Of all the school districts in metropolitan areas, about one-fourth have fewer than 300 pupils, and about one-third operate no more than a single school.

In physical size many of the local governments in metropolitan areas are extremely small. Of all the municipalities in SMSA's, about one-half have less than a single square mile of land area, probably 60 percent are smaller than 2 square miles, and four-fifths have a land area of under 4 square miles. Fewer than 200 SMSA municipalities include as much as 25 square miles of land area.

Most residents of metropolitan areas, then, are served by at least four separate local governments, i.e., a county, municipality, or township, and a school district, plus one or more special districts. The average SMSA central city has more than four overlapping local governments.

The abuses that such a multiplicity of governments work on a metropolitan area are many, and we need not list them all here. One is the discriminatory zoning that suburban towns adopt. Zoning, which is barely a body of law, very effectively keeps the poor and those with low incomes out of suburban areas by stipulating lot sizes way beyond their economic reach. Many suburbs prohibit or severely limit the construction of apartments, townhouses, or planned unit developments which could accommodate more people in less space at potential savings in housing costs. Even where apartments are allowed, they often are limited as to size of dwelling unit, effectively keeping out families with children who would presumably place a burden on school budgets. Zoning is also used by most suburban areas to keep out blue-collar industry which could go a long way in providing the types of jobs low-income people could take if they could afford to live in the suburbs.

Another bad effect of too many local governments comes from their competitive scramble to attract industry. To support faltering local economies, communities often put industrial plants in places where, according to sound planning, they do not belong. The favors held out to bring in industry then make it possible for companies to avoid their fair share of the metropolitan area tax burden.

Still another abuse is excessive strip zoning along main thoroughfares, sometimes used to increase the tax base with commerce. The resulting gaudy development is a major offender in urban ugliness.

All of the foregoing raises the question: How many local governments would there be in metropolitan areas if it were somehow possible, in each SMSA, to replace existing arrangements by a set of comprehensive units, each responsible for providing all local public services for its own defined territory and each serving a population of at least 50,000 persons?

Such an arrangement can be tested by reference to 1960 population figures for the 228 SMSA's as defined in 1967. On this basis, the metropolitan areas altogether would have approximately 1,300 local governments, or an average of less than six per area as compared with the present average of 90 per SMSA. If thus reorganized, about one-fourth of the SMSA's would each be served by only a single local government, and nearly as many by two local governments apiece. At the other extreme, this approach would involve more than 30 governments for each of seven very large metropolitan areas—58 for the Los Angeles-Long Beach SMSA (instead of 223); 55 for the New York SMSA (instead of 551); 52 for the Chicago SMSA (instead of 1,113); 46 for the Philadelphia area (instead of 876); 38 for the Detroit SMSA (instead of 242); 37 for the Pittsburgh SMSA (instead of 146).

Unless local units are large enough to function well, it is almost certain that the demands for better services will cause power over local affairs to be shifted to higher levels. This is not theory, but simply a statement of political fact that has been observed many times over the past generation. We should weed out many of the unnecessary, overlapping layers of local government, especially the very small units and special districts.

While we strongly favor consolidations to form larger city governments and would offer revenue incentives to political jurisdictions with 50,000 people or more in major urban areas, we should not overlook the counties. County governments have a largely undeveloped potential for handling many urban matters. This is understandably overlooked or flatly denied in many parts of the country because most counties still stick to obsolete procedures and programs. But they do cover broad geographical areas. They embrace substantial populations–whole cross sections, not just narrow interest groups. And they draw from a tax base spread over a whole spectrum of land uses. These advantages explain why a few urban counties already are taking the lead in restoring a unified approach to metropolitan affairs. One lesson is that counties must modernize if they are to exercise leadership on the local scene. At present they are a very weak reed, indeed. They do have a much greater potential.

A big key to the success of revising, enlarging, and rationalizing local boundaries is held by the State legislatures. Local governments can hardly be expected to do this by themselves; their lack of objectivity and perspective in these matters is one reason the urban areas are in such trouble already. Although many State legislatures have been indifferent to city problems, they have authority to cure many urban ills.

Recent metropolitan reorganization efforts have experienced more setbacks than successes. Public apathy has been more prevalent than outright opposition. In the record of attempts at a significant restructuring of local government in metropolitan areas—the handful accomplished as well as the unsuccessful efforts—one feature stands out; each was primarily a local undertaking, initiated and pursued uniquely in the areas concerned, even though basically authorized by State constitutional or statutory provisions and sometimes some specific State action. Because each metropolitan area has it own particular problems and attitudes, major structural changes should be tailor-made by local people.

Councils of governments in various places around the country are making genuine progress in giving local government a new perspective. Some students of government say that the councils do not move us along as swiftly or as far toward metropolitan government as they believe necessary. The fact is, however, that really comprehensive mergers will take a great deal of time. Meanwhile, many areas, spurred by Federal incentives, are combining metropolitan services, saving taxpayers' dollars, learning to work together, and developing loyalties beyond their own backyards. Councils of government should not be used as a sedative, however, to lull the public into indifference about consolidations of governments when that is needed.

Can a restructuring of local government, at the scale required, ever be done? The answer we believe is a highly qualified "yes." The need for change is too urgent to permit complacency on this score.

As one of the Nation's most thoughtful students of these matters said recently:

America's great urban regions lack the powers to guide their development. They cannot decide the use of their most precious commodity—open land; nor prevent the fouling of their air and water; nor assure equality in opportunity and education for their children. Until they have such authority—until suburb and central city acknowledge in these specific respects their common concern—we can blanket the present array of local jurisdictions in a blizzard of Federal cash and still fail to protect our urban heritage and upgrade our urban environment.[6]

How do these governmental issues relate to the problems of poverty, segregation, and civil rights, so explosively reflected by recent unrest and disorder in many cities? To oversimplify a complex question, it takes financially strong and structurally sound local governments to deal fairly and firmly with these social problems. The Commission was impressed by the number of highly motivated, conscientious local officials; but these officials often are ineffective because of the economic weakness and splintered authority of their local governments. Even worse, in other cases, the existing governmental patterns contribute to conflict and social discontent. So the growing public concern about the urban crisis should help overcome the apathy that often characterized efforts to modernize local government.

Those most likely to live in substandard housing are the poor nonwhites who have big families and are renters. But they are not alone. A third of our affluent Nation cannot afford adequate, nonsubsidized housing today, despite great gains in our housing stock.

Most measures of substandard housing include not only dilapidated housing but also standard or deteriorating housing with inadequate plumbing. Estimates of housing need in addition must take account of overcrowding or what might be called substandard occupancy, when the number of people in a household outnumber the number of rooms. (Bathrooms and closets do not count as rooms: kitchens do.) But as our report frequently emphasizes, we consider these measures inadequate, leading to a gross understatement of the Nation's housing needs.

Decent housing has a far more subjective definition. Almost no agreed standards exist for measuring what is decent housing, which is why the Commission proposes a system for arriving at useful standards. Definitions will change, of course, as the standards of living and expectations rise. For middle-class Americans at the end of the 1960's, decent housing implies a high level of amenity, both in the house and within its immediate environment, a level of amenity none of the rest of the world, outside the rich, enjoys in its housing.

6. Under-Secretary Robert C. Wood, Department of Housing and Urban Development, from a speech on October 24, 1968.

To meet middle-class aspirations, decent housing may mean, for instance, enough bathrooms so there are no morning lineups as the family gets ready for work and school; uncrowded bedrooms; and a kitchen with a sink, range, oven, refrigerator, counter space, and outlets for portable appliances. Many even would include as minimum requirements dishwashers, clothes washers and dryers, garbage disposals, and, in areas of hot climate, air conditioning.

Even such housing does not meet many people's idea of what is decent unless, in the neighborhood, there is recreation for children, shopping, and public transportation. Cultural or entertainment facilities within easy reach, trees, grass, flowers, and other features that make a neighborhood pleasant and livable are expected. In short, the house that is adequate in itself ceases to be adequate for the middle-class family when dropped in the middle of a slum or otherwise unsuitable surroundings.

On the other hand, the world of a slum child is a world of substandard housing, often without plumbing or heat, infested with rats and insects, and so packed with many more people than there are rooms that a child is happy to live on the streets all summer.

There are today at the very least 11 million substandard and overcrowded dwelling units in the United States. This is 16 percent of the total housing inventory. According to the census, three-fifths of all that substandard housing is said to be in rural areas— generally on farms and in towns of less than 2,500 persons. Thirty-six percent of all rural housing is substandard, compared with estimates of 10 percent of all urban housing. These are highly conservative figures. And they not only greatly understate the problem but tend to mask the critical aspect of the urban housing problem—the *concentration* of substandard housing and of poor people.

In metropolitan areas there are about 4 million substandard and overcrowded units. Almost that many more are so deteriorated they need constant repair. Another several million have serious code violations. Recent surveys in some inner city slums indicate, instead of improvement, a deterioration in this inventory. Not all of the people in these houses are poor. Many have moderate incomes—between $3,500 and $6,000—and are trapped in inadequate housing because there is no decent housing within their ability to pay. It should also be noted that just as all who live in bad housing are not poor, neither do all poor people live in bad housing.

In some places, there is a steady increase in substandard housing. In New York City, for example, the number of substandard units has risen since 1960. However, it is not only the size but the concentration of substandard urban housing which is the problem in city areas. In cities where the *general* average for substandard over-crowded units is only 10 percent, 40 percent of the housing in slum areas may be deficient.

Most important, poverty families in substandard housing have a high correlation with race. If you are *poor* and *nonwhite* and *rent* the chances are three out of four that you live in substandard housing.

To use another measure, 45 percent of all nonwhite *owner* household families had incomes of $3,000 or less or were poverty families. But these poverty families occupied 72 percent of the substandard, nonwhite, owner-occupied housing.

A similar but even bleaker picture was true for the nonwhite *renter*. Nonwhite households occupied a third (32 percent) of the Nation's substandard rented housing, although they made up only 16 percent of all rented households. If one were nonwhite and poor, the gap widened even more. Sixty-two percent of poor nonwhite families were in substandard rental units. Only 35 per cent of poor whites were living in substandard rental units. Almost 60 percent of all nonwhite renters were in the poverty income class in 1960. But they accounted for 75 percent of substandard housing which was lived in by nonwhite renters.

A seven-city Commission staff study showed that there were 103,000 large poor families in the seven cities who could not afford to rent standard housing of a suitable size at market rents. In these seven cities only 20,000 units with three or more bedrooms in publicly assisted housing of any kind was available to these families. The gap between the need and the units available was, therefore, 83,000 units, or over 80 percent. For the large poor family that also was nonwhite, the chances of escaping substandard housing were even more difficult. It is fair to conclude that one of the most desperate urban needs in the country is housing for the large poor family.[7]

In public housing, for a given amount of money, more units can be produced by building efficiency or one- or two-bedroom units. This fact explains, in part, why from 50 to 60 percent of all public housing units in recent years have been built for the elderly. From a bureaucratic point of view, the ability to list a housing unit for two people as equal to that of a housing unit for six or eight or 10 people, is one reason why such a large proportion of public housing is made up of smaller rather than large family-sized units.

7. Smart, Rybeck, Shuman, *The Large Poor Family—A Housing Gap*, National Commission on Urban Problems, 1968.

This has been a grave mistake. Besides the initial cost, many factors enter in the decision to build small or large units. This is seen in private as well as public housing. Larger units mean more kids, more maintenance problems, less tranquil apartments or neighborhoods, more local school costs, and usually more poverty. The decision to build small units unfortunately may have racial overtones as well as fiscal.

It is widely held that job programs, training programs and other anti-poverty programs will help increase the purchasing power of urban residents enough so that they can get their own housing without subsidy. Useful as these programs may be, the present level of funding for them is a relative drop in the bucket when measured against the actual need. In our big center cities where the need for job programs, higher incomes and better housing is greatest, the arithmetic of this need is staggering.

New multifamily housing, appropriate for some big cities, costs from $17,000 to $22,000 a unit, even with an urban renewal land writedown. Translating costs into rent, a $20,000 unit even with heavy subsidy, requires payments of roughly $150 a month. That figure would include maintenance, operating costs, interest (subsidized to a few points below market) and amortization (term up to 40 years), assuming a property tax abatement of about 50 percent and a two-thirds public writedown of the land cost.

Yet half of the low-income families in the slums can afford to pay only $65 to $110 a month, or $780 to $1,320 a year, for rent. And the other half cannot afford more than $35 to $60 a month, or $300 to $720 a year. The cities with their critical fiscal situation require higher taxes almost every year just at the time when the slum areas need the greatest tax abatement and subsidy. In the light of such considerations, to expect the free market to supply housing for all Americans without subsidy requires a flight from reality. We have to turn to government at every level to help finance an adequate supply of minimum standard housing, especially in the inner cities.

Misconceptions frequently obscure the problem of supplying decent housing, such as the notion that housing low-income families will take care of itself by the trickle-down or filter-down principle. This has it that as people move up the economic ladder, they leave behind them dwelling units which people moving up the ladder behind them can occupy. At the end of that chain of transferring residences, the poor in theory are provided with an inventory of available, lowest cost housing. Undeniably the trickle-down theory does work for part of the population, but it falls short of supplying enough housing for low-income families principally because: (1) the availability of the lowest cost housing is not always where the poor can get to it, and because (2) so much of the cheapest available housing is substandard, that is, lacking indoor plumbing and hot water, badly deteriorated, or overcrowded. In all conscience, housing that may have been suitable for one family cannot be counted as suitable when three or four families are sardined into it. Virtually all slum housing is filter-down housing—which is proof enough of its inadequacy.

In order to break the back of our minimum housing needs by 1980, we calculate that the Nation should build 2 to $2\frac{1}{4}$ million new housing units a year. That compares with the rate over the last 6 years of an average of 1.45 million (not counting mobile homes). In only 1 year, 1950, since the end of World War II have we even approached the rate of 2 million units a year. We are clearly dragging our feet.

Just building new housing at a certain rate is not enough. To make sure that the people who are now left with no alternative to substandard housing get relief, we feel it is important to specifically reserve 500,000 of the new housing units for people in the lower income brackets. We think a fair breakdown would be to designate 100,000 a year for the abject poor (incomes up to $2,200 a year for families of four); 100,000 for the poor (incomes up to $3,300); 100,000 for the near poor (incomes up to $4,500); and 200,000 units for families with incomes over $4,500 but who still cannot afford to buy or rent decent housing in the private market. In short, the increased housing over the present level of production should go to those who need it most.

We cannot pretend that this half million units of added housing over current production can help many of the poor unless there are subsidies to bring rents or sale prices down. Society must face up to this. But the amount of the subsidies can be reduced to the extent we find ways to bring down the costs of housing.

At present, subsidies are needed so the lower economic middle class can afford adequate housing. By reducing housing costs appreciably, so that the average family of four earning $6,000 a year could afford decent housing in the private market, then the upper limit requiring some subsidy could be brought further down the income scale. The main thrust could then be aimed at the really poor.

An important byproduct of building more dwelling units will be increased jobs—about 165,000 a year to construct the homes and about 330,000 a year in related supplier industries. These combined new workers could make a big dent in urban unemployment, especially among the young and minority groups.

Segregation has been a complex problem nagging at America for years. Foot dragging at all levels has not helped. The problem remains critical.

Segregation has been a fact of life in America for 300 years. While we make no pretense of having studied it exhaustively nor to having any unique insights into the problem, we cannot fail to mention it here.

The institution of slavery and its aftermath which we have inherited has poisoned relationships between many whites and Negroes. And the past pressures for racial separation were reinforced by complex cultural, social, and economic factors.

A commonly observed pattern in America has been the initial more or less voluntary flocking together for mutual protection and fellowship of migrant peoples of various ethnic, religious, and other ties in preference to venturing into a mixed, integrated society.

The traditional American hopes and attempts of the individual to rise to new stature without being bound to one's beginnings often lead to social exclusiveness. Many people try to reassure themselves that they have indeed achieved new heights by physically escaping from and then rejecting their origins. The white well-to-do exclude the middle class, and the middle class exclude the poor. Some Negroes who struggle to rise economically exhibit this characteristic, seeking to exclude poor Negroes from their neighborhoods, just as whites do. White middle and upper classes have been particularly anxious to keep out the black poor.

Prejudices are harder to erase when people are insecure about their jobs and status. Large numbers of Negroes have educated and prepared themselves to compete in most fields. But some whites fear that the trained Negro cannot be absorbed without threatening their jobs. Racial contempt, open or concealed, is encouraged by the resulting economic friction. Whites who try to keep their neighborhoods segregated often disguise their feelings, claiming instead that Negroes and the poor will lower property values, overtax the schools, and invite delinquency or crime.

Actions and attitudes of the whites inevitably create reactions within the black community. The result has been a tendency for society to become polarized, and by income group as well as by race. But the answers are enough jobs and enough housing for all. As the late President Kennedy often remarked, a rising tide floats all boats.

Elected officials at all levels found it hard to stand up against the prevailing pressure for segregated neighborhoods. Those at the Federal level were no exception. For years they made little effort to resist the pressure. They closed their eyes to the massive federally supported buildup of largely white suburbia in the period following World War II. In the North and in the South, reflecting dominant moods of the times, the Federal Housing Administration would not insure any mortgage where a black family bought a home from a white. It may fairly be charged that in line with the prevailing general attitude, Federal funds were so used for several decades that their effects were to intensify racial and economic stratification of America's urban areas.

Much of this was due to the emphasis that housing legislation placed on local control. When the Federal Government during the depression era become involved in housing and other matters affecting the general welfare, the stress was on stimulating the economy. And local control became a guiding principle. The Federal Government in the 1930's began to build housing for poor people, using its power of eminent domain and contracting directly for construction. But this gave way to an indirect approach: Federal subsidies to local housing authorities which had the full responsibility for site selection and operation, including racial policies.

Local control again was embodied and carried forward in the landmark Housing Act of 1949. The limitations on Federal action, as spelled out in the Senate report on that bill, stated that Federal assistance for clearing slums and blighted areas, under the bill, "shall be available only for projects where there has been a local determination by the governing body of the community that the project is needed and where the plans for such project are locally made and locally approved. This bill incorporates the basic philosophy that if the people of a local community take no interest in that community's housing problems, it is not for the Federal Government to impose a program upon them." If the fathers of housing legislation preferred more Federal muscle, the bow to local determination often was the only way to get their bills through Congress.

To recognize this emphasis on local control is not to say that Federal officials were powerless to alter the racial policies alluded to, or that they could not have prevented the abuses, for example, which led urban renewal in some places to be called Negro removal. The Federal administrators still controlled the funds and, in distributing them, they had the right and duty to insist that legislative purposes were adhered to locally. The purpose of the 1949 Housing Act, for instance, included assistance both for slum clearance and (what tended to be overlooked locally and federally) for low-rent public housing.

If the Federal bureaucracy often tended to be timid and to lack a robust faith in the programs and policies it was supposed to administer, the congressional pulling and tugging over these controversial issues, between the legislative committees, on the one hand,

and the appropriations committees, on the other, did not help. It weakened the will of the Federal bureaucracy. Not only in public housing and urban renewal, but also in rent supplements, leased housing, non-profit housing, and many other programs, these unresolved issues raged.

Top housing officials and recent administrations certainly have thrown themselves wholeheartedly behind freedom of choice in housing. The majority in Congress, by outlawing segregation in public facilities and insisting on equal opportunity in the use of Federal grants, put its weight behind a desegregated America. By the Open Housing Act of 1968, it prohibited discrimination in the sale and rental of housing.

The real test—whether or not these prescriptions actually will be carried out where people live—is yet to come. Because the Commission believes that evil days will fall upon the country if segregation policies are not wiped out, we present many recommendations aimed at reversing the past trends. We believe in the long run that the good sense and innate decency of the American people will triumph. We are encouraged by the socially minded groups and individuals who are struggling to create and maintain desegregated and integrated communities. We find indications that there probably are more persons who believe in freedom of choice and genuine democracy than is commonly believed. Major segments of society, ranging from the religious leadership to the business leadership, are attacking the problem with new vigor.

A story that should not be forgotten in these times is that in the past the American city had progressed a long way toward a balanced community, with people of many origins and occupations and wage levels living in the same neighborhoods, sending their children to the same schools, and working in the same sections. The city was the melting pot. And to many, the people living in these neighborhoods seemed far less burdened by the fears and phobias that haunt some citizens who today take such pains to wall themselves off from all shades of differences.

Putting our Nation back on the right track will not be easy. The difficulties are great. It is a struggle for the soul of America. . . .

Housing costs can be reduced if none of the many avenues for savings is dismissed as inconsequential. Add them all up and they promise to be substantial.

The Commission believes that housing costs can and must be reduced. We believe that substantial savings can be made short of the introduction of revolutionary new systems.

One way this can be done is to attack individual items of costs in housing. No opportunity to reduce tham should be ignored simply because, by itself, it may not result in dramatic overall reductions. Significant savings can be made through numerous small reductions.

Costs can also be cut if large-scale or industrialized production is combined with the most progressive existing products or techniques. To do this, we must also remove the barriers to large-scale distribution brought on by restrictive building codes and practices, subdivision regulations, and zoning ordinances.

We believe that a number of changes in national policy can help to cut housing costs. Government should provide an economic climate which promotes the continuity of housing production. This can be done through creating housing construction goals, carrying out the fiscal and monetary policies to achieve them, reducing the general level of interest rates, funding Government programs at high levels and with continuity over time, shifting the impact of the Federal income tax as it affects housing to encourage new construction, rehabilitation and maintenance, and to discourage the present practice of deductions for depreciation and maintenance when no maintenance is required and excessive depreciation is allowed; and by emphasizing housing to the same degree that economic growth and full employment have been emphasized in the past.

Costs could also be cut in the Federal programs by subsidizing in the most efficient and least costly methods, simplifying Federal programs and reducing the time for planning and construction.

We strongly urge prompt action of the Proxmire amendment to the 1968 Housing Act—calling for large-scale housing experiments on Federal sites as a test of potential cost savings while adding to the housing inventory.

At the local level, central city housing authorities should be able to lease housing outside their immediate jurisdictions to house some proportion of the poor on less costly sites and in housing which costs less to build than in central city locations.

The proportion which the property tax plays in the overall tax burden should be reduced by a variety of means in order to reduce the tax impact on housing. We believe both the Federal Treasury and the States should explore methods of taxing land value increases so that some proportion of the increase due to population growth and public policies might be recaptured for public purposes.

Costs could be cut by the public purchase of land in advance of development and by leasing rather than selling land acquired by governmental bodies. The States could use their powers to aid in the assembly of land. Removing zoning practices which prevent planned unit developments, and which restrict land supply and raise the cost of site improvements through excessive large-lot zoning, would help cut costs. More objective standards for site improvements and subdivision regulations could also reduce some excessive costs now required.

A major reform in the system of building codes would both permit new and less costly products and processes to be used and could provide uniformity of codes over metropolitan and State areas. The uniformity of codes is the most important step for it can bring greater specialization, mass production, and the reduction of costs. We suggest a series of steps to bring this about.

One of the most important ways to cut housing costs is to combine large-scale production with the most modern existing products and techniques. While new breakthroughs may some day bring a revolutionary change in the method of building, modern techniques are now widely used. Vast numbers of housing products are factory produced. The fabrication of panels, electrical harnesses and plumbing trees are already done in the factory. Assembly line methods are used both in the factory and on the site by large builders. Entire houses are fabricated in the factory for delivery to the site. If the best methods in the existing state of the art can become more widely used through the removal of restrictions which prevent their more general application, numerous savings could be made.

Among the savings are the reduction in the hours of labor needed and the substitution of industrial for craft labor, in short, fewer hours at lower hourly rates. This must be accompanied by large-scale continuing production both to cover the increased capital costs for the plant and machines, and to induce labor to cooperate through higher annual wages from more secure employment. Additional savings will come because work can thus be done independent of the weather. Costs can be cut through quantity purchases. Time savings should save on financing costs. Builders and professional fees, now paid on a percentage of costs, would be less as costs are reduced. Other savings such as the absence of extras, removal of delays due to material shortages, and reduction in vandalism and maintenance costs are possible.

Again let us emphasize that no savings should be overlooked. Because many cost items are calculated as a percentage or proportion of other costs, there is greater leverage in the housing field for cost savings than in most other fields.

Builders' profits are usually based on gross costs, not on the funds actually invested.

The benefits of mass production can be achieved if a mass market can be provided through, among other things, the removal of building code and zoning roadblocks and the removal of restrictive building practices.

Other means of reducing costs can come from the use of new financing provisions found in the 1968 Housing Act, notably those which will attract and expand the flow of mortgage funds into the housing industry; from the reform and reduction of closing costs, to which we address ourselves in some detail; and the expansion of cooperative ownership, which would provide savings to those who take part which would otherwise be unavailable to them.

All of these methods should be pursued. Large overall savings, or a smaller rise in costs than there would otherwise be in the face of a general price rise, can come from working on these and other individual items of costs in housing.

The Commission attaches great importance to the cutting of housing costs for two main reasons: so that more Americans can afford to rent or buy housing in the private market, and to reduce the public subsidies needed to help house those who cannot meet their basic shelter requirements.

Escalation of land prices adds an ever bigger increment in the price of housing, and further explains the squeeze on low-income families seeking decent housing.

The first and by the far the biggest cost booster of housing prices is the cost of building sites. Land acquisition and site preparation (streets, curb and gutter, storm drainage, and so forth) now run from 15 up to 32 percent of the price to the consumer of a finished dwelling unit, whether single or multifamily.

Raw land prices are soaring faster than any other component involved in homebuilding. Between 1956 and 1966, the market value of privately owned land in the United States approximately doubled. Careful estimates[8] for "ordinary taxable real estate" indicated a rise in land value from $269 billion to approximately $523 billion during that decade. The 10-year growth in land value amounted to more than $5,000 per American family. This indicated an average rate of increase of 6.9 percent, or somewhat more than the 6-percent rate of increase in gross national product. During the same 10-year

8. Manvel, *Three Land Research Studies*, National Commission on Urban Problems, 1968.

interval, wholesale commodity prices rose 1 percent annually and the consumer price index 1.8 percent annually.

A large portion of this trend, of course, results directly from increased urbanization, involving the shift of some land from rural to urban use. Between 1956 and 1966, for example, the number of separately valued parcels of "urban" property rose by a little over one-fourth, while the number of "acreage and farm" properties dropped off. The estimated value of urban land rose more than 130 percent, indicating an increase in average land value per urban parcel of about 83 percent, or 6.2 percent per year. Similar calculations for "acreage and farms" suggest an average annual rise in land value per property of about 5.6 per cent. The greatest increases occurred when there were shifts from rural to urban uses.

Our studies have shown that in relation to market value, land tends to be assessed at a lower percentage than are buildings and improvements. Housing therefore bears a larger proportionate share of the local tax burden than does land. To assess both at market value would therefore not only be more just, but by diminishing the relative burden borne by improvements, should lead to a greater investment in them and would encourage more construction in housing and hence, some reduction in rents, below what they would otherwise be.

While urging a *relative* deemphasis of the property tax, we would improve this bulwark of local finance by moving toward full value assessment, improving machinery for taxpayer appeals, public dissemination of data on assessment ratios, and strenuous efforts at uniform assessment.

Zoning was intended to control land development, but fiscal considerations often distort it, leading to economic and racial exclusion.

Zoning does not create land values. Population growth, community facilities and services, and the total community's commerce and industry create the values. Zoning determines whether landholders (or which landholders) may reap these values, setting up certain goals, presumably in the public interest, which take precedence over the real estate market as the sole arbiter of land uses.

Zoning is a "police power" regulation, deriving from the power of each state to legislate for health, safety, morals, and the general welfare. Since its earliest use, zoning developed as a system which leaves property in private hands while regulating its use. It attempts to guard the larger public interest while maintaining the sanctity of private property. This is widely accepted by private interests, and is an approach to land-use control that government easily can afford.

In the 1920's, when zoning became prevalent, it adapted to the small-scale ownership and development typical of that era. Builders then were unable to build 1,000 houses at a clip; they often built one at a time or three or four. And the owner of a single small lot then, as now, is almost wholly dependent on his neighbors for his environment—a dependence which is increased by the American tradition of using yards, rather than walls, as the dividers between properties. The buyers and sellers of lots needed some device to prevent a drop in property values, keep out unwanted intrusions, encourage investment in land and construction—in sum, to assure character. The fee simple land tenure, which gives owners a freedom of use that modern homeowners are frightened to have their neighbors possess, did not provide the needed protection. Zoning did.

Today, a basic problem results because of the delegation of the zoning power from the States to local governments of any size. This often results in a type of Balkanization which is intolerable in large urban areas where local government boundaries rarely reflect the true economic and social watersheds. The present indiscriminate distribution of zoning authority leads to incompatible uses along municipal borders, duplication of public facilities, attempted exclusion of regional facilities.

In short, the proliferation of zoning authorities in metropolitan areas can consign sound metropolitan planning to an often fruitless exercise. But this is only part of the story. The problems of local government are greatly magnified because each political subdivision within the fragmented metropolis, relying primarily on the local property tax and facing heavy financial burdens, tends to lean inordinately on this splintered zoning power to boost its tax base. This is known as "fiscal zoning," the use of zoning to achieve fiscal objectives rather than purely land-use objectives. Fiscal zoning seeks to exclude from a jurisdiction any proposed development that might create a net financial burden and to encourage development which promises a net financial gain. Fiscal zoners try to strike a balance so the tax revenue which new development will contribute to local coffers will at least pay for the public services which that development will entail. The result of such practice is often serious economic and social dislocation.

The most serious effect of fiscal zoning is the spate of exclusionary practices relating to residential development. The aim, of course, is to keep out the lower income groups, and especially large families which require significant public expenditures in education, public health and welfare, open space, recreational facilities, police and fire, and the like. Lower income housing produces relatively low tax revenues so these expenditures add to the community's fiscal strain. The effect, under present financing methods, is either a reduced level of public services for all segments of the community or a higher tax bill. Given such a choice, present residents of the community are usually loath to accept additional tax burdens. Looking at the matter in pocketbook terms, they support fiscal zoning. Usually nobody bothers to ask where the families who are being excluded should live.

Fiscal zoning also violates a basic administrative principle: that authority be equated with responsibility. In zoning, and the relationship between the Federal Government and local communities, there is no equating of authority and responsibility.

Most communities want all cream and no skim milk. They want the best, not only in physical structures and facilities, but also in the economic levels of people who will become their future citizens. They are willing to accept some industry for their tax base, but it has to be the cream—the research type—and not heavy industry. Each community engages in "one-upmanship," attempting to outdo its neighboring communities. In the communities' race for the cream they give little thought to a balanced community—to providing shelter for all economic levels that may wish to live in the community, for those who will teach in their schools, clerk in their supermarkets, and work in their industrial plants.

The community rigs its master plan and accompanying zoning ordinance, making sure that it is almost impossible for low- and moderate-income families to move into the community by requiring large lots and reduced density, by prohibiting multifamily apartments, and by other excessive standards that price out poorer people.

The Federal Government has assumed some responsibility for providing decent, safe, and sanitary shelter, but presently it exercises little authority in this matter in local communities. As if this were not bad enough, Federal programs often *reward* suburban communities which are "zoning out" the moderate-income buyer. The suburban communities, for instance, receive planning money to assist them in drawing up discriminatory general plans to do the job.

In some communities, there is a very real problem of corruption in zoning decisions. A property owner who could build a shopping center or a high-rise apartment suddenly discovers that his property is worth many times as much as the property owner who is relegated to low-density development. The values at stake are enormous, so it is not surprising, therefore, that the zoning system is subject to enormous pressures by landowners and developers and that outright corruption is more than simply an occasional exception. Newspaper exposés of this sort of corruption are dramatic testimony to many less dramatic and less well understood effects of the relation of the control process to private market forces. Pressures for the more lucrative forms of development are always present.

One of the country's foremost legal experts on zoning[9] notes that zoning is caught between two objectives, protection of the family home which requires positive Government action, and protection of the free market which requires Government refusal to take action. He questions the narrow court view of zoning as fitting into real estate law when, through subtle forms of discrimination, for instance, zoning affects people and the nature of society, not just land. In short, although the basic justification for zoning is to protect the overall public good, this often appears to be the last consideration as zoning is now practiced.

Orderly urban growth can be the result of a political commitment on land-use decisions, who makes them and how they are made, plus the will to spend money on cities.

Our crisis in urban growth springs from using 19th-century controls and attitudes in an attempt to mold and contain 20th-century cities faced with 21st-century problems.

Over the next 30 years about 18 million acres of land will come into urban use for the first time, and in present urban areas the processes of rebuilding and rehabilitation will continue. Just as land-use decisions made many years ago have affected the quality of today's urban environment, so decisions which we make today and tomorrow will shape the quality of urban life for future generations. We cannot delay many of the most important decisions until those who will be most affected by them can make their own choices. A reluctance to deal positively with the control of land development and redevelopment will not prevent development. Rather, it will allow it to take place in an undirected and haphazard fashion. That reluctance will represent just as much of a choice about our future urban environment as would careful, positive action.

We recognize that people and localities differ, that immutable principles about optimal urban form and character are largely illusory, and that variety and experimentation are important precepts of our federal system. For these reasons many of the Commission's proposals on land-use control are concerned with encouraging the creation of a governmental framework in which the

9. Richard Babcock, *The Zoning Game.*

legitimate choices of people can be formulated into public policy which, in turn, can then be translated into reality.

Land-use policies and practices are not limited in their effects to the quality of the physical environment, but have major social and economic implications as well. So we have tried to understand the total impact of present practices and to formulate recommendations within a broader scope of restoring fiscal and economic health to our cities and strengthening the currently fragile social fabric of our great metropolitan areas.

We propose State legislative action to improve local governmental framework for development control and to confine the exercise of such control to counties, regional governments (where they exist) and large municipalities. States should be required to undertake comprehensive studies of allocation of local government responsibilities for land-use controls if those States are to qualify for certain Federal planning grants.

We further call for the establishment of a framework for controlling urban development through establishment of a Council of Development Standards.

To point up the problem let us reiterate the estimate that over the next 30 years 18 million acres of land will come into urban use for the first time. This is about the size of all the urbanized land within the SMSA's right now. Between now and the year 2000, nearly all metropolitan area population growth, some 80 million people, will occur in the suburbs, which will use that next 18 million acres. We have come this far in our urban civilization in a haphazard way and the results surround us. We cannot afford to let our future urban growth occur the same way.

Implicit in our recommendations is a concern over the clutter and ugliness in our present urban environment. We are encouraged by the public support of efforts to remove or hide junkyards, to restrict highway billboards, and to plant more trees and flowers. It is imperative to deal not only with surface ugliness, but to incorporate esthetics as an essential element of all urban development. We see the results of unplanned growth in our metropolitan areas—congestion, unsightliness, blight, and unending ribbons of traffic. Both the courts and the legislatures need to support the people who are trying to halt the defacement of our cities and our land.

The sort of environment we should plan and build is an environment that includes all the aspects of a genuine community and that does not neglect any aspects of adequate housing. That will cost money and take careful planning and good design, not standardized design, but design to please the eye and the heart with a sense of variety.

The American people have a clear responsibility: They are both the consumers and the trustees of an environment. Only they can say whether we will have beautiful metropolitan areas or ugly ones. Beautiful cities of the past were beautiful because the trustees of these old environments—a few powerful princes and prelates—so ordered them. Today in a democracy, the men in the street have the power and responsibility for deciding what their environment will be like; they will only underwrite a good one if they know what has brought them our ugly one.

The Commission's recommendations in land use are extensive. We urge that land-use authority be in the hands of larger units of government. We call for giving the housing consumer a greater variety in the choice of location of his residence, with special attention to the convenience of housing to employment opportunities. We propose that planning and design of new neighborhoods be pursued in a unified manner and in a comprehensive way, but within the framework of large-scale development, we support maximum opportunity for participation by small businessmen. Holding zones and land banking to control the timing and nature of development, authorization of planned unit developments in built-up areas as well as in new subdivisions, and compensative regulations are among the broader types of control that we believe will help replace haphazard growth with communities that better serve those who live and work in them. . . .

To free the building industry, product manufacturers, planners, and the public from a hopeless maze of restrictions, we must develop a new system for codes and standards.

What we have seen in our separate studies of building codes, housing codes, subdivision regulations, zoning ordinances, and development standards, is a myriad of standards, many of them conflicting, often based on no objective data, a number of them excessively restrictive, some of them embodied in no formal code, and many the result of the whim of an inspector, mortgage company, or self-serving group.

In a number of areas, especially relating to the neighborhood or community environment, there are often no objective standards at all. This is usually the case in respect to noise, open space, school requirements, and recreation and park facilities.

In other matters, the standards seem unusually low, such as housing code requirements for dwelling and sleeping space.

In vast geographical areas of the country, there are no codes or standards which apply at all.

The main question is: How can order be brought out of this chaos? The Commission recommends a number of steps which should be taken.

First, we believe that some highly regarded institution, non-governmental in nature, should provide an umbrella under which research and testing of new products and building methods can take place. Represented in this work should be Government agencies, private companies, educational institutions, trade associations, private laboratories, and professional and scientific bodies.

This is needed to provide some objective basis either for keeping or changing existing standards. It is needed to develop new standards in those areas where none now exist. Further, it is needed to create a better climate for new products and techniques.

We believe that the National Academy of Science-National Academy of Engineering is the institution which could oversee these functions.

We further recommend that a Council of Development Standards should be established by the Academies, and that two Institutes under it be established for the purpose of coordinating or bringing together research and testing in the building and environmental fields. We advocate a National Institute of Building Sciences to coordinate the work of public and private institutions in the areas of building products, structures, and codes. We believe a companion institution, a National Institute of Environmental Sciences, should perform the same type of work in the area of housing occupancy, environment and community standards.

This structure would bring a series of objective standards which could then be incorporated into the various model building codes, housing codes, subdivision regulations, zoning ordinances, and neighborhood environmental codes. These should apply uniformly at the local, regional, and State levels. Where no code now exists, where a code is restrictive, where standard products and practices are prohibited, where either below minimum standards exist or where excessive requirements are made, and where codes and standards conflict, then the builder or architect or community should be guided by the standards developed under the auspices of the institutions we have suggested.

Since the powers to apply and enforce these standards are State police powers, the States by adopting the standards (developed either under the procedures we suggest, or an improved framework) could provide for uniform and objective treatment throughout their jurisdiction. The Federal Government could also help enforce them by providing incentives to localities to adopt them.

In addition, we envisage that these standards could be codified and made available to builders, developers, city officials, and private groups, through a single development standards guide. This should embody not only those standards found in the traditional codes as they are developed and upgraded, but also those practices by professional and other groups which are, in effect, standards or requirements for building, occupancy, and development.

The major objectives of the Council for Development Standards and its functioning Environmental and Building Institutes would be both to push the development of new standards where none now exist, and to rationalize those existing standards which are outdated or in conflict with others, and to bring all standards affecting development into one orderly system.

No broad attack on housing problems can ignore the sticky, myth-ridden issue of restrictive practices. Needed: More labor efficiency coupled with job security.

Labor costs in the building trades are rising as fast or faster than in other industries. Some hourly wage rates for construction workers cause horrors among the watchers of a balanced economy. Yet these high wages are offset by loss of work between jobs and especially during bad weather conditions. Instead of the normal 2,000 hours of work per year in other industries, the average building tradesman works between 1,400 and 1,600 hours. As a national average, construction workers received lower *annual* wages than workers in other manufacturing industries in 1967.

Restrictive building practices are not easily separated from the special insecurity facing the construction workers. Not only the workers, but the entrepreneurs and manufacturers in the competitive homebuilding field enjoy less security than is common in other industries. Restrictive practices, typically considered simply as union or labor matters, often result from pressure by contractors and producers. Construction work may be extremely hazardous, and only persons intimately familiar with actual working conditions are qualified to separate legitimate safety rules from excessive, cost-padding restrictions.

Restrictive practices do exist. They are frequently exaggerated and misconstrued by viewing them out of context of the peculiar problems of the industry. But labor officials themselves told the Commission that restrictive practices are a problem.

Some of the most serious restrictive practices are these: (1) on-site rules requiring work to be done on the premises, prohibiting or limiting the use of prefabricated products; (2) restrictions against the use of certain tools or devices; and (3) requirements for excessive manpower, including irrational limits on the kind of work certain workers may perform.

We do not quibble about how much restrictive practices add to the cost of housing. The Commission finds no single magical way to reduce the cost of housing. Therefore, whether it is pennies or dollars or thousands of dollars per unit, every potential way to achieve savings must be pursued with vigor. That is the only way decent housing can be brought within the price reach of millions of working Americans.

Onsite wages are a big factor in housing, accounting for 20 to 30 percent of the price of a single-family house in most areas. Significantly, this variation of 10 percentage points is linked to management efficiency rather than to union versus nonunion scale. Also, the average current portion of housing costs attributable to wages, about 23 percent, is a sharp drop from the 33 percent figure of 20 years ago. In the same period, studies show that allowances for overhead and profit more than doubled.

The most widely recognized and most urgent restrictive practice is not a cost factor—it is discrimination. Until recently, minority groups were kept out of many building trades. That pattern is beginning to change. Determined efforts to change the old pattern, which used to keep out many whites who did not have relatives in the trade as well as virtually all Negroes, although made too slowly, are finally showing signs of success.

Getting the unions to open the bars is only part of the struggle. Persuading Negroes to enter where they had not previously been welcome is not always easy. Many thorny problems of pretraining and apprenticeship also must be overcome.

Surprisingly, the big problem in the building trades could quickly shift to genuine trouble over getting enough qualified workers. In spite of the high hourly wages, young people are not drawn to them. Among high school students, few young men want to be carpenters. Or among most groups of parents in any metropolitan area, hardly any want their children to become carpenters.

So labor shortages loom on the horizon at the time the Government, this Commission, and many others are calling for a vast acceleration of new housing construction.

Challenging as this is, we think it offers an opportunity for dealing with restrictive building practices. Many onerous practices are almost insoluble in the framework of widely fluctuating employment and construction patterns. But a greatly expanded construction industry should offer opportunities to stabilize employment and to reduce the threat of seasonal unemployment. This means the use of more mass production techniques, which should simplify apprentice work to the extent more repetitive and routine assignments can be used. It should mean more indoor work, protecting workers from the rain and snow that often mean no pay. It should mean more opportunity for the trade unions to extend their membership into the prefabricating fields so that, as is already true in some unions, restrictive practices are thrown out because they begin to hurt fellow union members. Just enlarging the construction industry will not bring these things about automatically. But all those in government and private construction can use accelerated building programs as leverage to offer much more job security in exchange for abandonment of inefficient work practices.

The Federal Government, through its extensive contracting for housing and other construction, can exert considerable leverage to minimize the valleys of unemployment and peaks of labor shortages in the building trades. The Commission particularly recommends, as an appropriate measure in this direction, that the Congress authorize programs for a minimum of 3 years and in the case of public housing up to 10 years with the understanding that the local agencies will use their long-term scheduling to help stabilize building activities in their areas.

Labor is often described as blocking the path of new technology. Many instances can be cited. But labor has also accepted many modern building techniques. In the innovative or experimental fields, the Commission has found instances where labor was an active partner. If workers are brought into the planning at an early stage, there is every reason to expect they will not be obstructive, but will cooperate, working out jurisdictional problems and other matters before these lead to work stoppages or conflicts. Finding ways to do this better and more often should be the path of the future.

To cut costs and to prevent capricious interruptions of production, the Commission also strongly recommends that project agreements for public and publicly subsidized housing be negotiated between the unions, the contractors, and the Government, both national and local. These have proved successful in the TVA and the atomic energy and space efforts. These agreements should seek to guarantee a greater volume of employment and in return remove some of the obstacles to increased production and reduced costs. They should provide for an increased opportunity for minority groups to share in the provision of employment and the opportunity to acquire skills. The settling of jurisdictional disputes should also be carried out by the appropriate board within the building industry.

The Commission does not urge punitive legislative action or Government compulsion to gain the abandonment of restrictive building practices. But we do urge trade union leaders and builders to cooperate to promote efficiency, as in project agreements. We do think that Government can help in many constructive ways. We warn that if restrictive practices in the industry are not reduced, the people may well be forced to take stronger action.

Cost-benefit ratios of the programs we suggest are mere bickering in light of our need for a real political commitment to solve our problems.

Within a matter of hours after the publication of this report, the Commission's members—businessmen, builders, architects, lawyers, educators, and public officials—are likely to stand accused of asking for a program that costs more money. If so, we plead guilty. But the "defense" has one question to put to the "prosecution." Can we afford not to undertake these programs?

What will be the consequences if we permit present trends and policies to continue? One indirect answer is to count the costs we are paying now for the present state of affairs. A riot, for instance, may be accepted as a symptom of a problem, whether celebrated in a ghetto or around the administrative buildings of a university. In the 2 weeks following the death of the Reverend Martin Luther King, the Nation sustained many millions of dollars worth of insured property damage alone, not including the lost taxes on the burned and looted property. Nor does this include the loss of future sales because of fearful shoppers, higher costs of police and fire protection from increased crime and arson, jobs lost, and most importantly, the lives lost.

A riot is only the top end of the mercury, as it climbs past the fever line. The disease may be systemic, or it may be only a 1-day inflammation. No one, however, is betting on the latter.

The very idea of measuring the economic benefit of some programs against others, in the intangible area of "human investment," tends to stump those who try it. What does it cost and what are the benefits if society provides a college education for the brightest high school graduates? Taking one program at a time, if opportunties are opened up, convincing studies can show the economic payoff of a good education, on-the-job training, or vocational rehabilitation in terms of lifetime income, and the taxes paid over the working life of adults who have or who lack various types of education. This is generally true, but it is true for minority groups only when they can use their new skills.

What cannot be costed out are the myriad returns in dollars and cents as well as intangibles to a city that is relatively free of slums, that does not wall up its minority citizens in a ghetto, that has the economic health to be able to respond to the needs of its residents. We have to approach it from the other side, and count the cost of present inaction. The President's Crime Commission studies indicated that in 1 year, 1965, $300 million worth of property was destroyed by arson and vandalism; that "index crimes" (robbery, burglary, larceny, and auto theft) reached double that, and that the cost of public law enforcement (including punishment) added $4.2 billion. The highest cost of all, that for "illegal goods and services" —all typical of the ghetto—narcotics, loansharking, prostitution, alcohol, and gambling: a whopping $8.1 billion in 1965 alone.

A growing chorus of responsible, informed voices urges a change in policy. The programs this Commission advocates are not all-inclusive but are necessary companions to others, forming part of a web of actions to speed change in our urban areas.

However, the simple truth is that the Congress, the administration, State and local governments, and the general public have not yet had a sufficiently combined commitment to improve our cities. HUD appropriations for housing and community development in 1969 will not reach $3 billion, but money for defense and space will top $79 billion. Congress has no trouble authorizing $2 billion for an airplane that cannot land on any public airfield in the United States, but recently the House chopped out 30 percent of HUD's meager programs, killed rent-supplement appropriations for the year, and came within 20 votes of wiping out the model cities program. The House appropriations Committee this year cut the money allocated for model cities and funds to provide essential social services in public housing. The point is that we already have the legislation and the programs to do the job. It is now a question of commitment.

A lot of the rules of our society will have to be changed before anything meaningful can be done to make right the wrongs of our most disadvantaged and helpless citizens. We should do this in the name of justice. We should also do it in our own self interest. Over time, welfare costs could be cut, police protection diminished, and productive lives prolonged. Housing for low-income families in the suburbs might also attract industry needing unskilled and semi-skilled labor and hence increase the tax base and the economic well-being of the community. There are economic advantages in doing what is just.

But little will change without a political commitment from the larger society. It will not be enough simply to preach to the larger society that "perhaps the measure of a free, democratic society is the condition of life of its most abject citizens."

Perhaps the characteristic phenomenon of American politics in the *1960*'s will someday be seen as the emergence of the city as a political issue.

To be sure, government has long addressed itself to the separate components of the urban experience—unemployment, deteriorating housing, segregation, crime, disease—but only in this decade have we developed a sense of the effect of all of these forces working together in the modern metropolis.

This Commission does not believe that the Nation must choose either the policy of "gilding the ghetto" or "dispersing the ghetto." We are now doing neither. The Nation must do both. We must build decent housing in the slums, and we must provide freedom of residence for all Americans.

We advocate policies which not only promote freedom of residence but programs which would build low-rent housing in the suburbs as well as in the cities, provide sites in outlying areas, give States incentives to act where localities do not, lease houses for the poor in middle-class neighborhoods, and tie a locality's eligibility for Federal grants such as for highways, sewers, and water to that community's effort to house its share of the poor.

We also advocate a massive attack on substandard and overcrowded housing conditions which are concentrated in the core city among the poor, especially among the Negro poor. When we speak of housing conditions we also mean providing adequate city services, housing code programs, relocation payments, neighborhood improvements, recreation and open space, and good urban design, so that both a decent home and a suitable living environment are provided.

We view a larger governmental role as an absolute necessity in providing low-income housing.

Federal, State, and local governments share responsibility for urban problems. There is no question that cities must continue to rely on the Federal Government to carry a large part of the burden by providing the subsidies. The present fiscal resources of the city do not permit the scale of funding required to bring decent housing within reach of those at the bottom of the economic ladder.

The Federal Government also may have to play a more direct role. This may be particularly true when conflicting demands on local officials block effective action. Though city governments have considerable legal powers, city officials have limited political power and less money to deal with all the conflicts which are inherent in the rising expectations of the urban poor. Then, too, the politically potent objections to public housing, to rezoning for multifamily housing and to opening up previously all-white areas to Negroes have also constituted serious impediments to a rational and success- ful exercise of city powers. Metropolitan and State powers should be brought into play to the fullest possible extent. And at the Federal level there will be required more insight and determination than has been manifest in past years.

Meanwhile, there has been a growing cry for "community participation." Many communities within a city desire somehow to have self-determination and become the executors of their own policies in housing and other matters. The model cities program incorporates some of this philosophy, but it does not go as far as the supporters of advocacy planning and total community control believe; namely, that only the residents of a particular area can know what best serves their interests. They believe that any attempt on the part of the city, let alone the State or Federal Government, to impose new housing is per se arbitrary and undemocratic. Com- pliance with these demands may satisfy the prevailing or most vocal political sentiments of the moment. But it is not necessarily the most rational or effective or efficient way to create housing. For too long it has been forgotten that neighborhoods deserve a strong voice in public programs affecting them. But a distinction needs to be made between the right to be heard and the right to obstruct. The final power should be through elected officials, which gives the public the ultimate control via the ballot box. Not every community is in the best position to evaluate its needs in relation to the entire urban area. And that goes for suburban communities as well as for sections of the inner city.

Direct Federal intervention also raises serious policy questions. There is the risk of a uniformity and standardization that might result from a single Federal agency contracting for housing in many parts of the country. The size of the bureaucratic structure that could develop might stifle new developments, new techniques and local variations. Above all, it might curb local initiative and the proper exercise of community prerogatives. That is why we place such emphasis on local, regional, and State action to get the job done.

So, if our cities are to continue to play the decisive role in the formulation and development of their own housing supply, they will have to evolve new mechanisms for dealing with the disparity of local interests and they will have to incur the political risks of choosing between competing demands. Proper planning decisions can probably only be made on an area-wide basis, yet if they are done arbitrarily without any participation and consultation of the local community, they will not meet the public acceptance needed to carry them out.

There are no simple mechanisms, and it is inevitable that we will continue to search for the right blend of Federal, State, city, and neighborhood participation. A giant step was taken in that direction with the passage of the Housing Act of 1968, a landmark in housing legislation. President Johnson called it a "Magna Carta to liberate our cities."

The new act properly emphasizes housing for low-income people. It calls for action comparable to the need. How the mandates of that legislation are followed, of course, remains to be seen. But the Nation would be well on the right track if it followed the directives set forth. It has a great potential and does credit to those in the administration and Congress who framed it.

To do something about the urban crisis, as political commitment grows, we can start getting the rules changed: Revenue sharing, property tax modernization, Federal income tax revision. Tax incentives not an efficient means to solve slum problems.

Under present practices of taxation and financing, even with a subsidized interest rate and long-term mortgages, private enterprise cannot supply the low-income housing required in the inner city. Only public housing in some form can meet the needs of the families earning under $4,000 a year. For the localities themselves to underwrite the cost of land assembly, removal of buildings, and loss of property tax payments would bankrupt almost any city. Only a massive addition of public funds can meet the situation.

The money for this will have to be drawn from the increase in tax receipts coming from the gains in national productivity, a more humane reordering of public expenditures, and reforms in our system of taxation. Our willingness and ability to take these steps will be a test of the values of the men and women who comprise our society.

But many will ask: Why should we subsidize on such a massive scale? The question is largely based on an uninformed notion of how our economy grew. American enterprise has been fueled again and again with subsidies, starting with land grants from the 17th to the 19th century. We often subsidize the richest people in the country: There are more than 30 families in the United States who have annual incomes over $500,000 but who pay no taxes. Perhaps more relevant to the housing problem, about 3½ times as much in housing subsidies goes to those with middle or higher incomes through income tax deductions than the amount of the subsidies which go to the poor for housing.

In a recent year, the upper 20 percent of income groups got twice as much in housing subsidies as did the lower 20 percent.

Many businesses benefit from one or a number of subsidies, hidden or open: air travel, automotive, agriculture, communications, the oil business, research and aerospace industries, and just about anything else you can name. Each year in the United States, the Government finances reclamation for agriculture to the tune of millions a year on long-term loans at a zero rate of interest. Middle- and high-income homeowners also enjoy Federal subsidies.

We do not necessarily favor all of these subsidies, but they do show that vast quantities of economic aid have gone to powerful groups. Based on Lincoln's principle that government should do what private citizens cannot do or cannot do as well themselves, and on the principle that aid should go to those who need it most, the strongest case can be made for helping those at the bottom of the economic ladder.

Additional Federal assistance to the cities is urgent. About 54 percent of all local government expenses go toward education and welfare. Many education and welfare costs are dumped on cities by the immigration from small towns and rural areas. If the needs are not created locally, even less are the benefits local: In our mobile society, everybody everywhere benefits by a school system that turns out well-trained citizens, and by a welfare system that minimizes human suffering. Putting more of the burden of education and welfare costs on the Federal Government could be worked out equitably and would be one way of leaving local governments enough revenue to meet their other pressing needs.

Some new urban-oriented Federal programs may mean less funding for other worthwhile domestic programs. But not necessarily. The growth of the economy produces a greater than commensurate increase in Federal revenues. From June 30, 1967, to June 30, 1968, the gross national product is estimated to have increased by $60 billion and Federal revenues by $11.5 billion. Of course, a considerable proportion of the resulting increase in Federal revenues must go for increased costs of servicing an expanding economy and population. However, a significant proportion of the annual increase in Federal revenues should be available to help pay for urban development programs in general.

To this end, the Commission recommends that Congress adopt a system for regular revenue sharing with State governments and major cities and urban counties. The revenue-sharing system should be on a simple formula basis that (1) reserves to a Federal trust fund a sum for annual allocation consisting of a legally authorized percentage of the total net taxable income reported under the Federal individual income tax; (2) provides an allocation to each State area based primarily upon population, but with an adjustment for relative total State-local tax effort in relation to resources and additional crediting for State revenue from taxation of individual income; and (3) provides for a portion of the allocation for individual State areas to be paid directly to the cities according to their respective shares of all State and local tax revenue in the particular State. The system should leave a high degree of discretion with the recipient governments as to the use of the distributed funds.

It seems reasonable to expect that the proposed "new" revenue source would promote some shift in the overall composition of the base for domestic government financing. The increased use of Federal income taxation would permit either improvement and expansion of State-local services, or less increase than would otherwise occur in State and local taxes, or—most likely—some of both. The Federal tax system, with all its faults, is more progressive and equitable than the systems currently used by the State and local governments, so such a shift clearly would be in the public interest.

We strongly favor an increased reliance upon major multipurpose governments in large urban areas. For various reasons, however, some existing Federal and State grant programs do involve an effective bias against large cities and urban counties. We are proposing a comprehensive effort to identify and eliminate such conditions for grants which put multipurpose governments at a relative disadvantage.

While a shift of more Federal funding would be worthwhile, local taxation most likely will have to continue to rise, even if at a relatively slower pace. So it becomes increasingly important to perfect the property tax which remains the fiscal bulwark of local government.

We also favor a revision of the income tax rules which in the case of the older buildings would permit major repairs to be treated as an operating expense rather than penalized as an addition to capital value. To the extent that the income tax provisions discourage maintenance of old existing housing, the goal of better cities requires that these rules be changed.

While the Commission strongly urges the removal of income tax

features which now tend to discourage the owners of rental properties from conserving and improving their investments, we do not
advocate Federal tax incentives to solve slum problems. Our studies
indicate that such an approach would be inefficient and ineffective.
It is frequently forgotten that tax incentives may cause a drain on
the Treasury as great or greater than direct subsidies. The main
fiscal reform job is to make certain that the tax system poses no
pocketbook obstacles to socially desirable behavior. But to accomplish further goals, beyond what the private market system accom-
plishes within this framework, direct subsidy programs tend to be
superior to the tax incentives route for pinpointing benefits and
assuring alert supervision by governmental bodies.

**The Commission believes in a larger role for the cities. We must
improve local governments and then give them more authority and
more money.**

The Commission believes in a much larger role for the cities and
proposes numerous ways by which they can improve their structures
and exercise their authority in more efficient ways.

So that cities may have more money, we propose a Federal
revenue sharing plan in which funds would go not only to the States
but also directly to cities of 50,000 or more people. And they could
benefit from this system in proportion to their own local tax effort.

The further improvement of the local revenue system is the aim
of additional proposals: more user charges where appropriate; collection of school taxes on a county or multicounty basis to smooth
out big-city inequities; modernization of the property tax; and
arrangements for interstate metropolitan areas to "piggyback" on
the Federal income tax where the localities so desire.

To help cities do a better job of housing the poor, we propose
that the Federal programs they rely upon should be simplified and
speeded up. We urge the long-term funding of these Federal programs—from a minimum of 3 years and up to 10 years—so the
money spigot will not be turned on and off unpredictably. We want
communities that turn in a consistently good record on Federal
programs to be rewarded by an easing up of restrictions or red-tape.
To preserve and improve existing housing inventories, we urge that
housing codes, now often limited to gray areas, be expanded city-
wide to include slums and more affluent neighborhoods. We also
propose that cities make use of better, faster, and more humane code
enforcement methods.

To further help cities with their problems, we urge that cities
be given authority to lease housing for low-income families through-

out the entire metropolitan area, especially in suburban areas that have job opportunities for blue collar workers. We could also shield the right of local officials to act on these difficult matters by urging that public housing and urban renewal approvals not be subject to State or local referendums.

To assure more orderly development, we propose protection for the central city resident against excessive variances, rezonings and tolerance of nonconforming uses. For the protection of citizens in the outlying areas, and to help prevent wasteful, hodgepodge growth in areas moving from rural to urban uses, we offer a variety of local planning and land assembly tools. And we urge that very small jurisdictions be prevented from disrupting sound area-wide plans by giving broader surveillance and veto powers to governmental units with a larger perspective.

We urge leaving to the cities as much authority as they can competently handle. But we urge consolidation of the hundreds of tiny jurisdictions and special districts into larger and more efficient bodies. As this is done, even more authority can be exercised locally. Housing the poor and removing segregation are of such supreme national importance that States and the Federal Government must set guidelines for minimum performance. But competent city governments should have the added tools and money to carry out the programs and to make the day-to-day decisions.

The States are close enough to the people and yet enough removed from petty parochial interests to become major constructive forces in dealing with urban problems.

The Commission does not subscribe to the notion that all problems can be best solved or handled from Washington. That is why we give so much attention to improvement of local government. We also feel that the States have a special role to play.

Among the issues in which we urge the States to exert new leadership are the following:

Adoption of open housing legislation (by States not now having it) and the strengthening of existing laws.

State legislation to authorize housing assistance functions to be carried out by countywide or multicounty housing agencies.

The use of State powers of eminent domain to provide sites on which to build housing for low- and moderate-income families in those municipalities or counties which have received Federal or State assistance for urban renewal, planning grants, or water and sewer projects, but which have not built housing for these income groups.

Enactment or amendment of State housing laws to give municipal housing authorities the right to lease dwelling units for publicly assisted housing outside of their corporate boundaries under specified circumstances.

Operation of statewide housing programs funded jointly by Federal and State moneys.

Removal of the constitutional barriers (in some States) which prevent combined private-governmental ventures in housing and other urban activities.

As pointed out elsewhere, the Commission proposes many incentives to encourage the States to move vigorously in matters of zoning, land use and assembly, building codes, housing codes, development standards, reduction of housing costs, and the streamlining of local government. They can do much to bring order out of chaos in the codes field by helping to achieve uniformity, by providing State codes for areas that have no codes, and setting forth uniform standards to be used in areas where local codes are found to be too restrictive.

Codes are State police powers delegated to the localities. The States must reassert some of their authority through appeals bodies and other appropriate means in those areas (1) where no codes exist, (2) where they are restrictive, (3) where they lack uniformity and (4) where local boards or inspectors take too narrow a view.

We believe the States have tended to become forgotten members of the governmental family. By using powers they already possess, by assuming new authority when necessary, and in providing funds, they occupy a unique position to help bring urban areas out of confusion. State governments are close to the people and to the problems, but bring enough perspective to bear to help release urban areas from the excesses of localism. State action of the kind we recommend, where the States are willing to help pay a significant amount of the costs as well as to exercise their authority, can help restore a genuine sense of community to our cities and their surrounding areas.

The solutions we call for are a tall order, but they are in proportion to the enormity of the problems of our urban areas.

If there is a sense of urgency and even alarm in our report and our recommendations, it is because the Commission saw the cities of our country firsthand and listened to the voices of the people. The Commission members certainly were not less concerned or knowledgeable than the average citizen, but after our inspections, hearings, and research studies, we found problems much worse, more widespread, and more explosive than any of us had thought.

We do not want to lose our perspective nor cause others to do so. This is a remarkable country. The poor and so-called uneducated often speak with an eloquence and moral fervor reflecting an environment that cannot be entirely negative in its influence. Our huge metropolitan areas on the whole offer a wider range of choices for making a living, for type of residences, and for pursuit of happiness than has ever been available to so many people anywhere. The number of able and highly motivated local officials, often remaining optimistic and determined in the face of great odds, is impressive. The Federal response to criticisms and suggestions (including some of our own) often has been swift and to the point. The recent acceleration and quantitative advances in Federal housing programs to meet the domestic urban crisis, in the face of international distractions and political handicaps, has been creditable. The urban renewal program, for all its shortcomings, has given many cities a better appearance and a new lease on life. The country's balance of private production with only limited governmental restraints not only turns out a great abundance of goods and services, but demonstrates a strength and stability that should not be taken for granted. Americans show great initiative and industriousness

It is not because we are unmindful of these and other blessings, but because we want them to be conserved and extended, that we point so urgently to the various problems that threaten our society. We need not dwell on this point. The riots have dramatized it more than words can do. Even though they have slowed down we remind the public that the causes still remain.

The Nation can, if it will, remove many of the causes of unrest.

A glance at the specific assignments given to this Commission for study will show that they are weighted heavily on the technical side: zoning and land use, building codes and technology, housing codes, development standards, local and Federal taxes affecting housing and urban growth, housing for low-income families, and the governmental framework to deal with all of these. But the Commission could not lose sight of the relationship between these technical matters and social problems. We agreed from the start not to duck the tough issues of poverty and race. And we conclude that those who sincerely want to solve the big social problems cannot do so if they duck the tough technical matters.

We must put housing on the front burner. We must focus our housing programs on housing for poor people. We believe in giving local authorities the tools and the money to get the job done. The States must have an expanded role, especially in getting sites, providing for low-income housing, and in breaking down the barriers of codes and zoning. We need simpler programs, a speedup in processing, and more initiative from Federal agencies. We seek the utmost cooperation from builders, developers, and private industry. If all of these fail to bring an abundance of housing for poor people, then we believe that the Government must become the builder of last resort. We hope this is not necessary but past neglect, unfulfilled promises, misplaced priorities and the consequences of failing to act give us compelling moral and practical reasons for proposing no less.

We must ease the tension between central city and suburb, between rich and poor, and especially between black and white. Too few have recognized how these basic democratic issues are related to local government structure and finance, to zoning policies, land and housing costs, or to national housing policies. The recommendations we make in these areas are a test of our most fundamental beliefs. We are a wealthy Nation, so it is not really a question of whether we can afford to do such things as we recommend. It is simply a matter of whether we still have faith in freedom, in equality, in justice, enough to make sacrifices in their cause.

We are confident that the Nation can rededicate itself to these goals that have been the touchstones of national progress and success.

5   DANIEL P. MOYNIHAN

Toward a national urban policy[*]

In the spring of 1969, President Nixon met in the Cabinet room with ten mayors of American cities. They were nothing if not a variegated lot, mixing party, religion, race, region in the fine confusion of American politics. They had been chosen to be representative in this respect, and were unrepresentative only in qualities of energy and intelligence that would have set them apart in any company. What was more notable about them, however, was that in the interval between the invitation from the White House and the meeting with the President, four had, in effect, resigned. All but assured of reelection, they had announced they would nonetheless not run again. The Mayor of Detroit who, at the last minute, could not attend, announced *his* resignation in June.

Their decisions were not that uncommon. More and more, for the men charged with governance of our cities great and small, politics has become the art of the impossible. It is not to be wondered that they flee. But we, in a sense, are left behind. And are in trouble. And know it.

At a time of great anxiety—a time which one of the nation's leading news magazines now routinely describes as "the most serious

* Chapter 1 of TOWARD A NATIONAL URBAN POLICY edited by Daniel P. Moynihan, © 1970 by Basic Books, Inc., Publishers, New York.

domestic crisis since the Civil War," a time when Richard Rovere, writing of the 1972 elections, adds parenthetically "assuming that democracy in America survives that long"—these personal decisions may seem of small consequence, yet one suspects they are not. All agree that the tumult of the time arises, in essence, from a crisis of authority. The institutions which shaped conduct and behavior in the past are being challenged, or worse, ignored. It is in the nature of authority, as Robert A. Nisbet continues to remind us, that it is consensual, that it is not coercive. When authority systems collapse they are replaced by power systems, which *are* coercive. Our vocabulary rather fails us here: the term "authority" is an unloved one, with its connotations of authoritarianism, but there appears to be no substitute. Happily, public opinion is not so dependent on political vocabulary, certainly not on the vocabulary of political science, as some assume. For all the ambiguity of the public rhetoric of the moment the desire of the great mass of our people is clear. They sense the advent of a power-based society, and they fear it. They seek peace. They look to the restoration of legitimacy, if not in existing institutions, then in new or modified ones. They look for a lessening of violent confrontations at home and, in great numbers, for an end to war abroad. Concern for personal safety on the part of city dwellers has become a live *political* fact, while the reappearance —what, praise God, did we do to bring this upon ourselves?—of a Stalinoid rhetoric of apocalyptic abuse on the left and its echoes on the right have created a public atmosphere of anxiety and portent that would seem to have touched us all. It is with every good reason that the nation gropes for some means to weather the storm of unreason that has broken upon us and seems if anything to grow wilder.

It would also seem that Americans at this moment are much preoccupied with the issue of freedom, or rather with new, meaningful ways in which freedom is seen to be expanded or constrained. We are, for example, beginning to evolve some sense of the meaning of group freedom. This comes after a century of preoccupation with individual rights of a kind which were seen as somehow opposed to and even threatened by group identities and anything so dubious in conception as *group* rights.

The Civil Rights Act of 1964 was the culmination of the political energies generated by that earlier period. The provisions which forbade employers, universities, governments, or whatever to have any knowledge of the race, religion, or national origin of individuals with which they dealt marked in ways the high-water mark of Social Darwinism in America, and did not long stand unopposed. Indeed, by 1965 the Federal government had already, as best one can tell, begun to require ethnic and racial census of its own employees, of federal contractors and research grant recipients. To do so violated the spirit if not the letter of the Civil Rights Act, with its implicit model of the lone individual locked in equal—and remorseless—competition in the Mancunian market place, but very much in harmony with the emerging sense of the 1960s that groups have identities and entitlements as well as do individuals. This view is diffusing rapidly. (In Massachusetts, for example, legislation of the Civil Rights Act period that declared any public school with more than fifty percent black pupils to be racially "imbalanced" and in consequence illegal, is already being challenged—by precisely those who supported it in the first instance.) If so far these demands have been most in evidence among black Americans, there is not the least reason to doubt that they will now diffuse to other groups, defined in various ways, and that new institutions will arise to respond to this new understanding of the nature of community.

In sum, two tendencies would appear to dominate the period. The *sense of general community is eroding*, and with it the authority of existing relationships, while simultaneously a powerful *quest for specific community* is emerging in the form of ever more intensive assertions of racial and ethnic identities. Although this is reported in the media largely in terms of black nationalism, it is just as reasonable to identify emergent attitudes in the "white working class" as part of the same phenomenon. The singular quality of these tendencies is that they are at once complementary and opposed. While the ideas are harmonious, the practices that would seem to support one interest are typically seen as opposing the other. Thus one need not be a moral philosopher or a social psychologist to see that much of the "crisis of the cities" arises from the interaction of these intense new demands with the relative inability of the urban social system to respond to them.

Rightly or otherwise—and one is no longer sure of this—it is our tradition in such circumstances to look to the condition of government. Social responses to changed social requirements take the form in industrial democracies of changed government policies. This had led, in the present situation, to a reasonably inventive spate of program proposals of the kind the New Deal more or less began and which flourished most notably in the period between the Presidential elections of 1960 and 1968 when the number of domestic programs of the Federal government increased from 45 to 435. Understandably, however, there has been a diminution of the confidence with which such proposals were formerly regarded. To say the least, there is a certain nonlinearity in the relationship between the number of categorical aid programs issuing forth from Washington and the degree of social satisfaction that ensues.

Hence the issue arises as to whether the demands of the time are not to be met in terms of *policy*, as well as program. It has been said of urban planners that they have been traumatized by the realization that everything relates to everything. But this is so, and the perception of it can provide a powerful analytic tool.

Our problems in the area of social peace and individual or group freedom occur in urban settings. Can it be that our difficulties in coping with these problems originate, in some measure, from the inadequacies of the setting in which they arise? Crime on the streets and campus violence may mark the onset of a native nihilism, but in the first instance they represent nothing more complex than the failure of law enforcement. Black rage and white resistance, Third World separatism, and restricted covenants all may define a collapse in the integuments of the social contract; but, again, in the first instance they represent for the most part simply the failure of urban arrangements to meet the expectations of the urban population in the areas of jobs, schools, housing, transportation, public health, administrative responsiveness, and political flexibility. If all these are related, one to the other, and in combination do not seem to be working well, the question arises whether the society ought not attempt a more coherent response. In a word, ought a national urban crisis be met with something like a national urban policy? Ought not the vast efforts to control the situation of the present be at least informed by some sense of goals for the future?

The United States does not now have an urban policy. The idea that there might be such is new. So also is the Urban Affairs Council, established by President Nixon on January 23, 1969, as the first official act of his administration, to "advise and assist" with respect to urban affairs, specifically "in the development of a national urban policy, having regard both to immediate and to long-range concerns, and to priorities among them."

The central circumstance, as stated, is that America is an urban nation and has been for half a century.

This is not to say Americans live in *big* cities. They do not. Only slightly more than half (55 percent) of the population lives in cities of 50,000 persons or more, and the bulk of that group is concentrated in relatively small urban aggregations of a hundred thousand to a quarter million persons. Ninety-eight percent of the units of local government have fewer than 50,000 persons. In terms of the 1960 census only somewhat more than a quarter of Congressmen represented districts in which a majority of residents lived in central city areas. The 1970 census will show that the majority of Americans in metropolitan areas in fact live in what are known as suburbs, while a great many more live in urban settlements of modest size. But they are not the less urban for that reason, providing conditions of living and problems of government profoundly different from that of the agricultural, small-town past.

The essentials of the present "urban crisis" are simple enough to relate. Until about World War II the growth of the city, as Otto Eckstein argues, was "a logical, economic development." At least it was such in the northeastern quadrant of the United States, where most urban troubles are supposed to exist. The political jurisdiction of the city more or less defined the area of intensive economic development which more or less defined the area of intensive settlement. Thereafter economic incentives and social desires combined to produce a fractionating process which made it ever more difficult to collect enough power in any one place to provide the rudiments of effective government. As a result of or as a part of this process, the central area ceased to grow and began to decline. The core began to rot. This most primitive analogue began to suggest to us that in some way life itself was in decline.

Two special circumstances compounded this problem. First, the extraordinary migration of the rural southern Negro to the northern city. Second, a post-war population explosion (90 million babies were born between 1946 and 1968) which placed immense pressures on municipal services and drove many whites to the suburbs seeking relief. (Both these influences are now somewhat attenuating, but their effects will be present for at least several decades, and indeed a new baby boom may be in the offing.) As a result the problems of economic stagnation of the central city became desperately exacerbated by those of racial tension. In the course of the 1960s tension turned into open racial strife.

City governments began to respond to the onset of economic obsolescence and social rigidity a generation or more ago, but quickly found their fiscal resources strained near to the limit. State governments became involved, and much the same process ensued. Starting in the post-war period, the Federal government itself became increasingly caught up with urban problems. In recent years resources on a fairly considerable scale have flowed from Washington to the cities of the land and will clearly continue.

However, in the evolution of a national urban policy, more is involved than merely the question of national goals and the provision of resources with which to attain them. Too many programs have produced too few results simply to accept a more or less straight-forward extrapolation of past and present practices into an oversized but familiar future.

The question of method has become as salient as that of goals themselves. As yet the Federal government, no more than state or local government, has not found an effective *incentive* system—comparable to profit in private enterprise, prestige in intellectual activity, rank in military organization—whereby to shape the forces at work in urban areas in such a way that urban goals—whatever they may be—are in fact attained. This search for incentives and the realization that present procedures such as categorical grant-in-aid programs do not seem to provide sufficiently powerful ones must accompany and suffuse the effort to establish goals as such. We must seek not just policy, but policy allied to a vigorous strategy for obtaining results from it.

Finally, the Federal establishment must develop a much height-ened sensitivity to its "hidden" urban policies. There is hardly a department or agency of the national government whose programs do not in some way have important consequences for the life of cities, and those who live in them. Frequently—one is tempted to say normally!—the political appointees and career executives concerned do not see themselves as involved with, much less responsible for, the urban consequences of their programs and policies. They are, to their minds, simply building highways, guaranteeing mortgages, advancing agriculture, or whatever. No one has made clear to them that they are simultaneously redistributing employment opportunities, segregating neighborhoods or desegregating them, depopulating the countryside and filling up the slums, and so on: all these things as second and third order consequences of nominally unrelated programs. Already this institutional naïveté has become cause for, suspicion; in the future it simply must not be tolerated. Indeed, in the future, a primary mark of competence in a Federal official should be the ability to see the interconnections between programs immediately at hand, and the urban problems that pervade the larger society.

THE FUNDAMENTALS OF URBAN POLICY

It having long been established that with respect to general codes of behavior eleven precepts are too many and nine too few, ten points of urban policy may be set forth, scaled roughly to correspond to a combined measure of urgency and importance.

1. The poverty and social isolation of minority groups in central cities is the single most serious problem of the American city today. It must be attacked with urgency, with a greater commitment of resources than has heretofore been the case, and with programs designed especially for this purpose.

The 1960s have seen enormous economic advances among minority groups, especially Negroes. Outside the South, 37 percent of Negro families earn $8,000 per year or more, that being approximately the national median income. In cities in the largest metropolitan areas, 20 percent of Negro families in 1967 reported family incomes of $10,000 or over. The earnings of young married couples are approaching parity with whites.

Nonetheless, certain forms of social disorganization and dependency appear to be increasing among the urban poor. Recently, Conrad Taeuber, Associate Director of the Bureau of the Census, reported that in the largest metropolitan areas—those with 1 million or more inhabitants—"the number of black families with a woman as head increased by 83 percent since 1960; the number of black families with a man as head increased by only 15 percent during the same period." Disorganization, isolation, and discrimination seemingly have led to violence, and this violence has in turn been increasingly politicized by those seeking a "confrontation" with "white" society. Urban policy must have as its first goal the transformation of the urban lower class into a stable community based on dependable and adequate income flows, social equality, and social mobility. Efforts to improve the conditions of life in the present caste-created slums must never take precedence over efforts to enable the slum population to disperse throughout the metropolitan areas involved. Urban policy accepts the reality of ethnic neighborhoods based on choice, but asserts that the active intervention of government is called for to enable free choice to include integrated living as the normal option.

It is impossible to comprehend the situation of the black urban poor without first seeing that they have experienced not merely a major migration in the past generation, but also that they now live in a state almost of demographic siege as a result of population growth. The dependency ratio, in terms of children per thousand adult males, for blacks is nearly twice that for whites, and the gap widened sharply in the 1960s.

Table 5–1—Children per 1000 Adult Males

	1960	1966
White	1,365	1,406
Negro	1,922	2,216

It is this factor, surely, that accounts for much of the present distress of the black urban slums. At the same time, it is fairly clear that the sharp escalation in the number of births that characterized the past twenty-five years has more or less come to an end. The number of Negro females under age five is exactly the number aged 5 to 9. Thus the 1980s will see a slackening of the present severe demands on the earning power of adult Negroes and also on the public institutions that provide services for children. But for the decade immediately ahead, those demands will continue to rise—especially for central city blacks, whose median age is a little more than 10 years below that for whites—and will clearly have a priority claim on public resources.

Table 5-2—1967 Negro Female Population

AGE	NUMBER
Under 5	1,443,000
5 to 9	1,443,000
10 to 14	1,298,000
15 to 19	1,102,000
20 to 24	840,000

2. Economic and social forces in urban areas are not self-balancing. Imbalances in industry, transportation, housing, social services and similar elements of urban life frequently tend to become more rather than less pronounced, and this tendency is often abetted by public policies. The concept of urban balance may be tentatively set forth: A social condition in which forces tending to produce imbalance induce counterforces that simultaneously admit change while maintaining equilibrium. It must be the constant object of federal officials whose programs affect urban areas—and there are few whose do not—to seek such equilibrium.

The evidence is considerable that many Federal programs have induced sharp imbalances in the "ecology" of urban areas—the highway program, for example, is frequently charged with this, and there is wide agreement that other specifically city-oriented programs such as urban renewal, have frequently accomplished just the opposite of their nominal objectives. The reasons are increasingly evident. Cities are complex social systems. Interventions that, intentionally or not, affect one component of the system almost invariably affect second, third, and fourth components as well, and these in turn affect the first component, often in ways quite opposite to the direction of the initial intervention. Most Federal urban programs have assumed fairly simple cause and effect relationships which do not exist in the complex real world. Moreover, they have typically been based on "common sense" rather than research in an

area where common sense can be notoriously misleading. In the
words of Jay W. Forrester, "With a high degree of confidence we can
say that the intuitive solution to the problems of complex social
systems will be wrong most of the time."

*3. At least part of the relative ineffectiveness of the efforts of urban
government to respond to urban problems derives from the fragmented
and obsolescent structure of urban government itself. The Federal
government should constantly encourage and provide incentives for the
reorganization of local government in response to the reality of metropolitan conditions. The objective of the Federal government should be
that local government be stronger and more effective, more visible,
accessible, and meaningful to local inhabitants. To this end the Federal
government should discourage the creation of paragovernments designed
to deal with special problems by evading or avoiding the jurisdiction of established local authorities, and should encourage effective decentralization.*

Although the "quality" of local government, especially in large
cities, has been seen to improve of late, there appears to have been
a decline in the vitality of local political systems and an almost total
disappearance of serious effort to reorganize metropolitan areas into
new and more rational governmental jurisdictions. Federal efforts
to recreate ethnic-neighborhood-based community organizations, as
in the poverty program or to induce metropolitan area planning as in
various urban development programs have had a measure of success,
but nothing like that hoped for. The middle-class norm of "participation" has diffused downward and outward, so that Federal urban
programs now routinely require citizen participation in the planning
process and beyond, yet somehow this does not seem to have led to
more competent communities. In some instances it appears rather
to have escalated the level of stalemate.

It may be we have not been entirely candid with ourselves in this
area. Citizen participation, as Elliott A. Krause has pointed out, is
in practice a "bureaucratic ideology," a device whereby public
officials induce non-public individuals to act in a way the officials
desire. Although the putative object may be, indeed almost always
is, to improve the lot of the citizen, it is not settled that the actual
consequences are anything like that. The ways of the officials, of
course, are often not those of the elected representatives of the
people, and the "citizens" may become a rope in the tug-of-war
between bureaucrat and representative. Especially in a Federal
system, "citizen participation" easily becomes a device whereby the
far-off Federal bureaucracy acquires a weapon with which to battle
the elected officials of local government. Whatever the nominal
intent, the normal outcome is Federal support for those who would

diminish the legitimacy of local government. But it is not clear that Federal purposes are typically advanced through this process. To the contrary, an all-round diminishment rather than enhancement of energies seems to occur.

This would appear especially true when "citizen participation" has in effect meant putting citizens on the payroll. However much they may continue to "protest," the protest acquires a certain hollow ring. Something like this has surely happened to groups seeking to influence public opinion on matters of public policy which have been openly or covertly supported by the Federal government. This is a new practice in American democracy. It began in the field of foreign affairs, and has now spread to the domestic area. To a quite astonishing degree it will be found that those groups which nominally are pressing for social change and development in the poverty field, for example, are in fact subsidized by Federal funds. This occurs in protean ways—research grants, training contracts, or whatever—and is done with the best of intentions. But, again, with what results is far from clear. Can this development, for example, account for the curious fact that there seems to be so much protest in the streets of the nation, but so little, as it were, in its legislatures? Is it the case, in other words, that the process of public subsidy is subtly debilitating?

Whatever the truth of this judgment, it is nevertheless clear that a national urban policy must look first to the vitality of the elected governments of the urban areas and must seek to increase their capacity for independent, effective, and creative action. This suggests an effort to find some way out of the present fragmentation and a certain restraint on the creation of Federally-financed "competitive governments."

Nathan Glazer has made the useful observation that in London and Tokyo comprehensive metropolitan government is combined with a complex system of "sub-governments"—the London Boroughs—representing units of 200,000–250,000 persons. These are "real" governments, with important powers in areas such as education, welfare, and housing. In England they are governed through an electoral system involving the national political parties in essentially their national postures. (Indeed, the boroughs make up the basic units of the parties' urban structure.) It may well be there is need for social inventions of this kind in the great American cities, especially with respect to power over matters such as welfare, education, and housing which are now subject to intense debates concerning "local control." The demand for "local control" is altogether to be welcomed. In some degree it can be seen to arise from the bureaucratic barbarities of the highway programs of the 1950s, for example. But in the largest degree it reflects the processes of democracy catching up with the content of contemporary government. As government more and more involves itself in matters that very much touch on the lives of individual citizens, those individuals seek a greater voice in the programs concerned. In the hands of ideologues or dimwits, this demand can lead to an utter paralysis of government. It has already done so in dozens of urban development situations. But approached with a measure of sensitivity—and patience—it can lead to a considerable revitalization of urban government.

4. *A primary object of Federal urban policy must be to restore the fiscal vitality of urban government, with the particular object of ensuring that local governments normally have enough resources on hand or available to make local initiative in public affairs a reality.*

For all the rise in actual amounts, Federal aid to State and local government has increased only from 12% of State-local revenue in 1958 to 17% in 1967. Increasingly, State and local governments that try to meet their responsibilities lurch from one fiscal crisis to another. In such circumstances, the capacity for creative local government becomes least in precisely those jurisdictions where it might most be expected. As much as any other single factor, this condition may be judged to account for the malaise of city government, and especially for the reluctance of the more self-sufficient suburbs to associate themselves with the nearly bankrupt central cities. Surviving from one fiscal deadline to another, the central cities commonly adopt policies which only compound their ultimate difficulties. Yet their options are so few. As James C. Wilson writes, "The great bulk of any city's budget is, in effect, a fixed charge the mayor is powerless to alter more than trivially." The basic equation, as it were, of American political economy is that for each one percent increase in the Gross National Product the income of the Federal government increases one and one-half percent, while the normal income of city governments rises half to three-quarters of a point at most. Hence both a clear opportunity and a no less manifest necessity exist for the Federal government to adopt as a deliberate policy an increase in its aid to urban governments. This should be done in part through revenue sharing, and in part through an increase in categorical assistance, hopefully in much more consolidated forms than now exist, and through credit assistance.

It may not be expected that this process will occur rapidly. The prospects for an enormous "peace and growth dividend" to follow the cessation of hostilities in Vietnam are far less bright than they were painted. But the fact is that the American Gross National Product grows at better than a billion dollars a week, and we can afford the government we need. This means, among our very first priorities, an increase in the resources available to city governments.

A clear opportunity exists for the Federal government to adopt as a deliberate policy an increase in its aid to state and local governments in the aftermath of the Vietnam war. Much analysis is in order, but in approximate terms it may be argued that the present proportion of aid should be about doubled, with the immediate objective that the Federal government contribution constitute one-third of state and local revenue.

5. Federal urban policy should seek to equalize the provision of public services among different jurisdictions in metropolitan areas.

Although the standard depiction of the (black) residents of central cities as grossly deprived with respect to schools and other social services when compared with their suburban (white) neighbors requires endless qualification, the essential truth is that life for the well-to-do is better than life for the poor and that these populations tend to be separated by artificial government boundaries within metropolitan areas. (The people in between may live on either side of the boundaries and are typically overlooked altogether.)

As a minimum, Federal policy should seek a dollar-for-dollar equivalence in the provision of social services having most to do with economic and social opportunity. This includes, at the top of the list, public education and public safety. (Obviously there will always be some relatively small jurisdictions—"the Scarsdale school system"— that spend a great deal more than others, but there can be national or regional norms, and no central city should be forced to operate below them.)

Beyond the provision of equal resources lies the troubled and elusive question of equal results. Should equality of educational opportunity extend to equality of educational achievement (as between one group of children and another)? Should equality of police protection extend to equality of criminal victimization? That is to say, should there be not only as many police but also as few crimes in one area of the city as in another? These are hardly simple questions, but as they are increasingly posed it is increasingly evident that we shall have to try to find answers.

The area of housing is one of special and immediate urgency. In America, housing is not regarded as a public utility (and a scarce one!) as it is in many of the industrial democracies of Europe, but there can hardly be any remaining doubt that the strong and regular production of housing is very nearly a public necessity. We shall not solve the problem of racial isolation without it. Housing must not only be open, *it must be available.* The process of filtration out from dense center city slums can only take place if the housing perimeter, as it were, is sufficiently porous. For too long now the production of housing has been a function not of the need for housing as such, but rather of the need to increase or decrease the money supply, or whatever. Somehow a greater regularity of effective demand must be provided the housing industry, and its level of production must be increased.

6. *The Federal government must assert a specific interest in the movement of people, displaced by technology or driven by poverty, from rural to urban areas, and also in the movement from densely populated central cities to suburban areas.*

Much of the present urban crisis derives from the almost total absence of any provision for an orderly movement of persons out of the countryside and into the city. The Federal government made extraordinary, and extraordinarily successful, efforts to provide for the resettlement of Hungarian refugees in the 1950s and Cuban refugees in the 1960s. But almost nothing has been done for Americans driven from their homes by forces no less imperious.

Rural to urban migration has not stopped, and will not for some time. Increasingly, it is possible to predict where it will occur and in what time sequence. (In 1968, for example, testing of mechanical tobacco harvesting began on the East Coast, and the first mechanical grape pickers were used on the West Coast.) Hence, it is possible to prepare for it, both by training of those who leave and providing for them where they arrive. Doubtless the United States will remain a nation of exceptionally mobile persons, but the completely unassisted processes of the past need not continue with respect to the migration of impoverished rural populations. There are increasing indications that the dramatic movement of Negro Americans to central city areas may be slackening, and that a counter movement to surrounding suburban areas may have begun. This process is to be encouraged in every way, especially by the maintenance of a flexible and open housing market.

But it remains the case that in the next thirty years we shall add one hundred million persons to our population. Knowing that, it is impossible to have no policy with respect to where they will be located. *For to let nature take its course is a policy.* To consider what might be best for all concerned and to seek to provide it is surely a more acceptable goal.

7. *State government has an indispensable role in the management of urban affairs, and must be supported and encouraged by the Federal government in the performance of this role.*

This fact, being all but self-evident, tends to be overlooked. The trend of recent legislative measures, almost invariably prompted by executive initiatives, has been to establish a direct Federal-city relationship. States have been bypassed, and doubtless some have used this as an excuse to avoid their responsibilities of providing the legal and governmental conditions under which urban problems can be effectively confronted.

It has, of course, been a tradition of social reform in America that city government is bad and that, if anything, state government is worse. This is neither true as a generalization nor useful as a principle. But on the other hand, by and large, state governments, with an occasional exception such as New York, have *not* involved themselves with urban problems and are readily enough seen by mayors as the real enemy. But this helps neither. States must become involved. City governments, without exception, are creatures of state governments. City boundaries, jurisdictions, and powers are given and taken away by state governments. It is surely time the Federal establishment sought to lend a sense of coherence and a measure of progressivism to this fundamental process.

The role of state government in urban affairs cannot easily be overlooked: it is more typically *ignored* on political or ideological grounds. By contrast, it is relatively easy to overlook county government, and possibly an even more serious mistake to do so. In a steadily increasing number of metropolitan areas, the county, rather than the original core city, has become the only unit of government that makes any geographical sense. That is to say, the only unit whose boundaries contain most or all of the actual urban settlement. The powers of county government have typically lagged well behind its potential, but it may also be noted that in the few—the very few—instances of urban reorganization to take place since World War II, county government has assumed a principal, even primary role in the new arrangement.

8. The Federal government must develop and put into practice far more effective incentive systems than now exist whereby state and local governments, and private interests can be led to achieve the goals of Federal programs.

The typical Federal grant-in-aid program provides its recipients with an immediate reward for promising to work toward some specified goal—raising the educational achievement of minority children, providing medical care for the poor, cleaning up the air, reviving the downtown business district—but almost no reward for actually achieving such goals, and rarely any punishment for failing to do so.

It is by now widely agreed that what Federal grant-in-aid

programs mostly reward is dissimulation. By and large the approach of the Federal government to most urban problems is to provide local institutions with money in the hope they will perform but with no very powerful incentives to do so.

There is a growing consensus that the Federal government should provide market competition for public programs or devise ways to imitate market conditions. In particular, it is increasingly agreed that Federal aid should be given directly to the consumers of the programs concerned—individuals included—thus enabling them to choose among competing suppliers of the goods or services that the program is designed to provide.

Probably no single development would more enliven and energize the role of government in urban affairs than a move from the monopoly service strategy of the grant-in-aid programs to a market strategy of providing the most reward to those suppliers that survive competition.

In this precise sense, it is evident that Federal programs designed to assist those city-dwelling groups that are least well-off, least mobile, and least able to fend for themselves must in many areas move beyond a *services* strategy to an approach that provides inducements to move from a dependent and deficient status to one of independence and sufficiency. Essentially, this is an *income* strategy, based fundamentally on the provision of incentives to increase the earnings and to expand the property base of the poorest groups.

Urban policy should in general be directed to raising the level of political activity and concentrating it in the electoral process. It is nonetheless possible and useful to be alert for areas of intense but unproductive political conflict and to devise ways to avoid such conflict through market strategies. Thus conflicts over "control" of public education systems have frequently of late taken on the aspect of disputes over control of a monopoly, a sole source of a needed good. Clearly some of the ferocity that ensues can be avoided through free choice arrangements, that, in effect, eliminate monopoly control.

If we move in this direction, difficult "minimum standard" regulation problems will almost certainly arise and must be anticipated. No arrangement meets every need, and a good deal of change is primarily to be justified on grounds that certain systems need change for its own sake. (Small school districts controlled by locally elected boards may be just the thing for New York City. However, in Phoenix, Arizona, where they have just that, consolidation and centralization would appear to be the desire of educational reformers.) But either way, a measure of market competition can surely improve the provision of public services, much as it has proved an efficient way to obtain various public paraphernalia, from bolt-action rifles to lunar landing vehicles.

Here, as elsewhere, it is essential to pursue and to identify the *hidden* urban policies of government. These are nowhere more central to the issue than in the matter of incentives. Thus for better than half a century now, city governments with the encouragement of State and Federal authorities have been seeking to direct urban investment and development in accordance with principles embodied in zoning codes and not infrequently in accord with precise city plans. However, during this same time the tax laws have provided the utmost incentive to pursue just the opposite objectives of those incorporated in the codes and the plans. It has, for example, been estimated that returns from land speculation based on zoning code changes on average incur half the tax load of returns from investment in physical improvements. Inevitably, energy and capital have diverted *away* from pursuing the plan, *toward* subverting it. It little avails for government to deplore the evasion of its purposes in such areas. Government has in fact established two sets of purposes, and provided vastly greater inducements to pursue the implicit rather than the avowed ones. Until public authorities, and the public itself, learn to be much more alert to these situations and far more open in discussing and managing them, we must expect the present pattern of self-defeating contradictions to continue.

9. *The Federal government must provide more and better information concerning urban affairs, and should sponsor extensive and sustained research into urban problems.*

Much of the social progress of recent years derives from the increasing quality and quantity of government-generated statistics and government-supported research. However, there is general agreement that the time is at hand when a general consolidation is in order, bringing a measure of symmetry to the now widely dispersed (and somewhat uneven) data-collecting and research-supporting activities of the Federal government. Such consolidation should not be limited to urban problems, but it must surely include attention to urban questions.

The Federal government should, in particular, recognize that most of the issues that appear most critical just now do so in large measure because they are so little understood. This is perhaps especially so with respect to issues of minority-group education, but generally applies to all the truly difficult and elusive issues of the moment. More and better inquiry is called for. In particular, the

Federal government must begin to sponsor longitudinal research designed to follow individual and communal development over long periods of time.

It should also consider providing demographic and economic projections for political subdivisions as a routine service, much as the weather and the economy are forecast. (Thus, Karl Taueber has shown how seemingly unrelated policies of local governments can increase the degree of racial and economic differentiation between political jurisdictions, especially between central cities and suburbs.)

Similarly, the extraordinary inquiry into the educational system begun by the U.S. Office of Education under the direction of James S. Coleman should somehow be established on an ongoing basis. It is now perfectly clear that little is known about the processes whereby publicly-provided resources affect educational outcomes. The great mass of those involved in education, and of that portion of the public which interests itself in educational matters, continues undisturbed in the old beliefs. But the bases of their beliefs are already thoroughly undermined, and the whole structure is likely to collapse in a panic of disillusion and despair unless something like new knowledge is developed to replace the old. Here again, longitudinal inquiries are essential. And here also, it should be insisted that however little the new understandings may have diffused beyond the academic research centers in which they originated, the American public is accustomed to the idea that understandings do change and, especially in the field of education, is quite open to experimentation and innovation.

Much of the methodology of social science originated in clinical psychology and perhaps for that reason tends to be deficiency-oriented. Social scientists raise social problems, the study of which can become a social problem in its own right if it is never balanced by the identification and analysis of social successes. We are not an unsuccessful country. To the contrary, few societies work as hard at their problems, solve as many, and in the process stumble on more unexpected and fulsome opportunities. The cry of the decent householder who asks why the profession (and the news media which increasingly follow the profession) must be ever preoccupied with juvenile delinquency and never with "juvenile decency" deserves to be heard. Social science like medical science has been preoccupied with pathology, with pain. A measure of inquiry into the sources of health and pleasure is overdue, and is properly a subject of Federal support.

10. The Federal government, by its own example, and by incentives, should seek the development of a far heightened sense of the finite resources of the natural environment, and the fundamental importance of aesthetics in successful urban growth.

The process of "uglification" may first have developed in Europe, but as with much else the technological breakthroughs have taken place in the United States. American cities have grown to be as ugly as they are, not as a consequence of the failure of design, so much as of the success of a certain interaction of economic, technological, and cultural forces. It is economically efficient to exploit the natural resources of land, air, and water by technological means which the culture does not reject, albeit that the result is an increasingly despoiled, debilitated, and now even dangerous urban environment.

It is not clear how this is to change, and so the matter which the twenty-second century, say, will almost certainly see as having been the primary urban issue of the twentieth century is ranked last in the public priorities of the moment. But there *are* signs that the culture is changing, that the frontier sense of a natural environment of unlimited resources, all but impervious to human harm, is being replaced by an acute awareness that serious and possibly irreparable harm is being done to the environment, and that somehow the process must be reversed. This *could* lead to a new, non-exploitive technology, and thence to a new structure of economic incentives.

The Federal establishment is showing signs that this cultural change is affecting its actions, and so do State and city governments. But the process needs to be raised to the level of a conscious pursuit of policy. The quality of the urban environment, a measure deriving from a humane and understanding use of the natural resources, together with the creative use of design in architecture and in the distribution of activities and people, must become a proclaimed concern of government. And here the Federal government can lead. It must seek out its hidden policies. (The design of public housing projects, for example, surely has had the consequence of manipulating the lives of those who inhabit them. By and large the Federal government set the conditions which have determined the disastrous designs of the past two decades. It is thus responsible for the results and should force itself to realize that.) And it must be acutely aware of the force of its own example. If scientists (as we are told) in the Manhattan Project were prepared to dismiss the problem of long-lived radioactive wastes as one that could be solved merely by ocean dumping, there are few grounds for amazement that business executives in Detroit for so long manufactured automobiles that emitted poison gases into the atmosphere. Both patterns of decision evolved from the primacy of economic concerns in the context of the exploitation of the natural environment in ways the culture did not forbid. There are, however, increasing signs that we are beginning to change in this respect. We may before long evolve into a society in which the understanding of and concern about environmental pollution, and the general uglification of American life, will be both culturally vibrant and politically potent.

Social peace is a primary objective of social policy. To the extent that this derives from a shared sense of the value and significance of the public places and aesthetic value of the city, the Federal government has a direct interest in encouraging such qualities.

Daniel J. Elazar has observed that while Americans have been willing to become urbanized, they have adamantly resisted becoming citified. Yet a measure of this process is needed. There are not half a dozen cities in America whose disappearance would, apart from the inconvenience, cause any real regret. But to lose one of those half dozen would plunge much of the nation and almost all the immediate inhabitants into genuine grief. Something of value in our lives would have been lost, and we would know it. The difference between those cities that would be missed and those that would not be resides fundamentally in the combination of architectural beauty, social amenity, and cultural vigor that so sets them apart. It has ever been such. To create such a city and to preserve it was the great ideal of the Greek civilization, and it may yet become ours as we step back ever so cautiously from the worship of the nation-state with its barbarous modernity and impotent might. We might well consider the claims for a different life asserted in the oath of the Athenian city-state:

> We will ever strive for the ideals and sacred things of the city, both alone and with many;
> We will unceasingly seek to quicken the sense of public duty;
> We will revere and obey the city's laws;
> We will transmit this city not only not less, but greater, better and more beautiful than it was transmitted to us.

6 THE NATIONAL ADVISORY COMMISSION ON CIVIL DISORDERS

The Kerner Commission Report (Summary)

INTRODUCTION

The summer of 1967 again brought racial disorders to American cities, and with them shock, fear and bewilderment to the nation.

The worst came during a two-week period in July, first in Newark and then in Detroit. Each set off a chain reaction in neighboring communities.

On July 28, 1967, the President of the United States established this Commission and directed us to answer three basic questions:

What happened?

Why did it happen?

What can be done to prevent it from happening again?

To respond to these questions, we have undertaken a broad range of studies and investigations. We have visited the riot cities; we have heard many witnesses: we have sought the counsel of experts across the country.

This is our basic conclusion: Our nation is moving toward two societies, one black, one white—separate and unequal.

Reaction to last summer's disorders has quickened the movement and deepened the division. Discrimination and segregation have long permeated much of American life; they now threaten the future of every American.

This deepening racial division is not inevitable. The movement apart can be reversed. Choice is still possible. Our principal task is to define that choice and to press for a national resolution.

To pursue our present course will involve the continuing polarization of the American community and, ultimately, the destruction of basic democratic values.

The alternative is not blind repression or capitulation to law-lessness. It is the realization of common opportunities for all within a single society.

This alternative will require a commitment to national action—compassionate, massive and sustained, backed by the resources of the most powerful and the richest nation on this earth. From every American it will require new attitudes, new understanding, and, above all, new will.

The vital needs of the nation must be met; hard choices must be made, and, if necessary, new taxes enacted.

Violence cannot build a better society. Disruption and disorder nourish repression, not justice. They strike at the freedom of every citizen. The community cannot—it will not—tolerate coercion and mob rule.

Violence and destruction must be ended—in the streets of the ghetto and in the lives of people.

Segregation and poverty have created in the racial ghetto a destructive environment totally unknown to most white Americans.

What white Americans have never fully understood—but what the Negro can never forget—is that white society is deeply impli-cated in the ghetto. White institutions created it, white institutions maintain it, and white society condones it.

It is time now to turn with all the purpose at our command to the major unfinished business of this nation. It is time to adopt strategies for action that will produce quick and visible progress. It is time to make good the promises of American democracy to all citizens—urban and rural, white and black, Spanish-surname, American Indian, and every minority group.

Our recommendations embrace three basic principles:

To mount programs on a scale equal to the dimension of the problems.

To aim these programs for high impact in the immediate future in order to close the gap between promise and performance.

To undertake new initiatives and experiments that can change the system of failure and frustration that now dominates the ghetto and weakens our society.

These programs will require unprecedented levels of funding and performance, but they neither probe deeper nor demand more than the problems which called them forth. There can be no higher priority for national action and no higher claim on the nation's conscience. . . .

PART I—WHAT HAPPENED?

Chapter 1—Profiles of disorder

The report contains profiles of a selection of the disorders that took place during the summer of 1967. These profiles are designed to indicate how the disorders happened, who participated in them, and how local officials, police forces, and the National Guard responded. Illustrative excerpts follow:

Newark

. . . It was decided to attempt to channel the energies of the people into a nonviolent protest. While Lofton promised the crowd that a full investigation would be made of the Smith incident, the other Negro leaders began urging those on the scene to form a line of march toward the city hall.

Some persons joined the line of march. Others milled about in the narrow street. From the dark grounds of the housing project came a barrage of rocks. Some of them fell among the crowd. Others hit persons in the line of march. Many smashed the windows of the police station. The rock throwing, it was believed, was the work of youngsters; approximately 2,500 children lived in the housing project.

Almost at the same time, an old car was set afire in a parking lot. The line of march began to disintegrate. The police, their heads protected by World War I-type helmets, sallied forth to disperse the crowd. A fire engine, arriving on the scene, was pelted with rocks. As police drove people away from the station, they scattered in all directions.

A few minutes later a nearby liquor store was broken into. Some persons, seeing a caravan of cabs appear at city hall to protest Smith's arrest, interpreted this as evidence that the disturbance had been organized, and generated rumors to that effect.

However, only a few stores were looted. Within a short period of time, the disorder appeared to have run its course.

*   *   *

. . . On Saturday, July 15, [Director of Police Dominick] Spina received a report of snipers in a housing project. When he arrived he saw approximately 100 National Guardsmen and police officers crouching behind vehicles, hiding in corners and lying on the ground around the edge of the courtyard.

Since everything appeared quiet and it was broad daylight, Spina walked directly down the middle of the street. Nothing happened. As he came to the last building of the complex, he heard a shot. All around him the troopers jumped, believing themselves to be under sniper fire. A moment later a young Guardsman ran from behind a building.

The Director of Police went over and asked him if he had fired the shot.

The soldier said yes, he had fired to scare a man away from a window; that his orders were to keep everyone away from windows.

Spina said he told the soldier: "Do you know what you just did? You have now created a state of hysteria. Every Guardsman up and down this street and every state policeman and every city policeman that is present thinks that somebody just fired a shot and that it is probably a sniper."

A short time later more "gunshots" were heard. Investigating, Spina came upon a Puerto Rican sitting on a wall. In reply to a question as to whether he knew "where the firing is coming from?" the man said:

"That's no firing. That's fireworks. If you look up to the fourth floor, you will see the people who are throwing down these cherry bombs."

By this time four truckloads of National Guardsmen had arrived and troopers and policemen were again crouched everywhere looking for a sniper. The Director of Police remained at the scene for three hours, and the only shot fired was the one by the Guardsman.

Nevertheless, at six o'clock that evening two columns of National Guardsmen and state troopers were directing mass fire at the Hayes Housing Project in response to what they believed were snipers. . . .

Detroit

. . . A spirit of carefree nihilism was taking hold. To riot and destroy appeared more and more to become ends in themselves. Late Sunday afternoon it appeared to one observer that the young people were "dancing amidst the flames."

A Negro plainclothes officer was standing at an intersection when a man threw a Molotov cocktail into a business establishment at the corner. In the heat of the afternoon, fanned by the 20 to 25 m.p.h. winds of both Sunday and Monday, the fire reached the home next door within minutes. As residents uselessly sprayed the flames with garden hoses, the fire jumped from roof to roof of adjacent two- and three-story buildings. Within the hour the entire block was in flames. The ninth house in the burning row belonged to the arsonist who had thrown the Molotov cocktail. . . .

*   *   *

. . . Employed as a private guard, 55-year-old Julius L. Dorsey, a Negro, was standing in front of a market when accosted by two Negro men and a woman. They demanded he permit them to loot the market. He ignored their demands. They began to berate him. He asked a neighbor to call the police. As the argument grew more heated, Dorsey fired three shots from his pistol into the air.

The police radio reported: "Looters, they have rifles." A patrol car driven by a police officer and carrying three National Guardsmen arrived. As the looters fled, the law enforcement personnel opened fire. When the firing ceased, one person lay dead.

He was Julius L. Dorsey. . . .

*   *   *

. . . As the riot alternately waxed and waned, one area of the ghetto remained insulated. On the northeast side the residents of some 150 square blocks inhabited by 21,000 persons had, in 1966, banded together in the Positive Neighborhood Action Committee (PNAC). With professional help from the Institute of Urban Dynamics, they had organized block clubs and made plans for the improvement of the neighborhood. . . .

When the riot broke out, the residents, through the block clubs, were able to organize quickly. Youngsters, agreeing to stay in the neighborhood, participated in detouring traffic. While many persons reportedly sympathized with the idea of a rebellion against the "system," only two small fires were set—one in an empty building.

*   *   *

. . . According to Lt. Gen. Throckmorton and Col. Bolling, the city, at this time, was saturated with fear. The National Guardsmen were afraid, the residents were afraid, and the police were afraid. Numerous persons, the majority of them Negroes, were being injured by gunshots of undetermined origin. The general and his staff felt that the major task of the troops was to reduce the fear and restore an air of normalcy.

In order to accomplish this, every effort was made to establish contact and rapport between the troops and the residents. The soldiers—20 percent of whom were Negro—began helping to clean up the streets, collect garbage, and trace persons who had disappeared in the confusion. Residents in the neighborhoods responded with soup and sandwiches for the troops. In areas where the National Guard tried to establish rapport with the citizens, there was a smaller response.

New Brunswick

. . . A short time later, elements of the crowd—an older and rougher one than the night before—appeared in front of the police station. The participants wanted to see the mayor.

Mayor [Patricia] Sheehan went out onto the steps of the station. Using a bullhorn, she talked to the people and asked that she be given an opportunity to correct conditions. The crowd was boisterous. Some persons challenged the mayor. But, finally, the opinion, "She's new! Give her a chance!" prevailed.

A demand was issued by people in the crowd that all persons arrested the previous night be released. Told that this already had been done, the people were suspicious. They asked to be allowed to inspect the jail cells.

It was agreed to permit representatives of the people to look in the cells to satisfy themselves that everyone had been released.

The crowd dispersed. The New Brunswick riot had failed to materialize.

Chapter 2—Patterns of disorder

The "typical" riot did not take place. The disorders of 1967 were unusual, irregular, complex and unpredictable social processes. Like most human events, they did not unfold in an orderly sequence. However, an analysis of our survey information leads to some conclusions about the riot process.

In general:

The civil disorders of 1967 involved Negroes acting against local symbols of white American society, authority and property in Negro neighborhoods—rather than against white persons.

Of 164 disorders reported during the first nine months of 1967, eight (5 percent) were major in terms of violence and damage; 33 (20 percent) were serious but not major; 123 (75 percent) were minor and undoubtedly would not have received national attention as "riots" had the nation not been sensitized by the more serious outbreaks.

In the 75 disorders studied by a Senate subcommittee, 83 deaths were reported. Eighty-two percent of the deaths and more than half the injuries occurred in Newark and Detroit. About 10 percent of the dead and 38 percent of the injured were public employees, primarily law officers and firemen. The overwhelming majority of the persons killed or injured in all the disorders were Negro civilians.

Initial damage estimates were greatly exaggerated. In Detroit, newspaper damage estimates at first ranged from $200 million to $500 million; the highest recent estimate is $45 million. In Newark, early estimates ranged from $15 to $25 million. A month later damage was estimated at $10.2 million, over 80 percent in inventory losses.

In the 24 disorders in 23 cities which we surveyed:

The final incident before the outbreak of disorder, and the initial violence itself, generally took place in the evening or at night at a place in which it was normal for many people to be on the streets.

Violence usually occurred almost immediately following the occurrence of the final precipitating incident, and then escalated rapidly. With but few exceptions, violence subsided during the day, and flared rapidly again at night. The night-day cycles continued through the early period of the major disorders.

Disorders generally began with rock and bottle throwing and window breaking. Once store windows were broken, looting usually followed.

Disorder did not erupt as a result of a single "triggering" or "precipitating" incident. Instead, it was generated out of an increasingly disturbed social atmosphere, in which typically a series of tension-heightening incidents over a period of weeks or months became linked in the minds of many in the Negro community with a reservoir of underlying grievances. At some point in the mounting tension, a further incident—in itself often routine or trivial—became the breaking point and the tension spilled over into violence.

"Prior" incidents, which increased tensions and ultimately led to violence, were police actions in almost half the cases; police actions were "final" incidents before the outbreak of violence in 12 of the 24 surveyed disorders.

No particular control tactic was successful in every situation. The varied effectiveness of control techniques emphasizes the need for advance training, planning, adequate intelligence systems, and knowledge of the ghetto community.

Negotiations between Negroes—including your militants as well as older Negro leaders—and white officials concerning "terms of peace" occurred during virtually all the disorders surveyed. In many cases, these negotiations involved discussion of underlying grievances as well as the handling of the disorder by control authorities.

The typical rioter was a teenager or young adult, a lifelong resident of the city in which he rioted, a high school dropout; he was, nevertheless, somewhat better educated than his nonrioting Negro neighbor, and was usually underemployed or employed in a menial job. He was proud of his race, extremely hostile to both whites and middle-class Negroes and, although informed about politics, highly distrustful of the political system.

A Detroit survey revealed that approximately 11 percent of the total residents of two riot areas admitted participation in the rioting, 20 to 25 percent identified themselves as "bystanders," over 16 percent identified themselves as "counter-rioters" who urged rioters to "cool it," and the remaining 48 to 53 percent said they were at home or elsewhere and did not participate. In a survey of Negro males between the ages of 15 and 35 residing in the disturbance area in Newark, about 45 percent identified themselves as rioters, and about 55 percent as "noninvolved."

Most rioters were young Negro males. Nearly 53 percent of arrestees were between 15 and 24 years of age; nearly 81 percent between 15 and 35.

In Detroit and Newark about 74 percent of the rioters were brought up in the North. In contrast, of the noninvolved, 36 percent in Detroit and 52 percent in Newark were brought up in the North.

What the rioters appeared to be seeking was fuller participation in the social order and the material benefits enjoyed by the majority of American citizens. Rather than rejecting the American system, they were anxious to obtain a place for themselves in it.

Numerous Negro counter-rioters walked the streets urging rioters to "cool it." The typical counter-rioter was better educated and had higher income than either the rioter or the noninvolved.

The proportion of Negroes in local government was substantially smaller than the Negro proportion of population. Only three of the 20 cities studied had more than one Negro legislator; none had ever had a Negro mayor or city manager. In only four cities did Negroes hold other important policy-making positions or serve as heads of municipal departments.

Although almost all cities had some sort of formal grievance mechanism for handling citizen complaints, this typically was regarded by Negroes as ineffective and was generally ignored.

Although specific grievances varied from city to city, at least 12 deeply held grievances can be identified and ranked into three levels of relative intensity:

First Level of Intensity
1. Police practices
2. Unemployment and underemployment
3. Inadequate housing

Second Level of Intensity
4. Inadequate education
5. Poor recreation facilities and programs
6. Ineffectiveness of the political structure and grievance mechanisms

Third Level of Intensity
7. Disrespectful white attitudes
8. Discriminatory administration of justice
9. Inadequacy of federal programs
10. Inadequacy of municipal services
11. Discriminatory consumer and credit practices
12. Inadequate welfare programs

The results of a three-city survey of various federal programs—manpower, education, housing, welfare and community action—indicate that, despite substantial expenditures, the number of persons assisted constituted only a fraction of those in need.

The background of disorder is often as complex and difficult to analyze as the disorder itself. But we find that certain general conclusions can be drawn:

Social and economic conditions in the riot cities constituted a clear pattern of severe disadvantage for Negroes compared with whites, whether the Negroes lived in the area where the riot took place or outside it. Negroes had completed fewer years of education and fewer had attended high school. Negroes were twice as likely to be unemployed and three times as likely to be in unskilled and service jobs. Negroes averaged 70 percent of the income earned by whites and were more than twice as likely to be living in poverty. Although housing cost Negroes relatively more, they had worse housing—three times as likely to be overcrowded and substandard. When compared to white suburbs, the relative disadvantage is even more pronounced.

A study of the aftermath of disorder leads to disturbing conclusions. We find that, despite the institution of some post-riot programs:

Little basic change in the conditions underlying the outbreak of disorder has taken place. Actions to ameliorate Negro grievances have been limited and sporadic; with but few exceptions, they have not significantly reduced tensions.

In several cities, the principal official response has been to train and equip the police with more sophisticated weapons.

In several cities, increasing polarization is evident, with continuing breakdown of inter-racial communication, and growth of white segregationist or black separatist groups.

Chapter 3—Organized activity

The President directed the Commission to investigate "to what extent, if any, there has been planning or organization in any of the riots."

To carry out this part of the President's charge, the Commission established a special investigative staff supplementing the field teams that made the general examination of the riots in 23 cities. The unit examined data collected by federal agencies and congressional committees, including thousands of documents supplied by the Federal Bureau of Investigation, gathered and evaluated information from local and state law enforcement agencies and officials, and conducted its own field investigation in selected cities.

On the basis of all the information collected, the Commission concludes that:

The urban disorders of the summer of 1967 were not caused by, nor were they the consequence of, any organized plan or "conspiracy."

Specifically, the Commission has found no evidence that all or any of the disorders or the incidents that led to them were planned or directed by any organization or group, international, national or local.

Militant organizations, local and national, and individual

agitators, who repeatedly forecast and called for violence, were active in the spring and summer of 1967. We believe that they sought to encourage violence, and that they helped to create an atmosphere that contributed to the outbreak of disorder.

We recognize that the continuation of disorders and the polarization of the races would provide fertile ground for organized exploitation in the future.

Investigations of organized activity are continuing at all levels of government, including committees of Congress. These investigations relate not only to the disorders of 1967 but also to the actions of groups and individuals, particularly in schools and colleges, during the last fall and winter. The Commission has cooperated in these investigations. They should continue.

PART II—WHY DID IT HAPPEN?

Chapter 4—The basic causes

In addressing the question "Why did it happen?" we shift our focus from the local to the national scene, from the particular events of the summer of 1967 to the factors within the society at large that created a mood of violence among many urban Negroes.

These factors are complex and interacting; they vary significantly in their effect from city to city and from year to year; and the consequences of one disorder, generating new grievances and new demands, become the causes of the next. Thus was created the "thicket of tension, conflicting evidence and extreme opinions" cited by the President.

Despite these complexities, certain fundamental matters are clear. Of these, the most fundamental is the racial attitude and behavior of white Americans toward black Americans.

Race prejudice has shaped our history decisively; it now threatens to affect our future.

White racism is essentially responsible for the explosive mixture which has been accumulating in our cities since the end of World War II. Among the ingredients of this mixture are:

Pervasive discrimination and segregation in employment, education and housing, which have resulted in the continuing exclusion of great numbers of Negroes from the benefits of economic progress.

Black in-migration and white exodus, which have produced the massive and growing concentrations of impoverished Negroes in our major cities, creating a growing crisis of deteriorating facilities and services and unmet human needs.

The black ghettoes where segregation and poverty converge on the young to destroy opportunity and enforce failure. Crime, drug addiction, dependency on welfare, and bitterness and resentment against society in general and white society in particular are the result.

At the same time, most whites and some Negroes outside the ghetto have prospered to a degree unparalleled in the history of civilization. Through television and other media, this affluence has been flaunted before the eyes of the Negro poor and the jobless ghetto youth.

Yet these facts alone cannot be said to have caused the disorders. Recently, other powerful ingredients have begun to catalyze the mixture:

Frustrated hopes are the residue of the unfulfilled expectations aroused by the great judicial and legislative victories of the Civil Rights Movement and the dramatic struggle for equal rights in the South.

A climate that tends toward approval and encouragement of violence as a form of protest has been created by white terrorism directed against nonviolent protest; by the open defiance of law and federal authority by state and local officials resisting desegregation; and by some protest groups engaging in civil disobedience who turn their backs on nonviolence, go beyond the constitutionally protected rights of petition and free assembly, and resort to violence to attempt to compel alteration of laws and policies with which they disagree.

The frustrations of powerlessness have led some Negroes to the conviction that there is no effective alternative to violence as a means of achieving redress of grievances, and of "moving the system." These frustrations are reflected in alienation and hostility toward the institutions of law and government and the white society which controls them, and in the reach toward racial consciousness and solidarity reflected in the slogan "Black Power."

A new mood has sprung up among Negroes, particularly among the young, in which self-esteem and enhanced racial pride are replacing apathy and submission to "the system."

The police are not merely a "spark" factor. To some Negroes police have come to symbolize white power, white racism, and white repression. And the fact is that many police do reflect and express these white attitudes. The atmosphere of hostility and cynicism is reinforced by a widespread belief among Negroes in the existence of police brutality and in a "double standard" of justice and protection—one for Negroes and one for whites.

*   *   *

To this point, we have attempted to identify the prime components of the "explosive mixture." In the chapters that follow we seek to analyze them in the perspective of history. Their meaning, however, is clear:

In the summer of 1967, we have seen in our cities a chain reaction of racial violence. If we are heedless, none of us shall escape the consequences.

Chapter 5—Rejection and protest: an historical sketch

The causes of recent racial disorders are embedded in a tangle of issues and circumstances—social, economic, political and psychological—which arise out of the historic pattern of Negro-white relations in America.

In this chapter we trace the pattern, identify the recurrent themes of Negro protest and, most importantly, provide a perspective on the protest activities of the present era.

We describe the Negro's experience in America and the development of slavery as an institution. We show his persistent striving for equality in the face of rigidly maintained social, economic and educational barriers, and repeated mob violence. We portray the ebb and flow of the doctrinal tides—accommodation, separatism, and self-help—and their relationship to the current theme of Black Power. We conclude:

The Black Power advocates of today consciously feel that they are the most militant group in the Negro protest movement. Yet they have retreated from a direct confrontation with American society on the issue of integration and, by preaching separatism, unconsciously function as an accommodation to white racism. Much of their economic program as well as their interest in Negro history, self-help, racial solidarity and separation, is reminiscent of Booker T. Washington. The rhetoric is different, but the ideas are remarkably similar.

Chapter 6—The formation of the racial ghettos[1]

Throughout the 20th century the Negro population of the United States has been moving steadily from rural areas to urban and

1. The term "ghetto" as used in this report refers to an area within a city characterized by poverty and acute social disorganization, and inhabited by members of a racial or ethnic group under conditions of involuntary segregation.

from South to North and West. In 1910, 91 percent of the nation's 9.8 million Negroes lived in the South and only 27 percent of American Negroes lived in cities of 2,500 persons or more. Between 1910 and 1966 the total Negro population more than doubled, reaching 21.5 million, and the number living in metropolitan areas rose more than five-fold (from 2.6 million to 14.8 million). The number outside the South rose eleven-fold (from 880,000 to 9.7 million).

Negro migration from the South has resulted from the expectation of thousands of new and highly paid jobs for unskilled workers in the North and the shift to mechanized farming in the South. However, the Negro migration is small when compared to earlier waves of European immigrants. Even between 1960 and 1966, there were 1.8 million immigrants from abroad compared to the 613,000 Negroes who arrived in the North and West from the South.

As a result of the growing number of Negroes in urban areas, natural increase has replaced migration as the primary source of Negro population increase in the cities. Nevertheless, Negro migration from the South will continue unless economic conditions there change dramatically.

Basic data concerning Negro urbanization trends indicate that:

Almost all Negro population growth (98 percent from 1950 to 1966) is occurring within metropolitan areas, primarily within central cities.[2]

The vast majority of white population growth (78 percent from 1960 to 1966) is occurring in suburban portions of metropolitan areas. Since 1960, white central-city population has declined by 1.3 million.

As a result, central cities are becoming more heavily Negro while the suburban fringes around them remain almost entirely white.

The twelve largest central cities now contain over two-thirds of the Negro population outside the South, and one-third of the Negro total in the United States.

Within the cities, Negroes have been excluded from white residential areas through discriminatory practices. Just as significant is the withdrawal of white families from, or their refusal to enter, neighborhoods where Negroes are moving or already residing. About 20 percent of the urban population of the United States changes residence every year. The refusal of whites to move into

2. A "central city" is the largest city of a standard metropolitan statistical area, that is, a metropolitan area containing at least one city of 50,000 or more inhabitants.

"changing areas" when vacancies occur means that most vacancies eventually are occupied by Negroes.

The result, according to a recent study, is that in 1960 the average segregation index for 207 of the largest United States cities was 86.2. In other words, to create an unsegregated population distribution, an average of over 86 percent of all Negroes would have to change their place of residence within the city.

Chapter 7—Unemployment, family structure, and social disorganization

Although there have been gains in Negro income nationally, and a decline in the number of Negroes below the "poverty level," the condition of Negroes in the central city remains in a state of crisis. Between 2 and 2.5 million Negroes—16 to 20 percent of the total Negro population of all central cities—live in squalor and deprivation in ghetto neighborhoods.

Employment is a key problem. It not only controls the present for the Negro American but, in a most profound way, it is creating the future as well. Yet, despite continuing economic growth and declining national unemployment rates, the unemployment rate for Negroes in 1967 was more than double that for whites.

Equally important is the undesirable nature of many jobs open to Negroes and other minorities. Negro men are more than three times more likely as white men to be in low-paying, unskilled or service jobs. This concentration of male Negro employment at the lowest end of the occupational scale is the single most important cause of poverty among Negroes.

In one study of low-income neighborhoods, the "subemployment rate," including both unemployment and underemployment, was about 33 percent, or 8.8 times greater than the overall unemployment rate for all United States workers.

Employment problems, aggravated by the constant arrival of new unemployed migrants, many of them from depressed rural areas, create persistent poverty in the ghetto. In 1966, about 11.9 percent of the nation's whites and 40.6 percent of its nonwhites were below the "poverty level" defined by the Social Security Administration (currently $3,335 per year for an urban family of four). Over 40 percent of the nonwhites below the poverty level live in the central cities.

Employment problems have drastic social impact in the ghetto. Men who are chronically unemployed or employed in the lowest status jobs are often unable or unwilling to remain with their families. The handicap imposed on children growing up without fathers in an atmosphere of poverty and deprivation is increased as mothers are forced to work to provide support.

The culture of poverty that results from unemployment and family breakup, generates a system of ruthless, exploitative relationships within the ghetto. Prostitution, dope addiction, and crime create an environmental "jungle" characterized by personal insecurity and tension. Children growing up under such conditions are likely participants in civil disorder.

Chapter 8—Conditions of life in the racial ghetto

A striking difference in environment from that of white, middle-class Americans profoundly influences the lives of residents of the ghetto.

Crime rates, consistently higher than in other areas, create a pronounced sense of insecurity. For example, in one city one low-income Negro district had 35 times as many serious crimes against persons as a high-income white district. Unless drastic steps are taken, the crime problems in poverty areas are likely to continue to multiply as the growing youth and rapid urbanization of the population outstrip police resources.

Poor health and sanitation conditions in the ghetto result in higher mortality rates, a higher incidence of major diseases, and lower availability and utilization of medical services. The infant mortality rate for nonwhite babies under the age of one month is 58 per cent higher than for whites; for one to 12 months it is almost three times as high. The level of sanitation in the ghetto is far below that in high income areas. Garbage collection is often inadequate. Of an estimated 14,000 cases of rat bite in the United States in 1965, most were in ghetto neighborhoods.

Ghetto residents believe they are "exploited" by local merchants; and evidence substantiates some of these beliefs. A study conducted in one city by the Federal Trade Commission showed that distinctly higher prices were charged for goods sold in ghetto stores than in other areas.

Lack of knowledge regarding credit purchasing creates special pitfalls for the disadvantaged. In many states garnishment practices compound these difficulties by allowing creditors to deprive individuals of their wages without hearing or trial.

Chapter 9—Comparing the immigrant and Negro experience

In this chapter, we address ourselves to a fundamental question that many white Americans are asking: why have so many Negroes, unlike the European immigrants, been unable to escape from the ghetto and from poverty. We believe the following factors play a part:

The Maturing Economy : When the European immigrants arrived, they gained an economic foothold by providing the unskilled labor needed by industry. Unlike the immigrant, the Negro migrant found little opportunity in the city. The economy, by then matured, had little use for the unskilled labor he had to offer.

The Disability of Race : The structure of discrimination has stringently narrowed opportunities for the Negro and restricted his prospects. European immigrants suffered from discrimination, but never so pervasively.

Entry into the Political System : The immigrants usually settled in rapidly growing cities with powerful and expanding political machines, which traded economic advantages for political support. Ward-level grievance machinery, as well as personal representation, enabled the immigrant to make his voice heard and his power felt.

By the time the Negro arrived, these political machines were no longer so powerful or so well equipped to provide jobs or other favors, and in many cases were unwilling to share their influence with Negroes.

Cultural Factors : Coming from societies with a low standard of living and at a time when job aspirations were low, the immigrants sensed little deprivation in being forced to take the less desirable and poorer-paying jobs. Their large and cohesive families contributed to total income. Their vision of the future—one that led to a life outside of the ghetto—provided the incentive necessary to endure the present.

Although Negro men worked as hard as the immigrants, they were unable to support their families. The entrepreneurial opportunities had vanished. As a result of slavery and long periods of unemployment, the Negro family structure had become matriarchal; the males played a secondary and marginal family role —one which offered little compensation for their hard and unrewarding labor. Above all, segregations denied Negroes access to good jobs and the opportunity to leave the ghetto. For them, the future seemed to lead only to a dead end.

Today, whites tend to exaggerate how well and quickly they escaped from poverty. The fact is that immigrants who came from rural backgrounds, as many Negroes do, are only now, after three generations, finally beginning to move into the middle class.

By contrast, Negroes began concentrating in the city less than two generations ago, and under much less favorable conditions. Although some Negroes have escaped poverty, few have been able to escape the urban ghetto.

PART III—WHAT CAN BE DONE?

Chapter 10—The community response

Our investigation of the 1967 riot cities establishes that virtually every major episode of violence was foreshadowed by an accumulation of unresolved grievances and by widespread dissatisfaction among Negroes with the unwillingness or inability of local government to respond.

Overcoming these conditions is essential for community support of law enforcement and civil order. City governments need new and more vital channels of communication to the residents of the ghetto; they need to improve their capacity to respond effectively to community needs before they become community grievances; and they need to provide opportunity for meaningful involvement of ghetto residents in shaping policies and programs which affect the community.

The Commission recommends that local governments:

Develop Neighborhood Action Task Forces as joint community-government efforts through which more effective communication can be achieved, and the delivery of city services to ghetto residents improved.

Establish comprehensive grievance-response mechanisms in order to bring all public agencies under public scrutiny.

Bring the institutions of local government closer to the people they serve by establishing neighborhood outlets for local, state and federal administrative and public service agencies.

Expand opportunities for ghetto residents to participate in the formulation of public policy and the implementation of programs affecting them through improved political representation, creation of institutional channels for community action, expansion of legal services, and legislative hearings on ghetto problems.

In this effort, city governments will require state and federal support.

The Commission recommends:

State and federal financial assistance for mayors and city councils to support the research, consultants, staff and other resources needed to respond effectively to federal program initiatives.

State cooperation in providing municipalities with the jurisdictional tools needed to deal with their problems; a fuller measure of financial aid to urban areas; and the focusing of the interests of suburban communities on the physical, social and cultural environment of the central city.

Chapter 11—Police and the community

The abrasive relationship between the police and the minority communities has been a major—and explosive—source of grievance, tension and disorder. The blame must be shared by the total society.

The police are faced with demands for increased protection and service in the ghetto. Yet the aggressive patrol practices thought necessary to meet these demands themselves create tension and hostility. The resulting grievances have been further aggravated by the lack of effective mechanisms for handling complaints against the police. Special programs for bettering police-community relations have been instituted, but these alone are not enough. Police administrators, with the guidance of public officials, and the support of the entire community, must take vigorous action to improve law enforcement and to decrease the potential for disorder.

The Commission recommends that city government and police authorities:

Review police operations in the ghetto to ensure proper conduct by police officers, and eliminate abrasive practices.

Provide more adequate police protection to ghetto residents to eliminate their high sense of insecurity, and the belief of many Negro citizens in the existence of a dual standard of law enforcement.

Establish fair and effective mechanisms for the redress of grievances against the police, and other municipal employees.

Develop and adopt policy guidelines to assist officers in making critical decisions in areas where police conduct can create tension.

Develop and use innovative programs to ensure widespread community support for law enforcement.

Recruit more Negroes into the regular police force, and review promotion policies to ensure fair promotion for Negro officers.

Establish a "Community Service Officer" program to attract ghetto youths between the ages of 17 and 21 to police work. These junior officers would perform duties in ghetto neighborhoods, but would not have full police authority. The federal government should provide support equal to 90 percent of the costs of employing CSOs on the basis of one for every ten regular officers.

Chapter 12—Control of disorder

Preserving civil peace is the first responsibility of government. Unless the rule of law prevails, our society will lack not only order but also the environment essential to social and economic progress.

The maintenance of civil order cannot be left to the police alone. The police need guidance, as well as support, from mayors and other public officials. It is the responsibility of public officials to determine proper police policies, support adequate police standards for personnel and performance, and participate in planning for the control of disorders.

To maintain control of incidents which could lead to disorders, the Commission recommends that local officials:

Assign seasoned, well-trained policemen and supervisory officers to patrol ghetto areas, and to respond to disturbances.

Develop plans which will quickly muster maximum police manpower and highly qualified senior commanders at the outbreak of disorders.

Provide special training in the prevention of disorders, and prepare police for riot control and for operation in units, with adequate command and control and field communication for proper discipline and effectiveness.

Develop guidelines governing the use of control equipment and provide alternatives to the use of lethal weapons. Federal support for research in this area is needed.

Establish an intelligence system to provide police and other public officials with reliable information that may help to prevent the outbreak of a disorder and to institute effective control measures in the event a riot erupts.

Develop continuing contacts with ghetto residents to make use of the forces for order which exist within the community.

Establish machinery for neutralizing rumors, and enabling Negro leaders and residents to obtain the facts. Create special rumor details to collect, evaluate, and dispel rumors that may lead to a civil disorder.

The Commission believes there is a grave danger that some communities may resort to the indiscriminate and excessive use of force. The harmful effects of overreaction are incalculable.

The Commission condemns moves to equip police departments with mass destruction weapons, such as automatic rifles, machine guns and tanks. Weapons which are designed to destroy, not to control, have no place in densely populated urban communities.

The Commission recognizes the sound principle of local authority and responsibility in law enforcement, but recommends that the federal government share in the financing of programs for improvement of police forces, both in their normal law enforcement activities as well as in their response to civil disorders.

To assist government authorities in planning their response to civil disorder, this report contains a Supplement on Control of Disorder. It deals with specific problems encountered during riot-control operations, and includes:

> Assessment of the present capabilities of police, National Guard and Army forces to control major riots, and recommendations for improvement;

> Recommended means by which the control operations of those forces may be coordinated with the response of other agencies, such as fire departments, and with the community at large;

> Recommendations for review and revision of federal, state and local laws needed to provide the framework for control efforts and for the call-up and interrelated action of public safety forces.

Chapter 13—The administration of justice under emergency conditions

In many of the cities which experienced disorders last summer, there were recurring breakdowns in the mechanisms for processing, prosecuting and protecting arrested persons. These resulted mainly from long-standing structural deficiencies in criminal court systems, and from the failure of communities to anticipate and plan for the emergency demands of civil disorders.

In part, because of this, there were few successful prosecutions for serious crimes committed during the riots. In those cities where mass arrests occurred many arrestees were deprived of basic legal rights.

The Commission recommends that the cities and states:

> Undertake reforms of the lower courts so as to improve the quality of justice rendered under normal conditions.

> Plan comprehensive measures by which the criminal justice system may be supplemented during civil disorders so that its deliberative functions are protected, and the quality of justice is maintained.

Such emergency plans require broad community participation and dedicated leadership by the bench and bar. They should include:

Laws sufficient to deter and punish riot control.

Additional judges, bail and probation officers, and clerical staff.

Arrangements for volunteer lawyers to help prosecutors and to represent riot defendants at every stage of proceedings.

Policies to ensure proper and individual bail, arraignment, pre-trial, trial and sentencing proceedings.

Procedures for processing arrested persons, such as summons and release, and release on personal recognizances, which permit separation of minor offenders from those dangerous to the community, in order that serious offenders may be detained and prosecuted effectively.

Adequate emergency processing and detention facilities.

Chapter 14—Damages: repair and compensation

The Commission recommends that the federal government:

Amend the Federal Disaster Act—which now applies only to natural disasters—to permit federal emergency food and medical assistance to cities during major civil disorders, and provide long-term economic assistance afterwards.

With the cooperation of the states, create incentives for the private insurance industry to provide more adequate property-insurance coverage in inner-city areas.

The Commission endorses the report of the National Advisory Panel on Insurance in Riot-Affected Areas: "Meeting the Insurance Crisis of our Cities."

Chapter 15—The news media and the riots

In his charge to the Commission, the President asked: "What effect do the mass media have on the riots?"

The Commission determined that the answer to the President's question did not lie solely in the performance of the press and broadcasters in reporting the riots. Our analysis had to consider also the overall treatment by the media of the Negro ghettos, community relations, racial attitudes, and poverty—day by day and month by month, year in and year out.

A wide range of interviews with government officials, law enforcement authorities, media personnel and other citizens, including ghetto residents, as well as a quantitative analysis of riot coverage and a special conference with industry representatives, leads us to conclude that:

Despite instances of sensationalism, inaccuracy and distortion, newspapers, radio and television tried on the whole to give a balanced, factual account of the 1967 disorders.

Elements of the news media failed to portray accurately the scale and character of the violence that occurred last summer. The overall effect was, we believe, an exaggeration of both mood and event.

Important segments of the media failed to report adequately on the causes and consequences of civil disorders and on the underlying problems of race relations. They have not communicated to the majority of their audience—which is white—a sense of the degradation, misery and hopelessness of life in the ghetto.

These failings must be corrected, and the improvement must come from within the industry. Freedom of the press is not the issue. Any effort to impose governmental restrictions would be inconsistent with fundamental constitutional precepts.

We have seen evidence that the news media are becoming aware of and concerned about their performance in this field. As that concern grows, coverage will improve. But much more must be done, and it must be done soon.

The Commission recommends that the media:

Expand coverage of the Negro community and of race problems through permanent assignment of reporters familiar with urban and racial affairs, and through establishment of more and better links with the Negro community.

Integrate Negroes and Negro activities into all aspects of coverage and content, including newspaper articles and television programming. The news media must publish newspapers and produce programs that recognize the existence and activities of Negroes as a group within the community and as a part of the larger community.

Recruit more Negroes into journalism and broadcasting and promote those who are qualified to positions of significant responsibility. Recruitment should begin in high schools and continue through college; where necessary, aid for training should be provided.

Improve coordination with police in reporting riot news through advance planning, and cooperate with the police in the designation of police information officers, establishment of information centers, and development of mutually acceptable guidelines for riot reporting and the conduct of media personnel.

Accelerate efforts to ensure accurate and responsible reporting of riot and racial news, through adoption by all news gathering organizations of stringent internal staff guidelines.

Cooperate in the establishment of a privately organized and funded Institute of Urban Communications to train and educate journalists in urban affairs, recruit and train more Negro journalists, develop methods for improving police-press relations, review coverage of riots and racial issues, and support continuing research in the urban field.

Chapter 16—The future of the cities

In 1985, the Negro population in central cities is expected to increase by 72 percent to approximately 20.8 million. Coupled with the continued exodus of white families to the suburbs, this growth will produce majority Negro populations in many of the nation's largest cities.

The future of these cities, and of their burgeoning Negro populations, is grim. Most new employment opportunities are being created in suburbs and outlying areas. This trend will continue unless important changes in public policy are made.

In prospect, therefore, is further deterioration of already inadequate municipal tax bases in the face of increasing demands for public services, and continuing unemployment and poverty among the urban Negro population.

Three choices are open to the nation:

We can maintain present policies, continuing both the proportion of the nation's resources now allocated to programs for the unemployed and the disadvantaged, and the inadequate and failing effort to achieve an integrated society.

We can adopt a policy of "enrichment" aimed at improving dramatically the quality of ghetto life while abandoning integration as a goal.

We can pursue integration by combining ghetto "enrichment" with policies which will encourage Negro movement out of central city areas.

The first choice, continuance of present policies, has ominous consequences for our society. The share of the nation's resources now allocated to programs for the disadvantaged is insufficient to arrest the deterioration of life in central city ghettos. Under such conditions, a rising proportion of Negroes may come to see in the deprivation and segregation they experience, a justification for violent protest, or for extending support to now isolated extremists who advocate civil disruption. Large-scale and continuing violence could result, followed by white retaliation, and, ultimately, the separation of the two communities in a garrison state.

Even if violence does not occur, the consequences are unacceptable. Development of a racially integrated society, extraordinarily difficult today, will be virtually impossible when the present black ghetto population of 12.5 million has grown to almost 21 million.

To continue present policies is to make permanent the division of our country into two societies; one, largely Negro and poor, located in the central cities; the other, predominantly white and affluent, located in the suburbs and in outlying areas.

The second choice, ghetto enrichment coupled with abandonment of integration, is also unacceptable. It is another way of choosing a permanently divided country. Moreover, equality cannot be achieved under conditions of nearly complete separation. In a country where the economy, and particularly the resources of employment, are predominantly white, a policy of separation can only relegate Negroes to a permanently inferior economic status.

We believe that the only possible choice for America is the third —a policy which combines ghetto enrichment with programs designed to encourage integration of substantial numbers of Negroes into the society outside the ghetto.

Enrichment must be an important adjunct to integration, for no matter how ambitious or energetic the program, few Negroes now living in central cities can be quickly integrated. In the meantime, large-scale improvement in the quality of ghetto life is essential.

But this can be no more than an interim strategy. Programs must be developed which will permit substantial Negro movement out of the ghettos. The primary goal must be a single society, in which every citizen will be free to live and work according to his capabilities and desires, not his color.

Chapter 17—Recommendations for national action
Introduction

No American—white or black—can escape the consequences of the continuing social and economic decay of our major cities.

Only a commitment to national action on an unprecedented scale can shape a future compatible with the historic ideals of American society.

The great productivity of our economy, and a federal revenue system which is highly responsive to economic growth, can provide the resources.

The major need is to generate new will—the will to tax ourselves to the extent necessary to meet the vital needs of the nation.

We have set forth goals and proposed strategies to reach those goals. We discuss and recommend programs not to commit each of us to specific parts of such programs but to illustrate the type and dimension of action needed.

The major goal is the creation of a true union—a single society and a single American identity. Toward that goal, we propose the following objectives for national action:

Opening up opportunities to those who are restricted by racial segregation and discrimination, and eliminating all barriers to their choice of jobs, education and housing.

Removing the frustration of powerlessness among the disadvantaged by providing the means for them to deal with the problems that affect their own lives and by increasing the capacity of our public and private institutions to respond to these problems.

Increasing communication across racial lines to destroy stereotypes, to halt polarization, and distrust and hostility, and create common ground for efforts toward public order and social justice.

We propose these aims to fulfill our pledge of equality and to meet the fundamental needs of a democratic and civilized society—domestic peace and social justice.

Employment

Pervasive unemployment and underemployment are the most persistent and serious grievances in minority areas. They are inextricably linked to the problem of civil disorder.

Despite growing federal expenditures for manpower development and training programs, and sustained general economic prosperity and increasing demands for skilled workers, about two million—white and nonwhite—are permanently unemployed. About ten million are underemployed, of whom 6.5 million work full time for wages below the poverty line.

The 500,000 "hard-core" unemployed in the central cities who lack a basic education and are unable to hold a steady job are made up in large part of Negro males between the ages of 18 and 25. In the riot cities which we surveyed, Negroes were three times as likely as whites to hold unskilled jobs, which are often part time, seasonal, low-paying and "dead end."

Negro males between the ages of 15 and 25 predominated among the rioters. More than 20 percent of the rioters were unemployed, and many who were employed held intermittent, low status, unskilled jobs which they regarded as below their education and ability.

The Commission recommends that the federal government:

Undertake joint efforts with cities and states to consolidate existing manpower programs to avoid fragmentation and duplication.

Take immediate action to create 2,000,000 new jobs over the next three years—one million in the public sector and one million in the private sector—to absorb the hard-core unemployed and materially reduce the level of underemployment for all workers, black and white. We propose 250,000 public sector and 300,000 private sector jobs in the first year.

Provide on-the-job training by both public and private employers with reimbursement to private employers for the extra costs of training the hard-core unemployed, by contract or by tax credits.

Provide tax and other incentives to investment in rural as well as urban poverty areas in order to offer to the rural poor an alternative to migration to urban centers.

Take new and vigorous action to remove artificial barriers to employment and promotion, including not only racial discrimination but, in certain cases, arrest records or lack of a high school diploma. Strengthen those agencies such as the Equal Employment Opportunity Commission, charged with eliminating discriminatory practices, and provide full support for Title VI of the 1964 Civil Rights Act allowing federal grant-in-aid funds to be withheld from activities which discriminate on grounds of color or race.

The Commission commends the recent public commitment of the National Council of the Building and Construction Trades Unions, AFL-CIO, to encourage and recruit Negro membership in apprenticeship programs. This commitment should be intensified and implemented.

Education

Education in a democratic society must equip children to develop their potential and to participate fully in American life. For the community at large, the schools have discharged this responsibility well. But for many minorities, and particularly for the children of the ghetto, the schools have failed to provide the educational experience which could overcome the effects of discrimination and deprivation.

This failure is one of the persistent sources of grievance and resentment within the Negro community. The hostility of Negro parents and students toward the school system is generating increasing conflict and causing disruption within many city school districts. But the most dramatic evidence of the relationship between educational practices and civil disorders lies in the high incidence of riot participation by ghetto youth who have not completed high school.

The bleak record of public education for ghetto children is growing worse. In the critical skills—verbal and reading ability—Negro students are falling further behind whites with each year of school completed. The high unemployment and underemployment rate for Negro youth is evidence, in part, of the growing educational crisis.

We support integration as the priority education strategy; it is essential to the future of American society. In this last summer's disorders we have seen the consequences of racial isolation at all levels, and of attitudes toward race, on both sides, produced by three centuries of myth, ignorance and bias. It is indispensable that opportunities for interaction between the races be expanded.

We recognize that the growing dominance of pupils from disadvantaged minorities in city school populations will not soon be reversed. No matter how great the effort toward desegregation, many children of the ghetto will not, within their school careers, attend integrated schools.

If existing disadvantages are not to be perpetuated, we must drastically improve the quality of ghetto education. Equality of results with all-white schools must be the goal.

To implement these strategies, the Commission recommends:

Sharply increased efforts to eliminate de facto segregation in our schools through substantial federal aid to school systems seeking to desegregate either within the system or in cooperation with neighboring school systems.

Elimination of racial discrimination in Northern as well as Southern schools by vigorous application of Title VI of the Civil Rights Act of 1964.

Extension of quality early childhood education to every disadvantaged child in the country.

Efforts to improve dramatically schools serving disadvantaged children through substantial federal funding of year-round compensatory education programs, improved teaching, and expanded experimentation and research.

Elimination of illiteracy through greater federal support for adult basic education.

Enlarged opportunities for parent and community participation in the public schools.

Reoriented vocational education emphasizing work-experience training and the involvement of business and industry.

Expanded opportunities for higher education through increased federal assistance to disadvantaged students.

Revision of state aid formulas to assure more per student aid to districts having a high proportion of disadvantaged school-age children.

The welfare system

Our present system of public welfare is designed to save money instead of people, and tragically ends up doing neither. This system has two critical deficiencies:

First, it excludes large numbers of persons who are in great need, and who, if provided a decent level of support, might be able to become more productive and self-sufficient. No federal funds are available for millions of men and women who are needy but neither aged, handicapped nor the parents of minor children.

Second, for those included, the system provides assistance well below the minimum necessary for a decent level of existence, and imposes restrictions that encourage continued dependency on welfare and undermine self-respect.

A welter of statutory requirements and administrative practices and regulations operate to remind recipients that they are considered untrustworthy, promiscuous and lazy. Residence requirements prevent assistance to people in need who are newly arrived in the state. Regular searches of recipients' homes violate privacy. Inadequate social services compound the problems.

The Commission recommends that the federal government, acting with state and local governments where necessary, reform the existing welfare system to:

Establish uniform national standards of assistance at least as high as the annual "poverty level" of income, now set by the Social Security Administration at $3,335 per year for an urban family of four.

Require that all states receiving federal welfare contributions participate in the Aid to Families with Dependent Children—Unemployed Parents program (AFDC-UP) that permits assistance to families with both father and mother in the home, thus aiding the family while it is still intact.

Bear a substantially greater portion of all welfare costs—at least 90 percent of total payments.

Increase incentives for seeking employment and job training, but remove restrictions recently enacted by the Congress that would compel mothers of young children to work.

Provide more adequate social services through neighborhood centers and family-planning programs.

Remove the freeze placed by the 1967 welfare amendments on the percentage of children in a state that can be covered by federal assistance.

Eliminate residence requirements.

As a long-range goal, the Commission recommends that the federal government seek to develop a national system of income supplementation based strictly on need with two broad and basic purposes:

To provide, for those who can work or who do work, any necessary supplements in such a way as to develop incentives for fuller employment;

To provide, for those who cannot work and for mothers who decide to remain with their children, a minimum standard of decent living, and to aid in the saving of children from the prison of poverty that has held their parents.

A broad system of supplementation would involve substantially greater federal expenditures than anything now contemplated. The cost will range widely depending on the standard of need accepted as the "basic allowance" to individuals and families, and on the rate at which additional income above this level is taxed. Yet if the deepening cycle of poverty and dependence on welfare can be broken, if the children of the poor can be given the opportunity to scale the wall that now separates them from the rest of society, the return on this investment will be great indeed.

Housing

After more than three decades of fragmented and grossly under-funded federal housing programs, nearly six million substandard housing units remain occupied in the United States.

The housing problem is particularly acute in the minority ghettos. Nearly two-thirds of all non-white families living in the central cities today live in neighborhoods marked with substandard housing and general urban blight. Two major factors are responsible.

First: Many ghetto residents simply cannot pay the rent necessary to support decent housing. In Detroit, for example, over 40 percent of the non-white occupied units in 1960 required rent of over 35 percent of the tenants' income.

Second: Discrimination prevents access to many non-slum areas, particularly the suburbs, where good housing exists. In addition, by creating a "back pressure" in the racial ghettos, it makes it possible for landlords to break up apartments for denser occupancy, and keeps prices and rents of deteriorated ghetto housing higher than they would be in a truly free market.

To date, federal programs have been able to do comparatively little to provide housing for the disadvantaged. In the 31-year history of subsidized federal housing, only about 800,000 units have been constructed, with recent production averaging about 50,000 units a year. By comparison, over a period only three years longer, FHA insurance guarantees have made possible the construction of over ten million middle- and upper-income units.

Two points are fundamental to the Commission's recommendations:

First: Federal housing programs must be given a new thrust aimed at overcoming the prevailing patterns of racial segregation. If this is not done, those programs will continue to concentrate the most impoverished and dependent segments of the population into the central-city ghettos where there is already a critical gap between the needs of the population and the public resources to deal with them.

Second: The private sector must be brought into the production and financing of low and moderate rental housing to supply the capabilities and capital necessary to meet the housing needs of the nation.

The Commission recommends that the federal government:

Enact a comprehensive and enforceable federal open housing law to cover the sale or rental of all housing, including single family homes.

Reorient federal housing programs to place more low and moderate income housing outside of ghetto areas.

Bring within the reach of low and moderate income families within the next five years six million new and existing units of decent housing, beginning with 600,000 units in the next year.

To reach this goal we recommend:

Expansion and modification of the rent supplement program to permit use of supplements for existing housing, thus greatly increasing the reach of the program.

Expansion and modification of the below-market interest rate program to enlarge the interest subsidy to all sponsors and provide interest-free loans to nonprofit sponsors to cover pre-construction costs, and permit sale of projects to nonprofit corporations, cooperatives, or condominiums.

Creation of an ownership supplement program similar to present rent supplements, to make home ownership possible for low-income families.

Federal writedown of interest rates on loans to private builders constructing moderate-rent housing.

Expansion of the public housing program, with emphasis on small units on scattered sites, and leasing and "turnkey" programs.

Expansion of the Model Cities program.

Expansion and reorientation of the urban renewal program to give priority to projects directly assisting low-income households to obtain adequate housing.

Conclusion

One of the first witnesses to be invited to appear before this Commission was Dr. Kenneth B. Clark, a distinguished and perceptive scholar. Referring to the reports of earlier riot commissions, he said:

I read that report . . . of the 1919 riot in Chicago, and it is as if I were reading the report of the investigating committee on the Harlem riot of '35, the report of the investigating committee on the Harlem riot of '43, the report of the McCone Commission on the Watts riot.

I must again in candor say to you members of this Commission—it is a kind of Alice in Wonderland—with the same moving picture re-shown over and over again, the same analysis, the same recommendations, and the same inaction.

These words come to our minds as we conclude this report.

We have provided an honest beginning. We have learned much. But we have uncovered no startling truths, no unique insights, no simple solutions. The destruction and the bitterness of racial disorder, the harsh polemics of black revolt and white repression have been seen and heard before in this country.

It is time now to end the destruction and the violence, not only in the streets of the ghetto but in the lives of people.

PART II

Functional issues of our times

7. Poverty in Cities
Daniel P. Moynihan

8. Housing Conditions in Urban Poverty Areas
National Commission on Urban Problems

DANIEL P. MOYNIHAN

Poverty in cities*

Dr. J. H. Plumb of Christ's College, Cambridge, who is the most recent and with luck will be the most successful of those bold-hearted scholars who have undertaken to assemble a comprehensive record of man's experience, began his series with a proposition that will serve equally well to open a discussion of poverty in American cities. The theme of *The History of Human Society*, Plumb writes, is thus: "that the condition of man now is superior to what it was."[1]

Not to see that this is so with respect to the problem of poverty in the central cities is to risk a serious misinterpretation of the present concern over the issue. Things have not been getting worse. There are few groups in American cities who are not in fact considerably better off than they have been. In an entirely familiar pattern, however, the response to this situation has not been one of rising content, but, for many individuals and groups, rising *dis*-content. Many who suffered the worst deprivation in the past have begun to wonder why they need be deprived at all; many

* Reprinted by permission of the publisher from James Q. Wilson, editor, THE METROPOLITAN ENIGMA, Cambridge, Mass.: Harvard University Press, Copyright 1968, by the President and Fellows of Harvard College; 1967 by Chamber of Commerce of the United States of America.

1. J. H. Plumb, introduction to C. R. Boxer, *The Dutch Seaborn Empire: 1600–1800* (New York: Alfred A. Knopf, 1965), p. xvi.

who have now attained a quite considerable standard of living find that this has only brought new sets of problems, further compounded by puzzlement as to what the others are causing such disturbances about. Hence a pattern of demand and resistance seems to be rising within American cities that threatens instability of a potentially serious and damaging variety. The fact is that for the first time since the late nineteenth century American cities are experiencing mass violence, brought on as an expression of discontent and fury by the poorest of the working classes. The fact that these masses are Negro seems somehow to have lessened the impact of the rioting: the events seem somehow more "natural," more an understandable response to a racially prejudiced society than evidence of any deep social imbalance. One wonders, for example, what might be the response within the business community, if, instead of reporting Negro disturbances, the press were to inform the nation that the "workers" or the "proletariat" of Los Angeles had set fire to their quarter and had been suppressed only by the summoning of military force. Yet it is necessary to insist that these events take place in the context of steadily rising living standards and steadily improving public services.

It has always been the case that cities have been places of great extremes of wealth and poverty: some societies have rejoiced in the display and magnificence, others have been repelled by the degradation and inequality. American society has been ambivalent. Committed to the amassing of personal wealth (and endlessly adept at doing so), it has also had a persisting commitment to the ideal of social equality and a concern at the appearance of gross disparities between social classes—a concern commonly taken to the point of not wishing even to admit the fact of social stratification. Until very recently any discussion of the subject would be forced to depend heavily on impressions and measures made with fairly rudimentary instruments of uncertain coverage. However, income statistics have by now achieved a quality such that changes over time can be judged with increasing confidence. Moreover, since the enactment of the Economic Opportunity Act of 1964 a growing number of special surveys and studies have provided more new information on the subject than has ever before been available. We do not and likely never shall have as much or as good information as could be put to use, but the time has arrived when it is possible to state a number of general findings.

1. *Poverty in the United States is now largely an urban phenomenon.* This is a sharp break from the past, when the greatest proportion of poverty would invariably have been found in the countryside.

As of 1965, however, only 6 percent of all poor households were located on farms. There is still a large amount of small-town poverty in the nation. Of some 32.5 million poor persons, 12.5 were living outside the 227 Standard Metropolitan Statistical Areas. But 17.2 million live within the SMSA's (where 66 percent of the population resides), including 10.6 million in the central cities of the metropolitan areas.

It must be kept in mind that the poverty population is neither static nor fixed. In a given year a fairly considerable number of persons appears to move in and out of poverty, part of a larger "at risk" population whose incomes rise and fall with changing employment conditions, personal circumstances such as health, family status, and so forth. To the extent that it is likely that this group would be proportionately larger in the more volatile urban setting, the relative preponderance of urban poverty becomes even greater.

2. *Urban poverty is concentrated among Negroes and other ethnic minorities.* Almost 13 million nonwhites live in central cities. About one third of this group lives below the poverty levels specified by the Social Security Administration, which are currently an income of $3,200 a year for a family of four, with adjustments for size up to a cutoff point of seven persons. This incidence of poverty is three times that of the white population living in central cities, and would be even higher if the Oriental population were excluded from the nonwhite totals. Negroes do not make up a majority of poor persons living in central cities. There are roughly 4.6 million nonwhites as against 5.9 million whites. But if the poor Puerto Ricans and Mexican Americans, classified by the Census as white, were added to the Negroes, it is almost certain that the combined total would make up a majority of the central city poor. (A further point is that among the aged poor, whites greatly outnumber Negroes. For example, of the 1,061,000 elderly individuals living in central cities, that is to say persons not living in families, 909,000 are white and only 152,000 are Negro. Thus it may be said that Negroes and other minorities make up a large proportion of those growing up poor, or living in poverty during their most productive years.)

3. *Urban poverty is closely associated with large families and broken families.* Large families and to some degree broken families are commonly found among poor people. At the present time Negro Americans are the most conspicuous such group, but by no means the only group and in any event are merely the most recent in a long sequence of peasant migrants who have kept the slums of

American cities in teeming disarray. (In addition to which, of course, there is a large and prospering Negro middle class, now frequently to be encountered in suburban areas.) The average size of the poor nonwhite family is 5.1 persons, nationwide, and 4.8 in central cities. The statistical probability that a large Negro family will also be poor is very high indeed. Thus in 1964 only *one quarter* of all nonwhite families with one child in the home lived in poverty, but *three quarters* of all such families with five or more children were poor. White families living in poverty are significantly smaller than nonwhite families in that circumstance: 3.7 persons for each poor urban white family as compared to 4.8 for each poor urban nonwhite family. This suggests that it is children as well as low income that is a cause of a certain proportion of Negro poverty. In central cities there are 2,395,000 nonwhite children under 16 years of age growing up in poverty. This contrasts with only 1,905,000 white children in that circumstance. Whereas children under 16 make up less than a third of the poor white population in central cities, they account for slightly more than half the nonwhite poor.

The contrast is most pronounced for children in female-headed families. In 1965 there were 1,209,000 nonwhite children under 16 living in central-city families headed by a woman under 65, as against 723,000 white children in that circumstance (many of whom, of course, would be drawn from other ethnic minorities). In the nation as a whole, almost two thirds of all nonwhite female-headed families live below the poverty line, as against less than one third of white female-headed units.

These conditions are unmistakably associated with population growth. During the six-year period between 1960 and 1966, the number of children under age 14 in metropolitan areas increased by 3.3 million. *Nonwhite children accounted for one third of the gain.* The average annual rate of increase of nonwhite children (2.4 percent) was three times the rate for white children. Ninety-five percent of the nonwhite increase was in the central cities, where the proportion of all children who are nonwhite rose from 23 percent in 1960 to 29 percent in 1966.[2]

As the heartbreaking decade of the 1960s came to an end, Census data began to reveal more clearly the *demographic* basis of much of the internal stress of the black urban population, as well as the degree to which that portion of the population living in poverty

2. U.S. Bureau of the Census, *Current Population Reports*, series P-20, no. 163, *Population of the United States by Metropolitan and Nonmetropolitan Residence: April 1966 and 1960*, March 27, 1967, p. 2.

had become separated from the rest of the metropolis. Clearly a large proportion of the black city-dwellers of the nation had been and, for a decade at least would be living in a state of demographic siege, cut off by social and geographic barriers from their neighbors.

During this period the rate of increase of the Negro population was about three-fourths greater than that of the white population. And in the same period the concentration of blacks in central cities became steadily more pronounced. Between 1960 and 1968 the American population increased about 11 percent, and that of metropolitan areas about 13 percent, but this latter growth was almost entirely suburban. Central cities grew by only about 1 percent, while the population of the suburban surrounds grew by 25 percent.

The overall stability of the central city population conceals a pronounced change in the population mix. From 1960 to 1968 the number of whites declined 2.1 million and that of blacks increased 2.4 million. Negroes had by then become significantly more urbanized than whites, with 54 percent of the black population living in central cities, a proportion twice that of whites. It was a younger population; in 1968 the median age of Negroes was 21.3 years, contrasted with 28.6 years for whites. Where it was poor and urban, it tended to have a high incidence of disorganization. This exchange may be seen in Table 7–1. In the period 1960–1968 central cities

Table 7–1—Change in Number of Families by Sex of Head, 1960–1968
(Numbers in thousands)

	White		Negro	
	NUMBER	PERCENT	NUMBER	PERCENT
Central cities:				
Male head	−757	−7	172	11
Female head	155	12	294	60

Source: U.S. Bureau of the Census, *Current Population Reports*, Series P-23, No. 27, February 7, 1969, "Trends in Social and Economic Conditions in Metropolitan Areas."

lost three-quarters of a million white male-headed families. They gained 172,000 black male-headed families. But the number of black female-headed families increased by 294,000. These are the data behind "the crisis in welfare," indeed behind much of the "urban crisis" generally.

The most that can be said about this process is that it can be traced but not explained. The 1960s were a period of great economic gains for black workers. Income data for 1967 revealed almost spectacular advances for Negroes during the decade. In particular, families headed by a black male, aged 25–34, earned 79 percent of the median income of their white counterparts in that year. However, the median income for all families in the young age group was considerably lower for blacks than for whites. Female-headed families brought the proportion down further.[3] Between 1959 and 1967 the median income of male-headed Negro families in central cities rose 37 percent—twice the proportion for white families. In the latter year median earnings for such black families was $6,778. This was 78 percent of white earnings, and well above the median income of city dwellers anywhere else on earth. Simultaneously, the number of central city Negro families with earnings under $4,000 dropped from almost half (45 percent) in 1959 to a third (33 percent) in 1967.

Who was left behind in this surge of affluence? Fatherless children and abandoned or widowed women. In 1967 a full 95 percent

Table 7-2—Negro Money Income as a Percent of White

Males, Aged 25–34		
1949	1959	1967
57.3	58.9	84.4

of Negro children in families with incomes over $15,000 were living with both parents. For families with incomes under $4,000 the proportion was 24 per cent.

In the long perspective of economic development the case can readily be argued that the United States is working its way out of poverty, and doing so at a steady and probably increasing rate. The actual number of persons living in poverty has been declining at about one million persons per year of late, and the proportion of persons in poverty has dropped even more rapidly as the size of the total population grows. It would appear that the poverty population is made up of persons who are not "normal" but rather who suffer special disabilities. They are very old or very young, quite uneducated or else disabled, geographically or socially isolated, and most conspicuously of all, disabled by racial and ethnic practices that grievously diminish the life chances of millions of Negro Americans and numbers of other minority groups. A highly productive and increasingly well-managed national economy has offered exits from poverty to large numbers of persons who

3. See Jane Newitt, "Young Negroes' Income as an Indicator of Progress Toward Equalization of Employment Opportunities." Hudson Institute, Inc. Mimeographed. May 23, 1969.

needed no more than that: an opportunity. Those unable to take advantage of national prosperity have become an increasingly large proportion of the poor. Thus, Herman P. Miller notes that "In 1947 only 16 percent of the families with incomes under $3,000 had a female head as compared with 23 percent in 1960."[4]

Similarly, female-headed families accounted for about 18 percent of all families in the lowest fifth of income distribution in the period 1947–1949, but by 1950 they accounted for 23 percent. But even for persons in these situations, the chances of being poor in a city are much less than elsewhere, and for those who move to the city, the chances of remaining poor would seem also to diminish quite sharply. Fifty-nine percent of nonwhite, female-headed families in cities live in poverty, but for those on farms the proportion is 79 percent, and in the small towns outside the metropolitan areas it is at the three-quarters mark. Cities, in a word, continue to perform their ancient service of enhancing both the material as well as the social and intellectual life of those who come to and live in them.

At the same time it must be insisted that there *are* signs that the problem of poverty in American cities is becoming more difficult, that its steady diminishment can no longer simply be assumed. There are signs that American society lacks both the political will and the social inventiveness to keep up the momentum and to prevent the formation of what Gunnar Myrdal has graphically described as an "under class."

Any number of indications might be cited, but it would perhaps be most useful to take three quite disparate instances, each in its different way arguing the hardening of the lines.

The first concerns the rising number of persons supported by public welfare. There can be no question that the amount and, within the groups most affected, the incidence of welfare dependency is on the rise. The advent of Social Security—each month one American in ten receives a Social Security check—has reduced somewhat the number of older persons dependent on public assistance. Thus in 1955 the proportion of persons 65 and older receiving federal-state old-age assistance was 173 per 1,000. Ten years later this had declined to 119 per 1,000. But during the same decade, however, the proportion of youth under age 18 receiving Aid to Families of Dependent Children (AFDC) rose from 30 to 49 per thousand, while the actual number of such children rose, in round numbers, from one and a half million

4. Herman P. Miller, *Income Distribution in the United States* (Washington, D.C.: U.S. Government Printing Office, 1966), p. 58.

to three and a half million.[5] The lifetime incidence rate also appears to be increasing. Estimates by Robert H. Mugge suggest that about one white youth in ten and six nonwhite youths in ten will be supported by AFDC payments at one point or another before reaching 18.[6] It does not at all follow that the incidence of persons eligible to receive welfare assistance is in fact growing: no one knows what a "true" eligibility rate would look like. But the number and amount of payments continue to rise. This situation has created genuine problems for large cities such as New York. Thus by June of 1964 the number of persons receiving public assistance in New York City reached 448,097, almost exactly the same point (449,105) reached in November 1941, the month before Pearl Harbor. But despite the continued and unexampled economic growth of the 1960s, which toward the end of the decade produced a national economy growing at better than a billion dollars a week, the number of families dependent on welfare grew in New York (and in the nation generally) at wholly inexplicable rates. By the end of 1966 there were 600,000 persons on the welfare rolls in New York City. A study by the research division of the Teamster's Joint Council Number 16 of New York showed that where in 1956 the number of persons in the City receiving welfare assistance amounted to 8.9 percent of the nongovernment work force, by 1966 the proportion had risen to 17.9 percent. But still the increase in numbers continued. By the end of 1968 the million mark had been passed. At that point the rate of increase began to decline somewhat, but in the meantime the social structure of the city had sharply changed. The increase in the AFDC population in New York and in the nation could be partly attributed to rising rates of acceptance of applicants, to increased levels of payments which made more persons eligible, to rising illegitimacy ratios, and to some changes in Federal law. But *au fond* the matter remained a mystery: something had happened that no one understood.

A second indication of the seeming hardening of poverty lines within American cities can be had from the various special censuses that have been conducted in the aftermath of the rioting that swept many Negro slums during the summers of 1965 and

5. The Advisory Council on Public Welfare in its report of June 1966 estimated, however, that only 6.8 percent of the increase in the number of AFDC recipients from January 1961 to December 1965 could be classified as an "increase resulting from increase in rate of need for assistance among families in general population with female head and own children under 18 years of age." (p. 9).

6. Robert H. Mugge, "Demographic Analysis and Public Assistance," paper presented to the Population Association of America, New York, April 30, 1966 (mimeographed).

1966. These studies suggest most emphatically that despite steadily rising levels of income and general prosperity for the nation as a whole, the conditions of life in many slum areas of the great cities were becoming worse. Whatever might be the case for the population as a whole, the gap separating the lives lived in these areas from the rest of the city was widening.

Possibly the most dramatic evidence of the worsening trend emerges from the special census taken in South and East Los Angeles in November 1965, following the Watts riot of the previous summer. A mid-term census of this kind is rather unusual; the nation must normally wait from one decade to the next for such information. The survey showed that at a time of burgeoning national prosperity, when by many general economic indicators Negro families were making great progress, *things were getting worse in South Los Angeles*, an area of a quarter million Negroes. From 1959 to 1965 the typical nonwhite family's income rose 24 percent. But in South Los Angeles median family income *dropped* by 8 percent, from $5,122 in 1959 to $4,736 in 1965. In Watts, median family income dropped from $3,879 to $3,803.

It will be recalled that 1960 was a recession year, but shortly thereafter the nation began the longest peacetime economic expansion in history in the course of which unemployment more or less steadily declined. By 1965 the rate for adult men had dropped to its lowest point since the Korean War year of 1953, and for Negroes the over-all rate dropped to the level of the prosperous 1957. But for male Negro workers in South Los Angeles the unemployment rate dropped only from 12.4 percent to 10.9 percent. In Watts it dropped only from 16.0 percent to 14.2 percent. Significantly, the labor force participation rate for Negro males dropped from 78.7 percent to 69.6 percent for the area as a whole, and in Watts from 70.0 percent to 58.5 percent. This contrasts with an overall national labor force participation rate for males of 77.1 percent in November 1965. Inasmuch as persons not in the labor force are not classed as unemployed, it is at least possible that "true" male unemployment in the area went up during this period. During the five years the number of Negro males in the area declined slightly (by 998 persons), but the number of Negro males in the labor force dropped by 7,208. The number of Negro males holding jobs as craftsmen, foremen, and kindred workers increased during the period, but the number working as operatives and laborers decreased. Female unemployment rates were higher than male in both years, and the female labor force participation rate declined as well.

Inevitably, given these trends in employment and income, the proportion of Negroes living in poverty in South Los Angeles increased from 41 percent to 43 percent. Seemingly, just as inevitably, this was accompanied by family break-up and a trend toward female-based households. The proportion of the poverty population (to use a less than fortunate term that has emerged from the Economic Opportunity Act of 1964) living in families with a female head rose from 45.5 percent in 1960 to 56.2 percent in 1965. The proportion of Negroes under 18 living with both parents dropped from 64.1 percent to 58.6 percent for the area as a whole, and from 55.5 percent to 44.4 percent in Watts. The average number of children in female-based households living below the poverty line increased from 2.54 to 2.93. (In 1966 the average number of children per household for the United States was 1.45.)

During this period the median age of nonwhite males in the area dropped from 24.8 years to 20.3—at which point it was a full four years below the median age of 24.5 for nonwhite females. In Watts the median age for nonwhite males in 1965 was a fantastic 13.5, both rates reflecting the disappearance of Negro males and the high birth rate of the Negro poor. During this period the total population of Watts declined somewhat, but again it was the males who vanished most. In 1960 there were 5,058 nonwhite males aged 20 to 64 in Watts, and 6,748 nonwhite females, a surplus of 1,690. By 1965 there were only 3,930 males for 5,810 females, a surplus of 1,880. The proportion of adult nonwhite males, twenty years and older, to infant and teenage population correspondingly declined.

A similar range of findings emerges from a recent Census study of poverty neighborhoods in Cleveland, including Hough, where a riot occurred. In 1960, 91 per cent of Cleveland's Negro population, some 228,322 persons, lived in these areas. In the next five years the number of Negroes in Cleveland grew somewhat, but the proportion living outside the poverty neighborhoods grew to 15 percent, or 41,451 persons. During this period there was little change in the incidence of poverty among Negro families, which remained at about one quarter, but considerable change in the *concentration* of such families. For families living outside the poverty area the incidence of poverty dropped from 17.9 percent to 9.8 percent. Median family income rose $1,107 to a total of $7,285 in 1964. The number of female-headed families dropped from 13.9 percent in 1959 to 9.1 percent in 1964. The unemployment rate for males dropped to 8 per cent, and the labor force participation to an impressive 82.2 percent, seven percentage points above the national average for the nonwhite males, and five points above the average for all males in the labor force. In a word, this 15 per cent of the Negro population of Cleveland was made up overwhelmingly of hard-working, well-paid citizens on the way up in the world.

This made the contrast with the poverty areas all the greater. In these neighborhoods the incidence of poverty among Negro families *rose*, reaching 28.5 percent. Median family income (1959–1964) increased only $132, to a level of $5,085, while the proportion of female-headed households rose from 20 per cent to 25 percent, and the male labor force participation rate dropped to 73.1 percent.

Even these over-all figures conceal the deterioration in some of the worst neighborhoods. In the Hough section, for example, median family income *declined* $776 to $3,966 in 1964, and in nearby West Central it dropped to $2,984. This decline in income was closely associated, as it almost invariably will be, with a rise in the proportion of female-headed families. From 1959 to 1964 the ratio in Hough rose from 22.5 percent to 32.6 percent, and in West Central from 32.6 to 35.1 percent. In Hough, the number of children living in poverty increased by one third.

These Census surveys indicated astonishingly high unemployment rates in such neighborhoods. In the West Central area, for example, the male unemployment rate rose to 20.4 percent in 1965, and the labor force participation rate dropped to 58.7 percent. These data have been dramatically confirmed by a survey conducted in November 1966 by the U.S. Department of Labor in a number of poverty neighborhoods throughout the nation. The unemployment rate was found to be 10 percent, or three times the national average. The Department of Labor found that "one out of every three residents in the slum has a serious employment problem," and, while pointing out that the number of persons concerned was small enough that the problem is still manageable, it concluded that "no conceivable increase in the gross national product would stir these backwaters."

This is the heart of the issue: Have we run into structural defects in the distribution of income and opportunity in the nation such that continued and growing prosperity will not necessarily bring about *widening* prosperity? It would be foolish to assume that this is the case, as it has never been the case in the past, at least for any length of time, but there are surely many indications that at the present time the system is working somewhat imperfectly, and also that it may be changing, and beginning to work on a somewhat different level. In particular there is evidence that the power of employment conditions to "control" matters such as welfare dependency and family integrity may be weakening. During the late 1940s and the 1950s, the correlation between the nonwhite male unemployment rate and the number of new AFDC cases opened each month, or the number of nonwhite married women separated from their husbands, was quite close. The numbers rose and fell in what was sometimes almost perfect accord. Thus, between 1948 and 1962 the correlation between the unemployment rate and the AFDC case rate was a remarkable +.91. For the years 1953 to 1964 the correlation between the unemployment rate for nonwhite males aged 20 and over and the separation rate for nonwhite married women at the interval of four months was a no less remarkable +.73. However, with the onset of the 1960s these relations began to weaken, and by the mid-1960s they disappeared altogether.

The unemployment rates go down, but the rates of welfare dependency and family instability do not. It must be emphasized that here as elsewhere it is necessary to cite instances drawn from nonwhite data only because the high concentration of poverty among nonwhites makes it possible to get from over-all nonwhite statistics some indication as to what is happening in groups living in poverty. There is as yet no reason to suppose that the same phenomenon would not be found in white slums if separate statistics were collected in them, as hopefully as they will be in the future.

A tradition going back at least as far as de Tocqueville's 1839 report to the French Chamber of Deputies on the abolition of slavery in the French West Indies argues that family instability derives from forced servitude. W. E. B. DuBois, and later E. Franklin Frazier, presented this case with clarity and force. More recently, the researches of Herbert G. Gutman have cast great doubt on the validity of this thesis. Employment patterns that developed in the late 19th century would appear, at least with respect to the Negro American, to have had far more important consequences, and to be the true source of familial patterns so much to be encountered in the slums of the present time. And yet by this token, such patterns ought to have begun to respond to the much improved employment opportunities open to black workers in the 1960s. In the aggregate things got worse, not better. It is likely that a decade or two hence events will seem explicable enough—especially if what is involved in essence is time lag—but for the moment there is no satisfactory explanation.[7]

7. See Alexis de Tocqueville, *Report made to The Chamber of Deputies on The*

A third and final indication that poverty lines may be hardening in the United States is the simple fact that the teeming, disorganized life of impoverished slums has all but disappeared among the North Atlantic democracies—save only the United States. It requires some intrepidness to *declare* this to be a fact, as no systematic inquiry has been made that would provide completely dependable comparisons, but it can be said with fair assurance that mass poverty and squalor, of the kind that may be encountered in almost any large American city, simply cannot be found in comparable cities in Europe, or Canada, or Japan. A quarter century of full and over-full employment, income supplements, health services, and social insurance has simply put an end to it. It may be that a matter of priorities is to be found here: vast numbers of French families do without a telephone, but none does without work. Higher education is sharply restricted in Britain and Germany, but teenage unemployment is practically unknown. Income taxes are heavily progressive everywhere, but there is not one such nation that does not automatically provide a monthly payment to every family with minor children to help with the costs of rearing them.[8]

Whatever the reason, the fact does emerge with considerable clarity and force: the bleak industrial slums of Marxist lore have all but disappeared from the industrial democracies of Northern and Western Europe, but they continue to persist and even to worsen in the United States. Even were the United States among the weaker of these nations in economic terms, this matter would still have to be explained. But given the overwhelming American economic advantage, the persistence of mass poverty suggests that something more fundamental is amiss.

What? This is a far more troubled question than might at first be supposed, and accordingly as one chooses one answer or set of answers among the various options, program choices of quite different kinds will emerge. Walter B. Miller has noted that ex-

Abolition of Slavery in the French Colonies, July 23, 1839 (Boston: James Munroe & Co., 1840); W. E. Burghardt Du Bois, editor, *The Negro American Family* (Atlanta, Georgia: Atlanta University Press, 1908) [This edition is now out of print. It was reprinted by Negro Universities' Press in 1969 (New York), and a new edition, with a foreword by Daniel P. Moynihan, was to be published by The M.I.T. Press.]; E. Franklin Frazier, *The Negro Family in the United States* (Chicago: University of Chicago Press, 1939); Herbert G. Gutman and Laurence A. Glasco, "The Buffalo, New York, Negro, 1855–1875: A Study of the Family Structure of Free Negroes and Some of Its Implications," prepared for delivery at the Wisconsin Conference on the History of American Political and Social Behavior, May 16–17, 1968.
    8. In some countries family allowances are not provided for an only child.

planations of poverty tend to assign causative primacy to conditions the observer wishes to see changed, ranging from the innate sinfulness of the poor to the innate sinfulness of "the System." The most powerful hypothesis to emerge in the present age is Oscar Lewis' conception of "the culture of poverty," which he describes as "both an adaptation and a reaction of the poor to their marginal position in a class-stratified, highly individuated, capitalistic society."[9] The poverty Lewis describes is something considerably more tenacious than simply an absence of money. Indeed, poverty as such is almost an incidental aspect of the phenomenon, which is characterized principally by "the lack of effective participation and integration of the poor in the major institutions of the larger society"[10] and accompanied by the familiar patterns of unemployment, poor housing, disorganized family life, and strong feelings of helplessness and dependence. Lewis finds these traits in many parts of the Western world, but not at all, for example, among the lower castes in India, where despite the most relentless material poverty the integration of the individual into the caste system seems to produce a stable, well-organized personality. Lewis estimates the number of persons living in a culture of poverty in the United States at six to ten million people at most, but for them "the elimination of physical poverty *per se* may not be enough to eliminate the culture of poverty which is a whole way of life."[11]

It in no way detracts from the brilliance of Lewis' hypothesis to point out that it is as yet no more than that: the detailed study of life in American slums that his analysis requires has yet to be done. For the moment we must grope with a fairly limited understanding that nonetheless provides some guide to action. We know for the most part who the poor are; we know something about the "caste" lines by which they are kept apart from much of society; we know something of the effects of technology on the jobs the poor characteristically hold; and we are beginning to sense something of the surprisingly negative impact that portions of our welfare practices may be having.

In far the greatest number, the urban poor of the present time are made up of the urbanized agricultural proletariat. That is the overwhelming fact of life about Negro and Puerto Rican city dwellers of the present time: in bulk, they are the newcomers of this generation, and they bring with them all of the traditional

9. Oscar Lewis, *La Vida* (New York: Random House, 1966), p. xliv.
10. *Ibid.*, p. xlv.
11. *Ibid.*, p. lii.

burdens of refugees from a bankrupt, oppressive, and primitive agricultural society. There seems absolutely no question but that time and economic opportunity are the greatest elements in the transformation of such groups from displaced peasants into prospering city dwellers, a transformation that has already occurred many times in American history.

A second quality possessed by many of today's poor is that they are Negro. In contrast to the great success with which American cities have absorbed waves of Irish, Polish, and Italian peasants, to name but a few of the past migrations, American society has never yet been able to provide Negroes an equal place in social and economic arrangements, be they urban or rural. Negroes are seriously discriminated against on the basis of race, so that poor Negroes are almost locked in behind the double barriers of caste and class. The question of race is a new challenge; unless this issue is resolved, the question of poverty will inevitably remain.

A third quality of the present-day poor is that they are seeking employment in a job market that is becoming more and more difficult for them. It is not necessary to grow apocalyptic about the disappearance of low-skilled jobs in the American economy in order to admit that such jobs are relatively harder to find than they have been in the past and moreover seem increasingly to be located in areas beyond the suburban fringe, far from the homes of the central city poor. The question of providing guaranteed full employment is surely the one that should be easiest for the United States to solve, but unaccountably it has not been solved.

The fourth, and in ways the most frustrating, aspect of contemporary poverty has to do with the nature of the American social welfare system. The essence of this system is to assume that no one needs help until he is in trouble, after which it repeatedly emerges that no one in trouble can be helped. This exaggerates the case, to be sure, but the case can nonetheless be made. The most conspicuous quality of the poor is their relative lack of money, a quality which shows little change in recent years. Wealth and income in the United States are most unevenly distributed and are showing no tendency to become more equal. As Herman P. Miller writes, "For example, during 1947–1960, there was no change at all in the distribution of income groups among urban families; the top 5 percent and the top 20 percent received about the same share of the aggregate income in every year during the decade."[12] At the other extreme, as Christopher Jencks and David Riesman note, "The bottom 20 percent of all

12. Miller, *Income Distribution*, pp. 20–22.

families have had between 4 and 5 percent of all income for as long as we have had income statistics."[13] Recent federal fiscal policies have if anything confirmed and even possibly accentuated this condition. The plain fact is that the United States needs a measure of income redistribution. Unfortunately, the American social welfare system is wedded to the provision of *services* to the poor rather than *income* and, as Lee Rainwater has forcefully pointed out, the frequent result is neither the one nor the other.

Fortunately, the subject of income supports for the poor is being raised with increasing credibility. Proposals for some form of guaranteed minimum income are being put forward with increasing cogency and sophistication.[14] There is also a certain measure of interest in family allowances. The United States is one of the few industrial nations in the world that does not have a system of family allowances, which are small (or in countries such as France, not so small) monthly payments tendered to families with minor children. The particular attraction of family allowances is that they involve no means tests, go to all families so that there is no distinction made between the poor who receive the benefits and the remainder of society that pays for them, and not least, that they can be administered with a minimum of bureaucracy. Although family allowances have been shown in other nations to have no perceivable effect on birth rates, it is reasonable to assume that any such program in the United States should be accompanied by a genuinely adequate federal program to provide birth control services for all families desiring them.

In many important respects the United States would seem to be approaching a crossroads. The issue of poverty has been raised, and is now an open one. The fact confronts us that other nations with whom we would wish to be compared have themselves largely eliminated domestic poverty, at least in their cities. So also does the fact that the American nation is fully capable of eliminating the purely economic aspects of poverty by simple measures of full employment and income supplements, again of a kind familiar to most of the industrial democracies of the world. If in spite of these facts the conditions of impoverishment that are to be found in one American city after another should continue unchanged, the United States will be required to acknowledge that it is not what it has thought itself to be.

13. Christopher Jencks and David Riesman, "The American Negro College," *Harvard Educational Review*, vol. 37, no. 1, 1967, p. 11.
14. See James Tobin, "On Improving the Economic Status of the Negro," *Daedalus* (Fall 1965).

Housing conditions in urban poverty areas

INTRODUCTION

It is common knowledge—as such terms as "slums," "ghettos," and "blighted neighborhoods" attest—that urban social and economic problems tend to be geographically concentrated. However, few examples of data can be found that show how such poor or deprived areas compare with other parts of cities or metropolitan areas. One long-standing obstacle has been the lack of any set of consistent standards to identify especially poor areas.

An effort to meet that need has recently been made by the Bureau of the Census, for the Office of Economic Opportunity. The Bureau used findings of the 1960 Census of Population to define "poverty areas" within the largest metropolitan areas ("SMSA's")—i.e., those that had a 1960 population of 250,000 or more. (See "The Definition of Poverty Areas," below.) The Census Bureau has published some population data for such defined poverty areas, showing that in 1960 they included 4,795,000 families, or 19.6 percent of all families in the major SMSA's involved. This included 3,653,000 families in central-city poverty areas, or 29.7 percent of all central-city families; and 1,142,000 families in the outlying portions of these SMSA's, or 9.3 percent of all families residing there. Of course, the incidence of poverty averages much higher in these defined poverty areas than in other parts of major SMSA's, as indicated by the Census Bureau data in Table 8–1.

Table 8–1—Characteristics of Families in SMSA's of over 250,000 Population, by Poverty Area Status and Region: 1960

(in thousands)

Item	United States*	North- east	North Central*	South	West
Total	24,506	8,335	6,541	4,906	4,724
White	22,025	7,696	5,878	4,085	4,366
Nonwhite	2,481	639	663	821	358
Percent in poverty areas:					
Of all families	19.6	17.8	15.5	33.9	13.4
Of white families	13.7	13.6	8.8	24.5	10.4
Of nonwhite families	71.7	69.2	74.3	80.7	50.7
Percent of families below poverty level:					
In poverty areas	28.5	24.0	27.4	34.5	25.1
Outside poverty areas	8.5	8.0	7.5	11.0	8.9

* Excluding data for the Davenport–Rock Island–Moline SMSA, for which no poverty area was defined.

Source: U.S. Bureau of the Census, *Poverty Areas in the 100 Largest Metropolitan Areas*, Report PC(S1)-54, November 1967.

This report summarizes the results of two special tabulating efforts carried out by the Census Bureau at the request of the National Commission on Urban Problems, to supply (1) figures showing the geographic extent of these defined poverty areas, separately for the central city and outlying portions of each of the major SMSA's; and (2) findings of the 1960 Census of Housing on housing conditions in these SMSA's, separately for the poverty area portions and other portions of the respective central cities[1] and noncentral-city territory.

Before detailing the findings about housing conditions in poverty areas, we will first examine the data with respect to the geographic extent of the poverty areas.

GEOGRAPHIC FINDINGS

Each poverty area defined by the Bureau of the Census, as more fully explained below, consists of a group of adjoining Census tracts which ranked relatively low in terms of a composite index based on various measures from the 1960 Census of Population and Housing. Altogether, 193 such areas were delineated, including some terri-

1. The term "central city" refers to the entire area of the city or cities used in the name of the SMSA, and *not* merely to the "core" or "downtown" or "inner-city area" of a major city.

tory in all but one of the 101 SMSA's of 250,000 or over (the exception being the Davenport-Rock Island-Moline SMSA).[2]

Following is a summary distribution of the 101 largest SMSA's, in terms of the geographic incidence of poverty areas within and outside the central cities:

	Number of SMSA's
No poverty area	1
Poverty area only outside central city	1
Poverty area only within central city	43
Poverty area both within and outside, with poverty area proportion of territory:	
Higher in central city	28
Lower in central city than outside	28

Of the 203,303 square miles of land within the largest metropolitan areas, approximately one-fourth, or 52,073 square miles, lie within the defined poverty areas. However, as indicated by Table 8–2, this

Table 8–2—Territory within Poverty Areas of SMSA's of over 250,000 Population, by Region: 1960

Item	United States	North- east	North Central	South	West
Number of SMSA's	101	26	25	32	18
SMSA land area (sq. miles):					
Total	203,303	30,277	36,435	44,475	92,116
Within central cities	7,663	1,124	1,732	3,018	1,791
Outside central cities	195,640	29,153	34,703	41,457	90,325
Poverty-area land (sq. miles):					
Total	52,073	3,242	347	18,334	30,150
Within central cities	1,785	208	305	941	331
Outside central cities	50,288	3,034	42	17,393	28,819
Poverty area percentage of all land area:					
Entire SMSA's	25.6	10.7	1.0	41.2	32.7
Within central cities	23.3	18.5	17.6	31.2	18.5
Outside central cities	25.7	10.4	0.1	42.0	33.0

proportion differs widely among regions—from 41 percent for the 32 major SMSA's in the South and 33 percent for the 18 major SMSA's in the West down to only 1 percent for the 25 major SMSA's in the North Central region. This reflects the fact that the North Central poverty areas are found nearly entirely within central cities. In each of the other regions, there is far more poverty-area

2. The Office of Economic Opportunity has issued (in three volumes) a set of maps delineating the poverty areas for each of the largest SMSA's, under the title, *Maps of Major Concentrations of Poverty in Standard Metropolitan Statistical Areas of 250,000 or More Population.*

territory in the suburban parts of the major SMSA's than within the central cities.[3]

Poverty areas within the central cities themselves comprise 23 percent of the cities' total land area—i.e., 1,785 out of 7,660 square miles. Again, one region differs considerably from the others: the percentage of the central city land within poverty areas is 31 percent for the 32 major SMSA's in the South, as compared with about 18 percent for the SMSA's in each of the other three regions.

The poverty-area proportion of land averages about the same, nationwide, for the central cities and outlying parts of these large SMSA's. Again, however, this is the net result of marked inter-regional differences: the outlying-area proportion is considerably less in the Northeast and North Central regions, while the reverse is true in the South and West.

About one-third of all the entire SMSA's, and also of the central cities and outlying portions, have 30 percent or more of their territory within poverty areas. However, as Table 8–3 shows, the various regions differ a great deal, with these proportions running considerably higher in the South and West than in the Northeast and North Central regions for entire SMSA's and their outlying portions. On the other hand, for central cities as such, high poverty-area proportions of territory are especially evident in the South and Northeast.

POVERTY-AREA HOUSING CONDITIONS

In 1960, the SMSA's of over 250,000 population had 31.2 million housing units, or 53.5 percent of the Nation's total housing stock. Three million of these housing units in the largest metropolitan areas, or nearly 10 percent, were found to be "substandard" when that term is defined as "dilapidated" or, although better than this from a general structural standpoint, lacking hot water, running water, or a private toilet or bath. More than 2.9 million of the occupied housing units in these SMSA's were "overcrowded"—i.e., they averaged more than one resident per room. (A considerable fraction of these overcrowded units were also substandard by the definition above; so the two figures should not be added.)

Relation to area totals

The proportions of substandard and crowded housing—as defined above—were considerably higher in the poverty-area parts of the

3. This comparison, it should be emphasized, is entirely *geographic*. The population of poverty areas outside central cities, as suggested by the housing data in Table 8-4, is only about one-fourth that of the central-city poverty areas.

Table 8-3—Distribution of SMSA's of over 250,000 Population by Proportion of Territory within Poverty Areas—Total, Central City and Outlying Portions—by Region: 1960

PERCENT OF LAND IN POVERTY AREAS	Number of areas					Cumulative percent of areas				
	UNITED STATES	NORTH-EAST	NORTH CENTRAL	SOUTH	WEST	UNITED STATES	NORTH-EAST	NORTH CENTRAL	SOUTH	WEST
Entire SMA's										
Total	101	26	25	32	18	xxx	xxx	xxx	xxx	xxx
60 or more	16	1	—	11	5	16	4	—	34	28
50 to 59.9	9	1	—	6	2	25	8	—	53	39
30 to 49.9	6	1	—	4	1	31	12	—	66	44
20 to 29.9	3	2	—	2	—	34	19	—	72	44
10 to 19.9	4	21	24	2	—	38	100	96	78	44
0.1 to 9.9	62	—	1	7	10	99	100	100	100	100
None	1			—	—	100			100	100
Central cities										
60 or more	7	3	—	3	1	7	12	—	9	6
50 to 59.9	10	2	—	8	—	17	19	—	34	6
30 to 49.9	16	5	5	4	2	33	38	20	47	17
20 to 29.9	28	7	3	13	5	50	65	32	88	44
10 to 19.9	28	6	13	3	6	88	88	84	97	78
0.1 to 9.9	10	3	3	—	4	98	100	96	97	100
None	2	—	1	1	—	100	100	100	100	100
Outlying portions										
60 or more	16	1	—	11	5	16	4	—	34	28
50 to 59.9	10	1	—	6	3	26	8	—	53	44
30 to 49.9	4	1	—	3	—	30	12	—	63	44
20 to 29.9	4	1	—	3	—	34	15	—	72	44
10 to 19.9	3	8	5	2	—	37	46	20	78	44
0.1 to 9.9	20	14	20	3	4	56	100	100	88	67
None	44			4	6	100			100	100

major SMSA's. Substandard units made up 25.1 percent of the total in poverty areas, as against 5.2 percent elsewhere in these SMSA's; and 16.3 percent of the occupied units in poverty areas were overcrowded, compared with 7.4 percent elsewhere. These and other disparities can be seen in another way, as shown in Table 8–4.

Table 8–4—Poverty-Area Percentages of Land Area and of Various Housing Items, for all SMSA's of over 250,000 Population: 1960

Item	Percent of All-SMSA Totals			Poverty-area Percentages of	
	ALL POVERTY AREAS	CENTRAL CITY POVERTY AREAS	OUTLYING POVERTY AREAS	CENTRAL CITY TOTALS	OUTLYING AREA TOTALS
Land area	25.6	0.9	24.7	23.3	25.7
All housing units	22.4	17.6	4.8	33.3	10.3
All occupied units	22.0	17.3	4.6	32.6	9.9
Owner-occupied units	12.6	7.9	4.7	18.9	8.1
Renter-occupied units	35.0	30.5	4.5	43.9	14.8
Vacant units	28.7	20.8	7.9	45.0	14.6
Units occupied by nonwhites	73.6	65.6	8.0	79.2	46.7
Substandard units	58.2	44.8	13.4	75.8	32.7
Those occupied by nonwhites	83.3	68.0	15.3	90.9	60.6
Dilapidated units	57.6	42.7	14.9	76.0	34.0
Overcrowded housing units	38.9	30.5	8.4	54.2	19.1
Those occupied by nonwhites	77.6	66.7	10.9	83.5	54.1
Housing units in structures over 20 years old	31.4	26.7	4.7	40.8	13.6
Those occupied by nonwhites	78.8	72.9	5.8	83.1	47.8
Housing units in multi-unit structures	35.1	32.7	2.4	42.2	10.5
Those occupied by nonwhites	79.8	77.1	2.7	83.2	37.6

In 1960, the defined poverty areas had 25.6 percent of the land area and 22.4 percent of the housing units of the largest SMSA's, but—

58 percent of all the substandard units;
39 percent of all the overcrowded units;
31 percent of all the housing units in structures over 20 years old;
35 percent of the units in multi-unit structures; and
35 percent of all the renter-occupied units; but only
13 percent of all the owner-occupied units.

Also, the poverty areas accounted for 74 percent of all the housing units in the major SMSA's that were occupied by nonwhites.

POVERTY AREAS IN CENTRAL CITIES

Looking specifically at the central cities of these largest SMSA's, it is found that defined poverty areas, with 23.3 percent of the land area of the central cities, had in 1960—

33 percent of all the cities' housing units;
76 percent of the substandard units;
54 percent of the overcrowded units;
45 percent of the vacant housing units;
41 percent of the units in structures over 20 years old;
42 percent of the units in multi-unit structures; and
44 percent of the renter-occupied units; but only
19 percent of all the owner-occupied units in the central cities.

The defined poverty areas accounted for 79 percent of all the central city housing units occupied by nonwhite households.

Regional variations

In all except 4 of the 101 largest SMSA's, as indicated by Table 8–5, the defined poverty areas accounted for at least 10 percent of all housing units in 1960, and in 12 of the areas, this proportion was at least 50 percent. Again, a marked regional variation appears, with the Southern SMSA's typically showing a considerably larger fraction of poverty-area housing units.

When the comparison is limited to central-city territory, high proportions are also found among many Northeast areas: in half the 26 large SMSA's in that region, the poverty-area proportion of all housing units in the central cities was at least 35 percent in 1960, and in only 3 instances was this fraction less than 25 percent. The West, with relatively younger and often geographically larger metropolitan centers, offers a contrast: of the 18 central cities there, only 5 showed poverty areas accounting for 25 percent or more of all housing units.

Central city housing density

The poverty areas of the central cities typically have a considerably higher "housing density" than other parts of these cities. In 1960, the poverty areas had 3,071 housing units per square mile, or 64 percent more than the 1,874 per square mile average for the remainder of the cities. However, the poverty areas also had a higher proportion of vacancies, so that in terms of occupied housing units the disparity was not quite so great—2,839 per square mile in poverty areas, or 59 percent higher than the 1,787 per square mile elsewhere in these metropolitan cities.

This tendency toward a relatively higher housing density in poverty areas is found for most of the 97 metropolitan central cities for which a specific comparison can be made. In 4 cities, there are at least 4 times as many units per square mile in the poverty-area portion as

Table 8-5—Distribution of SMSA's of over 250,000 Population by Proportion of all Housing Units Located Within Poverty Areas—Entire SMSA's and Central City Portions, by Region: 1960

Percent of all Housing units Located in Poverty Areas	NUMBER OF AREAS					CUMULATIVE PERCENT OF AREAS				
	United States	North-east	North Central	South	West	United States	North-east	North Central	South	West
Entire SMSA's										
Total	101	26	25	32	18	xxx	xxx	xxx	xxx	xxx
50 or more	12	2	—	9	1	12	8	—	28	6
40 to 49.9	5	—	—	4	1	17	8	—	41	11
35 to 39.9	4	—	—	3	1	21	8	—	50	17
30 to 34.9	3	—	—	2	1	24	8	12	56	22
25 to 29.9	10	2	3	4	1	34	15	28	69	28
20 to 24.9	16	3	4	7	2	50	27	68	91	39
15 to 19.9	27	11	10	3	3	76	69	88	100	56
10 to 14.9	20	7	5	—	8	96	96	100	100	100
Less than 1.0	4	1	3	—	—	100	100	100	100	100
Central city portions										
50 or more	13	3	1	9	—	13	12	4	28	—
40 to 49.9	19	7	1	11	—	32	38	8	63	—
35 to 39.9	12	3	4	2	3	44	50	24	69	17
30 to 34.9	20	7	6	5	2	63	77	48	84	28
25 to 29.9	6	3	2	1	—	69	88	56	88	28
20 to 24.9	19	3	6	1	9	88	100	80	91	78
15 to 19.9	5	—	2	—	3	93	100	88	91	94
10 to 14.9	4	—	2	1	1	97	100	96	94	100
Less than 1.0	3	—	1	2	—	100	100	100	100	100

elsewhere; in 6 cities this ratio is between 3 to 1 and 4 to 1; in 33 cities, it is between 2 to 1 and 3 to 1; and in 32 cities, it is between 1.2 to 1 and 2 to 1. In 12 cities, there is relatively little difference in housing density between poverty areas and other city territory; and in 10 cities, the difference runs the other way.

However, it should not be concluded that all central city poverty areas involve a very high housing density. The poverty areas tend to share the general housing patterns of their respective regions—typically involving a higher proportion of multi-family housing and higher geographic densities in Northeast and North Central cities than in metropolitan central cities of the South and West. Accordingly, the poverty-area parts of some major cities are less "crowded" from a housing standpoint than even the non-poverty parts of numerous other major cities.

Nonetheless, there is a strong general tendency toward higher density for the poverty areas: as Table 8–6 shows, housing units in

Table 8–6—Housing Units per Square Mile Within and Outside Poverty Areas of Central Cities of the Largest SMSA's: 1960

Housing Units per Square Mile	Number of Cities POVERTY AREAS	Number of Cities OTHER AREA	Cumulative Percent POVERTY AREAS	Cumulative Percent OTHER AREA
Total*	97	97	xxx	xxx
8,000 or more	9	1	9.3	1.0
5,000 to 7,999	17	2	26.8	3.1
3,500 to 4,999	12	11	39.2	14.4
3,000 to 3,499	11	4	50.5	18.6
2,500 to 2,999	13	10	63.9	28.9
2,000 to 2,499	7	14	71.1	43.3
1,500 to 1,999	10	15	81.4	58.8
1,000 to 1,499	6	23	87.6	82.5
Under 1,000	12	17	100.0	100.0

* Counting each major SMSA only once (i.e., combining any "twin" central cities), and omitting 4 of the 101 largest SMSA's (2 without any central city poverty area and 2 for which precise geographic data are lacking).

1960 averaged at least 5,000 per square mile in the poverty-area parts of more than one-fourth of the central cities, while only 3 percent of the cities showed such a high density for their nonpoverty territory; and for half the cities, the poverty-area average was at least 3,000 units per square mile, while less than one-fifth of the cities showed this high a housing density for their nonpoverty territory.

The contrast between housing density in the central city poverty areas and the density outside the central city but within SMSA's is even greater. In the former it is 3,071 units per square mile, compared with 75 units per square mile in the suburbs of the central cities.

DETAILED CHARACTERISTICS

Table 8–7 provides nationwide totals and computed proportions for many types of housing characteristics. Especially because of the geographic variations discussed above, these findings obviously should not be taken to reflect closely the housing situation for any one metropolitan area. Nevertheless, they provide a useful summary background—in a form not previously available—on some major patterns and relationships of housing conditions within the largest metropolitan areas.

At the time of the 1960 Census, as Table 8–7 shows, the poverty areas of major SMSA's had:

A higher rate of vacant housing than other areas (8.2 versus 5.9 percent for entire SMSA's, and 7.6 versus 4.6 percent within central cities);

A far smaller proportion of homeownership (33 versus 65 percent of occupied units for entire SMSA's, and 26 versus 55 percent within central cities);

A far higher proportion of nonwhite occupancy (35 versus 3.5 percent for entire SMSA's, and 39 versus 5 percent within central cities);

A far higher proportion of substandard housing units (25 versus 5 percent for entire SMSA's, and 25 versus 4 percent within central cities);

A considerably higher proportion of overcrowded units (18 versus 8 percent for entire SMSA's, and 18 versus 7 percent within central cities);

A larger proportion of housing units in structures more than 20 years old (79 versus 50 percent for entire SMSA's, and 85 versus 62 percent within central cities); and

A considerably higher proportion of housing in multi-unit structures (54 versus 29 percent in entire SMSA's, and 64 versus 44 percent within central cities).

The direction of difference indicated in each of these instances might have been anticipated merely in terms of "common knowledge" and cursory observation of the urban scene, but until now explicit data have not been available. The reported data have translated such anticipations into explicit measures.

Table 8–7 also includes at least two sets of ratios that do not conform to common impressions. In the first place, no significant difference appears in the proportion of "substandard" units that

Table 8-7—Selected Housing Data for SMSA's of over 250,000 Population, Poverty Areas, Other Portions: 1960

(housing units in thousands)

ITEM	Entire SMSA's			Central Cities			Outside Central Cities		
	TOTAL	WITHIN POVERTY AREAS	OUTSIDE POVERTY AREAS	TOTAL	WITHIN POVERTY AREAS	OUTSIDE POVERTY AREAS	TOTAL	WITHIN POVERTY AREAS	OUTSIDE POVERTY AREAS
Land area (thousands of square miles)	203.3	52.1	151.2	7.7	1.8	5.9	195.6	50.3	145.4
All housing units	31,200	6,993	24,207	16,477	5,481	10,996	14,723	1,512	13,211
Owner-occupied	16,996	2,142	14,853	7,070	1,339	5,731	9,925	803	9,122
Occupied by nonwhites	1,039	639	400	1,767	520	247	271	119	152
Renter-occupied	12,217	4,281	7,936	8,487	3,728	4,758	3,730	552	3,178
Occupied by nonwhites	2,004	1,601	403	1,774	1,476	278	250	125	126
Vacant	1,987	570	1,418	920	414	507	1,067	156	911
Substandard housing units	3,018	1,755	1,263	1,784	1,352	432	1,235	404	831
Dilapidated	920	530	390	517	393	124	403	137	266
Other	2,098	1,225	873	1,267	959	308	832	267	565
Housing units occupied by nonwhites	3,044	2,240	803	2,522	1,997	525	522	244	278
Substandard housing units	765	637	128	572	520	52	193	117	75
Occupied housing units	29,212	6,423	22,789	15,557	5,067	10,489	13,655	1,356	12,300
With recent movers	9,564	2,326	7,238	5,149	1,863	3,286	4,414	463	3,951
Occupied by whites	26,168	4,183	21,986	13,035	3,070	9,964	13,133	1,112	12,022
With recent movers	8,437	1,510	6,927	4,191	1,123	3,067	4,245	387	3,859
Occupied by nonwhites	3,044	2,240	803	2,522	1,997	525	522	244	278
With recent movers	1,127	816	311	958	740	219	169	76	92
Overcrowded housing units	2,933	1,141	1,792	1,650	895	755	1,283	245	1,037
Occupied by whites	2,206	577	1,628	1,069	410	659	1,137	166	970
Occupied by nonwhites	727	564	164	581	485	96	146	79	67
Housing units in structures over 20 years old	17,478	5,492	11,986	11,449	4,674	6,775	6,029	818	5,210
Occupied by nonwhites	2,225	1,753	472	1,953	1,623	330	272	130	142
Housing units in multi-unit structures	10,690	3,750	6,940	8,283	3,497	4,786	2,407	253	2,154
Occupied by nonwhites	1,494	1,192	301	1,385	1,152	233	109	41	68

were classed in the Census of Housing as "dilapidated," as between poverty and other areas; in each instance, the dilapidated housing made up less than one-third of all the substandard units, with the remainder being so designated because of a deficiency in their plumbing facilities.

Secondly, Table 8–7 reflects only a slightly higher proportion of "recent movers" for occupied units in poverty areas than in other parts of metropolitan areas and their central cities. (The term refers to households that had moved into the dwelling where they were enumerated in April 1960 within the preceding 27 months—i.e., after December 1957.) This does not seem to conform with the common impression of a high turnover rate of tenancy for poor areas. Perhaps, however, that phenomenon would show up if a shorter interval than 27 months were being separately recorded. A word of caution is thus in order. It should also be remembered that poverty-stricken areas (both rural and urban) involve especially difficult problems of complete enumeration in the Census, with under-counting most likely to involve some of the transient elements of the population. . . .

DEFINITION OF POVERTY AREAS

The concepts and methods used by the Bureau of the Census to delineate poverty areas in the largest metropolitan areas are fully outlined in its report, *Poverty Areas in the 100 Largest Metropolitan Areas.*[4] In brief, the following steps were involved:

a. Ranking all the Census tracts in the 101 SMSA's that had a 1960 population of 250,000 or more in terms of a composite "poverty index" that gave equal weight to the following five characteristics:

1. Percent of families with cash incomes under $3,000 in 1959;

2. Percent of children under 18 not living with both parents;

3. Percent of males over 25 with less than 8 years of schooling;

4. Percent of unskilled males over 14 in the employed labor force;

5. Percent of substandard housing units.

b. Selecting the one-fourth of all the tracts which ranked lowest, in terms of this composite index, as "poor" tracts.

c. Adjusting the selection to add some nonpoor tracts completely surrounded by "poor" tracts, and to drop out some geographically isolated "poor" tracts, to arrive at tentative poverty-area groups of tracts.

4. See fn., Table 8–1.

    d. Deleting some tracts to take account of urban renewal operations of 1960–1966.

The net result was to derive 193 "poverty areas," in 100 of the 101 largest SMSA's, altogether comprising 4,660 of the 20,915 tracts in the 101 SMSA's. . . .

9 THEODORE R. SIZER

The schools in the city*

It is said that the schools of our largest cities are in trouble, inadequate and wanting in comparison with schools in the suburbs. Good schools, the argument goes, give children the chance to succeed in life and to be happy, law-abiding citizens. City schools, or at least slum schools, are successful if they provide people with the skills to leave the slum and its cultural misery. By this criterion, however, our big city school systems have over time been enormously successful institutions, one of the most staggeringly successful in American history. Millions have left the slums, and schools played a central part in making this possible.

But the slum remains and within it the people and their children who for one reason or another cannot leave. For these it appears that the schools have been failures; but here one confronts the chicken and the egg. Are these children, hostile to school and unsuccessful in its terms, so conditioned by their surroundings against entering middle-class culture that no institution could alter them? Is the fact of the frequent racial barriers to leaving the slum

* Reprinted by permission of the publisher from James Q. Wilson, editor, THE METROPOLITAN ENIGMA, Cambridge, Mass.: Harvard University Press, Copyright 1968, by the President and Fellows of Harvard College; 1967 by Chamber of Commerce of the United States of America.

one that schools cannot overcome? Are today's city schools trying to educate only the children of those who failed to pass or who cannot pass—and have they accordingly become barren institutions, cruelly symbolizing the inevitable despair of the situation? Put another way, can schools "succeed" for those whom society holds down irrespective of merit?

It is in this context that one must see the "trouble" in our urban schools—and, in an appreciation of their past roles, their opportunity. Lumping together all schools found in big cities distorts the picture—there is as much variety of quality and kind within "big city" school systems as within the country as a whole. Nonetheless, the schools in our central cities include among them those that serve a majority of our most desperately disadvantaged population.

It is at these schools that this essay is directed. Some simple facts show the extent of the present trouble of fifteen of our largest cities.[1]

31 per cent of the children who completed ninth grade in the big cities failed to receive their high school diplomas, against 24 per cent nationally.

At least 6 per cent of the childen who start fifth grade in the big cities never start tenth grade.

In one city, the rate of unemployment for male school-leavers sixteen to twenty-one is 15 per cent higher than the rate for high-school graduates.

In the same city, 48 per cent of the boys sixteen to twenty-one with high-school diplomas were unemployed; this pattern is found in other cities.

88.4 per cent of the applicants for General Assistance in Cook County (Chicago) for a six-week period had not completed high school; again, this is found elsewhere as well.

While difficult to demonstrate statistically, it is clear that a great

1. New York, Chicago, Boston, Los Angeles, Philadelphia, Detroit, Baltimore, Houston, Cleveland, Washington, D. C., St. Louis, Milwaukee, San Francisco, Pittsburgh, Buffalo. These communities have banded together, with the help of the Ford Foundation, in the "Great Cities Program for School Improvement." (San Diego has joined the program since the writing of this article, and others may join in the near future.) Sources for these figures—which are surprisingly spare—include R. A. Dentler and M. E. Warshauer, *Big City Drop-Outs and Illiterates* (New York, 1965); M. Harrington, *The Other America* (New York, 1964); "Facts on American Education," *NEA Research Bulletin*, May 1966; U.S. Office of Education, *Digest of Educational Statistics* (Washington, 1965); D. Schreiber, *Holding Power* (Washington, 1962); J. B. Conant, *Slums and Suburbs* (New York, 1961); and D. J. Brooks, *A Study to Determine the Literary Level of Able-Bodied Persons Receiving Public Assistance* (Chicago, 1962). For the searching out of these and other data and for excellent editorial advice, I am indebted to Lawrence Robertson, now of the Beverly, Massachusetts, Public Schools.

majority of school-leavers and a large percentage of high-school graduates are unemployable save for unskilled work.

While again difficult to document, there is considerable evidence that mental illness is higher among many of the groups which these schools serve.

These figures cannot be taken to prove the failure of schools alone or in part; they may reflect conditions which other agencies as well as the schools must seek to correct. But they do suggest that the urban schools face a task far harder than the suburban schools, a task requiring imagination, considerable resources, and the concern of all Americans, not just those who live in cities. These fifteen great cities enroll over five million children, over 10 per cent of the country's precollege student body. Further, these children's families are highly mobile, some leaving the city for the suburbs. Over two-thirds move within the city, some moving again and again. The former, if ill-educated, become other communities' wards. The latter, often drawn from groups that the suburbs inadequately absorb—the racial minorities—are only more frustrated and caught.

A typical inner-city school is on a slight rise in a previously "respectable" part of the city. Many of the houses nearby have a kind of late nineteenth century grandeur left, with high windows, bay turrets, and flights of imposing stone steps. Pressing in upon them are frame "triple deckers" thirty to fifty years old, with porches out back covered with drying laundry. The school's yard is very small and backs onto the houses. Trash is in abundance.

The door of the school is locked, not to keep the children in, as some critics would think, but to keep undesirables out. To get in, one pushes a button which rings in the classroom nearest the front door. An assigned student comes out, peers at those who wish admittance, and either lets them in or informs the office.

The building dates from Grover Cleveland's second administration. It is solid, high ceilinged; the floors are well polished, but the sickly green walls need paint badly; the rooms are surprisingly cool on a warm June or September day, but the antique steam heating system is raucous on winter days. The windows in each classroom are decorated pane by pane with colorful paper cutouts made by the teacher after school. Some rooms have new, tan-colored wood and steel movable table-desks; others have older, lift-top models. In each case, the desks are arranged in rows, though only the older ones are screwed to the floor. The hall outside has a line painted down the middle; during class breaks, "no talking" and "keep to the right." Teachers are on duty at each point where the hall turns.

The teachers are proud and defensive; devoted and cynical; in many ways the most interesting, important, and neglected part of the school. They are stereotyped as rigid and out-of-date, and they deeply resent this. They are local people, by and large, and locally trained, but they protest, quite rightly, that this does not necessarily mean that they are parochial and ill-informed. They look on most visitors much as they look on the battalion of behavioral scientists which has rushed forward to explain the "pathology" of the urban school—with the contempt for (and fear of) the witch doctor who never seems to get at the root of the illness. They are at once critical and loyal to the "central office," their own school administration, and they doubt the sincerity of a federal government which largely ignores them while it makes political hay out of a national "teachers' corps" scheme to send eager but wholly inexperienced youngsters for brief tours into their schools. There are superb professionals among them, more than most critics suspect, but buried in the impersonality of the system and under a staggering load of work.

The children are quiet, well-disciplined: no "Blackboard Jungle" here. The rein is tight and one can feel the pressure, but order and quiet are maintained. Few of the children are ragged, though some are clearly undernourished. Several of the teachers, at their own expense, keep packets of dry cereal and a bottle of milk to serve as breakfast for those youngsters who come hungry to school. Attendance at school is, however, poor. Many of the students' families are constantly on the move, from one rented space in the city to another, from one school district, inevitably, to another. Statistically, 50 per cent of the children in this school in September will not be there in June.

The children's studies are a mixture of the old and the new, all in basic subjects such as reading, writing, arithmetic, social studies, civics. The older authorities, "Dick and Jane," Muzzey, and the rest are there along with the new Science Research Associates reading kits, Elementary Science Study materials, and more. All are used, however, in almost identical ways, the teacher teaching and the child listening, recording, reviewing in a workbook, and taking tests. One is struck by the paradox that the key "teachers" are the materials—the books—and yet they "teach" only as the human teacher allows them. Ask classroom teachers about this paradox and why there seems to be largely a single pedagogy, and they respond that the conditions require it—elementary school teachers are responsible for from twenty to forty children without a break during the day and secondary teachers may see between 150 and 250 different children during a day's five or more periods. They assert either that "discovery" or "student-initiated" methods are unproven with "their" kinds of children or, when tried, require more time for preparation and more materials and space than are available. They also suggest that "discovery" and "non-directive" discipline rest necessarily on middle-class values which are relatively meaningless for their children who come from other backgrounds.

What strikes one is the feeling of irrelevance. The distance between much of what the children are asked to learn and what they perceive as their needs is great. The formality of the school doesn't mesh with the informality out of school. School language isn't their language. School music, school stories, school expectations aren't theirs. This disjunction could cause rebellion (and does, in the form of "discipline problems" and dropping out), but it more often causes lassitude. School in its irrelevant way is to be endured. It is a necessary ritual to the children, meaning little more than that.

While one gets in the halls and classrooms a feeling of order, an atmosphere of learning is virtually absent. The main worries of the teachers and the administrators are social worries: principally, control and regular attendance at school, less frequently trouble at home, inattentiveness and hostility, medical and dental problems. There are many children and few adults, considering the task, and the emphasis is on control. The front door bell interrupts teaching. The public address system interrupts. The principal, taking his visitors around, interrupts every class in turn. Interruption of learning is the rule; it suggests to all, teachers and students alike, that learning is not the prime purpose of school. The principal is not the principal teacher; he is the school's policeman and judge. The school's impossible teaching schedule clearly suggests that teachers need not really teach. The teachers claim that this is not anti-intellectualism, but that it is rather misplaced purpose. The school is in fact to control children, not to teach them. The locked door, the childish window cutouts made not by children but by teachers, the white line on glossy floors by walls ill-cared-for, the bitter and misunderstood teachers—all add to a feeling not so much of desperation as confusion.

What is the school for? To move children quietly from class to class? To teach them a basic curriculum resting on a set of values and expectations irrelevant for many of the children? All suggest that simple conclusions—this city school is "bad," or understaffed, or ill-staffed—are unwise. The problems here are more complex.

Ours is not the first period where the purposes and practices of schools, city schools among them, have been under scrutiny. Two other reform periods have occurred, both in conjunction with dislocating changes within the cities themselves. The first came in the

1840s and 1850s, led by a group of Whig reformers who saw schooling as a vehicle to maintain moral and political order. These men
were Jeffersonian in their fear and hatred of urban life, and they
sought to impose what can properly be called traditional agrarian
ideals through schools. They failed, of course: the children they
hoped to reach either remained employed at work, untouched by the
saccharine injunctions of McGuffey and his imitators or, if at school,
unmoved by their plea, irrespective of attendance. Legislators spoke
in favor of schools—and then failed to appropriate money for
their adequate support. And in only a limited sense did the families
of those for whom the new city schools were primarily intended
desire and support them.[2]

The second and far larger effort at reform occurred at the turn
of the present century. The urban problems of the 1840s pale in
comparison with the post-Civil War growth of cities. Industrialization, rapid foreign immigration, and agricultural failure combined
to cause a rush to closely populated centers. With rapid growth
came the inevitable range of problems—inadequate housing, rapidly
shifting political patterns, the breakdown of traditional family
structure, inadequate police and social welfare facilities—which in
turn spawned a group of reformers whom Teddy Roosevelt promptly
labeled muckrakers. Several of these focused in part on schools and
children, most notably Joseph Mayer Rice, Jacob Riis, and Robert
Hunter.[3] Where the reformers of the 1840s had been led by such
middle-class "insiders" as there were at the time—men actively
involved with schooling, Horace Mann, James Carter, Henry
Barnard, and the rest—turn-of-the-century protest was led largely
by journalists. The reforms they suggested were ameliorative: feed
and clothe the poor and teach them to get jobs and to hold these as
dignified working-men. Their allies were drawn from a narrow
group of academic politicians and progressives—Seth Low, Nicholas
Murray Butler, Woodrow Wilson, John Dewey, Charles Eliot—and
the middle- and upper-class readers of their journals. They had
their successes, largely through private philanthropy—*noblesse
oblige*—but their gains were small and briefly enjoyed. The particular success of the period was the absorption of the foreign and
native immigrant, and the mushrooming public school system played

2. See M. B. Katz, "The Irony of Urban School Reform," unpublished doctoral
dissertation, Harvard University, 1966; and L. A. Cremin, *The American Common
School* (New York, 1951).

3. For example, Riis, *Children of the Poor* (New York, 1892); J. M. Rice, *The Public-
School Systems of the United States* (New York, 1893); Robert Hunter, *Poverty* (New
York, 1905), Chapter V. On the progressives in education generally, see L. A. Cremin,
The Transformation of the School (New York, 1961); and S. Cohen, *Progressive Education
and Urban School Reform* (New York, 1964).

a central part in this. The Three R's, rote learning, and middle-class virtues were preached; those who learned well left the slum and entered the expanding middle-class mainstream of American life.

The schools in the twentieth century grew enormously in numbers and in the services they provided, but their essential purpose remained constant—to teach simple intellectual and social skills and the folkways of the dominant culture. By the 1920s they were staffed largely with the products of the system, those who had moved "up" in the world by means of their education. Their devotion to middle-class ideology was single-minded—no cultural pluralism here. Their leadership, both inside the system and among reformers, was middle and upper class and fundamentally afraid of the changes the new city dweller might bring. In a word, both school-men and their ideological leadership were essentially conservative, the label "progressive" notwithstanding.[4] They were devoted to social reform, but within an existing set of class and economic lines. Truly radical educational ideas that emerged in the 1930s had little effect. Concern for social adaptation and control were dominant.[5]

This background is important for two purposes—to explain the shape of today's city schools and to offer a contrast with the contemporary situation. Present community leadership is drawn from a far broader spectrum of society than previously and, most importantly, includes the concerned city dweller himself. Negro leadership, especially that of the civil rights movement, is centrally involved. The federal government's effort to give the "poor" a major stake in deciding program for themselves through the local committees of community action programs is striking evidence of the change in American social reform. The potential political force of the emerging (though still fragile) alliance of liberal middle-class reformers in the older tradition and the poor is considerable, and the chance that lasting gains may be possible is substantially greater than ever before. Schooling is important to this new alliance (though the purpose of that schooling is still unclear and a clash of traditional and radical positions inevitable). As it has political power, much increased resources will flow to it—as indeed they already have.

4. It is illuminating that most of the successful truly "progressive" educational experiment attempts before World War II took place in independent schools or their virtual equivalent within public school systems. Save in the extension of services, "progressivism" of a pedagogical sort reached neither city public nor parochial schools in any significant measure. See S. J. Clark, "Two Schools and Two Ideas: A Study of Progressivism in Boston, 1920–40," unpublished doctoral dissertation, Harvard University, 1965; and Cremin, *The Transformation of the School*, Chapter 7.

5. See, for an example of radical thought, George S. Counts, *Dare the Schools Build a New Social Order* (New York, 1932); and copies of *Social Frontier*, 1934–1939. See also R. Hofstadter, *Anti-Intellectualism in American Life* (New York, 1963), Chapter 7.

The strategy for reform demanded today is no different than heretofore: to decide what the schools should do and then to harness the men with the money to see that those ends are met. According to the conventional wisdom, educational goals are set by "lay" boards of education. This is far from what really happens. Like most policies, educational policy is largely shaped by clusters of interest groups and bureaucrats. Most boards of education and school committees react to ideas rather than create them.[6]

A new educational policy must meet certain constraints. First, the social, economic, and cultural problems of the city cannot be solved by schools alone, and school policy aimed at their alleviation must be closely locked into a plan that encompasses all social organizations. Evidence is overwhelming that schooling is but a minor influence on many children,[7] and while one might try to improve schools to alter this, at the same time one must take into account "nonschool" educational influences—the street corner, the union, church, job, television. The approach might be centered in the school department as in New Haven with its "community schools," or it might lead to a new kind of group such as New York's "human resource" agency under Mitchell Sviridoff. In sum, those educational ends best reached within schoolhouses should be worked toward there; but, in turn, those which are better handled elsewhere—for example, some aspects of technical education or of civics—put elsewhere.[8]

Second, the ends of education (*not* the organization and control of the largest number of children at the least cost) should govern the shape of schoolhouses. This sounds so obvious as to be absurd, yet even the most casual visit to many schools (suburban as well as urban, it must be admitted) demonstrates the irrelevance of much of what is going on. Such irrelevance is the *prime* blight on American education, far more grievous than understaffing, skimpy funding, and poor housing.

What policies are implied here? Clearly, some agency broader than present school departments (as they are now most usually constituted) must plan and direct educational programs, both those in schools and those out of schools. More difficult, however, is the

6. See Neal Gross, *Who Runs Our Schools?* (New York, 1958), and R. A. Dahl, *Who Governs?* (New Haven, 1961), for two case studies.

7. U.S. Office of Education, "Equality of Educational Opportunity" (Washington, 1966). This study, headed by James Coleman of Johns Hopkins University, raises a wide series of questions and is discussed below.

8. The inclusion of civics may surprise some. Donald W. Oliver and Fred M. Newmann deal with this issue in a chapter of *Religion in Public Education*, published in 1967 by Houghton Mifflin.

question of purpose. Insofar as is possible, I would like to argue, schooling should be deliberately pluralistic, primarily focused on teaching people alternatives and providing them the means to act upon them. One teaches not an American creed (as though there were only *one*) but the reasons for and the substance of the tensions that make American life viable (one studies Jefferson and Jackson less as presidents and more as representatives of different, important ideological positions). One tolerates a wide variety of views, and only insists on their rational justification. One teaches the skills children need to get ahead, not the skills tradition may impose. (This involves a list of priorities, for, as Benjamin Franklin observed on this topic over two hundred years ago, art is long and time is short. For example, one decreases the study of literary criticisms in favor of more work in exposition; slights the study of plane geometry for work in the binary number system; cuts back on cabinet making and upholstery in favor of electronics.) One deliberately rewards a variety of forms of expression—visual, spoken, musical—not just that of the written language.

While this argument for schools to teach "alternatives," for a deliberate educational pluralism, requires more discussion than can be made here, even in its simplest form it suggests a school of a clearly different character than that of the present. It would be a school where the child would move at his own pace and not be grouped necessarily by chronological age. The variety among teachers would be capitalized upon, and students would be exposed to and deal with many kinds of adults. The curriculum would not be "tracked," would be broad, and would accommodate itself to the progress of individual children. The vast resources of the city outside of the school rooms would be used.

This is hardly a radical conception. It has been suggested for sixty years or more and tried in a variety of guises. The Dalton Plan, briefly attempted in New York City among other places, is one partial experiment from the 1920s and there are others. The Pittsburgh schools are experimenting along these lines today, and there is much talk there and elsewhere of "individualized instruction," "flexible scheduling" and "team teaching."[9] All seek to loosen up the controlled school and to let the needs of the children chart the shape of the curriculum, and in this sense they are at fundamental

9. See J. T. Shaplin and H. Olds, eds., *Team Teaching* (New York, 1964); R. Bush and D. Allen, *A Design for High-School Education* (New York, 1964); T. I. Goodlad and R. H. Anderson, *The Nongraded Elementary School*, rev. ed. (New York, 1963); and various relevant articles in the special issue on computer technology of *Saturday Review*, July 23, 1966. In a somewhat different vein, see also Nat Hentoff, *Our Children Are Dying* (New York, 1966).

cross-purposes with the traditional school, in the city and elsewhere.

If these be the elements of present reform, two facets are yet lacking The issue of values has not been fully faced. Does the teacher accept the values of the child's parents or impose his own values? Does one acknowledge and encourage the rebellion of the children of aggrieved groups, such as many Negroes, or does one try to discourage a rebellious nature? Until this issue is faced, and until school authorities recognize the contradiction between a scheme for truly educating individuals in a pluralistic setting and the present system, the experiments going forward will founder. The second element lacking is the resources for a vast experiment, one which goes beyond one "computerized classroom" or one "team teaching" school. A cluster of ideas needs to be tried out together, supported by a clear, if tentative, ideology, the kind that most educators tend to avoid. Boston's proposed "sub-system" (a portion of the public school system set aside for experiment) could be a forerunner here, as could similar plans in other cities, but it would require several hundred times the resources now available and an autonomy not now provided. Education is expensive and, while much of it in its present form is inefficient, any truly effective form will cost substantial sums. Efficiency should be one test of an experiment, but experiments, with their false starts and wrong assumptions, are inherently expensive. Resources for a major trial must be found.

Whatever the trial, whatever the purpose or purposes freshly identified for schooling (urban *and* suburban it must be said), the need for a redefinition of this purpose is clear. Curiously we tend to shy away from it or we feel we can leave it to clichés or for philosophical fights in the academy. We miss the striking incongruity of the non-learning of our learning institutions, of the anti-intellectualism or the non-intellectualism of our supposed cradles of rationalism and intellect. The professionals in education and concerned laymen must confront this.

While long-range restructuring of the system is clearly necessary, there is yet worthwhile and badly needed intermediate-range work to be done. There is the central problem of people, the persons who staff the schools and those who, as "lay" representatives, serve supposedly as policy makers.

No large public service is so weakly staffed as is education. Teaching is a form of personal service, and the staff Americans employ is enormous, over two million in public and private elementary and secondary schools in 1965–66. But the average educator, on several counts, leaves a good deal to be desired. First, he is drawn from the lower academic levels of the colleges and hardly at all from highly selective undergraduate institutions.[10] Second, he stays at the game of teaching (or counseling or administering) but a short time, around five years. This is a result in part, of course, of the fact of many young women in the teaching profession, and it makes continuity in many schools difficult, city schools among them. Third, his training has focused not on the profound ethical issues which educating implies (in spite of courses in "philosophy" of education), but rather on the tools of an unexamined trade. And fourth, once on the job, he is largely cut off from contacts with the academic, political, and financial worlds by tradition and by the incredible time demand of his job.

What to do? Until professional leadership is strengthened, the situation in the schools will not be improved. First, the conditions of teaching must be improved—time demands, salaries, conditions of work, status. Considering the difficulty and subtlety of their tasks, teachers are grievously overworked. The average elementary school teacher has but a few minutes off a day from overseeing (much less seriously teaching) twenty-five or more pupils. The average secondary school teacher "teaches" over 150 different pupils a day, pupils he is supposed to understand and nurture as individuals. On top of their teaching, teachers have to keep up their subjects, prepare for future instruction, and correct and grade papers. Top this with the common practice of "moonlighting"—to earn extra money through odd jobs to help one's budget—and one sees the impossibility of the task. The psychic rewards of teaching clearly attract idealistic young people: if we can show them that in this job these rewards are fully attainable and that the teacher's self-respect and dignity are assured, the principal hurdle to recruiting will be overcome. Current public focus on big-city education makes these schools particularly attractive to many potential teachers. The conditions of employment— not the children, not the communities—presently give them pause. Perhaps the current militancy among big city teachers is a happy sign here. While the initial union-school board struggles were primarily over salaries, the raising for collective bargaining by some locals of the issue of conditions of work may spur school authorities to improve them. Militancy often spurs self-respect, and while unionization (or its virtual carbon copy among certain large-city National Education Association "professional" groups) has brought problems,

10. According to norms computed for the Miller Analogies Test, the mean score of prospective teachers on that test is lower than that of any other academic or industrial group with a college degree. W. S. Miller, *Miller Analogies Test Manual, 1960 Revision.* The Graduate Record Examination corroborates this finding.

on the whole it has been a constructive movement. Teachers are looking after their own interests, and if these can be held in most respects consonant with their children's interests, much can be achieved.

Recruiting new teachers is, of course, far more difficult and time-consuming than making better use of those of high quality already in the schools. The top career people now in service must be the principal keys to school reform, and communities should work hard to find them. Some form of team teaching will be necessary both to use them more effectively and to defend paying the extra sums they deserve. Sometimes, the ablest teachers are not the pleasantest and certainly not the most docile—precisely those whom many school systems identify and reward the least. Lay groups can play a part here in spotting these persons and rewarding them in one way or another, with sabbatical grants, extra stipends, and so forth, even though (or perhaps because) it embarrasses the formal administration of the system.

Third, experienced persons from other professions will have to be lured into careers in the schools and local school and state licensing authorities persuaded to accept them. Many of the problems of operating a large school system are only partially educational and cut across many aspects of public administration and law. Persons from those fields should be recruited. (Why, for example, should a first-class teacher who has been promoted to a principalship arrange bus schedules, keep accounts, struggle with custodians, and deal extensively with local political concerns? Why can't he concentrate on instruction and have an appropriately trained colleague handle these other matters under his supervision? The present waste of most principals'—and in like measure, high school department chairmen's—time is scandalous.)

Part-time help for non-teaching tasks is also an obvious step, but one used far less than one might expect. Many teachers apparently are ill at ease and distrustful of other adults in "their" classrooms, and there has been surprisingly little call for such help from the professionals. However, one can see a triple virtue for schools hiring mothers from, for example, poor families to work as aides: the women can well use the money, earned on a time schedule that will allow them to be at home when their children are at home; the jobs would provide them with experience and training in child care, the most appropriate concern for many of them; and the program would bring into the many classrooms which are staffed with middle-class teachers women familiar with the children's view of the world, their expectations, and their language.

In spite of teachers' and administrators' claim that a locally reared and trained staff is not unduly parochial, more variety of background is undoubtedly needed in many systems, if for no other reason than to allow children to meet adults from highly different backgrounds. Many large cities recruit hard: Los Angeles, for example, has several teams on the road constantly. By contrast, until the last few years the New York City schools had but one man to handle their entire recruiting effort in a city with a staff of over 40,000. Fortunately, that community has changed its recruiting policies substantially. Many cities have special examinations which are a nuisance for outsiders to take, and their administrative policies are hardly geared to lure strong personnel from other places. Salaries have improved in recent years, owing in part to pressure from organized teachers; beginning salaries for teachers with bachelor's degrees in the fifteen largest cities ranged from $4,590 to $6,120 with a median of $5,300 against a nationwide median of $5,000.[11] Top salaries are high, with that of Chicago's superintendent being one of the highest in the country.

These suggestions are neither novel nor radical; they just beg for resources and firm administration. Efforts at political reform, however, may be less obvious but perhaps more important. Where school board tenure is a rung on a ladder of political promotion, a position for party patronage, or a post of excessively short and impotent character, little progress is made. Education is a political matter as it touches on matters of great sensitivity and controversy. It *must* be a political matter, in the best sense: close to popular will and capable of change, not at popular whim but by a clear and studied popular mandate. Government must find devices to allow for this.

The fifteen Great City schools have a wide variety of governing bodies, from Boston's highly political, elected, and short-term committee to New York's long term, Mayor-appointed board. The latter, by the operation of its nominating commission, has much to commend it, the former only that it stays close to what it detects as local majority opinion. Much has been written on this subject, and various schemes such as that in New York have clear merit. It may take vigorous action by state governments, as it did in New York, to establish sound governing boards for those remaining cities seriously in need of them. Pressure must also be applied by local interest groups, such as New York's Public Education Association and

---

11. Research Council of the Great Cities Program for School Improvement, "Teachers' Salary Analysis of the Great Cities 1965–66" (1965); National Education Association, "Salary Schedules for Classroom Teachers, 1965–66" (1965).

Cleveland's PACE. These groups, if organized behind constructive and realistic programs and employed with political acumen, can have powerful effect. Too often they are dominated by middle-class ideals (rather than a commitment to pluralism), are unrealistic, and are politically naive.

If sound purposes and men are crucial to reform, so is money. The cities spend vast sums of it, and education is often the largest item on their budgets, though not to the overwhelming extent it is in the majority of suburbs. (Welfare in a few cities takes first place at the public trough.) New York spends $737.45 per child per year, Los Angeles $512.85, Miami (Dade County) $410.54, and Cleveland $434.16. The national average per-pupil expenditure is about $500.[12] Why, then, are the cities so in "trouble?" For the obvious reason that it costs more to school the city's children, so many of whom are culturally "disadvantaged," and on real estate and with services which come dear in congested settings. If one compares the number of citizens in elementary and secondary school—over fifty million in 1961, 26 per cent of the total population—the country's investment in their future is niggardly. The percentage of America's gross national product devoted to education has not appreciably risen in the last fifty years; surely we can tolerate a rise without discomfort.[13] The largest single federal program for education, Title 1 of the Elementary and Secondary Education Act of 1965, currently totals but one billion dollars a year, less than one month's expenditures on the war in Viet Nam. It is worth repeating in this context the point that schools are inefficient and must be made less so; but this does not mean that improvements in efficiency will end in a cost to taxpayers the same or less. To do the minimal job of schooling that is clearly called for may cost more, and we should be prepared for it.

Where are these resources to come from? More and more, surprising to say, from private industry in the form of vastly improved teaching materials and devices, in-plant "vocational" training jointly sponsored with public authorities, and sponsored materials over the mass media. Industry's stake in the education market is growing and is best evidenced by the entrance into it of previously uninvolved companies such as IBM, Raytheon, and General Electric. Their most important single short-range impact

12. National Education Association, "Expenditures of Large Local School Systems" (1966). It must be noted that inter-city comparisons indicate only a general tendency, and are misleading in detail.

13. Charles S. Benson, *The Economics of Public Education* (Boston, 1961), p. 53. In 1958–59, total public school expenditures were a mere 3.09 per cent of the gross national product.

may well be the pressure they put on public authorities, particularly the federal government, for the additional resources necessary for their wares to be purchased. They will be unaccustomed and powerful allies for the professional education lobby. The excellence of their wares will be a measure of their public responsibility.

Federal aid to the schools generally and to city schools in particular has been rapidly growing, but direct aid only accounted in 1965 for 1.3 per cent of total elementary and secondary public school expenditure in the Great Cities (except Washington).[14] The proportion was substantially higher in some cities, however, as they contain large numbers of the poor toward whom many of the programs are directed. Federal funds will have to increase, as, in many areas, state and particularly local funds have been pushed to the limit.

Better men and more money: obvious remedies, and a part of the present rhetoric of urban education. The prior condition of a clearly stated purpose which is directly met by the schools is less obvious and, perhaps, more important in the long run than the other two elements. Good men and vast sums are spent today controlling children and attempting to feed them a curriculum and a set of values which are in part irrelevant and, for some, insulting. The latent (or not so latent) hostility of many children to the so-called process of education is evidence not so much of a spirit to be broken as of the inadequate scope of schools.

It goes without saying that no particular issue is more pressing on many city school systems today than that of racial balance. Staffing, housing, finances—all are important but big-city school boards and administrators are more disturbed by this issue than by any other. And for good reason. In a country that is 11.4 per cent nonwhite, the fifteen Great Cities have total populations that are 21.1 per cent nonwhite. The school-age population of these cities is 24.8 per cent nonwhite, but the nonwhite public school population is even higher, as non-public schools are largely Caucasian and the nonwhite families in the cities tend to be larger than those of whites. In Philadelphia, which has a population that is 30 per cent nonwhite, 57 per cent of the public school enrollment is nonwhite. Seventeen per cent of Boston's public schools had over 90 per cent nonwhite pupils in a year (1960) when that city's nonwhite population was only 9.8 per cent. One city, Washington, D.C., has a nonwhite public school enrollment of 90 per cent, the highest in the nation. More striking is the fact that the percentage of nonwhites in most of these cities and especially in their public schools is steadily and rapidly

14. Research Council of the Great Cities Program for School Improvement, "Sources of Revenue for the Public Schools of the Great Cities" (1965).

rising. Owing to birth rates higher among Negroes than whites, the age cohort shortly to enter school will be between 15 per cent and 17 per cent Negro; given increasing white enrollments in private schools, the nation's elementary schools may be 25 per cent Negro by 1985. These are national figures; and clearly the cores of the majority of our great metropolitan areas will shortly be predominantly Negro.[15]

The issue here for schools—and it is a hotly contested issue—turns on the belief of many educators that children of different races must live and work together if they are going to learn to respect and tolerate one another. An open-minded attitude toward others, the argument goes, comes little from book learning or exhortation; it comes rather from real experience.[16] The best opportunity society now has to acquire the "mixing" of all persons is within the public schools. Accordingly those who would teach the virtues of full integration preach the necessity of starting this social revolution in classrooms.

There are, of course, opponents to this view, both Negro and white. Some argue what seems a higher virtue, the neighborhood school. Children, this argument goes, should attend school with those with whom they live all the time and not with relative strangers from other parts of town. Others see the problem as not primarily a racial one, but an economic one, calling not for a deliberate mixing of races in classrooms but rather a massive "compensatory" education program which will allow all children eventually to compete in the economy as equals. Still others, both Negro and white, argue for racially segregated schools on theoretical grounds, not unlike the arguments of early immigrant groups who wished to preserve their traditions against swamping by a majority culture.

The debate on this issue received a fillip (rather than a conclusion) with the publication in July 1966 of a massive study by the United States Office of Education entitled, *Equal Educational Opportunity* (otherwise dubbed the "Coleman Report" after its senior author).[17] The study, required by the Civil Rights Act of 1964, was on the effects of segregated and integrated schooling on Negro

15. U.S. Bureau of the Census, *U.S. Census of Population and Housing: 1960 Housing Tracts* (1962); Joseph M. Cronin, "Catholic Schools and Racial Balance," *Commonweal*, October 7, 1966; Commission on School Integration, National Association of Intergroup Relations Officials, "Public School Segregation and Integration in the North" (1963); (Pittsburgh) Board of Public Education, "The Quest for Racial Equality in the Pittsburgh Public Schools" (1965); and figures from a forthcoming volume on the Negro family by Daniel Patrick Moynihan.

16. See, for example, Kenneth Clark, *Dark Ghetto* (New York, 1965), Chapter 6.

17. U.S.O.E., "Equality of Educational Opportunity," *op. cit.* See, especially, Chapters 1–3.

children and their white colleagues. With all its imperfections, the massive study (750,000 children were tested, making the program the second largest social science survey in history) is highly suggestive. Social and economic class is found to be the overwhelming influence upon school learning (as defined by written achievement tests—and this is an admittedly narrow definition). Put more bluntly, your father and your mother control your education opportunity much more than do your teachers; it is difficult indeed, it appears, to break out from one's birthright. By and large, newer school buildings, more teachers, more materials, libraries, special programs, and the rest did not alter the central fact of socio-economic determinism. The school as the vehicle of upward social mobility did not seem to be operating in 1965–66.

These findings bear directly on the discrimination issue by suggesting that economic and social exclusion may be as powerful restraints on equal opportunity as is race. It is hard to overcome your ancestry whatever your color. The racial problem is compounded by this: Negro children from poor families tend not to achieve because they are poor—and their color clearly makes it difficult for their parents to become less poor.

Integrated schooling produces some gain, but it is small and uneven. When Negro children in the Northeastern states went to integrated schools, their achievement increased by roughly one year (that is, their reading level, for example, was one grade ahead of comparable children in segregated schools)—and this finding is consistent even when social class is controlled. Findings for other parts of the country are less hopeful or are confused. All one can say is that integrated schooling in some areas of the country seems to make a small difference for Negro children. It is a comfort, but small comfort, for those who wish to use the present schools to increase Negro rights.

The report supports another hypothesis: schools are but part of the process of socialization and present schools are considerably less powerful influences than family and friends. Perhaps this is because formal education is by its nature relatively impotent. But perhaps it is so because contemporary schools are a shadow of what they could be—irrelevant, shoddy, anti-intellectual. Perhaps powerful schools could make a difference. Cast within a large public effort to help children, they very well might be. We need a trial—and then another report.

Notwithstanding these positions, the social and political demand for the elimination of racially imbalanced schools is, not surprisingly, strong in many cities. Its realization founders on the simple fact of the imbalance of whole school systems. You cannot desegregate a predominantly Negro system if you do not have whites with whom to integrate. If ending imbalance is to be a goal, then the *only* long-range solution is to redraw system boundaries—to create, for the sake of racial balance, large metropolitan school systems of such variety as to allow desired "mixing" of racial (and, for that matter, of economic and social) groups.[18]

This prospect scares most people. It spells the end, they fear, of local control, and of schools close to the people. It would require, they argue, a vast bureaucracy which would ignore the individual even more than present bureaucracies. It would encourage, some even feel, greater federal control.

These worries are misplaced. At the same time that one centralizes some functions (such as the allocation of children to schools) one should also decentralize others. Curricular decisions, the choice of texts, the length of classes and sessions, the mix of teachers: these matters should be delegated directly to the school principal who, with the teachers and parents, knows the children best. A broadening of school boundaries should be accompanied by a plan to decentralize many purely educational decisions and to involve the directly served community in the reaching of these. Even a casual look at, for example, the London County Council schools in England will show that it can be done. Thus we need to move in two directions at once: to centralize some functions and to decentralize others. The former alone will lead to a deadening bureaucracy, as many of our present large school systems already demonstrate. The latter alone will lead to missed opportunities and parochialism.

Metropolitan allocation of children is a necessity if we are to have in communities any sort of racial or socio-economic balance: this is obvious. But there are other virtues, ones of possibly even greater long-term importance. New kinds of programs for children and adults may be possible. Certain economies may result from the elimination of small, duplicated offices. The wide area could easily support strong schools for special purposes that could concentrate on the problems of groups such as the deaf, the retarded, the blind, and those otherwise handicapped. The region might also be able to support, perhaps in conjunction with the state, systems of collegiate

---

18. This is not to suggest that other remedies—internal redistricting, educational "parks," busing, and the rest—will not serve well in some settings. For a metropolitan plan for racial balance purposes, see "Schools for Hartford," Center for Field Studies, Harvard Graduate School of Education, 1965. It is well also to note that some cities, such as parts of New York, Washington, and Chicago, may be so densely segregated as to be impossible to "balance."

and technical education which could be functionally related to lower schools. Of great importance is the possibility of far more diverse sources of local tax revenues, sufficient, perhaps, in many areas to maintain an independence of overwhelming state and federal aid.

Big-city schools have, since the turn of the century, provided millions of new and old Americans the means to move into the center of the economy and society. The schools' means for doing this were simple; today, with many persons in slum situations whom the society will not absorb, different and more flexible steps must be taken. Further, the inflexibility of traditional practice, with its control and order, stifles and warps. Schools, and all the other institutions which educate, should concern themselves first with learning in the broadest sense and with the learning most appropriate for each individual. Individual rights have become a cliché for educators; perhaps that is why they have never been fully respected. We must start with this respect, and reshape our institutions accordingly.

What, then, is a sound public policy for urban schools?

To demand of educators a fundamental review and recasting of present schools to eliminate the irrelevant and shoddy, as a condition for massive new funding;

to launch comprehensive educational planning across all agencies that teach, schools and others together;

to redefine educational communities, to capitalize upon the needs and strengths of entire metropolitan regions and, concurrently, to decentralize many educational matters to individual schools and to the particular communities which they serve.

10 JAMES S. COLEMAN AND OTHERS

Equality of educational opportunity (Summary)

SEGREGATION IN THE PUBLIC SCHOOLS

The great majority of American children attend schools that are largely segregated—that is, where almost all of their fellow students are of the same racial background as they are. Among minority groups, Negroes are by far the most segregated. Taking all groups, however, white children are most segregated. Almost 80 percent of all white pupils in 1st grade and 12th grade attend schools that are from 90 to 100 percent white. And 97 percent at grade 1, and 99 percent at grade 12, attend schools that are 50 percent or more white.

For Negro pupils, segregation is more nearly complete in the South (as it is for whites also), but it is extensive also in all the other regions where the Negro population is concentrated: the urban North, Midwest, and West.

More than 65 percent of all Negro pupils in the first grade attend schools that are between 90 and 100 percent Negro. And 87 percent at grade 1, and 66 percent at grade 12, attend schools that are 50 percent or more Negro. In the South most students attend schools that are 100 percent white or Negro (see Figures 10–1 through 10–4).

The same pattern of segregation holds, though not quite so

strongly, for the teachers of Negro and white students. For the nation as a whole, the average Negro elementary pupil attends a school in which 65 percent of the teachers are Negro; the average white elementary pupil attends a school in which 97 percent of the

Figure 10—1

WHITE PUPILS—ALL REGIONS
GRADE 1

**PERCENT OF WHITE STUDENTS IN SCHOOLS
OF DIFFERING RACIAL COMPOSITION**

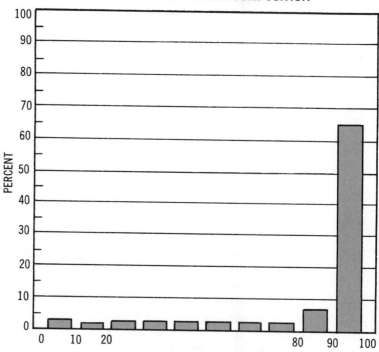

RACIAL COMPOSITION OF SCHOOL (PERCENT WHITE)

teachers are white. White teachers are more predominant at the secondary level, where the corresponding figures are 59 and 97 percent. The racial matching of teachers is most pronounced in the South, where by tradition it has been complete. On a nationwide basis, in cases where the races of pupils and teachers are not matched, the trend is all in one direction: white teachers teach Negro children but Negro teachers seldom teach white children; just as, in the schools, integration consists primarily of a minority of Negro pupils

in predominantly white schools but almost never of a few whites in
largely Negro schools.

In its desegregation decision of 1954, the Supreme Court held
that separate schools for Negro and white children are inherently

Figure 10—2

NEGRO PUPILS—ALL REGIONS
GRADE 1

**PERCENT OF NEGRO STUDENTS IN SCHOOLS
OF DIFFERING RACIAL COMPOSITION**

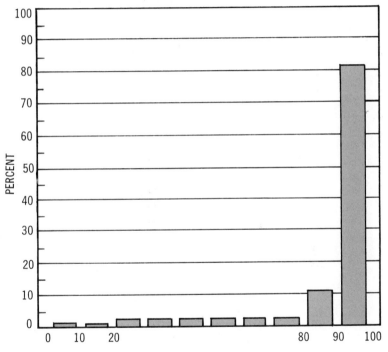

RACIAL COMPOSITION OF SCHOOL (PERCENT NEGRO)

unequal. This survey finds that, when measured by that yardstick,
American public education remains largely unequal in most regions
of the country, including all those where Negroes form any significant proportion of the population. Obviously, however, that is not
the only yardstick. . . .

THE SCHOOLS AND THEIR CHARACTERISTICS

The school environment of a child consists of many elements,
ranging from the desk he sits at to the child who sits next to him, and

including the teacher who stands at the front of his class. A statistical survey can give only fragmentary evidence of this environment.

Great collections of numbers such as are found in these pages—totals and averages and percentages—blur and obscure rather than

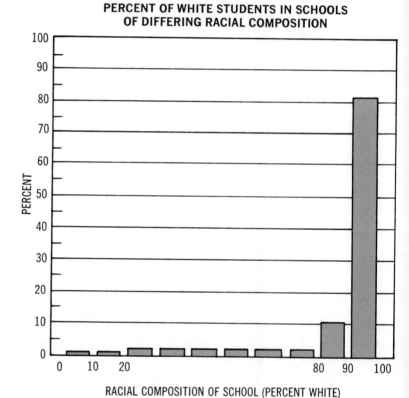

Figure 10—3
WHITE PUPILS—ALL REGIONS
GRADE 12

**PERCENT OF WHITE STUDENTS IN SCHOOLS
OF DIFFERING RACIAL COMPOSITION**

RACIAL COMPOSITION OF SCHOOL (PERCENT WHITE)

sharpen and illuminate the range of variation they represent. If one reads, for example, that the average annual income per person in the State of Maryland is $3,000, there is a tendency to picture an average person living in moderate circumstances in a middle-class neighborhood holding an ordinary job. But that number represents at the upper end millionaires, and at the lower end the unemployed, the pensioners, the charwomen. Thus the $3,000 average income should somehow bring to mind the tycoon and the tramp, the showcase and the shack, as well as the average man in the average house.

So, too, in reading these statistics on education, one must picture the child whose school has every conceivable facility that is believed to enhance the educational process, whose teachers may be particu-

Figure 10—4

NEGRO PUPILS—ALL REGIONS
GRADE 12

**PERCENT OF NEGRO STUDENTS IN SCHOOLS
OF DIFFERING RACIAL COMPOSITION**

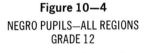

RACIAL COMPOSITION OF SCHOOL (PERCENT NEGRO)

larly gifted and well educated, and whose home and total neighborhood are themselves powerful contributors to his education and growth. And one must picture the child in a dismal tenement area who may come hungry to an ancient, dirty building that is badly ventilated, poorly lighted, overcrowded, understaffed, and without sufficient textbooks.

Statistics, too, must deal with one thing at a time, and cumulative effects tend to be lost in them. Having a teacher without a college degree indicates an element of disadvantage, but in the concrete situation, a child may be taught by a teacher who is not only without a degree but who has grown up and received his schooling in the local community, who has never been out of the State, who has a 10th-grade vocabulary, and who shares the local community's attitudes.

One must also be aware of the relative importance of a certain kind of thing to a certain kind of person. Just as a loaf of bread means more to a starving man than to a sated one, so one very fine textbook or, better, one very able teacher, may mean far more to a deprived child than to one who already has several of both.

Finally, it should be borne in mind that in cases where Negroes in the South receive unequal treatment, the significance in terms of actual numbers of individuals involved is very great, since 54 percent of the Negro population of school-going age, or approximately 3,200,000 children, live in that region.

All of the findings reported in this section of the summary are based on responses to questionnaires filled out by public school teachers, principals, district school superintendents, and pupils. The data were gathered in September and October of 1965 from 4,000 public schools. All teachers, principals, and district superintendents in these schools participated, as did all pupils in the 3rd, 6th, 9th, and 12th grades. First-grade pupils in half the schools participated. More than 645,000 pupils in all were involved in the survey. About 30 percent of the schools selected for the survey did not participate; an analysis of the nonparticipating schools indicated that their inclusion would not have significantly altered the results of the survey. The participation rates were: in the metropolitan North and West, 72 percent; metropolitan South and Southwest, 65 percent; non-metropolitan North and West, 82 percent; non-metropolitan South and Southwest 61 percent.

All the statistics on the physical facilities of the schools and the academic and extracurricular programs are based on information provided by the teachers and administrators. They also provided information about their own education, experience, and philosophy of education, and described as they see them the socioeconomic characteristics of the neighborhoods served by their schools.

The statistics having to do with the pupils' personal socioeconomic backgrounds, level of education of their parents, and certain items in their homes (such as encyclopedias, daily newspapers, etc.) are based on pupil responses to questionnaires. The pupils also answered questions about their academic aspirations and their attitudes toward staying in school.

All personal and school data were confidential and for statistical purposes only; the questionnaires were collected without the names or other personal identification of the respondents.

Data for Negro and white children are classified by whether the schools are in metropolitan areas or not. The definition of a metropolitan area is the one commonly used by government agencies: a city of over 50,000 inhabitants including its suburbs. All other schools in small cities, towns, or rural areas are referred to as nonmetropolitan schools. Finally, for most tables, data for Negro and white children are classified by geographical regions. . . .

Facilities

The two tables which follow (Table 10–1, for elementary schools, and Table 10–2, for secondary) list certain school characteristics and the percentages of pupils of the various races who are enrolled in schools which have those characteristics. Where specified by "average" the figures represent actual numbers rather than percentages. Reading from left to right, percentages or averages are given on a nationwide basis for the six groups; then comparisons between Negro and white access to the various facilities are made on the basis of regional and metropolitan-nonmetropolitan breakdowns.

Thus, in Table 10–1, it will be seen that for the nation as a whole white children attend elementary schools with a smaller average number of pupils per room (29) than do any of the minorities (which range from 30 to 33). Farther to the right are the regional breakdowns for whites and Negroes, and it can be seen that in some regions the nationwide pattern is reversed: in the non-metropolitan North and West and Southwest for example, there is a smaller average number of pupils per room for Negroes than for whites.

The same item on Table 10–2 shows that secondary school whites have a smaller average number of pupils per room than minorities, except Indians. Looking at the regional breakdown, however, one finds much more striking differences than the national average would suggest: In the metropolitan Midwest, for example, the average Negro has 54 pupils per room—probably reflecting considerable frequency of double sessions—compared with 33 per room for whites. Nationally, at the high school level the average white has 1 teacher for every 22 students and the average Negro has 1 for every 26 students. (See Table 10–6b.)

It is thus apparent that the tables must be studied carefully, with special attention paid to the regional breakdowns, which often provide more meaningful information than do the nationwide averages. Such careful study will reveal that there is not a wholly

Table 10-1—Percent (except where average specified) of pupils in *elementary* schools having the school characteristic named at left, fall 1965

Characteristic	Whole Nation						Nonmetropolitan						Metropolitan									
							NORTH AND WEST		SOUTH		SOUTH-WEST		NORTH-EAST		MID-WEST		SOUTH		SOUTH-WEST		WEST	
	MA	PR	IA	OA	Neg.	Maj.	Neg.	Maj.	Neg.	Maj.	Neg.	Maj.	Neg.	Maj.	Neg.	Maj.	Neg.	Maj.	Neg.	Maj.	Neg.	Maj.
Age of main building:																						
Less than 20 years	59	57	66	61	63	60	48	54	72	34	73	40	31	59	28	63	77	75	52	89	76	80
20 to 40 years	18	18	20	20	17	20	35	13	21	43	17	28	23	23	18	18	11	20	27	10	14	9
At least 40 years	22	24	13	18	18	18	17	32	4	20	9	29	43	18	53	18	12	4	21	1	7	7
Average pupils per room	33	31	30	33	32	19	25	28	34	26	21	31	33	30	34	30	30	31	39	26	37	31
Auditorium	20	31	18	21	27	19	3	5	16	40	14	19	56	40	27	10	20	21	11	1	47	12
Cafeteria	39	43	38	30	38	37	41	33	46	64	47	54	41	45	24	22	34	32	48	38	34	14
Gymnasium	19	27	20	14	15	21	9	8	15	31	15	21	46	49	36	19	6	5	13	17	0	8
Infirmary	59	62	64	77	71	68	52	52	49	44	38	39	74	74	74	79	81	76	59	48	93	96
Full-time librarian	22	31	22	24	30	22	4	13	32	22	5	11	46	43	22	15	38	50	11	12	19	13
Free textbooks	80	82	80	85	84	75	73	56	70	73	99	98	100	98	72	54	84	82	83	65	98	100
School has sufficient number of textbooks	90	87	91	93	84	96	97	99	76	94	97	96	90	97	97	99	74	98	82	84	95	90
Texts under 4 years old	66	68	60	52	67	61	66	51	60	60	47	85	57	56	67	59	71	91	76	53	77	77
Central school library	69	71	72	83	73	72	44	58	74	77	48	75	83	89	57	70	79	69	59	33	81	95
Free lunch program	64	73	66	52	74	59	61	50	87	94	83	70	50	43	42	48	90	85	74	82	65	47

Note: In this Summary section, the group identifications are abbreviated as follows: MA—Mexican American; PR—Puerto Rican; IA—Indian American; OA—Oriental American; Neg.—Negro; and Maj.—majority or white.

Table 10-2—Percent (except where average specified) of pupils in *secondary* schools having the school characteristic named at left, fall 1965

Legend: Column groups — **Whole Nation** (MA, PR, IA, OA, Neg, Maj); **Nonmetropolitan** (North and West, South, South-West — each Neg/Maj); **Metropolitan** (North-East, Mid-West, South, South-West, West — each Neg/Maj).

Characteristic	WN MA	WN PR	WN IA	WN OA	WN Neg	WN Maj	NM N&W Neg	NM N&W Maj	NM South Neg	NM South Maj	NM S-W Neg	NM S-W Maj	M N-E Neg	M N-E Maj	M Mid-W Neg	M Mid-W Maj	M South Neg	M South Maj	M S-W Neg	M S-W Maj	M West Neg	M West Maj
Age of main building:																						
Less than 20 years	48	40	49	41	60	53	64	35	79	52	76	44	18	64	33	43	74	84	76	43	53	79
20 to 40 years	40	31	35	32	26	29	15	26	13	33	22	46	41	20	38	37	18	14	16	56	46	19
At least 40 years	11	28	15	32	12	18	21	38	3	15	3	10	40	15	29	20	3	0	6	1	2	3
Average pupils per room	32	33	29	32	34	31	27	30	35	28	22	20	35	28	54	33	30	34	28	42	31	30
Auditorium	57	68	49	66	49	46	32	27	21	36	56	68	77	72	51	44	49	40	67	57	72	45
Cafeteria	72	80	74	81	72	65	55	41	65	78	78	97	88	73	55	54	77	97	75	63	77	79
Gymnasium	78	88	70	83	64	74	51	52	38	63	71	71	90	90	75	76	52	80	70	77	99	95
Shop with power tools	96	88	96	98	89	96	97	96	85	90	88	91	67	97	99	100	89	90	92	97	100	100
Biology laboratory	95	84	96	96	93	94	99	87	85	88	93	95	83	94	100	99	95	100	100	97	100	100
Chemistry laboratory	96	94	99	97	94	98	98	97	85	91	92	93	92	99	100	100	100	100	100	97	100	100
Physics laboratory	90	83	90	75	80	94	80	90	63	83	74	93	47	79	94	96	83	100	96	97	76	80
Language laboratory	57	45	58	69	49	56	32	24	17	32	38	19	96	99	68	57	48	72	69	85	95	87
Infirmary	65	77	77	70	70	75	47	56	53	45	23	47	97	99	70	83	83	83	74	63	71	99
Full-time librarian	84	93	85	88	87	83	53	58	69	76	67	61	98	99	99	94	96	99	71	97	100	99
Free textbooks	74	79	78	88	83	62	42	53	51	43	94	92	94	91	67	39	58	34	98	57	99	86
Sufficient number of textbooks	92	89	90	96	85	95	99	99	79	91	97	100	99	99	98	100	69	97	94	82	96	96
Texts under 4 years old	58	68	65	55	61	62	77	56	64	54	73	66	55	59	51	67	56	65	99	57	59	67
Average library books per pupil	8.1	6.2	6.4	5.7	4.6	5.8	4.5	6.3	4.0	6.1	8.1	14.8	3.8	5.3	3.5	4.8	4.5	5.7	5.6	3.7	6.5	6.3
Free lunch program	66	80	63	75	74	62	58	54	89	88	61	82	66	52	74	63	79	79	89	52	47	54

consistent pattern—that is, minorities are not at a disadvantage in every item listed—but that there are nevertheless some definite and systematic directions of differences. Nationally, Negro pupils have fewer of some of the facilities that seem most related to academic achievement: They have less access to physics, chemistry, and language laboratories; there are fewer books per pupil in their libraries; their textbooks are less often in sufficient supply. To the extent that physical facilities are important to learning, such items appear to be more relevant than some others, such as cafeterias, in which minority groups are at an advantage.

Usually greater than the majority-minority differences, however, are the regional differences. Table 10–2, for example, shows that 95 percent of Negro and 80 percent of white high school students in the metropolitan Far West attend schools with language laboratories, compared with 48 and 72 percent, respectively, in the metropolitan South, in spite of the fact that a higher percentage of Southern schools are less than 20 years old.

Finally, it must always be remembered that these statistics reveal only majority-minority average differences and regional average differences; they do not show the extreme differences that would be found by comparing one school with another.

Programs

Tables 10–3 and 10–4 summarize some of the survey findings about the school curriculum, administration, and extracurricular activities. The tables are organized in the same way as Tables 10–1 and 10–2 and should be studied in the same way, again with particular attention to regional differences.

The pattern that emerges from study of these tables is similar to that from Tables 10–1 and 10–2. Just as minority groups tend to have less access to physical facilities that seem to be related to academic achievement, so too they have less access to curricular and extracurricular programs that would seem to have such a relationship.

Secondary school Negro students are less likely to attend schools that are regionally accredited; this is particularly pronounced in the South. Negro and Puerto Rican pupils have less access to college preparatory curriculums and to accelerated curriculums; Puerto Ricans have less access to vocational curriculums as well. Less intelligence testing is done in the schools attended by Negroes and Puerto Ricans. Finally, white students in general have more access to a more fully developed program of extracurricular activities, in particular those which might be related to academic matters (debate teams, for example, and student newspapers).

Table 10–3—Percent of pupils in *elementary* schools having the characteristic named at left, fall 1965

Characteristic	Whole Nation						Nonmetropolitan										Metropolitan					
							NORTH AND WEST		SOUTH		SOUTH-WEST		NORTH-EAST		MID-WEST		SOUTH		SOUTH-WEST		WEST	
	MA	PR	IA	OA	Neg.	Maj.	Neg.	Maj.	Neg.	Maj.	Neg.	Maj.	Neg.	Maj.	Neg.	Maj.	Neg.	Maj.	Neg.	Maj.	Neg.	Maj.
Regionally accredited schools	21	27	25	22	27	28	38	29	16	22	59	39	34	24	52	49	21	35	42	23	22	9
Music teacher	31	34	41	33	24	35	22	43	26	17	37	42	34	49	38	32	21	17	23	61	9	13
Remedial reading teacher	41	45	35	41	39	39	37	46	15	11	12	26	73	58	60	17	28	31	18	29	66	70
Accelerated curriculum	34	32	42	37	29	40	47	26	28	24	32	13	34	47	21	28	19	41	34	76	43	73
Low IQ classes	43	44	44	56	54	48	54	48	30	29	47	25	60	51	73	45	48	33	63	66	77	75
Speech impairment classes	41	44	42	58	41	51	34	49	13	11	27	22	59	73	86	67	20	41	34	23	86	82
Use of intelligence test	93	77	90	95	88	95	85	93	80	91	92	90	73	91	97	99	92	100	97	98	98	99
Assignment practice other than area or open	6	11	9	5	12	6	6	1	27	20	26	2	7	4	1	2	12	22	0	0	4	1
Use of tracking	37	47	40	34	44	36	36	28	38	25	38	23	66	50	40	38	45	35	50	48	36	40
Teachers having tenure	68	68	69	79	70	64	70	64	34	49	7	36	100	98	94	76	51	58	64	39	92	90
Principal's salary $9,000 and above	51	52	56	69	51	51	45	34	12	12	22	36	95	86	92	72	30	26	35	14	98	99
School newspaper	23	29	35	37	28	29	39	43	25	26	8	6	28	31	31	24	29	27	22	11	31	31
Boys' interscholastic athletics	55	44	51	47	41	43	71	62	51	51	59	72	22	22	43	46	38	22	43	54	34	22
Girls' interscholastic athletics	35	29	36	32	26	26	37	35	39	38	40	44	19	14	17	17	2	6	29	43	25	18
Band	71	63	64	76	66	72	82	81	39	40	54	76	67	73	77	86	66	85	52	33	95	94
Drama club	26	37	32	33	38	29	43	33	50	31	25	25	34	32	36	29	35	23	33	2	37	36
Debate team	6	4	4	7	5	4	0	3	14	6	10	6	1	3	0	0	3	6	16	8	0	2

Table 10-4—Percent of pupils in secondary schools having the characteristic named at left, fall 1965

Characteristic	Whole Nation						Nonmetropolitan						Metropolitan										
							NORTH AND WEST		SOUTH		SOUTH-WEST		NORTH-EAST		MID-WEST		SOUTH		SOUTH-WEST		WEST	
	MA	PR	IA	OA	Neg.	Maj.	Neg.	Maj.	Neg.	Maj.	Neg.	Maj.	Neg.	Maj.	Neg.	Maj.	Neg.	Maj.	Neg.	Maj.	Neg.	Maj.
Regionally accredited schools	77	78	71	86	68	76	69	65	40	59	30	62	74	74	75	86	72	81	92	86	100	100
Music teacher, full-time	84	94	88	96	85	88	87	87	65	61	85	77	95	97	96	96	87	100	91	82	99	97
College preparatory curriculum	95	90	96	98	88	96	98	95	74	92	81	83	93	99	99	100	87	100	89	82	100	100
Vocational curriculum	56	50	55	68	56	55	49	64	51	62	52	34	42	35	60	60	58	21	89	80	65	65
Remedial reading teacher	57	76	55	56	53	52	35	32	24	20	4	9	81	66	62	57	46	65	63	62	100	97
Accelerated curriculum	67	60	66	80	61	66	42	46	46	58	25	25	60	82	64	78	72	81	87	55	74	73
Low IQ classes	54	56	50	85	54	49	44	47	23	20	46	12	75	62	86	59	37	34	64	14	98	98
Speech impairment classes	28	58	28	51	21	31	18	33	10	6	1	11	43	44	48	42	0	10	14	3	45	57
Use of intelligence test	91	57	84	86	80	89	87	93	83	90	97	100	59	87	86	86	78	100	94	75	89	92
Assignment practice other than area or open	4	20	9	3	19	4	5	0	32	14	2	0	14	5	0	0	36	9	4	0	0	0
Use of tracking	79	88	79	85	75	74	41	48	55	57	21	24	94	92	74	90	80	80	92	82	99	98
Teachers having tenure	65	86	71	85	61	72	47	73	33	41	2	3	100	98	97	83	50	79	24	15	96	88
Principal's salary $9,000 and above	73	89	73	91	66	72	54	64	31	37	59	63	99	99	76	91	61	46	86	18	100	100
School newspaper	89	95	86	97	80	89	71	72	50	81	67	71	95	93	99	97	87	100	66	94	100	100
Boys' interscholastic athletics	94	90	98	99	95	98	99	99	97	100	96	93	80	95	100	97	93	100	95	100	100	100
Girls' interscholastic athletics	58	33	59	37	57	54	32	32	80	69	89	81	51	60	50	43	45	80	89	97	38	35
Band	92	88	92	98	91	95	90	97	80	76	84	81	92	97	100	100	93	100	99	100	100	100
Drama club	95	93	89	92	92	93	75	91	87	75	91	88	92	88	93	99	94	94	100	97	100	100
Debate team	51	32	46	50	39	52	43	48	27	36	80	67	27	46	49	69	42	58	68	63	37	48

Again, regional differences are striking. For example, 100 percent of Negro high school students and 97 percent of whites in the metropolitan Far West attend schools having a remedial reading teacher (this does not mean, of course, that every student uses the services of that teacher, but simply that he had access to them) compared with 46 percent and 65 percent, respectively, in the metropolitan South—and 4 percent and 9 percent in the nonmetropolitan Southwest.

Principals and teachers

The following tables (10–5, 10–6a, 10–6b) list some characteristics of principals and teachers. On Table 10–5, figures given for the whole nation of all minorities, and then by region for Negro and white, refer to the percentages of students who attend schools having principals with the listed characteristics. Thus, line one shows that 1 percent of white elementary pupils attend a school with a Negro principal, and that 56 percent of Negro children attend a school with a Negro principal.

Tables 10–6a and 10–6b (referring to teachers' characteristics) must be read differently. The figures refer to the percentage of teachers having a specified characteristic in the schools attended by the "average" pupil of the various groups. Thus, line one on Table 10–6a: the average white student goes to an elementary school where 40 percent of the teachers spent most of their lives in the same city, town, or county; the average Negro pupil goes to a school where 53 percent of the teachers have lived in the same locality most of their lives.

Both tables list other characteristics which offer rough indications of teacher quality, including the types of colleges attended, years of teaching experience, salary, educational level of mother, and a score on a 30-word vocabulary test. The average Negro pupil attends a school where a greater percentage of the teachers appears to be somewhat less able, as measured by these indicators, than those in the schools attended by the average white student.

Other items on these tables reveal certain teacher attitudes. Thus, the average white pupil attends a school where 51 percent of the white teachers would not choose to move to another school, whereas the average Negro attends a school where 46 percent would not choose to move.

Student body characteristics

Tables 10–7 and 10–8 present data about certain characteristics of the student bodies attending various schools. These tables must be

Table 10-5—Percent of pupils in elementary and secondary schools having principals with characteristic named at left, fall 1965

Characteristic	Whole Nation						Nonmetropolitan								Metropolitan							
							NORTH AND WEST		SOUTH		SOUTH-WEST		NORTH-EAST		MID-WEST		SOUTH		SOUTH-WEST		WEST	
	MA	PR	IA	OA	Neg.	Maj.	Neg.	Maj.	Neg.	Maj.	Neg.	Maj.	Neg.	Maj.	Neg.	Maj.	Neg.	Maj.	Neg.	Maj.	Neg.	Maj.
Elementary schools:																						
Negro principal	16	27	11	12	56	1	13	0	86	2	69	1	9	1	28	0	94	2	64	0	3	0
Majority principal	79	71	80	77	39	95	79	90	7	91	24	97	86	97	69	94	1	97	29	100	95	99
Principal with at least M.A.	85	84	77	86	84	80	69	69	65	64	86	91	98	90	98	92	83	74	95	85	96	94
Principal would keep neighborhood school despite racial imbalance	62	52	58	52	45	65	58	67	39	67	58	67	38	53	61	80	48	71	78	67	29	53
Principal approves compensatory education	66	68	61	70	72	59	63	60	61	46	52	58	76	64	82	63	67	46	75	52	92	76
Principal would deliberately mix faculty for:																						
Mostly minority pupils	40	48	38	47	48	43	31	44	41	43	43	35	56	37	51	40	43	44	52	45	61	57
Mixed pupils	34	46	31	42	44	35	46	40	37	35	35	26	50	32	50	34	40	28	46	23	52	42
Almost all majority pupils	17	30	15	25	35	14	19	13	29	3	18	3	48	18	42	15	34	7	33	1	41	37
Secondary schools:																						
Negro principal	9	12	7	3	61	1	8	0	85	0	68	0	22	0	36	4	97	0	82	0	10	0
Majority principal	89	81	91	76	37	95	79	87	10	94	25	98	75	99	64	95	3	100	18	100	90	99
Principal with at least M.A.	91	97	94	94	96	93	89	85	92	90	90	90	97	97	100	100	97	93	94	86	100	100
Principal would keep neighborhood school despite racial imbalance	49	37	50	33	32	56	54	49	41	73	27	52	25	53	48	55	18	91	80	64	14	28
Principal approves compensatory education	80	83	73	94	78	71	73	59	66	55	81	49	75	79	71	79	80	57	100	80	100	100
Principal would deliberately mix faculty for:																						
Mostly minority pupils	56	47	61	70	54	58	50	53	41	49	57	43	41	50	46	71	53	42	85	86	92	65
Mixed pupils	35	41	45	57	46	40	40	39	36	19	37	7	37	37	18	56	57	32	47	46	82	55
Almost all majority pupils	22	32	23	43	39	14	17	9	23	1	32	1	35	20	14	29	48	0	70	1	78	26

— percent of teachers with characteristic named at left, fall 1965

| Characteristic | Whole Nation | | | | | | Nonmetropolitan | | | | | | Metropolitan | | | | | | | | | |
| | | | | | | | NORTH AND WEST | | SOUTH | | SOUTH-WEST | | NORTH-EAST | | MID-WEST | | SOUTH | | SOUTH-WEST | | WEST | |
	MA	PR	IA	OA	Neg.	Maj.	Neg.	Maj.	Neg.	Maj.	Neg.	Maj.	Neg.	Maj.	Neg.	Maj.	Neg.	Maj.	Neg.	Maj.	Neg.	Maj.
Percent teachers who spent most of life in present city, town, or county	37	54	35	39	53	40	34	40	54	55	40	31	64	51	55	39	69	37	35	18	24	24
Average teacher verbal score[1]	22	22	22	23	20	23	23	24	17	22	20	22	22	23	22	23	19	23	21	24	22	24
Percent teachers majored in academic subjects	19	18	17	21	17	16	16	18	12	14	16	22	19	17	17	15	18	16	9	7	23	22
Percent teachers who attended college not offering graduate degrees	39	41	37	32	53	37	48	38	63	47	44	30	45	38	39	40	72	46	44	26	22	21
Percent teachers attended college with predominantly white student enrollment	79	70	85	83	39	97	81	99	9	97	28	93	73	97	75	97	7	95	43	98	82	96
Average educational level of teacher's mother (score)[2]	3.7	3.5	3.7	3.8	3.5	3.7	3.4	3.5	2.9	3.5	3.6	3.7	3.6	3.7	3.7	3.6	3.5	4.2	3.8	3.8	4.1	4.2
Average highest degree earned[3]	3.1	3.1	3.1	3.1	3.2	3.0	2.8	2.8	3.1	3.0	3.4	3.3	3.2	3.1	3.1	3.0	3.2	3.0	3.5	3.2	3.3	3.1
Average teacher-years experience	13	12	12	12	13	12	12	13	14	16	14	13	11	11	11	11	14	10	13	11	11	10
Average teacher salary ($1,000's)	5.9	6.0	6.1	6.6	6.0	6.0	5.8	5.7	4.7	5.0	5.5	5.4	7.2	7.1	7.0	6.5	5.2	5.0	5.9	5.1	7.8	7.3
Average pupils per teacher	30	30	30	28	20	28	26	25	32	27	23	26	27	26	29	28	28	30	30	42	30	31
Percent teachers would not choose to move to another school	58	57	59	59	55	65	56	60	49	73	57	64	53	64	49	63	61	76	63	59	55	66
Percent teachers plan to continue until retirement	44	42	41	39	45	37	42	35	50	51	57	55	31	32	34	31	51	34	48	46	41	34
Percent teachers prefer white pupils	27	21	26	20	7	37	22	32	6	57	10	45	8	18	12	37	1	57	12	48	8	31
Percent teachers approve compensatory education	56	59	56	64	61	56	53	56	55	47	53	44	69	66	65	55	59	49	56	54	73	66
Percent Negro teachers	19	30	14	15	65	2	17	1	90	2	75	1	31	2	40	2	96	4	65	1	22	2
Percent White teachers	78	67	83	79	32	97	82	99	8	96	24	96	67	97	58	98	2	96	32	98	69	95

[1] Score is the average number of correct items on a 30-item verbal facility test.
[2] Educational attainment scored from 1–8 (lowest to highest); 4 represents high school graduate.
[3] Highest degree earned scored from 1–6 (lowest to highest); 3 represents a Bachelors degree.

Table 10-6b—Characteristics of teachers in the *secondary* schools attended by the average white and minority pupil, fall 1965

Characteristic	Whole Nation						Nonmetropolitan						Metropolitan									
							NORTH AND WEST		SOUTH		SOUTH-WEST		NORTH-EAST		MID-WEST		SOUTH		SOUTH-WEST		WEST	
	MA	PR	IA	OA	Neg.	Maj.	Neg.	Maj.	Neg.	Maj.	Neg.	Maj.	Neg.	Maj.	Neg.	Maj.	Neg.	Maj.	Neg.	Maj.	Neg.	Maj.
Percent of teachers who spent most of life in present city, town, or county	31	55	31	36	41	34	20	23	38	48	35	28	62	49	34	31	52	41	37	19	22	25
Average teacher verbal score[1]	23	22	23	23	21	23	23	24	19	23	22	24	22	23	22	23	21	23	21	24	23	24
Percent of teachers majored in academic subjects	37	40	39	40	38	40	36	39	37	35	30	32	40	46	35	41	42	41	25	36	38	41
Percent of teachers who attended colleges not offering graduate degrees	26	27	27	20	44	31	31	33	52	44	32	17	25	29	38	34	64	42	42	22	16	13
Percent of teachers who attended colleges with predominantly white student enrollment	90	86	92	86	44	48	99	90	15	99	31	98	85	98	75	97	8	97	29	99	90	95
Average educational level of teacher's mother (score)[2]	3.8	3.5	3.8	3.7	3.6	3.8	3.8	3.6	3.3	3.8	3.7	3.8	3.5	3.5	3.7	3.8	4.3	3.8	3.4	3.7	4.1	4.0
Average highest degree earned[3]	3.4	3.5	3.4	3.6	3.3	3.4	3.2	3.2	3.2	3.4	3.4	3.4	3.5	3.5	3.4	3.4	3.3	3.3	3.4	3.3	3.6	3.5
Average teacher years experience	11	11	10	11	11	10	10	9	10	11	11	11	12	11	11	10	12	8	11	9	11	11
Average teacher salary ($1,000's)	6.8	7.6	6.8	7.7	6.4	6.6	6.3	6.0	4.9	5.6	5.8	7.8	7.6	7.2	7.2	5.5	5.4	6.1	5.5	8.8	8.8	8.3
Average pupils per teacher	23	22	23	24	26	22	20	20	30	20	21	24	20	25	24	25	26	25	26	23	23	23
Percentage of teachers would not choose to move to another school	49	48	48	40	46	51	39	42	42	48	48	63	51	55	45	49	50	62	55	51	42	47
Percentage of teachers plan to continue until retirement	36	41	34	38	38	33	25	28	35	36	43	43	44	38	37	31	36	23	37	30	44	41
Percentage of teachers prefer white pupils	26	13	24	13	8	32	28	28	8	58	15	48	8	14	11	31	2	52	7	38	10	21
Percentage of teachers approve compensatory education	61	67	60	68	66	60	55	62	49	59	59	50	72	67	67	58	67	54	67	49	72	70
Percent Negro teachers	10	16	8	6	59	2	11	2	85	70	70	18	2	2	35	2	94	1	77	0	14	2
Percent White teachers	87	81	88	76	38	97	88	97	13	27	27	79	96	97	64	97	3	99	20	97	82	94

read the same as those immediately preceding. Looking at the sixth item on Table 10–7, one should read: the average white high school student attends a school in which 82 percent of his classmates report that there are encyclopedias in their homes. This does not mean that 82 percent of all white pupils have encyclopedias at home, although obviously that would be approximately true. In short, these tables attempt to describe the characteristics of the student bodies with which the "average" white or minority student goes to school.

Clear differences are found on these items. The average Negro has fewer classmates whose mothers graduated from high school; his classmates more frequently are members of large rather than small families; they are less often enrolled in a college preparatory curriculum; they have taken a smaller number of courses in English, mathematics, foreign language, and science.

On most items, the other minority groups fall between Negroes and whites, but closer to whites, in the extent to which each characteristic is typical of their classmates.

Again, there are substantial variations in the magnitude of the differences, with the difference usually being greater in the Southern States.

ACHIEVEMENT IN THE PUBLIC SCHOOLS

The schools bear many responsibilities. Among the most important is the teaching of certain intellectual skills such as reading, writing, calculating, and problem solving. One way of assessing the educational opportunity offered by the schools is to measure how well they perform this task. Standard achievement tests are available to measure these skills, and several such tests were administered in this survey to pupils at grades 1, 3, 6, 9, and 12.

These tests do not measure intelligence, nor attitudes, nor qualities of character. Furthermore, they are not, nor are they intended to be, "culture free." Quite the reverse: they are culture bound. What they measure are the skills which are among the most important in our society for getting a good job and moving up to a better one, and for full participation in an increasingly technical world. Consequently, a pupil's test results at the end of public school provide a good measure of the range of opportunities open to him as he finishes school—a wide range of choice of jobs or colleges if these skills are very high; a very narrow range that includes only the most menial jobs if these skills are very low.

Table 10–9 gives an overall illustration of the test results for the various groups by tabulating nationwide median scores (the score

Table 10-7—For the average minority and white pupil, the percent of fellow pupils with the specified characteristics, fall 1965

Level of school and pupil characteristic	Whole Nation						Nonmetropolitan						Metropolitan									
							NORTH AND WEST		SOUTH		SOUTH-WEST		NORTH-EAST		MID-WEST		SOUTH		SOUTH-WEST		WEST	
	MA	PR	IA	OA	Neg.	Maj.	Neg.	Maj.	Neg.	Maj.	Neg.	Maj.	Neg.	Maj.	Neg.	Maj.	Neg.	Maj.	Neg.	Maj.	Neg.	Maj.
Elementary schools:																						
Mostly white classmates last year	59	52	66	63	19	89	59	91	17	91	19	72	33	87	26	91	7	91	27	91	20	86
All white teachers last year	75	68	77	74	53	88	71	89	53	87	57	84	60	89	52	88	49	89	51	89	52	85
Encyclopedia in home	62	57	64	70	54	75	62	72	36	65	48	64	71	84	60	80	51	80	57	72	64	83
Secondary schools:																						
Mostly white classmates last year	72	56	72	57	10	91	77	96	12	94	23	88	41	90	40	89	4	95	14	96	35	81
All white teachers last year	73	57	75	57	25	89	79	93	11	93	23	90	44	84	45	88	3	92	16	95	46	79
Encyclopedia in home	77	76	75	82	69	82	76	78	52	75	66	75	82	87	80	86	67	88	73	83	78	83
Mother high school graduate or more	49	47	50	53	40	58	51	58	23	45	44	48	51	63	49	63	37	58	41	49	53	65
Taking college preparatory course	36	38	35	41	32	41	29	35	22	33	28	32	39	53	43	46	34	44	29	31	34	46
Taking some vocational course	27	30	28	32	27	23	22	24	23	20	25	20	30	20	28	25	27	16	37	38	35	30
2½ years or more of science	36	38	38	38	39	42	41	41	41	38	47	39	43	55	32	38	43	43	42	31	26	34
1½ years or more of language	37	41	35	43	35	40	29	30	25	26	19	23	49	60	36	44	38	44	34	23	37	50
3½ years or more of English	77	73	80	76	69	83	68	78	66	89	75	84	79	91	73	79	67	89	71	87	62	72
2½ years or more of math	47	45	44	47	44	49	40	39	43	46	50	52	47	63	41	50	46	55	58	45	37	47

Table 10-8—For the average minority and white pupil, the percent of fellow pupils with the specified characteristics, fall 1965

Secondary school pupil characteristic	Whole Nation						Nonmetropolitan						Metropolitan									
							NORTH AND WEST		SOUTH		SOUTH-WEST		NORTH-EAST		MID-WEST		SOUTH		SOUTH-WEST		WEST	
	MA	PR	IA	OA	Neg.	Maj.	Neg.	Maj.	Neg.	Maj.	Neg.	Maj.	Neg.	Maj.	Neg.	Maj.	Neg.	Maj.	Neg.	Maj.	Neg.	Maj.
Mother not reared in city	45	33	44	33	45	42	58	50	64	65	53	61	25	19	35	32	45	42	48	60	34	33
Real father at home	77	71	75	84	64	83	80	84	65	84	64	85	67	83	70	84	58	84	55	84	62	74
Real mother at home	90	88	90	89	85	92	90	92	82	93	82	94	88	92	90	92	83	92	83	94	86	88
Five or more brothers and sisters	28	27	30	27	44	20	30	24	56	23	54	23	25	15	34	19	48	13	47	17	36	21
Mother expects best in class	48	49	45	42	62	43	47	39	71	55	67	54	50	41	49	38	69	49	71	51	53	41
Parents daily discuss school	47	46	44	42	49	47	44	44	51	51	52	54	50	52	44	45	53	53	51	43	43	44
Father expects at least college graduate	38	34	35	37	38	37	36	32	33	37	39	44	33	39	36	38	39	44	45	45	37	40
Mother expects at least college graduate	41	39	39	41	44	41	41	35	42	40	48	45	38	42	43	41	48	45	52	50	43	44
Parents attend PTA	36	38	34	37	51	37	36	40	59	37	50	34	43	37	45	36	61	44	42	26	36	30
Parents read to child regularly before he started school	25	28	24	24	30	26	26	24	30	25	32	23	32	31	27	27	33	29	31	21	26	27

Table 10–9—Nationwide median test scores for 1st- and 12th-grade pupils, fall 1965

Test	PUERTO RICANS	INDIAN AMERICANS	Racial or ethnic group MEXICAN-AMERICANS	ORIENTAL AMERICANS	NEGRO	MAJORITY
1st grade:						
Nonverbal	45.8	53.0	50.1	56.6	43.4	54.1
Verbal	44.9	47.8	46.5	51.6	45.4	53.2
12th grade:						
Nonverbal	43.3	47.1	45.0	51.6	40.9	52.0
Verbal	43.1	43.7	43.8	49.6	40.9	52.1
Reading	42.6	44.3	44.2	48.8	42.2	51.9
Mathematics	43.7	45.9	45.5	51.3	41.8	51.8
General information	41.7	44.7	43.3	49.0	40.6	52.2
Average of the 5 tests	43.1	45.1	44.4	50.1	41.1	52.0

which divides the group in half) for 1st-grade and 12th-grade pupils on the tests used in those grades. For example, half of the white 12th-grade pupils had scores above 52 on the nonverbal test and half had scores below 52. (Scores on each test at each grade level were standardized so that the average over the national sample equaled 50 and the standard deviation equaled 10. This means that for all pupils in the nation, about 16 percent would score below 40 and about 16 percent above 60.)

With some exceptions—notably Oriental Americans—the average minority pupil scores distinctly lower on these tests at every level than the average white pupil. The minority pupils' scores are as much as one standard deviation below the majority pupils' scores in the 1st grade. At the 12th grade, results of tests in the same verbal and nonverbal skills show that, in every case, the minority scores are farther below the majority than are the 1st-graders. For some groups, the relative decline is negligible; for others, it is large.

Furthermore, a constant difference in standard deviations over the various grades represents an increasing difference in grade level gap. For example, Negroes in the metropolitan Northeast are about 1.1 standard deviations below whites in the same region at grades 6, 9, and 12. But at grade 6 this represents 1.6 years behind; at grade 9, 2.4 years; and at grade 12, 3.3 years. Thus, by this measure, the deficiency in achievement is progressively greater for the minority pupils at progressively higher grade levels.

For most minority groups, then, and most particularly the Negro, schools provide little opportunity for them to overcome this initial deficiency; in fact they fall farther behind the white majority in the development of several skills which are critical to making a living and participating fully in modern society. Whatever may be the combination of nonschool factors—poverty, community attitudes, low educational level of parents—which put minority children at a disadvantage in verbal and nonverbal skills when they enter the first grade, the fact is the schools have not overcome it.

Some points should be borne in mind in reading the table. First, the differences shown should not obscure the fact that some minority children perform better than many white children. A difference of one standard deviation in median scores means that about 84 percent of the children in the lower group are below the median of the majority students—but 50 percent of the white children are themselves below that median as well.

A second point of qualification concerns regional differences. By grade 12, both white and Negro students in the South score below their counterparts—white and Negro—in the North. In addition,

Southern Negroes score farther below Southern whites than Northern Negroes score below Northern whites. The consequences of this pattern can be illustrated by the fact that the 12th-grade Negro in the nonmetropolitan South is 0.8 standard deviation below—or, in terms of years, 1.9 years behind—the Negro in the metropolitan Northeast, though at grade 1 there is no such regional difference.

Finally, the test scores at grade 12 obviously do not take account of those pupils who have left school before reaching the senior year. In the metropolitan North and West, 20 percent of the Negroes of ages 16 and 17 are not enrolled in school—a higher dropout percentage than in either the metropolitan or nonmetropolitan South. If it is the case that some or many of the Northern dropouts performed poorly when they were in school, the Negro achievement in the North may be artificially elevated because some of those who achieved more poorly have left school.

RELATION OF ACHIEVEMENT TO SCHOOL CHARACTERISTICS

If 100 students within a school take a certain test, there is likely to be great variation in their scores. One student may score 97 percent, another 13; several may score 78 percent. This represents variability in achievement within the particular school.

It is possible, however, to compute the average of the scores made by the students within that school and to compare it with the average score, or achievement of pupils within another school, or many other schools. These comparisons then represent variations between schools.

When one sees that the average score on a verbal achievement test in school X is 55 and in school Y is 72, the natural question to ask is: What accounts for the difference?

There are many factors that may be associated with the difference. This analysis concentrates on one cluster of those factors. It attempts to describe what relationship the school's characteristics themselves (libraries, for example, and teachers and laboratories, and so on) seem to have to the achievement of majority and minority groups (separately for each group on a nationwide basis, and also for Negro and white pupils in the North and South).

The first finding is that the schools are remarkably similar in the way they relate to the achievement of their pupils when the socioeconomic background of the students is taken into account. It is known that socioeconomic factors bear a strong relation to academic achievement. When these factors are statistically controlled, however, it appears that differences between schools account for only a small fraction of differences in pupil achievement.

The schools do differ, however, in their relation to the various racial and ethnic groups. The average white student's achievement seems to be less affected by the strength or weakness of his school's facilities, curriculums, and teachers than is the average minority pupil's. To put it another way, the achievement of minority pupils depends more on the schools they attend than does the achievement of majority pupils. Thus, 20 percent of the achievement of Negroes in the South is associated with the particular schools they go to, whereas only 10 percent of the achievement of whites in the South is. Except for Oriental Americans, this general result is found for all minorities.

The inference might then be made that improving the school of a minority pupil may increase his achievement more than would improving the school of a white child increase his. Similarly, the average minority pupil's achievement may suffer more in a school of low quality than might the average white pupil's. In short, whites, and to a lesser extent Oriental Americans, are less affected one way or the other by the quality of their schools than are minority pupils. This indicates that it is for the most disadvantaged children that improvements in school quality will make the most difference in achievement.

All of these results suggest the next question: What are the school characteristics that are most related to achievement? In other words, what factors in the school seem to be most important in affecting achievement?

It appears that variations in the facilities and curriculums of the schools account for relatively little variation in pupil achievement insofar as this is measured by standard tests. Again, it is for majority whites that the variations make the least difference; for minorities, they make somewhat more difference. Among the facilities that show some relationship to achievement are several for which minority pupils' schools are less well equipped relative to whites. For example, the existence of science laboratories showed a small but consistent relationship to achievement, and Table 10-2 shows that minorities, especially Negroes, are in schools with fewer of these laboratories.

The quality of teachers shows a stronger relationship to pupil achievement. Furthermore, it is progressively greater at higher grades, indicating a cumulative impact of the qualities of teachers in a school on the pupil's achievements. Again, teacher quality seems more important to minority achievement than to that of the majority.

It should be noted that many characteristics of teachers were not measured in this survey; therefore, the results are not at all conclusive regarding the specific characteristics of teachers that are most important. Among those measured in the survey, however, those that bear the highest relationship to pupil achievement are first, the teacher's score on the verbal skills test, and then his educational background—both his own level of education and that of his parents. On both of these measures, the level of teachers of minority students, especially Negroes, is lower.

Finally, it appears that a pupil's achievement is strongly related to the educational backgrounds and aspirations of the other students in the school. Only crude measures of these variables were used (principally the proportion of pupils with encyclopedias in the home and the proportion planning to go to college). Analysis indicates, however, that children from a given family background, when put in schools of different social composition, will achieve at quite different levels. This effect is again less for white pupils than for any minority group other than Orientals. Thus, if a white pupil from a home that is strongly and effectively supportive of education is put in a school where most pupils do not come from such homes, his achievement will be little different than if he were in a school composed of others like himself. But if a minority pupil from a home without much educational strength is put with schoolmates with strong educational backgrounds, his achievement is likely to increase.

This general result, taken together with the earlier examinations of school differences, has important implications for equality of educational opportunity. For the earlier tables show that the principal way in which the school environments of Negroes and whites differ is in the composition of their student bodies, and it turns out that the composition of the student bodies has a strong relationship to the achievement of Negro and other minority pupils.

This analysis has concentrated on the educational opportunities offered by the schools in terms of their student body composition, facilities, curriculums, and teachers. This emphasis, while entirely appropriate as a response to the legislation calling for the survey, nevertheless neglects important factors in the variability between individual pupils within the same school; this variability is roughly four times as large as the variability between schools. For example, a pupil attitude factor, which appears to have a stronger relationship to achievement than do all the "school" factors together, is the extent to which an individual feels that he has some control over his own destiny. Data on items related to this attitude are shown in

Table 10-10—Percent of minority and white 12th-grade pupils having certain attitudes and aspirations, fall 1965

| | Whole Nation | | | | | | Nonmetropolitan | | | | | | Metropolitan | | | | | | | | | |
| | | | | | | | NORTH AND WEST | | SOUTH | | SOUTH-WEST | | NORTH-EAST | | MID-WEST | | SOUTH | | SOUTH-WEST | | WEST | |
Item	MA	PR	IA	OA	Neg.	Maj.	Neg.	Maj.	Neg.	Maj.	Neg.	Maj.	Neg.	Maj.	Neg.	Maj.	Neg.	Maj.	Neg.	Maj.	Neg.	Maj.
Do anything to stay in school	37	35	36	44	46	45	43	44	49	50	46	50	47	47	44	43	48	54	50	47	35	44
Desires to be best in class	33	36	38	46	58	33	48	35	69	46	68	48	48	36	48	33	63	45	70	45	50	35
3 or more hours per day study outside of school	22	21	17	42	31	23	26	21	32	23	36	23	33	27	27	19	33	27	33	22	27	23
No willful absence	59	53	60	76	76	66	72	65	84	75	86	73	68	61	73	66	78	69	77	69	64	56
Read at least 1 book last summer	69	72	73	74	80	75	76	74	83	73	82	75	81	79	75	74	83	73	80	72	76	75
Desires to finish college	43	43	42	46	46	45	43	38	42	41	51	47	43	49	46	47	52	52	57	45	42	51
Definitely planning to attend college next year	26	26	27	53	34	40	22	35	30	35	41	50	31	46	33	37	35	41	43	40	48	55
Have read a college catalog	46	45	50	70	54	61	51	57	49	50	54	64	59	73	55	59	57	67	59	63	54	65
Have consulted college officials	22	25	26	33	25	37	26	33	22	38	23	38	32	46	25	35	24	44	26	30	25	30
Believes self to be brighter than average	31	37	31	51	40	49	41	48	42	45	44	51	37	48	36	50	40	48	46	51	43	56
"I just can't learn"	38	37	44	38	27	39	31	39	24	37	21	35	29	39	34	40	23	37	25	39	28	38
"I would do better if teacher didn't go so fast"	28	31	26	26	21	24	23	23	22	25	19	24	22	22	22	24	20	24	19	25	20	25
"Luck more important than work"	11	19	11	8	11	4	14	4	15	4	14	4	9	4	9	4	10	4	11	4	10	4
"When I try, something or somebody stops me"	23	30	27	18	22	14	24	14	22	16	26	14	21	13	23	15	19	14	23	13	21	12
"People like me don't have much of a chance"	12	19	14	9	12	6	15	6	11	6	11	5	12	5	13	6	10	6	11	4	13	6
Expect professional career	18	21	21	43	27	37	26	34	25	31	26	38	31	46	31	37	27	37	28	37	22	38

Table 10-10 along with data on other attitudes and aspirations. The responses of pupils to questions in the survey show that minority pupils, except for Orientals, have far less conviction than whites that they can affect their own environment and futures. When they do, however, their achievement is higher than that of whites who lack that conviction.

Furthermore, while this characteristic shows little relationship to most school factors, it is related, for Negroes, to the proportion of whites in the schools. Those Negroes in schools with a higher proportion of whites have a greater sense of control. This finding suggests that the direction such an attitude takes may be associated with the pupil's school experience as well as his experience in the larger community.

Opportunity in institutions of higher education

The largely segregated system of higher education in the South has made comparison between colleges attended mainly by Negro students and mainly by majority students easy in that region. Elsewhere it has not been possible in the past to make comparison between educational opportunities because of the general policy in Federal and State agencies of not collecting data on race. In the fall of 1965, however, the Office of Education reversed this policy as a result of the interest of many agencies and organizations in the progress of minority pupils in gaining access to higher education. The racial composition of freshmen of all degree-seeking students was obtained from nearly all of the colleges and universities in the nation.

These racial compositions have been cross-tabulated against a variety of characteristics of the institutions in the report itself. Here we present only three such cross-tabulations which relate particularly to the overall quality of the institutions. First, there are presented three tables (10–11, 10–12, 10–13), showing the distribution of Negro students in number and by percentages over eight regions of the Nation. Over half of all Negro college students attend the largely segregated institutions in the South and Southwest. About 4.6 percent of all college students are Negro (11.5 percent of college-age persons are Negro).

Following the three distribution tables are three cross-tabulations showing, respectively: student-faculty ratio, percent of faculty with earned doctorate, and average faculty salary. Looking at Table 10-14, the upper column headings classify the institution by percent of Negro students in the total enrollment; for each of these the next column headings show the number of such institutions in the cate-

Table 10-11—Estimated number of college students by race and region, fall 1965[1]

	New England	Mideast	Great Lakes	Plains	South	Southwest	Rocky Mountains	Far West	Total
Majority	313,514	781,112	821,999	375,043	778,472	434,005	175,000	552,153	4,232,098
Negro	2,216	30,226	30,870	8,500	101,648	20,620	1,605	11,631	207,316
Other minority	1,538	6,542	10,822	2,885	4,996	7,012	1,968	16,092	51,855
Total	317,268	817,880	863,691	386,428	885,116	461,637	179,373	579,867	4,491,269

[1] Based on reports received on 2,013 institutions from among a total of 2,183.

Table 10-12—Percent distribution of college students by race across region, fall 1965[1]

	New England	Mideast	Great Lakes	Plains	South	South-west	Rocky Mountains	Far West	Total
Majority	7.41	18.46	19.42	8.86	18.39	10.26	4.15	13.05	100
Negro	1.07	14.58	14.89	4.10	49.03	9.95	.77	5.61	100
Other minority	2.97	12.62	20.87	5.56	9.63	13.52	3.80	31.03	100

[1] Based on reports received on 2,013 institutions from among a total of 2,183.

Table 10-13—Percent distribution of college students by race within region, fall 1965[1]

	New England	Mideast	Great Lakes	Plains	South	Southwest	Rocky Mountains	Far West
Majority	98.82	95.50	95.17	97.05	87.95	94.01	98.01	95.22
Negro	.69	3.70	3.57	2.20	11.48	4.47	.89	2.00
Other minority	.48	.80	1.25	.75	.56	1.52	1.10	2.78
Total	99.99	100.00	99.99	100.00	99.99	100.00	100.00	100.00

[1] Based on reports received on 2,013 institutions from among a total of 2,183.

Table 10-14—Student-faculty ratio by percent of Negro enrollment in institutions of higher education, fall 1963

Control and region	0%		0–2%		Negro enrollment 2–5%		5–10%		10–50%		50–100%	
	No. inst.	Wtd. avg.	No. inst.	Wtd. avg.	No. inst.	Wtd. avg.	No. inst.	Wtd. avg.	No. inst.	Wtd. avg.	No. inst.	Wtd. avg.
(1)	(2)	(3)	(4)	(5)	(6)	(7)	(8)	(9)	(10)	(11)	(12)	(13)
Public institutions:												
North Atlantic	8	22	64	21	15	23	5	21	2	69	6	16
Great Lakes and Plains	41	22	91	21	27	22	7	21	10	33	2	23
South	24	18	66	19	13	19	21	22	3	21	28	17
Southwest	3	26	46	23	24	27	8	28	(1)	(1)	3	20
Rocky Mountains and Far West	12	21	83	26	22	32	8	40	2	36	(1)	(1)
Private institutions:												
North Atlantic	70	12	265	20	58	16	11	25	14	13	2	11
Great Lakes and Plains	54	13	249	16	59	17	20	27	8	21	1	20
South	86	18	117	16	15	18	4	14	1	18	48	15
Southwest	9	19	33	18	10	18	1	22	(1)	(1)	6	16
Rocky Mountains and Far West	17	15	90	17	20	19	4	25	1	2	(1)	(1)
All public institutions	88	21	350	22	101	25	49	25	17	35	39	17
All private institutions	236	16	754	18	162	17	40	25	24	18	57	15
All institutions	324	18	1,104	20	263	22	89	25	41	31	96	16

[1] Data not available.

gory at the left of the table and the average number of students per faculty member; the average is weighted (abbreviated in col. head "Wtd. avg.") by the number of students in an institution, so that large colleges have large influence on the average. For example, the numbers 8 and 22 in the top line of the 0% column mean that there were 8 institutions in the North Atlantic region with no Negro students, and that there were on the average 22 students per faculty member in these 8 institutions. The bottom line shows that whereas the bulk of the institutions (1,104 in the 0–2% column) have on the average 20 students per faculty member, those with predominantly Negro enrollment (the 96 in the 50–100% column) have on the average 16 students per faculty member. Table 10-15 provides the same categories of information on the percent of faculty with Ph. D. degree. Negro students are proportionally in colleges with lower proportions of Ph. D. faculty (bottom line of Table 10-15); this is generally but not always true in the various regions.

Table 10-16 shows the average annual salary in dollars for faculty members in the same format as before. Negro students are in colleges with substantially lower faculty salaries. The institutions in the South and Southwest generally pay lower salaries than those in other regions, and the colleges serving primarily the Negro students are at the bottom of this low scale.

Other findings of the study are that (1) In every region Negro students are more likely to enter the State college system than the State university system, and further they are a smaller proportion of the student body of universities than any other category of public institutions of higher education, (2) Negro students are more frequently found in institutions which have a high dropout rate, (3) they attend mainly institutions with low tuition cost, (4) they tend to major in engineering, agriculture, education, social work, social science, and nursing.

Future teachers

Since a number of investigations of teacher qualification in the past few years have indicated that teachers of Negro children are less qualified than those who teach primarily majority children, this survey investigated whether there might be some promise that the situation may be changed by college students now preparing to become teachers. To this end, questionnaire and achievement test data were secured from about 17,000 college freshmen and 5,500 college seniors in 32 teacher training colleges in 18 States that in 1960 included over 90 percent of the Nation's Negro population.

Table 10–15—Percent faculty with earned doctorate by percent of Negro enrollment in institutions of higher education, fall 1963

Control and region	Negro enrollment 0%		0–2%		2–5%		5–10%		10–50%		50–100%	
	No. inst.	Wtd. avg.	No. inst.	Wtd. avg.	No. inst.	Wtd. avg.	No. inst.	Wtd. avg.	No. inst.	Wtd. avg.	No. inst.	Wtd. avg.
(1)	(2)	(3)	(4)	(5)	(6)	(7)	(8)	(9)	(10)	(11)	(12)	(13)
Public institutions:												
North Atlantic	3	47	47	38	5	54	2	30	(1)	(1)	6	22
Great Lakes and Plains	2	46	49	41	12	28	2	23	2	42	2	34
South	12	29	49	30	12	32	3	26	1	17	18	19
Southwest	2	22	25	37	8	39	1	45	(1)	(1)	3	26
Rocky Mountains and Far West	4	37	32	40	2	27	1	32	(1)	(1)	(1)	(1)
Private institutions:												
North Atlantic	13	25	175	37	31	35	7	17	3	30	2	26
Great Lakes and Plains	10	32	179	30	35	26	6	23	4	29	1	27
South	31	32	78	32	12	23	2	28	1	33	28	29
Southwest	1	41	24	34	5	27	(1)	(1)	(1)	(1)	3	31
Rocky Mountains and Far West	8	22	67	38	15	35	3	25	(1)	(1)	(1)	(1)
All public institutions	23	36	202	37	39	35	9	28	3	34	29	21
All private institutions	63	30	523	34	98	31	18	20	8	30	34	29
All institutions	86	34	725	36	137	34	27	25	11	31	63	24

[1] Data not available.

Table 10–16—Average annual salary, full professor through instructor in institutions of higher education by percent of Negro enrollment, fall 1963

Control and region	0%		0–2%		Negro enrollment 2–5%		5–10%		10–50%		50–10%	
	No. inst. (2)	Wtd. avg. (3)	No. inst. (4)	Wtd. avg. (5)	No. inst. (6)	Wtd. avg. (7)	No. inst. (8)	Wtd. avg. (9)	No. inst. (10)	Wtd. avg. (11)	No. inst. (12)	Wtd. avg. (13)
(1)												
Public institutions:												
North Atlantic	3	$8,577	38	$8,607	6	$10,601	2	$11,514	(1)	(1)	5	$8,152
Great Lakes and Plains	2	8,268	43	8,777	11	9,417	2	8,687	1	10,005	2	8,185
South	11	7,296	45	7,992	13	7,838	3	6,959	1	6,784	19	6,583
Southwest	2	7,041	24	8,176	7	7,777	1	7,419	(1)	(1)	2	6,806
Rocky Mountains and Far West	2	6,436	28	8,893	2	9,641	(1)	(1)	(1)	(1)	(1)	(1)
Private institutions:												
North Atlantic	7	6,513	156	8,268	27	8,867	6	8,040	3	5,947	1	8,309
Great Lakes and Plains	7	6,336	147	7,781	30	7,872	5	7,145	4	7,895	(1)	(1)
South	25	6,421	63	7,543	8	6,340	3	6,047	(1)	(1)	19	5,974
Southwest	1	5,816	23	6,770	5	5,784	(1)	(1)	(1)	(1)	2	5,473
Rocky Mountains and Far West	1	5,470	50	8,448	9	7,107	1	7,302	(1)	(1)	(1)	(1)
All public institutions	20	7,573	178	8,491	39	9,112	8	9,248	2	8,754	28	6,824
All private institutions	41	6,379	439	7,964	79	8,175	15	7,640	7	7,352	22	6,652
All institutions	61	7,165	617	8,279	118	8,756	23	8,643	9	7,795	50	6,773

[1] Data not available.

Some of the findings of this survey are:

1. At both the freshman and senior levels, future teachers are very similar to students in their colleges who are following other career lines. (It should be remembered that these comparisons are limited to students in colleges that have a primary mission in the training of teachers, and is not, of course, a random sample of all colleges.)

2. Majority students being trained at the college level to enter teaching have a stronger preparation for college than have Negro students; that is, they had more courses in foreign languages, English, and mathematics, made better grades in high school, and more often were in the highest track in English.

3. Data from the senior students suggest that colleges do not narrow the gap in academic training between Negro and majority pupils; indeed, there is some evidence that the college curriculum increases this difference, at least in the South.

4. Substantial test score differences exist between Negro and white future teachers at both freshman and senior levels, with approximately 15 percent of Negroes exceeding the average score of majority students in the same region. (This figure varies considerably depending on the test, but in no case do as many as 25 percent of Negroes exceed the majority average.)

5. The test data indicate that the gap in test results widens in the South between the freshman and senior years. The significance of this finding lies in the fact that most Negro teachers are trained in the Southern States.

6. The preferences of future teachers for certain kinds of schools and certain kinds of pupils raise the question of the match between the expectations of teacher recruits and the characteristics of the employment opportunities.

The preferences of future teachers were also studied. Summarized in terms of market conditions, it seems apparent that far too many future teachers prefer to teach in an academic high school; that there is a far greater proportion of children of blue-collar workers than of teachers being produced who prefer to teach them; that there is a very substantial number of white teachers-in-training, even in the South, who prefer to teach in racially mixed schools; that very few future teachers of either race wish to teach in predominantly minority schools; and finally, that high-ability pupils are much more popular with future teachers than low-ability ones. The preferences of Negro future teachers are more compatible with the distribution of needs in the market than are those of the majority; too few of the latter, relative to the clientele requiring service, prefer blue-collar or low-ability children or prefer to teach in racially heterogeneous schools, or in special curriculum, vocational, or commercial schools. These data indicate that under the present organization of schools, relatively few of the best prepared future teachers will find their way into classrooms where they can offset some of the environmental disadvantage suffered by minority children.

School enrollment and dropouts

Another extensive study explored enrollment rates of children of various ages, races, and socioeconomic categories using 1960 census data. The study included also an investigation of school dropouts using the October 1965 Current Population Survey of the Bureau of the Census. This survey uses a carefully selected sample of 35,000 households. It was a large enough sample to justify reliable nationwide estimates for the Negro minority but not for other minorities. In this section the word "white" includes the Mexican American and Puerto Rican minorities.

According to the estimates of the Current Population Survey, approximately 6,960,000 persons of ages 16 and 17 were living in the United States in October 1965. Of this number 300,000 (5 percent) were enrolled in college, and therefore, were not considered by this Census Bureau study. Of the remaining, approximately 10 percent, or 681,000 youth of 16 and 17, had left school prior to completion of high school.

Table 10–17—Enrollment status of persons 16 and 17 years old not in college by sex and race, for the United States: October 1965

[Numbers in thousands. Figures are rounded to the nearest thousand without being adjusted to group totals, which are independently rounded]

Enrollment status	Total	Both sexes WHITE	NEGRO	Male WHITE	NEGRO	Female WHITE	NEGRO
Total not in college, 16–17 years	6,661	5,886	775	3,001	372	2,885	403
Enrolled:							
Private school	588	562	26	281	11	281	15
Public school	5,198	4,588	610	2,363	299	2,225	311
Not enrolled:							
High school graduate	194	183	11	66	2	117	9
Non-high-school graduate	681	553	128	291	60	262	68
Nonenrollment rate[1]	10	9	17	10	16	9	17

[1] Percent "not enrolled, non-high-school graduates" are of "total not in college, 16–17 years."

The bottom line of Table 10-17 shows that about 17 percent of Negro adolescents (ages 16 and 17) have dropped out of school whereas the corresponding number for white adolescents is 9 percent. The following Table 10-18 shows that most of this difference comes from differences outside the South; in the South the white and Negro non-enrollment rates are much the same.

Table 10–18—Enrollment status of persons 16 and 17 years old not in college by sex, race, and region of residence, for the United States: October 1965

[Numbers in thousands]

Enrollment status and region of residence	Total	Both sexes WHITE	NEGRO	Male WHITE	NEGRO	Female WHITE	NEGRO
South							
Total not in college, 16–17 years	2,141	1,676	465	847	238	829	227
Enrolled:							
Private school	108	89	19	45	11	44	8
Public school	1,666	1,297	369	669	195	628	174
Not enrolled:							
High school graduate	36	29	7	8	0	21	7
Non-high-school graduate	331	261	70	125	32	136	38
Nonenrollment rate[1]	15	16	15	15	13	16	17
North and West							
Total not in college, 16–17 years	4,520	4,210	310	2,154	134	2,056	176
Enrolled:							
Private school	480	473	7	236	0	237	7
Public school	3,532	3,291	241	1,694	104	1,597	137
Not enrolled:							
High school graduate	158	154	4	58	2	96	2
Non-high-school graduate	350	292	58	166	28	126	30
Nonenrollment rate[1]	8	7	19	8	21	6	17

[1] Percent "not enrolled, non-high-school graduates" are of "total not in college, 16–17 years."

Table 10–19—Enrollment status of persons 16 and 17 years old by sex, race, and occupation of household head, for the United States: October 1965

[Numbers in thousands. Percent not shown where base is less than 40,000]

Enrollment status and occupation of household head	Total	Both sexes WHITE	NEGRO	Male WHITE	NEGRO	Female WHITE	NEGRO
White Collar							
Total not in college, 16–17 years	2,065	2,017	48	1,081	31	936	17
Enrolled:							
Private school	275	257	18	135	11	122	7
Public school	1,680	1,654	26	893	18	762	8
Not enrolled:							
High school graduate	44	42	2	14	2	28	0
Non-high-school graduate	65	63	2	39	0	24	2
Nonenrollment rate[1]	3	3	4	4	—	3	—
Non White Collar							
Total not in college, 16–17 years	4,596	3,869	727	1,920	341	1,949	386
Enrolled:							
Private school	313	305	8	146	0	159	8
Public school	3,517	2,933	584	1,470	281	1,463	303
Not enrolled:							
High school graduate	150	141	9	52	0	89	9
Non-high-school graduate	616	490	126	252	660	238	66
Nonenrollment rate[1]	13	13	17	13	18	12	17

[1] Percent, "not enrolled, non-high-school graduates" are of "total not in college, 16–17 years."

Table 10-19 is directed to the question of whether the dropout rate is different for different socioeconomic levels. The data suggest that it is, for whereas the nonenrollment rate was 3 percent for those 16- and 17-year-olds from white-collar families, it was more than four times as large (13 percent) in the case of those from other than white-collar families (where the head of household was in a blue-collar or farm occupation, unemployed, or not in the labor force at all).

Table 10–20—Nonenrollment rates of persons 16 and 17 years old not in college by sex, race, type of area, and region of residence, for the United States: October 1965

[Numbers in thousands. Percent not shown where base is less than 50,000]

Nonenrollment rate, type of area, and region of residence	Total	Both sexes		Male		Female	
		WHITE	NEGRO	WHITE	NEGRO	WHITE	NEGRO
Metropolitan South							
Total not in college, 16–17 years	715	545	170	295	95	250	75
Nonenrollment rate[1]	10	9	12	4	14	16	11
Metropolitan North and West							
Total not in college, 16–17 years	2,576	2,301	275	1,237	124	1,064	151
Nonenrollment rate[1]	8	6	20	7	23	6	17
Nonmetropolitan South							
Total not in college, 16–17 years	1,426	1,131	295	552	143	579	152
Nonenrollment rate[1]	18	19	17	21	13	17	20
Nonmetropolitan North and West							
Total not in college, 16–17 years	1,944	1,909	35	917	10	992	25
Nonenrollment rate[1]	8	8	—	9	—	7	—

[1] Percent "not enrolled, non-high-school graduates" are of "total not in college, 16–17 years."

Furthermore, this difference in nonenrollment by parental occupation existed for both male and female, Negro and white adolescents.

The racial differences in the dropout rate are thus sharply reduced when socioeconomic factors are taken into account. Then the difference of 8 percentage points between all Negro and white adolescent dropouts becomes 1 percent for those in white-collar families, and 4 percent for those in other than white-collar families.

Table 10-20 breaks the data down by metropolitan and nonmetropolitan areas as well as by South and non-South. The largest differences between Negro and white dropout rates are seen in the urban North and West; in the nonurban North and West there were too few Negro households in the sample to provide a reliable estimate. In the South there is the unexpected result that in the urban areas, white girls drop out at a greater rate than Negro girls, and in the nonurban area white boys drop out at a substantially greater rate than Negro boys.

Relation of integration to achievement

An education in integrated schools can be expected to have major effects on attitudes toward members of other racial groups. At its best, it can develop attitudes appropriate to the integrated society these students will live in; at its worst, it can create hostile camps of Negroes and whites in the same school. Thus, there is more to "school integration" than merely putting Negroes and whites in the

Table 10–21—Average test scores of Negro pupils, fall 1965

| Grade | Region | Reading comprehension Proportion of white classmates last year | | | | Math achievement Proportion of white classmates last year | | | |
		NONE	LESS THAN HALF	HALF	MORE THAN HALF	NONE	LESS THAN HALF	HALF	MORE THAN HALF
12	Metropolitan Northeast	46.0	43.7	44.5	47.5	41.5	40.6	41.1	44.5
12	Metropolitan Midwest	46.4	43.2	44.0	46.7	43.8	42.6	42.9	44.8
9	Metropolitan Northeast	44.2	44.8	44.8	47.1	43.1	43.5	43.7	47.2
9	Metropolitan Midwest	45.3	45.2	45.3	46.4	44.4	44.3	44.1	46.6
6	Metropolitan Northeast	46.0	45.4	45.8	46.6	44.0	43.4	43.6	45.6
6	Metropolitan Midwest	46.0	44.7	44.9	45.1	43.8	42.8	42.9	44.1

same building, and there may be more important consequences of integration than its effect on achievement.

Yet the analysis of school factors described earlier suggests that in the long run, integration should be expected to have a positive effect on Negro achievement as well. An analysis was carried out to seek such effects on achievement which might appear in the short run. This analysis of the test performance of Negro children in integrated schools indicates positive effects of integration, though rather small ones. Results for grades 6, 9, and 12 are given in Table 10-21 for Negro pupils classified by the proportion of their classmates the previous year who were white. Comparing the averages in each row, in every case but one the highest average score is recorded for the Negro pupils where more than half of their classmates were white. But in reading the rows from left to right, the increase is small and often those Negro pupils in classes with only a few white pupils score lower than those in totally segregated classes.

Table 10–22—Average test scores of Negro pupils, fall 1965

Grade	Region	Grade of first time with majority pupils	NONE	Proportion of majority classmates last year			Total
				LESS THAN HALF	HALF	MORE THAN HALF	
9	Metropolitan Northeast	1, 2, or 3	45.9	46.7	46.9	48.1	46.8
		4, 5, or 6	45.2	43.3	44.4	44.4	44.8
		7, 8, or 9	43.5	42.9	44.6	45.0	44.0
		Never	43.2	—	—	—	43.2
9	Metropolitan Midwest	1, 2, or 3	45.4	46.6	46.4	48.6	46.7
		4, 5, or 6	44.4	44.1	45.3	46.7	44.5
		7, 8, or 9	44.4	43.4	43.3	45.2	43.7
		Never	46.5	—	—	—	46.5
12	Metropolitan Northeast	1, 2, or 3	40.8	43.6	45.2	48.6	46.2
		4, 5, or 6	46.7	45.1	44.9	46.7	45.6
		7, 8, or 9	42.2	43.5	43.8	49.7	48.2
		10, 11, or 12	42.2	41.1	43.2	46.6	44.1
		Never	40.9	—	—	—	40.9
12	Metropolitan Midwest	1, 2, or 3	47.4	44.3	45.6	48.3	46.7
		4, 5, or 6	46.1	43.0	43.5	46.4	45.4
		7, 8, or 9	46.6	40.8	42.3	45.6	45.3
		10, 11, or 12	44.8	39.5	43.5	44.9	44.3
		Never	47.2	—	—	—	47.2

Table 10-22 was constructed to observe whether there is any tendency for Negro pupils who have spent more years in integrated schools to exhibit higher average achievement. Those pupils who first entered integrated schools in the early grades record consistently higher scores than the other groups, although the differences are again small.

No account is taken in these tabulations of the fact that the various groups of pupils may have come from different backgrounds. When such account is taken by simple cross-tabulations on indicators of socioeconomic status, the performance remains highest in those schools which have been integrated for the longest time. Thus, although the differences are small, and although the degree of integration within the school is not known, there is evident, even in the short run, an effect of school integration on the reading and mathematics achievement of Negro pupils.

11. The Financial Crisis of Our Cities
Thirty-three Panel Members

12. Impact of the Property Tax
National Commission on Urban Problems

11 THIRTY-THREE PANEL MEMBERS[1]

The financial crisis of our cities

CENTRAL CITY GOVERNMENTS ARE BURDENED

They are burdened with more than their share of welfare costs, education costs, and regional facility costs. They are paying costs that should more properly be borne by the federal government, paying costs that should more properly be borne by the state governments, paying costs that should at least be shared by their suburbs, paying many costs that should be met by private enterprise and should not be subsidized by any level of government—federal, state or local.

They are burdened with far more costs than they can meet with their present taxing powers or their present tax resources, more costs than they can meet under today's state-imposed restrictions on their taxing authority, more costs than they can meet without pushing their tax rates so high that they would drive still more people and more business to lower-tax shelters outside the city line. Perhaps worst of all, in every state except Hawaii, they are burdened with state-imposed property tax rules that make them subsidize obsolescence, blight, decay, slum formation, and sprawl by undertaxation at the same time that they penalize and inhibit improvements by taxing them more heavily than any other major product of American industry except hard liquor, cigarettes, and perhaps gasoline.

1. See list of panelists at conclusion of this study.

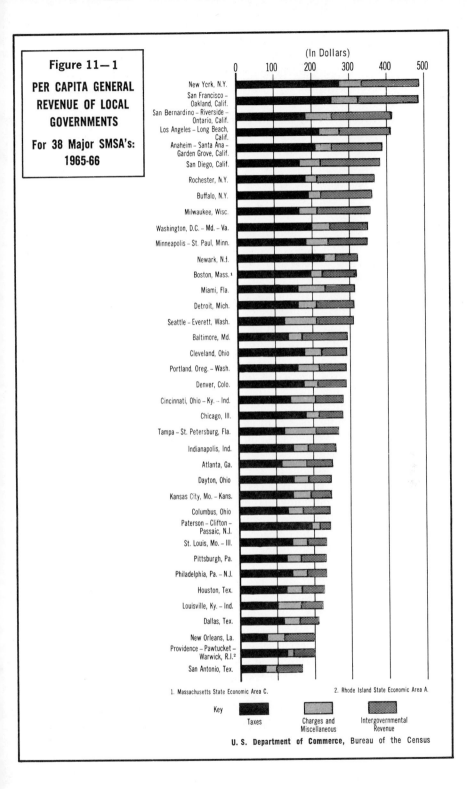

Figure 11—1

PER CAPITA GENERAL REVENUE OF LOCAL GOVERNMENTS

For 38 Major SMSA's: 1965-66

(In Dollars)

1. Massachusetts State Economic Area C.
2. Rhode Island State Economic Area A.

Key — Taxes — Charges and Miscellaneous — Intergovernmental Revenue

U. S. Department of Commerce, Bureau of the Census

They are burdened with costs so far beyond their own present revenue-raising powers that many mayors must spend far too much of their time begging grants-in-aid from the state and/or federal governments, so too many people seem to think the state and federal governments are subsidizing our cities. On the contrary, it might more truly be said that cities are subsidizing the state and federal governments by carrying heavy costs for functions which are a state or federal rather than a local responsibility.

The bigger the city the bigger the money squeeze is apt to be. New York spends for other-than-school costs 22 per cent as much as all other cities combined—half again as much per capita as the other cities over 1,000,000, nearly twice as much per capita as cities between 500,000 and 1,000,000, nearly three times as much as the other 288. But many smaller cities (especially older cities) with less than their share of taxables and more than their share of poverty problems, school problems, sprawl problems, tax exemption problems, and integration problems are in trouble too.

In some cities all the costs of local government are paid through the city itself; in others, the costs of welfare are paid through the county, the costs of education through the school board. But no matter how the local pay-out is handled, the same local taxpayers have put up the money and the city finance problem remains the same: more costs than its local tax base can afford, more costs than its local taxpayers should be asked to carry, more costs than the city government, the school system, and/or the county government can meet without help.

From World War II through 1967 local governments raised their local tax collections 499 per cent, but city costs have climbed nearly 10 per cent faster. Now more and more cities are beginning to face municipal union demands for pay scales well above the levels paid by private business. They may find these union demands hard to resist without backing from the states—and these demands threaten to make the city money problems still worse.

So the question of more state and federal aid for our cities is no longer whether, but how. The question is no longer whether the state and federal governments should allocate more of their own tax revenues to meet local government needs, but how that allocation can best be channelled and directed so it will reach those places where it is needed instead of being dissipated where it is not.

But central cities should not kid themselves that the state or federal governments or the suburbs can or will come through with enough aid and relief to close the whole gap between local spending at the present rate of increase and local revenue from today's local tax practice. Once again the question is not whether, but how; the question is not whether cities must do far more to help themselves financially, but how best the cities can hold down their own local costs and step up their own local revenues.

At today's growth rates of city spending vs. city tax revenue plus state and federal aid, the urban deficit for the next 10 years is estimated by the National League of Cities at $262 billion plus. If the gap is anything like that big, it is all too obvious that something must be done to close it; or, more correctly, many things must be done, beginning with a thorough reconsideration of what, if any, functions might better be performed and/or paid for by the federal government; what, if any, functions might better be performed and/or paid for by the state governments; and what functions might better be shifted to private enterprise. . . .

Two reasons cities can't finance themselves

Reason No. 1—Cities are creatures of the states, and the states have seen fit to limit the cities' taxing powers, partly because the states do not want the cities dipping deep into the same tax sources the states depend on for their own support, partly because some state legislators still do not trust their cities, and partly because state legislators do not always understand their cities' problems.

We are unanimous that every state should repeal its constitutional limitations on local taxing power, reconsider its statutory limitations, and remove or at least ease them whenever they find this easing would not be inconsistent with a sound, comprehensive state-local taxing program. The property tax is the one tax that has always been reserved for local use, so most specifically we recommend that every state should (1) be far more liberal about how much revenue its cities can raise by this levy, and (2) stop forbidding local governments to tax the location values created by community investment more heavily than they tax improvement values paid for by the owner. The only reason most of us can see why states should perhaps keep some control over local property tax rates is to keep the various layers of local taxing units (city, county, school district, etc.) from over-tapping the same tax source on which they all depend.

States set many of the standards local government must meet. Unless the states let local government collect locally the money needed to meet those standards, the states will have little choice but to assume the cost out of the states' own revenues. So instead of restricting local taxing powers the states might be wiser to encourage local governments to raise more money locally.

Reason No. 2—Local taxes (and state taxes too, for that matter) are "competitive," i.e., too many local governments feel (often mistakenly) that they must compete with other local governments to offer low local taxes as a decisive inducement to attract and hold business, industry, and population. The one and only reason the

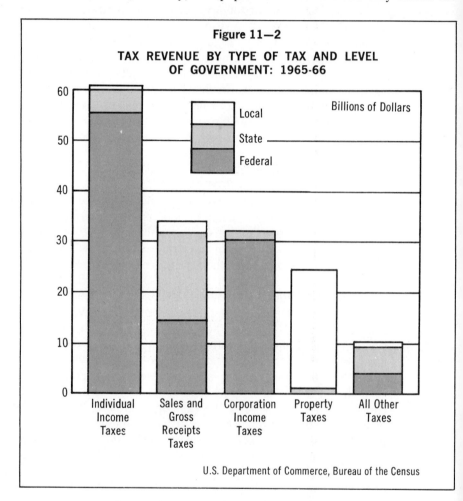

Figure 11—2

TAX REVENUE BY TYPE OF TAX AND LEVEL OF GOVERNMENT: 1965-66

U.S. Department of Commerce, Bureau of the Census

federal government can get away with an income tax schedule ranging from a minimum of 15.4 per cent to a high of 77 per cent is that no one can escape the tax without giving up his citizenship; but no city has dared raise its maximum income tax rate higher than 3 per cent for fear of speeding the upper-income and middle-income exodus to tax-cheaper suburbs. The federal government can get away with taxing business profits 52 per cent, but cities know that even a

10 per cent tax on business would drive out most of their business. Before New York City cut its sales tax back from 4 per cent to 2 per cent, a university research showed that each 1 per cent of tax was driving 6 per cent of all clothing and household furnishing sales out beyond the city line (along with thousands of jobs). Cities do not dare take full advantage of the one tax source that is everywhere reserved to them—the property tax—for fear of speeding the exodus of business and prosperous families to tax havens in the suburbs.

The biggest urban taxable that can't run away to tax shelters out of town is urban land. This could provide local government with an enormous captive tax base, estimated by the Douglas Commission at $320 billion for urban land alone; but every state except Hawaii and Pennsylvania forbids its cities to tax land more heavily than they tax improvements (and new construction is just about the easiest taxable to drive away).

Even with this restriction most cities could collect much more revenue from land if they could and would get the often shocking underassessment of idle and underused land corrected.

WHAT GOVERNMENT SHOULD DO OR PAY FOR

The central cities' need for more financial help from Washington and more help from the states is as urgent as it is obvious.

But we are also agreed that the need for a more rational method allocating that help is almost equally obvious and equally urgent.

The most significant achievement of the federal Constitution was its sensible allocation of what responsibilities (war, foreign relations, postal service, interstate commerce regulation, etc.) could best be met by the central government and what responsibilities could best be left to the state and local governments. For nearly 150 years this division, progressively modified to meet changing conditions, worked reasonably well without undue confusion.

But since the federal government began using the income tax to redistribute the wealth, the constitutional allocation of responsibilities and powers has been so eroded that nobody but nobody knows where the new dividing lines lie today or where else they will lie tomorrow. Under today's many-times-broader interpretation of the welfare clause, Congress has enacted so many splintered urban grant-in-aid and subsidy programs that even the federal agencies can't agree on how many there are. The Advisory Commission on Intergovernmental Relations counted 379 last summer, but the number changes almost from month to month. No matter what the exact count may be, there are so many that city officials must spend countless hours studying a 701-page *Catalog of Federal Aids to State and Local Governments.*

In Washington, responsibility for voting urban grants is scattered around nearly all the congressional committees and subcommittees and responsibility for their execution is scattered in hundreds of agencies and offices. For example, 50 different federal agencies are all working on the problems of water supply and water pollution (up from 25 found by the Hoover Commission in 1955). Grants for urban renewal come from one department, grants for roads come from another, grants for pollution come from a third.

Each of the 379 fragmented federal aid programs is developing its own federal bureaucracy with its own vested interest in self-perpetuation. These vested interests are growing so strong that it may already be too late to dislodge them and replace them with simple and coherent grant-in-aid programs.

With so many federal aids available to city officials who know how to find them and tap them, mayors must spend far too much of their time scheming for federal handouts. For example, Oakland, Calif., has landed 134 separate subsidy programs and keeping track of them is more than a full-time job.

With so many subsidies available to tap, the first question asked about any local spending proposal is too apt to be, not whether the spending would be wise, but "what are the chances of getting federal money to pay for it?" . . .

We are unanimous that today's proliferation of less-than-half-coordinated federal programs and subsidies should be stopped. It is much too wasteful and falls far short of meeting the cities' needs.

As a first step towards rationalizing them, most of us would recommend that all the federal categorical grants would be reorganized and consolidated along functional lines, so each city could choose, for example, whether to spend its health subsidy for mental health out-patient clinics or for venereal disease control, or whether to spend its transportation funds for harbor development, rapid transit, or airport improvement.

While we do recognize that the federal government must keep some reasonable control over how its grants-in-aid are spent, we believe local residents are better able to decide what they need most than officials far away in Washington. Who in Washington could have known that the people in Pittsburgh's Hill slum would assign their three top urban renewal priorities to (1) collect our garbage, (2) repave our streets, and (3) give us more street lights? And who would have dreamed that in Columbus, Ohio, the East Central

Citizens Organization would decide their most needed subsidy was money to inoculate all the neighborhood dogs for rabies!

Confusion is worse at the local level

Confusion in Washington over who should hand out aid is matched by local confusion over who should get it.

Confusion runs horizontally. Except in a few cities, there are at least three layers of government almost everywhere and often five or more (county, city, school district, fire district, water district, library district and what have you) all superimposed and all levying taxes on the same local property through 14,000 primary assessment districts, most of them too small to employ professional assessors.

Confusion runs vertically. Not counting thousands more outside, there are some 22,000 local governments inside the 228 standard metropolitan areas, including thousands of small school districts, thousands of small special districts, and 5,000 separate municipalities, half of which have less than 2,500 population and cover less than one square mile.

Some municipalities and some school districts (notably the central cities and their schools) have desperate need of far more state and federal aid. Other municipalities and school districts have less than their share of costly problems and can get along very well without it. But this we can predict for sure:

Regardless of local need or lack of need, any dramatic increase in state or federal aid (like revenue sharing) would start almost every municipality, every county, and every school district fighting for its full share and more.

So the first question raised by revenue sharing would be the very touchy political problem of how to direct the shared revenue where it is needed and keep it from flowing where it is not. Today the shocking fact is that, in most states, per capita state aid is greater to the suburbs than to the central cities whose need is so much greater!

State governments would like to have full control of allocating the federal money; city governments would like to get their hands on the money direct; county governments are pressing similar claims. So now the National League of Cities, the National Governors Conference, and the National Association of Counties are trying to work out a compromise revenue sharing proposal under which perhaps half the desired increase in federal-local aid would be channelled direct to cities of over a certain size under some allocation formula still to be worked out, a formula that would give weight both to the city's needs and to its own tax effort to meet those needs.

Cities should not set their subsidy hopes too high

There is no reason to believe, and little reason to hope, that the federal government will increase its urban grants-in-aid, which now total only about $2 billion directly to the cities and $4 billion more indirectly through the states, on a major scale with the end of the Vietnam conflict.

It is quite true that the federal government now gets 64 cents out of every tax dollar vs. the states' 19 cents and local governments' 17 cents.

It is also quite true that the federal tax on business profits is so high and the federal income tax rates are so steeply graduated that every new peak of inflation and every non-inflationary increase in the Gross National Product gives the federal tax collectors a bigger share of the GNP. It is quite true that at present rates federal income tax receipts are climbing $10 billion a year, with each $1 billion growth in GNP pouring some $200 million more into the federal treasury. It is quite true that at present rates federal receipts will climb so much faster than projected federal non-war costs that by 1975 the federal surplus could be running $54 billion a year. It is quite true that ending the Vietnam War would make more federal billions available for domestic programs, though not necessarily the $30 billion that is now being talked up.

It is also quite true that the federal government—and only the federal government—has unlimited borrowing capacity for operating as well as capital expenses.

But this easy forecast of federal opulence leaves three big questions unanswered:

Are these very stiff federal tax rates wise, or are they too big a drag on the economy?

The corporation tax takes 52 per cent of the admitted profits of corporate business (plus another 5 per cent or so in accelerated payments). On top of that the personal income tax takes an average of some 30 per cent of whatever corporate profits are paid out in dividends, so all told the federal government is now taking close to two-thirds of business profits from all but the smallest corporations.

Meanwhile the personal income tax takes a quarter of any taxable income the father of two can earn above $12,000 a year, a third of anything he can earn above $22,000, and half of anything he can earn above $40,000. Figuring out ways to escape these taxes has become big business. Corporate executives are getting more and more insistent on taking out their pay in tax-avoiding stock options and deferred compensation; labor unions are pushing more and more demands for tax-exempt fringe benefits.

Affirmative evidence that such stiff tax rates can be a heavy drag on the economy was given by how the small relief provided by the Kennedy tax reduction abetted an overnight acceleration in the GNP growth rate. Converse evidence was the widespread expectation that the 1968 tax surcharge would slow the rate of growth, an expectation that might well have come true if inflation psychology had not called off all bets.

Even at today's stiff tax rates the federal government has been able to balance its budget in only two years since the end of World War II. This gives small support to the idea that the federal government has unlimited money to spend.

Whether or not the present federal tax rates are wise, is the voting public willing to go on paying them?

The one thing we know for sure about today's public attitudes is that the public is angrily dissatisfied and clamoring for change. There is some reason to believe that tax reduction might be the most welcome change of all.

Even if the voters are willing to continue present federal taxes, how much of the increase can the cities hope to cut themselves in on in competition with all the other claimants for federal largesse?

For example, how much would be left over for the cities if the federal government votes some form of negative income tax at a cost of, say, $12 billion a year? And what reason is there to believe the alliance of big business and big military will not find ways to cut itself back in on a big share of any defense saving that may follow peace in Asia?

All of us agree the cities should get more financial help from Washington. All of us wish the cities well in getting it.

But most cities would be foolish to count on major federal help.

Some states are doing much more than others

Helping their cities meet their growing needs is much more than a challenge and a responsibility for the states. It is also an opportunity they cannot afford to pass up to reassert and re-establish their position as the foundation units on which creative federalism must be built.

Some states are seizing this opportunity; others are not. Too many states have been far too slow to recognize their role, responsibility, and stake in facing the problems raised by the urbanization of the nation.

States are now contributing some $16 billion to local government costs (not counting a $4 billion pass-through from Washington), but only a minor fraction of this is allocated to city governments and only a very small part is available to help the cities meet their peculiarly urban problems like pollution and mass transportation. Most state aid to local governments is earmarked for the long recognized needs of education (62 per cent in 1967) or for relief (16 per cent).

One big reason the federal government involved itself in so many different urban aids and programs was to fill the vacuum left by the states' slowness in recognizing many problems that are far more urgent in the cities than in rural areas. Conversely, this state inaction is one big reason (but by no means the only reason) why so many cities are now trying to bypass their state governments and carry their appeals for help direct to Washington.

Some states are doing much more than others to help their local governments, either by sizable grants-in-aid or by taking on responsibility for some activities and costs that would otherwise hit locally. For example, more than half the states provide for practically all public welfare expenditure that is not federally financed. But local taxes must foot much of this bill in California, New York, New Jersey, Ohio, and various smaller states, and since welfare costs are typically greatest in the central cities they are particularly hard hit.

Nationwide, the states and local governments contribute about 50-50 toward the combined cost of state-local services, and in most of the south the states' part is considerably more. But the state-provided share is far less than the national average in such urban states as California, Illinois, Ohio, and New Jersey—and even in New York, though payments to local governments make up more than half the New York state budget.

States set up the laws under which local governments must operate, including the laws by which local taxing powers are restricted and local government is allowed to stay fragmented, so all of us agree that all the states and not just a few should take a more active part in solving some of the resultant problems and pay more of the cost.

At the very least, even the less prosperous state governments could and should help out by giving city governments more authority to help themselves (including, for example, more authority to annex adjoining territory, more authority for some degree of extraterritorial planning, zoning, and subdivision control on the urban fringe, and more authority to ease the costly wastes of building code chaos by adopting uniform construction codes and standards by reference).

Today some states are actually making their cities' financial

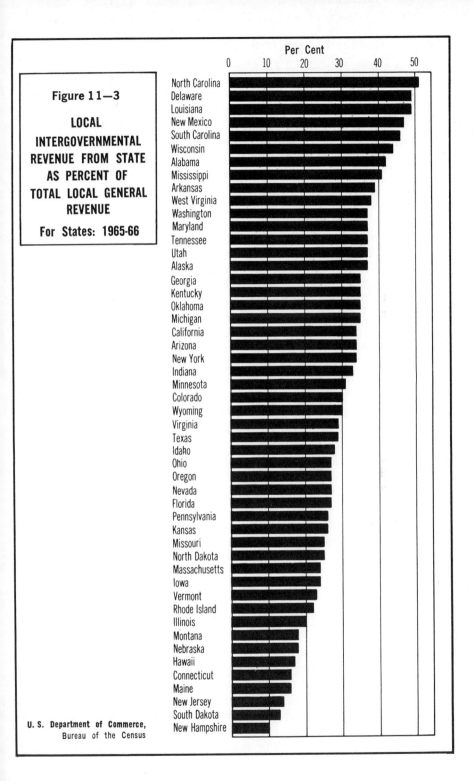

Figure 11—3

LOCAL INTERGOVERNMENTAL REVENUE FROM STATE AS PERCENT OF TOTAL LOCAL GENERAL REVENUE

For States: 1965-66

Per Cent

North Carolina
Delaware
Louisiana
New Mexico
South Carolina
Wisconsin
Alabama
Mississippi
Arkansas
West Virginia
Washington
Maryland
Tennessee
Utah
Alaska
Georgia
Kentucky
Oklahoma
Michigan
California
Arizona
New York
Indiana
Minnesota
Colorado
Wyoming
Virginia
Texas
Idaho
Ohio
Oregon
Nevada
Florida
Pennsylvania
Kansas
Missouri
North Dakota
Massachusetts
Iowa
Vermont
Rhode Island
Illinois
Montana
Nebraska
Hawaii
Connecticut
Maine
New Jersey
South Dakota
New Hampshire

plight worse instead of better by (1) mandating local expenditures like salary increases for police and firemen, mental outpatient clinics, and a host of other functions without providing any money or any added local taxing powers to pay for them, and/or by (2) voting tax exemptions at local expense to win support from favored voter groups like veterans and farmers.

The least the states should do is compensate local governments for any and all local revenue lost as a result of such state-ordered special exemptions. And we are almost unanimous that cities should no longer be expected to give the state and federal governments a free ride on local services by giving all state and federal property a multi-billion-dollar tax exemption. Why, for example, should New York City subsidize the Army with a $37,340,000 exemption on Fort Hamilton, or subsidize the Navy with a $50,940,000 exemption on Floyd Bennett Field?

Prior to 1959, when New York took the lead, no state had even set up an office or council for community affairs; and before the racial disorders began focusing voter attention on the "urban crisis" only Alaska, Rhode Island, California, and Tennessee had acted on the recommendation of the Council of State Governments and followed New York's lead. Now 21 states have established such an office; and eight, led by Pennsylvania and New Jersey, have up-graded it to department status. Their functions are still mostly coordinating and advisory (including advisory service on how to get more federal subsidies). Only half of these 21 states (less than a quarter of the total) give their urban offices any substantial money to contribute towards local costs.

As of the end of 1967, 20 states were helping local communities meet the local contribution required for federal waste treatment, sewage, and/or water facilities, eight were helping on urban renewal, 10 on urban mass transportation, and at least nine on air pollution control.

WHY EDUCATION COSTS SHOULD BE SHIFTED

Reason No. 1—The central city tax base just plain cannot afford to carry all the cost of city schools. For example, one big reason New York's finances are so critical is that its school costs have soared to equal nearly 80 per cent of the city's property tax take, despite New York's having three times as big a property tax roll as any other city and taxing it at a rate more than twice the national average.

Reason No. 2—The impact of school costs varies too widely

from one tax jurisdiction to the next, and it costs central cities much more than it costs the suburbs to give all children comparable schooling.

Some of this uneven impact is inevitable, because (1) slum families tend to have more children per family to educate at public expense, and because (2) it costs much more per pupil to educate children from "culturally deprived" slum families than it costs to give comparable education to children from educated families. New York City already spends more per pupil for the public schools in Harlem than the grade school tuition in the city's more expensive private schools—and even that is not enough.

Some of the uneven impact is accidental, because some tax jurisdictions just happen to have fewer children per assessment dollar to educate.

But much of the uneven impact is deliberate, the result of (1) suburban zoning conceived for the express purpose of zoning tax resources in and school costs out, and (2) tax shelters created with the express intention of attracting industry by the promise of low school costs and therefore low local taxes.

Whatever the cause, the consequences of this uneven impact are likely to get progressively worse as more and more substantial taxpayers, both business and individual, seek to escape from high taxes by moving to low-school-tax areas, leaving the heavy school costs behind in the city to be paid out of a tax base diminished by their flight.

Reason No. 3—With our increasingly mobile population it no longer makes sense to think of education as a local cost and treat it as a local cost to be paid for out of local taxes. Most of the children now being educated in central city schools will move somewhere else as soon as they grow up, and half the families whose children add most to central city school costs come from somewhere else. Furthermore, the need for an educated citizenry all capable of supporting themselves in an economy making more and more educational demands is a national need that knows no local limits. It is a need we cannot afford to slight, for a Committee on Economic Development study found that from 1929 to 1957 some 21 per cent of the growth in real income per worker was due to better education of the labor force and another 36 per cent to the advance of knowledge. Said the President's Council of Economic Advisers: "Education is the most important force behind economic growth."

Reason No. 4—If education costs were taken over by the states or heavily subsidized on a per pupil basis (instead of per average attendance), suburbs would have one less reason for restrictive

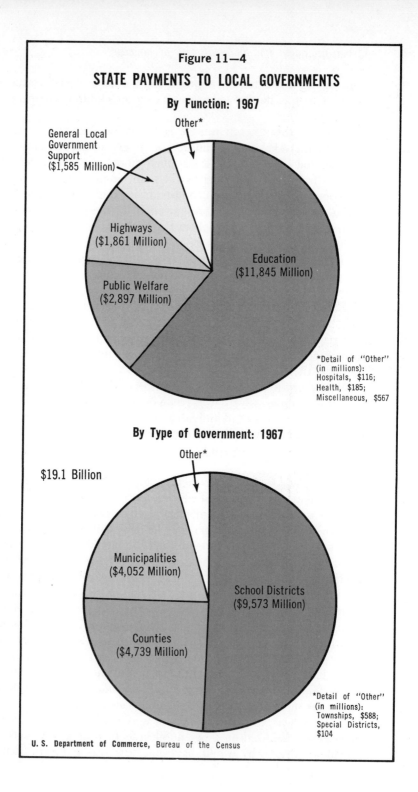

Figure 11—4

STATE PAYMENTS TO LOCAL GOVERNMENTS

By Function: 1967

Other*

General Local
Government
Support
($1,585 Million)

Highways
($1,861 Million)

Public Welfare
($2,897 Million)

Education
($11,845 Million)

*Detail of "Other"
(in millions):
Hospitals, $116;
Health, $185;
Miscellaneous, $567

By Type of Government: 1967

Other*

$19.1 Billion

Municipalities
($4,052 Million)

School Districts
($9,573 Million)

Counties
($4,739 Million)

*Detail of "Other"
(in millions):
Townships, $588;
Special Districts,
$104

U. S. Department of Commerce, Bureau of the Census

zoning to keep out children and one less reason to resist annexation or consolidation into larger and more functional governmental units.

For each and all of these four reasons, we believe that the costs of education should no longer be treated as local costs or paid for out of local revenues (except where local taxpayers may choose to impose additional taxes on themselves to pay for educational advantages for their children).

Instead, most of us would recommend that every state should assume a much bigger share of the basic costs of meeting the state-determined standard of education.

And we would also urge that the federal government should supplement the state effort by (1) assuming a much bigger share of the tax-supported costs of higher education, (2) paying the poverty-related costs of educating children from "culturally deprived" homes, and (3) recognizing that many states will need help to bring their educational standards up to an acceptable national form. (Mississippi, for example, spends a larger percentage of the total income of its population on education than almost any other state, but the income level there is so low that it can spend only $412 per pupil for its schools.)

We do not believe increased state financing of school costs should give the states increased control; on the contrary, we are almost unanimous that city people in each local school district should be encouraged to take a more active interest in how their children are educated and given a bigger voice in how their local schools are run.

If the states put up all or almost all the money for the public schools, many of us believe the states should keep some control over teachers' salary levels; otherwise local school boards might be too ready to yield to union pressures for higher pay on the general theory that the state will pay the bill anyway.

Without help for schools, central cities will lose more middle-income taxpayers

Poor families want more money spent for better schools in the slums. Middle-income families want more money spent for better schools for middle-income children. Both demands are justified, but where will the money come from?

Ghetto families are registering their discontent noisily by riots, sit-ins, and loud demands for neighborhood control of their neighborhood schools. Middle-income families are registering their discontent much more quietly but just as forcefully in two ways, both of which threaten to make the central city school problem worse:

Millions of middle- and upper-income families are moving out to suburbs where they can have some assurance that the heavy school taxes they pay will be spent to provide the particular kind and quality of education they want for their own children instead of being spent mostly to provide the often-quite-different kind of education needed by children from the slums. Families with school-age children account for most of the "flight to the suburbs," just as families whose children have finished school account for most of the move back to town. Desegregation is speeding this middle-income exodus but did not start it; the exodus began long before desegregation became an issue, and many middle-income non-white families are joining the exodus when they can. Its prime motivation is the strongest middle-income motivation of all: the desire to give their children a good start in life.

How much longer can the central cities afford to lose the school taxes of these upper- and middle-income taxpayers?

Millions of middle- and upper-income families, black as well as white, are taking their children out of public school and often paying high tuition to send them to private or parochial schools. In Washington less than a third of the white families who still live in the capital send their children to public school. In New York nearly 400,000 middle-class white and more than 25,000 non-white children now go to private or parochial schools. Racial desegregation has speeded this resegregation by incomes, but once again desegregation did not start it; it began long before racial desegregation became an issue.

How much longer will these upper- and middle-income families be willing to vote heavy school taxes for schools to which they are unwilling to send their own children?

Obviously someone must pay the extra costs of educating children from "culturally deprived" homes. But we sympathize with the unwillingness of the upper- and middle-income families who still live in the cities to pay a disproportionate share of these costs and we sympathize with their insistence that city schools should be as good as suburban schools for their own children.

All this adds up to one more big reason why school costs should be spread over a broader geographic tax base.

Some cities pay far more than their share for poverty

Poverty is highly localized, but poverty is not just a local problem. Its cause is more often national or regional, and it can seldom be cured by local action.

In some localities poverty costs are no problem at all. In most central cities they are a heavy drain. New York has a million people on welfare, with relief payments so generous that the unskilled and needy are attracted there from all parts of the country.

Much of the poverty in our big central cities is what got left behind when upper- and middle-income families moved out to the suburbs. And much of the poverty in our big central cities moved there from somewhere else as millions of workers displaced by farm or mine mechanization swarmed into the cities vainly hoping to find jobs.

All of us agree that all the tax costs of poverty should be spread over a broad geographic tax base and most of them should be borne by the federal government.

All of us favor this upward shift for the very practical reason that only the federal government has the tax resources needed to cover the cost.

Some of us also favor the upward shift for somewhat theoretical reasons, arguing that the federal government has formally assumed responsibility for maintaining national prosperity and full employment, so the federal government should also bear the responsibility for failures and pay the costs where poverty continues in the midst of plenty. They further argue that:

Only the federal government can formulate and activate a coherent national urbanization policy. Only the federal government can offer tax incentives to direct business and industrial location into poverty and unemployment areas, and only the federal government can direct the multi-billion dollar flow of its own purchases where it is needed most. Conversely, only the federal government can maintain a computerized national employment and information service to steer the flow of displaced workers to places where they would be most likely to find jobs. Only the federal government could be expected to provide interstate resettlement and new-job-training allowances. And only the federal government can even out the standards of relief payments so jobless families will have less cause to concentrate in high-relief-payment centers like New York, where monthly aid to dependent children averages $241.65 per family, New Jersey ($229.05) or Connecticut ($220.90), compared with $34.85 in Mississippi and $26 in Puerto Rico.

Half the states now pick up the check for all or nearly all the public assistance payments the federal government does not cover. We are almost unanimous that all the other states should do the same. But these welfare payments now borne by local government are only a small part of the local tax cost of poverty. They total today only about $1.5 billion, and the central cities need far more help than that to meet the other costs of poverty that are concentrating there.

EVEN IF CENTRAL CITY NEEDS WERE LESS URGENT, HERE ARE TWO REASONS FOR
MORE FEDERAL AID

Poverty and education are the two costs whose impact is least equally
divided, the two costs whose incidence bears least relation to the
local property tax base on which local government still depends,
on the average, for nearly 87 per cent of its local revenue. They are
the two costs for which a broader geographic and economic tax
base is most needed to lessen today's local inequities.

Freed from paying the costs of poverty and education, most cities
could raise through a better-applied property tax alone all the money
they would need to meet their remaining money needs, improve all
other services, and make city living more attractive.

This would still leave two big reasons why we would urge the
federal governments to continue making certain specific grants-in-
aid to city governments:

Reason No. 1—The hope of federal subsidies has proven a most
effective way to motivate local governments to tackle problems and
meet needs (like air pollution) they have too long neglected.

Reason No. 2—The hope of federal subsidies could be the most
effective inducement to get local governments to get together and
consolidate or at least combine their operations. Local government
needs to be broadly restructured to perform its proper functions
well, but this restructuring will be far too slow in coming without
the bait of federal aid. If metropolitan-area government units below
a certain size were declared ineligible for federal bloc grants, we
might be surprised by how many too-small units might decide to
get together.

Cities and states should do more taxing themselves

We recognize that the federal government is taking so much money
out of the cities and states that some way must be found to get some
of this revenue back to the lower levels of government. That is why
we favor some form of federal tax sharing.

We recognize that some cities need more tax sharing than others
because they are poorer and have less taxables; but we also recognize that some cities and some states are trying much harder than
others to meet their money needs by levying heavier taxes on their
own people, so we are unanimous that all cities and all states should
be encouraged to do as much of their own taxing as they can before
asking Washington to do the taxing for them.

To give them this incentive, all of us agree that:

Any allocation of urban aids and subsidies should give heavy consideration to how hard the needy local government is trying to meet its own needs.

How good a case for bigger state and federal subsidies can a city make if its property tax rate is well below the 2-per-cent-of-true-value national average and less than half the rate many other cities impose? Do cities where the state-plus-local tax burden is light rate the same increase in federal subsidies as cities where state-plus-local taxation takes half again as big a percentage of personal incomes? (viz New York 13.2 per cent vs. Illinois 8.5 per cent, California 12.2 per cent vs. Ohio 8.2 per cent, Wyoming 13.2 per cent and Arizona 12.8 per cent vs. Connecticut 9.1 per cent and New Jersey 9.3 per cent).

And most of us would recommend that:

Stimulation of greater state and local tax effort might start by letting federal income taxpayers take a credit for the state and local taxes they pay, including, specifically, a much larger credit for the state and local income taxes because the income tax is very much underutilized at the state and local levels. This would give state and local governments a big new reason to do more taxing themselves instead of asking Washington to do the taxing for them.

As things stand today the heavy federal income taxation actually seems to have discouraged state and local income taxation. As long as the federal income tax rates were low (i.e. before 1937), 32 states imposed income levies; since the federal rates soared only three more states have begun taxing incomes; until just recently only nine states had ventured to raise their rate above 2 per cent. Now six have actually lifted the top bracket above 10 per cent (New York 14 per cent, Minnesota 12 per cent, Delaware, Hawaii, and North Dakota 11 per cent, Vermont a quarter of the federal levy).

If all states had raised the level of their state and local income tax collections to take the same income percentage as the 1966 average of the top 10, their income tax take would have been more than twice as big ($11.2 billion in 1966 compared with an actual $4.8 billion). Similarly, if all states had raised the level of their state and local sales tax collections to the level of the top 10, they would have had $5.2 billion more of their own revenue to spend; and if all local governments had brought their property tax collections up to the average level that prevailed in the top 10 property-tax states, they would have had $9.3 billion more of their own to spend from this source ($33.8 billion vs. $24.5 billion).

We recognize that southern cities may have their own good and special reasons for needing more help from Washington, but most of us think that whoever allocates that aid should remember that there are big differences in local tax effort even in the south. For example, in 1966 Birmingham taxed its median homeowner .92 per cent of true value vs. .54 per cent in Montgomery; Memphis taxed

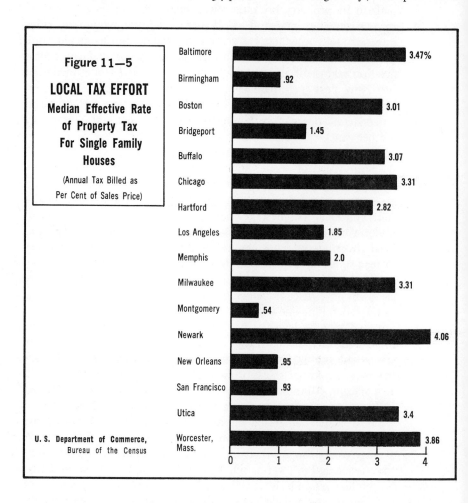

Figure 11—5

LOCAL TAX EFFORT

Median Effective Rate of Property Tax For Single Family Houses

(Annual Tax Billed as Per Cent of Sales Price)

U. S. Department of Commerce, Bureau of the Census

Baltimore	3.47%
Birmingham	.92
Boston	3.01
Bridgeport	1.45
Buffalo	3.07
Chicago	3.31
Hartford	2.82
Los Angeles	1.85
Memphis	2.0
Milwaukee	3.31
Montgomery	.54
Newark	4.06
New Orleans	.95
San Francisco	.93
Utica	3.4
Worcester, Mass.	3.86

its median homeowner 2 per cent vs. .95 per cent in nearby New Orleans. Outside the south, according to the 1967 Census of Governments, Los Angeles taxed its median homeowner twice as heavily as San Francisco—1.85 per cent vs. .93 per cent; Milwaukee almost three fourths more than Chicago—3.31 per cent vs. 1.94 per cent; Hartford nearly twice as heavily as Bridgeport—2.82 per cent vs. 1.45 per cent; and many other cities throughout the northeast made their median homeowners pay more than 3 per cent—

including Baltimore 3.47 per cent, Boston 3.01 per cent, Worcester 3.86 per cent, Buffalo 3.07 per cent, Utica 3.40 per cent, and Newark 4.06 per cent.

More states should follow the example set by Maryland which encourages its principal local governments (the counties) to piggyback a county income tax at up to half the state rate on the state income levy. This is one good way to discourage local competition to see which community can offer the lowest taxes as bait to catch more business and more people. (Incidentally, to avoid confusion and senseless duplication of collection machinery, most of us would recommend that all local income and sales taxes should always be piggybacked on state income and sales levies.)

Regardless of how hard a city may try to meet its money needs by heavier local taxation, we recognize that most central cities and all big cities will still need much more federal aid. In fact, many of the cities most in need of more help are already among the cities where local taxation is heaviest. For example, no big city imposes a higher local income tax than New York, no big city collects a higher local sales tax, and few cities impose a heavier property tax—and yet few cities are in more urgent and obvious need of more state and federal money help.

Correct what's wrong with the property tax

Wisely applied, the property tax on which local governments depend for 87 per cent of their tax revenue could be one of the wisest and fairest of all taxes; but as most cities apply it today it may well be the very worst—a weird combination of overtaxation and undertaxation, an incentive tax for what we don't want and a disincentive tax for what we do want. It harnesses the profit motive backward instead of forward to both urban renewal and urban development. Too often it makes it more profitable to misuse and underuse land than to use it wisely and fully, more profitable to let buildings decay than to improve them or replace them.

Too few tax levyers seem to understand that the property tax is not just one tax; on the contrary, it combines and confuses two completely opposite and conflicting taxes, and it would be hard to imagine two taxes whose consequences for urban renewal and urban development would be more different.

One of the two conflicting taxes fused and confused in the property tax is the tax on the improvement—the tax on what past, present, and future owners of the property have spent or will spend to improve it. And it must be obvious to anyone that heavy taxes on improvements are bound to discourage, inhibit, and often prevent improvements.

The other levy confused in the property tax is the land tax—the tax on the location value of the site, the tax on what the property would be worth if the owners had never done anything or spent anything to improve it, the tax on the value that derives mostly from an enormous investment of other peoples' money and other tax-payers' money to create the community around it and make the location accessible, livable, and richly saleable. And it must be obvious to anyone that heavy taxes on the location cannot discourage or inhibit improvements; on the contrary, heavy taxes on location could put effective pressure on the owners to put their sites to better use so as to bring in enough income to earn a good profit after paying the heavier tax.

All this is so obvious that you would think every city would try to tax land heavily and tax improvements lightly if at all; but just the opposite is the case. Almost every city collects two or three times as much money from taxes on improvements as from taxes on land. In fact, many cities tax improvements more heavily than the combined local, state, and federal taxes on any other product of American industry except hard liquor, cigarettes, and perhaps gasoline.

A 3-per-cent-a-year tax on improvements may not sound big compared with an income tax averaging, say, 30 per cent, but it sounds small only because it is expressed as a percentage of capital, whereas the income tax, as its name makes clear, is expressed as a percentage of income. The enormity of the improvement tax becomes self-evident when we restate it in income tax, in sales tax, and in consumer tax terms:

First in income tax terms:

A 3-per-cent-of-true-value tax on improvements is apt to tax away 75 per cent of the net income a new building would otherwise earn.

And now in sales tax terms:

A 3-per-cent-of-true-value tax on improvements is the instalment plan equivalent of a 52 per cent sales tax; i.e., it will cost the improver as much as a 52 per cent lump sum sales tax would cost him if he could finance it at 5 per cent interest over the 60-year life of the improvement.

And finally in consumer tax terms:

A 3-per-cent-of-true-value tax on improvements will cost the consumer more than a 25 per cent consumption tax; i.e. it will add more than 25 per cent to the rent a tenant must pay or more than 25 per cent to the carrying costs an owner must meet.

So no wonder New York's 4-per-cent-of-true-value tax on new improvements has stopped almost all private new construction in the city except for the seemingly unstoppable boom in never-mind-the-cost office buildings renting at $8 to $12 a sq. ft. and luxury apartments selling at $10,000 a room or renting at $100-plus a room.

And no wonder Boston's 6 per-cent-of-true-value tax on improvements brought all private construction to a halt until the law was changed so new improvements can be taxed only half as heavily as existing buildings.

The deterrent effect of the improvement tax is so obvious and so widely recognized that whenever government wants to encourage some favored project the first thought is to offer the builder tax exemption on the new construction. But this makes the city-wide problem worse by making it necessary to increase the improvement tax everywhere else, thereby increasing the tax deterrent for all other improvements.

Cities could help themselves by taxing land heavily

By definition, the value of unimproved urban and suburban land is created not by anything the owners have done to improve it, but by an enormous investment of other people's money to build the community around it and an enormous investment of other tax-payers' money to provide the infrastructure of roads, schools, water systems, sewage systems, mass transit facilities, parks, pollution controls, police facilities, fire protection, etc., etc., etc., needed to make the location easily reachable, pleasantly livable, and richly saleable.

The enormity of this other-taxpayer investment is suggested by a Regional Plan Association report indicating that near New York it is averaging well over $16,850 per lot in single-family locations, many times $16,850 in multi-family locations. This $16,850 figure is confirmed and given broader significance by studies for the Southern California Research Council that come within about a thousand dollars of the same figure for Los Angeles.

But the selling price of land is bound to be less than its total value. How much less will depend on how much or how little of this enormous community investment of other people's money and other taxpayers' money the local government chooses to recover for the community by taxation and/or special assessments, and how much it allows the landowner to convert to his private profit. If the community made landowners pay back 100 per cent of this investment, the price of their land would often fall to zero or less. Today most local governments assess and tax unused, underused, and misused land so lightly that the tax makes the owners repay only a trifling share (perhaps 5 per cent) of the community investment that multiplied the value of their land. The other 95 per cent they are free to capitalize into higher and higher land prices.

This practice of public improvements for private profit gives land speculation an enormous hidden subsidy, a hidden subsidy so big that it may actually be bigger than all the farm subsidies plus foreign aid combined. And this is perhaps the biggest reason why building-site prices have been going up much faster than the prices of everything else. The Douglas Commission found that from 1955 to 1965 land prices climbed six times as fast as the index of wholesale commodity prices.

The smaller the land tax the bigger the land subsidy and the higher the land price can go. So we are shocked but hardly surprised to hear the Tax Foundation report that most of the federal urban redevelopment subsidies have gone to enrich the owners of slum property by raising the price of slum land ($484,000 per average acre for the slum properties bought for demolition by the New York Public Housing Authority) and have done little to help the poor people living in the slums (just as the federal *Report on the Causes of Rural Poverty* found that the federal farm subsidies "have created a class of wealthy rural landowners but done little to improve the condition of the rural poor").

Here are a few of the many reasons why most of us believe the unimproved location value of urban and suburban land should be taxed much more heavily:

Quite simply, to help pay the cost of local government, including the cost of all the tax-paid improvements that make the location valuable.

To offset the cost of untaxing improvements. Local governments depend on property taxation for nearly 87 per cent of their local revenue, so the only way they can afford to tax improvements less is to tax unimproved land values more.

To slow down the pace of land price inflation.

To exert heavy pressure on the owners of underused and misused land (including most specifically slums) to put it to better use now instead of waiting for further subsidies and further investments of other peoples' money to raise its price still higher (land speculators call this "waiting for it to ripen"). With land prices for building soaring 8 to 15 per cent a year, millions of idle acres are now so underassessed and undertaxed that the owner can hold $1 million worth off the market for a property tax cost of as low as $5,000 a year, with up to 77 per cent of that $5,000 deductible from his federal income tax.

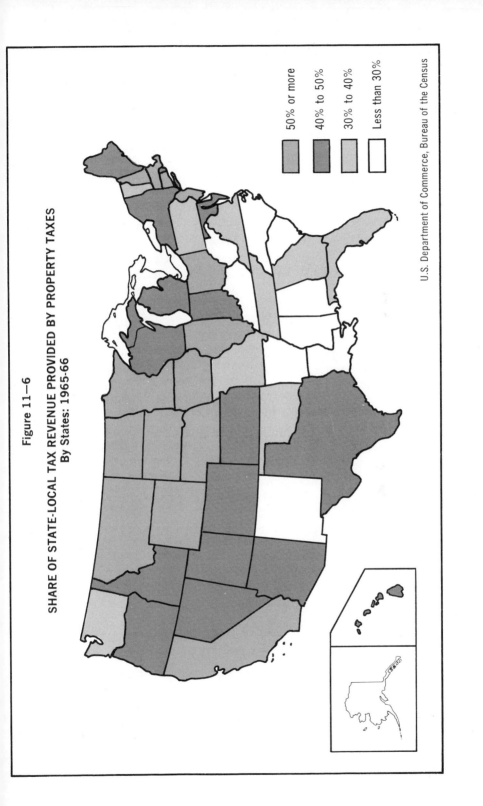

Figure 11–6

SHARE OF STATE-LOCAL TAX REVENUE PROVIDED BY PROPERTY TAXES
By States: 1965-66

50% or more

40% to 50%

30% to 40%

Less than 30%

U.S. Department of Commerce, Bureau of the Census

To let cities expand in an orderly manner instead of disintegrating in suburban sprawl and premature subdivision, with millions of close-in acres held off the market for speculation, thereby forcing homebuilders to leapfrog further and further out into the countryside to get land they can afford to build on and forcing industry to move further and further away from urban employment (and unemployment) centers to find enough land they can afford to build new plants on.

To save the tax waste of sprawl, which multiplies the cost of roads to reach sprawl-scattered homes, multiplies the cost of water distribution, multiplies the cost of sewage collection, multiplies the cost of mass transportation, inflates the cost of police and fire protection, and doubles the cost of getting children to and from school.

To stop and perhaps reverse the futile spiral in which the multibillion-dollar urban renewal subsidies are being capitalized into higher urban renewal land costs calling for bigger urban renewal subsidies that will in turn be capitalized into higher land costs requiring still bigger subsidies (land write-down subsidies, below-market-interest subsidies, tax exemption subsidies, or perhaps some new kind of subsidy). . . .

Cities should collect more user charges

Service charges can serve a double purpose: they can produce a substantial revenue and they can discourage costly and wasteful practices that need to be discouraged.

We are unanimous in urging more cities to make more use of service charges, including specifically and for example:

To discourage today's almost scandalous waste of water, all water service should be metered at rates high enough to cover the cost.

To discourage the on-street parking that is a main source of downtown congestion and traffic delays, parking meter rates should be raised at least as high as off-street parking charges in the same area. It is insane to let motorists park at the curb for 10¢ or 25¢ an hour where parking lots charge 50¢ or $1.

To discourage industrial water pollution, industries that pour pollutants into streams and sewers should be charged the full cost of purification. If this policy can keep the Ruhr in Germany safe for drinking there is no reason why the same policy should not do as much for the Hudson, the Mississippi, and Lake Erie.

To minimize air pollution, cities should charge property owners more for garbage collection than it would cost them to install and operate garbage incinerators equipped with water washers and electrostatic filters adequate to remove 99 per cent of all pollutants. The biggest reason New York cannot enforce its incinerator standards is that building owners just threaten to stop burning their trash and garbage and leave it for the city to collect and cart away free.

Instead of relying on the property tax to provide most of the local revenue, a few of us would even go so far as to favor abolishing this levy and substituting carefully-cost-accounted service charges to pay all the costs of local government except education, poverty, and traffic police (which they would shift to the state or federal levels).

Cities could get greater productivity

Private enterprise has been able to pay higher and higher wages only because over the years private enterprise has found ways to raise the level of labor productivity at least as fast as it raised the level of wages:

partly by taking full advantage of mechanization to let machines perform faster and better many functions that were formerly done by hand;

partly by job reassignment so skilled workers need no longer waste high-pay time on jobs that could just as well be handled by less skilled labor;

and partly by reviewing all their operations and eliminating work for which there is no longer any good reason.

Today, with far less productivity improvement, municipal pay scales are climbing nearly twice as fast as private industry's.

We are unanimous in urging that in most cities a broad review and reorganization of local government operations to improve productivity and hold down costs is now overdue. This review should also consider what savings could be achieved by making it worthwhile for private enterprise to take over many functions (like garbage collection) that are now performed by city employees.

Three examples we could cite to suggest that many cities could check their soaring costs by following the example of private business on mechanization, specification changes, and job reassignment:

Example No. 1—Cities could make it profitable for private enterprise to offer better equipment cheaper if they could and would coordinate and standardize their buying specifications. For example: today there is no such thing as a standard fire engine; almost every city allows its fire department to order something different and special. For another example: most cities could also save quite a lot of money rationalizing their fire hydrant purchases. What possible excuse can there be for tropical Honolulu's paying extra for hydrants that won't freeze in sub-zero temperatures?

Example No. 2—Most of us think it is time more cities began to coordinate police pay scales with police job requirements. It may well be true that many policemen are now underpaid for the dangerous and/or exacting work they are assigned to do; but it is also true that many jobs now done at full police pay (like ticketing parked cars and collecting tolls) could be done just as well at half the cost by persons with lesser qualifications. For some police functions like fighting organized crime the best is none too good; for other police jobs a high school graduate with courage, good health, and proper training can do at least as well as a Ph.D. So it makes no sense that in so many cities the starting requirements and pay scales for all police jobs should be so nearly alike. The end result of this leveling practice can only be higher costs for a mediocre police force.

Example No. 3—Cities could save much of the land cost for new schools on high-priced close-in land by following New York's example and sharing the site with an apartment tower, with the school occupying the lower floors entered from one side of the block and the apartments using the air rights above and entered through a lobby on the opposite side.

On outlying land cheap enough for one-story buildings, cities might save perhaps a third of the construction cost by not requiring fireproof construction where every classroom can have direct access to out-of-doors. (A fireproof building has been likened to a "stove whose contents can be burned up without damaging the container.")

Many cities could save much of their slum area school vandalism bill for broken glass ($1 million a year in New York) by specifying unbreakable glass.

A broad study of how municipal costs could be held down by rationalizing municipal labor assignments and equipment purchases would threaten many vested interests in waste, patronage, and job security, so it may well be beyond the capacity (let alone the means) of most local governing and spending bodies. So help in its direction and financing might well be one of the very best aids the federal and state governments could offer the cities. . . .

Schools are the biggest challenge to control costs

Many of us consider education a backward industry. It spends least for research, development, and evaluation of its own processes— only a small fraction of 1 per cent. It lacks any effective agency for getting schools to know and use what little research it does. (This is a job the schools of education should be doing but are not.)

Its standards of professional compensation, both starting pay and top salary, are the lowest and its professional turnover is the highest, with one-third of the teaching force dropping out every five years.

It lacks any accepted and reliable evaluation technique by which to judge the scope and quality of its service (which a CED study rates only 8 per cent better than in 1955, vs. a 32 per cent improvement in other public services). It applies no standard program accounting to identify costs and permit item by item comparisons with other schools.

It spends only 3.3 per cent of its budgets for all instructional materials, equipment, and supplies—compared with more than 60 per cent for salaries, whose level climbed 61.6 per cent from 1957 to 1968 with too little apparent gain in productivity.

It lacks any orderly pattern for effective cooperation among school districts, state school offices, universities, and the federal funding agencies.

Public school budgets have soared from $12 billion in 1957 to $28 billion in 1968, making education by far the biggest charge on local government. And now the U.S. Education Office says this cost will climb 37 per cent higher by 1975, mostly for the continuing rise in teachers' pay scales, the continuing (if slower) rise in enrollments (up 8 per cent in this decade vs. 37 per cent from 1955 to 1965), and a small continuing reduction in class size (from 26 to 24). It will climb much higher if our schools try to meet the growing demand for pre-schooling, longer schooling, vocational and technical training, and compensatory education. Pre-schooling alone will require another $2.8 billion just to give an urgently needed head start to 80 per cent of the children below the poverty level at $1,400 each.

Taxpayers have shown growing resistance to rising education costs by blindly voting down a third of the school bonds put on the ballot in 1966–67, and all of us believe a broad review of education costs and methods is long overdue. Up to now the semi-independence of most school boards has let them escape even the not-good-enough annual review and questioning to which city governments subject the operations of the various departments under their direct control.

We are particularly concerned lest too much of tomorrow's bigger school budgets be absorbed by across-the-board raises to teachers under seniority-based salary schedules and by indiscriminate—though costly—reductions in class size.

We recognize the need for more rather than less individual contact between teacher and pupil, including particularly the need for

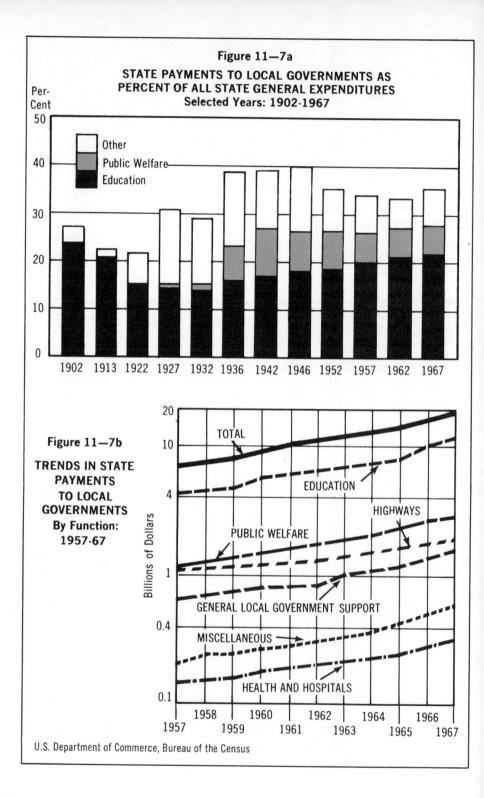

Figure 11—7a

STATE PAYMENTS TO LOCAL GOVERNMENTS AS PERCENT OF ALL STATE GENERAL EXPENDITURES
Selected Years: 1902-1967

Per-Cent

Other
Public Welfare
Education

1902 1913 1922 1927 1932 1936 1942 1946 1952 1957 1962 1967

Figure 11—7b

TRENDS IN STATE PAYMENTS TO LOCAL GOVERNMENTS
By Function: 1957-67

Billions of Dollars

TOTAL
EDUCATION
HIGHWAYS
PUBLIC WELFARE
GENERAL LOCAL GOVERNMENT SUPPORT
MISCELLANEOUS
HEALTH AND HOSPITALS

1957 1958 1959 1960 1961 1962 1963 1964 1965 1966 1967

U.S. Department of Commerce, Bureau of the Census

more small-group discussions. But many teaching functions can be performed just as well with much larger groups than the present 26 average; in some advanced schools the basic instructional unit has been increased to 90 or even 120 students and the certified-teacher ratio increased as high as 50 to 1, with staff dollars redeployed to employ assistants and buy better teaching equipment, and permit higher pay for top teachers.

Instead of expecting all teachers to be all things to all pupils and paying all teachers more or less alike, we think it is high time to recognize the great diversity of teaching talent and qualification by putting instruction on a team basis and introducing such categories as master teacher, teacher, assistant teacher, intern, and media technician, with differential and incentive pay for each gradation. We deplore today's simple standardization of teacher classification, certification, and pay scales, with teacher salaries based mostly on seniority and the accumulation of college credits.

Obviously any such educational reform as this is far beyond the means or the capacities of any single city or school district. It can be achieved only under the leadership of the state and federal education offices working together. We can think of no greater service the state and federal governments can perform at this time to help local governments—and most particularly central city governments.

And we hope it is not too much to expect that the educational establishment will cooperate instead of obstructing the needed changes.

The panel members who discussed the financial crisis of our cities were:

From the National League of Cities and the U.S. Conference of Mayors:

PATRICK HEALY   *Executive Director of the League*
JOHN GUNTHER   *Executive Director of the Conference*
HENRY W. MAIER   *Mayor of Milwaukee, Past President of the League of Cities*
JOHN R. COLLINS   *Ex-Mayor of Boston, Past President of the League of Cities, Professor of Urban Affairs, M.I.T.*
TRAVIS H. TOMLINSON   *Chairman, Revenue & Finance Committee, Mayor of Raleigh, N.C*
NATHAN B. KAUFMAN   *Vice Chairman, Revenue & Finance Committee, Mayor of University City, Mo.*
WAYNE ANDERSON   *City Manager, Evanston, Ill.*
ROBERT W. SWEET   *Deputy Mayor of New York City*

From the Council of State Governments and the National Governors Conference:

BERNARD CRIHFIELD   *Executive Director*

SEN. EDWARD L. MARCUS (Connecticut)   *Chairman of the Governing Board*

SEN. JOHN J. MARCHI (New York)   *Chairman, Committee on State Urban Relations*

T. N. HURD   *New York State Budget Director*

ALBERT G. GILES   *Director, Ohio Department of Urban Affairs*

WAYNE F. MCGOWN   *Secretary, Wisconsin Department of Administration*

JULIAN STEELE   *Massachusetts Commissioner of Community Affairs*

From the National Association of Counties:

BARNARD HILLENBRAND   *Executive Director*

From the Advisory Commission on Intergovernmental Relations:

WILLIAM G. COLMAN   *Executive Director*

From the National Commission on Urban Problems:

ALLEN D. MANVEL   *Associate Staff Director*

From the Small Business Administration:

HOWARD J. SAMUELS   *Administrator*

From the Committee for Industrial Development:

ALFRED C. NEAL   *President*

From the National Association of Manufacturers:

A. WRIGHT ELLIOTT   *Vice President, Industrial Environment Department*

From the U.S. Chamber of Commerce:

CARL MADDEN   *Chief of Economics*

From the National Industrial Conference Board:

JOHN MURPHY   *Director, Department of Business and Government Relations*

From the N.Y. Economic Development Council:

PAUL BUSSE   *Executive Vice President*

From the Tax Foundation Inc.,

HERBERT J. MILLER   *Federal Affairs Counselor*

For Public Education:

FRANCIS KEPPEL   *Ex-Commissioner of Education, HEW*

From the Universities:

RAYMOND J. SAULNIER   *Columbia University (former Chairman, Council of Economic Advisers)*
DICK NETZER   *New York University*
MASON GAFFNEY   *University of Wisconsin*

From the National Housing Center:

THOMAS P. COOGAN   *Past Chairman*

From the Regional Plan Association Inc.:

JOHN P. KEITH   *Executive Vice President*

From the Ford Foundation:

LOUIS WINNICK   *Deputy Vice President for National Affairs*

From the Schalkenbach Foundation:

ALBERT PLEYDELL   *President*

Moderator and Rapporteur

PERRY PRENTICE   Time, Inc.

Impact of the property tax

In recent years, as throughout the twenty years following World War II, local and state government public expenditures have been increasing more rapidly than has the Nation's total output and income (see Table 12–1). Public expenditures in urban areas have always been significantly higher, in relative terms, than those in non-urban areas, and recently have been increasing slightly faster, in dollar terms, within the urban areas. This is to be expected, since nearly all the Nation's population growth has been occurring in urban areas. But urban population growth alone does not explain the rate of increase in public spending. Indeed, the increase in per capita local government expenditures in metropolitan areas was more rapid than the increase in aggregate gross national product between 1957 and 1962.

Perhaps most striking, public expenditures in the larger central cities have been climbing steeply, despite their losses or slow growth in population. In the most recent four-year period for which data are available, expenditures of municipal governments in the larger cities rose by 27 percent, as shown in Table 12–1, about three-fourths as rapidly as expenditures of all other local governments combined.

To be sure, substantially more external aid to central cities in the provision of public services has been forthcoming in recent years. State and Federal aid to central city governments has risen considerably more rapidly than have central city expenditures. Also, the direct role of state governments in the provision of public services in and for the central cities has expanded considerably. Since the passage of the Interstate Highway Act in 1956, the states have been far more active in the construction of central city highways than previously. In a growing number of states, the state

Table 12-1—Percentage Increases in Nonfederal Public Expenditures, 1957-1962 and 1962-1965/66

	Percentage Increase	
	1957–1962	*1962–1965/66*
Gross National Product[a]	27%	33%
Total Expenditures:		
All State and Local Governments	48	35
All Local Governments	46	35
Local Governments in Metropolitan Areas—All SMSA's[b]	47	N.A.
38 Largest Areas	N.A.	34
Central City Governments in Large Cities[c]	31	27
Per Capita Expenditure:[d]		
All State and Local Governments	36	28
All Local Governments	34	28
Local Governments in Metropolitan Areas—All SMSA's	30	N.A.
38 Largest Areas	N.A.	24

Source: Adapted from various publications of the U.S. Census Bureau, Governments Division.

N.A.: Not Available.
[a] For calendar years 1957–1962 and 1962–1966.
[b] For identical collections of metropolitan areas in 1957 and 1962.
[c] Includes only the municipal government (excludes separate overlapping county, school district and special district governments); for the 42 cities with a 1960 population of more than 300,000 excluding Honolulu.
[d] Based on estimated 1957, 1962, and 1966 populations.

government is directly involved in urban mass transportation, in park and open space activities, and in housing programs. In some states in the Northeast, expansion of state higher education programs has had an important effect on central city populations. Despite all this, the taxes imposed by central city governments, collected from static populations and slowly growing central city economies, continue to rise sharply.

The explanation for rising public expenditures in urban areas is not hard to find. In the central cities, local-tax-financed outlays for services directly linked to poverty (in the health and welfare fields) have not been static; the central cities of the 12 largest metropolitan areas account for one-eighth of the country's population, but nearly two-fifths of health and welfare outlays financed from local taxes. For central city governments, the problems associated with poverty and race are by far the most urgent of public problems.

Neither poverty nor racial disabilities can be eliminated solely by governmental action, and still less by action by local or state and local governments combined (that is, governments other than the Federal government). But local governments do have a major responsibility to grapple with these problems and can make a major contribution toward their alleviation. In the American system of government, it is local governments which are responsible for providing educational services that over time will have a major bearing on the chances the poor and racially disadvantaged have to overcome their disadvantages. Local governments are also responsible for a wide range of health and welfare services, which are almost entirely oriented toward the poor in American cities. They have had, since the late forties, major responsibilities in connection with the housing of the poor. And, as far as the poor are concerned, local government recreational facilities are about the only recreational facilities available.

A second major set of problems confronting the older central cities lies in the fact that they have a huge legacy of obsolescence. Their stock of housing and other social capital—that is, public, and quasi-public facilities of all kinds—is old, often physically deteriorated, and generally far from competitive with the newer parts of the same urban areas. It may be, as some have argued, that the best national policy would be to allow this obsolescence to continue, and allow further deterioration of the older parts of the older cities. In this case, population would decline in these sections and, presumably at some stage, values would be so low that private renewal of such areas would become possible. Or, if desirable, public renewal could be undertaken, but on the basis of exceedingly low values.

Developments in recent years suggest that this is hardly a likely course of action. For one thing, there is the plight of those who, because they are poor, or Negro, or both, have little chance to escape the deteriorating areas. Amelioration for these hundreds of thousands of people is both politically and morally necessary. Quite apart from moral issues, most cities and the Federal government appear to have decided that it is necessary to replace obsolete social capital and to compete for residents and businesses in an atmosphere of rising expectations. That is, the cities feel they must offer an environment of public facilities and services which, together with other attractions that the central locations may have, offset the blandishments of the newer and presumably more modern sections of the metropolitan areas where standards of public services and amenity are high indeed.

In the newer sections of metropolitan areas—the new portions of central cities as well as the urbanizing fringes of the metropolitan area—the main governmental problem is the provision of the new social capital needed by a rising population, and a population which has peculiarly heavy demands for public services and facilities, notably schools.

In the aggregate, these urban problems have caused a diversion of resources from private to public use, via tax increases. This relative expansion of the public sector is costly in another way. If local governments are to command resources, they must pay prices for these resources which are competitive with those prevailing in the economy, notably salaries of public employees. If they are to expand *more rapidly* than the private sector, they must bid away resources by paying even more. This they are doing, as is shown by the rapid increase in urban government salary levels, especially for occupational groups whose talents are in heavy demand in the private sector.

As Table 12-1 suggests, the rate of increase in the expenditure of urban governments is not tapering off; if anything, it is increasing. This is consistent with our observations of the urban fiscal scene (with almost continual fiscal crises), and our observations of the urban social scene, with the huge unmet needs for new and improved public services. But these trends do conflict with some of the recent projections of the outlook for state and local finances in the decade ahead. These projections are generally optimistic, in that they foresee no great fiscal strains, largely because of an expected tapering off of the rate of increase in expenditure.

The projections may be right, but there is room for skepticism. For example, the projections have not allowed for the recent surge in expenditure for public assistance programs. Between 1962 and 1965–66, local government public welfare expenditures rose by nearly 50 percent, a rate of increase nearly double that found in the more comprehensive sets of projections; in New York State, public welfare expenditures will be more than double those implied by the projections sponsored by the Council of State Governments.[1] . . .

POSSIBLE REMEDIES

To the extent that the defects of the property tax are inherent ones, the principal remedies must take the form of some reduction in the reliance on the property tax for the financing of urban public

1. For a recent evaluation of the projections, see *Revenue Sharing and Its Alternatives*, Hearings before the Subcommittee on Fiscal Policy of the Joint Economic Committee, U.S. Congress, July 31–August 3, 1967, especially pp. 65–106.

services.[2] The alternative financing is by higher levels of government which do not use the property tax, or by other local government revenue sources. Reduced reliance on the property tax will also diminish the importance of the other types of defects, mainly related to the fragmented local government patterns. But these latter defects can also be remedied in part by reforms within the institution of the property tax itself.

Increase state-Federal responsibilities

The increase of state and Federal government responsibilities is an obvious route toward reduced reliance on the property tax, and one which is in keeping with developments in fiscal federalism since the 1920s.

These developments include both the transfer of direct responsibility for the actual performance of some functions from the local to state and Federal levels of government, and increased state and Federal financing of functions still performed at the local level.

Consider four of the major functional classes of civilian public expenditure: education; highways; public welfare; and health and hospitals. In each case, the local government share of total direct public expenditure by all three levels of government declined appreciably from 1927 to 1965–66; for example, from 71 percent to 32 percent for highways and from 69 percent to 52 percent for welfare. But there were even larger declines in the proportions of local government expenditure financed from local, rather than state and Federal, revenue sources. As a result of this (and of another much less important factor, the expansion of local nonproperty revenue sources), the property tax now finances half or less of local expenditure for these functions, compared to 75 percent or more in 1927.

The combined effect of functional transfers, increased grants-in-aid, and increased use of local nonproperty revenue sources is indicated by the following estimates of the percentages of total public expenditure of all levels of government financed by the property tax:[3]

	1965–66	1927
Education	37%	73%
Highways	13	56
Public Welfare	8	61
Health and Hospitals	15	32

2. This does not necessarily mean a roll-back in property tax levies or rates. In practice it will mean a reduction in the *relative* role of the property tax; that is, financing increased expenditures in future years from revenue sources other than the property tax.

3. These are very rough estimates based on Census Bureau data; they somewhat overstate the decline for education.

Suppose the 1927 percentages prevailed today, and expenditure levels were no different than they are. To finance these four functions, local governments would have needed, in 1965–66, an additional $23 billion in property tax revenue, above and beyond the $23.8 billion they actually received ($12.5 billion more for education; $5.5 billion more for highways; $5.1 billion more for health and welfare services). Thus, we can say that during this period, there has been an upward shift of nearly half the potential property tax burden.

But a strong argument can be made for further upward shifts, in two functional areas. One is education; very small portions of the eventual benefits from education are recaptured within the confines of individual school districts, since our population is so mobile—perhaps no more than 20 percent on the average. This argues for a much increased role for external financing, especially at the Federal level. Since education now absorbs slightly over half of current property tax revenues, such shifts could greatly reduce reliance on the property tax.

A second area is that of poverty-linked services, notably welfare and health services, which now absorb roughly 10 percent of total property tax revenues, but substantially more for the large central cities. A good case can be made for relieving the property tax of the job of financing all public services linked to the existence of poverty. Since this burden is concentrated in central cities, it would alleviate central city-suburban disparities and the property tax problems these create; it would also alleviate the regressivity problem in the sense of taxing the poor for services to the poor.

This is very much in keeping with the historic trends. During the last 30 years, each of the important institutional changes which reduced pressures on the property tax has been associated with redistributive services. These include the Federal and state assumption of most public welfare costs in the thirties, via grants-in-aid, transfers of functional responsibilities, or direct Federal social insurance programs; the steady expansion of the state government role in financing education in the past 20 years; the gradual increase in Federal financing of health services (either directly or through grants-in-aid), culminating in Medicare and the 1965 Social Security amendments; the Federal role in the provision of housing for low-income people; and most recently, the new Federal participation in anti-poverty programs and in the costs of education where there are extensive pockets of poverty. All of these Federal-state aids combined have not been sufficient to keep effective property tax rates from rising at a fairly rapid rate. But without external aid to urban-area local governments, the rise might have been far more rapid.

Some evidence on the extent to which complete external financing of poverty-linked services would have alleviated central-city-suburban tax effort (tax revenue divided by personal income) disparities, had this been in effect in 1962 in 22 of the largest SMSA's, is presented in Table 12-2. The estimates are those of Professor

Table 12-2—Measures of Tax Effort in Central Cities and Suburbs in 22 Largest SMSA's, 1962[a]

(Per capita tax revenue, 1962, divided by per capita income, 1960)

SMSA	Actual Tax Revenue		Adjusted Tax Revenue I[b]		II[c]	
	Cities	Suburbs	Cities	Suburbs	Cities	Suburbs
New York	9.5	7.5	7.8	7.0	7.3	6.8
Chicago	7.4	6.1	6.6	5.8	6.2	5.6
Los Angeles	8.4	7.0	7.3	6.0	6.8	5.6
Philadelphia	7.4	4.9	6.6	4.6	6.1	4.4
Detroit	7.5	5.7	6.2	4.9	5.5	4.6
Baltimore	6.9	4.4	6.0	4.3	5.3	3.9
Houston	5.9	5.6	5.4	5.4	4.7	4.9
Cleveland	7.4	5.2	6.1	4.4	5.5	4.2
St. Louis	7.6	5.1	5.9	4.8	5.2	4.4
Milwaukee	8.4	6.5	6.8	5.4	6.3	5.2
San Francisco	7.4	7.2	6.1	6.0	5.6	5.6
Boston	11.2	7.4	8.9	6.8	8.3	6.4
Dallas	5.7	3.7	5.2	3.1	4.8	2.7
Pittsburgh	7.2	4.9	6.8	4.7	6.3	4.5
San Diego	6.3	6.7	5.3	5.6	4.7	4.9
Seattle	5.0	3.6	4.5	3.2	4.2	2.9
Buffalo	7.5	7.0	6.2	6.2	5.7	5.9
Cincinatti	8.2	4.5	6.5	4.2	5.7	3.8
Atlanta	6.3	3.7	5.1	2.8	4.5	2.4
Minneapolis	7.0	6.5	5.3	5.6	4.8	5.3
Kansas City	6.0	5.4	5.1	5.0	4.5	4.6
Newark	12.3	7.0	9.5	6.5	8.9	6.2
Mean	7.6	5.7	6.3	5.1	5.8	4.8

[a] Data computed by and presented in Woo Sik Kee, "City-Suburban Differentials in Local Government Fiscal Effort" (mimeo., Regional Research Institute, West Virginia University, October 1967).
[b] Total tax revenue minus the estimated locally financed portion of expenditure for public welfare, health and hospitals.
[c] Total tax revenue minus the estimated locally financed portion of expenditure for public welfare, health, hospitals, and for education of children in families with incomes of less than $3,000.

Woo Sik Kee of West Virginia University. On the average, the tax effort disparities would have been cut in half: central city tax burdens would have been nearly 25 percent lower, while suburban tax burdens would have been 15 percent lower. Converted to effective property tax rate terms, this would have reduced central city tax rates to levels equal to or less than those in suburban areas in a number of cases.

To some extent, Professor Kee's estimates understate the reduction in the disparity. He is looking at tax effort as if all local taxes were charges against personal incomes received by residents of the communities levying the taxes. But some part of the burden of taxes paid by businesses is "exported" to other communities, via higher product prices or reductions in the profits accruing to nonresident owners of businesses.[4] And generally speaking, the export percentage is higher for central cities than for suburban areas, if for no other reason than the lesser role of housing in the central city tax base.

Estimates made for New York City suggest that 25 percent of its tax burden was exported in the early 1960s.[5] Similar estimates for suburban counties in the New York SMSA suggest that only about 15 percent of their tax burden was exported. Applying this correction to Kee's estimates, actual tax burdens on residents can be said to have been 7.1 percent of central city residents' personal incomes in 1962 and 6.3 percent for suburbanites. Had the poverty-linked services been entirely financed from external sources, the percentages would have been 5.5 for the city and 5.7 for the suburbs. Since effective property tax rates in central city and suburbs in this SMSA are roughly equivalent, the upward shift would have resulted in effective suburban rates nearly one-fifth above those in the central city, if the entire effect of the transfer fell on the property tax.

Other local revenue sources

Changes in intergovernmental fiscal arrangements of the types proposed here could have a potent impact. Kee and other observers have asserted that much of the remaining disparity in tax burdens—where any does remain, after correction for tax exports—can be associated with the extent to which the central city accommodates the surrounding suburban population with places of employment, shopping and cultural facilities and, presumably, the public services supportive of these activities.

To the extent that this is in fact the case, it strengthens the argument for greater reliance on other local government revenue sources, notably direct charges for the use of public services and facilities (paid by actual users wherever they may live) and local income taxes paid by residents and commuters alike.

4. For comprehensive estimates of this, see Charles E. McLure, Jr., "Tax Exporting in the United States: Estimates for 1962," *National Tax Journal*, Vol. 20 (March 1967), pp. 49–77.

5. See Alan D. Donheiser, "The Incidence of the New York City Tax System," in *Financing Government in New York City* (1966), Graduate School of Public Administration, New York University. Table II, p. 162.

User-Charges for Public Services

Local governments do currently employ user-charges; they obtain roughly 18 percent of their locally raised general revenue from charges for services (other than utility services) and from special assessments. About half of this amount comes from school lunch and similar charges, hospital charges and public housing rental payments, but charges apply to a wide range of other services. Despite this, there is considerable potential for greater exploitation of user-charges, in connection with activities which do *not* have significant income-redistribution objectives. The case for this has been put as follows:

... many of the public services provided by local governments are in many ways like those provided by public utility companies. That is, they are not provided uniformly to the entire population, but rather in distinguishable quantities and qualities to individual families in the population, who consume them in accord with their personal preferences. For example, not all families use the same amount of water, not all use the same amount of highway transportation, and so on. There is a strong case for financing such services in the same way public utility services are financed—that is, via user charges which are like prices, rather than through general taxes.

If the purpose of providing the public service is to offer different consumers the services they want, and place some value on, then they ought to pay for such services in proportion to the costs. Otherwise, governments will be called upon to provide a great deal more of the service than people would be willing to consume if they did have to pay for it, which is a wasteful use of resources; or the service will be in such short supply that a form of non-price rationing will be employed to allocate the service among consumers. The outstanding example of this is street congestion in cities: users pay for highways in the aggregate but not for specific individual uses of the streets, and therefore, not surprisingly, treat highways as a free good. The only deterrent to use of the streets at the most crowded times and in the most crowded places is the value one places on time; the rationing in effect then results in those who place a low value on time pre-empting the street space from those who place a high value on time. Ordinarily, in our society, rationing is on the basis of price. Somebody who values a service highly bids it away from someone who places a lower value on that service and would rather use his income for alternative kinds of consumption.[6]

The most striking opportunities for greater utilization of user-charges, as this would suggest, are in connection with financing of urban highway and parking facilities and services, waste collection and disposal, and recreational activities; the potential revenue in these areas alone equals roughly one-tenth of property tax revenue on a nationwide basis. The potential is relatively larger in urban

6. Netzer, "Financing Urban Government," in James Q. Wilson, editor, *The Metropolitan Enigma* (Chamber of Commerce of the United States, 1967), p. 65.

areas, especially the larger ones, which provide more of these services and are generally less effective exploiters of user-charges.

Local Income Taxes

The case for local income taxation does not rest on the argument that it is a good device for central city taxation of commuters. To be sure, the potential here is a large one. The municipal governments of the 43 largest cities collected $3.3 billion in property tax revenue in 1965–66. Excluding Washington, D. C., their local income tax revenue was $242 million, largely made up of the collections in Detroit, Louisville, and the larger cities in Pennsylvania, Ohio, and Missouri. But if all 43 cities had a flat 1 percent tax on income earned within the central cities, revenue would have amounted to perhaps $1.3 billion, probably $300 million of this from commuters. This is a substantial fraction of property tax revenue for these units of government.

The more general case for income taxation is that it does *not* have an especially adverse effect on housing, as does the property tax. It escapes the regressivity charge. Moreover, for central cities, it is superior to local sales taxes and other local business taxes, since unlike the latter, it is highly unlikely to encourage migration of economic activity away from the central cities.

Local income taxation heretofore has been largely a large city affair, except in Pennsylvania. However, in time, it may become more like the widespread use of local sales taxes, which in states like California and Illinois, are virtually universally used supplements to the state sales tax, collected by the state. As such, local non-property taxes have the general character of the state tax, since, if universally applied, they have no impact on the intra-state location of economic activity. They may be thought of as a substitute for outright grants-in-aid from State tax revenue, with the distribution of the funds based on the origin of the tax collections rather than on the traditional kinds of state-aid formulas. The latter can permit much more adequate reflection of differences in needs among communities (although state-aid formulas frequently do not realize this potential). On the other hand, the local tax supplements permit much more local government discretion in the use of the funds.

Land Value Taxation

An entirely different type of alternative revenue source would be a heavy tax on land values in urban areas as a partial substitute for currently collected property tax revenues.

As the name implies, land value taxation is a tax on the value of land alone, irrespective of the value of buildings or the lack of buildings on a site. A step in this direction is the graded or differential tax—the application of a higher tax rate to the land portion than to the improvement portion of property valuations.

The argument for exclusive taxation of site values, or for substantially heavier taxation of land than of buildings, is an old one, and differential site value taxation is widely practiced—in western Canada, Australia, New Zealand, and South Africa, for example. The merits of the case have been submerged for many years by the extravagant claims of the proponents of site value taxation. Moreover, skepticism has been bolstered by the apparent absence of discernible effects in the places where site valuation is utilized.

However, the case for site value taxation is a good one. The argument, on equity grounds, is that most of the value of land is a consequence, not of actions by individual owners, but of collective investment, community development, and population growth. Individual land owners therefore can realize large "unearned increments" over time. It is entirely appropriate for the community to recapture these unearned increments by taxation, and use them for community purposes. There are complications in this equity argument, related to the fact that most land owners have already paid, in their purchase prices, for at least some of the unearned increment, but by and large the equity argument makes sense.

The economic argument is even more compelling. A tax on site value which is independent of the improvements on the site will not affect entrepreneurial decisions as to the use of the site: the best (most profitable) use before tax remains the best use after the tax is imposed. In other words, the tax is neutral with regard to land use decisions. Since the present property tax, on both land and improvements, is *not* neutral but tends to discourage investment in buildings, a switch from the present tax to exclusive site value taxation (or to a tax heavily weighted on the land portion) would tend to have strong land use effects.

Provided that demand permits, it would encourage owners to develop their sites more intensively, in an effort to minimize tax liability as a percentage of current receipts, since additional investment in buildings would not increase tax liability. Within individual urban jurisdictions, taxes on vacant land would tend to rise, thereby increasing the holding costs of vacant land and making the speculative withholding of land from development a less attractive proposition. Thus, a switch to site value taxation is likely to have its maximum impact in two parts of a metropolitan area—in the central areas, where it would encourage more investment in buildings, and in the outlying sections, where it would tend to discourage land speculation and the resulting patchy patterns of land development (less "leapfrogging" over sites withheld from the market).

In theory, there are few if any legitimate economic arguments against site value taxation. On an operational level, there are grounds for hesitation.

First of all, one may doubt the actual strength of the positive tendencies associated with a switch to site value taxation. It is, after all, a major institutional change, and major institutional changes should not be pressed unless their positive effects are also expected to be major in extent. However, it should be noted that effective property tax rates in most American metropolitan areas are high and rising. The negative land use effects of the present tax are likely to become increasingly apparent in time, and the likely benefits from a change in the basis of taxation will correspondingly increase.

Second, there is some question about the revenue adequacy of site value taxation. Some calculations suggest that the present yield of property taxes on nonfarm realty substantially exceeds the total rental value of privately owned nonfarm land. Thus, even a 100 percent site value tax might not yield enough to fully replace the existing property tax (on real property, exclusive of personalty). This suggests that only a partial, rather than a complete, shift is possible, diluting the possible advantageous land use effects.

Third, there are administrative problems if both land and buildings are taxed, but at differential rates—the "graded tax" concept applying in Pittsburgh, Hawaii and western Canada, for example. This makes it very important to accurately value land and buildings *separately*. Under a pure system of site value taxation, the building value is irrelevant. Under the conventional property tax, the distinction between land and building for any individual site is also irrelevant, although the statutes may require the assessor to make some statement about the notional separation. It seems likely that joint administration of the two different types of taxes will produce bad administration of the site value tax, in that assessors will tend to relate land and building valuations as they often do at present. Therefore, the proposal here is for a *separate* system of land value taxation, levied and administered, if possible, over a wide geographic area—a whole state or SMSA.

Taxation of Land Value Increments

The equity argument for taxation of *increases* in land values is at least as strong as that for annual taxes on total land values. This kind of tax is aimed at recapturing for the government a higher proportion of what economists call the unearned increment—the rise of land value that occurs, not through efforts of an owner but through governmental action (new highways, subway lines, zoning changes, etc.) and through growth of the population and industry of the community.

Land value increment taxes strike directly at the unearned increments realized by specific individual owners, and do not penalize present owners who have *not* realized substantial land value increments. The claim in this case is not that community improvements *tend* to enrich land owners in general; tax liability occurs only when enrichment is demonstrated by the realization of capital gains on land.

Variants of this approach to taxation are used in a number of countries. In some Hispanic countries, specific public improvements are financed from taxes on the estimated (although not necessarily realized by sale) increase in the value of adjacent properties; this is done on a very large scale in some of the major cities in Colombia. In our own country, special assessments to finance street and sewer projects have a similar rationale. In a number of European countries, this approach shows up in the income tax treatment of capital gains on land, which is much less favorable than that of other types of capital gains.

Thus, land value increments could be taxed in a number of ways and at different levels of government. Perhaps the easiest method might be through state income taxation, by a special supplemental rate on capital gains on land or by including a larger portion of the gain as ordinary income (rather than the 50 percent now included in most states, following the Federal practice). This seems easiest, because the gains are already reported and legal definitions do exist and are applied.

Like annual land value taxation, this form of taxation would be largely neutral with respect to the use of land and would not discourage new construction. However, its economic impact and revenue potential would be somewhat less. Presumably, the land value increment tax would apply only to gains actually realized (including constructive realization at the death of the owner). Very high tax rates would tend to postpone realization of gains, although closing the transfer-by-death loophole would reduce this. Nevertheless, the economic impact would be in the right direction and the equity effects appropriate. Therefore, this seems good policy, especially if straightforward annual land value taxation does not prove acceptable.

Improvement of the existing institution

Since some of the major defects in the existing institution relate to the fragmented structure of local government in urban areas, an obvious direction for reform is application of the property tax over wider geographic areas, thereby reducing tax rate disparities by evening out the differences in tax base per capita or per pupil. There are two approaches to this.

Tax Base Consolidation

One would be to regionalize a segment of the tax base—eliminate local taxes on some types of property and levy property taxes on these types over a broader area, with either use of the proceeds for region-wide (or state-wide) functions or distribution of the proceeds to local government units on the basis of some measure of need. A frequent suggestion along these lines is for regional or state-wide taxation of business property, to eliminate local competition for economic activity and attendant pressures on land use planning.[7]

Fiscal Federation

A second approach is to regionalize the financing (and perhaps administration) of part or all of selected local government functions, but still utilize the property tax to the extent it is now used. The most dramatic proposal along these lines is to employ a state-wide property tax for the great bulk of (non-federal) school funds.[8] There also have been proposals for metropolitan-area-wide school financing in, perhaps, some kind of fiscal federation. Under this scheme, state school aid would continue as at present, but paid to an area-wide authority. The area authority would then levy a uniform area-wide property tax and distribute this revenue and the state aid on a per pupil basis. For most school districts, this would provide adequate program levels. However, they would be free to supplement the levels with local levies, but presumably only few districts would do so. Since property taxes for schools amount to roughly half of total property taxes, there would be an appreciable reduction in property tax disparities.

Smaller, but real, reductions in disparities would result from

7. It should be noted that the planning difficulties could be accommodated in another way—by regionalizing land use controls rather than taxation. There is much to be said for this course of action; indeed, there is hardly anything to be said in defense of land use planning by a huge number of small jurisdictions. But this is an entirely separate subject.

8. This has been proposed by Lynn A. Stiles of the Federal Reserve Bank of Chicago.

metropolitan-area-wide financing of functions with a fundamentally regional character, like transportation and waste disposal. Within single-county SMSA's, this could be done on a county basis. In fact, even in multi-county SMSA's, significant reductions in disparities could be achieved by increased county-wide financing. An indication of the potential can be found in aggregate data for SMSA's from the 1962 Census of Governments.

Consider a few functions with a regional character, or for which county-wide administration is common in some parts of the country. Expenditure for these functions can be divided into that handled by county-scope units of government (counties, combined city-county governments like New York, Philadelphia, and Baltimore, and large special districts) and that handled by sub-county units. The following is the approximate proportion of SMSA local government expenditure in 1962 handled by sub-county units:

Highways	55%
Waste disposal	60
Parks and recreation	60
Health and hospitals	30
Public welfare	15

Now, had these functions been financed *entirely* on a county-wide basis, roughly $1.7 billion of property taxes collected on a sub-county basis in 1962 would have been collected county-wide. This is roughly *half* the total property tax revenue of the sub-county units (excluding school districts) in that year.

Better Administration

The position in this report is that improved assessment of most types of complex business property is a Utopian goal, but that it is possible to do a much better job with respect to housing, vacant lots and the simpler, more common types of business property, like small store buildings. The basis for this argument is that there are fairly frequent sales of such property to provide a basis for assessment. The requirements for realization of such improvements as are achievable are professionalization and adoption of truly systematic procedures—indeed, full computerization of the primary assessment process.[9] These in turn imply large-scale assessment organizations.

Except in the very largest states, this may very well imply state-wide assessment; it surely is not consistent with assessment districts having populations of very much less than 500,000. The general rule

9. This has been done on an experimental basis with extraordinarily good results in California.

seems to be, if full use is to be made of the possibilities for computer-ization, the bigger, the better. This, then, is no less radical a pro-posal than the others advanced in this report, since this country has been firmly wedded over many decades to the notion that small local assessment districts are an essential component of local self-govern-ment.

Hardship adjustments

One way in which the burdensomeness of the propety tax, including its regressivity, has been attacked has been through the device of special exemptions and abatements for various kinds of "hardship" cases. The homestead exemptions which became popular in the 1930s were one manifestation of this. More recently, there have been adoptions of devices to relieve property tax burdens for older people. Almost without exception, exemptions and abatements have proven to be clumsy and inefficient methods of relieving hardship. If a partial tax exemption is offered to a whole class of property-owners— such as the aged—it is likely to relieve the real hardship cases only if it is very generous, and hence very costly in foregone tax revenue. Meanwhile, many property owners who are not hardship cases benefit. If the generosity of the provision is tempered by revenue-loss considerations, it may be of trivial value for those really hard hit, and administratively complex as well. Moreover, tax relief for homeowners, whether aged or not, tends to ignore the frequently worse-off cases among renters.

One way out of this is to offer carefully tailored credits for very burdensome property tax payments under state income tax laws. Such credits can be restricted to those whose income status makes it clear that the burdens are real ones. An example of this is the provision in Wisconsin, adopted in 1963, for income tax credits for the aged, both homeowners and tenants, who have *both* low incomes *and* pay high proportions of their incomes in property taxes, directly or through rents.[10] This kind of provision parallels the spreading use of income tax credits to offset the regressivity of state sales taxes, and could be usefully employed on a widespread basis.

Housing Tax Incentives

The obvious deterrent effects of high property taxes on housing has led to the use of tax exemptions and abatements for specific kinds of new housing construction and rehabilitation, most notably in New

10. Billy Dee Cook, Kenneth E. Quindry, and Harold M. Groves, "Old Aged Homestead Relief—The Wisconsin Experience," *National Tax Journal*, 19 (September 1966), pp. 319-324.

York State. The New York programs have had some success in stimulating construction of middle-income housing, with real though indirect effects on the housing status of poorer families.

Even from the standpoint of an exclusive emphasis on increasing the supply of housing, the tax abatement programs now being used have a serious drawback—they are administratively very cumbersome, and therefore slow-moving. When governments single out particular groups in the population for extraordinarily favorable treatment, they are likely to try very hard to ensure that the benefits do in fact accrue to the worthy target population, rather than to unintended freeloaders with no special claim on the public purse. The attendant restrictions can greatly complicate matters.

New York's most generous tax abatement scheme is a good example of this. Under this plan, designed to encourage rehabilitation of older housing occupied by lower-income people, an owner can recover 75 percent of the cost of the improvements through tax reductions over nine years. However, the improved property is subject to rent control, and the owner typically must forego rent increases he might otherwise be entitled to. As a result of this and other complications, the program is little used.

The administrative difficulties could be overcome by a general tax abatement or exemption for *all* new housing investment, not just that which satisfies complex administrative requirements. The selective tax abatement programs are moderate in size,[11] and therefore the reduction in taxes has a negligible effect in increasing property taxes on other types of housing. But an effective across-the-board exemption program for all new investment would be a different matter. It could result in a significant shift in the tax burden to older properties, including older properties occupied by relatively low-income households. Therefore, such a program is a questionable one unless it is linked to steps to reduce the reliance on the property tax in general, such as those suggested in the preceding section of this study. And if there is a substantial reduction in reliance on the property tax in general, the need for special housing exemptions will be greatly reduced.

De-emphasis

In summary, the highest priority would seem to attach to de-emphasis of the property tax *per se*. It is a generally inferior tax instrument, although not the worst of all possible taxes. But an

---

11. The various New York City programs as of the end of 1965 covered 75,000 units, 2.5 percent of the city's housing inventory. City of New York, Committee on Housing Statistics, *Housing Statistics Handbook* (August 1966), Table 1–3.

inferior tax becomes a monstrous one if applied at high enough rates.

There *are* alternatives to ever-increasing property tax rates in urban areas, alternatives which require a willingness to accept real change in that most conservative of all institutions, local government.

13. Housing and National Urban Goals: Old Policies and New Realities

Bernard J. Frieden

14. The Shape of the Nation's Housing Problems

The President's Committee on Urban Housing

13 BERNARD J. FRIEDEN

Housing and national urban goals: old policies and new realities*

Federal housing programs in the past thirty years have helped
millions of American families to improve their living conditions.
Housing policy today, however, must be reconsidered in the broad
context of contemporary urban problems, for it is becoming clear
that the solutions of the past are no longer adequate. Housing
standards remain important: several million families are still living
in slum conditions that should no longer be tolerated in the United
States. But new housing strategies are needed that will recognize
more complex goals: freedom of residential choice, the elimination
of racial barriers, and a chance for all families to have access to good
schools, good public services, and job opportunities.

The housing problem, in its most basic and traditional form,
can be defined as one of assuring an adequate living environment for
people too poor to pay for decent housing at market prices. Other
groups than the poor have also laid claim to a housing problem,
however. Considerable government aid has in fact gone to middle-
income families whose problem is not that of reaching minimum
living standards but rather having a wide range of choice in the

* Reprinted by permission of the publisher from James Q. Wilson, editor, THE
METROPOLITAN ENIGMA, Cambridge, Mass.: Harvard University Press, Copy-
right 1968, by the President and Fellows of Harvard College; 1967 by Chamber of
Commerce of the United States of America.

housing market or meeting the terms of home ownership. The most urgent conflicts over housing policy center on the still unmet needs of the poor and of Negroes and other minorities victimized by discrimination in the housing market. The issues at stake have important implications for the future of central cities, metropolitan development, racial equality, and the elimination of poverty. Serious conflicts over neighborhood change, the enforcement of fair housing laws, and the management of urban development programs arise directly from the shortage of decent low-cost housing in metropolitan areas.

This paper will focus on housing problems confronting the poor and minority groups—the nature and dimensions of these problems, the progress that has been made in dealing with them, and housing policies that may bring faster results. Although there has been substantial improvement in American housing since World War II, there are disturbing signs that progress so far has exposed a hard core of remaining issues that call for new approaches. In addition, housing policies that have worked in the past are now coming into conflict with other national objectives. Thus a review of past experience and a reconsideration of goals and strategies are in order.

EFFECTS OF SLUM HOUSING

To earlier urban reformers, the elimination of slum housing was essential to cope with many social evils. Slums were thought to cause family breakdown, personal disorganization, crime, disease, and poverty. Contemporary social scientists are skeptical of such claims, and current research findings do not bear out simple causal relationships between physical housing conditions and social behavior. Experience with public housing also provides grounds for skepticism: families who move from run-down tenements into sanitary apartment projects do not necessarily resolve their other problems. In rejecting earlier simplistic views, however, there is a danger of falling into the equally questionable conclusion that housing conditions have no impact on social life. It is clear that housing interacts with other elements of the social and physical environment in influencing patterns of human behavior.

Current research suggests that crowding, inadequate plumbing and ventilation, and insufficient wiring and lighting clearly contribute to the spread of respiratory and digestive diseases and to home accidents.[1] Morbidity and mortality rates are sensitive to housing

1. For a review of evidence concerning the effects of substandard housing, see Alvin L. Schorr, *Slums and Social Insecurity* (Washington: U.S. Department of Health, Education, and Welfare, 1963). The following discussion is based on Schorr's findings.

conditions; studies indicate that improved housing reduces the incidence of illness and death. Evidence on the psychological effects of crowding and the extent of stress resulting from dilapidated and poorly maintained housing is less clear-cut. Lack of space and of privacy appear to interfere with children's study and with parental control. There is evidence that housing is an important factor in self-perception. Houses that convey an obvious image of neglect and inferior status have been found to influence the self-evaluation and motivation of people who live there, leading to feelings of pessimism and passivity.

This quick sketch of the research evidence on effects of substandard housing is subject to two important qualifications. First, the amount of research focusing directly on housing conditions has been very limited. Much of what is known is deduced indirectly or as a byproduct of studies focused on different subjects. It is possible that stronger connections do exist between housing and behavior, but that research to date has not been adequate to identify them. Second, such factors as morale, self-perception, and motivation appear to be related to a broader environment than the housing unit alone. Neighborhood surroundings, both social and physical, are extremely important—possibly more so than the living quarters. In recognition of the importance of the neighborhood, programs to improve slum conditions have given increasing attention to providing better local facilities and services—schools, parks, clinics—and to involving the residents more directly in planning their own communities. Although this paper is concerned primarily with housing, it should be understood that improvements in housing must be accompanied by related community development if they are to have significant impact on the lives of people who are now in inadequate housing.

One unmistakable aspect of the low-income housing problem is a simple matter of economics. Families living in poverty are often forced to spend a substantial share of their income—one third or more—for housing, thus cutting heavily into their budget for other necessities, such as food and health care. Other dissatisfactions resulting from inadequate heat and maintenance, rats and insects, and the many hazards and discomforts of slum housing have been compelling enough to lead to political action and direct pressure for improvement.

Rent strikes, demonstrations, protests, and local demands focused specifically on housing conditions, have attracted national attention. A recent poll of Harlem residents put the need for better housing near the top of the list of "worst problems" (second only to drug addiction).[2] The Office of Economic Opportunity has found poor housing so frequent a concern in poverty areas that it has modified its antipoverty programs to give more attention to housing. Housing also ranked high among the problem areas identified by the first group of cities applying for aid under the model cities program. Communities entering this program were encouraged to survey the needs of their poverty areas broadly and to give attention to such subjects as education, employment, welfare, and health. Although many cities assigned first priority to a subject other than housing, housing was nevertheless ranked among the high priority items more often than any other problem.[3] Further, governmental activities that demolish housing—urban renewal, highway construction, other public works—have met with increasing resistance because they add to the housing problems of the poor. Thus the people who live in slums have made it clear that they are not there by choice and that they want a chance to improve their living conditions.

DIMENSIONS OF THE PROBLEM

Defining and measuring the quality of housing raises many difficulties. A good definition would reflect our society's consensus as to what constitutes decent living conditions, and it would permit clear classification of housing units by field observers. We do not now have such a definition. Studies of housing since World War II have, however, made use of fairly consistent standards that allow reasonable approximations of housing quality to be made. Since these standards first came into use, society has upgraded its concept of adequate housing. By today's standards, the application of these measures thus yields a rock-bottom estimate of the extent of substandard housing, but it does make possible an estimate of change in the supply and distribution of housing from a single set of benchmarks.

Four aspects of housing enter into this set of standards: structural condition, presence or absence of plumbing facilities, crowding, and cost in relation to the income of the occupant. Surveys by the U.S. Census Bureau provide the basic data on all these subjects. National housing censuses were taken in 1950 and 1960 and national housing inventories, based on a more limited sample, were conducted in 1956 and 1959. Substandard structural condition is reported as "dilapidated" housing, which according to Census definition "does not provide safe and adequate shelter and in its

2. "Negroes in Poll Ask for More Police," *New York Times*, Sept. 4, 1966, p. 1.
3. U.S. Department of Housing and Urban Development, *Content Analysis of First Round Model Cities Applications* (Washington, April 18, 1968), pp. 2-4.

present condition endangers the health, safety, or well-being of the occupants." To be classified as dilapidated, a house must have one or more "critical defects"—holes over large areas of the foundation, walls, roof, floors, or chimney; substantial sagging of floors, walls, or roof; external damage by storm, fire, or flood—or a combination of lesser defects sufficient to require considerable repair or rebuilding; or must be of inadequate original construction, such as shacks with makeshift walls or roofs or dirt floors. The absence of a private toilet, bath or shower, and hot running water is reported separately. In interpretations of the Census data, housing is generally classified as substandard if it is dilapidated or lacks one or more of these plumbing facilities.[4]

The other measures concern crowding and cost. The usual measure of overcrowding is an occupancy ratio of more than one person per room. The point at which the cost of housing becomes an unacceptable burden depends upon a judgment of the proportion of a family's income that can be allocated to housing without creating other deprivation. Welfare administrators and others concerned with low-income family budgets make widespread use of a norm of 20 per cent of income as the maximum that can be spent for housing without cutting into expenditures on other necessities.

Condition, crowding, and cost are all related as measures of housing welfare and guides to public policy. Discussions of housing are often distorted when one or more of these factors are neglected. Thus slum clearance has been advocated as a way of eliminating the problem of substandard housing; instead, it may replace the slum problem with an overcrowding problem. Or strict enforcement of local housing codes may reduce the number of substandard and crowded housing units, while raising the price of housing so that high costs create fresh problems.

Taken together, information on substandard conditions, crowding, and cost provides a picture of current housing deficiencies in the United States. According to the 1960 Census of Housing, 8.5 million families (including one-person households) were living in substandard housing—in dilapidated conditions or lacking one or more plumbing facilities. This number constituted 16 per cent of all families in the United States. At the same time, 6.1 million families —12 per cent of the total—were overcrowded; we do not know how many were both overcrowded and in substandard housing.

Substandard housing is clearly a problem of low-income families.

4. For a fuller discussion of Housing Census definitions and their interpretation, see Leonore R. Siegelman, "A Technical Note on Housing Census Comparability, 1950-1960," *Journal of the American Institute of Planners*, 29 (February 1963), pp. 48-54.

Households with annual (1959) incomes of $4000 or less constituted 38 per cent of all households in 1960, but this low-income group accounted for three fourths of the total families in substandard units and for 42 per cent of all families in overcrowded housing. Nor is this prevalence of inadequate housing among the poor a result of insufficient spending for housing. Among families who earned less than $4000 and lived in rental dwellings, more than 80 per cent were paying 20 per cent of their income or more for rent. Nearly half (46 per cent) paid 35 per cent or more of their income for rent, clearly an excessive amount to spend. It is sometimes alleged that the majority of people who live in slums are there because they place a low value on housing and do not spend much for it and that many slum dwellers can actually afford to live in better housing. The information at hand indicates, to the contrary, that low-income people strain their budgets to pay higher rents than they can afford, but that there is not enough decent cheap housing available to meet their needs.

Contrary to popular impression, there is more substandard housing in rural than urban areas. About 40 per cent of the families in substandard housing in 1960 were living within metropolitan areas. Overcrowding is more an urban than a rural problem, however: almost 60 per cent of the overcrowded families lived in metropolitan areas.

These figures add up to a very conservative estimate of inadequacies in American housing. They exclude a large amount of deficient housing reported in the Census as "deteriorating"; that is, having complete plumbing facilities but needing more structural repairs than would be provided in the course of normal maintenance. In 1960, 4.1 million families were living in housing of this type, 2.5 million of them inside metropolitan areas. Many other families live in housing that lacks central heating; still others live in housing that is sound but located in substandard surroundings, near heavy industry or truck terminals for example. Several million families live in quarters that are not dilapidated by Census standards but that are in violation of the higher standards set by local housing codes. In sections of Philadelphia, the number of units in violation of the building code has been found to exceed Census counts of deficient housing by as much as two to one.[5] Thus it has been estimated that at least one fourth of the American people are living in inadequate housing or an inadequate environment.[6]

5. William Grigsby, *Housing Markets and Public Policy* (Philadelphia: University of Pennsylvania Press, 1963), p. 253, n. 2.
6. *Ibid.*, p. 253.

RECENT TRENDS

In the Housing Act of 1949, Congress declared as national policy "the realization as soon as feasible of the goal of a decent home and a suitable living environment for every American family." This goal is still far from achievement, and the situation today must be considered disappointing in view of the vast resources of the American economy. Yet the dynamics of the American housing market are more encouraging than a static overview would suggest.

Housing conditions in the United States improved substantially in the 1950s. The improvement was not only in percentage terms, but also involved a reduction in the actual number of families living in substandard and overcrowded housing. Thus the national housing problem is not a matter of an unyielding quantity of occupied slums, irreducible even by massive new homebuilding and unresponsive to public policies. Still less is it a matter of slums growing faster than efforts to improve them, though the rhetoric of slum reform is filled with such assertions. Instead, the problem confronting policy makers is one of maintaining or accelerating present rates of improvement—a difficult task in itself but more manageable than fighting a losing battle.

Since the extent of improvement in American housing is still debated and not yet widely acknowledged, it is useful to review the evidence gathered by the Census Bureau in 1950, 1959, and 1960. Because of certain changes in Census definitions, technical difficulties in making Census comparisons have opened the way for misinterpretations that tend to obscure the substantial changes that have occurred. I shall cite data from the Housing Census of 1950 and from two separate surveys at the end of the 1950s: a 1959 Census survey on a sampling basis (covering approximately 180,000 units) which used exactly the same definitions as the 1950 Census; and the 1960 Housing Census, which counted for the first time a number of single-room housing units and which changed certain definitions of housing condition. Data for 1960 have been adjusted to approximate the same categories of housing condition used in 1950 and 1959. The three surveys show declines in both substandard and overcrowded (1.01 or more persons per room) housing:[7]

	1950	1959	1960
families in substandard housing (millions)	14.8	9.1	8.4
families in overcrowded units (millions)	6.6	6.0	6.1

7. For the method used in making Census comparisons, see Leonore R. Siegelman,

(A further post-enumeration survey differed only slightly from the 1960 Census results, estimating 8.5 million occupied substandard units. A later restudy of the 1960 data undertaken by the Census Bureau found that the national trends in substandard housing from 1950 to 1960 were measured accurately, despite widespread errors in block statistics: measurement errors at the block level tended to cancel out at the tract and city levels, and errors in structural condition classification were corrected by plumbing facilities data.[8]) The various sources of data are not far out of line with one another. They all indicate that the number of families living in substandard housing was reduced by about 40 per cent in the 1950s, and the number of overcrowded families was reduced by 8 or 9 per cent.

Comparable national surveys of housing conditions have not been undertaken since 1960, but FHA housing market analyses of some 65 cities in 1965–66 indicated continuing reductions in substandard housing.[9] On the basis of preliminary data, the Census Bureau has estimated that the national total of families in substandard housing dropped from 8.5 million in 1960 to 5.7 million by 1966.[10]

Some observers who continue to question whether housing conditions improved in the 1950s have based their argument on that portion of substandard housing consisting of dilapidated units. Robert P. Groberg, formerly Assistant Director of the National Association of Housing and Redevelopment Officials, has contended that post-enumeration surveys conducted by the Census Bureau following the Censuses of 1950 and 1960 "revealed that there was no significant change in the number of dilapidated housing units over the decade. There were 4.1 million dilapidated units in 1950 and the same number in 1960!"[11] This statement conveys a misleading image of unchanging and seemingly incurable slum housing.

"A Technical Note." The relevant sources of data for 1950, 1959, and 1960 are: *U.S. Census of Housing: 1950*, vol. I, *General Characteristics*, pt. 1, U.S. Summary, tables 7, 11; *U.S. Census of Housing: 1960*, vol. IV, *Components of Inventory Change*, Final Report HC (4), pt. 1A-1, 1950–59 Components, U.S. and Regions, table 1; *U.S. Census of Housing: 1960*, vol. I, *States and Small Areas*, U.S. Summary, Final Report HC (1)-1, table 9.

8. U.S. Bureau of the Census, *Measuring the Quality of Housing: An Appraisal of Census Statistics and Methods*, Working Paper no. 25 (Washington, 1967).

9. U.S. Congress, Senate, Subcommittee on Executive Reorganization of the Committee on Government Operations, *Hearings, Federal Role in Urban Affairs*, 89th Cong., 2nd sess., 1966, pt. 1, pp. 148–149.

10. U.S. Bureau of the Census, *Current Population Reports*, series P-23, no. 24, "Social and Economic Conditions of Negroes in the United States" (October 1967), p. 55.

11. Robert P. Groberg, "Urban Renewal Realistically Reappraised," in *Urban Renewal: The Record and the Controversy*, ed. James Q. Wilson (Cambridge, Mass.: M.I.T. Press, 1966), p. 528.

It appears to refer to total dilapidated housing units, including those that are vacant. A more accurate measure of housing welfare is the number of occupied units; empty structures may be an eyesore but they should be distinguished from inadequate living conditions. Groberg's figures are derived from the post-enumeration surveys that supplied corrected estimates of the 1950 and 1960 Housing Censuses. These corrected estimates, for occupied dilapidated units, are 3,709,000 in 1950 and 3,485,000 in 1960.[12] The improvement indicated here is slight, to be sure, but dilapidated housing constituted only a fourth of all substandard units in 1950. The post-enumeration surveys provide no evidence for doubting the substantial reduction in other substandard housing. In fact, while the post-1950 survey indicated that the Census had overstated the number of occupied dilapidated units (thus exaggerating the apparent improvement registered in 1960), the same survey indicated that the 1950 Census had understated the number of units with plumbing deficiencies, which constitute the remainder of the substandard housing. On balance, the several Census surveys confirm the impressive decrease in inadequate housing during the 1950s.

Further, it is important to note that the stock of dilapidated and other substandard housing does not consist of the same houses over time. Many units are improved every year, while others are neglected or altered so that they decline in quality. Between 1950 and 1959, 4,250,000 dwelling units were upgraded from substandard to standard condition, while 965,000 went from standard to substandard.[13] In this respect as well as others, the housing policy problem is more complex than mounting an attack on enduring slums; it involves promoting the maintenance of sound housing as well as encouraging the renovation or replacement of inadequate dwellings.

EXTENT OF IMPROVEMENT

How widespread were these improvements in housing in the 1950s? Several issues are important in evaluating recent housing trends: their impact on urban areas, the extent to which Negroes shared in housing gains, and the distribution of housing improvement among different income levels. One significant dimension of housing

12. U.S. Bureau of the Census, *The Post-Enumeration Survey: 1950*, Bureau of the Census Technical Paper no. 4 (Washington, 1960), table 14; U.S. Bureau of the Census, *Evaluation and Research Program of the U.S. Censuses of Population and Housing, 1960: Accuracy of Data on Housing Characteristics*, series ER 60, no. 3 (Washington, 1964), table 2A.

13. *U.S. Census of Housing: 1960*, vol. IV, *Components of Inventory Change*, Final Report HC (4), pt. 1A-1, table 5.

welfare—changes in cost—has so far been omitted from this account of the housing market, but will appear as a key issue in weighing the benefits received by different income groups.

Housing conditions improved more rapidly in metropolitan areas than in the rest of the country, despite the very large migration of low-income rural people into the cities in the 1950s. Because of the redefinition of many metropolitan areas between 1950 and 1960, aggregate information on metropolitan housing is not available on a consistent basis. Information on several key aspects of metropolitan area housing does tell a clear story, however. The major element in reducing substandard housing in the 1950s was renovation. Of the substandard units occupied in 1950, the number renovated to standard condition by 1959 exceeded the number removed by demolition or other means (fire, flood, and the like) by more than two to one, both in the country at large and in metropolitan areas. Inside metropolitan areas, more than half the housing that was substandard in 1950 had been put in sound condition by 1959 through structural repairs or plumbing additions. In the rest of the country, about a third of the substandard housing was similarly improved.[14]

Table 13-1 presents more complete information for the twelve largest metropolitan areas, with comparable data for 1950 and 1959. In all these areas, the proportion of substandard and overcrowded housing declined notably. In absolute numbers, the gains are substantial for housing condition but less impressive for overcrowding. The number of overcrowded families decreased in eight cities, but increased in four others. Statistics for both years make use of the 1950 definition of a dwelling unit, thus excluding a number of single-room units counted for the first time in the 1960 Census. As a result, figures for both years slightly understate both the total quantity of housing and the amount of substandard or overcrowded housing; but this qualification does not affect the basic trend toward improvement.

Further confirmation that the urban slums are yielding comes from New York City, where the image of constantly spreading slums has been nurtured for a long time. As recently as 1960, an official report to the mayor concluded that all the construction activity in New York in the 1950s added up to no progress in meeting the city's need for sound housing to replace slums and ease overcrowding.[15] In

14. *Ibid.*, tables 3, 5. For a fuller analysis of the improvement in urban housing, see Bernard J. Frieden, *The Future of Old Neighborhoods* (Cambridge, Mass.: M.I.T. Press, 1964), pp. 19–26.

15. J. Anthony Panuch, *Building a Better New York: Final Report to Mayor Robert F. Wagner* (March 1, 1960), p. 35.

Table 13-1—Substandard and Overcrowded Housing in Twelve Largest Metropolitan Areas, 1950 and 1959

METROPOLITAN AREA (STANDARD CONSOLIDATED AREA OR STANDARD METROPOLITAN STATISTICAL AREA)	Substandard dwelling units[a]				Overcrowded dwelling units[b]			
	1950		1959		1950		1959	
	Number	Per cent of total	Number	Per cent of total	Number	Per cent of total	Number	Per cent of total
New York SCA	482,737	12.2	356,035	7.4	528,766	14.0	477,981	10.2
Chicago SCA	371,002	22.0	202,220	9.4	224,639	13.8	198,677	9.7
Philadelphia SMSA	151,451	14.3	97,626	7.3	90,342	8.9	84,458	6.7
Los Angeles–Long Beach SMSA	136,799	9.1	61,981	2.6	149,125	10.3	202,016	9.2
Detroit SMSA	112,760	13.1	70,831	6.2	91,337	11.0	97,286	9.0
Baltimore SMSA	89,248	22.1	29,916	5.8	45,834	12.0	50,245	10.5
Cleveland SMSA	49,415	11.3	41,235	7.3	35,819	8.4	41,288	7.7
St. Louis SMSA	181,204	34.9	102,990	15.6	93,254	18.4	84,869	13.5
Washington, D.C. SMSA	54,069	13.0	29,820	5.0	52,063	12.8	49,680	8.6
Boston SMSA	85,590	12.1	57,346	7.4	63,781	9.6	52,410	7.1
San Francisco–Oakland SMSA	70,333	9.5	46,391	5.0	66,917	9.5	65,439	7.3
Pittsburgh SMSA	201,992	32.2	102,114	14.2	95,730	15.6	65,323	9.4

Source: U.S. Census of Housing: 1960, Vol. 4, Components of Inventory Change; Final Report HC (4), Part 1A, for respective metropolitan areas, Table 1.

[a] Substandard units are either dilapidated or lacking one or more plumbing facilities.
[b] Overcrowded units are defined as those with 1.01 or more occupants per room.

a subsequent study, Frank Kristof (formerly Assistant Chief of the U.S. Census Bureau Housing Division and then research director of the New York City Housing and Redevelopment Board) made the necessary adjustments in Census data and other sources to permit a definitive comparison of housing conditions in 1950 and 1960. Kristof's calculations indicate that substandard housing was reduced from 367,000 units in 1950 to 276,000 by 1960, and overcrowded standard housing from 87,000 to 73,000 units. Using a concept of housing need that takes into account substandard condition, over-crowding, and a desirable vacancy reserve, Kristof concluded that in the 1950s the city progressed about one-quarter of the way toward achieving this goal.[16] (As of 1965, a special Census Bureau survey indicated a further reduction of some 40,000 units of sub-standard housing in New York City.[17])

A fundamental question in appraising recent improvements in housing is the extent to which Negroes shared in the over-all gains. Negroes do not participate in the nation's housing market on the same terms as whites. They are victimized by widespread discrimi-nation in the sale or rental of housing, their choices are limited, and their need for additional housing in urban areas is especially pressing. Particularly for Negroes, criteria other than condition, crowding, and cost are relevant, including freedom of locational choice, especially opportunities to leave segregated areas. These issues will be discussed later; for the moment it is useful to continue focusing directly on the housing unit and its characteristics.

In the country at large, the number of nonwhite families living in substandard housing was cut by about one-fifth, from 2.8 million in 1950 to 2.3 million in 1960. Proportionally, the gain was greater. In 1950 Negroes were so poorly housed that 72 per cent of all non-white families were living in substandard dwellings; by 1960 the proportion was down to 44 per cent. Despite this improvement, the gap between Negroes and whites actually widened in the 1950s. Comparable figures for white families were 32 per cent in 1950 and 13 per cent in 1960.[18] Preliminary Census Bureau estimates for 1966 show further reductions in the proportion of both white and non-white families living in substandard housing, with whites down to 8

16. Frank S. Kristof, "Housing Policy Goals and the Turnover of Housing," *Journal of the American Institute of Planners*, 31 (August 1965), pp. 232–245.

17. U.S. Congress, Senate, Subcommittee on Executive Reorganization of the Committee on Government Operations, *Hearings, Federal Role in Urban Affairs*, 89th Cong., 2nd sess., 1966, pt. 1, pp. 147–148.

18. U.S. Housing and Home Finance Agency, *Our Nonwhite Population and Its Housing* (Washington: Government Printing Office, 1963), table 24 (based on U.S. Census data).

per cent and nonwhites down to 29 per cent nationally.[19] Information on changes in overcrowding is not available by race for the entire country, but Table 13–2 summarizes the urban situation for both crowding and condition.

Table 13–2—Characteristics of Occupied Urban Housing Units

	1950	1960
Nonwhite:		
Unsound condition or lacking plumbing facilities	60%	46%
With 1.01 or more persons per room	30%	25%
White:		
Unsound condition or lacking plumbing facilities	18%	14%
With 1.01 or more persons per room	12%	8%

Source: U.S. Housing and Home Finance Agency, *Our Nonwhite Population and Its Housing* (Washington: Government Printing Office, 1963), Table 32 (from U.S. Census data).

The gains for nonwhites indicated in Table 13–2 are solely proportional; with the great increase of black population in the cities, the number of nonwhite families in inadequate housing increased even though their proportion dropped. In 1950, 1.4 million nonwhite families in urban areas lived in housing that was unsound or lacked plumbing facilities; in 1960, 1.8 million. During the same period, the number of overcrowded nonwhite families increased from 700,000 to one million.[20] Further, even the proportional gains failed to narrow the differential between white and nonwhite housing conditions.

A look at the distribution of housing gains among different income groups is also in order. In evaluating current trends in housing, it is important to know whether the benefits of improved housing reach low-income groups as well as those who are in a better position to pay for improvements. Figure 13–1 depicts the proportion of families at different income levels who lived in substandard housing in 1950 and in 1960.[21] At every income level, including the lowest, smaller proportions lived in substandard housing in 1960 than in 1950. Of course, incomes rose substantially for most of the population between 1950 and 1960; thus the actual distribution of

19. U.S. Bureau of the Census, *Current Population Reports*, series P-23, no. 24, "Social and Economic Conditions of Negroes in the United States" (October 1967), p. 53.

20. U.S. Housing and Home Finance Agency, *Our Nonwhite Population and Its Housing* (Washington: Government Printing Office, 1963), table 32.

21. Figures 13–1 to 13–3 involve a minor inconsistency in the data reported for 1950 and 1960. Information for 1950 covers 34.0 million occupied nonfarm units but omits the 5.7 million farm dwellings that were occupied at that time. Information for 1960 covers all occupied housing, including 3.6 million farm units of a total 53.0 million. This compromise was necessary in order to obtain cross-classifications of housing characteristics by the income of residents; it does not appear to introduce errors of a magnitude that would change the findings significantly.

Figure 13-1
PERCENT OF FAMILIES IN SUBSTANDARD HOUSING,
BY INCOME GROUP, 1950 AND 1960

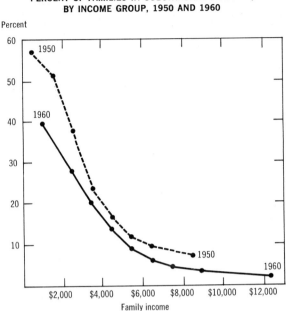

Source: Calculated from *U.S. Census of Housing: 1950*, Vol. II, *Nonfarm Housing Characteristics*, Part 1, U.S. and Divisions, Table A-4; and *U.S. Census of Housing: 1960*, Vol. II, *Metropolitan Housing*, Part 1, U.S. and Divisions, Table A-4.

Information for 1950 covers only occupied nonfarm housing; information for 1960 covers all occupied housing, including 3.6 million farm units of a total 53.0 million. Income is that of primary families and individuals in 1949 and 1959.

Substandard housing is classified as dilapidated or lacking one or more plumbing facilities.

Figure 13-2
PERCENT OF FAMILIES IN OVERCROWDED HOUSING,
BY INCOME GROUP, 1950 AND 1960

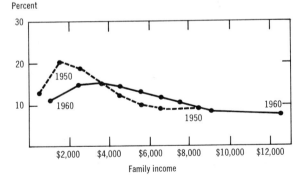

Source: Calculated from *U.S. Census of Housing: 1950*, Vol. II, Part 1, Table A-7; *U.S. Census of Housing: 1960*, Vol. II, Part 1, Table A-3.

Information for 1950 covers only occupied nonfarm housing; information for 1960 covers all occupied housing, including 3.6 million farm units of a total 53.0 million. Income is that of primary families and individuals in 1949 and 1959.

Overcrowded units are defined as those with 1.01 or more persons per room.

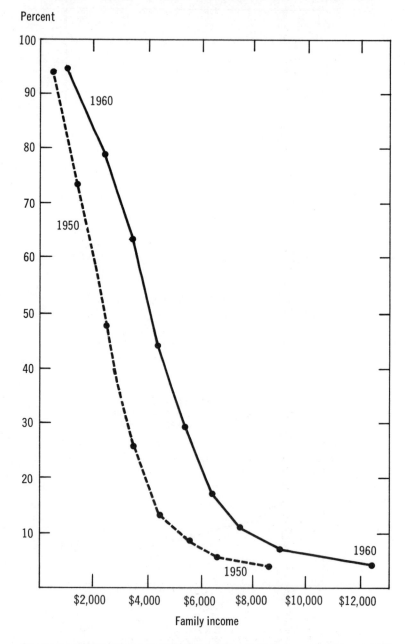

Figure 13-3

PERCENT OF FAMILIES PAYING MORE THAN ONE–FIFTH OF INCOME FOR RENT, BY INCOME GROUP, 1950 AND 1960

Source: See note to Figure 13-2. Gross rent is reported as a percentage of 1949 and 1959 income for primary families and individuals in renter-occupied housing. Gross rent includes utility costs where the tenant pays for these.

families along the income curve shifted to the right. To take account of changes in income, I have divided the Census income categories into groupings representing roughly the bottom third ($0–1999 in 1950, $0–2999 in 1960), middle third ($2000–3999 in 1950, $3000–5999 in 1960), and upper third ($4000 and above in 1950, $6000 and above in 1960) of the population in each year. The proportion of families in each third who were living in substandard housing was:

	1950	*1960*
Upper third	12%	4%
Middle third	30%	14%
Lower third	53%	36%

Thus the lowest income groups did share substantially in the improved housing conditions of the 1950s, but middle- and upper-income groups made greater proportional gains.

Figure 13–2, dealing with changes in overcrowding by income level, tells a somewhat different story. Here the improvements are not distributed across the board but are most evident at the low income levels. Between $4000 and $8000, the proportion of families living in overcrowded housing actually increased between 1950 and 1960. Once again, the graph itself does not take account of the changing distribution of income, which alters the picture. Divided into thirds, the proportion in overcrowded housing becomes:

	1950	*1960*
Upper third	10%	9%
Middle third	17%	14%
Lower third	17%	12%

At all income levels, the proportional reduction in overcrowding is less than the reduction in substandard occupancy. When the changing distribution of income is considered, however, the proportional reductions in overcrowding are greatest for the low-income group, less for the middle-income group, and still less for the top third.

The other key element in housing welfare—cost—is the subject of Figure 13–3. This graph reports the proportion of families at different income levels who spend more than 20 per cent of their income for rent. It is therefore limited to renter-occupied housing in 1950 and 1960, and covers gross rent, including utilities where the tenant pays for them himself. The general upward shift in the curve from 1950 to 1960 answers the question of who is paying for the widespread renovation and general improvement in housing conditions. At every income level, a higher proportion of families paid more than one fifth of their income for rent in 1960 than in 1950. An analysis in terms of changing distribution of income indicates the extent of the upward shift for each of the three income divisions:

	1950	*1960*
Upper third	9%	10%
Middle third	37%	46%
Lower third	81%	89%

The greatest proportional increase was thus in the middle-income group, but the greatest hardship undoubtedly occurred in the low-income group, where extra dollars for housing are most certain to deprive the family of income needed badly for other expenses.

FUTURE PROSPECTS

The experience of the 1950s shows considerable progress in improving housing welfare in the United States, but the performance of the housing market was unimpressive in some important respects. In urban areas, the improvement that did take place was not sufficient to cope with the growing numbers of black families, and in the country at large an increasing number of families at all economic levels were forced to spend more than a reasonable share of their income for rent in order to better their housing conditions. Despite these qualifications, the trends of the 1950s have provided grounds for optimism about the future. William Grigsby has concluded his careful study of changes in the 1950s with a prediction that substandard housing in the United States will be eliminated by 1980.[22] Frank Kristof, in the study of New York City already mentioned, indicates that New York's housing needs can be met within the normal functioning of the housing market (including the continued use of public policy in support of this goal) by 1980.[23] In a subsequent study for the National Commission on Urban Problems (Douglas Commission), Kristof applied the same concept of housing needs to the country at large and concluded that the rate of progress of the 1950s has continued into the early 1960s and can reasonably be expected to continue in the decades ahead. Kristof's projections, which assume no significant increase in the federal role in housing, show a steady reduction from 20.5 million units needed in 1950 (to replace substandard housing, end overcrowding, and provide a 5

22. William Grigsby, *Housing Markets*, p. 322.
23. Frank S. Kristof, "Housing Policy Goals."

per cent vacancy reserve of sound housing) to 5.7 million units needed by 1990.[24]

If these expectations are reasonable, they still pose the question of whether reaching the national housing goal by the 1980s is an acceptable rate of progress. There is widespread dissatisfaction with housing conditions now, particularly among Negroes and low-income groups. The prospect of waiting another twenty years to reach the goal of the Housing Act of 1949 will not evoke great enthusiasm in the slums. Further, the definition of substandard housing that enters into these projections is a minimal one, based on Census categories that do not include such factors as central heating, adequacy of light and air, blighted surroundings, or violations of local housing codes. In addition, our notion of what constitutes acceptable housing will continue to reflect constantly rising expectations. By the 1980s, much of the old housing that meets today's concept of minimum standards will be considered obsolete in size, layout, or appearance. In this sense, postponing the replacement of today's inadequate housing until then means that large numbers of people will continue indefinitely to live in conditions that they and the rest of society consider unacceptable.

Whether the rate of housing improvement can be accelerated depends upon many circumstances, including some that are independent of housing policies. The close connection between low incomes and inadequate housing has already been stressed. The elimination of poverty in the United States would go a long way toward eliminating substandard living conditions. Short of this goal, rising incomes for those who are now poor will be essential to maintain—if not increase—the rate of progress that was achieved in the 1950s. But aside from a general growth of income or the provision of a guaranteed annual income, the operation of the housing market will have much to do with future rates of improvement. The market mechanisms that contributed to improvement in the 1950s will not necessarily operate the same way in the future. A closer look at the components of housing change is helpful in assessing future prospects.

A high volume of new housing construction has been one of the main forces for improvement. Total housing production between 1950 and 1959 (excluding farm units) averaged slightly more than 1.5 million units started per year.[25] This new construction more

24. Frank S. Kristof, *Urban Housing Needs Through the 1980's: An Analysis and Projection* (Washington: National Commission on Urban Problems, Research Report no. 10, 1968).

25. U.S. Department of Commerce, *Construction Statistics, 1915–1964* (Washington: Government Printing Office, 1966), pp. 17–18.

than kept pace with population growth, and triggered a series of changes in the rest of the housing supply. Two-thirds of the new homebuilding took place inside metropolitan areas, mostly in the suburbs. Millions of middle-income families moved from the central cities to new suburban developments, leaving behind a large stock of vacant housing. These vacancies freed the tight housing situation of the late 1940s and made it possible for other families to move out of crowded or unsatisfactory quarters. The turnover of existing housing was sufficient to provide living space for new migrants arriving in the cities as well as older city residents and newly formed families. In most large cities, the movement out to suburbia was greater than population growth resulting from migration plus natural increase. With this decline of central city population, crowding was eased considerably in the dense slum neighborhoods. Crowding was also reduced within the dwelling units: large households, in which grown children lived together with their parents and other relatives, split up to live in separate quarters. Since the population pressure was easing, many small units were merged to form larger apartments. Each wave of movement freed some housing that became available to others. Accompanying this turnover of housing was the impressive amount of renovation noted earlier. Housing that formerly lacked plumbing facilities or bathrooms or needed repairs was put in sound condition.

The indirect effects set in motion by new construction emerged very clearly from a pilot study of housing turnover in New York City.[26] In the study sample, 64 new units gave rise to a chain of turnover involving 90 additional units. At each successive link in the chain, families with lower incomes moved into turnover units, improving the space or quality of their housing and in a few cases moving from a substandard to a standard unit. Most families increased their rent bill as a result of the move, though the new median rent generally remained about one-fifth of family income. This turnover process is not necessarily the same as "filtering," a concept that implies a drop in the cost of old housing as a result of vacancies triggered by new construction. Nevertheless, the turnover of existing housing is a means of supplying additional sound housing for income groups unable to afford the price of new construction. Turnover can involve higher rent-income ratios for the movers, as indicated in the New York study and in the national data cited earlier. The widespread effectiveness of the turnover process in providing sound housing for lower-income groups can be seen in the fact that

26. Frank S. Kristof, "Housing Policy Goals," pp. 241–242.

even at the lowest income levels in 1960 (Figure 13–1), a majority of families were living in standard housing.

Turnover is thus the basic process by which low-income groups improve their housing in the cities. It also has special significance as the way in which Negroes find places to live. Between 1950 and 1960, the nonwhite population grew from 9 million to 13.2 million in metropolitan areas, with more than 80 per cent of this increase occurring in the central cities. Living space for this growing population came almost entirely from older housing formerly occupied by white people. Only a small proportion of Negroes who need housing manage to buy or rent new housing, or move into newly built public housing. Between 1950 and 1960, almost a million metropolitan housing units went from white to nonwhite occupancy; fewer than 100,000 went from nonwhite to white occupancy during the same period. Thus in 1959, as many as 30 per cent of all nonwhite families in metropolitan areas were living in housing where white families had lived in 1950.[27]

Successful operation of the turnover process depends upon three major factors: a high volume of new construction, a low volume of demolition of existing units, and adequate maintenance and upgrading of older housing. During the 1950s all these factors interacted to produce a substantial improvement in housing in urban areas and in the country at large. Within metropolitan areas, 9.8 million new units were built and only 1.0 million were lost through demolition and another 700,000 through such means as fire and flood; 1.8 million dwellings were upgraded from substandard to standard condition and 600,000 downgraded from standard to substandard.[28]

These same components of housing change do not look as promising for the late 1960s and beyond. An increased volume of new construction is needed to keep pace with population growth and mobility, to offset demolitions and losses at the 1950s rate, to continue progress in eliminating substandard and overcrowded conditions, and to allow for a reasonable vacancy reserve. Current estimates, prepared by both governmental and private studies, are that at least 2 million new units per year are needed now and 2.5 million within a few years.[29] Actual production continued to average

27. *U.S. Census of Housing: 1960*, vol. IV, *Components of Inventory Change*, Final Report HC (4), pt. 1A–1, table 2.

28. *Ibid.*, pp. 21–24.

29. U.S. Congress, House, Committee on Banking and Currency, Subcommittee on Housing, *Hearings, Demonstration Cities, Housing and Urban Development, and Urban Mass Transit*, 89th Cong., 2nd sess., 1966, pp. 66, 246; U.S. National Commission on Technology, Automation, and Economic Progress, *Technology and the American Economy*, vol. 1 (Washington: Government Printing Office, 1966), p. 87; Charles Abrams, *The City Is the Frontier* (New York: Harper and Row, 1965), p. 277.

about 1.5 million units a year through 1965, but dropped starting in 1966 and is unlikely to recover during the high interest rate period at the end of this decade. Further, housing demolition in urban areas will increase substantially in the late 1960s and 1970s. The acceleration of urban renewal and of highway construction alone is expected to result in 100,000 demolitions a year, mostly in urban areas.[30] The total effect may be to double the yearly demolition of 100,000 units in metropolitan areas in the 1950s, when urban renewal and federally aided highway construction were just getting under way. Nor is demolition limited to substandard housing: in the 1950s, more than 40 per cent of the units demolished in metropolitan areas were in sound condition with all plumbing facilities.

The third major component—renovation of substandard housing—is more difficult to anticipate. Home repairs and improvements constitute a major industry in the United States. By 1967, outlays for maintenance, repairs, and improvements to nonfarm housing reached $11 billion per year.[31] We do not know, however, what proportion of the total is spent on improving substandard housing. Almost two thirds of the expenditures were for owner-occupied single-family houses,[32] and a large part of the remainder was undoubtedly for maintaining and improving rental housing already in sound condition. There is some evidence to suggest that the high rate of renovation in the 1950s has already taken care of many of the easy jobs, and that property owners will be slower to renovate the remaining substandard housing that is in poorer condition.[33] One careful analysis of the hardcore slums of Newark, New Jersey, has found disturbing signs that most slum-owners have little interest in property improvements, regardless of market conditions, tax policies, or the availability of financing. When the demand for tenement apartments is very strong, the landlord sees no need to improve his property; when the demand is weak, he does not improve because he fears for his investment.[34]

Thus the current outlook is for a slowing of the rate of housing improvement that occurred in the 1950s. In the 1950s, we built more than enough new housing to keep pace with new household for-

30. U.S. Congress, House, *Study of Compensation and Assistance for Persons Affected by Real Property Acquisition in Federal and Federally Assisted Programs*, printed for use of the Committee on Public Works, 88th Cong., 2nd sess., 1964, p. 258; Alvin L. Schorr, *Slums and Social Insecurity*, p. 61.

31. U.S. Department of Housing and Urban Development, *Housing and Urban Development Trends*, 22 (May 1969), p. 29.

32. *Ibid.*, p. 30.

33. William Grigsby, *Housing Markets*, p. 269.

34. George Sternlieb, *The Tenement Landlord* (New Brunswick, N.J.: Rutgers–The State University, Urban Studies Center, 1966).

mation, we demolished relatively little old housing, and we renovated a large number of substandard units. In the 1960s, new construction appears to be falling behind the needs created by urban population growth and housing losses, the volume of demolition is increasing, and the prospects for maintaining a high level of renovation are uncertain.

PROBLEMS WITH THE TURNOVER PROCESS

Among possible strategies for meeting the national housing goal, one approach would be to accelerate the forces that operated successfully in the 1950s. Policies could aim at stimulating a higher volume of new construction, faster turnover of existing units, and greater investment in maintenance and renovation of low-cost housing. But exclusive reliance on this turnover process creates other problems and leads to some bewildering dilemmas for public policy.

Urban growth in the United States has been pushing outward from the core of the central city, with new housing added in a series of rings wrapping around the central city and covering more and more suburban territory. Each ring of development tends to contain housing built at about the same time. Thus the old housing that middle-income families abandon when they move to new quarters is generally concentrated in the inner part of the metropolitan area. Some years ago, these areas of declining middle-class occupancy constituted only a small part of the central city just beyond the downtown business district. By the 1950s, with more housing considered obsolescent, and with a larger number of middle-income people able to move to newer housing, the area of declining middle-class occupancy blanketed very large parts of the central cities and even a number of the oldest suburbs just beyond the city boundary. With low-income people relying almost entirely on older housing abandoned by more affluent groups, it was inevitable that the economic and racial composition of the central cities and some adjoining suburbs would undergo drastic changes.

As a result, the same process that brought about a striking improvement in national housing conditions yielded a plentiful harvest of acute social and economic problems in the central cities. The combination of new suburban development and housing turnover in the older cities led to a massive dispersal of the population along racial and economic lines. By the late 1950s, the suburbs had succeeded in attracting a concentration of white, young, middle- and upper-income families with children; while the central cities were left with higher proportions of the elderly, broken families, Negroes, low-income workers, and the unemployed. These social and economic disparities between central cities and suburbs do not hold true throughout the country, but they do apply to virtually all the large metropolitan areas and to urban areas of all sizes in the Northeast.[35]

The consequences have been severe, both for the people involved and for city governments. One result has been a growing social and cultural isolation of the poor from the rest of society. In neighborhoods where the poor are concentrated, models of success are few and unemployment among youth is sometimes so prevalent that it becomes the normal pattern. It is difficult to judge just how significant this type of isolation is for the poor, and social science evidence is by no means definitive. Other effects of the same social separation are more direct. Workers in the central cities are increasingly cut off from blue-collar jobs in expanding suburban industrial centers, while manufacturing and related lines of employment continue to decline in the central cities. Transportation is difficult to the new industrial parks, and central-city workers are not sufficiently in touch with suburban firms to learn about job opportunities.

For Negroes, these problems are intensified. Even many of those who can afford to move to new housing in suburbia are blocked by discrimination or hostility, and are forced to stay in central-city ghettos. One recent analysis of 1960 data makes it clear that white families with low and moderate incomes are finding their way to the suburbs, but black families in the same income brackets are not. Richard Langendorf carried out calculations for eleven large metropolitan areas to test where Negro families would be living if, at every income level, an identical proportion of Negroes and whites were home-owners and an identical proportion of Negroes and whites in both homeowner and tenant categories lived in the suburbs. Under these assumptions, which imply that household income is the key determinant of where people live, the proportion of Negroes in the suburbs would increase substantially. For all eleven areas combined, 16 per cent of nonwhites actually lived in the suburbs in 1960; under the new assumptions this figure would rise to 40 per cent. The number of suburban nonwhites in New York, Los Angeles, Pittsburgh, and St. Louis would double; in Washington and Baltimore it would more than triple; in Detroit it would increase four times; in Chicago five times; and in Cleveland it would increase about twenty times.[36]

35. For documentation and analysis of central city-suburban differences, see U.S. Advisory Commission on Intergovernmental Relations, *Metropolitan Social and Economic Disparities: Implications for Intergovernmental Relations in Central Cities and Suburbs* (Washington: ACIR, 1965).

36. Richard Langendorf, "Residential Desegregation Potential," *Journal of the American Institute of Planners*, 35 (March 1969), pp. 90–95.

Where people live has much to do with the quality of public services available to them, and this connection leads to one of the most fundamental problems posed by current urban development: the gap between local needs and local resources. Disadvantaged groups in the central cities are highly dependent upon public services. They need high-quality educational programs for both children and adults, they have special needs for health and welfare assistance, recreation facilities, and police and fire protection. Central cities face high service demands, but many of their prosperous taxpayers have left and their commerce and industry are also moving to the suburbs. The cities have been struggling to cope with this gap between service needs and local tax resources. One result has been steady pressure for state and federal help; the recent proliferation of federal aid programs for the cities is a direct consequence. Another typical city strategy has been to develop urban renewal programs intended to win back (or hold onto) middle-income families, retail stores, and industrial firms. Despite the increase in federal aid and the more questionable effects of renewal programs, public services in the cities have had to be held far below the levels that are needed to enable disadvantaged groups to compete with others on equal terms.

In this sense, it is fair to say that our solution to the national housing problem has been creating a national urban problem. Federal housing policies seem to be at odds with other federal objectives. Some programs—chiefly FHA mortgage insurance, federal aid for highways that stimulate suburban growth, and aid for suburban water and sewer systems—accelerate the pace of new housing construction in the suburbs and the turnover of central-city housing. Others—principally urban renewal and aid for mass transit—aim at reviving the central cities and stemming the flight to the suburbs. Urban renewal in turn depletes the supply of low-cost housing and thus slows the turnover effects stimulated by national housing policy. The programs that favor suburban growth promote population dispersal along racial and economic lines, setting the stage for race segregation between central cities and suburbs, which runs counter to civil rights goals. This same dispersal handicaps the central cities in their efforts to supply adequate services for low-income groups, countering other national goals of eliminating poverty and providing equality of educational opportunity.

Continued dependence upon the turnover process to accommodate low-income groups is also producing open social and racial conflict in many central-city neighborhoods. In the 1950s, the growing black population of the central cities was able to take over a great deal of housing left behind by mobile white families who chose to move to suburbs. Even in the 1950s, however, this turnover process failed to reduce the number of urban Negro families living in substandard and overcrowded housing. The continued growth of black population in the cities means that many Negro families have nowhere to go but into whatever vacancies turn up in white areas. But as the more mobile white families have departed, a core of deeply rooted people have remained in old neighborhoods—people who cannot afford to move to the suburbs or who want to stay where they are. Many established ethnic neighborhoods remain in the central cities, where people are tied to friends, family, churches, clubs, and the other loyalties that develop in a close-knit community. Often they are fearful of invasions by Negroes or other newcomers. Some neighborhoods have tried to stabilize the situation by supporting urban renewal programs designed to remove pockets of low-cost housing and price out potential invaders. Others express their fears in backlash voting or open hostility to black newcomers.

The time has come to diversify our mechanisms for meeting the housing needs of low-income groups. The turnover system is working, but it is producing too many objectionable byproducts. These byproducts in turn have generated new policies that will interfere with the future turnover of old housing. In particular, many central cities have found their changing population composition unacceptable and have developed urban renewal programs to stabilize existing neighborhoods or to attract back middle-income families—both of which will sacrifice low-income housing needs in order to diversify the city's population.[37]

Still another reason for supplementing the turnover process with other approaches lies in the nature of national housing goals. The goal of a decent home and a suitable environment for every family is too limited for the needs of urban life today. In our spreading metropolitan areas, mobility is a prerequisite for equal opportunity. Families need to be able to move to keep up with changing work locations, to have access to specialized services or institutions, and to have some measure of freedom in choosing a type of housing or type of community. Most middle-income families now enjoy this freedom of movement through the operation of the housing market, though many middle-income Negroes still do not. Most low-income families have very limited freedom of movement: the turnover process restricts their choice to areas where old housing is concentrated. A more adequate statement of national housing goals would

37. See Bernard J. Frieden, "Toward Equality of Urban Opportunity," *Journal of the American Institute of Planners*, 31 (November 1965), pp. 320–330.

go beyond decent shelter and surroundings, and would include diversity of choice in housing and freedom of movement throughout metropolitan areas.[38] New strategies are needed to achieve this more complex goal. . . .

38. See *ibid.*

The shape of the nation's housing problems

INTRODUCTION

Nineteen years ago the 81st Congress passed the National Housing Act of 1949, calling for "the realization as soon as feasible of the goal of a decent home and a suitable living environment for every American family." In August of this year, the 90th Congress in its Housing and Urban Development Act of 1968 reaffirmed this historic national housing goal but found it "has not been fully realized for many of the nation's lower income families."

A study of this Committee[1] estimated the current number of "lower-income families" for whom a "decent home" is still unaffordable (the "noneffective demand" in the U.S. housing market):

About 7.8 million American families—one in every eight—cannot now afford to pay the market price for standard housing that would cost no more than 20 percent of their total incomes. (The average ratio of housing costs to gross income for the total population is 15 percent.) About half of these 7.8 million families are surviving on less than $3,000 a year—the Federal poverty level.

The study projected the size of this gap 10 years from now, assuming no marked changes in current economic trends, national

1. "United States Housing Needs; 1968–1978" by TEMPO, General Electric's Center for Advanced Studies.

policies and priorities among Federal programs. The projection showed that the prevalence of poverty can be expected to decline only slightly:

In 1978, about 7.5 million families—1 in every 10—would still be unable to afford standard housing.

Urban and rural housing problems

These estimated and projected housing needs among "lower-income families" encompass the entire nation, urban and rural. According to TEMPO's study:

About 56 percent (4.37 million) of today's 7.8 million house-poor families live in urban areas with 50,000 or more population (Standard Metropolitan Statistical Areas).

By 1978, in comparison, about 60 percent (4.5 million) of all families expected to require housing assistance will be urban dwellers. The numbers of urban poor will remain almost constant while the numbers of rural poor will decline.

Although the charge to this Committee was to concentrate on urban housing problems, it is not this report's intention to minimize those problems in rural America. Both are tightly interrelated. Sharecroppers' shacks and Appalachia's shanties are shaping environments for many poor migrants to the cities.

Characteristics of house-poor families

Taking the 1960 U.S. Census and other available data as sources, TEMPO's study group projected the demographic characteristics of 1978's families lacking sufficient income to afford standard housing:

About 70 percent will be white.

About one in four nonwhite families will need housing assistance, compared to 1 in 12 white families.

About half the nonwhite families will be living in the nation's central cities.

According to 1960 census statistics, nonwhites—regardless of income—must earn one-third more than whites in order to afford standard housing (based on allocation of 20 percent of earnings for mortgage payments or rent).

After projecting the characteristics of age and family size, TEMPO estimated these conclusions:

Among the urban white families too poor to afford decent housing in 1978, about half will be elderly (head of the household 65-years-old or more).

Among nonwhite urban families needing housing assistance, only 27 percent will be elderly.

Among needy urban white families, about 70 percent will be small households of one or two persons.

Among nonwhite families, only 43 percent will consist of one or two persons.

Housing conditions in the United States

What happens to the millions of families too poor to afford decent housing? Part of the answer is apparent in Harlem, Cleveland's Hough District, Chicago's Lawndale, other central cities' slums and the shanties of rural poverty areas.

TEMPO's estimates of the characteristics and conditions of the nation's total housing inventory suggest a fuller picture. There are about 66 million housing units and 60 million households.

Although there appear to be more than enough rooftops:

An estimated 6.7 million occupied units are substandard dwellings—4 million lacking indoor plumbing and 2.7 million in dilapidated condition.

6.1 million units (both standard and substandard) are overcrowded with more than one person per room.

Among the six million vacant units, only about two million are in standard condition and available for occupancy—the nation's lowest available vacancy rate since 1958.

These estimates suggest a growing shortage of decent housing, not only for lower-income families but for the entire population. TEMPO's projections bear out this assumption. In order to provide enough standard housing for the entire population by 1978, TEMPO estimates the American economy will need to:

Build 13.4 million units for new, young families forming during the decade ahead.

Replace or rehabilitate 8.7 million units that will deteriorate into substandard conditions.

Replace three million standard units that will be either accidentally destroyed or purposefully demolished for non-residential land reuses.

Build 1.6 million units to allow for enough vacancies for our increasingly mobile population.

Based on these and other available projections of the nation's housing needs, this Committee reached a fundamental conclusion: there are two distinct and definable but inseparably interdependent housing problems:

There is an immediate and critical social need for millions of decent dwellings to shelter the nation's lower-income families.

Overlying this need is one raising an unprecedented and challenging production problem. The nation is heading toward a serious shortage of housing for the total population, unless production is sharply increased.

These two problems—housing needs of the poor and total national housing needs—are parts of the same equation. They must be tackled together. So long as there is a severe shortage of housing among all income levels, the goal of meeting the housing needs of the poor will not only be more difficult but in this Committee's judgment, it is also unlikely that it will be politically, socially and economically attainable.

We recommended that the nation commit itself to a goal of producing at least 26 million new and rehabilitated housing units by 1978, including six to eight million Federally subsidized dwellings for families in need of housing assistance.

The remainder of this report addresses itself to attainment of this 10-year total goal. The goal is nearly a 40 percent increase in the current housing stock, better than 10 percent more than the total housing production for the 20 years from 1940 to 1960, and 70 percent more than the total production for the decade of the 1950's. It will require an average of 2.6 million units annually, compared to the nation's current rate of 1.5 million new housing starts per year.

As a principal requisite for attaining the above goal, we recommend that the Congress over the next decade appropriate the public funds necessary for at least six million Federally subsidized housing units.

The new Housing and Urban Development Act of 1968 set a national goal of six million more subsidized units over the next 10 years. During the entire 30-year history of Federal housing subsidies, only 800,000 subsidized units have been built. Recent annual production rates were only around 50,000.

COSTS FOR ADEQUATELY HOUSING THE NATION'S LOWER-INCOME FAMILIES

In the past fiscal year, it cost the Federal Government $303.7 million to subsidize the 800,000 existing housing units for low- to moderate-income families. The Department of Housing and Urban Development estimates that its annual budget for housing subsidy costs must increase to a peak of $2.8 billion in order to add six million units to the existing stock of subsidized housing. This peak level of annual expenditure would occur in 1978, after which the level of appropriations would start declining steadily for more than 30 years beyond 1978, until total development costs for all of these six million additional units were fully amortized.

In analyzing the peak budgetary impact of six million more subsidized dwellings, the Committee took an arbitrarily conservative viewpoint and added a 20 percent contingency factor to HUD's own estimates. By our estimates, the annual cash subsidy requirements for six million units in 1978, the year of peak costs when all units would be completed or near ready for occupancy, would be $3.4 billion. For eight million units in that same peak year, the required appropriations would approach $4.5 billion.

Comparing this multi-billion dollar demand with other recent Federal expenditures may help place the budgetary impact in perspective. From fiscal 1962 through 1967, $356.3 billion was spent for national defense, $33.2 billion for stabilizing farm prices and income, $24.2 billion for space exploration, and $22.2 billion for Federal highway construction. In contrast, $8.1 billion was budgeted for *all* programs under Housing and Urban Renewal, and only $1.25 billion for Federal housing subsidies.

In such a comparison, the Committee must point out that any commitment for housing subsidies generally requires a continuing annual appropriation (for up to 40 years in the case of projects financed under interest rate subsidy programs). By contrast, expenditures for national defense, space programs, highways and agriculture are subject to annual Congressional reaffirmation and appropriation.

The national price for neglecting the housing needs of the poor is equally impossible to estimate accurately. Slums impose economic costs and sociological drains that sap national welfare and unity. Social injustices and inequities carry their moral costs which may far exceed the material costs of subsidy programs.

Considering all the factors, the Committee believes our nation can and must afford the price for building at least the six million subsidized housing units called for by the President and established by the 1968 Housing Act as a national goal.

We further believe, as discussed later, that the U.S. economy possesses the resources for accomplishing the total 26 million unit goal. A national commitment to its attainment is required. Other requisites include responsible fiscal and monetary policies to keep the total economy balanced on a steady growth course between inflation and recession.

THE U.S. HOUSING MARKET AND PUBLIC POLICIES

Americans spend about $50 billion a year to buy, rent, and maintain our dwellings, and about another $50 billion on utilities, furniture, and other housing expenses. Residential land and structures represent about a third of our total national wealth. More than a quarter of new annual capital investment goes into all the elements that constitute the broadly defined housing industry.

Yet more than 12 percent of American families cannot afford decent housing and at least 10 percent of the nation's existing shelters are in substandard condition. This gap may imply some gross inefficiency in the American housing market. To the contrary, the Committee has found that such is not the case.

When consumers create an effective demand, the U.S. home-building industry and housing market have proven their capabilities for producing a quality product and delivering it at reasonable prices. The staff's comparative analyses of U.S. and foreign housing shows that the prevailing standards of American housing generally equal or surpass housing standards in other nations. Moreover, U.S. consumer price indexes point up that housing and all other items, excepting sharply rising medical care costs, rose roughly in line from 1950 to 1960, after which time all other consumer prices began climbing at a faster rate than housing costs.

Contrary to widespread belief, homebuilding is not a technically stagnant industry, resistant to new ideas. Studies for this Committee by consultants and staff concur in characterizing homebuilding and construction not as a highly organized national industry, but as a fractionated and highly localized one, subject to constraints and vagaries of local markets, widely varying local building codes and zoning ordinances and local labor practices.

The largest single on-site homebuilder produces less than 1 percent of the nation's annual new housing starts. The 50 largest producers of all types of housing (single and multi-family, site erected or factory built including mobile homes) together account for less than 15% of the nation's annual housing production.

A chart prepared by the staff dissects the housing delivery process into four distinct phases: preparation, production, distribution and service. Each phase requires inputs from 6 to 14 different sources, from architects to zoning officials, and each operates within the constraints set up by 5 to 11 separate and different sources for impediments and restrictions. In total, there are 23 major public and private direct participants in the housing production process (some involved in more than one phase) and 17 major public and private sources for laws, rules and practices that restrict and influence the process practically every step of the way.

The Committee concluded that within these sets of existing characteristics and constraints, housing producers operate with greater efficiency and response to innovations than commonly thought. The builder, however, can directly influence only a relatively small portion of housing costs.

Tables 14-1 and 14-2 taken from a consultant's report (McGraw-Hill Information System's Technical Report) show the cost components in building and occupying housing, and demonstrate that the real costs for housing are spread among more ingredients than the cost for constructing the dwelling itself.

Table 14–1—Rough Breakdown of Initial Development and Construction Costs

	Conventional single-family unit (percent)	Elevator apartment unit (percent)
Developed land	25	13
Materials	36	38
On-site labor	19	22
Overhead and profit	14	15
Miscellaneous	6	*12
	100	100

* The cost of hiring an architect is one principal reason for this higher figure.

Table 14–2—Rough Breakdown of Monthly Occupancy Cost of Three Kinds of Housing

	Conventional single-family home (percent)	Mobile home (percent)	Elevator unit (percent)
Debt retirement (mortgage payment)	53	55	42
Site rent		28	
Taxes	26	4	14
Utilities	16	11	9
Maintenance and repair	5	2	6
Admin. and similar costs			13
Vacancies, bad debts, and profit			16
Total	100	100	100

Later in this report, recommendations are made calling for broad reaching, new levels of public investment and private activities in research and development efforts aimed at reducing the costs all along the way in the complicated process that delivers housing to American consumers. The National Commission on Urban Problems is studying the complex impacts of building and housing codes, zoning regulations and state and local taxes on housing costs. This Committee, therefore, did not explore these areas in depth but we do note their critical effect on the costs for housing construction, rehabilitation and occupancy.

After analyzing the work of our consultants and staff, the Committee reached these major conclusions regarding the cost of housing:

Even with implementation of effective policies to squeeze out every practically attainable cost reduction, we can realistically expect a reduction in monthly housing costs of only about 10 percent in the foreseeable years ahead.

Although a 10 percent reduction in consumer's housing costs would save billions of dollars in resources annually, it would *not* be enough to bring new standard housing within economic reach of lower-income families.

Private enterprise, alone, cannot solve the nation's problems of housing the poor.

Federal housing assistance remains essential for lower-income families.

PUBLIC POLICIES IN HOUSING

Among the world community of nations, the United States has been a latecomer in providing adequate levels of housing subsidies for its disadvantaged poor. The first Federal housing assistance program (Public Housing) was enacted in 1938. Since that time, some 35 different Federal housing programs have been developed to serve these three broad income groups:

Families below the Federal poverty line (low-income).

Families above the poverty line but who would otherwise have to pay more than 20 to 25 percent of their gross incomes for standard housing (moderate-income).

Families able to pay the economic costs for standard housing under a Federal mortgage insurance or guaranty program, such as FHA or VA (middle-income).

Families in the first two groupings comprise those whose total housing needs could be met by national implementation of our recommended goal of six to eight million subsidized dwellings by 1978. Families in the third grouping are among the self-supporting housing occupants whose total projected housing needs call for 18 to 20 million new and rehabilitated units during the same timespan....

Among the inadequacies of these programs in this Committee's opinion are:

A slippage in program direction and Congressional funding, up and away from serving families in the most dire need of assistance.

A woefully inadequate scale of all Government housing subsidy programs.

Statutory restrictions and administrative practices which have raised unnecessary red tape barriers to private developers and sponsors and have limited their latitude for innovation and decision-making in project design, location and economic mix of tenants.

Underlying the structures of all Federal housing assistance programs are four basic questions of public policy:

How much housing subsidy should a family receive?

What percentage of their earnings should lower-income families be required to spend for standard housing?

What should be the standards in design and amenities for Federally assisted housing?

Where should subsidized housing be located?

On the question of housing subsidies . . . the Committee concluded:

Existing programs offer too little help to the neediest families, particularly families earning less than $2,500 a year who too frequently are beyond reach of Public Housing or Rent Supplement assistance (the deepest-reaching subsidy programs).

In attempts to give priority to lowest-income families, the Congress has often unintentionally undermined these programs' workability. The tendency has been to set family income eligibility limits at unrealistically low levels in relation to inadequate subsidies. The result is that required rentals are often beyond economic reach of the poorest families.

The Committee recommends that subsidy limitations generally be expanded so that programs are capable of serving the poorest families in need of housing assistance.

On the second question regarding allocation of income for housing, all existing Federal programs generally apply income eligibility formulas based on arbitrarily flat percentages of family income. All programs generally require a family to spend either 20 or 25 percent of their income for monthly housing costs. Some permit deductions for children.

White families earning $4,000 to $5,000 a year are spending an average of 20 percent of their income for housing, according to TEMPO's study. This figure of 20 percent was the determinant that TEMPO employed in projecting there will be 7.8 million families unable to afford standard housing by 1978. In many European countries, the percentage of income paid for rent by families in subsidized housing is considerably less than here in the United States.

Housing costs vary from city to city or region to region. Living expenses differ by family size, age and general health of its members. The Committee concluded that no flat percentage of lower-income families' income to be allocated for housing costs can possibly be equitable.

In order to develop better and more equitable formulas for Federal housing subsidies:

The Committee recommends that the Department of Health, Education and Welfare and the Department of Housing and Urban Development should undertake a joint study on patterns of family expenses, to determine the percentage of income the poor should be expected to allocate for housing. The study should determine how housing expenses are affected by such variables as age and size of families and the household's location in metropolitan or rural areas.

On the subject of quality and location of subsidized housing, the Committee shares Secretary Weaver's publicly expressed concern that such housing should not be "storage bins for the poor."

Certainly all housing built with Federal subsidies should conform to minimum health and safety standards, should be positive additions to the immediate environments and should avoid the dangers of early economic obsolescence and tenant stigmatization. As the staff study on "Federal Housing Programs" indicates, limitations on design and amenities in existing Federal housing programs not only vary from program to program but also are not always compatible with the latter two recommended criteria for avoidance of early obsolescence and tenant stigmatization. These limitations may often be partly responsible for generating local resistance to subsidized housing projects.

The Committee recommends that the quality of all housing developed with Federal subsidies should be equal to but should not exceed the quality of new, modest-cost unsubsidized housing constructed in the same locality during the same time period. We further recommend that within such developmental cost limitations, private builders and sponsors should have freedom to choose to furnish certain amenities at the sacrifice of others.

The location of one's place of residence determines the accessibility and quality of many everyday advantages taken for granted by the mainstream of American society. Among these commonplace advantages are public educational facilities for a family's children, adequate police and fire protection, and a decent surrounding environment, to name a few. In any case, a family should have the choice of living as close as economically possible to the breadwinner's place of employment.

It makes little sense for Federally subsidized housing to be concentrated in and around central cities' slums where social and environmental disadvantages can negate the uplifting qualities of decent housing. On the question of where subsidized housing should be located, the Committee submits the following recommended objectives:

Subsidized housing should be built wherever locally feasible under economics of land and development costs and maximum allowable subsidy programs.

Any artificial or discriminatory restrictions imposed by Federal housing programs and local codes and ordinances on the location of subsidized housing should be removed or overcome.

SHAPING HOUSING PROGRAMS FOR BETTER SERVING THE NEEDS

With passage of the Housing and Urban Development Act of 1968, the Federal Government possesses a variety of housing subsidy programs. There are two major programs for low-income families—Public Housing and Rent Supplements—and two for families with somewhat higher incomes but who still require housing assistance—the Section 235 Homeownership program and Section 236 (meant to replace 221 (d) (3) Below Market Interest Rate and 202). Some program gaps still exist. For example, there is no major program which would enable low-income families to purchase their own single-family homes; neither are there any programs which, in and of themselves, can serve the needs of the poorest of the poor who are often too poor even for public housing.

Although a single form of housing subsidy technique applicable for all income groups and for both rental and owner-occupied housing could probably be developed, the Committee concluded that continued reliance on a variety of programs is preferable, at least until production levels of subsidized housing have substantially increased and there is a record of working experience with the newer programs to determine their effectiveness.

The Committee is aware of past criticisms of the Department of Housing and Urban Development and its agencies responsible for administration of housing subsidy programs. Many of these criticisms were valid; others should have been properly redirected at legislative requirements and Congressional pressures imposed on the Department.

The Housing and Urban Development Act of 1968 frees HUD from many past constraints. During the past year, the three-year-old Department has demonstrated that many past valid criticisms are no longer just, although there is still room for further improvement. After thorough consideration:

The Committee recommends that all subsidized housing programs remain under HUD's administration but that they be consolidated under one Assistant Secretary (rather than two as is presently the case) *for maximum efficiency and coordination in their administration.*

For better serving the needs of both the families requiring housing assistance and, indirectly, the tax-paying public, the Committee has identified the following additional shortcomings in these programs and recommends these changes or new directions:

Experience under various housing programs indicates that lower-income families are prone to place such high priority on decent housing that they are willing to move into subsidized housing in neighborhoods lacking adequate community facilities, shopping centers, job opportunities and neighborhood conveniences. To help in correcting any such deficiencies in neighborhoods surrounding concentrations of subsidized housing:

The Committee recommends that HUD provide financing for needed commercial or job-producing facilities in the vicinity of subsidized housing developments. In the cases of interest-rate subsidy programs, such financing should be included in the total mortgage. Occupants of commercial and employment-generating space would be required to pay the prevailing market rate for rental of such space.

Studies indicate that subsidized housing developments are generally more successful if families in surrounding areas are involved to the maximum degree possible in project development and planning. It is only human nature that participants in any sort of venture are likely to develop a feeling of having a stake and pride in its success. The Model Cities and Urban Renewal programs recognize the advantages of citizen participation in planning and employment opportunities generated by Federal housing programs. The construction and rehabilitation of six to eight million more subsidized dwellings would open many more opportunities, both economic and social, for the nation's lower-income families.

To encourage citizen participation in all housing assistance programs to the maximum degree feasible:

The Committee recommends that HUD should encourage sponsors and owners of projects to consult area residents during the planning process.

The Committee further recommends that a $10 million fund be established under HUD's administration to underwrite promising public and private programs for training resident real estate managers, developing tenant management councils, creating resident maintenance *contractors, and for similar socioeconomic ventures.* Experiences of such efforts should be documented and evaluated.

Additionally, the Committee recommends that housing programs should emphasize the entrepreneurial and employment opportunities inherent in them for minority group contractors, subcontractors and construction employees.

As cited earlier, assistance under all Federal housing programs is tied to specific dwelling units or projects, not to specific needy families. If the recipient family vacates their subsidized dwelling for whatever reason, they lose their housing subsidy.

Again, as stated earlier, the Committee believes that project subsidies offer the best tool for directly and rapidly increasing the volume of housing construction and rehabilitation for needy lower-income families. Along with this belief, we recommended against imminent replacement of project subsidy programs with new and simplified forms of subsidy.

In the staff's supportive papers, a persuasive argument is presented for a housing allowance subsidy technique. The staff suggests that such allowances could be made available directly to needy families according to their individual needs and would be earmarked for expenditures on standard housing only. The most compelling arguments supporting this technique, in our judgment, are:

A housing allowance would allow a recipient family greater freedom of choice in location and type of housing.

Such a system would enable the free market in housing to operate in the traditional manner of supply and demand, with greater use of existing standard dwellings for housing lower-income families.

Freed from most Federal administrative restrictions, homebuilders could respond to a new and effective demand market for standard housing units.

Apart from many socioeconomic implications beyond this Committee's capability to assess or evaluate, one principal shortcoming of a broad-scale housing allowance program is its likelihood to inflate the housing economy by interjecting too much new purchasing power too quickly. After weighing its pros and cons:

The Committee recommends that a housing allowance program be introduced on an experimental basis, subject to full and careful analysis of its results.

Federal programs, particularly urban renewal through slum clearance or substantial rehabilitation, often result in dislocations or disruptions in the lives of area residents, generally lower-income families. Past inequities in compensating displaced property owners and assisting displaced tenants and small businessmen in relocating are now partially overcome by new Federal laws.

To assure fair compensation and assistance to all persons displaced or disrupted by Federal urban renewal or housing programs:

The Committee recommends the enactment and implementation of whatever additional Federal compensatory programs may be necessary, together with affirmative action by local public agencies to assure that such persons receive all the benefits available to them.

The Federal Government can help to assure a better flow of information to eligible families regarding the availability of Federal housing assistance and program qualifications for recipients. In 1967, HUD introduced a Home Counseling Service in 15 of its 76 FHA local insuring offices to advise prospective homeowners on mortgage procedures and housing opportunities under FHA programs.

The Committee recommends further strengthening and expansion of such educational and counseling programs for housing consumers. Specifically, the number of such offices should be increased and should be located among lower-income neighborhoods, and the programs should be expanded to include counseling in general financing and home maintenance.

Generally the Committee has found that most communities have yet to assess adequately their local housing needs or to develop affirmative action programs aimed at assuring that local needs will be met. Often, Federal housing programs are locally implemented by separate and uncoordinated local public agencies, with no single public official responsible for coordinating or overseeing the community's total housing efforts.

The Committee recommends that the Federal Government should provide funding to local governments for financing the preparation of plans aimed at meeting local housing needs. Regulations governing existing Federal programs could be modified so that Federal funds for local planning could be provided under existing authority.

Local housing authorities in some communities may lack the technical staff to plan and supervise the development of Public Housing projects. This lack of local expertise can seriously delay and impede local implementation of the Public Housing program.

The Committee recommends that HUD be granted the necessary authority to take full responsibility for preparation of plans and supervision of bidding and construction of public housing projects, or negotiating a turnkey proposal when requested by a local housing authority to do so.

INVOLVING THE PRIVATE SECTOR IN SUBSIDIZED HOUSING PROGRAMS

The principal charge to this Committee was to find the necessary incentives and mechanisms for attracting more private participation in the development of subsidized housing. The national goal of six million additional subsidized dwellings over the next 10 years represents nearly an eightfold increase in the subsidized stock developed over the past 30 years. We are convinced that attaining such a goal depends on full participation by the profit-oriented private sector, as well as by nonprofit and local public institutions.

The nation's homebuilding industry, except during the economic constraints of wartime and other adverse conditions, has demonstrated its capability to meet the market's demands for housing. The private sector has not yet developed much housing for the poor because until recent years the subsidies required to make such efforts feasible and reasonably profitable have been lacking in scale and attractiveness. Expansion of opportunities for private enterprise to enter the field—such as the relatively new Turnkey programs in Public Housing—has demonstrated that profit-motivated entrepreneurs can build and manage subsidized housing more efficiently and at less cost than public bodies.

In considering the means for attracting more private participation in the nation's efforts to provide every lower-income family with a decent home, the Committee concentrated on forming recommendations to meet these two objectives:

Attracting more existing homebuilders and developers into sponsoring, building and rehabilitating subsidized housing.

Developing new instruments or institutions capable of attracting new sources for entrepreneurial talent and capital.

The Committee found that most businesses not already directly active in housing development and even many homebuilders, themselves, were unfamiliar with the opportunities for participation in Federal housing programs. They were directing all their talents and resources to fields more familiar to them and, in their judgments, less complex and risky. . . .

We have examined those Federal programs currently available and have assessed their profitability, their requirements of participants and their workability, from the participants' viewpoints. We have consulted with participants in all of these programs and have considered their successes and difficulties.

The Committee has found a number of important and imaginative Federal programs designed to encourage participation by private enterprise. In many cases we found specific shortcomings in the details of such programs, and we have recommended means to remedy these problems. In the administration of subsidized housing programs, we found areas requiring changes in practice and pointed out these difficulties to the White House and to appropriate Federal agencies.

During our opportunity to help shape the Housing and Urban Development Act of 1968, we recommended the creation of a new private instrument to stimulate the participation of private enterprise in the massive housing task that lies ahead in the National Housing Partnership, now being brought into existence pursuant to Title IX of the new Housing Act.

Public housing programs

The Committee examined the "turnkey" public housing program under which a private developer sells the site and completed building to a local housing authority, as compared with the conventional process including public acquisition of a site followed by public design and public bidding of construction and was favorably impressed by initial reports of its success. While the Committee realized that a comprehensive appraisal of this new program may take several years, we believe that the desirability of the turnkey approach has been demonstrated from the standpoints of private developers, public housing tenants, and the American taxpayers at large. The Committee was particularly interested in the flexibility afforded under the turnkey program in allowing, for example, the sale or lease of individual units in a large project.

The Committee recommends that HUD urge and encourage local housing authorities to solicit turnkey proposals from private developers before undertaking the construction of public housing in the conventional public works manner (which limits the private participants to a contractor's role).

The Committee examined the programs for leasing all or portions of privately developed residential properties for public housing (sections 10 (c) and 23 of the United States Housing Act). We believe these programs provide an effective means for involving the private sector in low-income housing programs, and most importantly, in producing housing quickly for low-income families. Certain existing restrictions, however, unnecessarily impede the workability of these programs which could otherwise offer substantial opportunities for the private sector to develop public housing.

The section 23 program precludes lease terms in excess of five years. As a result of these short terms for leasing, private developers often find difficulties in securing financing of new units which would increase the stock of housing for low-income families. In both programs, Congress has limited the use of Federal subsidies to existing structures. In order to encourage more private participation in these programs and to enable developers to plan and finance such projects without unnecessary additional risk:

The Committee recommends that these barriers be removed. Specifically, HUD should permit lease renewal options between the developer and the local housing authority to extend for whatever time period would facilitate project financing. Secondly, the Congress should remove the restrictions that limit both programs to use of existing structures.

Rent supplement program

The Rent Supplement program, enacted in 1965, requires tenant families to pay 25 percent of their income toward rent with the Federal Government paying the difference between economic rent levels and the tenant's payments directly to the landlord. In essence, this program tries to shift responsibility for building and operating lower-rent housing projects from the local housing authorities to private, profit-motivated and nonprofit groups.

Among the Congressionally imposed regulations which hamper the Rent Supplement program's effectiveness are establishment of specific dollar limits on maximum fair market rentals and on construction costs. These low maximum rentals and construction costs make the program generally unworkable for new construction in major central cities outside the South and Southwest. Even where construction is feasible, builders often are hesitant to use this program tool. They are concerned that its limitations on construction costs will handicap them in developing a project that will be marketable to non-subsidized tenants able to afford the market rate rents.

The Committee recommends that the maximum monthly rent levels and unrealistic construction limits on the Rent Supplement Program should be removed.

Moderate-income housing programs

The Committee examined the FHA homeownership program, the new section 235 of the National Housing Act and the major rental programs, sections 221 (d) (3) Below Market Interest Rate and 236. While it is too early to evaluate the section 235 program, there has been substantial experience in project development and operation under section 221 (d) (3), and the Committee focused on this program as a measure of private involvement in moderate-income housing.

The Committee made a detailed analysis of the profitability of the section 221 (d) (3) BMIR Program, as it may be employed by a limited distribution, profit-seeking mortgagor. While the Committee favors the limited distribution mechanism:

We recommend that the current permissible cash flow to the limited distribution mortgagor (sponsor) be increased from 6% to a more realistic rate, for example, 8 percent, reflecting the return currently available to investors in alternative and less risky businesses or instruments.

As source material for the above recommendation, the staff developed a pro forma annual operating statement (after construction and start-up) for an illustrative project. If the permissible cash return were increased to 8 percent, the annual cash income in the staff's illustrative case would increase from $24,500 to a new figure of $32,600. An increase to 8 percent would raise the project's rentals an average of $2.50 per month. The Committee believed that this slight rise in rents would be justified by the need to bring about realistic profit potentials that would attract the necessary scale of private participation under these programs.

The Committee concluded that investors in 221 (d) (3) BMIR projects can obtain an overall yield, including tax savings to those in the 50 percent tax bracket, approximating that required by many industrial corporations—better than 15 percent per year. However, the return decreases markedly with time, as the substantial initial tax savings from accelerated depreciation starts to decline. Moreover, the Committee recognizes that existing tax law would substantially reduce overall yields if a project were sold in the early years at a price sufficiently low to avoid a rent increase.

Private developers of unsubsidized housing often avoid this dilemma by sale at a price sufficient to allow the retirement of their mortgage, payment of their taxes, and recovery of their equity. Such a sales price normally assumes substantial appreciation in the property's value and is reflected in higher rents. The objective of maintaining low rent schedules precludes sale at an increased price that would cause the subsequent owners to increase rents. But the need to allow a reasonable profit on these projects requires a mechanism giving the builder-sponsor a reasonable chance to liquidate his interest in the early years at a price sufficient to recover his equity after retirement of the mortgage and payment of taxes.

One means of accomplishing this objective, recommended by the Committee, is contained in the Housing and Urban Development Act of 1968. This provision would allow a limited distribution sponsor to sell to a tenant cooperative or nonprofit group at a price reflecting the objectives discussed above, at a price which would permit the seller to recover his equity. With 100 per cent mortgage financing (rather than the 90 percent financing to limited distribution entities), a cooperative or nonprofit group can meet the sales price set without increasing rents, if the remaining mortgage term is extended.

The Committee recommends that the Secretary take immediate action to implement the approach discussed above, as contained in the 1968 Housing Act.

It may be that experience will show that the most broadly effective solution to the above problem will require another approach. If so, the Committee makes two recommendations in this area:

First, the Committee recommends that a 3 percent tax credit be extended to limited distribution mortgagors (sponsors) on the completion of a low- or moderate-income housing project. This tax credit would be identical to that now available for companies placing into service public utility equipment and machinery. It would be less than the 7 percent investment tax credit available for the construction of buildings. The 3 percent tax credit, even with the existing tax treatment on sale, would appear to provide for a realistic level of profitability without the necessity for a rent increase or an extension of mortgage term upon sale. As a second alternative approach, *the Committee recommends the use of a tax forgiveness if the project is sold to a tenant's cooperative or non-profit group.*

All the above proposed approaches would have the advantage of encouraging developers to form tenants' associations and to assist them in gaining the experience and skill needed to manage and own their own housing. Early sale to such a group would achieve many of the desirable social objectives of homeownership by lower-income families, while allowing the builder-sponsor to free his capital and management skill for construction of other needed subsidized housing . . .

15 HERBERT J. GANS

The failure of urban renewal: a critique and some proposals*

INTRODUCTION

Suppose that the government decided that jalopies were a menace to public safety and a blight on the beauty of our highways and therefore took them away from their drivers. Suppose, then, that to replenish the supply of automobiles, it gave these drivers a hundred dollars each to buy a good used car and also made special grants to General Motors, Ford, and Chrysler to lower the cost—although not necessarily the price—of Cadillacs, Lincolns, and Imperials by a few hundred dollars. Absurd as this may sound, change the jalopies to slum housing, and I have described, with only slight poetic license, the first fifteen years of a federal program called urban renewal.

Since 1949, this program has provided local renewal agencies with federal funds and the power of eminent domain to condemn slum neighborhoods, tear down the buildings, and resell the cleared land to private developers at a reduced price. In addition to relocating the slum dwellers in "decent, safe, and sanitary" housing, the program was intended to stimulate large-scale private rebuilding, add new tax revenues to the dwindling coffers of the cities, revitalize

* Chapter 18 of PEOPLE AND PLANS by Herbert J. Gans, © 1968 by Herbert J. Gans, Basic Books, Inc., Publishers, New York. Reprinted from *Commentary*, by permission; Copyright © 1965 by the American Jewish Committee.

their downtown areas, and halt the exodus of middle-class whites to the suburbs.

For some time now, a few city planners and housing experts have been pointing out that urban renewal was not achieving its general aims, and social scientists have produced a number of critical studies of individual renewal projects. These critiques, however, have mostly appeared in academic books and journals; otherwise there has been remarkably little public discussion of the federal program. Slum dwellers whose homes were to be torn down have indeed protested bitterly, but their outcries have been limited to particular projects; and because such outcries have rarely been supported by the local press, they have been easily brushed aside by the political power of the supporters of the projects in question. In the last few years, the civil-rights movement has backed protesting slum dwellers, though again only at the local level, while rightists have opposed the use of eminent domain to take private property from one owner in order to give it to another (especially when the new one is likely to be from out of town and financed by New York capital).

Slum clearance has also come under fire from several prominent architectural and social critics, led by Jane Jacobs, who have been struggling to preserve neighborhoods like Greenwich Village, with their brownstones, lofts, and small apartment houses, against the encroachment of the large, high-rise projects built for the luxury market and the poor alike. But these efforts have been directed mainly at private clearance outside the federal program, and their intent has been to save the city for people (intellectuals and artists, for example) who, like tourists, want jumbled diversity, antique "charm," and narrow streets for visual adventure and aesthetic pleasure. (Norman Mailer carried such thinking to its furthest point in his recent attack in *The New York Times* magazine section on the physical and social sterility of high-rise housing; Mailer's attack was also accompanied by an entirely reasonable suggestion— in fact, the only viable one that could be made in this context—that the advantages of brownstone living be incorporated into skyscraper projects.)

NEW CRITICISM EMERGES

But if criticism of the urban-renewal program has in the past been spotty and sporadic, there are signs that the program as a whole is now beginning to be seriously and tellingly evaluated. At least two comprehensive studies, by Charles Abrams and Scott Greer, are nearing publication,[1] and one highly negative analysis—by an ultra-conservative economist and often free-swinging polemicist—has already appeared: Martin Anderson's *The Federal Bulldozer*.[2] Ironically enough, Anderson's data are based largely on statistics collected by the Urban Renewal Administration. What, according to these and other data, has the program accomplished? It has cleared slums to make room for many luxury-housing and a few middle-income projects, and it has also provided inexpensive land for the expansion of colleges, hospitals, libraries, shopping areas, and other such institutions located in slum areas. As of March 1961, 126,000 dwelling units had been demolished and about 28,000 new ones built. The median monthly rental of all those erected during 1960 came to $158, and in 1962, to $192—a staggering figure for any area outside of Manhattan.

Needless to say, none of the slum dwellers who were dispossessed in the process could afford to move into these new apartments. Local renewal agencies were supposed to relocate the dispossessed tenants in "standard" housing within their means before demolition began, but such vacant housing is scarce in most cities and altogether unavailable in some. And since the agencies were under strong pressure to clear the land and get renewal projects going, the relocation of the tenants was impatiently, if not ruthlessly, handled. Thus, a 1961 study of renewal projects in 41 cities showed that 60 per cent of the dispossessed tenants were merely relocated in other slums; and in big cities, the proportion was even higher (over 70 per cent in Philadelphia, according to a 1958 study). Renewal sometimes even created new slums by pushing relocatees into areas and buildings which then became overcrowded and deteriorated rapidly. This has principally been the case with Negroes who, for both economic and racial reasons, have been forced to double up in other ghettos. Indeed, because almost two-thirds of the cleared slum units have been occupied by Negroes, the urban-renewal program has often been characterized as Negro clearance, and in too many cities this has been its intent.

Moreover, those dispossessed tenants who found better housing usually had to pay more rent than they could afford. In his careful study of relocation in Boston's heavily Italian West End,[3] Chester

---

1. Charles Abrams, *The City is the Frontier* (New York: Harper and Row, 1965); Scott Greer, *Urban Renewal and American Cities* (Indianapolis: Bobbs Merrill, 1965).
    2. Cambridge: Massachusetts Institute of Technology Press, 1964.
    3. "The Housing of Relocated Families," *Journal of the American Institute of Planners*, XXX (November 1964), 266–286. This paper also reviews all other relocation research and is a more reliable study of the consequences of renewal than Anderson's work.

Hartman shows that 41 per cent of the West Enders lived in good housing in this so-called slum (thus suggesting that much of it should not have been torn down) and that 73 per cent were relocated in good housing—thanks in part to the fact that the West Enders were white. This improvement was achieved at a heavy price, however, for median rents rose from $41 to $71 per month after the move.

According to renewal officials, 80 per cent of all persons relocated now live in good housing, and rent increases were justified because many had been paying unduly low rent before. Hartman's study was the first to compare these official statistics with housing realities, and his figure of 73 per cent challenges the official claim that 97 per cent of the Boston West Enders were properly rehoused. This discrepancy may arise from two facts: renewal officials collected their data after the poorest of the uprooted tenants had fled in panic to other slums; and officials also tended toward a rather lenient evaluation of the relocation housing of those actually studied in order to make a good record for their agency. (On the other hand, when they were certifying areas for clearance, these officials often exaggerated the degree of "blight" in order to prove their case.)

As for the substandard rents paid by slum dwellers, these are factual in only a small proportion of cases, and then mostly among whites. Real-estate economists argue that families should pay at least 20 per cent of their income for housing, but what is manageable for middle-income people is a burden to those with low incomes who pay a higher share of their earnings for food and other necessities. Yet even so, low-income Negroes generally have to devote about 30 per cent of their income to housing, and a Chicago study cited by Hartman reports that among non-white families earning less than $3,000 a year, median rent rose from 35 per cent of income before relocation to 46 per cent afterward.

To compound the failure of urban renewal to help the poor, many clearance areas (Boston's West End is an example) were chosen, as Anderson points out, not because they had the worst slums, but because they offered the best sites for luxury housing—housing which would have been built whether the urban-renewal program existed or not. Since public funds were used to clear the slums and to make the land available to private builders at reduced costs, the low-income population was in effect subsidizing its own removal for the benefit of the wealthy. What was done for the slum dwellers in return is starkly suggested by the following statistic: *only one-half of 1 per cent* of all federal expenditures for urban renewal between 1949 and 1964 was spent on relocation of families and individuals, and 2 per cent if payments to businesses are included.

Finally, because the policy has been to clear a district of all slums at once in order to assemble large sites to attract private developers, entire neighborhoods have frequently been destroyed, uprooting people who had lived there for decades, closing down their institutions, ruining small businesses by the hundreds, and scattering families and friends all over the city. By removing the structure of social and emotional support provided by the neighborhood, and by forcing people to rebuild their lives separately and amid strangers elsewhere, slum clearance has often come at a serious psychological as well as financial cost to its supposed beneficiaries. Marc Fried, a clinical psychologist who studied the West Enders after relocation, reported that 46 per cent of the women and 38 per cent of the men "give evidence of a fairly severe grief reaction or worse" in response to questions about leaving their tight-knit community. Far from "adjusting" eventually to this trauma, 26 per cent of the women remained sad or depressed even two years after they had been pushed out of the West End.[4]

People like the Italians or the Puerto Ricans who live in an intensely group-centered way among three-generation "extended families" and ethnic peers have naturally suffered greatly from the clearance of entire neighborhoods. It may well be, however, that slum clearance has inflicted yet graver emotional burdens on Negroes, despite the fact that they generally live in less cohesive and often disorganized neighborhoods. In fact, I suspect that Negroes who lack a stable family life and have trouble finding neighbors, shopkeepers, and institutions they can trust may have been hurt even more by forcible removal to new areas. This suspicion is supported by another of Fried's findings: that the socially marginal West Enders were more injured by relocation than those who had been integral members of the old neighborhood. Admittedly, some Negroes move very often on their own, but then they at least do so voluntarily and not in consequence of a public policy which is supposed to help them in the first place. Admittedly also, relocation has made it possible for social workers to help slum dwellers whom they could not reach until renewal brought them out in the open, so to speak. But then only a few cities have so far used social workers to make relocation a more humane process.

These high financial, social, and emotional costs paid by the slum dwellers have generally been written off as an unavoidable by-product of "progress", the price of helping cities to collect more

4. Marc Fried, "Grieving for a Lost Home," in Leonard J. Duhl, ed., *The Urban Condition* (New York: Basic Books, 1963), pp. 151–171.

taxes, bring back the middle class, make better use of downtown land, stimulate private investment, and restore civic pride. But as Anderson shows, urban renewal has hardly justified these claims either. For one thing, urban renewal is a slow process: the average project has taken twelve years to complete. Moreover, while the few areas suitable for luxury housing were quickly rebuilt, less desirable cleared land might lie vacant for many years because developers were—and are—unwilling to risk putting up high- and middle-income housing in areas still surrounded by slums. Frequently, they can be attracted only by promises of tax write-offs, which absorb the increased revenues that renewal is supposed to create for the city. Anderson reports that, instead of the anticipated four dollars for every public dollar, private investments have only just matched the public subsidies, and even the money for luxury housing has come forth largely because of federal subsidies. Thus, all too few of the new projects have produced tax gains and returned suburbanites or generated the magic rebuilding boom.

Anderson goes on to argue that during the fifteen years of the federal urban-renewal program, the private housing market has achieved what urban renewal has failed to do. Between 1950 and 1960, twelve million new dwelling units were built, and fully six million substandard ones disappeared—all without government action. The proportion of substandard housing in the total housing supply was reduced from 37 to 19 per cent, and even among the dwelling units occupied by nonwhites, the proportion of substandard units has dropped from 72 to 44 per cent. This comparison leads Anderson to the conclusion that the private market is much more effective than government action in removing slums and supplying new housing and that the urban-renewal program ought to be repealed.

A CRITIQUE OF ANDERSON

It would appear that Anderson's findings and those of other studies I have cited make an excellent case for doing so. However, a less biased analysis of the figures and a less tendentious mode of evaluating them than Anderson's leads to a different conclusion. To begin with, Anderson's use of nationwide statistics misses the few good renewal projects, those which have helped both the slum dwellers and the cities, or those which brought in enough new taxes to finance other city services for the poor. Such projects can be found in small cities and especially in those where high vacancy rates assured sufficient relocation housing of standard quality. More important, all the studies I have mentioned deal with projects carried out during the 1950s and fail to take account of the improvements in urban-renewal practice under the Kennedy and Johnson administrations. Although Anderson's study supposedly covers the period up to 1963, many of his data go no further than 1960. Since then the federal bulldozer has moved into fewer neighborhoods, and the concept of rehabilitating rather than clearing blighted neighborhoods is more and more being underwritten by subsidized loans. A new housing subsidy program, known as 221 (d) (3), for families above the income ceiling for public housing has also been launched, and in 1964 Congress passed legislation for assistance to relocatees who cannot afford their new rents.

None of this is to say that Anderson would have had to revise his findings drastically if he had taken the pains to update them. These recent innovations have so far been small in scope—only 13,000 units were financed under 221 (d) (3) in the first two years—and they still do not provide subsidies sufficient to bring better housing within the price range of the slum residents. In addition, rehabilitation unaccompanied by new construction is nearly useless because it does not eliminate overcrowding. And finally, some cities are still scheduling projects to clear away the nonwhite poor who stand in the path of the progress of private enterprise. Unfortunately, many cities pay little attention to federal pleas to improve the program, using the local initiative granted them by urban-renewal legislation to perpetuate the practices of the 1950s. Yet even with the legislation of the 1960s, the basic error in the original design of urban renewal remains: it is still a method for eliminating the slums in order to "renew" the city, rather than a program for properly rehousing slum dwellers.

Before going into this crucial distinction, we first need to be clear that private housing is not going to solve our slum problems. In the first place, Anderson conveniently ignores the fact that if urban renewal has benefited anyone, it is private enterprise. Bending to the pressure of the real-estate lobby, the legislation that launched urban renewal in effect required that private developers do the rebuilding, and most projects could therefore get off the drawing board only if they appeared to be financially attractive to a developer. Thus, his choice of a site and his rebuilding plans inevitably took priority over the needs of the slum dwellers.

It is true that Anderson is not defending private enterprise per se, but the free market, although he forgets that it only exists today as a concept in reactionary minds and dated economics texts. The costs of land, capital, and construction have long since made it impossible for private developers to build for anyone but the rich, and some form of subsidy is needed to house everyone else. The building boom of the 1950s which Anderson credits to the free market was subsidized by income-tax deductions to homeowners and by FHA and VA mortgage insurance, not to mention the federal highway programs that have made the suburbs possible.

To be sure, these supports enabled private builders to put up a great deal of housing for middle-class whites. This in turn permitted well-employed workers, including some nonwhites, to improve their own situation by moving into the vacated neighborhoods. Anderson is quite right in arguing that if people earn good wages, they can obtain better housing more easily and cheaply in the not-quite-private market than through urban renewal. But this market is of little help to those employed at low or even factory wages, or the unemployed, or most Negroes, who, whatever their earnings, cannot live in the suburbs. In consequence, 44 per cent of all housing occupied by nonwhites in 1960 was still substandard, and even with present subsidies, private enterprise can do nothing for these people. As for laissez faire, it played a major role in creating the slums in the first place.

A NEW MANDATE

The solution, then, is not to repeal urban renewal, but to transform it from a program of slum clearance and rehabilitation into a program of urban rehousing. This means, first, building low- and moderate-cost housing on vacant land in cities, suburbs, and new towns beyond the suburbs and also helping slum dwellers to move into existing housing outside the slums; and then, *after* a portion of the urban low-income population has left the slums, clearing and rehabilitating them through urban renewal. This approach is commonplace in many European countries, which have long since realized that private enterprise can no more house the population and eliminate slums than it can run the post office.

Of course, governments in Europe have a much easier task than ours in developing decent low-income projects. Because they take it for granted that housing is a national rather than a local responsibility, the government agencies are not hampered by the kind of real-estate and construction lobbies which can defeat or subvert American programs by charges of socialism. Moreover, their municipalities own a great deal of the vacant land and have greater control over the use of private land than do American cities. But perhaps their main advantage is the lack of popular opposition to moving the poor out of the slums and into the midst of the more affluent residents. Not only is housing desperately short for all income groups, but the European class structure, even in Western socialist countries, is still rigid enough so that low- and middle-income groups can live near each other if not next to each other and still "know their place."

In America, on the other hand, one's house and address are major signs of social status, and no one who has any say in the matter wants people of lower income or status in his neighborhood. Middle-class homeowners use zoning as a way of keeping out cheaper or less prestigious housing, while working-class communities employ less subtle forms of exclusion. Consequently, low-income groups, whatever their creed or color, have been forced to live in slums or near-slums and to wait until they could acquire the means to move as a group, taking over better neighborhoods when the older occupants were ready to move on themselves.

For many years now, the only source of new housing for such people, and their only hope of escaping the worst slums, has been public housing. But this is no longer a practical alternative. Initiated during the Depression, public housing has always been a politically embattled program; its opponents, among whom the real-estate lobby looms large, first saddled it with restrictions and then effectively crippled it. Congress now permits only 35,000 units a year to be built in the entire country.

The irony is that public housing has declined because, intended only for the poor, it faithfully carried out its mandate. Originally, sites were obtainable by slum clearance; after the war, however, in order to increase the supply of low-cost housing, cities sought to build public housing on vacant land. But limited as it was to low-income tenants and thus labelled and stigmatized as an institution of the dependent poor, public housing was kept out of vacant land in the better neighborhoods. This, plus the high cost of land and construction, left housing officials with no other choice but to build high-rise projects on whatever vacant land they could obtain, often next to factories or along railroad yards. Because tenants of public housing are ruled by a set of strict regulations—sometimes necessary, sometimes politically inspired, but always degrading—anyone who could afford housing in the private market shunned the public projects. During the early years of the program, when fewer citizens had that choice, public housing became respectable shelter for the working class and even for the unemployed middle class. After the war, federal officials decided, and rightly so, that public housing ought to be reserved for those who had no alternative and therefore set income limits that admitted only the really poor. Today, public housing is home for the underclass—families who earn less than $3,000 to $4,000 annually, many with unstable jobs or none at all, and most of them nonwhite.

Meanwhile the enthusiasm for public housing has been steadily dwindling and, with it, badly needed political support. Newspaper reports reinforce the popular image of public housing projects as huge nests of crime and delinquency—despite clear evidence to the contrary—and as the domicile of unregenerate and undeserving families whose children urinate only in the elevators. The position of public housing, particularly among liberal intellectuals, has also been weakened by the slurs of the social and architectural aesthetes who condemn the projects' poor exterior designs as "sterile," "monotonous," and "dehumanizing," often in ignorance of the fact that the tightly restricted funds have been allocated mainly to make the apartments themselves as spacious and livable as possible and that the waiting lists among slum dwellers who want these apartments remain long. Be that as it may, suburban communities and urban neighborhoods with vacant land are as hostile to public housing as ever, and their opposition is partly responsible for the program's having been cut down to its present minuscule size.

The net result is that low-income people today cannot get out of the slums, either because they cannot afford the subsidized private market or because the project they could afford cannot be built on vacant land. There is only one way to break through this impasse, and that is to permit them equal access to new subsidized, privately built housing by adding another subsidy to make up the difference between the actual rent and what they can reasonably be expected to pay. Such a plan, giving them a chance to choose housing like all other citizens, would help to remove the stigma of poverty and inferiority placed on them by public housing. Many forms of rent subsidy have been proposed, but the best one, now being tried in New York, is to put low- and middle-income people in the same middle-income project, with the former getting the same apartments at smaller rentals.

Admittedly, this approach assumes that the poor can live with the middle class and that their presence and behavior will not threaten their neighbors' security or status. No one knows whether this is really possible, but experiments in education, job-training, and social-welfare programs do show that many low-income people, when once offered *genuine* opportunities to improve their lives and given help in making use of them, are able to shake off the hold of the culture of poverty. Despite the popular stereotype, the proportion of those whom Hylan Lewis calls the clinical poor, too ravaged emotionally by poverty and deprivation to adapt to new opportunities, seems to be small. As for the rest, they only reject programs offering spurious opportunities, like job-training schemes for nonexistent jobs. Further, anyone who has lived in a slum neighborhood can testify that whatever the condition of the building, most women keep their apartments clean by expenditures of time and effort inconceivable to the middle-class housewife. Moving to a better apartment would require little basic cultural change from these women, and rehousing is thus a type of new opportunity that stands a better chance of succeeding than, say, a program to inculcate new child-rearing techniques.

We have no way of telling how many slum dwellers would be willing to participate in such a plan. However poor the condition of the flat, the slum is home, and for many it provides the support of neighborhood relatives and friends and a cultural milieu in which everyone has the same problems and is therefore willing to overlook occasional disreputable behavior. A middle-income project cannot help but have a middle-class ethos, and some lower-class people may be fearful of risking what little stability they have achieved where they are now in exchange for something new, strange, demanding, and potentially hostile. It would be hard to imagine an unwed Negro mother moving her household to a middle-income project full of married couples and far removed from the mother, sisters, and aunts who play such an important role in the female-centered life of lower-class Negroes. However, there are today a large number of stable two-parent families who live in the slums only because income and race exclude them from the better housing that is available. Families like these would surely be only too willing to leave the Harlems and Black Belts. They would have to be helped with loans to make the move and perhaps even with grants to buy new furniture so as not to feel ashamed in their new surroundings. They might be further encouraged by being offered income-tax relief for giving up the slums, just as we now offer such relief to people who give up being renters to become homeowners.

Undoubtedly there would be friction between the classes, and the more affluent residents would likely want to segregate themselves and their children from neighbors who did not toe the middle-class line, especially with respect to child-rearing. The new housing would therefore have to be planned to allow some voluntary social segregation for both groups, if only to make sure that enough middle-income families would move in (especially in cities where there was no shortage of housing for them). The proportion of middle- and low-income tenants would have to be regulated, not only to minimize the status fears of the former but also to give the latter enough peers to keep them from feeling socially isolated and without emotional support when problems arise. Fortunately, nonprofit and limited-dividend institutions, which do not have to worry about showing an immediate profit, are now being encouraged to build moderate-income housing; they can do a more careful job of planning the physical and social details of this approach than speculative private builders.

If the slums are really to be emptied and their residents properly housed elsewhere, the rehousing program will have to be extended beyond the city limits, for the simple reason that that is where most of the vacant land is located. This means admitting the low-income population to the suburbs; it also means creating new towns—self-contained communities with their own industry which would not, like the suburbs, be dependent on the city for employment opportunities and could therefore be situated in presently rural areas.

To be sure, white middle-class suburbanites and rural residents are not likely to welcome nonwhite low-income people into their communities, even if the latter are no longer clearly labeled as poor. The opposition to be expected in city neighborhoods chosen for mixed-income projects would be multiplied a hundredfold in outlying areas. Being politically autonomous, and having constituencies who are not about to support measures that will threaten their security or status in the slightest, the suburbs possess the political power to keep the rehousing program out of their own vacant lots, even if they cannot stop the federal legislation that would initiate it. On the other hand, experience with the federal highway program and with urban renewal itself has demonstrated that few communities can afford to turn down large amounts of federal money. For instance, New York City is likely to build a Lower Manhattan Expressway in the teeth of considerable local opposition, if only because the federal government will pay 90 per cent of the cost and thus bring a huge sum into the city coffers. If the rehousing program were sufficiently large to put a sizable mixed-income project in every community, and if the federal government were to pick up at least 90 per cent of the tab, while also strengthening the appeal of the program by helping to solve present transportation, school, and tax problems in the suburbs, enough political support might be generated to overcome the objections of segregationist and class-conscious whites.

Yet even if the outlying areas could be persuaded to co-operate, it is not at all certain that slum dwellers would leave the city. Urban-renewal experience has shown that for many slum dwellers there are more urgent needs than good housing. One is employment, and most of the opportunities for unskilled or semiskilled work are in the city. Another is money, and some New York City slum residents recently refused to let the government inspect, much less repair, their buildings because they would lose the rent reductions they had received previously. If leaving the city meant higher rents, more limited access to job possibilities, and also separation from people and institutions which give them stability, some slum residents might very well choose overcrowding and dilapidation as the lesser of two evils.

These problems would have to be considered in planning a rehousing program beyond the city limits. The current exodus of industry from the city would, of course, make jobs available to the new suburbanites. The trouble is that the industries now going into the suburbs, or those that would probably be attracted to the new towns, are often precisely the ones which use the most modern machinery and the fewest unskilled workers. Thus, our rehousing plan comes up against the same obstacle—the shortage of jobs—that has frustrated other programs to help the low-income population and that will surely defeat the War on Poverty in its present form. Like so many other programs, rehousing is finally seen to depend on a step that American society is as yet unwilling to take: the deliberate creation of new jobs by government action. The building of new towns especially would have to be co-ordinated with measures aimed at attracting private industry to employ the prospective residents, at creating other job opportunities, and at offering intensive training for the unskilled after they have been hired. If they are not sure of a job before they leave the city, they simply will not leave.

The same social and cultural inhibitions that make slum residents hesitant to move into a mixed-income project in the city would, of course, be even stronger when it came to moving out of the city. These inhibitions might be relaxed by moving small groups of slum residents en masse or by getting those who move first to encourage their neighbors to follow. In any case, new social institutions and community facilities would have to be developed to help the erstwhile slum dweller feel comfortable in his new community, yet without labeling him as poor.

Despite its many virtues, a rehousing program based on the use of vacant land on either side of the city limits would not immediately clear the slums. Given suburban opposition and the occupational and social restraints on the slum dwellers themselves, it can be predicted that if such a program were set in motion it would be small in size and would pull out only the upwardly mobile—particularly the young people with stable families and incomes—who are at best a sizable minority among the poor. What can be done now to help the rest leave the slums?

The best solution is a public effort to encourage their moving into existing neighborhoods within the city and in older suburbs just beyond the city limits. Indeed, a direct rent subsidy like that now given to relocatees could enable people to obtain decent housing in these areas. This approach has several advantages. It would allow low-income people to be close to jobs and to move in groups, and it would probably attract the unwed mother who wanted to give her children a better chance in life. It would also be cheaper than building new housing, although the subsidies would have to be large enough to discourage low-income families from overcrowding—and thus deteriorating—the units in order to save on rent.

There are, however, some obvious disadvantages as well. For one thing, because nonwhite low-income people would be moving into presently white or partially integrated areas, the government would in effect be encouraging racial invasion. This approach would thus have the effect of pushing the white and middle-income people further toward the outer edge of the city or into the suburbs. Although some whites might decide to stay, many would surely want to move, and not all would be able to afford to do so. It would be necessary to help them with rent subsidies as well; indeed, they might become prospective middle-income tenants for rehousing projects on vacant land.

Undoubtedly, all this would bring us closer to the all-black city that has already been predicted. For this reason alone, a scheme that pushes the whites further out can be justified only when combined with a rehousing program on vacant land that would begin to integrate the suburbs. But even that could not prevent a further racial imbalance between cities and suburbs.

Yet would the predominantly nonwhite city really be so bad? It might be for the middle class which needs the jobs, shops, and culture that the city provides. Of course, the greater the suburban exodus, the more likely it would become that middle-class culture would also move to the suburbs. This is already happening in most American cities—obvious testimony to the fact that culture (at least of the middle-brow kind represented by tent theaters and art movie houses) does not need the city in order to flourish; and the artists who create high culture seem not to mind living among the poor even now.

Nonwhite low-income people might feel more positive about a city in which they were the majority, for if they had the votes, municipal services would be more attuned to their priorities than is now the case. To be sure, if poor people (of any color) were to dominate the city, its tax revenues would decrease even further, and cities would be less able than ever to supply the high-quality public services that the low-income population needs so much more urgently than the middle class. Consequently, new sources of municipal income not dependent on the property tax would have to be found; federal and state grants to cities (like those already paying half the public-school costs in several states) would probably be the principal form. Even under present conditions, in fact, new sources of municipal income must soon be located if the cities are not to collapse financially.

If nonwhites were to leave the slums en masse, new ghettos would eventually form in the areas to which they would move. Although this is undesirable by conventional liberal standards, the fact is that many low-income Negroes are not yet very enthusiastic about living among white neighbors. They do not favor segregation, of course; what they want is a free choice and then the ability to select predominantly nonwhite areas that are in better shape than the ones they live in now. If the suburbs were opened to nonwhites— to the upwardly mobile ones who want integration now—free choice would become available. If the new ghettos were decent neighborhoods with good schools, and if their occupants had jobs and other opportunities to bring stability into their lives, they would be training their children to want integration a generation hence.

In short, then, a workable rehousing scheme must provide new housing on both sides of the city limits for the upwardly mobile minority and encouragement to move into older areas for the remainder. If, in these ways, enough slum dwellers could be enabled and induced to leave the slums, it would then be possible to clear or rehabilitate the remaining slums. Once slum areas were less crowded and empty apartments were going begging, their profitability and market value would be reduced and urban renewal could take place far more cheaply and quickly. Relocation would be less of a problem, and with land values down, rebuilding and rehabilitation could be carried out to fit the resources of the low-income people who needed or wanted to remain in the city. A semi-suburban style of living that would be attractive to the upper-middle class could also be provided.

At this point, it would be possible to begin to remake the inner city into what it must eventually become: the hub of a vast metropolitan complex of urban neighborhoods, suburbs, and new towns in which the institutions and functions that have to be at the center— the specialized business districts, the civil and cultural facilities, and the great hospital complexes and university campuses—would be located.

Even in such a city, there would be slums—for people who wanted to live in them, for the clinical poor who would be unable to make it elsewhere, and for rural newcomers who would become urbanized in them before moving on. But it might also be possible to relocate many of these in a new kind of public housing in which quasi communities would be established to help those whose problems were soluble and to provide at least decent shelter for those who cannot be helped except by letting them live without harassment until we learn how to cure mental illness, addiction, and other forms of self-destructive behavior.

CONCLUSIONS

This massive program has much to recommend it, but we must clearly understand that moving the low-income population out of the slums would not eliminate poverty or the other problems that stem from it. A standard dwelling unit can make life more comfortable, and a decent neighborhood can discourage some antisocial behavior, but by themselves, neither can effect radical transformations. What poor people need most is decent incomes, proper jobs, better schools, and freedom from racial and class discrimination. Indeed, if the choice were between a program solely dedicated to rehousing and a program that kept the low-income population in the city slums for another generation but provided for these needs, the latter would be preferable, for it would produce people who were able to leave the slums under their own steam. Obviously, the ideal approach is one that co-ordinates the elimination of slums with the reduction of poverty.

As I have been indicating, an adequate rehousing program would be extremely costly and very difficult to carry out. But its complexity and expense can both be justified, however, on several grounds. Morally, it can be argued that no one in the Great Society should have to live in a slum, at least not involuntarily.

From a political point of view, it is urgently necessary to begin integrating the suburbs, and to improve housing conditions in the city before the latter becomes an ominous ghetto of poor and increasingly angry Negroes and Puerto Ricans and the suburbs become enclaves of affluent whites who commute fearfully to a downtown bastion of stores and offices. If the visible group tensions of recent years are allowed to expand and sharpen, another decade may very well see the beginning of open and often violent class and race warfare.

But the most persuasive argument for a rehousing program is economic. Between 50 and 60 per cent of building costs go into wages and create work for the unskilled who are now increasingly unemployable elsewhere. A dwelling unit that costs $15,000 would thus provide as much as $9,000 in wages—one and a half years of respectably paid employment for a single worker. Adding four and half million new low-cost housing units to rehouse half of those in substandard units in 1960 would provide almost seven million man-years of work, and the subsequent renewal of these and other substandard units yet more. Many additional jobs would also be created by the construction and operation of new shopping centers, schools, and other community facilities, as well as the highways and public transit systems that would be needed to serve the new suburbs and towns. If precedent must be cited for using a housing program to create jobs, it should be recalled that public housing was started in the Depression for precisely this reason.

The residential building industry (and the real-estate lobby) would have to be persuaded to give up their stubborn resistance to government housing programs, but the danger of future under-employment, and the opportunity of participating profitably in the rehousing scheme, should either convert present builders or attract new ones into the industry. As for the building-trades unions, they have always supported government housing programs, but they have been unwilling to admit nonwhites to membership. If, however, the rehousing effort were sizable enough to require many more workers than are now in the unions, the sheer demand for labor—and the enforcement of federal nondiscriminatory hiring policies for public works—would probably break down the color barriers without much difficulty.

While the federal government is tooling up to change the urban-renewal program into a rehousing scheme, it should also make immediate changes in current renewal practices to remove their economic and social cost from the shoulders of the slum dwellers. Future projects should be directed at the clearance of really harmful slums, instead of taking units that are run down but not demonstrably harmful out of the supply of low-cost housing, especially for downtown revitalization and other less pressing community-improvement schemes. Occupants of harmful slums, moreover, ought to be rehoused in decent units they can afford. For this purpose, more public housing and 221 (d) (3) projects must be built, and relocation and rent-assistance payments should be increased to eliminate the expense of moving for the slum dweller. Indeed, the simplest way out of the relocation impasse is to give every relocatee a sizable grant, like the five hundred dollars to one thousand dollars paid by private builders in New York City to get tenants out of existing structures quickly and painlessly. Such a grant is not only a real incentive to relocatees but a means of reducing opposition to urban renewal. By itself, however, it cannot reduce the shortage of relocation housing. Where such housing now exists in plentiful supply, renewal ought to move ahead more quickly, but where there is a shortage that cannot be appreciably reduced, it would be wise to eliminate or postpone clearance and rehabilitation projects that require a large amount of relocation.

EPILOGUE

Nothing is easier than to suggest radical new programs to the overworked and relatively powerless officials of federal and local renewal agencies who must carry out the present law, badly written or not, and who are constantly pressured by influential private interests to make decisions in their favor. Many of these officials are as unhappy with what urban renewal has wrought as their armchair critics and would change the program if they could—that is, if they received encouragement from the White House, effective support in getting new legislation through Congress, and, equally important, political help at city halls to incorporate these innovations into local programs. But it should be noted that little of what I have suggested is very radical, for none of the proposals involves conflict with the entrenched American practice of subsidizing private enterprise to carry out public works at a reasonable profit. The proposals are radical only in demanding an end to our no less entrenched practice of punishing the poor. Yet they also make sure that middle-class communities are rewarded financially for whatever discomfort they may have to endure.

Nor are these suggestions very new. Indeed, in March 1965 President Johnson sent a housing message to Congress which proposes the payment of rent subsidies as the principal method for improving housing conditions. It also requests federal financing of municipal services for tax-starved communities and aid toward the building of new towns. These represent bold and desirable steps toward the evolution of a federal rehousing program. Unfortunately, however, the message offers little help to those who need it most. Slum dwellers may be pleased that there will be no increase in urban-renewal activity and that relocation housing subsidies and other grants are being stepped up. But no expansion of public housing is being requested, and to make matters worse, the new rent subsidies will be available only to households above the income limits for public housing. Thus, the President's message offers no escape for the mass of the nonwhite low-income population from the ghetto slums; in fact it threatens to widen the gap between such people and the lower-middle-income population which will be eligible for rent subsidies.

On the other hand, as in the case of the War on Poverty, a new principle of government responsibility in housing is being established, and evidently the President's strategy is to obtain legislative approval for the principle by combining it with a minimal and a minimally controversial program for the first year. Once the principle has been accepted, however, the program must change quickly. It may have taken fifteen years for urban renewal even to begin providing some relief to the mass of slum dwellers, but it cannot take that long again to become a rehousing scheme that will give them significant help. The evolution of federal policies can no longer proceed in the leisurely fashion to which politicians, bureaucrats, and middle-class voters have become accustomed, for unemployment, racial discrimination, and the condition of our cities are becoming ever more critical problems, and those who suffer from them are now considerably less patient than they have been in the past.

Home remedies for
urban cancer*

INTRODUCTION

Ever since 1948, when the national Urban Renewal Act was passed, the cities of this country have been assaulted by a series of vast federally aided building operations. These large-scale operations have brought only small-scale benefits to the city. The people who gain by the government's handouts are not the displaced slum dwellers but the new investors and occupants. In the name of slum clearance, many quarters of Greater New York that would still have been decently habitable with a modest expenditure of capital have been razed, and their inhabitants, along with the shopkeepers and tavern keepers who served them, have been booted out, to resettle in even slummier quarters.

Even in municipal projects designed to rehouse the displaced slum dwellers or people of equivalent low income, the physical improvements have been only partial and the social conditions of the inhabitants have been worsened through further social stratification—segregation, actually—of people by their income levels. The standard form of housing favored by the federal government and big-city administrators is high-rise slabs—bleak structures of ten to

* Copyright © 1962 by Lewis Mumford. Reprinted from his volume, THE URBAN PROSPECT by permission of Harcourt, Brace and World, Inc.

twenty stories. Superficially, these new buildings are an immense improvement over both the foul Old Law Tenements of New York and the New Law (1901) Tenements that covered the newer sections of the Bronx and the Upper West Side up to 1930. The latest model buildings are only two rooms deep; all the flats have outside exposure; the structures are widely spaced around small play areas and patches of fenced grass spotted with benches. Not merely are the buildings open to the sun and air on all sides but they are also as bugproof and verminproof as concrete floors and brick walls can make them; they have steam heat, hot and cold water, standard bathroom equipment, and practically everything a well-to-do family could demand except large rooms and doors for their closets; the absence of the latter is an idiotic economy achieved at the expense of the tenants, who must provide curtains.

These buildings, with all their palpable hygienic virtues, are the response to a whole century of investigation of the conditions of housing among the lower-income groups in big cities, particularly New York. Shortly after 1835, when the city's first deliberately congested slum tenement was built, on Cherry Street, the Health Commissioner of New York noted the appallingly high incidence of infant mortality and infectious diseases among the poor, and he correlated this with overcrowding of rooms, overcrowding of building plots, poor ventilation, and lack of running water and indoor toilet facilities. For a large part of the nineteenth century, in all big cities, housing conditions worsened, even for the upper classes, despite the common boast that this was 'the Century of Progress.' It was only because of the most massive effort by physicians, sanitarians, housing reformers, and architects that legislation established minimum standards for light, air, constructional soundness, and human decency.

Unfortunately, it turned out that better housing was more expensive housing, and at the rents the lower-income groups could afford no landlord could be tempted to invest. The most profitable rentals came from congested slum housing. So pressing were the economic and sanitary problems in urban housing that when finally government aid on a large scale was secured, the dominant conception of good lower-income housing was naturally centered on physical improvements. Our current high-rise housing projects find their sanction in the need to wipe out more than a century of vile housing and provide space for people who have been living in slums holding three hundred to seven hundred people an acre. On sound hygienic terms, this demand can be met within the limited areas provided only by tall buildings whose grim walls are overshadowing ever-larger sections of Manhattan.

There is nothing wrong with these buildings except that, humanly speaking, they stink. What is worse, after a few years of occupancy, some of them stink in an olfactory sense, for children, out of mischief or embarrassment, often use the elevators as toilets. And the young have found the automatic elevators marvellous instruments for annoying adults; putting them out of order or stalling them has become a universal form of play. London County Council administrators have told me the same story about the conflict between high-rise urban esthetics and the spirit of youth in city elevator shafts. By the very nature of the high-rise slab, its inhabitants are cut off from the surveillance and protection of neighbors and passers-by, particularly when in elevators. In some housing projects, the possibility of casual violence, rape, even murder, a rising menace in all our big cities, is conspicuously present. The daily life of the inhabitants, besides being subject to the insistent bureaucratic regulation of the management, labors under a further handicap. Because of a long-standing rule, only lately removed, urban renewal projects could not provide marketing facilities to replace those they had wiped out; often the housewife had to trundle her heavy shopping bags many blocks and was denied the convenience of sending a small member of the family to the corner store.

In short, though the hygiene of these new structures was incomparably superior to anything the market had offered in the past —and in sunlight, air, and open view definitely superior to the congested superslums of the rich on Park Avenue—most of the other desirable facilities and opportunities had descended to a lower level.

THE THEORIES OF JANE JACOBS

From time to time in 'The New Yorker' I have pointed out these deficiencies in public housing in New York; as far back as 1942, when one of the first high-rise projects opened in the Navy Yard area of Brooklyn, I foretold that it would become the slum that it now notoriously is. But the person who has lately followed through on all the dismal results of current public housing and has stirringly presented them is Jane Jacobs, whose book *The Death and Life of Great American Cities* has been an exciting theme for dinner-table conversation all over the country this past year. Though her examples of desirable urban quarters are drawn chiefly from New York—indeed, largely from a few tiny pockets of New York—the bad fashionable patterns she points to are universal.

A few years ago, Mrs. Jacobs stepped into prominence at a planners' conference at Harvard. Into the foggy atmosphere of professional jargon that usually envelops such meetings, she blew like a fresh, offshore breeze to present a picture, dramatic but not distorted, of the results of displacing large neighborhood populations to facilitate large-scale rebuilding. She pointed out a fact to which many planners and administrators had been indifferent—that a neighborhood is not just a collection of buildings but a tissue of social relations and a cluster of warm personal sentiments, associated with the familiar faces of the doctor and the priest, the butcher and the baker and the candlestick maker, not least with the idea of "home." Sanitary, steam-heated apartments, she observed, are no substitute for warmhearted neighbors, even if they live in verminous cold-water flats. The chat across the air shaft, the little changes of scene as a woman walks her baby or tells her troubles with her husband to the druggist, the little flirtations that often attend the purchase of a few oranges or potatoes, all season the housewife's day and mean more than mere physical shelter. It is no real gain to supplant the sustaining intimacies of long neighborhood association with the professional advice of a social worker or a psychiatrist, attempting by a wholly inadequate therapy to combat the trauma of social dislocation.

Mrs. Jacobs gave firm shape to a misgiving that many people had begun to express. But she saw more deeply into the plight of both those who were evicted and those who came back to living in homogenized and sterilized barracks. These barracks had been conceived in terms of bureaucratic regimentation, financial finagling, and administrative convenience, without sufficient thought for the diverse needs of personal and family life, thus producing a human void that matched the new architectural void. In this process, even valuable buildings, though cherished landmarks in the life of the community, are often destroyed, so that the operation may "start clean," without any encumbrances.

Mrs. Jacobs' criticism established her as a person to be reckoned with. Here was a new kind of "expert," very refreshing in current planning circles, where minds unduly fascinated by computers carefully confine themselves to asking only the kinds of questions that computers can answer and are completely negligent of the human contents or the human results. This able woman had used her eyes and, even more admirably, her heart to assay the human result of large-scale housing, and she was saying, in effect, that these top-lofty barracks that now crowd the city's skyline and overshadow its streets were not fit for human habitation. For her, the new pattern of high-rise urban housing was all one—whether undertaken by municipal authorities to rehouse low-income groups displaced from their destroyed slum quarters, or by insurance companies to house, somewhat more spaciously and elegantly, carefully selected members of the middle classes and provide a safe, reasonably high return—or finally, by speculative investors and builders taking advantage of state aid and state subsidies to feather their private nests.

From a mind so big with fresh insights and pertinent ideas, one naturally expected a book of equally large dimensions. But whereas "Sense and Sensibility" could have been the title of her Harvard discourse, what she sets forth in *The Death and Life of Great American Cities* comes close to deserving the secondary title of "Pride and Prejudice." The shrewd critic of dehumanized housing and faulty design is still evident, and has applied some of her sharp observations and her political experience to the analysis of urban activities as a whole. But this excellent clinical analyst has been joined by a more dubious character who has patched together out of the bits and pieces of her personal observation nothing less than a universal theory about the life and death of our great—by "great," Mrs. Jacobs seems always to mean "big"—American cities. This new costume of theory, though not quite as airy as the Emperor's clothes, exposes such large areas of naked unawareness that it undermines many of Mrs. Jacobs' sound statements. Some of her boldest planning proposals, indeed, rest on faulty data, inadequate evidence, and startling miscomprehensions of views contrary to hers. This does not make her book easy to appraise.

Before seeking to do justice to Mrs. Jacobs' work as a whole, I must say a word about her first chapter, in which she does not do justice to herself. Ironically, this doughty opponent of urban renewal projects turns out to have a huge private urban renewal project of her own. Like a construction gang bulldozing a site clean of all habitations, good or bad, she bulldozes out of existence every desirable innovation in urban planning during the last century, and every competing idea, without even a pretense of critical evaluation. She is sensibly opposed to sterile high-rise projects, but she is even more opposed to the best present examples of urban residential planning, such as Chatham Village, in Pittsburgh, and she seems wholly to misunderstand their nature, their purpose, and their achievement. Her misapprehension of any plans she regards as subversive of her own private concepts of urban planning leads her to astounding statements, and she even attempts to liquidate possible opponents by treating anyone who has attempted to improve the design of cities by another method as if such people were determined enemies of the city. To wipe out her most dangerous rival, she concentrates her attack on Sir Ebenezer Howard, the founder of the New Towns (Garden City) movement in England. Her handling of him is, for those who know anything of his biography, comic. Howard, it happens, devoted the last quarter century of his life to the improvement of cities, seeking to find by actual experiment the right form and size, and the right balance between urban needs and purposes and those of the rural environment. Under the rubric of the "garden city," he reintroduced into city building two important ideas: the notion that there was a functional limit to the area and population of a city; and the notion of providing for continued population growth by founding more towns, which would form "town clusters," to perform the more complex functions of a metropolis without wiping out the open recreational spaces and the rural activities of the intervening countryside. Fifteen such communities exist in England today as embodiments of his principle, mostly with populations ranging from sixty to ninety thousand people—a group of towns that will eventually hold a vast number of people working not as commuters to London but in their local factories and business enterprises. During the last year three more such towns have been founded in Britain alone.

Ebenezer Howard, Mrs. Jacobs insists, "set spinning powerful and city-destroying ideas. He conceived that the way to deal with the city's functions was to sort and sift out of the whole certain simple uses, and to arrange each of these in relative self-containment. He focused on the provision of wholesome housing as the central problem to which everything else was subsidiary." No statement could be further from the truth. Mrs. Jacobs' wild characterization contradicts Howard's clearly formulated idea of the garden city as a balanced, many-sided, urban community. In the same vein, Mrs. Jacobs' acute dislike of nearly every improvement in town planning is concentrated in one omnibus epithet expressive of her utmost contempt: "Radiant Garden City Beautiful." Obviously, neither radiance (sunlight), nor gardens, nor spaciousness, nor beauty can have any place in Mrs. Jacobs' picture of a great city.

I shall say no more of Mrs. Jacobs' lack of historical knowledge and scholarly scruple except that her disregard of easily ascertainable facts is all too frequent. An English reviewer has charitably called her an *enfant terrible*; terrible or not, she has become a rampant public figure in the cities movement, and she has a sufficiently large uncritical following even among supposedly knowledgeable professors of planning like Charles Abrams to require a rigorous appraisal of her work lest all of it be accepted as holy writ.

"This book is an attack on current city planning and rebuilding."

With these words Mrs. Jacobs introduces herself. An exhaustive critical analysis and appraisal of the torrent of urban renewal that has been reducing areas of New York and other cities to gargantuan nonentities of high-rise buildings has been long overdue. To have someone look over the situation with her rude fresh eye seemed almost a gift from heaven. Unfortunately, her assault on current planning rests on an odd view of the nature and function and structure of big cities. Underneath her thesis—that the sidewalk, the street, and the neighborhood, in all their higgledy-piggledy unplanned casualness, are the very core of a dynamic urban life—lies a preoccupation that is almost an obsession, the prevention of criminal violence in big cities.

Despite the grandiloquent title of her book, Mrs. Jacobs' obsession prevents her from presenting a total view of the great metropolis, in life or in death: she beholds it just in fragments, especially the rundown fragment of Greenwich Village she has lived in and sentimentally overvalues. While she exults in the mere size of New York and the immense diversity of its activities, she overlooks even the most obvious price of that size in millions of dismal man-hours of daily bus and subway transportation and even longer commuter journeys by rail and car, just as she overlooks the endless rows and blocks and square miles of almost identical houses, spreading from Brooklyn to Queens, from Queens over Long Island, that have not the least touch of the diversity she finds so valuable in her own familiar Village quarters.

When the inhabitants of Greenwich Village go to work each day, they have the unique grace, in Mrs. Jacobs' rose-spectacled eyes, of performers in a ballet. But she has no epithet and no image for the daily walk to the subway station, or for the tense scrimmage and grim incarceration of the subway ride. She recognizes the existence of "gray areas," with their overpowering monotony. But she dogmatically attributes this to the low density of population, even though the post-1904 Bronx, one of the grayest of gray areas, is a high-density borough. And she ignores the appalling prison routine that most of the inhabitants of a great city have to follow, a state that in some measure accounts for some of the aggressive reactions that are now visible. Her great American city has as its sole background the humble life of a very special, almost unique historic quarter, Greenwich Village: for long a backwater whose lack of dynamism accounts for such pleasant features as it has successfully retained.

With Greenpoint and East New York, with the Erie Basin and Harlem, with Flatbush and Canarsie, Mrs. Jacobs' analysis has nothing to do. She does not even trace to its turbid source the violence overflowing into the area around Columbia University. Had Mrs. Jacobs been more aware of urban realities that long antedated high-rise housing, she would have admitted that the crime rate on Morningside Heights is not, as she suggests, the result of recently planning superblocks or segregating urban functions. What is more, one solitary walk through Harlem should have made Mrs. Jacobs revise her notions of the benefits of high density, pedestrian-filled streets, crosslines of circulation, and a mixture of primary economic activities on every residence block, for all these "ideal" conditions are fulfilled in Harlem—without achieving the favorable results she expects of her prescription.

Mrs. Jacobs gives the show away on the first page, in introducing her new principles of town planning. "I shall mainly be writing about common ordinary things: for instance, what kinds of city streets are safe and what kinds are not; why some city parks are marvellous and others are vice traps and death traps," Mrs. Jacobs says. This sentence reveals an overruling fear of living in the big city she so openly adores, and, as all New Yorkers know, she has considerable reason for fear. Her underlying animus fosters some of her most sensitive interpretations of the quality of life in a genuine neighborhood, but it also fosters a series of amateurish planning proposals that will not stand up under the most forbearing examination.

From her point of view, one of the chief mischiefs of contemporary planning is that it reduces the number of streets by creating superblocks reserved almost exclusively for pedestrian movement, free from through wheeled traffic, with the space once pre-empted by unnecessary paved streets turned into open areas for play or provided with benches and plantations for the sedentary enjoyment of adults. Such a separation of automobile and pedestrian walks runs counter to her private directives for a safe and animated neighborhood; namely, to multiply the number of cross streets, to greatly widen the sidewalks, to reduce all other open spaces, and to place many types of shops and services on streets now devoted solely to residences. The street is her patent substitute for the more adequate meeting places which traditional cities have always boasted.

What is behind Mrs. Jacobs' idea of assigning exclusively to the street the mixed functions and diverse activities of a well-balanced neighborhood unit? The answer, I repeat, is simple: her ideal city is mainly an organization for the prevention of crime. To her, the best way to overcome criminal violence is such a mixture of economic and social activities at every hour of the day that the streets will never be empty of pedestrians, and that each shopkeeper, each householder, compelled to find both his main occupations and his recreations on the street, will serve as watchman and policeman, each knowing who is to be trusted and who not, who is defiant of the law and who upholds it, who can be taken in for a cup of coffee and who must be kept at bay.

This is indeed an "original" theory of the city, and a new order of city planning. It comes pretty close to saying that if the planners had kept blocks as small and irregular as they are in many old quarters of Manhattan below Fourteenth Street, and had made universal the mixture of shops and tenement houses that long characterized the main avenues, the blight and corrosion and violence that have now spread over the whole city could have been avoided. By concentrating upon the street and upon such neighborhood activities as the street promotes, Mrs. Jacobs holds, we shall go a long way toward producing a metropolis that shall be at once "fantastically dynamic"—the adjective is hers—and humanly safe. But if this remedy were a sound one, eighteenth-century London, which met all of Mrs. Jacobs' planning prescriptions, would not have been the nest of violence and delinquency it actually was.

In judging Mrs. Jacobs' interpretations and her planning prescriptions I speak as a born and bred New Yorker, who in his time has walked over almost every street in Manhattan, and who has lived in every kind of neighborhood and in every type of housing, from a private row house on the West Side to an Old Law dumbbell railroad flat, from a grim walkup apartment off Washington Square to the thirtieth floor of an East Side Hotel, from a block of row houses with no shops on Hicks Street in Brooklyn Heights to a two-room flat over a lunchroom in the same general neighborhood, with the odor of stale fat filtering through the windows, and with a tailor, a laundry, a florist, grocery stores, and restaurants—Mrs. Jacobs' favorite constellation for "urban liveliness"—immediately at hand. Like a majority of my fellow citizens, I am still unregenerate enough to prefer the quiet flat with a back garden and a handsome church beyond it on Hicks Street to all the dingy "liveliness" of Clinton Street as it was back in the twenties. Finally, for ten years I lived in Sunnyside Gardens, the kind of well-planned neighborhood Mrs. Jacobs despises: modestly conceived for people with low incomes, but composed of one-, two-, and three-family houses and flats, with private gardens and public open spaces, plus playgrounds, meeting rooms, and an infants' school. Not Utopia, but better than any existing New York neighborhood, even Mrs. Jacobs' backwater in Greenwich Village.

As one who has spent more than fifty years in New York, speaking to a native of Scranton who has not, I must remind Mrs. Jacobs that many parts of the city she denounces because they do not conform to her peculiar standards—and therefore, she reasons, are a prey to violence—were for over the better part of a century both economically quite sound and humanly secure. In the urban range of my boyhood, there were occasional rowdy gangs even half a century ago—we always ran for cover when the West Ninety-eighth Street gang invaded our street—but their more lethal activities were confined largely to their own little ghettos and nearby territory, like Hell's Kitchen or the Gas House District. With the policeman on his beat, a woman could go home alone at any hour of the night on a purely residential street without apprehension. (She could even, astonishingly, trust the policeman.) As for the great parks that Mrs. Jacobs fears as an invitation to crime, and disparages as a recreation space on the strange ground that no one any longer can safely use them, she treats as a chronic ailment a state that would have seemed incredible as late as 1935. Until the Age of Extermination widened the area of violence, one could walk the eight hundred acres of Central Park at any time of the day without fear of molestation.

Certainly it was not any mistake of Frederick Law Olmsted's in laying out Riverside Drive, Morningside Park, and St. Nicholas Park that has made these large parks unusable shambles today. What is responsible for their present emptiness is something Mrs. Jacobs disregards—the increasing pathology of the whole mode of life in the great metropolis, a pathology that is directly proportionate to its overgrowth, its purposeless materialism, its congestion, and its insensate disorder—the very conditions she vehemently upholds as marks of urban vitality. That sinister state manifests itself not merely in the statistics of crime and mental disorder but in the enormous sums spent on narcotics, sedatives, stimulants, hypnotics, and tranquillizers to keep the population of our "great" cities from coming to terms with the vacuous desperation of their daily lives and with the even more vacuous horrors that their more lunatic rulers and scientific advisers seem to regard as a reasonable terminus for the human race. Lacking any sense of an intelligible purpose or a desirable goal, the inhabitants of our "great American cities" are simply "Waiting for Godot."

THE MATTER OF SCALE

Mrs. Jacobs is at her best in dealing with small, intimate urban areas. She understands that the very life of a neighborhood depends upon the maintenance of the human scale, for it fosters relations between visible people sharing a common environment, who meet face to face without intermediaries, who are aware of their personal identity and their common interests even though they may not exchange a word. This sense of belonging rests, however, not on a metropolitan dynamism but on continuity and stability, the special virtues of the village. These virtues remain conspicuous features of Greenwich Village, the area in New York Mrs. Jacobs favors as a model of healthy urban activity. By the beginning of the nineteenth century this part of the city, the old Ninth Ward, was so well defined, so individualized, that the City Planning Commissioners of 1811 did not dare to make it conform to the gridiron pattern they imposed with geometric rigor on the rest of the city.

The larger part of this homogeneous area consisted of two- and three-story red brick houses with white porticoes, some of the best of which, those on Varick and King Streets, were destroyed to make way for the Seventh Avenue extension. For long, a loyal population clung to these quarters partly because—as an old friend of mine who lived there remembers—though the residents of the oldest houses had to draw their supply of water from a common pump in the back yard, they were far cheaper than more up-to-date accommodations. This historic enclave, a weedy backwater left behind in the tide of urban growth, would have lost most of the very features Mrs. Jacobs admires, including its short streets, if it had been sufficiently "dynamic." The Village's two special characteristics, indeed, make mock of her "new" principles—its original low density of population and its well-defined architectural character, which graciously set it off from the up-and-coming brownstone-front city that leaped beyond it. In short, old Greenwich Village was almost as much a coherent, concrete entity, with definite boundary lines, as a planned neighborhood unit in a British New Town.

The contradiction between Mrs. Jacobs' perceptions of the intimate values of neighborhood life and her unqualified adoration of metropolitan bigness and activism remains unreconciled, largely because she rejects the principles of urban design that would unite these complementary qualities. Her ultimate criteria of sound metropolitan planning are dynamism, density, and diversity, but she never allows herself to contemplate the unfortunate last term in the present series—disintegration. Yet her concern for local habits and conventions points her in the right direction for overcoming this ultimate disintegration: the recognition of the neighborhood as a vital urban entity, with an inner balance and an inner life whose stability and continuity are necessary for rebuilding the kind of community that the metropolis, in all its cataclysmic economic voracity —"cataclysmic" is Mrs. Jacobs' happy epithet—has destroyed.

She recognizes that a city is more than buildings, but she fails to perceive that a neighborhood is more than its streets and street activities. The new street system she proposes, with twice the number of intersecting north-and-south streets, would do nothing to give visible reality to the social functions of a neighborhood— those performed by school, church, market, clinic, park, library, tavern, eating house, theater. Mrs. Jacobs has no use for the orderly distribution of these activities or the handsome design of their necessary structures; she prefers the hit-and-miss distribution of the present city. No wonder she opposes the admirable work of Clarence Stein and Henry Wright. These pioneer planners have repeatedly demonstrated—in Sunnyside Gardens, on Long Island; in Radburn, New Jersey; in Chatham Village, Pittsburgh—how much superior a well-planned, visibly homogeneous neighborhood can be to the sort of random community she advocates.

In the multi-dimensional order of the city Mrs. Jacobs favors, beauty does not have a place. Yet it is the beauty of great urban cathedrals and palaces, the order of great monastic structures or the university precincts of Oxford and Cambridge, the serenity and spaciousness of the great squares of Paris, London, Rome, Edinburgh, that have preserved intact the urban cores of truly great cities over many centuries. Meanwhile, the sordid dynamism of the dingier parts of these same cities has constantly proved uneconomic, inefficient, and self-destructive.

Instead of asking what are the best possible urban patterns today for renovating our disordered cities, Mrs. Jacobs asks only under what conditions can existing slums and blighted areas preserve their congenial humane features without any serious improvements in their physical structure or their mode of life. Her simple formula does not suggest that her eyes have ever been hurt by ugliness, disorder, confusion, or her ears offended by the roar of trucks smashing through a once quiet residential neighborhood, or her nose assaulted by the chronic odors of ill-ventilated, unsunned housing at the slum standards of congestion that alone meet her ideal standards for residential density. If people are housed in sufficiently congested quarters— provided only that the buildings are not set within superblocks—and if there is a sufficiently haphazard mixture of functions and activities, her social and esthetic demands are both satisfied. She has exposed these convictions in a flat statement: "A city cannot be a work of art." The citizens of Florence, Siena, Venice, and Turin will please take note! But of course Mrs. Jacobs would have her own smug answer to this: if these places are beautiful they are not and never were cities.

What has happened is that Mrs. Jacobs has jumped from the quite defensible position that good physical structures and handsome design are not everything in city planning to the callow notion that they do not matter at all. That beauty, order, spaciousness, clarity of purpose may be worth having for their direct effect on the human spirit even if they do not promote dynamism, increase the turnover of goods, or reduce criminal violence seems not to occur to Mrs. Jacobs. This is esthetic philistinism with a vengeance.

HIGH DENSITY AND SMALL UNITS

Mrs. Jacobs' most original proposal, then, as a theorist of metropolitan development, is to turn its chronic symptom of disorganization—excessive congestion—into a remedy, by deliberately enlarging the scope of the disease. It is her belief, unshaken by irrefutable counter-evidence, that congestion and disorder are the normal, indeed the most desirable, conditions of life in cities. But it is now a well-established fact in biology that overcrowded quarters produce conditions of stress even in animals, a state marked by anxiety and hostility. Elbow room is a general condition for even animal health. Since her obstinate belief in high population density underlies Mrs. Jacobs' entire argument, it gratuitously vitiates even her valid contributions.[1]

Yet despite blind spots and omissions, this book at times offers valuable insights into the complex activities of the city—especially those urban functions that flourish precisely because of all the interchanges that take place, by chance no less than by plan, most frequently in cities that have reached a certain order of bigness and complexity. Mrs. Jacobs recognizes how much of value they will leave behind, unlike the big corporations and research laboratories that are stampeding into suburbia, in exchange for temporary access to a golf course, a private airfield, or a few domestic acres. She also recognizes, by observation and experience, the communal nucleus of the city—the spontaneous "primary" association of families and neighbors, upon which all the later complexities of urban life are based. And though she dislikes the notion of a planned "neighborhood unit," she chooses for her normal neighborhood the size that Clarence Perry, in his studies for the Regional Plan of New York back in the twenties, hit upon as roughly the proper size for such a unit—about

1. See Edward T. Hall, *The Hidden Dimension*. New York: Doubleday & Company, Inc., 1966.

five thousand people. "We shall have something solid to chew on," she observes, "if we think of city neighborhoods as mundane organs of self-government. Our failures with city neighborhoods are, ultimately, failures in localized self-government. And our successes are successes at localized self-government. I am using self-government in its broadest sense, meaning both the informal and formal self-management of society." Excellent. But as against Mrs. Jacobs many of us hold that such activities would be furthered by visible structures and that a planned architectural neighborhood unity will give firmness to its common functions, as it does in the classic example of Venice.

Venice was one of the few cities that, from the Middle Ages onward, were deliberately planned and practically organized on the neighborhood principle, each parish with the little *campo* at the center—occupied by a café and shops, and fountain—and its guildhall and its church, a building that might boast as fine a Tintoretto as the Ducal Palace. There is still plenty of variety and domestic vitality in such neighborhoods despite their long decay, but they do not follow Mrs. Jacobs' formula of shops and factories strewn all over the quarter. Her overvaluation of the street as a social rendezvous leads to her naïve remedy for combating random violence. And her prescription ("eyes on the street") is a result of wishful thinking. Since when has the idea of shopkeepers as substitute policemen kept even themselves from being held up and knifed? And what makes Mrs. Jacobs think that policemen are immune to murderous attack?

But about the long-term remoralization of this demoralized metropolitan community, she is emphatically right: the stabilities of the family and the neighborhood are the basic sources of all higher forms of morality, and when they are lacking, the whole edifice of civilization is threatened. When no one cares for anyone else, because we have all become mere computer digits or Social Security numbers, the elaborate fabric of urban life breaks down. Out of this rejection and isolation and emptiness comes, probably, the boiling hostility of both juvenile and adult delinquent.

Mrs. Jacobs' concern for the smallest unit of urban life is, then, pertinent and well directed. Unhappily, the main tendency of the metropolitan economy Mrs. Jacobs zealously supports is to turn all business over to big commercial enterprises, increasingly automatic in operation and automatically increasing in size. The huge, impersonal supermarket is symbolically the ultimate goal of unregulated metropolitan expansion. Mrs. Jacobs wishes to fight new forms of economic organization that are wiping out choice and variety. But the notion of achieving this by multiplying the number of short streets and increasing the population of marginal small business enterprises absurdly ignores the larger forces that must be controlled and humanized. The dominant economic institutions in our cities deliberately work to curtail freedom and reduce autonomy. There is no dividing line between the dynamic forces Mrs. Jacobs favors and the cataclysmic forces she opposes, for they have the same origin— an obsessive concern for power and profit, and an indifference to more humane interests.

In passing from that now barely recognizable unit of urban life, the neighborhood, to the larger problems of the city, Mrs. Jacobs again approaches but never reaches a desirable goal. She has had enough political experience to recognize that the city, by its very size, has got out of hand, particularly out of the hands of its own citizens, and that its hugeness causes it to be misplanned and maladministered. Because they lack any integral organs for formulating policies or making decisions, or even contesting the proposals of the Mayor, the City Planning Commissioners, the Borough Presidents, or Mr. Moses, the political pressure exerted by local areas is feeble and sporadic, and achieved only with great effort through *ad-hoc* organizations. The result has been a docile conformity by our governing agencies to other more powerful financial influences, unconcerned with the common good.

Mrs. Jacobs realizes that if public officials are to be made more responsive to public opinion and to be prevented from making wanton changes in neighborhoods to favor lending institutions, big contractors, and rich tenants instead of the old residents, politics must be organized on a local basis. So too, her proposed new neighborhood organ of government, like the English borough and unlike the purely formal area of an Assembly District, must have some coherence and integrity as an economic and social unit. Functions that were once pushed to the periphery of the city, or packed into specialized enclaves, like the Seventh Avenue garment district, should be distributed over wider areas in these local-government units. For smaller metropolises like Pittsburgh, she suggests that thirty thousand would be the right population for such units, while for cities as big as Chicago and New York, she chooses a hundred thousand, and she recognizes that to form these boroughs into active municipal entities industry and business must be established in these sub-centers. (See "The Roaring Traffic's Boom," in *The New Yorker* of April 16, 1953, for a similar proposal.)

I take a certain mischievous delight in pointing out that the thirty thousand she has hit on for a self-governing "district" is precisely the figure Leonardo da Vinci, the first advocate of New Towns, suggested to the Duke of Milan when he proposed to overcome the congestion and disordor of that city of three hundred thousand people by designing ten component cities of thirty thousand, and that thirty thousand is the number Ebenezer Howard—the arch-villain in Mrs. Jacobs' private urban melodrama—tentatively chose for his original Garden City. Nor do I think less of her proposals because the great Leonardo and the wise Howard got there before Mrs. Jacobs. But the recent Royal Commission in Great Britain on the government of London, which included such a masterly interpreter of urban government as Professor William Robson, concluded that a hundred thousand to two hundred and fifty thousand was the desirable population for the boroughs of Metropolitan London. If Mrs. Jacobs errs in laying down the ideal number for a borough, she errs in favor of the smaller unit. I salute her as a reluctant ally of old Ebenezer Howard.

Mrs. Jacobs innocently believes that complexity and diversity are impossible without the kind of intense congestion that has in fact been emptying out the big city, hurling masses of people into the vast, curdled Milky Ways of suburbia. In the desire to enjoy amenities impossible at even a quarter of the density of population she considers desirable, millions of people are giving up the delights and stimulations of genuine city life. It is millions of quite ordinary people who cherish such suburban desires, not a few fanatical haters of the city, sunk in bucolic dreams. Now, it is this massive century-old drift to suburbia, not the building of superblocks or garden cities, that is mainly responsible for the dilapidation and the near-death of big cities. How could Mrs. Jacobs ignore this staring historic fact?

This movement toward the rural periphery in search of things that were the proud possession of every premechanized city has been helped by the most active enemies of the city—the overbudgeted highway programs that have riddled metropolitan areas with their gaping expressways and transformed civic cores into parking lots. Those who leave the city wish to escape its snarling violence and its sickening perversions of life, its traffic in narcotics and its gangster-organized lewdness, which break into the lives even of children. Not least, the suburban exiles seek to find at least nightly surcease from constant bureaucratic regimentation: Punch the time clock! Watch your step! Curb your dog! Do not spit! No parking! Get in line for a ticket! Move on! Keep off the grass! Follow the green line! Wait for the next train! Buy now, pay later! Don't buck the system! Take what you get! The refugees who leave the metropolis may not keep even the fleeting illusion of freedom and security and a normal family life for long: all too soon rising land values and high rents bring high-rise housing, asphalted parking lots, and asphyxiating traffic jams. But their reaction is evidence of their own spontaneous vitality and a quickened desire for autonomy, which most of the rest of their existence as members of a gigantic, overcongested, necessarily impersonal hive defeats. Strangely, the city that so insistently drives its population into the suburbs is the very same city that Mrs. Jacobs quaintly describes as "vital." She forgets that in organisms there is no tissue quite so "vital" or "dynamic" as cancer growths.

But if *The Death and Life of Great American Cities*, taken as a critique of modern city planning, is a mingling of sense and sentimentality, of mature judgments and schoolgirl howlers, how does it stand as an interpretation of the larger issues of urban development and urban renewal, which the title itself so boldly points to? Here again Mrs. Jacobs heads her argument in the right direction, toward matters that have been insufficiently appreciated or misinterpreted. No one has surpassed her in understanding the reasons for the great metropolis' complexity and the effect of this complexity, with its divisions of labor, its differentiations of occupations and interests, its valuable racial, national, and cultural variety, upon its daily activities. She recognizes that one cannot handle such a multi-dimensional social organization as one might handle a simple machine, designed for a single function. "A growing number of people have begun, gradually," she notes, "to think of cities as problems in organized complexity—organisms that are replete with unexamined, but obviously intricately interconnected, and surely understandable, relationships."

That is an admirable observation, but the author has forgotten the most essential characteristic of all organic growth—to maintain diversity and balance the organism must not exceed the norm of its species. Any ecological association eventually reaches the "climax stage," beyond which growth without deterioration is not possible.

Despite Mrs. Jacobs' recognition of organic complexity in the abstract, she has a very inadequate appreciation of the ecological setting of cities and neighborhoods; she brusquely turns her back to all but the segregated local environment. Yet the overgrowth of our big cities has destroyed those special environmental qualities that made their setting desirable and fostered their growth in the first place. The obvious result of the large-scale metropolitan congestion she advocates she flatly ignores—the poisoning of the human system with carbon monoxide and the two hundred known cancer-producing substances usually in the air, the muffling of the vital ultra-violet rays by smog, the befouling of streams and oceanside (once used for fishing and bathing) with human and industrial waste. This is something worse than an oversight; it is willful blindness.

Mrs. Jacobs approvingly quotes Dr. Karl Menninger's observation that the best remedies for delinquency are "plentiful contacts with other people, work, including even drudgery, and violent play." But the kind of congested conglomeration she advocates would provide no room for violent play, and no sufficient opportunity to find relief from the monotonous and depressing regimentation of the big city. From the days of Ur onward, city dwellers have always had the countryside close at hand. There their homicidal impulses could be exorcised by digging and delving, or by shooting at destructive animals, and there their need for spontaneous muscular exercise could be satisfied by swimming and boating and climbing rather than by knives, brass knuckles, and rumbles. (Emerson long ago prescribed a pasture and a wood lot as the best cure for juvenile village mischief; they didn't call it "juvenile delinquency" in his day.)

When they have reached a point long ago overpassed by New York, Chicago, London, Tokyo, and Moscow, big cities are under the necessity to expand their operations to a more capacious container—the region. The forces that have formed our cities in the past are now almost automatically, by their insensate dynamism, wrecking them and threatening to destroy whole countries and continents. Against this background, the problem of policing public thoroughfares against violence is minor; violence and vice are symptoms of those far graver forms of disorder that Mrs. Jacobs rules out of consideration because they challenge her rosily sentimental picture of the "great American city."

To blame the conditions in the congested, overgrown metropolis of today on the monumental scale and human hollowness of its urban renewal projects is preposterous, for this draws attention from the grim, enveloping realities that our whole metropolitan civilization confronts. The prevailing economic and technological forces in the big city have broken away from the ecological pattern, as well as from the moral inhibitions and the social codes and the religious ideals that once, however imperfectly, kept them under some sort of control, and reduced their destructive potentialities.

Just as there is no limit to the power assigned to those who build nuclear weapons and rockets, who plan space shots and lunatic-cool mass exterminations, so there is no limit to those who multiply motor roads for the sake of selling more motorcars and gasoline and road-building machinery, who push on the market every variety of drug, narcotic, chemical, and biotic agent, without regard to their ultimate effect on the landscape or upon any form of organic life. Under this "cataclysmic" eruption of power, with its lack of any goal but its own expansion, as Henry Adams presciently predicted half a century ago, "law disappears as a priori principle and gives place to force: morality becomes police: disintegration overcomes integration." The present metropolitan explosion is both the symbol and agent of this uncontrolled power.

Failing to appraise the larger sources of urban disintegration, or to trace the connection between our major adult and our minor juvenile forms of delinquency, Mrs. Jacobs mistakenly regards those who may have a better grasp of the situation as enemies of metropolitan life. Now, under more normal circumstances, the special virtue of the great city was that it did, in fact, tend to keep any one idea or institution or group from becoming dominant. Today, military power, scientific power, technical power, financial power, and, in fact, "cataclysmic" power in every manifestation operate most successfully, on their own terms, by wiping out diversity and doing away with every mode of organic growth, ecological partnership, and autonomous activity.

"Silent Spring" came to the big city long before it visited the countryside. No planning proposal now makes sense unless it is conceived in terms of truly human purposes—self-chosen, self-limited, and self-directed. The command of this unlimited, automatically expanding power is, again as Henry Adams wisely pointed out half a century ago, the central problem of our civilization. For Mrs. Jacobs to imagine that the horrifying human by-products of the city's disordered life can be eliminated by a few tricks of planning is as foolish as for her to imagine that a too generous supply of open spaces and superblocks fostered these symptoms.

If our urban civilization is to escape progressive dissolution, we shall have to rebuild it from the ground up. Certainly we shall have to do far more than alter street plans, humanize housing projects, or give wider geographic distribution to economic activities. Since such a general transformation will affect every aspect of life, urban politics and planning must of course play an active and significant part. But it is the formative, stabilizing, coherent, order-making forces, not the overdynamic ones, that now need special encouragement.

One cannot control destructive automatisms at the top unless one begins with the smallest units and restores life and initiative to them—to the person as a responsible human being, to the neighborhood as the primary organ not merely of social life but of moral behavior, and finally to the city, as an organic embodiment of the common life, in ecological balance with other cities, big and little, within the larger region in which they lie. A quick, purely local answer to these problems is no better than applying a homemade poultice for the cure of a cancer. And that, I am afraid, is what the more "original" Jacobsean proposals in *The Death and Life of Great American Cities* come to.

17. Urban Transportation Planning: An Overview

Ralph A. Gakenheimer

18. Transportation in Cities

John W. Dyckman

17 RALPH A. GAKENHEIMER

Urban transportation planning: an overview[*]

INTRODUCTION

The problems of urban transportation are the most obvious problems of the city. Virtually every urban dweller participates in the city's systems of movement and suffers directly from their inefficiencies. Other problems may be equally serious and enduring, but their discovery, their explanation, and the extent to which they are viewed with alarm and made the object of corrective policy are subject to more subtle influences. They may be uncovered by new intellectual currents, brought to wide attention by the appearance of new social commitment, or suddenly detected in the unarticulated preferences of urban dwellers. They may be problems of a minority which become general concerns only when the majority is educated to a responsibility toward them or to the indirect benefits realized by solution. Through these changing patterns of concern for problems like housing, automation, poverty, economic growth, integrity of the natural environment and revitalization of downtowns, the transportation problem continues as one of the longest recognized of the "serious urban problems." Its most visible dimension, loss

* "Urban Transportation: An Overview" by Ralph Gakenheimer from TAMING MEGALOPOLIS, edited by H. Wentworth Eldredge. Copyright © 1967 by H. Wentworth Eldredge. Reprinted by permission of Doubleday and Company, Inc.

of time and money through inefficiencies imposed on the normal movements of people and goods, is modified and yields to more advanced interpretations when related to current perspectives on the other problems to which it is linked.

Thus the gravity of the transportation problem depends on relative concern for the others. During periods of relative slack in social commitment, such as the 1950s, transportation is regarded as the prominent urban problem. During times of greater commitment and new fears, like the late sixties, it assumes a more modest place. Because there are at present other significant social concerns, it has become current to think of transportation as a luxury problem which can be given priority only by an affluent society that has solved its more fundamental ones, but in view of the linkages between transportation systems and other troubled urban activities this position must be accepted with great qualification.

The question of whether the problem is getting worse at the present time, and if so in what sense, bears some attention. Taking the simplistic concept that the transportation problem is the one that gets worse as movements in the city are slowed down by congestion and other impairments, there is no firm evidence that the situation is currently getting worse. The major traffic problems have been associated with central business districts, where in most major cities the number of entering and leaving trips has been slightly reducing,[1] reflecting losses in employment and resident population in them. Thus while rapid urban growth in the outer rings of the metropolis would reduce travel speeds if destination preferences remained the same, it seems that this growth has taken a sufficient number of the downtown functions with it to adjust the movement systems away from the central focus and largely avoid this consequence.

Perhaps the problem takes its most extreme form when we consider the speeds of urban movement in contrast to the maximum speeds offered by available transportation technology. This form of the problem may be more intuitive to the urban dweller, and it exposes great limitations in the movement networks. We have a far greater capacity to build machines that move fast than to remove the external constraints on their speed in practical use. The automobile has a much higher ratio of maximum speed to speed in urban use than any previous mode. Horse-drawn urban vehicles probably had only a slightly lower average real in-town speed at less than a quarter of the maximum speed. It is necessary to emphasize this point because of the cultural inclination of Americans to assume that our

1. J. R. Meyer, J. F. Kain and M. Wohl, *The Urban Transportation Problem* (Cambridge: Harvard University Press, 1965), p. 35.

transportation problems are rapidly getting worse and that their only salvation lies in our rapidly improving technology. In fact, the technology itself is in large measure defining the problem.

Given the limitations to reducing these constraints on automotive travel, only partly mitigated by increasing the capacities of facilities and limiting access to them, the obvious answer seems to lie with vehicles on independent rights of way, where they are isolated from most of these external effects. Thus the transportation problem becomes easily interpreted as one of how to make rapid transit work. With trends toward the loss of transit ridership in some cities and little gain in any of the others, maintaining present levels of service is often regarded as the more feasible problem.

There has been much discussion and research on the matter of consumer choice between modes of travel, based on relative costs, length of trip, time of travel, waiting time, psychic responses to the modes, and so forth. But the various interests which affect this choice are underlain by the evolving pattern of the city. Though there are undoubtedly social, economic, and psychological attractions to independent vehicles, the choice is primarily for a living environment which requires the use of automobiles to be accessible. The values that have motivated people to move to the urban periphery have been largely independent of consideration of transportation costs or conveniences. On the level of public policy, also therefore, the balance between modes of transportation is in good measure a residual of the primary choice, that of the structure of the city which best provides for the preferences and maximum opportunities of the people as created by policy and the independent locational decisions of urban dwellers. It is at that point, land use and activities patterns, that transportation planning must begin.

RESPONSIBILITIES OF URBAN TRANSPORTATION PLANNING

As reflected by the various perceptions of the problem, urban transportation is a superficially simple activity whose planning is subject to a multitude of interpretations, owing to its linkages with other urban problems. The nature of this series of linkages with other urban problems is clarified by considering the participation of transport in the most basic purpose of the city, that of creating proximity. Many advanced forms of human accomplishment are complex in the sense that they require close interrelations among large numbers of people in order to be achieved. Since long-distance communication is not a satisfactory form presently for many of these interrelations, people resort to locations of dense habitation in order to facilitate them. In the city an individual has access from his bases of operation to the maximum number of participants in other activities, thus maximizing potential interaction. Without the need or desire for this access there would be no cohesion within densely populated areas, and, our sentimentalities notwithstanding, we would resume the dispersed pattern of living which has been the overwhelmingly dominant style of living throughout human history.

The primary function of urban transportation, then, is to provide the characteristic of accessibility to locations in the city, and the objective of transportation planning is to increase it. This accessibility is unevenly spread because some locations are necessarily closer to the rest than others are, because it depends on the use of a network of facilities which cannot provide completely uniform coverage, and because of externalities which impede movement unevenly on the network. For similar reasons public policy cannot be effectuated to increase accessibility uniformly. In any case there is no reason why it should. The value of an increment in accessibility varies widely among the various users of urban locations; some benefit from it much more than others. Consequently, we can define transportation planning as the selective distribution of access in urban space.[2]

The more familiar objective, expediting projected movement flow where it is expected most seriously to overload the existing network (or reducing congestion), can be regarded as derivative from the access concept. But this requires the implicit assumption that future expressed desire for movement will conform in pattern to the relative levels of benefit from access derived by the involved locations. It is nonetheless useful in approaching much of the problem and is tempting to policy action because it makes the problem subject to direct measurement. It also requires fewer normative judgments, since solution becomes a matter of correcting visible malignancy rather than weighing the relative merits of increased access at various locations. But this is dangerous for a variety of reasons. A person's concept of his opportunities, for example, may be very much controlled by his current reach. Further, it is not a completely politically acceptable interpretation because pressures for public action reflect the need for greater access by particular urban establishments, their forcefulness in demanding it, or their increasing loss of it because of growing externalities. In the case of the transportation industries, pressures arise from the desire of each to provide for a greater share of the movement.

2. Lowdon Wingo, Jr., and Harvey S. Perloff, "The Washington Transportation Plan: Technics or Politics?" *Papers of the Regional Science Association*, Vol. 7, 1961, pp. 249–62.

As a result, the operational objectives of transportation planning reflect the relative strengths of these access-seekers and public sympathies toward them, as well as the need to facilitate movement where the network is found or expected to be overloaded. The loudest voice among the access-seekers in most cities is that of the central business district interests, who are becoming less accessible to the urban populations spreading over larger areas, and who are affected by the externalities that work upon the extended radial routes to the center. These effects are, of course, also subject to direct observation, so solution to this problem may also stem from an effort to treat network overload. But given the current decrease in trips to most CBDs, the strongest influence is usually the voices of access-seekers or a public determination that the core be saved. The voices of other, less unified, access-seekers are added to these, such as those of industries desiring to expand their access to labor or those of the electorate in general, who are usually concerned with facilitating the trip to work, which is their most troublesome one. The spatially un-unified nature of these latter interests normally requires that they be solved by analysis of network overloading. Similarly, the objective of gaining a larger share of the trips for transit (or providing a greater choice between modes) reflects the industry's concern for its survival or an effort to relax network overload by a mode that uses urban space more efficiently in moving people.

Combinations of these objectives, together with others less closely related to transportation, can be represented by comprehensive decisions as to the way the form of the city should develop. This level of solution is preferable because in its comprehensiveness it establishes a balance among the immediate objectives and represents related interests outside this framework which are likely to be equally important, if not more so.

No matter how the objectives are approached, effort is made to provide specific levels of network service at least cost.

Though transportation planning has not yet been accomplished on a systematic basis for a mix of all the goals implied above, it has, in a qualified sense, been more systematic and internally logical than other aspects of planning.[3] This is true in the sense that minimum cost solutions (although within rigid limitations of benefit-cost measurement) have been sought and attained within stated criteria, lending more logical consistency to this aspect of the planning field than to many others. This accomplishment has been possible largely

3. Britton Harris, Roger L. Creighton and Edward F. R. Hearle, "Have We Learned Anything from Transportation Studies," *Planning 1963*, American Society of Planning Officials, 1963, pp. 175-91.

because of the nature of transportation—traffic on the streets—which can be easily and directly measured. This gives rise to an exact calculus for the field that also enables some measurement of the effects of policy and tends to define future change as tractable. That is, the unpredictability of human behavior patterns notwithstanding, direct dealings with the uncertainties that complicate other aspects of planning have to some extent been avoided, partly because the field has a fairly elaborate and standard analytical approach which permits the systematic entry of change estimates into the process. Moreover, the fact that most causes of urban movement are fundamental, and to some extent irreducible, makes these systems less liable to unpredictable change than others which depend more on popular tastes or more changeable commitment. Finally, the facilities which constitute the physical recommendations of the plan are provided by reliable sources (mostly the federal government) and are mainly within the public domain. This provides opportunity for direct cost measurement, which is not the case for planning in the private sector where effectuation is limited to indirect encouragement and controls.

This is not to say that transportation planning is without great uncertainties. Its confidence comes in good measure from a misleading specificity in its analytical methods; the ability to project systematically does not insure accuracy. Indeed, its uncertainties ultimately represent those of all the other urban systems to which transportation is related. Perhaps the greatest unreliability lies in our poor understanding of change in transportation and communication technology, where elemental changes have telling impacts on urban movement and location patterns.

THE PLANNING OF TRANSPORTATION

Regular professional attention to urban transportation problems began in the early years of the twentieth century. Street-cars had played major roles in the large cities for a sufficient length of time to create active concern for their standards of service, management effectiveness and effects on the urban physical structure. At this time contentions between the viabilities of private and public ownership began. Within the first fifteen years of the century methods were worked out for the measurement of origin-destination patterns, time of travel, and traffic volumes and changes in these with alteration of the route patterns and standards of service. The effects of transit routing on land value also received considerable attention, but only hortatory remarks were made about the capabilities of the transit systems for building or structuring cities. The orientation was toward providing service to meet demand.

By virtue of this development, concern for problems of automobile traffic, beginning in the late 1920s, could call upon sources of diagnostic method. The adjustment of these methods to the relative flexibility of automobile movement and the less centralized pattern of origins and destinations was eventually accomplished. More developed means of measurement and prediction appeared, but the prevailing understanding through the 1930s, that the populations of U.S. cities would cease to grow within the following twenty-five years, kept the problem from being dealt with as a crucial one.[4] Partly for this reason, the rapid increases in population and car ownership after World War II caused the transportation problem to reach professional as well as public recognition with explosive force. Aided by automatic data processing equipment, traffic flow characteristics and origin-destination studies were accomplished at increasing levels of detail. This greater capacity for detail made it possible to break down trip-making recorded in the origin-destination surveys by purposes of trips and characteristics of the trip-makers to understand the systems more clearly, thus introducing the possibility of the quantitative behavioral study of transportation.

In 1954 the analytical basis for studying interdependencies between land use and transportation was presented by Robert B. Mitchell and Chester Rapkin.[5] The concept was not entirely new that use of transportation facilities is determined by activities on proximate land and that the use of land is partially determined by its level of accessibility. But systematic means for the analysis of these relationships was a powerful tool that reset the approach of transportation planning. It provided a means for relating movement systems with other systems of activity in the city, represented as generators of person trips from fixed locations. This brought transportation analysis into the potentiality of full contact with planning concerns for land development and complex sets of activities of urban dwellers.

An operational form for this relationship was soon determined in a basic four-step procedure for the analysis and projection of transportation systems. The generation of trips from specific subareas is explained by its correlations to the values of variables representing the trip-making inclinations of the subareas' occupants; their

4. This understanding was expressed in many reports of the 1920s and '30s. See, for example, Ernest P. Goodrich, "Transit Facilities and Urban Development," unpublished ms. at the Library of the University of Pennsylvania, 1936, p. 54.

5. Robert B. Mitchell and Chester Rapkin, *Urban Traffic: A Function of Land Use* (New York: Columbia University Press, 1954).

purposes for making trips, income, car ownership, family size, distance from the CBD, and other measures. The variables are chosen as suitable for predicting the generation of trips at a future date when the occupation of the zones and other trip generation characteristics have changed. These trips are then distributed; their origins or destinations in other subareas are considered and interchanges between pairs of zones are simulated by equations. Trips which form the interchange between each pair of subareas are then divided between available modes of transportation. Finally, the interchange by modes is assigned to existing traffic facilities and thereby represented as traffic on the streets. This whole set of procedures is done once to reliably simulate the existing pattern of movement by use of equations which can take future changes in trip-making characteristics as input variables to predict future systems of travel based on a new pattern of land use and new trip-making characteristics.

The procedure for analyzing transportation systems, even in this simplistic form, suggests the principal problems met in an effort to establish future needs for transportation facilities. The predictive reliability of the process depends upon (1) the usefulness of the variables involved (or of any available) to properly register change in trip-making, (2) the extent to which principles of movement, reflected by the mathematics of the analysis, sufficiently approximate forces in the real world, and (3) the extent to which each variable can be usefully predicted. Considerable attention has been given to these topics. Comparisons of the fit of variables to generation equations, for example, have been made.[6] Controversy has continued for several years on the usefulness of alternative equations for predicting trip distribution, which assume different responses of generated trips to the availability of new origins and destinations. Limited verifications have been developed,[7] but since the equations are applied on the basis of assumptions which cannot be directly verified, only extensive review of their success in prediction can suggest their value. The predictability of variables is even more difficult to examine, but efforts have been made to understand the stability and change characteristics of some of the better behaved ones.[8] All of these assurances are, of course, circumscribed by the relatively unknown shape of matters such as future life styles, technology, and changes

6. See Walter Y. Oi and Paul W. Shuldiner, *An Analysis of Urban Travel Demands* (Evanston, Northwestern University Press, 1964).

7. Donald M. Hill and Norman Dodd, "Studies of Trends of Travel Between 1954 and 1964 in a Large Metropolitan Area," *Record of the Highway Research Board*, forthcoming.

8. J. F. Kain and M. E. Beesley, "Forecasting Car Ownership and Use," *Urban Studies*, Vol. 2, No. 2, November 1965, pp. 163–85.

in other elements of public policy, which forbear against the view that any projection of travel can be regarded as accurate. Still, an understanding of knowable trends provides a stronger base to underlie consideration of the open questions, and leads to an answer useful in the absence of major impingements by unknowns on the present course of events.

A second set of problems emerges from the need to recognize the interdependency between changes in movement systems and changes in activities taking place at fixed urban locations. A concomitant to the basic analytic procedures of the field is the interpretation that a transportation facility network cannot be designed merely to serve a previously devised or predicted land-use pattern because the network itself will stimulate trip-making that will change the future of that pattern. Correspondingly, a land-use pattern cannot be projected after a transportation plan, because the existence of these new activities will alter the requirements for the transportation network. This situation requires that the planning of the two areas be somehow simultaneous in order that the effects of each on the other be properly accounted for. The obvious means for doing this by current methodology is to pass several times through the planning of each in turn in order to absorb the effects upon each of the planning of the previous one. That is to say, land development can be planned or projected; then the transportation system can be designed for it; then the land-use plan is revised for transportation impacts upon it; in turn the transportation plan is revised to meet the new demands upon it, and so forth. This procedure would presumably achieve a reasonably stable relationship between the two components within a short number of iterations. This process has actually never been accomplished for a transportation study, but the impediments have been lack of time and money. It contains few fundamental technical problems.

Another problem, symptomatic of the relationship between transportation planning and other aspects of urban planning, stems from the hesitancy of transportation planners to accommodate planned change in other urban systems when they establish future facility networks. Transportation planning is based primarily on projections rather than plans. One of the reasons for this is that the specificity of transportation planning analysis requires more detailed statements of the policy objectives of other system plans than is normally provided, or can be provided by those aspects of the process. Even projections of land use provided by municipal agencies have generally been found unsatisfactory, so that the transportation agencies have made their own. But more significant than this is the orientation of transportation planning to directly purchased facilities in the public domain, which are less frequently obstructed politically than other planning recommendations. The relatively high assurance of effectuation offered by these conditions, when compared to the indirect means by which other urban systems must be planned, leaves transportation planners in the position of needing to cover rather long shot bets by other components of planning. They are not generally disposed to do this. Problems arise on account of this which are related to the interdependency argument above. Transportation planning based on a projection tends to "implement" the projection as though it were policy statement. Correspondingly, if based on a plan, the projected network would tend to validate that statement. Still, in view of the poor record of comprehensive planning, the risks are considered too high.

A final basic problem is the difficulty in measuring consequences of investment.[9] By virtue of the links between movement systems and other systems of urban activities, transportation investments cause a wide array of benefits and disbenefits in the city which are impossible to evaluate fully by the present state of knowledge on this subject. Further, facilities of this type have long lives, remaining parts of the urban plant through considerable changes in the conditions which determine their usefulness. Moreover, these facilities represent series of large single investments with considerable economies of scale, so that the level of effect from different series of such expenditures becomes a matter of difficult balance. The absence of a conventional market for these facilities also confuses the analysis. Most importantly, the widely different approaches to the accomplishment of objectives and broad choice among mixes of objectives themselves make it very difficult to identify an optimum investment mix among one set of investments, to which optima of others can be compared. There is, nonetheless, a substantial amount of work being done on this topic to describe workable boundaries for the effects of network changes,[10] to estimate network costs,[11] to clarify network planning principles implied by cost-benefit relationships,[12]

---

9. Britton Harris, comment on Tillo E. Kuhn, "The Economics of Transportation Planning in Urban Areas," *Transportation Economics* (New York: Columbia University Press, 1965) pp. 321–22.

10. A. R. Prest and R. Turvey, "Cost-Benefit Analysis: A Survey," *Economic Journal*, December 1965, see pp. 711–14. Also, Herbert Monring and Mitchell Harwitz, *Highway Benefits; an Analytical Framework* (Evanston: Northwestern University Press, 1962).

11. Abe Gottlieb, "The Economic Context of 1985: Transportation Costs in the PJ Region," Penn-Jersey Paper No. 23, 1965.

12. R. L. Creighton, I. Hock and N. Schneider, "Estimating Efficient Spacing for Arterials and Expressways," Highway Research Board *Bulletin 253.*

to better understand movement system costs,[13] and to explore broader series of network effects.[14]

The surest thing about the future shape of transportation planning is its growth as an active process in metropolitan areas. The present trend of federal legislation in this field bears similarities to the development of urban renewal legislation during the last two decades, which has been a decisive force in the expansion of planning work in that area. Since 1961 the Department of Commerce and the former HHFA have encouraged the use of the $1\frac{1}{2}$ percent highway survey planning funds for metropolitan transportation planning, thus joining the interests of urban transportation with urban renewal and paving the way for financial participation by the Department of Housing and Urban Development in the major transportation studies. The Federal Aid Highway Act of 1962 formally joined the transportation and urban planning efforts by requiring that highway projects since mid-1965 be based on continuing comprehensive planning. The trend represented by these and other federal acts will increase the amount of transportation planning activity and, hopefully, the store of useful experience in solving its difficult problems.

Current development of models for the allocation of new land uses promises to provide for transportation planning based on less limited policy assumptions, and to provide more understanding of the effects of relations between transportation and other urban systems. Past models for this purpose have normally predicted change in terms of aggregate behavioral data with changes in the land-use system stated in the same aggregate structural terms. A new generation of models is now being operationalized which focuses instead on the action of the individual decision unit—for example, the household, or single industrial plant—and adds these elemental decisions into a net effect.[15] In view of the close contact of these concepts with the real course of policy impact, response to policy by individual actors in the city, they should facilitate predictions which are better conditioned to changes which are expected to occur or are considered

13. J. R. Meyer, J. F. Kain and M. Wohl, *op. cit.*, Part II, "Comparative Costs," pp. 171–308.

14. Morris Hill, "Evaluation of Plans in One Sector," doctoral dissertation, University of Pennsylvania, Department of City and Regional Planning, 1966.

15. J. Herbert and B. Stevens, "A Model for the Distribution of Residential Activity in Urban Areas," *Journal of Regional Science*, Vol. 2, No. 2, 1960, pp. 21–36.

as policy alternatives. This would provide for removal of some of the unfortunate rigidities in transportation planning which are characteristic of the process to the present time.

Considerable work is also being done in the development and qualification of methods for the projection of zonal interchanges. Though the work in this area has tended to be more incremental than in that of land-use projection, some additional concepts in the systematic study of trip-making have appeared.[16]

More generally, improvements of this type offer an increased capacity to simulate entire series of urban systems. The model-building has been done in each of these subareas of the problem with the assumption that the various analyses can be linked together to provide a full picture of interactions between the subsystems. This development is countercyclical to the previous tendency to aggregate knowledge of the interactions from a more and more detailed knowledge of intuitively related parts. At this level, of course, the development is not fundamentally one of transportation planning, since its involvements are comprehensive within the field of urbanism. Nevertheless, most of the development has come from efforts in transportation planning because of the particular needs and analytical style of the field.

Problems may soon beset trip-making analysis on account of changes of balance among trip types. At the present time work trips dominate planning considerations because they are the most numerous single type, are highly convergent in pattern, and occur during very limited periods of the day. They therefore tend to fix the minimum capacity of transport networks. But with workplaces dispersing as the city grows, and with increased affluence and leisure time, work trips will become a less significant network determinant. Unfortunately, the trip purposes which are rising in significance, especially recreational, have different and less tractable characteristics. They are closely related in quantity and pattern to current fashions; they are flexible for time of travel and so can be made during off-peak hours (within serious limitations); they can be discouraged or diverted by congestion. In short, their patterns are far less reliable than those of work trips, and their projection requires dangerous assumptions about very changeable motivations. Though studies on these movements to the present time mostly emphasize travel at the supraurban scale,[17] where changes in volume will

16. Anthony R. Tomazinis, "A New Method of Trip Distribution in an Urban Area," (mimeo) Penn-Jersey Transportation Study Research Paper, 1963.

17. Outdoor Recreation Resources Review Commission, *Projections to the Year 1976 and 2000: Economic Growth, Population, Labor Force and Leisure, and Transportation* (Washington, D.C.: Government Printing Office, 1962), Part III, pp. 73-119.

probably be greatest, the concern for their planning in urban areas is bound to increase.

Technology

The technologies of transportation and of other urban activities present perhaps the most difficult problems in estimating future facility needs and urban structure. A considerable amount of research is going on toward the improvement of intra-urban transportation vehicles and networks, but the inconclusive likelihoods of particular innovations have made it impossible for planning to be based on assumptions of changed future technology. No public urban transportation plan to the present time has been based on technology other than that now existing and in common use.

Work in transportation technology is emphasizing the objectives of increased speed and acceleration, more economical power, abatement of noise and other nuisances, more comfort, more efficient use of urban space, lowering operating costs through automation, and increasing the efficiency of movements through systems design of networks and control of networks. Although most of this work is not likely to affect the dimensions of urban trip-making to the extent that it would invalidate projections of trip-making and locational choices, some of it seems to offer potentialities for this. Discounting possibilities of intracity air travel as leading to insurmountable traffic control problems, the research on very high speed ground transit systems could have considerable impact.[18] Though it is being considered primarily for intercity movement, the limitations of single-point destinations in major cities are likely to encourage two-scale networks with intra-urban distribution systems. Operational designs for acceleration and deceleration ramps would reinforce this impact enormously.[19] These ramps, off the main trunk of a transit system, would store small cars which would be boarded by a few passengers headed for the same destination. The car would accelerate to full cruising speed before entering the trunk line, and maintain that speed until it reached the deceleration ramp at its destination. By eliminating the intermediate stops, which seriously limit the speed of any current urban transit mode, high speed vehicles could be used to great effect.

Resistance against this type of innovation is offered by a number of factors, including the vested interests in other modes, need for

18. Project Transport, M.I.T., *Survey of Technology for High Speed Ground Transport* (Washington, D.C.: U.S. Department of Commerce, 1965).

19. This feature is not presently operational, but has been suggested by the Industrial Systems Group at Westinghouse.

large-scale initial network construction, and especially the increasingly dispersed location patterns of residences in American cities. In any case, current construction of the Bay Area Rapid Transit System in the San Francisco area and the recent Toronto subway construction serve to remind us that local introduction of a different technology is not impossible, even without the unique advantages of some of the developing forms.

With respect to transportation planning, the greatest question about future transport technology seems not the details of speed, economy and external effects upon transportation vehicles, but innovations which sharply affect preference between individual and mass movement. The important difference between these two is that individual movement encourages dispersed residential location patterns, while an overwhelmingly superior transit system could conceivably restructure the city into a series of density peaks at the transit stops, or onto a larger-scale version of the star-shaped streetcar-dominated city of the late nineteenth and early twentieth centuries.

This conflict between the two basic modes is fundamentally between automotive life style and transit technology. Three decades of increasing use of individual vehicles has induced location and trip-making patterns that are increasingly resistant to service by transit which requires heavy patronage along a single line. The locational dispersion will undoubtedly increase. On the other hand, individual vehicles are not susceptible to much technological improvement. Their usefulness can be measurably increased only by greater dispersion of the population. Thus technological impacts are sure to be on the side of transit. It seems quite possible that restructuring of Eastern U.S. urban areas might occur through the local distribution systems of very rapid transit designed primarily as an inter-city mode.

At the present time, most professionals in urban transportation planning do not consider major change in technology likely during the next twenty to thirty years, and adherence to this position seems to become more definite as time goes on. This is understandable as a working assumption since no specific alternative to it would be really viable at present. And it is surely to some extent reinforced by increasing vested professional interests in a detailed series of analytical methods whose value would be seriously limited by expectations of change in this magnitude. But as feasibilities of innovation become clearer, new demands for major policy decisions in the planning process will occur.

Communications—the movement of ideas rather than people

or goods—is another aspect of technology that is gradually altering the shape of urban activity. It is clear that transportation and communication are to some extent substitutable as means of completing transactions. In parts of the world where telephones are uncommon there is much street traffic incurred for purposes that would elsewhere be met by phone calls. Since transactions which can be accommodated by communications media are almost always less costly by that means, increasing adjustment of activity to the media usually follows their introduction. Extensive reliance on communications media partly releases the participant from the need for proximity to locations at which he interacts since the cost of communication, within broad bounds, does not increase with distance. Thus increasing reliance on mass media for information and recreation and on personal electronic media for individual transactions has in some measure made possible the dispersed pattern of suburban residences at the present time.[20] This effect is sure to continue in the future, reinforced by increasing social and physical mobility. Increased availability of closed-circuit television, telephone conference call arrangements, expansion of coverage by the mass media and so forth will be significant.

The trend for dispersing location patterns, however, is based not so much on additional innovation as on continued adaption to presently available media. Many transactions are now accomplished by the physical presence of people only because social propriety seems to demand it, because a feeling of trust is conveyed by personal contact, or in order to control the actions of a participant (to make sure he works a full eight hours a day, for instance). Yet the increasing complexity of bureaucratic and administrative networks served by improving communications networks tends to overcome these barriers. Central control of management functions is expedited, and systems of activity lap over each other such that collateral checks on facts and obligations become increasingly available. The effect is to regularize activity and "keep people honest," such that personalized control and intuitive assurances become less necessary. As a result more transactions can be accomplished by the more efficient means of communication. (Comparisons of business methods between underdeveloped and developed countries show differences partly explained by this.) To the extent that we cling to personal means of transaction because they are more pleasant and sociable,

20. Melvin M. Webber, "The Urban Place and the Nonplace Urban Realm," in Melvin M. Webber, *Explorations into Urban Structure* (Philadelphia: University of Pennsylvania Press, 1964). For comments on the details of substitutability see Frederick W. Memmott, III, "The Substitutability of Communications for Transportation," *Traffic Engineering*, Vol. 33, No. 5, February 1963, pp. 20–24.

the transition can be slowed; but since some participants in every relevant activity will seek to maximize their efficiency through communication, the others will be forced to follow in order to remain competitive.

It is not clear how far trends in this direction will go, particularly since they imply gross changes in social style. Since they involve change of well-ingrained patterns of activity, their advance, as in the past, is apt to be slow. Nonetheless, they present difficult problems to transportation planning, in which it would be useful to consider transportation and communications systems together and develop a better understanding of the partial substitutability between them. Unfortunately, this is very difficult because of the measurement problems in communications. Though there is theoretical basis for these measurements, meaningful empirical survey of transmission is not possible at the present time.

As a joint result of increased mobility and reliance on communications, it is clear that many people will take the option of greater physical isolation to gain a larger living space at less expense. Thus the city will continue to regionalize; to spread over larger areas with looser ties to its central locations and require a more even pattern of access to its various parts. Friedmann and Miller[21] have suggested a pattern of this type, in which the metropolitan area is circumscribed by a radius of two hours' driving time from the core (about a hundred miles by today's technology), urban facilities are widely dispersed, and a much broader series of interaction possibilities available, whether in the central metropolis or in the non-metropolitan periphery now fused to the city. A trend in this direction is presently in motion. Its advanced stages will present transportation network requirements of a different type from those of the core-dominated city. Required networks will convey more even access, rather than the unified converging radial network of the traditional city. With the access-seekers more widely distributed, problems of multiple point access and relative location will rise in significance; and current problems of congestion, minimization of the use of scarce central city land for transportation facilities, and damage by proximity of incompatible activities should decline.

Spread of the boundaries of concern

Aside from developments within the field, transportation planning is subject to change because of altered approaches to other urban problems. The existence of a much greater and more detailed

21. John Friedmann and John Miller, "The Urban Field," *Journal of the American Institute of Planners*, Vol. 31, No. 4, November 1965, pp. 312–20.

quantity of diagnostic data than in many other areas is encouraging the study of many urban activities through their access and movement characteristics. This has included studies in commercial location, urban land values,[22] the locational consequences of racial segregation,[23] alternatives in urban physical structure[24] and a number of other topics. Some of this work is filtering back into the planning of transportation in the form of new methods for analysis and qualification of objectives. The work in urban structural alternatives is particularly promising for transportation planning, since it approaches more closely the basic alternatives in life style and economic character which are the most fundamental impacts of transportation networks. Beginnings in this direction have been made.[25]

Along with this continual broadening and detailing of the analytical net, there are reactions against the increasing complexity and cost of comprehensive studies which are likely to increase. These take the form of militant conservatism, narrowly circumscribed simplistic solutions, or ad hoc solutions. Desire for the simplistic solution seems symptomized by the popularity of the recent Buchanan Report[26] on urban traffic planning in Great Britain. Ad hoc solutions to localized problems or to specific viewpoints on broader problems will, of course, always be necessary, at least as detailed solutions within larger policy frameworks. It seems likely, however, that efforts will arise to devise specific detailed solutions and then link them together, in the manner of social action trends, in order to avoid the complexities of the over-all job.

In the end, these rapidly expanding bounds of the applicability of transportation analysis and planning threaten on one hand to engulf a good part of the planning field, and on the other to disappear by assimilation. Broadening efforts in the projection and planning of urban activities by the major transportation studies (as necessary background to fulfill their responsibility of recommending

---

22. Stanislaw Czamanski, "Effects of Public Investment on Urban Land Values," *Journal of the American Institute of Planners*, Vol. 32, No. 4, July 1966.

23. John F. Kain, "The Effect of the Ghetto on the Distribution and Level of Nonwhite Employment in Urban Areas," paper presented to the annual meeting of the American Statistical Association, Chicago, December 1964.

24. Work on this topic is being pursued at the Department of City and Regional Planning at M.I.T. under the leadership of Professor Aaron Fleisher. See George C. Hemmens, "An Analysis of Urban Travel and the Spatial Structure of Urban Activities," doctoral dissertation, Department of City and Regional Planning, M.I.T., 1966.

25. The New York Regional Plan Association has developed such structural alternatives and related them to the particular transportation networks they imply.

26. Great Britain, Ministry of Transport, *Traffic in Towns: A Study of the Long Term Problems of Traffic in Urban Areas* (London: H.M. Stationery Office, 1963). See also remarks on the book by John W. Dyckman, "Transportation in Cities," *Scientific American*, Vol. 213, No. 3, September 1965, p. 169.

facilities networks) and the unusual formative strength of the networks, have caused some observers to believe that soon little may
be left to the rest of planning but residual tasks outside these
interests. It seems more likely, however, that as the methods are
diffused into other urban policy professions the broad urban structure analyses and decisions may become the responsibility of other
fields, leaving to transportation planning only its more fundamental
concern for network development. Their use in the recent Community Renewal Plans of San Francisco, Philadelphia, New York,
and other cities is symptomatic. Should this happen, urban transportation planning in its present sense will have disappeared. This is
no reason for concern, since it is only part of a larger current trend
toward the redefinition of professionalized activity by problem
areas, rather than skill areas. The contributions and skills of transportation planning would continue developing in the decision sectors where maximum use could be made of them.

18 JOHN W. DYCKMAN

Transportation in cities*

INTRODUCTION

Problems of urban transportation are not new in the world. In the first century A.D. the municipal government of Rome was obliged to relieve congestion in its streets by restricting vehicular traffic (with the exception of chariots and state vehicles) to the night hours. Rome was then the only truly "big" city in the Western world, however, and for many centuries thereafter its transportation problem remained the exception rather than the rule. It was not until the process of industrialization was well under way in the 19th century that vehicular traffic began to present serious problems in cities. Today descriptions of the conditions of movement in cities express the alarm of the observer with words such as "choke" and "strangle." Not only are there now more big cities; some of them are tending to consolidate into huge megalopolitan networks, further compounding the comparatively elementary difficulties that faced the Romans.

Among the complaints commonly heard about modern systems of urban transportation are congestion, the overloading of routes and facilities, the overlong trips, the irregularity and inconvenience of those services that are publicly provided and the difficulty of parking private vehicles at desired destinations. These are problems that arise not only out of the sheer size of modern cities but also out of the organization of their land uses, the rhythm of their activities, the balancing of their public services with private rights of access and movement, and the tastes and preferences of their citizens with respect to mode of travel, route, comfort and cost. There is in fact no isolated "transportation problem" in the modern metropolis; there are problems of the spatial organization of human activities, the adaptability of existing facilities and investments, and the needs and aspirations of the people in moving themselves and their goods. For the individual city dweller, nonetheless, the contemporary transportation problem remains in large measure a "traffic" problem.

The origins of the modern traffic problem are rooted in the very nature of industrialization in an open society. For example, the modern journey to work, which accounts for a large part of the urban traffic problem, is the product of a comparatively free choice of residence and place of work, made freer in industrialized societies by the greater number and variety of both. In the early industrial centers of the Western countries workers were grouped in dwellings close to their respective places of work. In the U.S. even employers did not commute long distances but typically drove to work in carriages from houses within convenient reach of their factories.

Improvements in living standards have contributed almost as much as the growth of cities to contemporary urban traffic conditions. Expectations of greater comfort and convenience, as well as the ability to sustain higher costs, have affected the choice of both residence and mode of travel. The transportation plight of cities—at least in the prosperous, developed countries of the world—is a condition people have themselves brought about by taking advantage of individual opportunities. Accordingly if major changes are to be achieved in the present condition of transportation, deliberate individual and collective decisions on the whole question of the quality of urban life must first be made.

THE TRANSPORTATION FUNCTION

The task of an urban transportation system is to move people and goods from place to place. This elementary statement of purpose is useful because it reminds one that the task is defined by the location of the terminal points as well as by the channels of movement. For this reason the problem of urban transportation is one of city layout and planning as well as one of transportation technology.

The city planner's approach to the transportation problem can be viewed as having two aspects: (1) the definition of the tasks and requirements of the system and (2) the devising of socially acceptable and economically feasible means of achieving those objectives. This approach depends on the existence of basic studies of the use of land in cities in order to relate these uses to transportation needs. Fortunately such basic data on land uses have been available in several U.S. cities, notably Philadelphia. Robert Mitchell and Chester Rapkin of the University of Pennsylvania drew on the Philadelphia data for a prototype "city planning" study of urban transportation in 1954. Their thesis was that different types of land use generate different or variable traffic flows. Such work shifted the emphasis from the study of the flows themselves to the study of the land uses that give rise to the flows. It underlined the basic city-planning proposition that traffic can be manipulated by controlling and rearranging the land uses that represent the destinations and purposes of transportation.

This approach—sometimes called the functional approach because it emphasizes the relation between city functions and transportation—has come to dominate large urban transportation studies supported by the U.S. Bureau of Public Roads and other public agencies. The approach has been applied in the Detroit Area Transportation Study, the Chicago Area Transportation Study, the Penn-Jersey Transportation Study and the Tri-State New York Metropolitan Transportation Study. These elaborate investigations (costing approximately $1 per capita in the regions mentioned) have done much to organize existing information about urban transportation, in spite of a heavy preoccupation with automobile traffic and road networks. Surveys of travel behavior are usually made at the homes and places of work of commuters. In addition, the Bureau of Public Roads has long conducted surveys to sample the purposes of householders' trips as well as their actual travel behavior; these data are integrated in the large transportation studies with such information as the addresses of workers by place of work, and sample origins and destinations of travelers en route.

The customary unit of travel—the "trip"—takes many forms, and in these studies the purposes of various kinds of trip must be differentiated. Shopping trips and recreational trips, for example, have many characteristics that distinguish them from trips to and from work. From an analysis of such characteristics the possibility of replacing one mode of travel (perhaps the automobile) by another (perhaps mass transit) can be considered.

The outstanding contributions of the major transportation studies, apart from the accumulation and organization of data, have

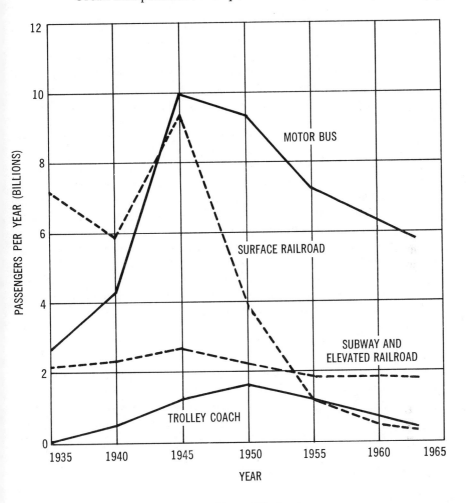

Figure 18—1

DECLINE IN USE OF MASS TRANSIT in the U.S. since the end of World War II is depicted in this graph. Gasoline and tire rationing, together with booming employment, led to an all-time high in the use of public transit during the war years; since 1945 total transit use has declined nearly 64 percent. In the same period overall route-miles of transit service have increased by 5 percent. The loss of transit riders is largely attributable to enormously increased use of private automobiles for commutation to and from work.

been (1) the approach to transportation as a comprehensive system of interrelated activities; (2) the recognition of the importance of land uses, demographic and social characteristics and consumer choices in determining transportation requirements; (3) an appreciation of the role of transportation itself in shaping the development of cities and metropolitan areas, and (4) the acceptance of the inevitably metropolitan scale of transportation planning in a society in which daily activities that generate travel move freely across the borders of local government and form the functionally interdependent fabric of the metropolitan region.

In focusing on the whole system of relations between users and facilities these elaborate studies should furnish the material for the solution to the two major problems of urban transportation: how to obtain efficient movement and how to promote new activities. The promotion of new urban activities is the province of city planning, but the city-planning results of the major transportation studies have not yet clearly emerged. The studies reflect the current condition of the planning profession, which is ambivalent toward the automobile and split on the issue of centralization v. dispersal.

FORM FOLLOWS FUNCTION

The city-forming role of transportation facilities is well known to city planners. The New York subway of 1905 opened up the Bronx; the radiating street-railway systems of the late 19th and early 20th centuries created the working-class suburbs of Boston, Chicago and Philadelphia. Today, of course, expressways are opening up at a far greater number of new suburban housing developments and shopping centers than the subway and street railways did.

To many city planners the central contemporary problem is one of conserving cities "as we have known them." These planners believe the issue is between centrality and spread, between efficient downtowns and disorganized ones. They see the present use of the automobile for the bulk of urban trips as destroying the amenities of the established downtown by contributing to congestion, eating up real estate for parking and storage, interfering with pedestrian flow and poisoning the air of the central city. Almost equally bad from their standpoint, the automobile makes possible the scattering of residences, of auxiliary commercial facilities and ultimately even of the downtown headquarters function. The planners' views are shared by many realtors holding downtown property, by some established merchants and by civic leaders who see the new emphasis on highway building as inevitably creating competing centers in outlying areas. If we are to have compact cities with centrally located places of work, relatively high-density residential zones, concentration of shopping and public facilities as well as employment, the currently dispersive effects of the automobile will have to be checked.

Other planners, not opposed to dispersal on these grounds, believe the growth of urban population itself is likely to produce a situation in which scale effects rule out present modes of transportation. These observers believe the congestion that will be faced by cities containing upward of 15 million people will be such as to require greatly enlarged capacity for traffic channels, the restriction of vehicles to specialized lanes, controlled timing and phasing of movement and many other adaptations more drastic than those proposed in present transportation plans.

In spite of the fact that every major transportation study has projected an increase in the ownership of automobiles, in the volume of automobile traffic to be accommodated in central cities, in the construction of new expressways and in the spread of metropolitan population, a number of the larger cities in the U.S. are taking steps in the direction of reinvestment or new investment in public mass transportation. In many cases this takes the form of building or expanding subways and related rail systems; in every case a major portion of the system is characterized by fixed routes and separate rights-of-way.

Public transportation systems are frequently a combination of "rapid transit," which uses for high-speed service rights-of-way that are separated by grade crossings, and "local transit," which uses public streets (with or without rail lines) and makes local stops. A truly effective transportation system must offer a full range of service, from the rapid-express system to the local-distribution system. Cities as far apart as San Francisco and Washington intend to build new subways; New York, Chicago and other cities propose to extend their existing systems; in the Northeast particular attention is being given to the problem of resuscitating privately owned commuter railroads and reviving the relation between these roads and the city transit systems. The Federal Government has shown interest in supporting these efforts, but as yet it has mounted no program comparable in scope to its highway-building effort.

City planners and transportation experts have turned to mass-transportation systems at a moment of grave difficulty for the established transportation companies. Transit franchises, which at the turn of the century were prized plums for entrepreneurs and investors, have long since ceased to be notably profitable. In most cases the companies have either been taken over by the cities or have gone

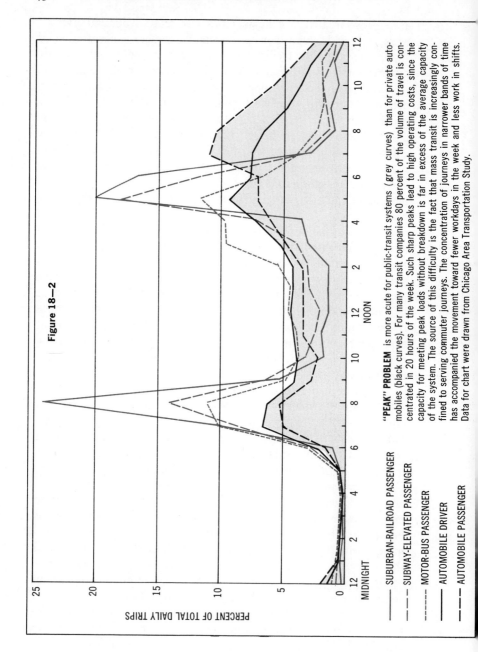

Figure 18–2

"PEAK" PROBLEM is more acute for public-transit systems (grey curves) than for private automobiles (black curves). For many transit companies 80 percent of the volume of travel is concentrated in 20 hours of the week. Such sharp peaks lead to high operating costs, since the capacity for meeting peak loads without breakdown is far in excess of the average capacity of the system. The source of this difficulty is the fact that mass transit is increasingly confined to serving commuter journeys. The concentration of journeys in narrower bands of time has accompanied the movement toward fewer workdays in the week and less work in shifts. Data for chart were drawn from Chicago Area Transportation Study.

—— SUBURBAN-RAILROAD PASSENGER

––– SUBWAY-ELEVATED PASSENGER

······ MOTOR-BUS PASSENGER

—— AUTOMOBILE DRIVER

–·– AUTOMOBILE PASSENGER

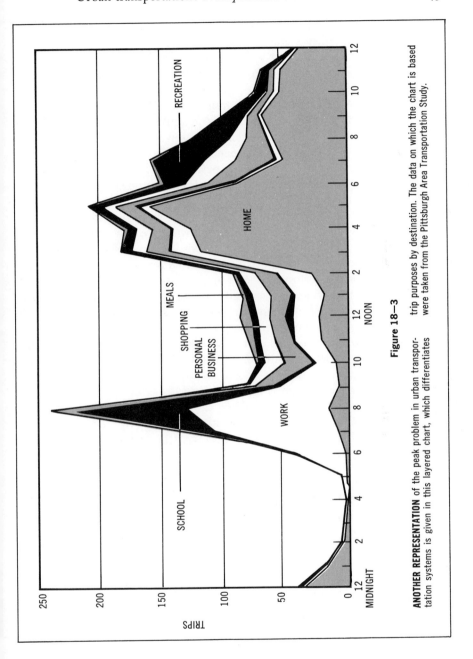

Figure 18–3

ANOTHER REPRESENTATION of the peak problem in urban transportation systems is given in this layered chart, which differentiates trip purposes by destination. The data on which the chart is based were taken from the Pittsburgh Area Transportation Study.

out of business. Although the very large cities could scarcely function without transit systems, the systems in these cities too have over the past decade suffered a decline in riders. The share of total commutation accountable to the automobile has risen at the expense of the transit systems.

The difficulties of urban transit companies have been the subject of many studies and need not be recapitulated here. Some of these are difficulties of the systems themselves; others are problems of urban growth and development only slightly related to the systems. The three major difficulties posed for transit by the pattern of growth of our cities are (1) the collection problem, (2) the delivery problem and (3) the "peak" problem.

The collection problem arises largely from the diffuse pattern of urban "sprawl" made possible by widespread ownership of automobiles and ready access to highways. Density of settlement is one of the most important variables in accounting for urban transit use, and for the performance and profitability of the systems. The New York subways are made possible by the heavy concentration of riders in areas served by the system, just as the system itself makes possible the aggregation of population at these densities. It is obviously difficult for a fixed-route system to collect efficiently in a highly dispersed settlement pattern. Not only is a commuter train unable to collect people door-to-door; the number of stops required to accumulate a payload is increased by a dispersed residential pattern. More stops in turn slow down the performance of the system and hurt it in terms of both operating costs and attractiveness to the rider. The operating disadvantages of the fixed-rail transportation system—relatively low efficiency at low operating speed, the high cost of braking and acceleration, the problems of scheduling, the minimum profitable payload required by fixed costs—all create conflicts between efficient service and low collection densities.

The problem of delivery has been exacerbated by changes in the scale and distribution of activities within the downtown areas as well as the general dispersal of places of work. Within metropolitan areas industries have moved increasingly toward the outskirts in search of larger sites; this movement has tended to disperse places of work and so reduce the usefulness of the highly centered, radial transit systems. Circumferential systems moving through predominantly low-density areas have been less attractive to the transit companies. Within the downtown areas dispersal of places of work and of central points of attraction (brought about by changes such as the shift of a department store to the fashionable fringe of the area) has greatly lengthened that portion of the trip between arrival at the terminal and arrival at the final destination. The lengthening of the walk or taxi ride from station to destination has made the whole transit ride less attractive. These developments can be summed up in the observation that the general dispersal of activities and functions within metropolitan areas has made the fixed-rail system less efficient in point-to-point delivery of passengers.

The "peak" problem arises almost entirely from the organization of journeys in time. For many transit companies 80 percent of the volume of travel is concentrated in 20 hours of the week. This results in the underutilization of rolling stock and other equipment necessary for meeting peak loads. The source of this difficulty is the fact that mass transit is increasingly confined to serving commuter journeys. The concentration of journeys in narrower bands of time has been a steadily evolving phenomenon, accompanying the movement toward fewer workdays in the week and less work in shifts.

It is axiomatic to the performance of any system—transportation or otherwise—that sharp peaks lead to high operating costs. The capacity needed for meeting peak loads without breakdown of the system is far in excess of the average capacity required by the system. The need for excess capacity is aggravated by the fact that in transportation accounting the obsolescence cycle and the amortization cycle are out of phase: mass-transportation systems in cities are rarely able to amortize investments in rolling stock and equipment before they are obsolete as a result of technical competition, of shifts in land use or of changes in employment patterns.

Finally, a whole set of factors arising from changes in consumer tastes and expectations have worked to the disadvantage of the fixed-rail system. Comfort, convenience, privacy, storage capacity, guaranteed seating, freedom from dependence on scheduled departure times and a number of intangible satisfactions all favor the use of private automobiles.

MODE OF TRAVEL

In view of the marked advantages of the automobile over other types of carrier, what can the public-transit system be expected to do to alter the present drift in commuter habits? Under what conditions would the transit system be able to compete with the automobile? The engineering efficiency of trains, which can move many times more people and much more cargo for a given road space and energy output than automobiles can, has persistently held out the promise that mass transportation would lower costs. One may ask, however, Costs for whom? Real costs, out-of-pocket costs to users and public costs have all been cited from time to time to make points for and against mass transit. It is particularly important to distinguish the public costs of the respective operations from the private costs and the average costs from the so-called marginal costs.

A recent study by economists at the RAND Corporation concluded that the automobile is competitive with other available modes of travel to work in large American cities. Under the assumptions made by these economists—including a relatively high rate for the driver's or passenger's time—it appears that the one-way hourly cost is lower for the automobile than for most competing modes of travel up to about 15 miles of commuting distance from door to door. In the framework of this analysis the behavior of commuters who choose to commute by automobile is rational.

When one compares the average cost per mile of automobile operation against the cost of transit fares per ride, the comparison may be misleading. The average cost of operating an automobile driven about 10,000 miles a year is close to 10 cents per mile. The marginal cost (the daily out-of-pocket operating cost) is much lower. A sizable fraction of the cost of operating an automobile lies of course in depreciation, insurance, registration, taxes and other fixed-cost items. Gasoline and oil account for only about 15 percent of the total cost. The cost of parking which might be significant if it were entirely passed on to the consumer at the point of destination, is frequently subsidized by private merchants and public authorities or is provided free by the community on the street. Similarly, the rights-of-way provided in highway programs are financed by gasoline taxes paid by all users, so that long journeys help to subsidize the shorter in-city trips.

As long as private incomes continue to rise, some substitution of private automobile travel for transit is probably inevitable under present competitive conditions. In analyzing the findings of the Detroit Area Transportation Study, John Kain, then at RAND, related much of the change in transit use in Michigan to changes in median family incomes of Michigan residents. His findings disposed him to the view that changes in income were more important in the decline in transit use than deteriorating service. In sum, although the automobile is not a technically elegant solution to the urban transportation problem, it is a socially engaging one because of its adaptability, social prestige and acceptability.

TRANSPORTATION STRATEGIES

Given these realities, what strategies are being developed for dealing

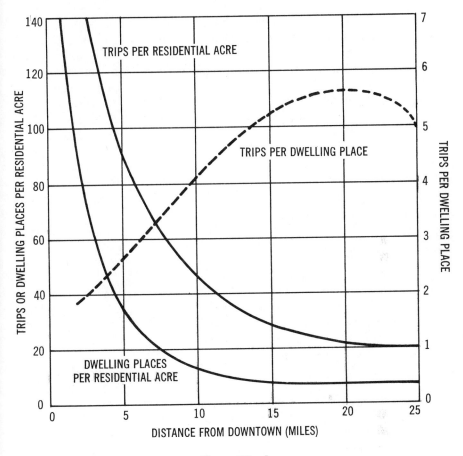

Figure 18—4

RELATION between density of dwelling places and trips generated by a given acre of land varies according to distance from the central business district, or downtown, of a city (in this case the Loop in Chicago). Why more trips are made to dwelling places that are at greater distances from the downtown area is not completely understood. One explanation may be that the proportion of income spent for travel rises slightly as income rises. It may also be cheaper and is probably easier to make trips in low-density areas, because of greater congestion and difficulty in parking in high-density areas. Families are also larger in suburban areas and so create a greater potential of trip-making per dwelling place.

with the overall problem of urban transportation? The two "pure" strategies are (1) all-out accommodation of the automobile and (2) a strategy of banning the automobile from the center city and replacing it on a large scale with rail transit as a mode of journey-to-work travel. Between these two positions are numerous mixed strategies.

Europeans, who are on the verge of entering the automobile age that has enveloped the U.S., have not as yet reacted so strongly to the automobile and are given to accommodative strategies. A firm statement of this view, albeit one tinged with ambivalence and irony, is to be found in the report entitled *Traffic in Towns*, prepared for the British government by Colin Buchanan. The Buchanan report proposes a general theory of traffic based on separation of express and local motor traffic, pedestrian traffic and certain freight movements. Buchanan holds that potential urban amenity is measured by the volume of traffic, since traffic is a measure of the use of buildings and spaces. His proposal for downtown London is based on a vertical separation of traffic: expressways are sunk below street level or are completely automobile subways, the street level is chiefly given over to the storage of vehicles, and pedestrians are lifted to a mezzanine level above the storage level. The principle is the same as the old architectural notion of arcaded shops above the major service lanes.

Although the presuppositions of the Buchanan report, as much as its analyses, lead to a drastic reshaping of cities to accommodate the automobile, similar efforts on a more modest scale are already to be seen in many of the large cities of the world. The downtowns of major U.S. cities have been attempting to adjust to the increasing number of automobiles by various internal adaptations. The process of adaptation has been going on for many years, with the widening of streets, the construction of garage spaces, the building of expressways to speed the exit and entry of cars, and alternating permission to park with restrictions on parking. Large investments in underpasses, bridges, tunnels and ramps have been made in order to integrate the local street systems with the high-speed expressways and to reduce local bottlenecks in the increasing flow of cars.

Calculations made by Ira Lowry of RAND and the University of California at Los Angeles on the basis of the Pittsburgh Transportation Study suggest that gains in transportation efficiency resulting from improved routes and automobile-storage capacity are almost immediately absorbed by the further dispersal of places of work and particularly of residences. This dispersal enables the consumer to indulge his preference for more living space; it also increases the advantage of the automobile over the fixed-route system, and it does not significantly relieve the center-city traffic problem. To borrow a concept from economics, in motoring facilities there is a "Say's law" of accommodation of use to supply: Additional accommodation creates additional traffic. The opening of a freeway designed to meet existing demand may eventually increase that demand until congestion on the freeway increases the travel time to what it was before the freeway existed.

The case for supplementary transportation systems, such as mass transit, arises from the conviction that measures to accommodate the demands of the automobile are approaching the limit of their effectiveness. The primary aim of improved transit systems is to relieve the conditions brought about by the success of the automobile. The issue for many years to come will not be trains v. automobiles but how to balance the two systems, and it may lead to new designs in which both systems complement each other.

The very scale of the effort to transform our cities to accommodate the automobile has, in view of the problems created by such investment, raised serious doubts in the minds of public officials and transportation experts about the efficacy of making further investments of this kind. The cost of building urban freeways in the interstate system has averaged $3.7 million per mile. This is not the entire real cost, however. Freeways are prodigal space-users that remove sizable tracts of land from city tax rolls. Among other costly consequences are the need for storage space for vehicles brought by freeways to the center city, for elaborate traffic-control systems and for the policing of vehicles. Freeway construction frequently displaces large numbers of urban residents; the freeway program accounts for the biggest single share of the residential relocation load resulting from public construction in the U.S. Moreover, automobiles are a prime contributor to air pollution, which can be viewed as the result of private use of a public air sewer over a central city by motorists from the entire metropolitan area.

These aspects of automobile transport in our cities have intensified public interest in alternative schemes and have expanded the political appeal of such schemes. At government levels a great deal of support has been mustered for the strengthening of rail systems, both local transit systems and the suburban lines of interstate railroads. Privately, however, consumers continue to vote for the use of the automobile. . . .

TECHNOLOGY AND THE FUTURE

As cities evolve into supercities, transportation planners must reckon with future urban form and scale as well as with future technology. The change is not occurring overnight. Even now, however, we have clear evidence of population overspill into the

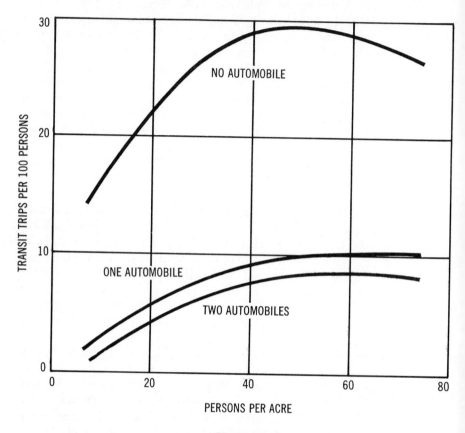

Figure 18—5

AUTOMOBILE OWNERSHIP, a function of personal income, appears to be more important in the decline of transit use than deteriorating service. This graph, based on data from the Pittsburgh Area Transportation Study, relates density of an area to transit use by residents of the area, according to the number of automobiles owned per household.

interstices between cities, of the growth of industry in outlying, low-density portions of the linear connections between cities, of the stabilization of employment in the central business districts, of the growth of circumferential and loop connections between employment centers and of the growing share of metropolitan employment and business outside the central city.

If the transportation systems serving these new agglomerations are to grow out of the present systems, the emphasis will have to be placed on the consolidation and rationalization of present operations, on the building of links now missing in the networks and on the development of new systems that will complement existing ones. To provide one example, in the San Francisco Bay Area the Golden Gate crossing is vital to the integration of Marin County into the district and could become the focus for technical work on light-weight cars that could be suspended from monorails on the existing bridge. An important step in the recognition of the modern urban transportation problem is represented by recent proposals in Boston, New York, Philadelphia and Chicago to integrate various transit companies, railroad operations, bridge and tunnel authorities and other elements in local transport. Coordinated development of high-ways and rail transit of local and express service, of private auto-mobiles, trucks and buses will be the hallmark of any forward-looking transportation plan. In this article there has been little mention of freight: the facilities for handling freight have in many instances far outstripped the performance of those for handling pas-sengers.

Finally, of course, transportation planning will proceed in the context of social choice and individual values, which in the U.S. set the priorities for planning and also the limits on it. Government officials have decided to push the development of supersonic aircraft well in advance of decisions to develop the high-speed surface facilities that will be needed to connect the increasingly remote airports with the destinations of passengers and cargo—even though 2,000-mile-per-hour aircraft will need 300-mile-per-hour ground connections to make any economic sense. Yet we may have both before we have effective integration of the Long Island Railroad, the New York City subway system and the Triborough Bridge Authority.

URBAN DESIGN

19 DAVID A. CRANE

The public art of city building*

INTRODUCTION

Few will quarrel with urban beauty as an ideal, but fewer still will value it highly or grant it a place in government programs for the American city. Even some with an enlightened social interest, who long ago accepted public intervention in a great variety of urban problems, suspect that the architect-planner seeks to strait-jacket free choice and variety in private tastes. As a people, we Americans are still a little closer to the old than to the New Frontier. A hint of what we believe to be legitimate in the realm of art and culture is given in the familiar national ideal: "It's a free country!" Our heroes in art, like our other idols, are those who pursue the individual private liberties of virtuosity, initiative, or courage.

With the American community in this frame of mind, it is not surprising that the pursuit of the city beautiful as a matter of public government endeavor is still suspect activity. The courts have sanctioned beauty of urban design as a public purpose, notably in the case of *Berman* v. *Parker*.[1] But as yet there is almost no political sanction for public programs in urban design. A few urban renewal

* Reprinted by permission of the author, and of the publisher of *The Annals* of the American Academy of Political and Social Science.

1. *Berman* v. *Parker*, 348 U.S. 26, 75 Sup. Ct. 98, 99 L. Ed. 27 (1954).

and planning administrators have taken determined design initiatives without benefit of public mandate. One can list William Slayton of the United States Urban Renewal Administration, Edmund Bacon of the Philadelphia City Planning Commission, Edward J. Logue of the Boston Development Program, and Justin Herman of the San Francisco Redevelopment Agency as exponents of this kind of political courage. Moreover, one can be warmed by the example of John and Jacqueline Kennedy's support of the arts as a public purpose.

Since we as a people have not pressed for a share in the art of city building, it remains at a very vulgar and primitive level. We do not yet possess a potent and universal theory of what makes the city beautiful and well ordered. Despite the tools at our disposal, we also lack a philosophy for approaching community design and do not have a systematic strategy for bringing about an aesthetic order even if we could agree on what kind.

THE UTILITY OF BEAUTY

With what aesthetic notions should government venture into the art of city building?

August Hechscher, commenting on the impermanent aspect of much that our civilization builds, has suggested that the greatest attention should be lavished upon those public works which are most permanent and most loved. He emphasizes the need for public sponsorship of the widest common good in the larger urban community, hinting that works merely serving large aggregates of special interests—for example, highways serving owners of automobiles—might receive lower priority.[2] In a related vein, Lewis Mumford has implied that civic design as an art emerges when a civilization enjoys some surplus and can aspire toward institutions and forms that are more than merely utilitarian.[3]

It is difficult to quarrel with Athenian views of the city as an instrument chiefly dedicated to that which is divine in human nature. Mumford's vision of the city as an instrument of human development is our best hope for leaving behind the drab life and designs of the industrial city and for establishing in its place the creative city called to view by John Galbraith's Affluent Society. This prospect of a city more devoted to an economy of ideas and men than to

2. August Hechscher, "Public Works and the Public Happiness," *Saturday Review*, August 4, 1962, pp. 8–10, 46.

3. Lewis Mumford, as quoted in *Civic Design Symposium I*, University of Pennsylvania Graduate School of Fine Arts, January 1963, pp. 10–13.

material production is already affecting the urban regions that are ready to grow in this direction; "The City of Ideas" has been taken as its slogan by the Boston Development Program.

But a great modern city *is* utilitarian, and much of its indispensable physical equipment does not evoke conscious community love. A serious failing of professional designers of cities and their clients is that they prefer to deal only with the more obvious, simple, and continuing sources of personal comfort and delight. Thus, parks and plazas, recreation and relaxation centers, places of commerce, government centers, and centers for performing arts—these fall into the professional architect's favorite realm. Urban oil tank farms, automated industrial districts, freight terminals, utilities and streets, or great highways, bridges, and tunnels—things not primarily dedicated to delight—are most often the work of engineers.

Even if some city essentials are not consciously loved, nonetheless they must become legitimate objects of public design concern if anything is to be done about abhorrent urban appearances. That is not to say that everything about a great city must be "beautiful," "human-scaled," or "comfortable." The modern "cult of the comfortable" does not take into account the relativity of beauty or scale. This cult has not recognized the highest mission of the functional artist: to employ art not merely to satisfy purpose but to dramatize purpose in some outward expression. If a great highway intersection is to facilitate a transaction of many vehicles, the design should go out of its way to be intolerable to pedestrian occupancy and vividly express this fact of inner purpose.

If beauty is relative, so is necessity. One man's need is another's surplus; the requirements of the American masses certainly exceed the subsistence levels of primitive societies. Yet existing examples of town-building in primitive societies show that they determined and clothed their needs and their surpluses in a rich and constantly evolving communal art. Admittedly, primitive town-building arts belong to societies in which individual liberty is more suppressed than we tolerate in America, and our people are far from the salutary aesthetic discipline of limited means. However, there is still a public responsibility for determining the basic common necessities and ensuring that such common surplus as may exist is not misused for passing baubles but is devoted to new objectives and forms, exalting the human condition and defining tomorrow's "necessities."

When there is an artificial distinction between architecture as an art and architecture as a utilitarian function, this limitation of design possibilities deprives us of a larger accomplishment and deep human satisfactions.

Our streets and highways, for example, are almost exclusively designed for their "carrier" role, or the mechanically efficient movement of vehicles and goods, to the exclusion of at least three other roles which they often serve in reality, albeit badly. The urban street, depending upon location and scale, might also do a better job of meeting these additional purposes: as a "shelter," providing different kinds of public living rooms; as a "city-builder," creating land values, uses, and architectural scale (or destroying these if improperly regarded); as a "communicator," providing visual impressions and meaningful signals. Each of these four purposes—carrier, shelter, city-builder, and communicator—makes its own demands upon the design. It can be demonstrated that conscious thought given to all these purposes will augment efficiency of traffic, not to mention the efficiency of men.

This example of the bonuses of multipurpose design merely illustrates the many opportunities for the public to satisfy a broader common good, with love, in those systems and elements which have in the past been treated in specialized ways for specialized interests. Great art rarely lacks comprehensiveness and emphasis. As made visible in their stones and steel, will the values in our cities merely emphasize mechanical needs?

One can rather hope that the public authority will choose, if only as a practical matter of greater total efficiency, to apply art and love not only to the most divine places of civilized culture but to all our needs and surpluses. With this broadening of the Athenian ideal, we may then be on the road toward a building culture appropriate to the heterogeneous demands of our time.

GROWTH AND FALL OF AN URBAN DESIGN TRIAD

Our city building culture and community design processes are less civilized than those which produced the wonderful preindustrial cities of Europe or Asia many of us admire so much today. Cities like Rome, Florence, Paris, or Peking resulted from the mutually supporting creative endeavors of a triad of design participants. The head of state ordained places and buildings of communal importance and laid in the utilitarian systems of movement, water, sewage, shipping, or recreation—the "bone and sinew"—on which the life and works of individuals depended. Professional designers and builders provided style and technique through pacesetting works of architecture as a formal art. The vernacular design of the unified masses filled in the urban fabric on a scale and in a harmonious variety which no king or architect could manage by himself.

We have no such creative partnership of processes in modern American city building.

Gone is the creative power of the vernacular under an affluent barrage of sophisticated materials and techniques; gone is the ability of the masses to exercise judgments of equal sophistication.

Gone is the responsible stylist, in a reaction and withdrawal from mass banality and public squalor. In their crusade, today's architects and critics carry a variety of patent medicines and nice motives. Urban cosmetologists rail against suburban "chromium and borax" or eclectically rediscover medieval "cityscapes" and "human scale" downtown. Unapplied theoretical diagrams of the city are abundant, but consistent development of urban architectural idioms is lacking. Each new opportunity in design is seized as license for experiment and self-satisfaction rather than as an opportunity to make a disciplined contribution to a communal culture. Partly because of this attitude, trained designers have had a diminishing role in decisions affecting city design—mass housing, shopping centers, industrial building, or urban renewal.

There is, to be sure, a very recent consciousness of the city among architects. This has led to a few notable civic design accomplishments, such as Boston's City Hall, now under construction, or Denver's Mile-High Center, completed a few years ago. The contemporary stylist is becoming more skilled and sensitive in the design of discrete city complexes, but there is so far no encompassing art or process of the whole.

The head of state, too, is no longer taking the direct creative action that he once did in the placement, timing, and design of public works as a generative framework for city form. Our city-building king still tries to do some of the things people cannot do for themselves, but he is a Hydra-headed designing monster of overlapping and unco-ordinated governments, regulations, and public works. He gives lip service to the democratic ideal and leaves art to the private sphere, but his activities affect the form of cities out of all proportion to his good intentions. The unseen city-making hands of the United States Federal Housing Administration property manuals, the United States Bureau of Roads funds and standards for highways, and local zoning and other powerful controls over private building—all provide graphic testimony to the absurdity and lack of creativity in this pretense of democratic spirit. Even where capital improvement programs might serve a direct value in controlling form, speculative subdivisions are built long before local government exercises its role as a builder and maintainer of utilities and roads.

We need a new basis for the disciplines and participation of vernacular, stylist, and king in a common building culture. Of the three, the role of modern government is most crucial.

A POINT OF DEPARTURE IN THE CITY DYNAMIC

The city-making king of the sixties must control an entirely different and more dynamic city organism than those on which Sixtus V of Rome or Napoleon III of Paris left their autocratic marks. It is no longer a matter of creating abstract public benefits with the quiet assurance that, in due course, private creativity and conformity will follow. Indeed, one can doubt whether the modern metropolis is subject to abstract plans or principles of any kind, let alone those of Sixtus V or Napoleon III.

Today's city tends to make and remake itself. The same vibrant forces that alter distribution and connections of people and enterprises in the human city also create a dynamic equality in the physical city. Perhaps we should not go so far as to claim immutability for these forces, for government and the designer can partially influence them and certainly cannot ignore them.

Today's city-building is not a still-life art. It is more like composing a painting on a flowing river that will not be still. In this sense, the symmetry and formality of Brasilia's design belongs to a rather autocratic and static age, not to ours.

The dynamic fact of city form-making is neither evil nor good, depending on how well we can design with rather than against the moving stream.

The dynamics of the city and their physical consequences can be described in terms of three kinds of images: (1) the city as a volume of motion, the "City on Wheels"; (2) the city as a volume of time, the "City of Change and Permanence"; and (3) the city as a volume of building participants and processes, the "City of a Thousand Designers."

The City on Wheels is not merely a way of life. It is also a factor in an evolving physical scheme of urban spaces, a force in urban growth and deterioration, and a fundamental conditioner of the aesthetic experience. Designing for the four faces of the modern city street—carrier, shelter, city-builder, and communicator—is like designing motion itself. It is an entirely new problem and potential delight, and it offers a new tool for land development.

The influence of advanced communication and transportation technology upon building and land use also creates entirely new dimensions for creative urban design. Because people and enterprises

combine and recombine in relation to available and needed communications, a communication change can bring about entirely new
inventions of space and cause substantial city-wide redistribution of
activity. We can no longer rely on planning the whole macrocosm of
the city on the basis of discrete microcosms—for example, office
building, theater, or shopping center. By the same token, the public
authority might come closer to affecting the whole by encouraging
the evolution of selected parts.

DESIGN OF THE CITY AS A PROCESS STATE

The City on Wheels is only part of a larger story of the city as a
dynamic process state. This process state gives our cities an air of
impermanence and a certain aesthetic grain and texture. It requires
new criteria and principles of physical design and imposes upon the
public authority a need to choose and order its artistic role in an
effective and not overly patronizing way.

The City of Change and Permanence is most often seen by the
planner as a horrible matter of excessive and unbalanced growth and
blight. Yet both phenomena are inherent in a living, cyclical
organism such as we must assume the city to be. Prevalent practices
of urban renewal tend to treat the symptoms but not the causes of
blight, as if the physical replacement of the cut-out disease will last
forever. Even new things must age, obsolesce from conditions of use,
suffer from physical wear and tear, and finally give way to new
growth.

Blight is not the absolute surface symptom planners and framers
of urban-renewal legislation seem to think it is. As Robert B.
Mitchell has suggested, there is a potentially ordered relativity
between conditions and locations of physical *containers* and requirements and distribution of their human *contents*.[4] Much that we do is
discarded or built impermanently because we do not solve the
logistics of human contents in relation to their containers. Thus, a
blighted community designed for large families but now overcrowded with transient groups might be less hurtfully renewed by
adapting existing houses and facilities to suit the needs of either the
former or present occupants.

In attempting to balance facilities with activities, and distribution of growth with locations of deterioration, we can perhaps
never achieve a painless renewal process. The problem is not quite
as simple as the One Hoss Shay that was made to fall apart at the

4. Robert B. Mitchell, "The New Frontier in Metropolitan Planning," *Journal of
the American Institute of Planners*, Vol. 27, No. 3 (August 1961), pp. 169–175.

right time and place and all together. But surely we could do with less concentrated slum clearance and have much more spread and continuity of public benefits to regenerate private change.[5] The new dimensions of urban growth and deterioration surpass the limited building powers of government. Government must multiply its city building influence with strategic distributions of public acts calculated to induce a suitable match between facilities and human contents, between blight and private energy.

The aesthetics of small changes flung broadly could be no worse than present project appearances.

The City of Change and Permanence—even more the City of a Thousand Designers—requires the use of structural patterns which are capable of accommodating or resisting stresses of the process state. It is possible through design to give land and facilities more physical permanence while at the same time accommodating unforeseen changes of use. Likewise, we can make things physically malleable under the will of multiple designers and deciders. These design possibilities exist at every level, from buildings to whole cities.[6]

Designers, builders, and governments, for various motives, aesthetic and otherwise, seem to resist the idea of letting people in on city building. The tendency toward total prefabrication and physical control is often upset by the creative will of the Thousand Designers. Witness the new homeowners who overlay their own embellishments on the predecorated subdivision house. Where this will is lost, slum symptoms will not be far away.

Designing for maximum creative participation of the more sophisticated public and private decision-makers is just as important as harnessing the "do-it-yourself" potential of the citizenry. Large plans have remained on dusty shelves and decision-makers have been left to follow expedients. Perhaps this was because the static projection of the future could not survive changes of mind and policy, or because there was no workable and sensitive program for their implementation. As this author has suggested, more use of trial runs for development ideas could provide a less abstract and more creative basis for deciding on far-reaching public programs.[7]

5. It is to be noted that "reconditioning" treatments in urban renewal, or the process of localities installing public improvements and taking minimal action against deteriorated structures, was recently discouraged by the federal government. Presumably this was done because a public expenditure of funds without immediate returns is intolerable to contemplate. Are our governments short-term enterprises?

6. For discussion of designs amenable to a process state, see David A. Crane, "Chandigarh Reconsidered," *Journal of the American Institute of Architects*, Vol. 33, No. 5 (May 1960), pp. 32–40.

7. *Ibid.*

The issue raised by August Hechscher is not whether we can but how much do we want to be designed permanently. Greater physical permanence combined with user adaptability would waste fewer physical resources and provide greater visual history. However, waste of physical facilities is, in a sense, a vehicle toward certain kinds of improved living standards.

Since governments are long-term financial institutions, though short-lived politically, one can hope the public sphere will be the first to build permanently at higher first costs. But government's living standards can also outgrow fixed facilities. Since we have but few acropolises in a living city, the search for permanence and symbolic meaning might be better directed toward a permanence of land, places, and relationships between general attributes of buildings, rather than toward buildings themselves. This would require a consciousness of relative adaptability or permanence in each step of an ordered building process.[8]

STRUCTURE AND PROGRAMS OF PUBLIC DESIGN

The activities of the city planner, the public and private developer, and the architect are on the verge of merging in an entirely new kind of urbanistic industry. Their increasing operational integration and professional interdependence are already having an impact on their individual approaches. Different kinds of planners emerge, and some are acquiring an unaccustomed interest in art and concrete action. Architects are working for public and private interests of larger scale for longer time ranges. Most importantly, urban-renewal specialists and agencies have begun to appear as the focus for a complete integration of local planning and development.

The only example in a major American city where all these evolving elements have been brought together in one agency is Mayor John F. Collins' Boston Development Program. Under this umbrella, the Boston Redevelopment Authority contains the functions of the former Planning Board as well as urban renewal. Development Administrator Edward J. Logue also serves as the Mayor's Development Coordinator for related municipal development activities. If still incomplete and imperfect, this approach toward total integration of planning and building offers a prototppe for the new industry of urbanism.

The significance of this alignment in professions, programs, and

8. For discussion of aesthetic principles and sequential development processes involved in this idea, see David A. Crane, "The City Symbolic," *Journal of the American Institute of Planners*, Vol. 26, No. 4 (November 1960), pp. 280–292.

processes is that it will offer, for the first time, *versatility* of city design and *strategy* for city building.

City design is no longer a matter of the generalized scale of whole districts versus the particular scale of buildings, but both. A versatile design system with built-in feedbacks can now embrace all subjects of aesthetic attention, all participants in city building, and all periods of time for achievement.

Similarly, the new public integration will provide a more effective democratic basis for local government influence and strategy. With its direct building powers relatively diminished in today's society, local government—and its federal and state helpers—must choose its design tools for maximum effect and minimum fiat.

A strategic public design program could take a leaf from India, where the Sanskrit word for "space," literally translated, means "opportunity for things to happen." Thus, to make public designs is to *leave* and *make* creative opportunities for the private sphere. Such a strategy should contain some of the following forms of direct public design initiatives: (1) *platform works*, demonstrating improved and practicable design standards—for public or private facilities; (2) *multiplication programs*, facilitating widespread use of new standards and techniques on a scale consonant with industrialization potentials and overwhelming needs; and (3) *generative works*, using "capital design" as an artful system of shaping and deploying public works in time and space for maximum encouragement and creative control of private development.[9]

Direct public design actions of these types cannot entirely preempt the need for public design review and controls, but at least these "policeman" functions could be turned in a more creative and discretionary direction. More flexible zoning and building codes, administered by full-time public servants qualified to render design judgments, would help. Perhaps zoning should be less a mediation between conflicting private developments and more a bulwark against private encroachment on the common good in public streets and open spaces. We could also improve on the design follow-through lying dormant in our rarely convened or reappointed city art commissions.

A more effective and helpful public policing of private design is beginning to emerge through urban-renewal experience. Although it has proved difficult to administer, design competitions for awarding land to private developers have improved quality. More important are the new day-to-day working relationships between re-

9. For further background on the "capital design" concept, see Crane, "Chandigarh Reconsidered" and "The City Symbolic."

development design staffs and consultants, on one hand, and, on the other hand, developers and their architects. Needless to say, this trend cannot become dominant unless the privateness of architecture diminishes and talented designers are made welcome in City Hall. American cities are still far behind European counterparts in this respect.

The new possibilities for a versatile and strategic public design program will open the way for the local authority to recognize the place for art in all aspects of its normal planning and building. If art is isolated from this role, it has little political value and even less weight in public affairs. The full spectrum of an agency's design activities could include:

1. *Design at the level of long-range master planning of public and private development.* This program should go beyond the typical long-range generalized plans of land use and transportation. A concrete architectural image of the city in immediate view, plus alternate long-range diagrams, should be included. The work should express the synthesis of typical physical units emerging from prototype research and development programs. The staging and distribution of public design commitments should be included in a plan of the "capital web."

2. *Capital design at the level of operating departments of local government.* Capital design should be amalgamated with existing capital improvements budgeting, thus defining public building standards and providing land and building integration of municipal services. Unco-ordinated execution activities of city departments should be brought together in one administrative center. Co-ordination should emphasize removal of architect selection from political patronage, space programing, economy of construction, and application of design talent within the exclusive domain of engineering.

3. *Design at the level of large-scale development projects.* This program should include over-all design framework preparation affecting urban renewal, subdivision, or any large-scale development within which public services and facilities will be built. The specific demands of this scale of public design will provide feedback to master planning and capital design. The use of the extralegal illustrative site plan in urban renewal shows it can provide a take-it-or-leave-it creative stimulus for private architects and also guide the defining of legal controls in the official development plan.

4. *Design research and development.* Although most local governments cannot afford pure research and experimentation, there are many opportunities to carry out normal building programs on a prototype basis. Regular renewal subsidies, plus special federal and

foundation research and demonstration funds, can often make possible certain studies or construction which financially strapped municipalities or private interests could not otherwise afford. This program should include various types of public assistance to enable mass application of tested prototypes throughout the city and the building industry.

5. *Design services for citizen participation in development.* Where the burden of neighborhood renewal is to be shared by homeowners and local groups, help may be necessary in the form of public education, technical services, or materials and equipment. Architectural advisory services can be incorporated in these programs, as in the redevelopment programs in New Haven or Boston. Private design organizations and services, similar to legal-aid societies, might also be mustered to guide the citizen's efforts of self-help.

6. *Design review as an adjunct to action and code-enforcement programs.* In the more advanced agencies, urban-renewal design review is beginning to include assistance to private developers and designers, in co-ordinating and expediting design, helping them to understand government procedure, and speeding them through separate barriers of red tape. Similar services should be incorporated into subdivision, zoning, and other activities regarding large-scale development.

The six-pronged local public design program resembles, at least in categories, the design targets of the Boston Development Program. It is a little broader in scope than the spectrum of local public design aims advocated in policy statements of the federal Urban Renewal Administration.[10] Undoubtedly, the six targets are still more demanding than any great American city can as yet carry out with practical creativity. However, the embryonic industry of urbanism could enable realization of such local design programs within this decade.

THE NEW GRANDEUR OF CITY-BUILDING KINGS

Of all potential public excursions into the art of building cities, the most promising is a pace-setting capital design of government's own stones and steel. Here lies the clearest obligation and the most visible opportunity. It is through capital design that beauty and symbol can be most easily woven into the common necessities of all the people.

10. William L. Slayton, Commissioner, Urban Renewal Administration, "Design Goals for Urban Renewal," *Architectural Record*, November 1963, pp. 149-152. Also See Slayton, "Design Considerations in Urban Renewal" (mimeographed lecture), Annual Conference on Urban Renewal, National Association of Housing and Redevelopment Officials, University of Oregon, Eugene, Oregon, July 9, 1962.

The public capital web offers an opportunity to express unique character and identity of the locality. Most American cities will indeed require essentially the same architectural elements: highways, maintenance plants, municipal buildings, libraries, health and welfare facilities, schools, and open spaces. But climate, materials, topography, and other indigenous problems, attitudes, and opportunities should furnish a point of departure for aesthetic expression of local public values. The flat, endless plains of Chicago and the expansive attitudes of its people inspired a giant, formal scale in the early twentieth-century public works of Daniel Burnham's plan.

Boston's capital web must be more complex and informal to reflect its hills, water, and unique historic neighborhoods. But even Boston has great cleavages in the development pattern left by topography, harbor filling, and now-obsolete facilities. Here the city can stimulate rejuvenation of adjacent neighborhoods by building the lifesaving things of heroic scale—a football stadium, highways, or services for new economic development. In San Juan, capital design can mean great drainage canals with jungle-sized parks, adjacent boulevards, and major concentrations of density-inducing community facilities. These would reflect the present development problems of undifferentiated sprawl, leapfrogging of unbuildable low lands, and leveling of hills for fill.

The public works of our times will not have the predictable simplicity of over-all pattern or building style that characterized the work of Baroque kings. But they can have equal greatness of scale. Nor should our works give exclusive attention to the pleasures of the eye or to the cultural needs of the few. But the American city has a new opportunity for public grandeur and munificence of design.

Will we continue to accept mediocrity in art from an otherwise superior form of government?

The pattern of the metropolis[*]

INTRODUCTION

The pattern of urban development critically affects a surprising number of problems, by reason of the spacing of buildings, the location of activities, the disposition of the lines of circulation. Some of these problems might be eliminated if only we would begin to coordinate metropolitan development so as to balance services and growth, prevent premature abandonment or inefficient use, and see that decisions do not negate one another. In such cases, the form of the urban area, whether concentrated or dispersed, becomes of relatively minor importance.

There are other problems, however, that are subtler and go deeper. Their degree of seriousness seems to be related to the particular pattern of development which has arisen. To cope with such difficulties, one must begin by evaluating the range of possible alternatives of form, on the arbitrary assumption that the metropolis can be molded as desired. For it is as necessary to learn what is desirable as to study what is possible; realistic action without purpose can be as useless as idealism without power. Even the range of

* Reprinted by permission from *Daedalus*, Journal of the American Academy of Arts and Sciences, Boston, Massachusetts, Volume 90, Number 1.

what is possible may sometimes be extended by fresh knowledge of what is desirable.

Let us, therefore, consider the form of the metropolis as if it existed in a world free of pressures or special interests and on the assumption that massive forces can be harnessed for reshaping the metropolis for the common good—provided this good can be discovered. The question then is, how should such power be applied? We must begin by deciding which aspects of the metropolitan pattern are crucial. We can then review the commonly recognized alternative patterns, as well as the criteria that might persuade us to choose one over another. Finally, we may hope to see the question as a whole. Then we will be ready to suggest new alternatives and will have the means of choosing the best one for any particular purpose.

THE CRITICAL ASPECTS OF METROPOLITAN FORM

There are at least three vital factors in our judging the adequacy of the form of the metropolis, once its total size is known. The first of all is the magnitude and pattern of both the structural density (the ratio of floor space in buildings to the area of the site) and the structural condition (the state of obsolescence or repair). These aspects can be illustrated on a map by plotting the locations of the various classes of density ranging from high concentration to wide dispersion, and the various classes of structural condition ranging from poor to excellent. Density and condition provide a fundamental index of the physical resources an urban region possesses.

A second factor is the capacity, type, and pattern of the facilities for the circulation of persons, roads, railways, airlines, transit systems, and pathways of all sorts. Circulation and intercommunication perhaps constitute the most essential function of a city, and the free movement of persons happens to be the most difficult kind of circulation to achieve, the service most susceptible to malfunction in large urban areas.

The third factor that makes up the spatial pattern of a city is the location of fixed activities that draw on or serve large portions of the population, such as large department stores, factories, office and government buildings, warehouses, colleges, hospitals, theatres, parks, and museums. The spatial pattern of a city is made up of the location of fixed activities as well as the patterns of circulation and physical structure. However, the distribution of locally based activities, such as residence, local shopping, neighborhood services, elementary and high schools, is for our purpose sufficiently indicated by mapping the density of people or of buildings. Hence, if we have already specified structural density and the circulation system, the remaining critical fact at the metropolitan scale is the location of the city-wide activities which interact with large portions of the whole.

When we come to analyze any one of these three elements of spatial pattern, we find that the most significant features of such patterns are the *grain* (the degree of intimacy with which the various elements such as stores and residences are related), the *focal organization* (the interrelation of the nodes of concentration and interchange as contrasted with the general background), and the *accessibility* (the general proximity in terms of time of all points in the region to a given kind of activity or facility). In this sense, one might judge that from every point the accessibility to drugstores was low, uneven, or uniformly high, or that it varied in some regular way, for example, high at the center and low at the periphery of the region. All three aspects of pattern (focal organization, grain, and accessibility) can be mapped, and the latter two can be treated quantitatively if desired.

It is often said that the metropolis today is deficient as a living environment. It has suffered from uncontrolled development, from too rapid growth and change, from obsolescence and instability. Circulation is congested, requiring substantial time and a major effort. Accessibility is uneven, particularly to open rural land. The use of facilities is unbalaced, and they become increasingly obsolete. Residential segregation according to social groups seems to be growing, while the choice of residence for the individual remains restricted and unsatisfactory. The pattern of activities is unstable, and running costs are high. Visually, the city is characterless and confused, as well as noisy and uncomfortable.

Yet the metropolis has tremendous economic and social advantages that override its problems and induce millions to bear with the discomforts. Rather than dwindle or collapse, it is more likely to become the normal human habitat. If so, the question then is, what particular patterns can best realize the potential of metropolitan life?

The dispersed sheet

One alternative is to allow the present growth at the periphery to proceed to its logical conclusion but at a more rapid pace. Let new growth occur at the lowest densities practicable, with substantial interstices of open land kept in reserve. Let older sections be rebuilt at much lower densities, so that the metropolitan region would rapidly spread over a vast continuous tract, perhaps coextensive with adjacent metropolitan regions. At the low densities of the outer suburbs, a metropolis of twenty million might require a circle of land 100 miles in diameter.

The old center and most subcenters could be dissolved, allowing

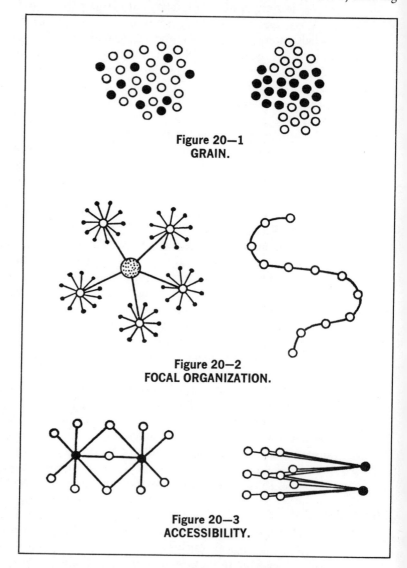

Figure 20—1
GRAIN.

Figure 20—2
FOCAL ORGANIZATION.

Figure 20—3
ACCESSIBILITY.

city-wide activities to disperse throughout the region, with a fine grain. Factories, offices, museums, universities, hospitals would appear everywhere in the suburban landscape. The low density and the dispersion of activities would depend on and allow circulation in individual vehicles, as well as a substantial use of distant symbolic communication such as telephone, television, mail, coded messages. Accessibility to rural land would become unnecessary, since outdoor recreational facilities would be plentiful and close at hand. The permanent low-density residence would displace the summer cottage.

The system of flow, concerned solely with individual land (and

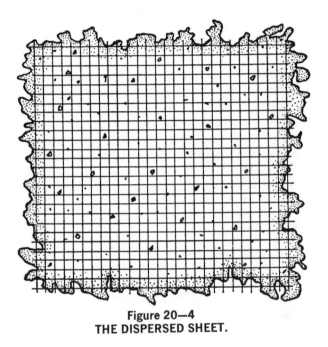

Figure 20—4
THE DISPERSED SHEET.

perhaps air) vehicles, should be highly dispersed in a continuous grid designed for an even movement in all directions. There would be no outstanding nodal points, no major terminals. Since different densities or activities would therefore be associated in a very fine grain, the physical pattern similarly might encourage a balanced cross-section of the population at any given point. Work place and residence might be adjacent or miles apart. Automatic factories and intensive food production might be dispersed throughout the region.

Frank Lloyd Wright dreamed of such a world in his Broadacre City.[1] It is this pattern toward which cities like Los Angeles appear to be moving, although they are hampered and corrupted by the vestiges of older city forms. Such a pattern might not only raise flexibility, local participation, personal comfort, and independence

1. Frank Lloyd Wright, "Broadacre City," in *Taliesin*, October 1940, vol. 1, no. 1.

to a maximum, but also go far toward solving traffic congestion through the total dispersion and balancing of loads. Its cost would be high, however, and distances remain long. Accessibility would be good, given high speeds of travel and low terminal times (convenient parking, rapid starting); at the very least it would be evenly distributed. Thus communication in the sense of purposeful trips ("I am going out to buy a fur coat") might not be hindered, but spontaneous or accidental communication ("Oh, look at that fur coat in the window!"), which is one of the advantages of present city life, might be impaired by the lack of concentration.

Although such a pattern would require massive movements of the population and the extensive abandonment of equipment at the beginning, in the end it might promote population stability and the conservation of resources, since all areas would be favored alike. It gives no promise, however, of heightening the sense of political identity in the metropolitan community nor of producing a visually vivid and well-knit image of environment. Moreover, the choice of the type of residence would be restricted, although the choice of facility to be patronized (churches, stores, etc.) might be sufficiently wide.

The galaxy of settlements

We might follow a slightly different tack while at the same time encouraging dispersion. Instead of guiding growth into an even distribution, let development be bunched into relatively small units, each with an internal peak of density and each separated from the next by a zone of low or zero structural density. Depending on the transport system, this separation might be as great as several miles. The ground occupied by the whole metropolis would increase proportionately; even if the interspaces were of minimum size, the linear dimensions of the metropolis would increase from thirty to fifty percent.

City-wide activities could also be concentrated at the density peak within each cluster, thus forming an over-all system of centers, each of which would be relatively equal in importance to any of the others. Such a metropolitan pattern may be called an "urban galaxy." The centers might be balanced in composition or they might vary by specializing in a type of activity, so that one might be a cultural center, another a financial center.

The system of flow would also be dispersed but would converge locally at the center of each cluster. It might be organized in a triangular grid, which provides such a series of foci while maintaining an easy flow in all directions over the total area. Since median densities remain low, while the centers of activity are divided into relatively small units, the individual vehicle must be the major mode of transportation, but some supplementary public transportation such as buses or aircraft running from center to center would now be feasible.

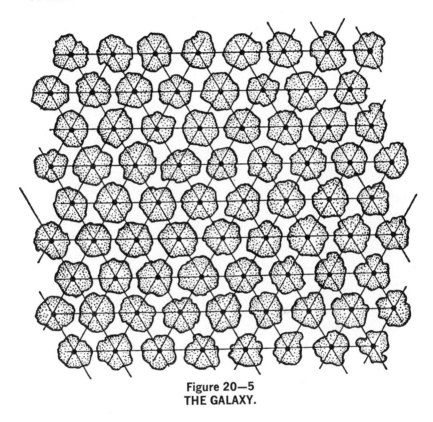

Figure 20—5
THE GALAXY.

While it retains many of the advantages of the dispersed sheet, such as comfort, independence, and stability, this scheme probably enhances general communication, and certainly spontaneous communication, through creating centers of activity. It would presumably encourage participation in local affairs by favoring the organization of small communities, though this might equally work against participation and coordination on the metropolitan scale. In the same sense, the visual image at the local level would be sharpened, though the metropolitan image might be only slightly improved. Flexibility might be lost, since local clusters would of necessity have relatively fixed boundaries, if interstitial spaces were preserved, and the city-wide activities would be confined to one kind of location.

The factor of time-distance might remain rather high, unless people could be persuaded to work and shop within their own cluster, which would then become relatively independent with regard to commutation. Such independent communities, of course, would largely negate many metropolitan advantages: choice of work for the employee, choice of social contacts, of services, and so on. If the transportation system were very good, then "independence" would be difficult to enforce.

This pattern, however, can be considered without assuming such local independence. It is essentially the proposal advocated by the proponents of satellite towns, pushed to a more radical conclusion, as in Clarence Stein's diagram.[2] Some of its features would appear to have been incorporated into the contemporary development of Stockholm.

The pattern of an urban galaxy provides a wider range of choice than does pure dispersion, and a greater accessibility to open country, of the kind that can be maintained between clusters. This pattern has a somewhat parochial complexion and lacks the opportunities for intensive, spontaneous communication and for the very specialized activities that might exist in larger centers. Local centers, too, might develop a monotonous similarity, unless they were given some specific individuality. That might not be easy, however, since central activities tend to support and depend on one another (wholesaling and entertainment, government and business services, headquarters offices and shopping). A compromise would be the satellite proposal proper: a swarm of such unit clusters around an older metropolitan mass.

The core city

There are those who, enamored with the advantages of concentration, favor a completely opposite policy that would set median structural densities fairly high, perhaps at 1.0 instead of 0.1; in other words, let there be as much interior floor space in buildings as there is total ground area in the city, instead of only one-tenth as much. If we consider the open land that must be set aside for streets, parks, and other such uses, this means in practice the construction of elevator apartments instead of one-family houses. The metropolis would then be packed into one continuous body, with a very intensive peak of density and activity at its center. A metropolis of

2. Clarence Stein, "City Patterns, Past and Future," *Pencil Points*, June 1942.

twenty million could be put within a circle ten miles in radius, under the building practice normal today.

Parts of the city might even become "solid," with a continuous occupation of space in three dimensions and a cubical grid of transportation lines. (The full application of this plan could cram a metropolis within a surprisingly small compass: twenty million people, with generous spacing, could be accommodated within a cube less than three miles on a side.) Most probably there would be a fine grain of specialized activities, all at high intensity, so that apartments would occur over factories, or there might also be stores on upper levels. The system of flow would necessarily be highly specialized, sorting each kind of traffic into its own channel. Such a city

Figure 20—6
THE CORE.

would depend almost entirely on public transport, rather than individual vehicles, or on devices that facilitated pedestrian movement, such as moving sidewalks or flying belts. Accessibility would be very high, both to special activities and to the open country at the edges of the city. Each family might have a second house for weekends; these would be widely dispersed throughout the countryside and used regularly three or four days during the week, or even longer, by mothers and their young children. The city itself, then, would evolve into a place for periodic gathering. Some of the great European cities, such as Paris or Moscow, which are currently building large numbers of high-density housing as compact extensions to their peripheries, are approximating this pattern without its more radical features.

Such a pattern would have an effect on living quite different from that of the previous solutions. Spontaneous communication would be high, so high that it might become necessary to impede it so as to preserve privacy. Accessibility would be excellent and time-distance low, although the channels might be crowded. The high density might increase discomfort because of noise or poor climate, although these problems could perhaps be met by the invention of new technical devices. As with the previous patterns, the choice of habitat would be restricted to a single general type within the city proper, although the population could enjoy a strong contrast on weekends or holidays. The nearness of open country and the many kinds of special services should on the whole extend individual choice. Once established, the pattern should be stable, since each point would be a highly favored location. However, a very great dislocation of people and equipment, in this country, at least, would be required to achieve this pattern.

Such a metropolis would indeed produce a vivid image and would contribute to a strong sense of the community as a whole. Individual participation, on the other hand, might be very difficult. It is not clear how running costs would be affected; perhaps they would be lower because of the more efficient use of services and transportation, but initial costs would undoubtedly be very high. The segregation of social groups, as far as physical disposition can influence it, might be discouraged, although there is a level of density above which intercommunication among people begins to decline again. Certainly this solution is a highly rigid and un-adaptable one in which change of function could be brought about only by a costly rearrangement.

The urban star

A fourth proposal would retain the dominant core without so drastic a reversion to the compact city. Present densities would be kept, or perhaps revised upward a little, while low-density develop-ment at the outer fringe would no longer be allowed. Tongues of open land would be incorporated into the metropolitan area to produce a density pattern that is star-shaped in the central region and linear at the fringes. These lines of dense development along the radials might in time extend to other metropolitan centers, thus becoming linear cities between the main centers. The dominant core, however, would remain, surrounded by a series of secondary centers distributed along the main radials. At moderate densities (less than the core pattern, and more than the sheet), the radial arms of a metropolis of com-parable size might extend for fifty miles from its own center.

The metropolitan center of the star pattern would again contain the most intensive types of city-wide activity. Elsewhere, either in the subcenters or in linear formations along the main radials—whichever proved the more suitable—these activities would be car-ried on at a less intense level. The system of flow would logically be organized on the same radial pattern, with supplementary con-centric rings. An efficient public transportation system of high capacity could operate along the main radials, whereas the ring roads could accommodate public transport of lower intensity. To some degree, travel by individual vehicles, although discouraged for centrally bound flows, would be practicable in other directions.

This pattern is a rationalization of the manner in which metropolitan areas were developing till the individual vehicle became the usual means of travel. It is the form the city of Copenhagen has adopted as its pattern for future growth;[3] Blumenfeld has discussed it at length.[4] This form retains the central core with its advantages of

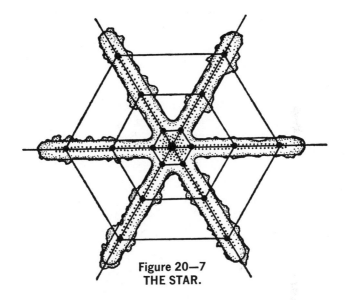

Figure 20—7
THE STAR.

rapid communication and specialized services yet permits the location of other kinds of major activities. Lower residential densities are also possible. Individual choice should be fairly wide, both in regard to living habitat, access to services, and access to open land— this land lies directly behind each tongue of development, even at the core, and leads continuously outward to rural land.

Movements along a sector would be fairly fast and efficient, although terminals at the core might continue to be congested and, with continued growth, the main radials might become overloaded. Movement between sectors, however, would be less favored, especially in the outer regions; there distances are great, transit hard to maintain, and channels costly, since they would span long distances

3. *Skitseforslag til egnsplan for Storkobenhaven:* Copenhagen regional plan. Summary of the preliminary proposal, 1948–1949, with list of contents and notes explaining all illustrations of the preliminary proposal, translated into English.

4. Hans Blumenfeld, "A Theory of City Form," *Society of Architectural Historians Journal,* July 1949.

over land they do not directly serve. Accessibility to services would
be unequal as between inner and outer locations.

The visual image is potentially a strong one and should be conducive to a sense of the metropolis as a whole, or at least to the sense
of one unified sector leading up to a common center. Growth could
occur radially outward, and future change would be accomplished
with less difficulty than in the compact pattern, since densities would
be lower and open land would back up each strip of development.
The principal problems with this form are probably those of circumferential movement, of potential congestion at the core and along the
main radials, and of the wide dispersion of the pattern as it recedes
from the original center.

The ring

In the foregoing, the most discussed alternatives for metropolitan
growth have been given in a highly simplified form. Other possibilities certainly exist—e.g., the compact high-density core pattern

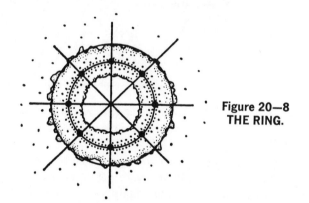

**Figure 20—8
THE RING.**

might be turned inside out, producing a doughnut-like form. In this
case the center would be kept open, or at very low density, while
high densities and special activities surround it, like the rim of a
wheel. The principal channels of the flow system would then be a
series of annular rings serving the high-intensity rim, supplemented
by a set of feeder radials that would converge at the empty center.
In fact, this is essentially a linear system, but one that circles back on
itself and is bypassed by the "spokes" crossing the "hub." This
system is well-adapted to public transportation, both on the ring
roads and the cross radials, while individual vehicles might be used
for circulation outside the rim.

Densities within the rim would have to be rather high, while those beyond the rim could be low. A system of weekend houses might also be effectively employed here. The central area could either be kept quite open or devoted to special uses at low densities. City-wide activities could be spotted round the rim in a series of intense centers, supplemented by linear patterns along the annular roadways. There would be no single dominant center but rather a limited number of strong centers (an aristocracy rather than a monarchy). These centers might also be specialized in regard to activity—finance, government, culture, etc.

This pseudo-linear form, like the radial tongues of the star plan, has the linear advantages: a high accessibility, both to services and to open land; a wide choice of habitat and location of activities; and a good foundation for efficient public transit. Congestion at any single center is avoided, yet there is a high concentration. In contrast to the galaxy or satellite form, the variety and strong character inherent in the specialized centers would have some hope of survival because of the relatively close proximity of these centers.

The visual image would be strong (though perhaps a little confusing because of its circularity), producing a particularly clear impression of the centers around the rim, in contrast to the central openness, and of their successive interconnections. The whole metropolis would seem more nearly like one community. One of the most difficult problems would be that of growth, since much development beyond the rim would soon blur the contour and require a new transportation system. A second concentric ring might be developed beyond the first, but it would negate some of the advantages of the first ring and would demand massive initiative by the central government to undertake its development. Another difficulty would be that of control. How can the belts of open land or the accessible center be kept free of building? Even if this problem were solved satisfactorily, a dilemma is also likely to arise in regard to the size of the ring: should it be small enough for the major centers to be in close proximity to one another or big enough to allow all the residences and other local activities to be related to it?

One classic example of this form exists, although on a very large scale—the ring of specialized Dutch cities that surround a central area of agricultural land, Haarlem, Amsterdam, Utrecht, Rotterdam, The Hague, and Leiden. This general pattern is now being rationalized and preserved as a matter of national policy in the Netherlands. In our own country, the San Francisco Bay region appears to be developing in this same direction.

The ring tends to be rather rigid and unadaptable as a form. It would require an extreme reshaping of the present metropolis, particularly with regard to transportation and the central business district; but it might dovetail with an observable trend toward emptying and abandoning the central areas. The plan could be modified by retaining a single major center, separated by a wide belt of open space from all other city-wide activities to be disposed along the rim. It may be noted that this use of open land in concentric belts ("green belts") is exactly opposite to its use as radial tongues in the star form.

THE OBJECTIVES OF METROPOLITAN ARRANGEMENT

Many other metropolitan forms are hypothetically possible, but the five patterns described (the sheet, the galaxy, the core, the star, and the ring) indicate the variation possible. One of the interesting results of the discussion is to see the appearance of a particular set of values as criteria for evaluating these forms. It begins to be clear that some human objectives are intimately connected with the physical pattern of a city, while others are very little affected by it. For example, there has been little discussion of the healthfulness of the environment or of its safety. Although these factors are influenced by the detailed design of the environment, such as the spacing of buildings or the provision for utilities, it is not obvious that the specific metropolitan pattern has any significant effect on them so long as we keep well ahead of the problems of pollution and supply. Psychological well-being, on the other hand, may be affected by the shape of the urban environment. But again, we are too ignorant of this aspect at present to discuss it further.

We have not referred to the efficiency of the environment in regard to production and distribution. This represents another basic criterion that probably is substantially affected by metropolitan pattern, but unfortunately no one seems to know what the effect is. "Pleasure" and "beauty" have not been mentioned, but these terms are nebulous and hard to apply accurately. A number of criteria have appeared, however, and it may well be worth while to summarize them. They might be considered the goals of metropolitan form, its fundamental objectives, either facilitated or frustrated in some significant way by the physical pattern of the metropolis.

The criterion of choice heads the list. As far as possible, the individual should have the greatest variety of goods, services, and facilities readily accessible to him. He should be able to choose the kind of habitat he prefers; he should be able to enter many kinds of environment at will, including the open country; he should have the maximum of personal control over his world. These advantages appear in an environment of great variety and of fine grain, one in which transportation and communication are as quick and effortless as possible. There may very likely be some eventual limit to the desirable increase of choice, since people can be overloaded by too many alternatives, but we do not as yet operate near that limit for most people. In practice, of course, to maximize one choice may entail minimizing another, and compromises will have to be made.

The ideal of personal interaction ranks as high as choice, although it is not quite so clear how the optimum should be defined. We often say that we want the greatest number of social contacts, so as to promote neighborliness and community organization, minimize segregation and social isolation, increase the velocity and decrease the effort of social exchange. And yet, while the evils of isolation are known, we are nevertheless beginning to see problems at the other end of the scale as well. Too much personal communication may cause breakdown, just as surely as too little. Even in moderate quantities, constant "neighborliness" can interfere with other valuable activities such as reflection, independent thought, or creative work. A high level of local community organization may mean civic indifference or intergovernmental rivalry when the large community is involved.

In this dilemma, a compromise could be found in saying that potential interaction between people should be as high as possible, as long as the individual can control it and shield himself whenever desired. His front door, figuratively speaking, should open on a bustling square, and his back door on a secluded park. Thus this ideal is seen as related to the ideal of choice.

Put differently, individuals require a rhythmical alternation of stimulus and rest-periods when personal interchange is high and to some degree is forced upon them, to be followed by other periods when stimulus is low and individually controlled. A potentially high level of interaction, individually controlled, is not the whole story; we also need some degree of spontaneous or unpremeditated exchange, of the kind that is so often useful in making new associations.

The goal of interaction, therefore, is forwarded by many of the same physical features as the goal of choice: variety, fine grain, efficient communication; but it puts special emphasis on the oscillation between stimulus and repose (centers of high activity versus quiet parks), and requires that communication be controllable. In addition, it calls for situations conducive to spontaneous exchange. Storehouses of communication, such as libraries or museums, should be highly accessible and inviting, their exterior forms clearly articulated and expressive of their function.

These two objectives of choice and interaction may be the most important goals of metropolitan form, but there are others of major importance, such as minimum first cost and minimum operating cost. These seem to depend particularly on continuous occupation along the major transportation channels, on a balanced use of the flow system, both in regard to time and direction of flow, a moderately high structural density, and a maximum reliance on collective transport.

Objectives of comfort, on the other hand, related principally to a good climate, the absence of distracting noise, and adequate indoor and outdoor space, may point either toward generally lower densities or toward expensive ameliorative works, such as sound barriers, air conditioning, and roof-top play areas. The important goal of individual participation may also indicate lower densities and an environment that promotes an active relation between an individual and his social and physical milieu, thus giving him a world that to some extent he can manage and modify by his own initiative.

We must also consider that the urban pattern will necessarily shift and expand, and therefore it is important to ask whether the adjustment to new functions will be relatively easy, and whether growth, as well as the initial state, is achievable with a minimum of control and central initiative and intervention. Adaptability to change seems to be greater at lower densities, since scattered small structures are readily demolished or converted. Both an efficient transport system and some form of separation of one kind of activity from another are also conducive to flexibility. Discontinuous forms like the galaxy or the ring require special efforts to control growth, for these patterns raise problems such as the appearance of squatters and the preservation and use of intervening open land.

Stability is a somewhat contradictory goal; it takes into account the critical social and economic costs of obsolescence, movement of population, and change of function. It is very possible that stability in the modern world will be impossible to maintain, and it runs counter to many of the values cited above. Yet stability may be qualified in this light: if change is inevitable, then it should be moderated and controlled so as to prevent violent dislocations and preserve a maximum of continuity with the past. This criterion would have important implications as to how the metropolis should grow and change.

Finally, there are many aesthetic goals the metropolis can satisfy. The most clear-cut is that the metropolis should be "imageable," that is, it should be visually vivid and well structured; its component parts should be easily recognized and easily interrelated. This objective would encourage the use of intensive centers, variety, sharp grain (clear outlines between parts), and a differentiated but well-patterned flow system.

THE RELATION OF FORMS TO GOALS

We have now treated a number of objectives that are crucial, that are on the whole rather generally accepted, and that seem to be significantly affected by the pattern of the metropolis: the goals of choice, interaction, cost, comfort, participation, growth and adaptability, continuity, and imageability. Other goals may develop as we increase our knowledge of city form. What even these few imply for city form is not yet obvious; moreover, they often conflict, as when interaction and cost appear to call for higher densities, while comfort, participation, and adaptability achieve optimal realization at lower levels. Nevertheless, we have immediate decisions to make regarding the growth of urban areas, and if we marshall our goals and our alternatives as best we can, we can the better make these decisions.

The clarifying of alternatives and objectives has an obvious value, for this will permit public debate and the speculative analysis of the probable results of policy as related to any given form. Yet this kind of approach will soon reach a limit of usefulness unless it is supported by experimental data. Such experimentation is peculiarly difficult in regard to so large and complex an organism as a metropolis. To some degree we can form judgments drawn from such different urban regions as Los Angeles, Stockholm, and Paris, but these judgments are necessarily distorted by various cultural and environmental disparities. Possibly we can study certain partial aspects of city form, such as the effects of varying density or the varying composition of centers, but the key questions pertain to the metropolitan pattern as an operating whole. Since we cannot build a metropolis purely for experimental purposes, we can only build and test models, with some simplified code to designate pattern. By simulating basic urban functions in these models, tests might be run for such criteria as cost, accessibility, imageability, or adaptability. Such tests will be hard to relate to the real situation, and it is difficult to see how certain objectives (such as interaction or participation) can be tested, yet this technique is our best current hope for experimental data on the implications of the total metropolitan pattern.

DYNAMIC AND COMPLEX FORMS

Until we have such experimental data, what can we conclude from our imaginary juxtaposition of metropolitan form and human goals?

Each of the alternatives proposed has its drawbacks, its failures in meeting some basic objectives. A radical, consistent dispersion of the metropolis appears to restrict choice, impair spontaneous inter-action, entail high cost, and inhibit a vivid metropolitan image. A galaxy of small communities promises better, but would still be substandard as regards choice, interaction, and cost, besides being harder to realize. A recentralization of the metropolis in an intensive core appears to entail almost fatal disadvantages in cost, comfort,

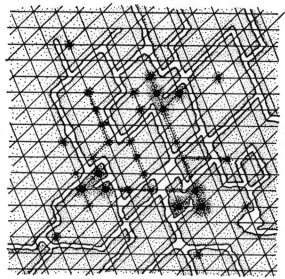

Figure 20—9
THE POLYCENTERED
NET.

individual participation, and adaptability. The rationalization of the old metropolis in a star would work better if central congestion could be avoided and free accessibility maintained, but this form is less and less usable as size increases. The ring has many special advantages but raises great difficulties in cost, adaptability, and continuity with present form.

Of course, these are all "pure" types that make no concessions to the complications of reality and they have been described as though they were states of perfection to be maintained forever. In actuality, a plan for a metropolis is more likely to be a complex and mixed one, to be realized as an episode in some continuous process, whose form involves rate and direction of change as well as a momentary pattern.

For example, let us consider, on the basis of the little we know, a form that might better satisfy our aspirations, if we accept the fact of metropolitan agglomeration: this form is in essence a variant of the dispersed urban sheet. Imagine a metropolis in which the flow system becomes more specialized and complex, assuming a triangular grid pattern that grows at the edges and becomes more specialized in the interior. Many types of flow would be provided for. Densities would have a wide range and a fine grain, with intensive peaks at junctions in the circulation system and with linear concentrations along major channels, but with extensive regions of low density inside the grid. Through the interstices of this network belts and tongues of open land would form another kind of grid. Thus the general pattern would resemble a fishermen's net, with a system of dispersed centers and intervening spaces.

City-wide activities would concentrate in these knots of density, which would be graded in size. In the smaller centers the activities would not be specialized but the larger centers would be increasingly dominated by some special activity. Therefore the major centers would be highly specialized—although never completely "pure"— and would be arranged in a loose central cluster, each highly accessible to another.

A metropolis of twenty million might have, not one such cluster, but two or three whose spheres of influence would overlap. These clusters might be so dense as to be served by transportation grids organized in three dimensions, like a skeletal framework in space. Elsewhere, the network would thin out and adapt itself to local configurations of topography. This general pattern would continue to specialize and to grow, perhaps in a rhythmically pulsating fashion. With growth and decay, parts of the whole would undergo periodic renewal. Such a form might satisfy many of the general criteria, but each particular metropolis is likely to encounter special problems. Even so, the description illustrates the complexity, the indeterminacy, and the dynamic nature of city form that are inherent in any such generalization.

Perhaps we can make such a proposal more concrete by stating it as a set of actions rather than as a static pattern. If this were the form desired, then the agencies of control would adopt certain definite policies. First, they would encourage continued metropolitan agglomeration. Second, they would begin to construct a generalized triangular grid of channels for transportation, adapting its interspacing and alignment to circumstances, but aiming at raising accessibility throughout the area as a whole. This grid would provide for many different kinds of flow and would have a hierarchy of its own—that is, the lines of circulation would be differentiated with respect to the intensity and speed of their traffic. Third, peaks of activity and density would be encouraged, but in sharply defined areas, not in rings whose density gradually declines from the center. The present metropolitan center would be encouraged to specialize and thus loosen into a cluster, while one or two major rival centers might develop elsewhere in the network, rather than allowing a general dispersal of city-wide activities. Such major specialized centers might be given even greater local intensity, with multi-level circulation, perhaps as a three-dimensional system of public rights-of-way.

Fourth, every effort would be made to retain, acquire, or clear a system of linked open spaces of generous size that pervaded the network. Fifth, a wide variety of activities, of accommodation and structural character, dispersed in a fine-grained pattern, would be encouraged. Once the concentration of special activities and the arrangement of higher densities in centers and along major channels had been provided for, then zoning and other controls would be employed only to maintain the minimum grain needed to preserve the character and efficiency of the various types of use and density, and large single-purpose areas would be avoided. Sixth, the form of centers, transportation channels, and major open spaces would be controlled so as to give as vivid a visual image as possible. Seventh, the agency would be committed to continuous rebuilding and re-organization of successive parts of the pattern.

Such a set of policies would mean a radical redirection of metropolitan growth. Whether this plan is feasible or worth the cost would require serious consideration. Even if this pattern were chosen, there would still be many crucial questions of relative emphasis and timing to be weighed. If life in the future metropolis is to be worthy of the massive effort necessary to build it, the physical pattern must satisfy human values. The coordination of metropolitan development, however obligatory, will not of itself ensure this happy result. Coordination must be directed toward some desired general pattern, and, to define this, we must clarify our alternatives and the goals they are meant to serve.

URBAN LIFE

The culture of urban America*

> "When a man is tired of London, he is tired of life."
>
> *Samuel Johnson*[1]

INTRODUCTION

It was an inquiring reporter, and he stopped one of three. "What is your opinion of contemporary American urban culture and its future?", he asked, now and again.

Said the young man with the green carnation in his buttonhole, "Nothing but roses. Did you catch Margo and Rudy the other night in their exquisite Romeo? Did you notice how the hippies tossed them flowers—anti-establishment flowers? Did you hear how much the Ford Foundation and the National Humanities Foundation are going to give to support dance next year? Soon we will teach dance in all the schools, and everyone will learn about ballet and crave to see it. And we will dance and dance and dance and spend and spend and spend—I don't go so far as to look for a choreographer President—but oh my!"

Said the balding taxi driver, "Lousier every day. It isn't only the traffic jams and the well-dressed muggers and the group riders who won't tip. The wife and I look at a lot of television, and it's getting weaker every night. There's practically no wrestling anymore, or

* Reprinted from ENVIRONMENT AND CHANGE edited by William Ewald Jr., by permission of Indiana University Press.

1. Samuel Johnson. *Life of Johnson* (Boswell) Vol. VI, Ch. IX (1777).

prize fights; the things you could count on regularly like *Perry Mason* and *Have Gun Will Travel* are disappearing. The other week they shelved a lot of good stuff for four nights to spiel about the Warren Commission. Who cares? And all those Ebans and Goldbergs at the UN! Phooie!"

Said the prosperous subdivider hastening to cut the ribbon on another bulldozer, "How could it be better? The population's growing, isn't it? And all those babies have to live somewhere, don't they? We have some troubles with the conservationists, but we can handle them. And we're getting more professional all the time. Have you seen any of our late-model purple-tiled bathrooms, or our cookouts, or our front door bell that plays Annie Laurie, or the new little green plaza in Sunshine Acres with sculpture, yet?"

Said the resident of Mill Valley,[2] "I see nothing but threats to the Marin County Way of Life. It isn't only the subdividers. We know how to keep them down to our standards of not more than $3\frac{1}{2}$ families per acre. But there are all those other people who want to come in here and leave us a lot of unused land but increase our density with high-risers. Imagine that! What will happen to our way of life if we have a lot of old people and childless families around here, even if they have managed to stay married for forty years? We've got to stop all this immigration, that's all. And if the San Franciscans think they are going to get any of our money to get them out of their troubles, they are crazy. Probably the Anguillans really have something.[3] Oh, of course we all go over there every day."

Said the engineer carrying blueprints and a black box, "I'm glad you asked. A lot of people have been clobbering us with the accusation that we don't care what we do to the countryside. Well, let me tell you that is not the attitude of the Highway Department. Of course, our main job is to give the people what they want at a cost they can afford. What they want is more lanes going more places. Most of them don't want all this prettification that the planners and the architectural nuts write about. And if they did, they couldn't afford it. I'm a bird watcher myself. If there were money for it, I'd be glad to specify beauty in. For instance, we can't do much planting because we can't afford to maintain it. Today I picked up some plastic flowers. Look at them, mister. Highway beauty's on the way."[4]

2. A small suburb in Marin County, California, north of San Francisco, which likes to believe it has a special way of life.

3. For those with short memories, these were the secessionists of the Antilles.

4. Plastic flowers are no joke. Not only do they exist, as we all know, but engineers are speculating about them; or so the *San Francisco Chronicle* asserts.

Said the lean, clean, long-limbed man with the brown face, "I'm afraid there isn't much hope, really. My club has been pretty effective up to now in stopping bad things that might invade the wilderness anywhere, and that means practically everything.[5] But we don't win them all, and every natural resource lost is one never to be regained. But there are worse difficulties with the ones we've saved. Look at the Yosemite Valley. Think of the future of the Point Reyes Seashore.[6] We saved that, but now too many humans are going to want to go there. It's been made too easy. And too many humans are going to mean too few birds, or the wrong kinds. But we don't know how to stop these people—we want to be democratic about it and are opposed to a nature-test qualification for a ticket. And we don't know how to stop the bishops from giving all this bad advice, either, so there will be more and more people to foul up no more wilderness. What has the wilderness got to do with the city? Well, more than you think.[7] Sorry, I've got to run to stop a power plant."

Said the Ford worker who had just bought his second General Motors car: "This is a great culture, and it's getting better. I turn up bolts on an assembly line. They've got an automatic machine about ready to do it, but I can arrange to watch the machine. And Walter's going to get us all $25,000 a year guaranteed annual wage. How can you beat that? Of course, there'll be a lot of spare time, but let the writers worry about that. I can probably find another job to keep from being bored. Maybe I won't be bored anyway, what with beer and bowling. Maybe I'll even invent a machine."

Said the young black drop-out: "It never has been any good, and it ain't about to get better. I never had much of a job, and I haven't got any now. Nobody's talking about paying me $25,000 to sit on my fanny. The only fun I get is to burn something, and the only way for me to get anywhere is to burn it all down and then maybe something will happen. It couldn't be worse. Anyway, looting nights is fun, isn't they?"

Said the incumbent mayor, "I look for great things from the federal government next year."

Said the opposition candidate, "Less is better."

We are all blind men trying to describe an elephant. What we think about American urban culture depends upon where we sit. It takes a great deal of gall for any one person to propose that he knows

---

5. I might be thinking of the Sierra Club, and again, I might not. It is, however, the most ruthless and therefore the most successful conservationist group. On balance it deserves much praise, as does the organization *Cry California*.

6. A fine piece of wild beach and bird refuge just north of San Francisco, eloquently memorialized by Ansel Adams and Nancy Newhall in *Island in Time*.

7. And he was right as right could be.

much about it, has seen much of it, or has seen with unprejudiced eyes.

When I was a lad, we were told to avoid writing in the first person. It was considered to be pretentious egotism. This was bad advice. As a lesser consequence, it was probably responsible for many bad writing styles, such as Pentagonese.[8] But it concealed a greater danger. The real egotism ran the other way. By the use of the third person, writers were able to conceal their personalities and present their work as objective, scholarly, and of universal import. I shall avoid this from time to time.

THE STATUS OF OUR URBAN CULTURE

American urban culture is obviously the summation of an enormous variety of subcultures. We have to cope with the details sooner or later. Few of us have any real perception of many. It is probably easier to conjecture the truth about the coming of age in Samoa after a serious sojourn there than after a comparable effort in Hollywood or Watts, even if a comparable effort is, in fact, possible. As Doctor Johnson said, "Nobody can write the Life of a man, but those who have eat and drunk and lived in social intercourse with him." We ought to be suspicious of "China experts" who have never been to Cathay and have to read Confucius and Mao in translation.

I am not a teenage Negro dropout, and have never had a visceral sense of poverty. I can photograph the beards and the bangles and the beads and the bells of Haight-Ashbury[9] and even wander on the fringes of it, but I cannot really understand it, and should not pretend that I think it is all good fun when the natives hold up my car. I cannot do much better with the other, possibly less important set of parasites, the jet set. Observation is possible; interpretation is tricky; generalization is dangerous; prophecy is absurd. Prophets, however, are safe. The world forgets what they guessed wrong and remembers in gratitude the times when they were prescient.

This will surely be clear to each of us if we consider recent writing by pontiffs we know. It is a common trick to compare fairly solid data of today with shaky or nonexistent data from yesteryear. Some use this method to show how much we have improved; others, how much we have deteriorated; others, including me, to suggest how nearly we have come to standing still. It is a common fallacy to use history as what we choose to remember. I happen to agree with

8. E.g., "It is not believed that."
9. Haight-Ashbury is a district in San Francisco which has presumably become nationally notorious as the Mecca of the hippies. The word is bells. There are no belles.

Montaigne about the cat, and am prone to overlook the occasional historical details which might make me think otherwise.

But our condition is quite as difficult when we leave history out altogether. Several equally intelligent, equally serious, equally honest men can deal with essentially the same data and draw conflicting conclusions. Within three months, I have encountered papers of this sort on housing; the future of neighborhoods; whether there is or is not a Negro crisis; whether there is or is not a "cultural boom." The interpretations most of us choose to make are much like what we do when we select what we want to remember from history. Those pundits who reinforce our opinions are the "sound" ones, though we may concede others to be bright. Intellectuals who scold tycoons for reading only *The Wall Street Journal* ought to reexamine their own reading lists. All of us may be all too prone to read what we like to hear. We are, after all, human beings. This is not a bad thing if we can remember it from time to time.

In such circumstances, though, we need many more dispassionate articles, reviewing the literature, than we are getting. Writing them is not a fashionable exercise, nor one likely to win promotion, since it is regarded as unoriginal. Reviews of the literature can be done successfully only by the wisest and most experienced scholars. They are worse than useless if done by hacks. But doing them seldom appeals to the wise or the experienced.[10] It is just a lot easier and more applauded to drone on over new tables and charts, or if one is endowed with literacy, as few social scientists and fewer planners really are, to engage in polemics and predictions of disaster. So the needed literature is sparse; and it becomes more sparse in direct proportion to the number of conferences and panels the scholar attends.

What I am suggesting is that even our most famous social interpreters need to be read skeptically and examined as to their credentials every step of the way. Each may have experienced much less than he seems to profess. Each may be more valuable as a poet than as an observer, as an observer than as a philosopher, as a philosopher than as a prophet. As things are, it is not impossible that novelists may give us better insights than statisticians, Zola more than the Lynds; in turn it may be so that social scientists with sensitively tuned radars like Daniel Lerner or Harold Isaacs may come nearer the truth than the data processors. But of course we do not know this for sure; and there are not many such men around;

10. Nathan Glazer, "Housing Problems and Housing Policies," in *The Public Interest*, Number 7, Spring, 1967, pp. 21 and following, has provided a model of what such things should be, though his piece is not technically a review of the literature.

while whom among them to believe may, again, become a matter of personal taste.

This does not lead me to despair. I cannot accept it as a plea to defer major investments in cities until we "know." We may never "know." We can hope for more and better studies. We can hope for more sympathetic attention to many of the details of our subcultures, comparable to those which have been lavished on the family of Sanchez or a village in the Vaucluse. Such studies may be harder to make because the cultures we need to know about are only marginally exotic, and the telephone is too near, and the jet plane to Washington too easy to board. The marginal stranger-student may be less welcome in Watts or Marin County than in Gilgit or Timbuktu. The fact remains that we need more and better studies; that we need them now; that, in the meantime, we need to be wary of generalizations; and that we are not going to get them now.

But this is not an argument for postponement of action. I was astonished to read that Lewis Mumford had urged the Congress to wait for five years before spending big money so that research might be done. Surely not much more can be expected to be known by then in a society where change often outmodes a study before it is published. The urban landscape is burning now, and we need hoses now. We may even have to risk that a few will carry gasoline, not water, which is, of course, a gross hyperbole for the sort of failures that might ensue.

What I mean to have said here is that we need to be wary of sweeping propositions about American urban culture; that we need much more serious studies of all the component cultures than we now have; that we must not wait for these studies to engage in massive efforts in our city. We could not possibly be flying so blind, for example, as the makers of foreign policy.

The Secretary of State talks almost scornfully of niggardly senators who hesitate to spend a mere 1 percent of our GNP on foreign aid; and the Secretary of Defense has no doubt that the much larger percentages spent in Vietnam are something the nation can easily endure in stride. I would like to see some leader, preferably the President, assert that the urban problem has more priority than space exploration and at least as much priority as foreign aid, and back up this homily by asking for the corresponding money. I would like this, even though I should not expect him to get it from Congress, or the public to approve a Congress which gave it to him.[11]

Were such a miracle to occur, and were planners and other urban architects suddenly to be endowed with this embarrassment of

11. Note the derision with which the House initially disposed of the "Rat" Bill.

riches, they would certainly have to fly without many instruments. The one prediction I can safely make is that it will be decades at least—and maybe never—before there will be a science of city planning and urban design in any way comparable to the science which predicts the course of a spacecraft after it leaves Cape Kennedy, or for that matter designs a spacecraft which is almost certain to get off the pad and fly true.[12] In the meantime, urban experiments on the large scale cannot wait for that great day. They should be as amply financed as rockets, and there should be no moanings of dismay when they fail, as some of them will.

The risk in such a bold course is that a few opinionated men (of like opinion) might cluster around to prepare a standard program of the sort which has so circumscribed our public housing in the United States. For as long as I should think anyone would dare foresee, our cities are going to consist of a multitude of highly mobile groups for whom quite different satisfactions must be provided and who are a little more likely to stay put if the satisfactions satisfy *them* rather than the man who planned them. So the urban programs must be as diverse as the urban necessities, the experiments as wideranging. I would hope that people appointed to the planning task would approach it, not on the defensive, but with a sense of personal humility and lack of confidence in other pundits. I would hope they could add something more difficult in what is, at bottom, a humorless nation—to wit, a feeling of gayety. Gayety is not the same thing as levity, and gayety is not inappropriate to a serious problem. There is nothing more radiant than a person or a city that smiles.

Rapid transit, for example, will be better when the designers learn to watch the people as carefully as the statistics. This is not easy. You may never have felt the need to tote several bulky and heavy bags from one airline to another at Kennedy International via the airport bus. It may seem extraordinary that anyone would. But if you board the bus, you can see that people do, and wonder why the bus was not designed, as it easily could have been, to make this journey easier. It must now approach a gruesome experience. You do not have to carry the bag to notice the problem, but you probably have to ride the bus. You will not see it in a taxicab, and you may miss it as well from Parnassus. So for every other element of urban design.

12. It may be possible, of course, to apply tough-minded operations analysis to some more primitive but as yet unresolved problems such as the design and control of traffic flow; but in matters of urban joy, the questions seem as yet too subtle to be resolved by digital responses and quite unprepared for more sophisticated computer treatments, if, indeed, they ever can be prepared on anything other than a statistical basis, which will clamp a sort of supply and demand gauntlet on the future of urban joy for most of us.

To argue for experiencing the individual's experience is not the same thing as asking him what he thinks he would like to experience and building a program on that. It may be good to know what he does not like in his present experience and what he likes, but a diminution of the one and augmentation of the other may offer too limited a projection.

I am quite sure that grass-roots consensus must come after the event and not before. You can be as hypersensitive and romantic as you want to be about the grass roots, but if you are realistic you will know that lots of the grass is neither long nor green. The great things in our great cities have come from the courageous, often dictatorial, decisions of individuals. When things have come out well, they have been approved after the event. Regretfully, from Central Park to Rockefeller Center, they have been more widely approved than emulated.

If one were to try to create a new Central Park by an enormous land-taking, even in another borough of New York, and were to have a pre-taking plebiscite, I think any of us can guess that the verdict would be a resounding "no". We can see examples of this all around us. The Bay Area Rapid Transit District,[13] for example, is allowed to take the land necessary for a station and its "needed" parking lots and the like, but "need" does not include plazas or other urban amenities. This is short-sighted, but it is the general view: millions for concrete but not a cent for fountains. It is much the view of the possibly aprocryphal banker from Fort Worth who snorted that he did not want to conduct business in a palm garden.[14]

On the other hand, suppose there were to be a plebiscite on turning Central Park over to developers with great tax advantages to the citizens. It might be hard to predict that the people even of the Borough of Manhattan, who gain the most from the Park, would vote to keep it, despite the support of *The New York Times*. But we can guess, I am sure, that the vote for keeping it would be much greater than the vote for establishing another, much as another is surely needed by Greater New York.

My conclusions from this set of musings are that we do not know enough about our subcultures to be wise about them or perhaps even sympathetic to them; that we need much more sensitive explorations of them both in quantity and in quality; that we cannot, however, wait until the returns are in; that we need national

---

13. The district was established to serve Contra Costa, Alameda, and San Francisco Counties with Marin County and San Mateo County abstaining.

14. This is supposed to have been said when he was opposing Victor Gruen's design for downtown Fort Worth. Apocrypha are often more truthful than the truth.

expenditures on our cities in amounts comparable to those on foreign aid, space, and war, and with at least as high a priority; that when we come to spend such sums much will have to be spent intuitively and therefore cannot be entrusted to the intuition of any one group, however noble its sentiments and strong its convictions; that we will need a great diversification of ideas to meet the needs of the subcultures; that the experiments will need to be on a large scale and costly; that they will be much criticized at every stage; that one should seek consensual approval after the demonstrations rather than grass-roots agreement in advance;[15] that those who do this planning will need imagination, courage, tenacity, humility and a considerable sense of humor. Planning the good life should be entrusted to those who, themselves, have a relish for it, and not to those who enjoy it only vicariously under the lamp.

Having thus slipped into the sort of generalizations I deplore, let me try again. I must begin to limit my scope by saying that it is presently idle to talk about a national urban culture. I hope it always will be.

THE UBIQUITY OF OUR URBAN CULTURE

There are some American traits, not, to be sure, universal, which are widely enough held to be observed from north to south and from coast to coast so that they may be called characteristic. Most of these have been pointed out long ago by shrewd observers from de Tocqueville to Bryce and Lasky, and there is little need to recapitulate them at length. Probably we still act as though it were more interesting to conquer nature than to live with her; we are still painfully belligerent and painfully pious about our belligerence; we are still frugal and suspicious of exuberance in dress or language or architecture; we are even suspicious of those who display good public or literary manners; we are humorless; we are unsure about art and artists; we would like to believe that men around the cracker barrel have more common sense than the experts; we remain hostile to the notion of national decisions about local matters. We still look for a frontier to which we can escape from the damage we, ourselves, have wrought; but we are capable of great, even heroic, effort when the occasion seems to arise. But we are also a little prone, like the Australians, to wait until the fire is really big enough to be worth

15. Note that the word is *agreement*. Advice should be sought and listened to in the neighborhoods, of course. However, the notion, often advanced in depressed areas scheduled for redevelopment, that the people who live there should control the decisions, is unrealistic. They are, as of now, quite unprepared to make good ones.

fighting before assembling to put it out. For most of us money is, if not the measure of all things, at least the measure of competence. The market place is still the preferred test of meaning.

In this value system we know there are regional differences. Southerners may be more belligerent, for example, than northerners. Some parts of our land are more responsive to artists than other parts; in some there is less suspicion of literacy than in others. But still the attitudes remain broadly the same. The differences between rural and urban attitudes, though, may no longer be significant. Not only is the city the dominant American culture, statistically. The city itself is largely rural in composition.

This does not apply only to the immigrants in the new ghettos; it applies to suburbs and to large numbers of people living downtown who, in their hearts, are silently crooning, "Why oh, why, oh why oh, why did we ever leave OHIO?" There are more hicks strolling on Broadway than are to be found in Keokuk and a good many of the hicks live, not in Iowa, but in one or another of the boroughs.

Each of the positions may have been somewhat softened by time and experience. de Tocqueville stated the early case about the American and nature with eloquence.[16] Our attitude, or at least our relation to nature, has been somewhat improved by zealous individual and organizational conservationists from Gifford Pinchot to the Sierra Club. But the struggle continues to be an uphill one, harassed by tax interrogators, confronted by recent glamor governors who have openly said that a tree is a tree is a tree and that once you have seen one, you have seen them all. Since de Tocqueville's assessment we have made great national and state parks. The total of national land under national control today is about one-third of all the acreage. We have even reforested some of the devastated strip-mined slopes of West Virginia. Despite large gains, the basic posture is unchanged. We will defer the landscaping of the highway but get the asphalt laid. A straight line remains for us the shortest distance between two points, especially at several million dollars a mile. It is easier to build a new town than to refrain from cutting a nice old one in two. The cost of only a handful of miles of California highway would pay for all the landscaping of 75 miles in the communities served by the Bay Area Rapid Transit District, but this switch is unlikely to be made.

The Yosemite Valley has become hideous. It is overcrowded by

16. "The Americans themselves ... are insensible to the wonders of inanimate nature, and they may be said not to perceive the mighty forests that surround them till they fall beneath the hatchet. Their eyes are fixed upon another sight; the American people views its own march across these wilds, draining swamps, turning the course of rivers, peopling solitudes and subduing nature."

people who have brought city habits and banalities with them; their radios blare the Beatles in unison, and this has sent the wild life high-tailing into the highwayless wilderness. The day may come when that obscene urban bird, the pigeon, will be the only survivor on the valley floor, taking it over as it has taken over Union Square.[17]

On the one hand we have a stronger force to prevent further erosion of our limited natural resources and domains; on the other hand we have greater demands for them, and corruption moves as fast as acquisition. It is hard to imagine anything more than a gentle linear projection of present mildly favorable trends, by no means likely to match the population curve.[18] It is not a thrilling prospect. The result is certain to be too little and too late, and a technique for fairly rationing the urban exoduses is almost certain to be demanded. Wilderness redevelopment is not impossible, but it can never be as fast as urban redevelopment and development.

Of the other subjects, much the same can be said. The exception is probably that of piety in foreign policy, which seems to continue to be non-partisan and interdenominational no matter whose sancti-mony is being displayed. Even here there is a gentle wind of dissent. It does not seem about to blow a gale. In all our other traits there may have been a gentle melioration in what might, with trepidation, be called more sensible and sensitive directions. A few of us are now willing to approve the antics of very strange people in our midst. There is a little more attention to the arts by the White House than perhaps there has been between Thomas Jefferson and John F. Kennedy.[19] The President can keep an adviser on the arts. There can be a National Council and a National Foundation though their budgets are smaller than the cost of a sophisticated military aircraft. But I fear this still remains a fragile element in the national budget. No one is going to be elected to the Congress through his sponsorship

17. Another San Francisco allusion. There are too many of them in this paper. It only goes to show the impact the area has on a fifty year New Englander who has been here only a short time; there is something absolutely fascinating about Baghdad on the Bay, the City which cannot make up its mind whether it most admires Babie Doe Tabor or Madame de Sevigné. Oh yes, Union Square is the most downtown of the squares, fronted by most of the airline ticket offices, a major hotel, and some of the most expen-sive stores, and perching on top of a very useful parking garage. It is no Place Vendôme or Piazza San Marco.

18. There are certainly some upper limits on what more can be done by the "Feds" given their already enormous holdings. The state by state count is even more spectacular:

Alaska 98%	Nevada 86%	Utah 67%	Idaho 64%
Oregon 52%	Wyoming 48%	Arizona 44%	California 44%

19. General Eisenhower's Sunday painting is not relevant. Fortunately, he seldom tried to interfere in aesthetic matters which he did not understand. This has happily been the usual situation. Think what catastrophes have been averted by the fact that Grant, Cleveland, McKinley, Coolidge, and Harding were not avid proponents of what they doubtless liked.

of the arts, and in a close election might be defeated if his opponent exposed the fact that he was a card-carrying art-lover. The national taste would still rather hear Senator Dirksen reciting "The Night Before Christmas."

I am pretty sure I am right about the public suspicion, even rejection, of establishment-art which, given the present antics of most art-dealers and many "movements," perhaps shows the public to have more sensitivity than the cognoscenti. Is there more to be made of a new thing for us, the sidewalk artist and the "paint-in"? Paul Goodman seems to think so:

There is an odd explosion in the arts, with an immense number of amateurs, of a kind of urban folk art in all genres. It is entirely unauthentic in style, combining misunderstood fragments of international culture with commercialized mountain music and stereotyped urban naturalism; yet it is authentic to the actual urban confusion. [20]

This accurate description may predict something good. Except for its possible cathartic value, I doubt it.

An increase in the number of specialists has no doubt increased the prestige of the specialist and decreased the prestige of the cracker-barrel philosopher, literally construed. But we have other cracker-barrels, in the clubs and groves where "common sense" reigns. Still, we must not be catty about this. There is an increase in the intelligent use of the specialist, and this may say something important to city planners and to the future of education in city planning.

The hope for a frontier in the sky or in the next outlying development or in the new remade downtown may be now merely vestigial, but I would not be too sure. In the next fifty years, though, I imagine hard facts will make it disappear, and this should improve the chance that planners might be seriously accepted and allowed to be influential in the thousands of cities where this is still not the case.

Local resistance to national requirements in the solution of national problems is likely to diminish, if only because there is an increasing local dependence on what is ludicrously called federal financial support, because the piper is likely to have his tunes called by the one who pays. The ironic point of this is that it is, of course, the locals who supply the federal funds, and that the only reason they are not collected locally is that the local politicians have for a long time had no stomach for a direct encounter with the people on the cost of government. When a mayor gloats to his constituents that he has wheedled 90 per cent of it out of the federal government, he should be fooling no one. There are only a few communities in America where this kind of money grows on trees. But I can see no

20. Paul Goodman, *Like a Conquered Province* (New York: Random House, 1967).

reason for this ritual dance to be changed much as the years go by.[21]

In any event, the national tune-caller has advantages to us as well as disadvantages. The main advantage is that better advice will be obtained by communities which are unwilling to pay for or unable to command the services of the best professionals. That is no trivial number of communities. The main disadvantage is that such big organizations tend to get thin as one moves away from the top, especially in a system where security of employment is a sine qua non. But there is also the equally dangerous probability that it will accelerate the decay of regional differences. The leveling forces, the standardizing pressures of national production and distribution and national communications are incessant. So we have moved much farther along the road of a uniform national culture than de Crevecoeur anticipated, and farther than men such as Goodman like:

> Anarchism is grounded in a rather definite social-psychological hypothesis; that forceful, graceful and intelligent behavior occurs only when there is an uncoerced and direct response to the physical and social environment; that in most human affairs, more harm than good results from compulsion, top-down direction, bureaucratic planning, pre-ordained curricula, jails, conscription, states.[22]

This is an eloquent description of a deep-rooted American instinct. As a curb to "mindless" big government, it has value; as a way of life, it is impossible.

THE HETEROGENEITY OF OUR URBAN CULTURE

Still, no sensitive observer who gets around much can really believe that there is a consistent national style. The images evoked by Boston, Washington, Miami, Chicago, St. Louis, Dallas, Denver, Salt Lake City, San Francisco, Los Angeles, Seattle, Honolulu, and Fairbanks are not the same; nor are they merely legendary or mythical; they are not even solely the result of different stages of development, although I suppose every city has to go through its Ruggles of Red Gap stage, and some are still in it. In these thirteen cities and in New York, Philadelphia, Pittsburgh, Baltimore, and Portland as well, there is by no means a uniform distribution of highbrows: nor an equal affection or disaffection for them; the existence of wealth and its open display is not equally admired; the dominant religious expressions are very different; the power elites are differently composed; the approved modes of dress are different as is

21. In the first place, it would be very hard to reverse the situation even if some brave mayor dared to try.
22. See Paul Goodman.

the tolerance for deviation from the approved; the best seller lists are different; the extent of visits by distinguished foreign performers of all kinds varies, as does the importance of the local professional baseball team; some regions use Mrs. Kennedy to raise money for charity, others prefer Danny Kaye; some are interested in second-class dukes divorced from their duchies; there are differences in the refinement of language, in the accent, in the topics of animated conversation, in the attitudes toward pornography or toward drinking before the sun is over the yardarm; the contents of the newspapers are different; the approved columnists from local gossip mongers to national Cassandras vary; and among the Cassandras some prefer the liberals and some the tories.

These and other similar traits are no doubt more noticeable in the middle to lower upper brow cultures. But if professors are high brows, then the differences among the high brows are also real. The contrast between the styles of Cambridge and New Haven is at once noticeable, although the scholarly values are more nearly held in common. But these two societies look alike when contrasted with the styles of, say, New York, Charlottesville, Chicago, Minneapolis, Houston, Fargo, and Berkeley. You do not have to have been long on the west coast after living in the east to notice the differences and believe that they are real. Nor do you have to decide which one is better or whether any one is better until you have to decide where to live.

Whether there are so many differences at the level of the Bonanza Culture or the culture of the genuinely poor, I would naturally not know. I suspect there are differences, but perhaps fewer and less dramatic. Still, if the upper culture affects the lower and not the other way around, there is no reason to suspect that these cultural differences will change very soon. And I am not disposed to dismiss them as trivial.

There will, perhaps, be a tide to wash away the little things. There might be even less lag, for example, in the national adoption of fashions of all kinds, whether in dress or in architecture, thanks to the instantaneous distribution of national news and picture magazines and network television. Even here there are at least time lags. By the time the skirts are really short in Portland Oregon, they will be quite long in London and then get a little shorter as you go west, just as at the moment they get a little longer.

The fashions in architecture are more easily adopted now since climatic conditions are taken as less determining than they once were, thanks to an abundant technology which on the face of it makes it possible to do anything given enough technical aid. This is undoubtedly a delusion, but it is widely held; and we can expect, on the one hand, that our downtowns will look more and more alike and, on the other hand, that our residential areas will on the whole become more and more eclectic. (You can be just as eclectic about the architecture of Sea Ranch as about the architecture of the Petit Trianon or the Parson Capen house.) Thus the visual evidence may suggest a considerable ironing out of regional differences, although local botany will perhaps always betray the camouflage. But even so, the visual evidence may be a mirage.

Here, then, is a limitation in talking about a national urban culture today. It exists only in part. In fifty years. . . ? Probably more things will be the same, yet perhaps there will also be more dissent, and it may be more vocal. I can only hope that things will not be too much the same. The problem is much the same as that of emulation, preservation, restoration. On the one hand, romantic insistence on maintaining the Texas way of life against all comers will not work unless the Texas way becomes the American way. On the other hand, one ought to hope that enough unsentimental differences could be noted. It would be a pity if, in the process of trying to make everything up to date in Kansas City, the updaters could think only of emulating New York, which they will never be able to succeed in doing. The New York style is not merely a consequence of its size. The maintenance of reasonable regional differences offers a considerable challenge to planners. If they are unable to detect the differences and to foster them at the regional level, they are quite unlikely to be sympathetic to the less palpable but equally important diversity, which, in my view, is essential to the good life of a single city.

CENTRAL CITY CULTURE

Surely I should long ago have said what I mean by the city. I mean the whole metropolis and even the megalopolis. Its primary characteristic and significance for us today, measured in cultural terms, is that it envelops a large number of people who can, with more or less ease, travel to the wide variety of encounters they wish to make with schooling, with work, with political and social action, with merchandise, with entertainment and recreation. The number of people is presumed to be large enough to make it at least statistically possible for the congeries to support activities and merchandise which only a small percentage of the population wants. If the city does not offer these opportunities, its size is meaningless, even a disaster. If it makes it too hard to reach the desired places, then they may cease to be desired. No matter how great the urge, there is some point at which the doctrine of *per aspera* falls down.

Looked at in these terms, it seems clear that the old stereotypes will not do. There is not a central city in which all the sophistication and much of the true affluence and patronage resides. The suburb is not only the home of the barbecue and the golf club; the grey area is not mainly the support of the pin ball and the numbers racket. Even the new peripheral plasmoids are harder to categorize. For a time they could be symbolized by the supermarket, the communal Bendix, the drive-in movie, the shrimp in the rough, and the car-hop for a lot of families who were so well adjusted and so adjustable that they could swing across the country from one tract house to another without dropping a stitch or in any real sense losing a neighbor. I doubt this is valid anymore, much as I am depressed by the sight of the new Palo Alto electricians, whose grey flannel suits consist of shiny narrow metal attache cases and sleeveless white shirts. Even they too seem to travel somewhere sometime for something other than the call of professional work or a visit to the nearest bowling alley and hamburger parlor.

If it were still necessary to think of the central city as the only place to which we would repair for many of the most important marginal cultural needs, then the distinction between the central city and the rest on the basis of its role as a culture-diffuser might be tenable. It is still tenable if it collects on a daily working basis, those who hold the culture of the metropolis.

I suspect this is still so and is likely to remain so. But it may not be relevant to the needs of the consumers of culture. Central City, for them, is no longer necessarily central, since centrality must be measured in time and not in miles. Lincoln Center might perhaps be as prosperous in Connecticut as in Manhattan, nearer perhaps to the center of gravity of patronage.

The vestigial elements of the old great downtowns, representing large investments of money and sentiment, can keep the activity alive so long as the investment is not destroyed or about to be destroyed by the wrecking ball. But this ball swings with ever increasing vigor in the American downtown, and when it begins to swing it is at least time to wonder whether the old cultural magnet belongs there any more, perhaps not even in the old city at all.

I am happy to be able to guess that large-scale electronic production and some mysterious and as yet unimagined distribution of exotic goods, or even their abolition altogether in favor of algae, will not meet the cultural needs of our people in the next fifty years, and that they will still want to do all the things they now do and many more, and not all by the now non-existent fireside. So Rosinante will still be on the road, and there will be adventures to be sought outside the home; I should think more rather than less. The question is where the road will lead those who have such objectives in mind.

In only a few cases of old and well stocked cities—practically all in the East or in cities where the strategic center remains downtown or in a few (how few) places like San Francisco where the sheer thrill of the place forces you to go downtown now and then, even if there is nothing much to do—only in these cases can I foresee a future of this sort for a revived downtown; and for those with great present advantages, it is going to be touch and go. For the rest, younger cities like Dallas or Los Angeles may in the end turn out to be holding the trump cards, even to having enough land to support an enormous and autonomous convention hotel. (The non-political convention, by the way, is a new phenomenon of American urban culture, more to be honored in the breach than in the observance, and by all means to be isolated from the daily lives of the citizens who are entitled to some protection.)

But all this redistribution of urban magnets is quite impossible to imagine in the present state of metropolitan political chaos. I would be quite pessimistic about the outcome of people's failures to be willing to hang together instead of hanging separately. Nonetheless, I expect the topic will be vigorously and wisely discussed in many other sessions, and I need not expose my ignorance or my prejudices on this topic, except to say that I am convinced that the urban culture of America's tomorrow will have to be defined in terms of at least the metropolitan culture and not in the terms of the culture of downtown.

Now that we have expanded the city, perhaps we can shrink the culture. Certainly I am not to be expected to deal with all the elements of city life that add up to culture. Lewis Mumford listed them brilliantly in his master-work of almost thirty years ago:

To describe the modern community, one would have to explore in detail the potentialities of life for modern man. In brief, the care of those whose labors and plans create the solid structure of the community's life must be to unite culture in all its forms; culture as the care of the earth; culture as the disciplined seizure and use of energy toward the economic satisfaction of man's wants; culture as the nurture of the body, as the begetting and bearing of children, as the cultivation of the human being's fullest capacities as a sentient, feeling, thinking, acting personality; culture as the transformation of power into policy, of experience into science and philosophy, of life into unity and significance of art, of the whole into that tissue of values that men are willing to die for rather than foreswear. . . . [23]

23. Lewis Mumford, "The Culture of Cities" (New York: Harcourt Brace, 1938), p. 492.

There could not be a better statement, nor one less possible for me to deal with, within the limits of my competence and my time. Fortunately, most of the questions appear slated for some discussion on some other meeting.

What then does he think he can talk about, you are more than ready to ask, and with some acerbity. I do not look for the solution in Aristotle: "the best way of life (for the majority of men) is one which consists in a mean, and a mean of the kind attainable by every individual."[24] I should find a computerized Benthamism, a better-engineered utopia, an unattractive denouement. Nor am I capable of Aristotelian or Platonic detachment. This might say of the city that "it grows for the sake of mere life, (but) it exists for the sake of a good life."[25] As a matter of fact, this is precisely what I shall in the end propose, but it would falsify Aristotle to suggest that by "good" I am going to mean what he means. Nor does Augustine help me. He is beyond my reach. "The love of self," he says, "even unto the contempt of God, made the earthly city, whereas the love of God, even unto the contempt of self, made the heavenly city."[26] Who could deny this, were he allowed to define God?

I can be concerned only about the earthly city of today and not the new Jerusalem of tomorrow, on some great come-and-get it day. Euripides has said it best for me, or at least Ernest Barker quoting out of *Medea*: "*polis* ... *our* city; the visible-crowned city of the Virgin Goddess, 'with its citizens ever delicately walking, through the most pellucid air.' "[27] So I shall not try to discourse on the city of justice or the city of God, though my city of the good life cannot survive if it is a good life for only a few, and hence must be a city of justice; it might even approach a city of God on earth, which is quite enough to try for.

I do not enjoy the consolation of revealed religion as Winston Churchill once put it;[28] I do not look for solace for my disappointments here, in some later repose in Abraham's Bosom, or by cool Siloam's shady rill; nor do I fear the scales of Michael or consignment to the jaws of Leviathan for my errors on earth. I do not believe that man was put on earth solely to toil or destined to mourn in atonement for the errors of some early and quite undocumented ancestor. I believe that when the Church sets out to refute some well established biological fact, it will, in the end, have

24. *Politics*, Vol. 4, No. 11, p. 3.
25. Ibid. I II 5.
26. *The City of God*, Book XIV, CL 28.
27. Sir Ernest Baker, tr., *The Politics of Aristotle* (New York: Oxford University Press, 1958), p. lxiii. The Euripidean quotation is from a chorus in *Medea*, l. 824.
28. In his 1949 address at M.I.T. See *Mid Century* (1950).

to recant, but that meanwhile a disciplined priest can do a great deal of harm.

It is easier for me to accept the fact that man may be only an accident of the Cosmos, doomed surely in the end to the fate predicted by the second law of thermodynamics. But this still leaves the question of how he is to occupy himself along the way. He may try for justice and good will, but surely he needs also to live while he tries. It is hard to believe that all our aim should be to increase the Gross National Product; or to gloat over new toys as this poet of technology did a year or so ago.

Today's newspaper . . . is a mosaic of bright colors and sound, in the rush of which can be glimpsed the unimaginable feats of a generation—the silvery dot of a space capsule, carrying men around the globe, the awesome array of nuclear needles pointing at each other across continents, the tiny trickling fluids that are synthesizing life in a glass tube, the piercing white beam of a laser cutting through the hardest metals, the clamorous march of people demanding their equal rights, the quick flicker of a multi-colored television picture, the liquid swish of a huge jet transport. [29]

The writer, you will notice, spoiled a perfect eulogy to what he really admires by a single bow to social conscience. The wonders are real but they are not real enough, except for a very limited scientific or engineering mind. They can quite as easily be dismissed as merely an expensive array of highly ingenious toys, a glorified expression of "look ma, I'm dancing." These brilliant human achievements are no more ends in themselves than the GNP.

For a limited number of professional men, it must be said, the concentration on making any one of these ventures come true is an exciting way of life. The interest may provide a sufficiently full life so that the only task of the city for them is not to act as an inhibitor: Los Alamos may be quite as attractive as San Francisco. In the future, the number of professional men so engaged may actually increase in more than an absolute sense. But there never will be a large proportion of urban workers who find, as you and I may that our work is the best play. And very few of us are that single-minded or that dedicated.

This may be just as well for, from such preoccupations, one might conclude that the only successful city is the one which serves as "an instrument for accelerating change."[30] The notion that change is a good in itself is a peculiarly American notion. Insofar as it serves to make us more willing to experiment with the new, it is good.

29. Anonymous, in Kaiser Aluminum News, Vol. I, 1966, p. 6.
30. Ibid., p. 15.

Insofar as it makes the new seem to be the only good, it is not only one of the most absurd delusions of the day, but it is positively harmful.

Although the pleasures of professional arete may be a substitute for the consolations of revealed religion, this still leaves most urban people, church attenders or not, quite up in the air. I am convinced that for all such people and, indeed, for all of us, the city is meaningless and even menacing unless it permits—or offers—pleasure throughout life. The pleasure is to be positive, not mere absence of pain. The enjoyment should be relatively unabandoned, not all premeditated and intellectual. The thing enjoyed may be very simple or very esoteric, from a bird call to a symphony, from a bill board to a Leonardo, from peanut butter to pressed duck, from something that happens every day, like my good breakfast, to a performance of *Traviata* by Tebaldi in her prime, such as I shall never encounter again.

Much of this pleasure must and should be low-keyed, and some of the pleasures should be those of routine and some those of accident. How have I slept? Was the night noisy or quiet? Did I have to use sleeping pills? Or Flents? What did the air feel like as it brushed my cheeks at dawn? Or did it brush me at all? Were the birds awake a little before me and did their chorus help to bring me to consciousness? Or were there no birds at all? Did I see something charming when my eyes first opened? Or only a broken window pane across a dirty street? Could I feel the sun on my back? Or was there no sun? Was it a pleasure to wash? Was it a joy to don the clothes I donned and to see myself in the morning mirror? Was breakfast a positive pleasure or a standard routine of two items whose merit was that they had no distinctive flavor but were supposed to contain the right amount of vitamins? When I left my home, did I walk or ride in pleasant quarters, among trees and verdure, or only in dingy streets; was my public conveyance clean, safe, even pleasant, the driver courteous? Did I see anything amusing on the way? Was my work a place to admire? Did I feel like singing at my work, or was the coffee break the only anticipated activity of the day?

Certainly I do not need to plough on until Morpheus kisses me good night. What this much enumeration signifies must be clear. All of our cities should offer all of these contentments—these simple things. As it is, no city offers all of them for any of its people all of the time; some cities offer some of them for some of the people some of the time; but in every city there are many people for whom none of them is offered any of the time.

AN URBAN AMENITY MATRIX

Beyond these gentle pleasures, some larger ones are available in some cities, American and foreign. There are, for example, the countless pleasures of various neighborhood "do's," organized or spontaneous.[31] Beyond these there are the specialized and grander pleasures we associate with "great cities."

I think it undebatable that one set of the "grander" pleasures involves what is often called the high culture. Of course there are other sources of urban joy: bird-watching, street dancing, hot-rodding, fishing in the Seine, going to a rally in Trafalgar Square, quiet pleasures and loud ones, gentle ones and vulgar ones. It would not be right to say that the pleasures of the high culture are the most important at all. I shall say a little more about them because I know more about them than I do about street fun and games, and because I have had a chance to savor them in many parts of the world.

The first and perhaps the only thing to be said about them is that in the present state of our knowledge, it is quite impossible to quantify them to anyone's satisfaction or to crank them into an urban cost-benefit analysis. I made the attached table of Urban Amenity with precisely that in mind. I began by drawing up a list of 24 things generally of the high culture (in my book as in the Greek book, big sports can easily be more important than little theater). Of course it is a highly personal and subjective list. Of course the items may not be of equal weight; there may be duplications; there may be inconsistencies. Then I drew up a list of sixteen cities, eight foreign, eight domestic, with which I had more than a casual familiarity. All of these cities I regard as positively pleasurable, viewed only from the standpoint of more or less traditional culture. This does not mean I can think of no others which *might* be individually more pleasurable than some one on the list (e.g., Lisbon, Mexico City, Kyoto, Melbourne, and maybe Philadelphia). Save that I included no "bad" cities, the list made no pretensions to being decisive. The presence of any city on the list did mean that I thought well of it; the absence of any city did not mean that I thought ill of it; nor was there any implication that this particular foreign set were the best eight foreign cities, or this particular American set the best eight American cities. It would have involved only labor to extend the list as far as one wanted to include all cities, but the thing I sought to show would not have justified it.

Having established this faulty matrix, I put a 1, a $\frac{1}{2}$, and a 0

31. These are difficult terms. Some of the most spontaneous-seeming happenings have in fact been highly organized.

opposite each characteristic and simply totalled the subjective results. I need no Ph.D. candidate to tell me this was terrible technique. I would only say that the nature of the problem is so subjective that more sophisticated techniques would be unlikely to produce more sophisticated answers. Then I published the results. The consequence of this confirmed my purpose, though it produced more angry correspondence than I craved. How could I really have left out City X? Did I really think Boston was "better" than Philadelphia? (Yes) Had I ever been to Mexico City? (Yes) Do I know how Venice smells at low tide on a hot day? (Yes) Do I really think Pittsburgh's *site* is more spectacular than Rome's? (Yes) How could I say there are no great restaurants in Washington? (I can and do.) What was good about it was that so many people seemed to care. What was also good was that the correspondence confirmed my convictions about the qualitative nature of the whole affair. What was bad was that scholars seemed quite as prone as the journalists to go off half-cocked.

As things turned out in the table—for which, it must by now be evident, I claim not even personal, let alone consensual validity—I probably would have rated the factors in a somewhat different order than they came out. On the other hand, I did not need to make the table to learn that, measured by this particular set of characteristics and on an Occidental scale, Paris, London, Rome, and New York were the greatest cities in our present world.

It should be clear also that this rubric is not enough even if it could be soberly and reliably constructed. It does not even suggest that the "greatest" cities would always be the ones in which it might be the most pleasant to live. I myself, for example, have chosen to live the best part of fifty years in Boston and San Francisco, which come out only in the middle of this score card. What is not so certain is whether this could have been the choice had Paris, Rome, London, and New York not existed and been reasonably accessible at that.

It would be interesting to see more serious research on quantifying the amenities. I doubt that the results will be qualitatively convincing. As long as they are not, there is a very serious risk that hardheaded but unhedonistic planners will leave them out of the urban calculation altogether.

As I have remarked elsewhere, there is no certainty that urban beauty spots may offer any solace to the discontented. Would the gardens of the Tuileries have satisfied the sansculottes of the Faubourg St. Antoine had they been public instead of royal gardens?[32] It is to be doubted. There is even the chance that, given enough

32. The respectable public, indeed, use them, respectably.

anger, the rioters might turn against the city's beauty as a better symbol of the target of the wrath than their own districts can ever be. But these seem to me risks that must be run. In our urgent solicitude to make our cities reasonable places for 10 percent of us, we must not neglect the other 90 percent.

Table 21-1—Urban Amenity Score Sheet[33]

	Paris	*Rome*	*London*	*New York*	*Stockholm*	*Chicago*	*Boston*	*Rio*	*San Francisco*	*Sydney*	*Venice*	*Washington*	*Istanbul*	*Pittsburgh*	*Los Angeles*	*Dallas/Ft. Worth*	*Totals*
Fine river, lake, etc.	1	1	1	1	1	1	1	1	1	1	1	½	1	1	0	0	13½
Great park(s)	1	1	1	1	1	1	½	1	1	1	0	1	0	1	½	1	13
Distinguished buildings	1	1	1	1	½	1	1	1	½	½	1	1	1	½	½	½	13
Distinguished museum(s)	1	1	1	1	½	1	1	½	0	0	1	1	1	1	1	½	12½
Readable plan	1	½	1	1	1	1	½	1	1	½	1	1	½	1	½	0	12½
Great university	1	½	1	1	1	1	1	0	1	1	0	½	1	1	1	½	12½
Diverse neighborhoods	1	1	1	1	½	½	½	1	1	½	1	½	½	½	½	0	11
Great eating	1	1	½	1	½	½	½	1	1	½	1	½	½	0	1	½	11
Fine music	½	1	1	1	½	1	1	½	1	½	0	½	0	1	1	½	11
General boscage	1	1	1	½	1	½	1	1	½	1	0	1	0	0	½	½	10½
Glamorous site	½	½	½	1	1	½	½	1	1	1	1	0	1	1	0	0	10½
Great sports	1	1	1	1	0	1	1	1	1	1	0	0	0	0	1	½	10½
Great avenue(s)	1	½	1	1	½	1	½	1	0	½	1	1	½	0	0	0	9½
Fine squares	1	1	1	½	1	0	½	0	½	½	1	0	½	½	0	0	8
Important visible past	1	1	1	1	½	0	1	0	0	0	1	½	1	0	0	0	8
Good air	0	1	0	0	1	0	0	1	1	1	1	0	1	0	0	½	7½
Fine libraries	1	1	1	1	0	1	1	0	0	0	0	1	0	0	0	0	7
Exciting shop windows	1	½	1	1	0	½	0	½	0	0	0	0	0	½	0	1	6
Generally pleasant climate	½	1	0	½	½	0	½	½	1	1	0	0	0	0	½	0	6
Fountains	1	1	1	0	1	1	0	0	0	0	0	0	0	0	0	0	5
Theater	1	1	1	1	½	0	0	0	0	0	0	0	0	0	0	½	5
Art in the streets	1	1	0	0	1	0	0	0	½	0	1	0	0	0	0	0	4½
Private galleries	1	½	1	1	0	½	½	0	0	0	0	0	0	0	0	0	4½
Many opportunities for participatory recreation	0	0	0	½	1	½	½	½	0	1	0	0	0	0	0	0	
Totals	20½	20	19	19	15½	14½	14	13½	13	12½	12	10	9½	9	8	6½	

Beyond delectability, there may, rarely, be ecstasy. Ecstasy is not something to be desired too much of the time; nor is it long prolonged. One needs always to ask whose ecstasy, and to remember that it cannot be charted in advance. It is impossible to predict the moment when one's heart will stand still, and I am not sure that planners can do anything to increase the probability of an ecstatic experience.

33. Correspondents have convinced me I have done some underrating. San Francisco, for example, might have had ½ for theater and 1 for recreation and thus have totalled 14½; Washington might have had 1 for its river, ½ for squares, 1 for air and ½ for fountains and so stretched to 13; and so on. If I *had* listed Philadelphia, it might have scored 12½ or so; and Mexico City might have scored an easy 18. No matter how hard I try, I can't raise Miami above 5. But to engage in such jostling for position is to miss the point of the exercise.

But the other urban amenities can be planned for and struggled for. They may be beautiful or just fun. None of the traditional urban beauties is really obsolete. Most of these are the result of past planning and architecture. The retreat from the Grand Plan, mainly on ideological grounds, created an antagonism to formal beauty that has not yet died away and that has mortgaged the future very heavily, since the great spaces of the older cities will seldom be duplicated now; new ones are not proliferating, and the inexorable march of the urban numbers means that each we have, like the parks and the wilderness, are desperately striving to serve more people without being drowned. The planner's traditional aversion to beauty is not something to look back upon with pride.

Beyond these, the other amenities are certainly necessary in great variety. Probably the problem is more one of offering an opportunity for local amenity than of fully designing it. A park for downtown Chinese, for example, might better be designed as a park without assumptions as to what kind of decoration downtown Chinese would find happy. They might bring these to the park themselves.

In embracing this problem, the first need of the planner is to realize that his is unlikely to be the general taste; that there is no such thing as "right" taste. Our urbanite has a right to sleep peacefully in Rittenhouse Square unmolested by the din of the Hippies; if only the Hippies too have their places. Neither Haight-Ashbury nor Rittenhouse Square has a right to possess the whole town; and this is a difficult point for that part of our culture which is young and rebellious and nomadic to understand.

IN CONCLUSION

In that great classic of his of 1938, Lewis Mumford also wrote:

Already, in the architecture and layout of the new community, one sees the knowledge and discipline that the machine has provided, turned to more vital conquests, more human consummations. Already, in imagination and plan, we have transcended the sinister limitations of the existing metropolitan environment. We have much to unbuild and much more to build; but the foundations are ready; the machines are set in place and the tools are bright and keen; the architects, the engineers, and the workmen are assembled. None of us may live to see the complete building and perhaps, in the nature of things, the building can never be completed: but some of us will see the flag of the fir tree that the workers will plant aloft in ancient ritual when they cap the topmost story.[34]

"Bliss was it, in that day, to be alive."[35]

34. Lewis Mumford, p. 493.
35. William Wordsworth, *Prelude*, Book VI.

Lewis Mumford no longer takes the rosy view he did thirty years ago. I still do, and would be prepared to end on his own eloquent note of so long ago were it not for some very dark clouds on the American urban sky.

The budgetary clouds consist of our disproportionate commitments to Vietnam, to space, and to foreign aid. The urban clouds say that the cities are broke, that their traffic tangles are suffocating, their pollution nearly so; and the darkest ones rumble with the use of LSD and with the lightning of the agonies of Watts, Cleveland, Newark, and Detroit which bid to be experienced and re-experienced in almost every American city.

Great cities will not be made by escapists, parasites, people on a trip, or by angry and impoverished rebels who are no more fit to govern themselves unaided than the people of Indonesia or the Congo, and for much the same reasons of past neglect and even contempt by those who essayed to carry the "white man's burden" too long and did not take the "burden" part of the challenge seriously enough.[36]

I think it is more important to save Cleveland than it is to save Saigon. I think it is more important to rescue young Americans from the wish to escape than to prepare the Vietnamese for a democracy they have not demanded. Magna Cartas that are not written by the people of a nation are not likely to endure. I think it is more important to give proper chances to our own black population than to any number of East Indians. The most expensive programs suggested by Senator Robert Kennedy or Daniel Moynihan are substantially smaller in cost than our Vietnam fiasco; there is no reason to believe they would have to last any longer.

The easy retort to this is, of course, that it is a cry of ignorant isolationism. But it is clear to me that the first American victory over Communism had better be scored in the American city streets and not by the police or the National Guard. Whether or not it seems relevant to his subject, and no matter how impolite it may seem to say these things in Washington, it seems to me imperative now that every American should declare himself publicly on these issues every time he has an opportunity to be heard. The things *are* relevant to my topic, indeed central to it.

Everything we are talking about here is no more than amiable conversation so long as funds and manpower are not available to cities in really large amounts; and so long as so much of the scientific and technological resource of the country is engaged elsewhere.

36. Consider, for example, the unworkable conclusions of the Black Power Conference held in Newark, July 23, 1967.

Neither the money nor the minds will be available under present foreign policy or until we are magnanimous enough and courageous enough to settle for peace without "*Victory.*"

It is probably true that we tend to see some other cities through more rosy glasses than we view our own (unless we persist in believing we can learn nothing anywhere else—"I wouldn't trade Shreveport for Rome any day"). This is no doubt because we are tourists with more time and even more daily money to spend on urban joy than we will allow ourselves at home.

Happy the citizen whose city is so abounding in diverse opportunities for personal pleasure that he has never quite explored them all and thus can approach them in some senses as a tourist. But the things one is used to matter too. One can get used to anything. It is only a matter of faith that it is better to get used to a thrush than to a pigeon. To make this possible is a task, not for narrow-nosed reformers, but for the planners with sympathy. They must not think it pandering to open opportunities for activities which they do not understand, or, if understanding, do not approve. The computers may provide such men with some information they need, but the projections have to come from not only the lucubrations of the mind, but also from the beatings of the heart.

Criteria for judging the quality of the urban environment[*]

INTRODUCTION

A sudden and general awakening of interest in "the urban problem" has taken place in America during the past decade. Some critics have said that the greatest threat to the future of mankind, next to nuclear war, lies in "the problems of the cities." Statements of this kind, however, mistake problems *in* the cities for those *of* the cities. Poverty, unemployment, racial discrimination, crime, alcoholism, drug addiction, and other social maladies certainly are to be found in the urban communities, but they are problems of society, not of the cities. They happen to have their locus in the cities because that is where people are. Since these problems are more visible in the cities, because of their concentrated populations, they force themselves on the consciousness and conscience of society. Were the same problems scattered in many small pockets, public attention would not be so forcefully directed to them; they could even be swept under the rug more easily.

While most of the so-called "urban problems" are, in fact, those

* "Criteria for Judging the Quality of the Urban Environment" by Hans Blumenfeld is reprinted from *The Quality of Urban Life* (1969) Volume III, *Urban Affairs Annual Reviews*, pp. 137–163, edited by Henry J. Schmandt and Warner Blumberg, Jr., by permission of the publisher, Sage Publications Inc.

of the larger society, there are some which refer to a smaller unit within the total urban environment: the "city" as a political entity in contradistinction to the "suburbs." A good deal of semantic confusion has arisen from the widening gap between socioeconomic fact and legal fiction. Until the turn of the present century, the legal boundaries of the city followed its socioeconomic boundaries fairly closely. Philadelphia, for example, expanded its corporate limits in 1854 from two to 130 square miles; and half a century later, five counties united to form the city of New York. Since then, the local body politic in the United States has suffered a hardening of the arteries. Canada, as well as several European countries, has, on the other hand, given recognition to the transformation of the city into a much larger and looser metropolitan area.

The expansion of cities into metropolitan areas, usually seen merely in quantitative terms, has resulted in a profound qualitative change, in the emergence of an entirely new form of human settlement which is indeed, as it is frequently accused of being, "neither city nor country." It differs profoundly from the city as it has been known throughout history. Although its peripheral sections show some of the aspects traditionally associated with a "rural" environment, low densities and extensive open areas, it is nonetheless "urban" in its totality. The entire area forms a single functional unit, a single labor market and a single housing market. The division into "city" and "suburbs" is obsolete and obscures the reality.

Urban growth

There has been, and continues to be, considerable hostility toward urban growth. "The intellectual versus the city" has become a fashionable theme of scholarly studies in contemporary America. This hostility, however, is by no means exclusively American nor is it new. It appeared in the Western World with the first appearance of the big city: in Anakreon's shepherd poetry in Alexandria and in Cicero's praise of "rustic" Tusculum in Rome. It disappeared temporarily with the dissolution of urban life in the "Dark Ages," only to surface again during the Renaissance. Both Elizabeth I and Cromwell tried to stop the growth of London by establishing a "Green Belt." The French kings left Paris for Versailles and the kings of Prussia left Berlin for Potsdam.

At the other end of the political spectrum, socialists like Karl Marx and anarchists like Peter Kropotkin, were even more emphatic in their condemnation of the big city and in their call for dispersal of industry over the countryside. Both they and later critics advocating "decentralization" were alarmed by the increasing centralization of decision-making and the consequent alienation of the individual from participation in the determination of his own fate and that of his fellow beings. However, given a complex economy, integrated and interdependent on a national and even international scale, it is inevitable that many decisions vitally affecting the local community will be made elsewhere—and the smaller the community, the more this will be the case. Moreover, it is evident that spatial decentralization can be brought about only by a powerful central decision-making body. Only such a center can decide to locate the many various elements of economic and cultural activities simultaneously in one place—be it a "new" or an "enlarged" town. Where decision-making is decentralized, as it largely is in the United States, each individual decision-maker of necessity locates where he can find the supplementary facilities and institutions which he needs—in existing large urban areas.

Louder than the warnings of the decentralizers that "bigger is worse"—and more typically American—have been the "bigger and better" barkings of chambers of commerce and other spokesmen of the business class. What both groups have in common is the emphasis on quantity. What ultimately matters, however, is the quality of life in urban areas, be they large or small.

THE "GOOD LIFE"

Few writers on urban affairs fail to quote Aristotle's dictum that "men come together in cities for security; they stay together for the good life." Considering that many people in American cities fear to walk on the streets and few dare to walk in a park at night, one might feel that we have come full circle and that our cities fail by the most basic and elementary criterion. The modern city is far better protected than its predecessors against "acts of God"—fires, floods, earthquakes, and hurricanes; but not against acts of man.

Do people remain in the city because of the good life? It is not too difficult to define the good life in general terms: health, happiness, wisdom, and virtue. An environment may be defined as "good," if it produces healthy, happy, wise, and good men and women. But it is difficult to measure these general qualities. Perhaps life expectancy can serve as a yardstick of health, but what are the indexes of happiness, wisdom, and virtue?

Mortality is no higher in our cities than in the countryside. This is in itself a quite remarkable achievement, because for centuries the cities have been the breeding places of deadly epidemic diseases, in particular of water-borne diseases. Indeed, the universal provision of an ample and safe supply of water—also decisive for the control of fires—is an essential precondition for the very existence of the modern city. However, as Frederic L. Osborn, the head of the British Town and Country Planning Society, remarked, after having been treated to many glasses of chlorinated water on the occasion of his visit to the United States: "The American engineers seem to be more concerned that I should live as long as possible than that I should enjoy the time that I am alive." Increased life expectancy means an increased quantity of life; it still tells us nothing about its quality and the quality of the environment.

Social and physical environment

The old school of environmental geographers attempted to explain human characteristics and human behavior as direct effects of the physical environment, of climate, soil, and nurture. To some extent this notion still persists. The crumbling buildings of slums are supposed to "breed" crime and vice. But serious study leaves no doubt that a far stronger influence is exercised by the social environment, by the totality of human relations into which an individual enters in his lifetime—in the family, in work and business, in school and church and neighborhood—formal and informal, from person to person, and mediated by various modes of communication. This all-pervasive human environment is determined by the structure of the total society, by its "culture." The man-made or man-modified physical environment is the effect rather than the cause of the quality of the life of human society. But the physical environment reacts on the social, indirectly influencing it by limiting or facilitating human relations. In addition, it has a direct influence on health and may have, through its aesthetic aspects, an influence on happiness.

THE CITY AS AN ECONOMIC MACHINE

Of all the social relations into which men enter, one with another, probably none are more basic and more variable than the economic, the arrangements for the production and distribution of wealth. "Wealth" was not mentioned among the four aspects by which we tried to define "the good life." This is at variance with the predominant American attitude which tends to regard the Gross National Product as the be-all and end-all of the life of society, by which all other aspects are measured. Many products forming part of the GNP may be useless and even positively harmful to health, happiness, wisdom, and virtue—as is the strain of accumulating them. Yet, it remains true that there can be no life without the material means of life. There can be no living without "making a living."

The millions of people who have been and are still pouring into American cities from the countryside and from all over the world have not been attracted primarily by the prospect of "living" in the city, but by the hope of "making a living." In the context of a fully developed money economy this means "making money." Essentially American cities developed as money-mining camps, with the mentality characteristic of such camps: a sense of impermanence and an indifference to the despoiling of the environment by the waste products of the mining process.

The negative aspects of the industrial city should not obscure the profound significance of the fact that for the first time in history the urban areas have become the main producers of the wealth of society. Pre-industrial cities were largely, sometimes exclusively, consumer cities, places in which the ruling elite consumed the wealth which they extracted from the countryside. It is, therefore, hardly realistic to expect in the working cities of today the kind of "urbanity" which graced the life of the Kaloi-k-Agathoi in classical Athens, of the Princes of the Church and their retinue in Papal Rome, or of the gentry in Georgian Bath.

Before discussing the quality of the urban environment as a place for living, it may therefore be appropriate to consider its qualities as a place for making a living; to evaluate the contemporary American urban area on its own terms, as an economic machine.

The productivity of the urban area

Urbanization is the product of the interacting processes of rising productivity and increasing division and specialization of labor. As productivity increased in "primary" production (agriculture and mining), and as more and more goods and services previously produced on the farm were supplied from the outside by specialized factories and institutions, an increasing portion of the total labor force was shifted to "secondary" production (manufacturing and construction). And as productivity in the secondary sector increased, as more and more functions previously carried out by the manufacturer—research and development, selling, accounting—were performed by outside specialists, and as many other services were similarly transferred from the household to other specialized enterprises, an increasing portion of the labor force was shifted to the "tertiary" or "service" sector.

The highly advanced specialization and division of labor

characteristic of modern society requires a complex and many-sided cooperation between an ever growing number of specialized establishments, as well as a growing number of specialists within each establishment. Moreover, changes both of product and of production process become more frequent as technical progress accelerates and as a rising level of living leads to more differentiated and variable demand for consumer goods and services. These changes can proceed effectively only if the enterprise can draw on a broad and deep assortment of specialized goods, services, and skilled workers—resources usually found only in the larger urban areas.

From the point of view of the urban worker, these developments mean a wide range of job opportunities. In a small community an employee who leaves his job because of a change in product or process is generally faced with a choice of pulling up stakes and seeking employment elsewhere, or to accept being "a square peg in a round hole," working at a job which does not utilize his best skills and talents. For the total economy, this means a loss of productivity; for the individual, a loss of income.

There is considerable evidence that productivity and income per person do indeed increase with population size. As census data show, per capita income tends to be highest in the largest urban areas. This relationship is based in part on the concentration of high-income occupations in these areas. However, wages and salaries for the same occupations also tend to be higher. A recent study of the Stockholm Region[1] concluded that the size factor alone accounted for a fifteen to twenty percent difference between Stockholm and the rest of Sweden. This variance must be ascribed to higher productivity resulting from the wider range of choice.

A wide range of mutual choice between employer and employee and between buyers and sellers is certainly the decisive criterion for the urban area as an economic machine, as a place for making a living. But it is hardly less important for the city as a place for living: a wide range of choice for location and type of residence, of shopping and consumer facilities, of educational, cultural, and recreational opportunities, of medical services, of voluntary associations, and, last but not least, of personal contacts.

ACCESSIBILITY AND TRANSPORTATION

Without accessibility, however, the mere existence of a wide range of choice within an urban area is only an empty promise. This was

1. Folke Kristensson, *People, firms, and regions.* Stockholm: The Economic Research Institute, Stockholm School of Economics (Sept., 1967), pp. 1–10.

dramatically illustrated by the fact that the unskilled workers of Watts who did not own a car could not avail themselves of those jobs in the Los Angeles area which might have been open to them.

Accessibility can be brought about in two ways (which are not mutually exclusive): by locating points of potential origin and destination close together, and by decreasing the friction of space between them. It is possible to reduce the need for commuting to work by providing within each section of an urban area an approximate balance between the number of residents in the labor force and the number of jobs. A purely quantitative balance, however, is not sufficient; a combination of residences in a price range accessible only to white-collar workers with an equal number of blue-collar jobs in manufacturing plants (a situation found in some large real estate developments misnamed "New Towns") will be of little value. A fairly broad range of types of jobs as well as of types of residence is required. Similarly, a distribution of a broad range of shopping and public and private service facilities in balance with the demands of the surrounding residential population can substantially increase accessibility. Minimizing the need for travel is a valid criterion for the arrangement of the physical environment.

Ample data on travel in urban areas confirm that the percentage of residents of a given area travelling to a given number of potential destinations for work or other purposes decreases with increasing travel distance. Other things being equal, people prefer to locate their residence as close as possible to their place of work. But other things are not equal, and are becoming less so. The more work becomes specialized, the more some jobs become more attractive than others. The more the level of living rises, the more some types of residences and of neighborhoods become more attractive than others. In other words, people avail themselves increasingly of the wide range of choice, which is the very hallmark and raison d'être of the large urban area.

For these reasons, the second method of improving accessibility, "decreasing the friction of space," is of growing significance. Even more important than minimizing the need for travel is the criterion of maximizing the possibility of travel; or, expressed differently, increasing mobility. It is, therefore, quite natural that in the public mind demands for "improving transportation" outweigh all others.

Criteria for urban transportation: mobility

Mobility or mutual accessibility is as important for goods and for messages as for persons. The problem is less with messages since for the most part they are equally accessible throughout the urban area.

Goods transportation, however, deserves more attention than it is usually accorded. To a greater extent than is generally realized, it has been relieved by substituting movement by pipeline and, for fossil fuels in the form of electricity, by wire for surface movement. Minimization of surface transportation by wider use of such substitution, as well as by proximate location of establishments which generate substantial interchanges of goods, is an important, if secondary, criterion for the arrangement of the urban physical environment.

The main problem, however, remains the reduction of the friction of space for the movement of persons. Friction of space cannot be adequately measured in terms of miles, but only in terms of time, money, and inconvenience. It is possible, though difficult, to express these three aspects by a common denominator—time or money—by a systematic analysis of the "trade-offs" between these different aspects, in which people actually engage. Although quantification of inconvenience has not yet been achieved, translation of time into terms of money—at present usually $1.55 per man hour—is common practice. It is on this basis that proposals for investment in road and transit facilities are considered justified. "Saving time" is generally regarded as the goal and product of a good transportation system.

There is considerable evidence that, in the long run, the benefits of increased mobility are taken out not so much in terms of less time, but of more space and of wider choice. It seems that the time people are willing to spend on a trip for a given purpose is fairly constant. Even in large urban areas the median duration of the journey to work has been found to be no more than half an hour. If walking at a speed of 3 m.p.h. is the predominant mode of movement, about half of all people will live within 1.5 miles of their place of work; if streetcars at 9 m.p.h. are universally used, within 4.5 miles; if car driving at 18 m.p.h. is predominant, within 9 miles. The area within which destinations can be reached within a given time is enlarged thirty-six times. If the density of potential destinations were the same, the range of choice would also be increased thirty-six times. In fact, the overall density of American urban areas is about one-fifth to one-sixth of the density prevailing a century ago, when walking was the predominant mode of transportation. It seems that the benefit of increased mobility is being taken out about equally in terms of more space and in terms of wider choice, each being increased more than five-fold.

The direct result of increased mobility is an enormous increase in the number of person-miles (and ton-miles). Once this new pattern is established, many trips require more time, money, and inconvenience than is acceptable. In particular, any unusual circumstances lead to congestion and delays. At many places and times movement is far slower than "normal." Thus, the "traffic problem" constantly reproduces itself; it is never "solved." It might appear from this that all improvements of transportation are futile; the expected saving of time does not materialize. However, if people take out the benefits of increased mobility in terms of more space and wider choice, it means that they value these higher than they value savings in travel time, cost, and inconvenience. The benefits of mobility are real, both for "living" and for "making a living."

It may, however, well be asked: How much space? How much choice? Is there not a point where "enough is enough"? Even if there are millions of jobs in an area, a man can only occupy one at a time; and he can have social contacts with only an infinitesimal fraction of the persons living in the area. The New York Regional Plan Association raised exactly this question: "Isn't there a maximum beyond which it becomes more of the same?" Its answer was: "Apparently not."[2] The appearance may not be entirely conclusive; there may well be a diminishing return. Certainly many people come to the New York region, but many others live happily in smaller cities. Yet whatever the population size of the urban area, broadening the range of choice by increased mobility remains a valid criterion.

The value of "more space" is not so easily resolved. Its desirability insofar as manufacturing and warehousing are concerned raises little doubt. The modern landscaped one-story plant with ample space for loading, parking, and expansion is superior to the multi-story loft building, in terms both of productivity and of environment for the life of the workers. Nor is there much doubt as to the desirability of more space for schools and playgrounds, parks, and sport facilities. Somewhat more questionable is the rapidly increased land absorption by residences. Some of this increase is forced by zoning requirements which many municipalities enact in order to keep taxes low by making it impossible for low income families to live within their boundaries. Some is due to the fact that each individual, in making his own decision, does not consider the combined effect of similar decisions made by all other individuals. People move to the "suburbs," in the expectation of being close to both "the city" and "the country." But the more people who make this choice, the further they have to move away from the city and the

2. New York Regional Plan Association, *Regional Plan News*, 86 (October, 1967), 15.

further the country moves away from them. Viewed in this light, the general move to the low-density urban periphery is self-defeating.

The "city-country" location is not the main reason for low-density suburban development. The desire for ample private outdoor space is deep-seated and the satisfactions derived from its various uses are real, as surveys all over the world have shown time and again. Thus, making an ample and growing supply of land per capita accessible, not only by road and rail, but also by pipeline and wire, is an important criterion for a good urban environment. However, with the presently prevailing methods of ownership, control, and development, much of the land made accessible is not used. The "overall density" previously referred to relates population to *all* land within a given area. This includes not only that actually used for any urban purposes (including parks), called "developed" in the planners' language, but also "undeveloped" or "open" land. Much could be gained if both types were held together instead of being scattered haphazardly. The cost of accessibility—of all types—within the developed areas would be reduced and the open spaces would be far better suited for recreation as well as for agriculture and forestry. The criterion of more accessible land must, therefore, be supplemented by that of compact and continuous urban development, at whatever density.

Criteria for urban transportation: safety

Reducing the friction of space not only has costs in terms of time, money, and inconvenience, it also exacts its price in accidents. The toll in human life and personal injury on the streets and highways of America is rightly a cause for alarm. It is important to realize that whatever may be achieved in reducing this toll by improvement of the road, the vehicle, and the driver, the individually directed fast movement of many heavy bodies is inherently dangerous. If 60 persons travel in two buses, the probability of a collision is one. If the same 60 persons travel in 40 cars, the probability is 40×39, or 1,560. Considering that the buses have been assumed to carry 20 times as many persons than the cars, the danger to persons is still 78 times greater in cars than in buses.

For reasons of safety alone—aside from many other considerations which will be discussed later—minimizing automobile and maximizing transit usage is an important criterion. Collisions between vehicles, as well as delays, occur almost exclusively because of two kinds of friction, cross-friction and side-friction (weaving). Provision of a separate, grade-separated right-of-way eliminates both types completely in public transportation; for vehicular movement, freeways eliminate the former completely and greatly reduce the latter. Hence, minimizing movement of all types of vehicles on surface streets and maximizing use of grade-separated facilities, subways for transit, and especially freeways for cars and trucks, as well as buses, is an additional criterion for a safe environment.

Criteria for urban traffic: indirect effects

So far this discussion has dealt only with the benefits and costs to the user of transportation; that is, with the bargain between seller and buyer which, according to classical economics, is supposed to result in maximizing the benefits of both. However, in an urban environment, any "deal" affects not only the seller and buyer, but third persons on whom it confers benefits—and malefits.

Third-person benefits of vehicular traffic are few; third-person malefits are many and overwhelming. The latter may be divided into two groups: interference with other movements, and dangers to pedestrians. The first includes the interference of private cars with the movement of transit vehicles and of trucks, and in particular the interference of all vehicular movements with that of pedestrians. Pedestrian movement suffers considerable delay by being forced to make detours and to wait for traffic lights. But delay is not the only and not the most serious malefit inflicted on the pedestrian. He is in almost constant danger. Noise and vibration, as well as the glare of headlights, disturb rest and sleep in adjacent houses. Exhaust fumes pollute the air. These factors, together, increase nervous tension. It has been rightly said that in our eagerness to "go places" we are in danger of destroying places worth going to.

The fact that traffic interferes with a good living environment has long been recognized. Even before the advent of the automobile, separation of residential streets and traffic arteries was an accepted principle of city planning, a principle which has developed further into the concept of the "superblock" of "precinct." The most complete and systematic statement of this concept was developed by the famous "Buchanan Report"[3] which proposed to establish standards of amenity for each built-up precinct. These standards, designed to preserve a "civilized" living environment, would determine the number of cars which would be permitted to move within the boundaries of each precinct.

Protection of the pedestrian realm

Traditionally the public domain of streets and squares has been a

3. Buchanan Report, *Traffic in Towns*, London: Her Majesty's Stationery Office (1963).

communal outdoor living room. It served for the play of children, for informal chats and meetings, for assemblies, demonstrations, and processions, and simply for sitting, standing, and walking around to enjoy the sun or the shade, to see and be seen. More and more the upper- and middle-income groups have transferred most of these activities into off-street enclosed and open spaces, at some loss of contact among neighbors. The lower-income groups, however, still rely on the street as their outdoor living room.

Large volumes of speeding automobiles have destroyed the age-old amenities of this pedestrian realm. It should be noted—and was recognized by the Buchanan Report—that a limited volume of cars moving at moderate speed is quite compatible with street life. Indeed, it may enhance it as one can appreciate by watching the use made of cars by boys and girls on Saturday night on any small town main street. In many cases, however, complete separation of cars and pedestrians is desirable. This separation can be achieved in three ways: in time, horizontally, and vertically.

Separation in time was practiced in Imperial Rome and is now being successfully applied to Copenhagen's main shopping street, Strøget; but its applicability is limited.

The first systematic attempt at complete horizontal separation of vehicular and pedestrian movement was the "Radburn Plan," developed around 1930. Radburn also uses vertical separation in the form of pedestrian underpasses under arterial streets. However, its most discussed and copied feature is the horizontal separation between cul-de-sacs for vehicular "service" access and walkways leading to the front door on the other side of the houses. Ironically, separation has here been applied where it is definitely not needed, because the numbers of cars serving the dozen or so houses on each cul-de-sac is minimal. As a consequence, the pathways and front doors are little used and most pedestrian life, including the play of children, occurs on the "service" roads.

Separation is needed where traffic volumes are high, particularly in city centers and shopping districts and in concentrations of high-density apartments. Shopping centers owe their success largely to this separation. Strangely, the example they provide has been followed more widely in Europe than in America, by transforming parts of the city center into pedestrian malls, sometimes extended to whole pedestrian precincts.

Horizontal separation can cover only a limited area, because access from the rear must be provided and because the network of streets cannot be interrupted for too long a distance. Over a large area complete separation can be achieved only by establishing separate levels. Ideally, pedestrians should move on arcaded side-walks above the vehicular levels. In built-up areas it is, however, generally easier to accommodate them on a lower level, as has been done in Philadelphia's Penn Center and in Montreal's Place Ville Marie.

A combination of horizontal and vertical separation is also possible by a system of walkways in the interior of blocks, with overpasses or underpasses crossing the streets. Whatever the method, protection of the pedestrian realm by total or partial segregation of vehicular traffic is an increasingly important criterion of the quality of the urban environment as a place for living.

While separation eliminates most of the malefits inflicted on the environment by the motor vehicle, it cannot overcome what may be the most serious one: the pollution of the air by the waste products of the internal combustion engine. This by-product of the motor age affects not only the immediate environment, but entire urban areas extending over hundreds of square miles.

WASTE AND POLLUTION

The mentality of the money-mining camp led its inhabitants to dispose of waste by dumping it in the easiest and cheapest way, whether on the soil, in the water, or into the air. But production and consumption have increased and are daily augmenting the volume of wastes of all kinds, to such a degree that life itself is endangered. The situation has been aptly described by a West German scholar in the following words: "No satisfactory solution has yet been found for disposal of the accumulated waste resulting from living standards brought by industrialization. Despite purification systems, rivers and canals can no longer eliminate the pollution; they are becoming biologically dead—sluggishly flowing cesspools. . . . The atmosphere all over the world is contaminated by certain technical robots that are part of the equipment of all civilized states and are regarded as indispensable." And he continued: "While on the one hand the findings of a number of research groups in the field of biology and geophysics have given us an added insight into this liaison between human existence and natural preconditions, on the other we are using technical means to abuse nature in a horrifying way. But, by destroying vital biological systems we are contriving our own destruction."[4]

Too many attempts to dispose of waste merely shift its incidence

4. Bodo Manstein, "Shaping the future in a rational manner." *Perspectives*, 6 (June, 1968), 26–27.

from one element of the environment to another. If garbage is dumped, it pollutes the earth; if it is incinerated, it pollutes the air; if it is run through grinders and flushed down the drain, it pollutes the water.

Water pollution may be the most immediate problem. Great concern is caused by the proliferation of algae. This is ironic when it is considered that many nutritionists see in the growing of chlorella algae the best hope to supply mankind with an adequate protein diet. The algae in our sewage effluent are, unfortunately, not chlorellae. But their exuberant growth testifies to the wealth of plant nutrients contained in sewage. Plants are the ultimate source of food for all animals, including humans; and the excrements—and ultimately the bodies—of animals are food for plants. The Chinese have become the most numerous nation on earth by carefully husbanding this natural cycle—at the risk of the spread of waterborne diseases. Modern technology should be able to reestablish this natural cycle without this risk and on a larger scale.

With a chemical technology able to make almost anything out of anything and something out of everything, the entire concept of "waste" is becoming obsolete and should be replaced by the concept of recycling. Rather than thinking in terms of "disposal" of waste, we must learn to think in terms of the reuse of by-products. The by-products of industry and transportation which pollute the water and interfere with its natural biological cleaning process, and also those which pollute the air such as particles of fossil fuels resulting from incomplete combustion, consist of usable materials. However, the cost of recapturing them generally exceeds their market price and their re-use and is, therefore, not worthwhile for the enterprises which dump them. But such action may be very much worthwhile for the community as a whole. A difficult problem of cost allocation arises here.

Although water pollution may be the most immediate problem, in the long run air pollution may be even more serious. Here, too, a natural ecological balance is involved. Plants absorb carbon dioxide and produce oxygen; animals absorb oxygen and produce carbon dioxide. But so does combustion of fossil fuels, and in vastly greater amounts. Concern has been expressed that continuation of the rapidly rising trend of combustion may reach a point where the volumes absorbed and produced may adversely affect the earth's climate.

A more immediate danger lies in the pollution of the atmosphere by the poisonous exhaust fumes of motor vehicles. Some reduction can be achieved by measures to encourage a shift from private to public transportation and from surface streets to freeways (which minimizes exhaust-producing starts and accelerations) and by the installation of after-burners. But the only complete and satisfactory solution lies in the replacement of the internal combustion engine by a different type of power plant. Electric batteries with a greatly improved power-to-weight ratio or thermo-electric cells hold some promise. Some research and development in these fields is going on, but far too slowly. If an effort comparable to that of putting one man on the moon were made to allow all men to breathe freely on earth, results would quickly be produced.

The list of human actions endangering the biosphere could be extended indefinitely. They all are expressions of the mentality of the money-mining camp which in its "pragmatic" single-purpose pursuit of immediate gains brings about unforeseen and often catastrophic results. The floods which for the first time in seven centuries reached and heavily damaged the priceless art treasures of Florence certainly were the combined result of many such single-purpose actions in the watershed of the Arno River. What is needed is replacement of the single-purpose approach by ecological thinking. Preservation of the biosphere by maintaining and restoring the ecological balance of nature is the most basic criterion for the urban environment, as indeed of any environment for human life.

MICRO-CLIMATE

While the climate in urban areas generally differs from that of the surrounding countryside by higher temperature and humidity and a severe deficiency of ultra-violet rays, there are very great climatic differences within each urban area. Ancient Greek and Chinese city planning was far ahead of contemporary practice in paying attention to sunshine, wind, and humidity in the selection of sites. In our cities the wealthy, who have a choice, generally have occupied the west end where, thanks to the predominance of western winds, air pollution is less. They have also preempted the higher altitudes where the air is cleaner and the heat of summer nights less oppressive. Less favorable climatic conditions obtain in most areas occupied by the non-airconditioned dwellings of the mass of the population.

In addition to judicious selection of sites, many other means are available to improve the micro-climate. Water and plants, in particular trees and shrubs, mitigate extremes of temperature and absorb dust and soot, as well as noise. The placing and shape of buildings greatly influence the movement of air and can create or prevent both violent gusts and complete stagnation. Much of our present built environment adversely affects the micro-climate by shutting out sunshine and air and by radiating until deep into the night the heat stored in walls and pavements during a hot day. In narrow street canyons, this may even produce local inversion. Replacement of moisture-absorbing soils by the hard surfaces of pavements and roofs often leads to a harmful lowering of the water table in the immediate area and to flash floods downstream. Creation of the best possible micro-climate in all parts of the urban area, but especially in its residential sections, is an important criterion for a physical environment conducive to health and happiness.

Recreational facilities

Health and happiness require not only passive freedom from disturbing effects of the environment, but, even more importantly, opportunities for active exercise of the body and mind. Although many American cities can boast of large parks, there is still a dearth of parks and playgrounds where they are most needed: in the densely populated low-income areas. Moreover, facilities and programs are often not geared to the real needs and demands of the population. Playgrounds, for instance, generally attract only a small section of the age groups which they are intended to serve. There is also a lack of small outdoor spaces in the immediate vicinity of the dwellings, easily accessible to preschool children and to the aged and the physically handicapped. Few immigrants from European countries, east or west, fail to comment on the lack of swimming pools to cool off in during our long, hot summers, and also of indoor facilities for physical exercise and for cultural activities.

Adequate provision of community facilities, geared to the needs of the surrounding population, is an essential element determining the quality of the urban environment.

IMPACT OF THE PHYSICAL ENVIRONMENT ON THE SOCIAL ENVIRONMENT

The aspects of the physical environments so far discussed certainly have an impact not only on physical health and well-being, but also on mental and moral health. However, in this respect, their impact can only be peripheral; the human environment is decisive. Obviously, large sections of America's urban population are spiritually sick, tossed around between overactive aggression and passive despondency, expressed in a constantly rising rate of violence, crime, and delinquency, race and class hatred and strife, alcoholism, drug addiction, clinically definable mental sickness, and other symptoms of anomie. While the root cause of this state lies in social, economic, and political conditions, these are exacerbated by certain aspects of the physical environment. Before discussing these, a general analysis of the typical structure of our urban areas may be in order.

The structure of urban areas

The structure of urban areas has developed—starting from the original and generally continuing center—in a fairly logical response to market forces. As an area increases at the square of the distance, the increasing supply of land with increasing distance from the center results in a rapid falling of land prices, and consequently of densities for all types of uses, toward the periphery. This density gradient is universal and inevitable, and in itself not unhealthy.

As Ebenezer Howard, the father of the "Garden City" idea noted, people are attracted by two magnets: city and country. Whatever one may think of Howard's therapy, his diagnosis is certainly correct. Hence, a basic criterion for the urban area as a place for living is the contradictory pair of requirements of accessibility to both the urban center and the country at its periphery.

While all people to some extent are attracted by both "magnets," the relative strength of the two varies greatly, not only with personal preferences, but primarily with the composition of the household. Single persons and childless couples, especially those in which both partners are working in white-collar jobs, are most strongly attracted by the occupational, educational, recreational, and cultural opportunities of the city center. They can satisfy their desire for "the country" by driving out to it. Preadolescent children do not have this mobility; they need open space right at their doorstep or in their neighborhood, and they have no use for the central city. Nor are their housewife-mothers generally attracted to the center for more than an occasional trip. The concentration of small dwelling units, generally in apartments, at the core of the urban areas, and of larger units, generally in single-family houses at the periphery, is therefore a perfectly logical response to entirely rational and voluntary decisions.

What is not rational and voluntary, but largely the result of arbitrary zoning, is the absence of dwellings suitable for those small households who want to live at the periphery; notably older couples and widows, whose children have left home, and who want, or have, to give up their homes, but do not want to give up their neighborhood. At the same time, many families with numerous children now live in and immediately around the core of cities, in areas called "slum," "blighted," or "gray." They live there not voluntarily, but because lack of money and lack of mobility leave them no other choice. Just as second-hand cars are cheaper than new ones, second- or twenty-second-hand dwellings are less expensive than new ones. This is the only housing that one-third to one-half of the American urban population can afford, and it is, with few exceptions, to be found only in the older inner areas of the central cities.

The result is an increasing territorial division by class. Separate residential locations for different income groups are, of course, not new. In the typical American small town the poor lived "on the wrong side of the tracks." However, the scale of the entire community was so small that all its inhabitants inevitably "rubbed shoulders." But the children growing up in the vast peripheral areas of our urban agglomerations never see "how the other half lives." In the United States this general class segregation is immeasurably aggravated by race segregation which confines the rapidly growing urban "nonwhite" population in overcrowded ghettos.

The remedy is evident: provide in all sections of the area dwelling units of various types accessible to all classes and races. This objective is an important criterion of a good environment. Its achievement will, of course, require the massive use of public funds to bridge the gap between the price or rent of a new dwelling and the amount low-income households can pay. It will also require the massive use of public power to break down the resistance of white prejudice.

The opposite approach, propagated under the fashionable slogan "bring the middle-income families back to the city," is utterly wrong. First, because the often repeated statement that "only the very rich and the very poor" live in the center is simply not true. Even in Manhattan, in 1959, over one-third (34.4%) of all families were in the $5,000-$10,000 income bracket.[5] Second, and far more important, "bringing the middle-income families back to the city" means displacing low-income families. Under such a policy more families would be pushed out than brought in, because the middle-income families demand more space, both inside and outside the dwelling. There are, moreover, better reasons for the poor than for anybody else to live close to the center. Their households frequently contain several persons looking for work, much of which is casual, part-time, or at unusual hours. The employment open to them may be either in the center—which does and will continue to contain the greatest concentration of such jobs—or at varying points at the periphery which can be reached by public transportation only from the center.

5. New York Regional Plan Association, *The Region's Growth* (1967), Table 39, p. 121.

These observations are not meant to imply that no low-income families would live at the periphery, if dwellings within their means were available. Those with a steady job at a peripherally located establishment could live close to it. Those who own a car could reach employment in any part of the outlying area (as well as at the center) from any other part of the periphery. The number of families in these categories may increase; but at present, and for a long time to come, very many low-income families will be forced to live in the center because of lack of mobility as well as of income. To force them out by "slum clearance" is, in the words of Patrick Geddes, "a pernicious blunder." Yet, the practice continues. Though the verbiage has changed from "slum clearance" to "redevelopment" to "renewal," it is still the same old bulldozer, with rare exceptions, which is expected to "eliminate slum and blight." It is obvious that demand for low-rent dwellings greatly outruns the supply when rooms are overcrowded and families are forced to share bathrooms, and when landlords can find tenants for dwellings in need of major repairs. Slum clearance makes this condition worse by further decreasing the supply of housing. Instead, it should be increased both by new low-rent and low-price units at the periphery and by maintenance, improvement, and rehabilitation of old ones, without raising their rents or prices. This action should be combined with addition of facilities and services in the "blighted" areas.

"Urban renewal," as it has been and is being practiced in North America, is harmful not only because it decreases the scant supply of low-rent housing, but also because it completely destroys the social fabric of the neighborhood. The displaced persons not only are forced to pay higher rents or prices for dwellings often no better and sometimes worse than those that have been destroyed, but are also deprived of the support of neighborhood friends and families, stores, and institutions on which they rely far more than wealthier people. The time is long overdue to stop this criminal folly. Maintenance and constant improvement of existing houses and neighborhoods is one of the most important and most neglected criteria for a good urban environment.

PRIVACY AND NEIGHBORLINESS

It has already been noted that for the lower income groups the street is an indispensable outdoor living room, an extension, indeed an integral part, of their home. By contrast, the higher the economical, social, and educational level of the group, the more it identifies the home with their own dwelling and yard, and the greater the value it attaches to privacy, the protection from sight and sound. At the same time, its human contacts are selective over an ever widening area.

While both privacy and ease of contact are desired by everyone, rising income and education make more unrealistic than ever the dream of reproducing the "community feeling" of the old village by surrounding "neighborhoods" of 5,000 to 10,000 people with green belts. This unlikelihood does not invalidate the desirability of organizing residential areas in units of approximately this size, for which the Russians use the more modest term "mikro-rayon," with all community facilities of daily use, notably elementary schools, easily and safely accessible to pedestrians. But neighboring in any meaningful sense occurs only in much smaller groups of perhaps a dozen or so households. Actually, neighboring depends little on the physical environment. The widespread notion that it can be promoted by increasing densities is not borne out by the facts. A survey in the New York Region showed that far more neighboring occurred among people living at densities of two or three houses per acre than among apartment dwellers and even among inhabitants of two- to three-family houses.[6]

Density

The current obsession with raising density by packing more people on top of each other in higher and higher apartment towers seems to be the result of a Leibnitzian preestabilized harmony between the urge of the land owner to squeeze the last square foot of rentable space out of his property and the compulsion of the architect to erect a steep monument to his prowess. It leads to such strange rationalizations as: "We wish more people would face up to the obvious fact that as our population doubles, the only way to bring low density close in is to develop much higher density at the center. . . ."[7] The obvious fact is that at a distance of three miles from the city center there is only one-ninth as much land as at a distance of nine miles. Yet we find proposals, such as the one reported in the *Nations Cities*, calling for the razing of most buildings inside of the present low-density belt, and the accommodation of all uses presently found in the intermediate "grey" belt by piling them up in the inner core. Even if this fantastic proposal were carried out, only a very small proportion of low-density dwellers could live closer in than they do now. It is impossible to believe that all of the very outstanding members of the panel, whose discussions this report purports to

6. New York Regional Plan Association, *Public Participation in Regional Planning* (October, 1967), Table 48, p. 52.
7. "What kind of city do we want?" *Nation's Cities* (April, 1967), pp. 17–47.

summarize, have checked this totally irresponsible statement of their reporter.

A wide variety of densities, between about 8,000 and 40,000 persons per square mile of residential area, can and should be achieved by a mixture of housing types of varying height. Beyond these limits excellent accommodation at higher densities can be provided for households of one or two adults who can afford to pay for airconditioned apartments in tall structures with underground parking, swimming pools, and other amenities. Excellent accommodation at much lower densities can be provided in single-family houses on large lots for people who can afford to pay for two or more cars and for hundreds of feet of streets and utilities.

Some observers believe that with rising incomes the proportion of these two extreme densities will greatly increase. This may well happen if the present extreme inequality in the distribution of the national income continues. However, should we develop sufficient economic rationality to maximize the utility of personal disposable income—which decreases exponentially with increase in volume—by distributing it more evenly, the intermediate densities will accommodate the vast majority of the population during the lifetime of houses presently on the drawing boards.

Lively centers

While neither higher density nor green belts or other boundaries have any noticeable effect on human relations, centers at which people meet and engage in common activities can promote community identification. It is difficult to define the most appropriate population size to be served by such centers; probably a hierarchy is required. The traditional "neighborhood" size appears to be too small in a typically urban environment. Some have advocated groups of 20,000 to 30,000 persons.[8] Those of this size will undoubtedly have a role. But at least in large urban areas of millions of people, spread out over hundreds of square miles, there is a need for larger centers, veritable "secondary downtowns," serving populations of 25,000 to 500,000 and more. The functions traditionally concentrated downtown—public, private and professional offices, a great variety of retail stores and consumer services, hotels and restaurants, theatres and concerts, museums and exhibitions—are more and more to be found also on the periphery, but in scattered locations. By concentrating them in major centers, their attraction and accessibility would be greatly increased; and the infrastructure, notably

8. Humphrey Carver, *Cities in the Suburbs.* Toronto: University of Toronto Press (1962).

public transportation, would be more fully utilized and could, therefore, provide a higher level of service.

Common use of such subcenters of various sizes and the contacts developed by their use may indeed provide identification with a unit which is closer to the individual citizen, more comprehensible, and more conducive to active participation in public affairs. Yet it should not be overlooked that identification with an ingroup implies a certain degree of rejection of outgroups. This may take such extreme forms as gangs of youths defending their "turf" with knives and guns against intruding outsiders; or the less violent, but far more vicious and harmful, zoning policies of exclusive suburbs.

Identification with a part of the urban area must, therefore, be supplemented by identification with the whole. Here we have another pair of contradictory criteria. The whole of the urban area is symbolized by its center, visually by the dominance of the silhouette of its skyscrapers and functionally by its uniqueness. Only in the largest center can those "highest-order" functions, which need the support of the entire metropolitan market, be located. In American cities this is often overshadowed by the second function, that of private and public management and their advisers, to whom easy accessibility to each other is even more important than accessibility to the entire urban area.

Because mutual accessibility is the very essence of the center, it is doubtful whether it is wise to dilute it by residential uses, although a concentration of apartment houses close to it certainly is desirable. In large centers the office towers, the seat of top management, tend to concentrate so highly that little space is left in or between them for other functions. The fact that such districts are dead and deserted after office hours has greatly alarmed some observers. Yet in itself this is no more alarming than the fact that a baseball stadium is dead and deserted when no game is on. What is important is that there should be at the center an area with a rich mixture of uses, vertically as well as horizontally, which attract life and movement in the evening as well as during the day and thereby support the infrastructure and those uses, such as restaurants, which operate during both periods. As previously mentioned, the center should be as far as possible a pedestrian realm, including plazas as outdoor living rooms, enclosed and shaped by the walls of the surrounding buildings, with the sky as the ceiling and with a sensitively patterned floor, furnished by plants, fountains, and sculpture.

Separation and integration

Development of the finely grained mixture of uses which gives variety and interest to the urban environment is frequently prevented by zoning. Zoning is essentially a device to protect property values from being impaired by the vicinity of incompatible uses and building types. Such incompatibilities do exist and do require separation. At the same time, integration of complementary functions, such as residence and retail trade, and of different housing types is also required. Separation and integration are another pair of contradictory criteria which call for judicious balance.

All too often, the desire for protection, implemented not by an administrative device such as the British "development permit" but by the legal instrument of zoning with its inevitable requirement of "equality before the law," has produced a deadening uniformity and monotony in our residential areas. A well-designed mixture of buildings of different height, type, and use could produce far more attractive districts. Certainly the mixture should not be the same in each district; otherwise, the uniformity now found within each would be reproduced on a larger scale by uniformity among them. A strong individual character of each district is indispensable for identification.

Continuity and change

Nobody can identify with an environment which constantly changes its identity. Without a sense of stability and continuity, one cannot feel at home. But incessant change is inherent in modern urban life. Here we identify a final and most profound pair of contradictory criteria: continuity and change.

The realization of continuing and unpredictable change has led to the notion that "planning a product" should be replaced by "planning as process." Plans, it is said, must be flexible. But the artifacts which are the objects of planning and which constitute the physical urban environment just do not flex. They can be modified only in a minor way; the possibilities for "plug-in-cities," are in fact, quite limited. The only way to leave all possibilities open for future development would be to develop nothing at present.

The most that can be done in this respect is to leave some land open for future development, notably in transportation corridors. Leaving substantial areas open would mean scatteration, which has indeed been advocated as a means of providing flexibility and encouraging efficient adaptation to change.[9] But such a policy would also mean an eternally unfinished environment burdened with severe costs in terms of both money and travel time. It might have the

9. Jack Lessinger, "The case for scatteration." *Journal of the American Institute of Planners*, 28 (August, 1962), 159-169.

advantage of ultimately producing the mixture of old and new buildings so strongly advocated by Jane Jacobs,[10] but it would completely destroy the compactness which the same author values even more highly, and correctly so.

PERCEPTION OF THE ENVIRONMENT

The newness of an environment built all at one time is certainly one of the reasons for the "inhospitability" ("Unwirtlichkeit") of which the Germans at present bitterly and passionately accuse the new or rebuilt sections of their cities. Probably a more decisive reason is scale. Not only is the contemporary urban area as a whole of such vast scale that it defies visual comprehension, but in all of its parts there is a conflict of two different scales.

The pre-industrial city could be and was comprehended in two ways: from the outside as a silhouette and from the inside as a sequence of various enclosed spaces formed by streets and squares, all of them on a human scale, the scale of the man standing or walking on his own feet. To some extent, the structure of the modern urban community can perhaps still be expressed by the silhouette of the group of skyscrapers at its center and of smaller such groups at its subcenters; but these can hardly ever be seen together. However, the city's streets run on to infinity and its squares are torn apart by wide openings required for vehicular movement. Only within islands reserved for the pedestrian realm is the experience of urban space and of expressively detailed structure possible, an experience mediated not only by the eye, but by all the senses, in particular by the varo-motoric sensation of moving and turning, climbing and descending. Within these islands the rich heritage of the design principles of the historical town—not, of course, their specific formal expression—is still valid.

The vast urban area, however, cannot be experienced in this way. It can be comprehended only as what it is, not a city, but an urbanized landscape, a sequence of built-up and open areas and districts of different character. And it can be experienced only by using the means that have brought this vast new landscape into being—fast vehicular movement. Driving through it can be a rich and meaningful experience, as described by a sensitive Danish visitor to the United States: "On and on flows the traffic, across bridges and down broad ramps, farther and farther in sweeping curves out into the country,

10. Jane Jacobs, *The Death and Life of Great American Cities.* New York: Random House (1961).

without stop, continuously rising and falling in time with the contours of the earth."[11]

We have scarcely paid any attention to using our freeways and rail lines to make the urban landscape visible and comprehensible. Most of our freeways run in straight lines and, as the cone of vision of the driver is quite narrow, he sees hardly anything but the pavement and the sky.[12] Ideally a freeway should consist exclusively of large sweeping curves. In Germany, Hans Lorenz designed the Nuernberg-Aschaffenburg Autobahn on this principle. It is beautiful to look *at* and to look *from*.

In the urban environment these two requirements tend to conflict. From the point of the driver or rider looking *from* them, it is preferable that roads be above or at least at grade level. But the person looking *at* them (and hearing their noise) would rather have them below level in a cut or a tunnel. Occasionally, an escarpment offers a possibility to locate a freeway so that it will articulate, rather than violate, the natural form of the earth, and at the same time offer the rider a view over the lower part of the urban landscape. Wide transportation corridors would open up further possibilities to reconcile both requirements.

The German term for the verb "to experience" is "erfahren." "Fahren" means "to drive"; and the prefix "er" indicates accomplishment of the purpose of an activity. The urban environment as a whole cannot be "seen"; but it can be "erfahren" and identified and thereby become a meaningful part of the citizen's identity.

CONCLUSION

In recent years, as the realization that urbanization is here to stay has sunk in, the old money-making camp attitude has begun to give way to the insight that the city is not merely a place for making a living but for living. Care for the urban environment is growing rapidly. Freeways destroying the urban landscape are rejected and even literally stopped in mid-air. Protests are mounting against pollution of air and water, against noise and ugliness.

Kenneth Galbraith hit a responsive chord when he pointed out the glaring disparity between the plethora of—often useless or even harmful—goods and services, which are bought and sold at a profit for private consumption and the dearth of publicly consumed goods

11. Steen Eiler Rasmussen, *Experiencing Architecture*, p. 147. Cambridge: MIT Press (1962).

12. Christopher Tunnard, and Boris Pushkarev, *Man-Made America : Chaos or Control*. New Haven: Yale University Press (1963).

and services which can only be sold and bought "wholesale" with public funds. A generation ago an American president said: "The business of America is business." Strangely enough, this man, who saw the *res privatae* as the be-all and end-all of society, considered himself a Republican. But the sum of the *res privatae* does not add up to the res publica; accumulation of private wealth does not create a commonwealth.

Only if the res publica is given priority, can a good urban environment be created. This is not a criterion for its quality, but it is the basic condition, both necessary and sufficient, for the successful application of any criteria by which quality may be measured.

INDEX